PRAISE FOR
Basics of Sahidic Coptic

Dr. Chappell's book is a definite welcome addition to those seeking to learn Sahidic Coptic. It can be used for individual instruction as well as classroom instruction at the university level, undergraduate as well as graduate level. It has a comprehensive grammatical treatment of the language in a simple yet academic way. Students are provided with vocabulary lists and translation exercises after each section, and for more advanced work, a nice selection of original texts are provided with a comprehensive and simple glossary that covers all the texts given.

—**Hany N. Takla**, Lecturer of Coptic Studies,
St. Athanasius and St. Cyril Coptic Orthodox Theological School

Basics of Sahidic Coptic is an ideal grammar for the university classroom or for independent study. A. Josiah Chappell's writing masterfully blends up-to-date scholarship with a witty pedagogical method. Students and professors alike will appreciate this expertly researched yet user-friendly introduction to the Sahidic Coptic language.

—**Joseph E. Sanzo**, Professor of History of Religions,
Ca' Foscari University of Venice

The value and advantage of *Basics of Sahidic Coptic* is that it is aimed at enthusiastic users with little or no prior knowledge of ancient languages or grammar and linguistics who wish to learn the basics of Sahidic Coptic on their own or with a teacher.

—**Frank Feder**, Niedersächsische Akademie der Wissenschaften zu Göttingen,
Arbeitsstellenleiter,
Akademievorhaben,
Digitale Gesamtedition und Übersetzung des
koptisch-sahidischen Alten Testamentes

BASICS of SAHIDIC
COPTIC

BASICS *of* SAHIDIC COPTIC

A COMPLETE GRAMMAR WITH EXERCISES, READINGS, AND LEXICON

A. JOSIAH CHAPPELL

ZONDERVAN ACADEMIC

Basics of Sahidic Coptic
Copyright © 2025 by A. Josiah Chappell

Published by Zondervan, 3950 Sparks Drive SE, Suite 101, Grand Rapids, Michigan, 49546, USA. Zondervan is a registered trademark of The Zondervan Corporation, L.L.C., a wholly owned subsidiary of HarperCollins Christian Publishing, Inc.

Requests for information should be addressed to customercare@harpercollins.com.

Zondervan titles may be purchased in bulk for educational, business, fundraising, or sales promotional use. For information, please email SpecialMarkets@Zondervan.com.

Library of Congress Cataloging-in-Publication Data

Names: Chappell, A. Josiah, 1975- author
Title: Basics of Sahidic Coptic: a complete grammar with exercises, readings, and lexicon / A. Josiah Chappell.
Description: Grand Rapids, Michigan: Zondervan Academic, 2025. | Series: Zondervan language basics series | Includes
    bibliographical references and index.
Identifiers: LCCN 2025004982 (print) | LCCN 2025004983 (ebook) | ISBN 9780310160304 paperback | ISBN 9780310160311 ebook
Subjects: LCSH: Sahidic dialect--Grammar--Textbooks | LCGFT: Textbooks | Introductory works
Classification: LCC PJ2035 .C47 2025 (print) | LCC PJ2035 (ebook) | DDC 493/.27--dc23/eng/20250520
LC record available at https://lccn.loc.gov/2025004982
LC ebook record available at https://lccn.loc.gov/2025004983

Any internet addresses (websites, blogs, etc.) and telephone numbers in this book are offered as a resource. They are not intended in any way to be or imply an endorsement by Zondervan, nor does Zondervan vouch for the content of these sites and numbers for the life of this book.

All rights reserved. No part of this publication may be reproduced, stored in a retrieval system, or transmitted in any form or by any means—electronic, mechanical, photocopy, recording, or any other—except for brief quotations in printed reviews, without the prior permission of the publisher.

Without limiting the exclusive rights of any author, contributor or the publisher of this publication, any unauthorized use of this publication to train generative artificial intelligence (AI) technologies is expressly prohibited. HarperCollins also exercise their rights under Article 4(3) of the Digital Single Market Directive 2019/790 and expressly reserve this publication from the text and data mining exception.

HarperCollins Publishers, Macken House, 39/40 Mayor Street Upper, Dublin 1, D01 C9W8, Ireland (https://www.harpercollins.com)

Cover design: LUCAS Art & Design
Interior design: Kait Lamphere

Printed in the United States of America

---

25 26 27 28 29 30 31 32 33 34 35 /TRM/ 15 14 13 12 11 10 9 8 7 6 5 4 3 2 1

CONTENTS

Expanded Table of Contents vii
Preface xvii
Abbreviations xix
Introduction to Coptic xxi

THE SAHIDIC WRITING SYSTEM

1. Letters and Sounds 3
2. Scribal Marks and Syllables 10

THE SAHIDIC NOUN SYSTEM

3. Nouns and the Definite Article 17
4. The Indefinite Article and Ownership 21
5. Adjectives and Nominal Sentences 25
6. Pronouns and More Articles 31
7. Prepositions, Conjunctions, and Relative Clauses 36
8. Compound Prepositions and Adverbs 42
9. Numbers and Time 47
10. Odds and Ends 53

THE SAHIDIC VERB SYSTEM

11. Introduction to Sahidic Verbs 61
12. Forms of the Verbal Stem 66
13. The Durative Pattern: The Present 72
14. The Future 77
15. The Non-Durative Pattern: Main Clause Conjugations ... 81
16. The Past 85
17. The Aorist 90
18. The Optative and the Jussive 94
19. Conversions: The Relative Converter 100

20. The Circumstantial Converter 107
21. The Preterite Converter 114
22. The Focalizing Converter 120
23. The Non-Durative Pattern: Subordinate Clause Conjugations 127
24. The Conjunctive and the Future Conjunctive 132
25. The Precursive and the Limitative 137
26. The Conditional and the Causative Infinitive 142
27. Verboids and Impersonal Predicates 148
28. Conclusion and Next Steps 152

Bibliography and Resources 157
Reading Selections 161
Sahidic-English Lexicon 195
Appendix 1: Survey of "the ⲛ̄-s" 247
Appendix 2: Verb Classes 248
Appendix 3: Verb Paradigms 251
Appendix 4: Prepositions and Directional Adverbs 260
Index of Verbal Forms 265

EXPANDED TABLE OF CONTENTS

Preface xvii
    Acknowledgments xvii
    A Note on Terminology xviii
Abbreviations xix
Introduction to Coptic xxi

THE SAHIDIC WRITING SYSTEM

  1. Letters and Sounds 3
      The Coptic Alphabet 3
          1.1 Origins 3
          1.2 The Sahidic Alphabet 4
      Sahidic Pronunciation 5
          1.3 Proper Pronunciation 5
          1.4 (De-)aspiration 6
          1.5 Uncommon Letters 6
          1.6 Monograms 6
          1.7 Vowels and Glides 7
          1.8 Diphthongs 8

  2. Scribal Marks and Syllables 10
      The Sahidic Overline 10
          2.1 The Overline 10
          2.2 Scribal Abbreviations 11
      Rightly Dividing the Words 11
          2.3 Word and Syllable Divisions 11
          2.4 Main Stress 12
          2.5 Other Divisions 13
      Spelling Changes 13
          2.6 Letter Changes 13
          2.7 Greek Spellings 14

THE SAHIDIC NOUN SYSTEM

3. Nouns and the Definite Article.. 17
   Nouns 17
      3.1 Noun Gender.. 17
      3.2 Noun Number... 18
   The Definite Article 18
      3.3 Forms of the Definite Article 18
      3.4 Translating the Definite Article 19

4. The Indefinite Article and Ownership..................................... 21
   The Indefinite Article.. 21
      4.1 Forms of the Indefinite Article 21
      4.2 Translating the Indefinite Article 21
   Connecting Nouns 22
      4.3 Showing Ownership 22
      4.4 "The ⲛ̄-s"... 22

5. Adjectives and Nominal Sentences 25
   Adjectives 25
      5.1 Modifying Nouns 25
      5.2 Egyptian "Adjectives".. 25
      5.3 Greek Adjectives 26
      5.4 Adjectives as Nouns.. 27
   Nominal Sentences 27
      5.5 Forming Nominal Sentences..................................... 27
      5.6 Negation of Nominal Sentences 28

6. Pronouns and More Articles... 31
   Personal Pronouns... 31
      6.1 Independent Personal Pronouns 31
      6.2 Nominal Sentences with Pronouns 31
   Possessive Articles and Demonstratives 32
      6.3 Possessive Articles 32
      6.4 Demonstrative Articles and Pronouns 33

7. Prepositions, Conjunctions, and Relative Clauses 36
   Simple Prepositions... 36
      7.1 Basic Prepositions 36
      7.2 Personal Suffixes 37
   Conjunctions 39
      7.3 Saying "And".. 39
      7.4 Other Conjunctions... 39

    Relative Clauses 39
        7.5 Saying "Who/Which" 39
        7.6 Relative Clauses as Nouns. 40

8. Compound Prepositions and Adverbs. 42
    Compound Prepositions 42
        8.1 Formation of Compound Prepositions 42
        8.2 Categories of Compound Prepositions 42
    Adverbs 43
        8.3 Nouns as Adverbs 43
        8.4 Directional Adverbs 44
        8.5 Adverbially Enhanced Prepositions 44

9. Numbers and Time. 47
    Numbers 47
        9.1 Usage of Numbers. 47
        9.2 Forms of Numbers. 47
    Time 49
        9.3 Terms 49
        9.4 Days of the Week. 50
        9.5 Months of the Year 50

10. Odds and Ends 53
    Asking Questions 53
        10.1 Interrogative Pronouns 53
        10.2 Indefinite Pronouns. 54
        10.3 Pronouns and Possession 54
    Quantities and Compounds 55
        10.4 Quantities 55
        10.5 Compounds. 55

THE SAHIDIC VERB SYSTEM

11. Introduction to Sahidic Verbs. 61
    Sahidic Verbs 61
        11.1 Verbal Functions 61
        11.2 Verbal Forms. 61
    Survey of the Verbal System 62
        11.3 The Two Patterns 62
        11.4 The Durative Pattern 62
        11.5 The Non-Durative Pattern 62
        11.6 Converters 63

12. Forms of the Verbal Stem 66
Infinitives (and Imperatives) 66
12.1 Verbal Listings in the Lexicon 66
12.2 The Three Forms of the Infinitive 67
12.3 The Imperative 68
12.4 Infinitives as Nouns 68
Statives and Conjunct Participles 68
12.5 The Stative 68
12.6 The Conjunct Participle 69

13. The Durative Pattern: The Present 72
The Present Conjugation 72
13.1 Conjugating the Present 72
13.2 Syntax of the Present 73
13.3 Translating the Present 74
Negation of the Present 74
13.4 The Negative Present 74
13.5 Translating the Negative Present 75

14. The Future 77
The Future Conjugation 77
14.1 Conjugating the Future 77
14.2 Translating the Future 78
14.3 The Negative Future 78

15. The Non-Durative Pattern: Main Clause Conjugations 81
The Non-Durative Pattern 81
15.1 The Two Non-Durative groups 81
15.2 Syntax of the Main Clause Conjugations 81
15.3 Negations of the Main Clause Conjugations 82
15.4 Survey of the Main Clause Auxiliaries 82

16. The Past 85
The Past Conjugation 85
16.1 Conjugating the Past 85
16.2 Translating the Past 86
Negation(s) of the Past 86
16.3 The Negative Past 86
16.4 The "Not Yet" Past 87

17. The Aorist 90
The Aorist Conjugation 90
17.1 Conjugating the Aorist 90
17.2 Translating the Aorist 91

    17.3 The Negative Aorist. 91

18. The Optative and the Jussive 94
  The Optative Conjugation 94
    18.1 Conjugating the Optative 94
    18.2 Translating the Optative. 95
    18.3 The Negative Optative 95
  The Jussive Conjugation (and the Imperative) 96
    18.4 Conjugating the Jussive. 96
    18.5 The Negative Jussive and Imperative 97

19. Conversions: The Relative Converter. 100
  Conversions. 100
    19.1 The Four Conversions. 100
    19.2 Conversion Possibilities 100
  Relative Conversion 101
    19.3 The Relative Converter. 101
    19.4 Translating the Relative 101
  The Relative Converter with the Durative Pattern 102
    19.5 Relative Present. 102
    19.6 Relative Future 103
  The Relative Converter with the Non-Durative Pattern 103
    19.7 Relative Past 103
    19.8 Relative Aorist. 104

20. The Circumstantial Converter 107
  Circumstantial Conversion 107
    20.1 The Circumstantial Converter 107
    20.2 Translating the Circumstantial. 107
  The Circumstantial Converter with the Durative Pattern. 109
    20.3 Circumstantial Present 109
    20.4 Circumstantial Future. 110
  The Circumstantial Converter with the Non-Durative Pattern. 110
    20.5 Circumstantial Past. 110
    20.6 Circumstantial Aorist 111

21. The Preterite Converter 114
  Preterite Conversion 114
    21.1 The Preterite Converter 114
    21.2 Translating the Preterite 114
  The Preterite Converter with the Durative Pattern 115
    21.3 Preterite Present 115
    21.4 Preterite Future 116
  The Preterite Converter with the Non-Durative Pattern 116

  21.5 Preterite Past 116
  21.6 Preterite Aorist. 117

22. The Focalizing Converter 120
 Focalizing Conversion. 120
  22.1 The Focalizing Converter 120
  22.2 Translating the Focalizing 120
 The Focalizing Converter with the Durative Pattern. 122
  22.3 Focalizing Present 122
  22.4 Focalizing Future 123
 The Focalizing Converter with the Non-Durative Pattern 123
  22.5 Focalizing Past 123
  22.6 Focalizing Aorist 124

23. The Non-Durative Pattern: Subordinate Clause Conjugations 127
 Overview of the Subordinate Clause Conjugations 127
  23.1 Subordinate Clause Conjugations. 127
  23.2 Negation of Subordinate Clause Conjugations. 128
 Causative Verbs. 128
  23.3 ⲧ- Causative Verbs 128
  23.4 ⲭ- Causative Verbs 128

24. The Conjunctive and the Future Conjunctive 132
 The Conjunctive Conjugation 132
  24.1 Conjugating the Conjunctive 132
  24.2 Translating the Conjunctive 133
 The Future Conjunctive Conjugation. 134
  24.3 Conjugating the Future Conjunctive 134
  24.4 Translating the Future Conjunctive 134

25. The Precursive and the Limitative 137
 The Precursive Conjugation 137
  25.1 Conjugating the Precursive. 137
  25.2 Translating the Precursive 138
 The Limitative Conjugation 139
  25.3 Conjugating the Limitative. 139
  25.4 Translating the Limitative 139

26. The Conditional and the Causative Infinitive 142
 The Conditional Conjugation. 142
  26.1 Conjugating the Conditional. 142
  26.2 Translating the Conditional 143
 The Causative Infinitive 144
  26.3 Conjugating the Causative Infinitive 144

  26.4 Translating the Causative Infinitive 145

27. Verboids and Impersonal Predicates 148
  Verboids 148
    27.1 Verboids 148
    27.2 ⲛⲁ- Verboids 148
  Impersonal Predicates 149
    27.3 Impersonal Expressions 149
    27.4 Greek Impersonals 150

28. Conclusion and Next Steps 152
  28.1 The End and the Beginning 152
  28.2 Reading Texts 152
  28.3 Learning Words 154
  28.4 Further Studies 154

Bibliography and Resources 157
  Online Projects and Resources 157
  Grammars (Print) 157
  Lexica/Dictionaries/Concordances (Print) 158
  Text Editions (Print) 158
  Other Studies 159

Reading Selections 161
  ⲡϫⲱⲱⲙⲉ ⲛ̄-ⲉ̓ⲝⲟⲇⲟⲥ Exodus 1.1–5.21 161
  ⲡϫⲱⲱⲙⲉ ⲛ̄-ⲛⲉⲯⲁⲗⲙⲟⲥ Psalms 2, 22(23), 90(91), 109(110), and 151 168
  ⲙ̄ⲡⲁⲣϩⲟⲓⲙⲓⲁ ⲛ̄-ⲥⲟⲗⲟⲙⲱ́ⲛ Proverbs 22.17–23.12 172
  ⲡⲉⲩⲁⲅⲅⲉⲗⲓⲟⲛ ⲛ̄-ⲕⲁⲧⲁ-ⲓ̈ⲱϩⲁⲛⲛⲏⲥ John 1.1–2.12 174
  ⲡⲉⲩⲁⲅⲅⲉⲗⲓⲟⲛ ⲛ̄-ⲕⲁⲧⲁ-ⲙⲁⲑⲑⲁⲓⲟⲥ Matthew 5.1–7.29 177
  ⲧⲁⲡⲟⲕⲁⲗⲩⲯⲓⲥ ⲛ̄ⲧⲉ-ⲓ̈ⲱϩⲁⲛⲛⲏⲥ Revelation 4.1–8.1 183
  ⲡⲉⲩⲁⲅⲅⲉⲗⲓⲟⲛ ⲡⲕⲁⲧⲁ-ⲑⲱⲙⲁⲥ The Gospel of Thomas 1–42 187
  ⲡⲃⲓⲟⲥ ⲛ̄-ⲁⲛⲧⲱⲛⲓⲟⲥ The Life of Antony 11–13 192

Sahidic-English Lexicon 195
Appendix 1: Survey of "the ⲛ̄-s" 247
Appendix 2: Verb Classes 248
Appendix 3: Verb Paradigms 251
Appendix 4: Prepositions and Directional Adverbs 260
Index of Verbal Forms 265

PREFACE

ACKNOWLEDGMENTS

I am deeply grateful to the many people who have contributed to *Basics of Sahidic Coptic* along the way, first to my amazing editor at Zondervan Academic, Nancy Erickson. Nancy has expertly shepherded this project from first pitch to finished product. I'm honored to have this text become part of the Zondervan Language Basics series under her guidance. I must also thank the rest of the team at Zondervan Academic: Kait Lamphere (who typeset this bilingual text), Matthew Miller (cover design and marketing), and the anonymous reviewers and readers who've helped to sculpt this book into its final form. Any remaining errors and quirks are my own.

Over the years, I've been fortunate to have had a number of gifted teachers and peers in the course of my own Coptic studies. Foremost of all is ⲡⲁⲥⲁϩ, Hany Takla, president of the St. Shenouda the Archimandrite Coptic Society in Los Angeles. My formal study of Coptic began when I took his Sahidic class at UCLA nearly seventeen years ago. I would go on to study Bohairic with him at the Society and to assist the Society as a research associate in the years after. I've always been grateful for his help and encouragement and inspired by his passion for the Coptic heritage.

Last of all, I'm extraordinarily thankful for my community of friends and family, who've had the dubious honor of listening to me yammer away about obscure aspects of Coptic for years. I'm blessed every day to have two bright and talented children, Ava and Isaac—and a wonderful, supportive, and patient wife, Abby. I truly couldn't have done it without you, ⲧⲁⲙⲉⲣⲓⲧ.

A. Josiah Chappell
Lá Fhéile Pádraig/The Feast of St Patrick, 2025
Los Angeles

A NOTE ON TERMINOLOGY

Every effort has been made to use current terminology for the various grammatical categories and structures of Sahidic Coptic. Older grammars and works often have different terms, and these have been footnoted for your refence as these categories are discussed.

With the definitions of vocabulary words, I have attempted to supply clear, functional, modern English equivalents. Naturally, the long tradition of English biblical translations has bequeathed us with a number of traditional renderings, but I have resisted this reflex and to provide "normal," common translations of the core meanings of these words. Some traditional renderings are recognizably (eroded) transliterations of Greek originals, not actually true translations ("apostle," "epistle," "christ," "baptize," "prophet," etc.). Some come from a Latin intermediary ("disciple," "savior," "gentile," "miracle," etc.). Some are older English ("lord," "heaven," "soul," "behold!," etc.). One can, of course, translate with one's choice of more traditional synonyms—but there is a real value in reconsidering and reimagining better ways to express these important terms in modern English.

ABBREVIATIONS

adj	adjective	nm	noun, masculine
adv	adverb	nmf	noun, masculine/feminine
art	article	neg	negative
circum	circumstantial	num	numeral, number
conj	conjunction	part	particle
cp	conjunct participle	pers	personal
def	definite	pl	plural
dem	demonstrative	poss	possessive
f	feminine	prep	preposition
fpl	feminine plural	pron	pronoun
fsg	feminine singular	rel	relative
impv	imperative	sg	singular
ind	independent	v	verb
indef	indefinite	vi	verb, intransitive
inf	infinitive	vr	verb, reflexive
inter	interrogative	vs	verb, stative
interj	interjection	vt	verb, transitive
m	masculine		
mpl	masculine plural	cf.	compare with
msg	masculine singular	†	stative form of verb
n	noun	<	derived from
nf	noun, feminine	>	by extension

INTRODUCTION TO COPTIC

Coptic is the final phase of the native Egyptian language—a language that has one of the longest recorded histories, stretching back to hieroglyphic inscriptions attested in the final centuries of the fourth millennium BCE. Egyptian is a member of the Afro-Asiatic superfamily of languages and a more distant cousin to Semitic languages such as Hebrew, Aramaic, and Arabic. The term "Coptic" is used both for the final language phase and for the massive change in the way Egyptian was written. Breaking from millennia of tradition (the complex hieroglyphic, hieratic, and demotic writing systems), Coptic is Egyptian written with a modified Greek alphabet. In the aftermath of Alexander the Great's conquests in the Mediterranean and ancient Near East in the fourth century BCE, Egypt was exposed to Greek culture and language—including the Greek alphabet. In the following centuries, Egyptian scribes would experiment with this far simpler system of writing. By the early first millennium CE, these attempts would become standardized as the Coptic alphabet. The scribes borrowed a few additional letters from the cursive demotic script to more accurately represent the sounds of the language: unlike Greek, Coptic has a "sh" sound, affricatives like English "j" and "ch," and a variety of grades of "h" sounds. Greek also influenced Egyptian beyond the adoption of an alphabet: many Greek words made their way into the language—contributing as much as 40 percent of Coptic vocabulary.

Importantly, because Greek has vowels, Coptic writing could also now effectively designate Egyptian vowels, something which was largely unmarked under the older writing systems. Throughout the millennia, the long, linear Nile Valley naturally created an entire continuum of Egyptian dialects between the Delta and the First Cataract. Much of the variation between these local dialects comes from the articulation of vowel sounds, something the old, traditional writing systems aren't capable of fully rendering (and not something with which official, prestige forms of the language like classical Middle Egyptian were concerned). Coptic finally allows us to see and hear the differences—people from different ends of the Nile would likely have had some difficulty understanding each other's local speech.

Some of the earliest and primary examples of Coptic literature are the translations of biblical literature from Greek. These were translated from the Greek texts of the New Testament but also from the pre-Christian Greek translations of the Hebrew Bible[1] (which formed the Old Testament

---

1. Commonly, but not entirely accurately, called the Septuagint (from the Latin for "Seventy," this name technically just applies to the Old Greek translation of the Pentateuch said to have been made by seventy[-two] scholars in the third century BCE). "Old Greek" encompasses this and all the other initial Greek translations of the rest of the Hebrew Bible (and the apocryphal/deuterocanonical texts), many of which would have later Greek revisions.

for Greek-speaking Christians). Because of the wide spectrum of dialects, a single Coptic biblical translation would not suffice for Christian missionary efforts along the Nile. Biblical texts, especially the Gospels and the Psalms, were translated into multiple dialects by the middle of the first millennium CE, most notably Sahidic[2] (probably originating near modern-day al-Ashmunayn[3]), Fayyumic (modern-day Fayyum), Oxyrhynchite (modern-day al-Bahnasa), Lycopolitan (modern-day Asyūṭ), Akhmimic, and Bohairic[4] (the Western Delta and surroundings).

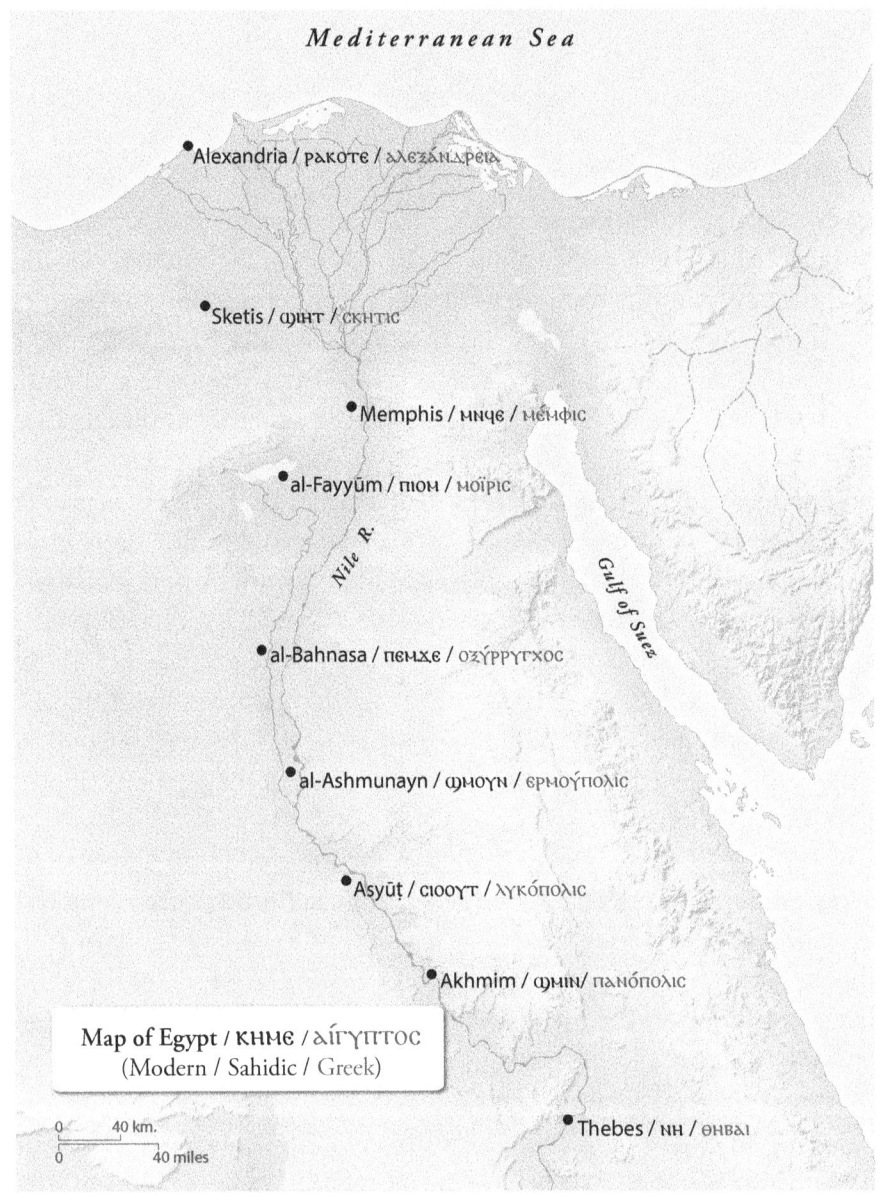

Map of Egypt with main dialectical hubs
(Sahidic names are in black, Greek names are in grey)

Map by International Mapping. Copyright © 2025 by Zondervan. All rights reserved.

---

2. The name of this dialect is derived from the Arabic name for Upper Egypt (the southern part, up the Nile), *aṣ-Ṣaʿīd*.

3. James P. Allen considers it to have been centered in Thebes. See his *Coptic: A Grammar of Its Six Major Dialects*, Languages of the Ancient Near East: Didactica 1 (University Park, PA: Eisenbrauns, 2020), 1.

4. Derived from the Arabic name for Lower Egypt (the northern part, down the Nile by the Mediterranean), *al-Buḥayrah*.

INTRODUCTION TO COPTIC

After imperial legalization of Christianity by Constantine in the fourth century CE, Egyptian church authority was able to focus its attention on the Sahidic dialect, a geographic "superdialect" that could be used throughout much of Christian Egypt. Sahidic was suited for this purpose, as it has the fewest distinctive differences—it works well as an approachable common denominator among all the dialects. Sahidic's ascendance and the standardization of Sahidic biblical literature slowed most literary production in other dialects in the following centuries. The arrival of Islam in the seventh century CE and the subsequent spread of Arabic throughout all parts of Egyptian culture would have a similar impact on Sahidic, which would wane in the following centuries.[5] Arabic largely supplanted the native language of Egypt, with Sahidic (and other dialects) becoming more and more relegated to remote and rural communities—and especially to the minority Egyptian Christian population (to whom the term "Coptic" was now applied). At the dawn of the second millennium CE, the Coptic ecclesial hierarchy was transitioning to the Bohairic dialect, which was used in the monasteries of Wādī al-Naṭrūn and the seat of the Coptic patriarch in the recently founded city of Cairo, the new capital of Egypt. The prevalence of Arabic throughout Egyptian society—including the Coptic population—saw an increasing use of parallel Arabic translations alongside Bohairic biblical texts.

Sahidic is thus the "classic" superdialect eventually superseding all other first millennium CE Coptic dialects; Bohairic represents the surviving dialect of the Coptic Church through the second millennium CE. These two major dialects tend to have different audiences: Sahidic is more often studied by Egyptologists (who can use its evidence to reconstruct earlier forms of the language), biblical scholars interested in text critical issues (Sahidic is an important early version, one step away from the Greek biblical texts), and scholars of early Christianity and gnostic movements in Egypt (especially after the 1945 discovery of the Nag Hammadi manuscripts). Bohairic is studied by scholars of the later Coptic Church and its literature—and by the Copts themselves, who have continued to employ Bohairic as a liturgical language to this day. The echoes of the language of the pharaohs can still be heard today in Coptic Christians' worship services around the world.

Sahidic, the first millennium classic superdialect, is the focus of this grammar. The core of *Basics of Sahidic Coptic* comprises twenty-seven chapters, most accompanied by vocabulary lists and translation exercises. After introducing the Coptic writing system, the chapters first work through the Sahidic noun system and associated topics before turning to the somewhat more complex topic of the Sahidic verb system. The main grammar chapters are followed by a discussion of further directions for study (including important online and print resources), a selection of extended readings from biblical and extrabiblical sources, a comprehensive lexicon, and other aids for reference.

My intent is for *Basics of Sahidic Coptic* to be accessible, even for those who have never learned an ancient language. Greek and Middle Egyptian are *not* prerequisites! Informed by current research yet avoiding overly complicated linguistic jargon, this grammar is designed to be of use for undergraduate and graduate level Coptic language classes.[6] But this guide is also for

---

5. The final copies of Sahidic manuscripts were made around the fourteenth century CE, long after the rise of Bohairic.
6. As a course, the grammar chapters could be worked through over the course of a semester (depending on students' pace), with a second semester devoted to working through reading selections.

interested students and scholars (and lovers of ancient languages in general) who want to learn Coptic on their own. It is my hope that *Basics of Sahidic Coptic* will be of great use in introducing new generations of students to the world of Coptic language and literature.

ⲭⲁⲓⲣⲉ!

THE SAHIDIC WRITING SYSTEM

CHAPTER 1

LETTERS AND SOUNDS

OVERVIEW

Each chapter in this book will begin with an overview of the topics to be covered. In this chapter, you will learn:

- The letters and names of the Coptic alphabet
- Sahidic pronunciation of these letters

THE COPTIC ALPHABET

1.1 **Origins.** As we discussed in the Introduction, the Coptic alphabet is an adaptation and expansion of the Greek alphabet. If you've studied Greek, you already have a significant advantage! You will notice immediately that there's no distinction between upper and lowercase forms in Coptic (something that Greek scribes only begin to develop later in the first millennium CE). Coptic forms are similar to Greek uncial letters, with many letters having curved, rounded shapes. Also be sure to take note of the differences in how some of the letters are pronounced in Coptic. While Koine Greek pronunciation undergoes a number of changes through the early first millennium CE, the Coptic letter values tend to be conservative: they seem to be inherited from earlier Greek pronunciation and are often closer to classical values. Because Greek has sounds that aren't as common in the native Egyptian language, some of those Greek letters are rarely used, aside from words borrowed from Greek (of which, as you will see, there are a lot). And because Egyptian has a number of other sounds that don't occur in Greek, additional letters were borrowed from the demotic script and added at the end of the alphabet (see fig. 1). Different phases and dialects of Coptic have variations in these bonus letters, but in standard Sahidic there are six.

Fig. 1. Coptic letters derived from hieroglyphic > demotic script

THE SAHIDIC WRITING SYSTEM

1.2   **The Sahidic Alphabet.** Below you will find the entire Sahidic Coptic alphabet listed, each letter with its name,[1] a general English transliteration value, and a more precise International Phonetic Alphabet value [in brackets],[2] followed by an example of how each letter should be pronounced. Some letters sound just like their English counterparts, but many (marked with *) can be trickier for English speakers and will be given further explanation in 1.3–1.7. Learn this alphabet and its sounds!

letter	name	transliteration	[IPA]	example (pronounced like the bold letters)
ⲁ	ⲁⲗⲫⲁ	a	[a]	Spanish g**a**to* (1.7)
ⲃ	ⲃⲏⲧⲁ	b	[β]	Spanish ca**b**o* (1.3)
ⲅ	ⲅⲁⲙⲙⲁ	g	[k]	s**k**ill* (1.5)
ⲇ	ⲇⲁⲗⲇⲁ	d	[t]	s**t**ill* (1.5)
ⲉ	ⲉⲓ	e	[ɛ][3]	b**e**t
ⲍ	ⲍⲏⲧⲁ	z	[s]	**s**ee* (1.5)
ⲏ	ϩⲏⲧⲁ	ē	[e]	h**ey**
ⲑ	ⲑⲏⲧⲁ	th	[th]	monogram for ⲧϩ* (1.6)
ⲓ	ⲓⲱⲧⲁ	i, y	[i], [j]	b**ee**t and **y**et; often spelled as the digram ⲉⲓ* (1.7)
ⲕ	ⲕⲁⲡⲡⲁ	k	[k]	s**k**ill* (1.4)
ⲗ	ⲗⲁⲩⲇⲁ	l	[l]	**l**ay
ⲙ	ⲙⲏ	m	[m]	**m**ay
ⲛ	ⲛⲉ	n	[n]	**n**ay
ⲝ	ⲝⲓ	ks	[ks]	monogram for ⲕⲥ* (1.6)
ⲟ	ⲟⲩ	o	[o][4]	n**o**te
ⲡ	ⲡⲓ	p	[p]	s**p**ill* (1.4)
ⲣ	ⲣⲱ	r	[r]/[ɾ]	Spanish pe**rr**o/pe**r**o* (1.3)
ⲥ	ⲥⲏⲙⲙⲁ	s	[s]	**s**ee
ⲧ	ⲧⲁⲩ	t	[t]	s**t**ill* (1.4)
ⲩ	ϩⲉ	u, w	[u], [w]	b**oo**t and **w**et; usually spelled as the digram ⲟⲩ* (1.7)
ⲫ	ⲫⲓ	ph	[ph]	monogram for ⲡϩ* (1.6)
ⲭ	ⲭⲓ	kh	[kh]	monogram for ⲕϩ* (1.6)
ⲯ	ⲯⲓ	ps	[ps]	monogram for ⲡⲥ* (1.6)
ⲱ	ⲱ	ō	[o]	n**o**te
ϣ	ϣⲁⲓ	š (sh)	[ʃ]	**sh**e
ϥ	ϥⲁⲓ	f	[f][5]	**f**oot

---

1. These names are generally attested in later Coptic (alongside other variant names). As you can see, many are derived from the familiar Greek letter names (with some interesting differences).

2. If you're not familiar with the IPA, the International Phonetic Association's website has a complete chart of these sounds (including audio recordings so you can hear precisely how they should be pronounced) at https://www.internationalphoneticassociation.org/IPAcharts/inter_chart_2018/IPA_2018.html. Other IPA websites have similar charts with letters you can click for sound recordings. If there's a need to clarify specific pronunciation, I will use the IPA.

3. This likely could also be pronounced as a shwa, like [ə] t**a**ken, when unstressed.

4. Conventionally, this is often pronounced like [ɔ] n**o**t, differentiating it from ⲱ. See discussion below in 1.7.

5. James P. Allen considers this to be the bilabial fricative [ɸ], "like *f* pronounced with the two lips rather than the teeth

LETTERS AND SOUNDS

ϩ	ϩορι	h	[h][6]	**h**ope
ϫ	ϫανϫια	č (ch)	[tʃ][7]	**ch**ild; also monogram for ⲧϣ* (1.6)
ϭ	ϭιμα	kʲ	[kʲ]	**c**ute
ϯ	ϯ	ti	[ti]	monogram for ⲧⲓ* (1.6)

SAHIDIC PRONUNCIATION

1.3 **Proper Pronunciation.** Despite Sahidic being an extinct dialect of an effectively dead language, it is worth getting as close as possible to how Sahidic was actually pronounced by native speakers of its time.[8] Try your best to be accurate and consistent, but fortunately you won't have to worry about offending any native speakers (just perhaps your teacher)! Again, if you've studied Greek in some form, it will be important to note the differences in Sahidic pronunciation.[9]

To begin our discussion of pronunciation, a number of consonants are easy for English speakers, requiring no further explanation. They sound just like the examples given:

ⲗ	ⲗαυⲇα	l	[l]	**l**ay
ⲙ	ⲙⲏ	m	[m]	**m**ay
ⲛ	ⲛⲉ	n	[n]	**n**ay
ⲥ	ⲥⲏⲙⲙⲁ	s	[s]	**s**ee
ϣ	ϣⲁι	š (sh)	[ʃ]	**sh**e
ϥ	ϥⲁι	f	[f]	**f**oot
ϩ	ϩορι	h	[h]	**h**ope
ϫ	ϫανϫια	č (ch)	[tʃ]	**ch**ild
ϭ	ϭιμα	kʲ	[kʲ]	**c**ute

The letters ⲃ and ⲡ require a bit more explanation for English speakers, as these aren't part of usual English pronunciation.

ⲃ	ⲃⲏⲧⲁ	b	[β]	Spanish ca**b**o

This is a softer *b* sound made without the lips completely closing, allowing it to be sustained. Try pronouncing a *b* sound with your lips in the position they would be when

---

and lower lip" (*Coptic: A Grammar of Its Six Major Dialects*, Languages of the Ancient Near East: Didactica 1 [University Park, PA: Eisenbrauns, 2020], 5).

6. Allen considers this to be [ħ], a rougher *h* like Arabic ح (*Coptic*, 5).

7. Some scholars define this as [tʲ], almost identical in practice to [tʃ]. See Allen, *Coptic*, 5 and Thomas O. Lambdin, *Introduction to Sahidic Coptic* (Macon, GA: Mercer University Press, 1983), xi.

8. And by this, of course, I mean as close as scholars are able to determine. Certain points in Coptic phonology are still debated.

9. For students of Greek, I will footnote concurrent differences in Koine Greek pronunciation of certain letters during the first millennium CE heyday of Sahidic Coptic. For further information on *historically accurate* Koine Greek pronunciation, see Randall Buth's Ἡ Κοινὴ Προφορά *Koiné Pronunciation 2012*, available online at: https://www.biblicallanguagecenter.com/wp-content/uploads/2012/08/Koine-Pronunciation-2012.pdf.

making a *w* sound. This sound is close to the *v* in *voice*, so default your pronunciation to that if you need to—and *not* to the *b* in *boy*.

| ⲣ | ⲣⲱ | *r* | [r]/[ɾ] | Spanish *perro/pero* |

This is a rolled or trilled *r* (like Spanish *perro*), and/or a tapped or flapped *r* [ɾ] (like Spanish *pero*). It is *not* like the common English *r* [ɹ] as in *road*. Spice up your *r*!

1.4 **(De-)aspiration.** Aspiration is the puff of air you sometimes make when pronouncing certain consonants (specifically stops or plosives). In English, this is conditioned by position: we usually aspirate *k*, *p*, and *t* if they begin words but not otherwise, such as when preceded by an *s*.[10] Sahidic very likely did not aspirate *k*, *p*, and *t* in any position.

ⲕ	ⲕⲁⲡⲡⲁ	*k*	[k]	*skill*
ⲡ	ⲡⲓ	*p*	[p]	*spill*
ⲧ	ⲧⲁⲩ	*t*	[t]	*still*

This can be tricky for English speakers to be aware of and avoid at the beginnings of words. Say *kill*, *pill*, and *till* while holding your hand in front of your mouth when you speak. You will feel a puff of air you probably didn't even realize you were making. Try to say the words without making that puff of air to deaspirate (you'll notice they sound almost like *gill*, *bill*, and *dill* when you do).

1.5 **Uncommon Letters.** Some letters inherited from Greek are rarely used in Coptic except with words that are themselves borrowed from Greek. The reason for this is that these sounds used in Greek had fallen out of the Egyptian phonological inventory (sounds used in the language) before the Coptic period. Greek loanwords do make up a sizable portion of Coptic vocabulary and still retained these letters in their spelling—even if most native Coptic speakers probably didn't pronounce them in the Greek manner (unless they were also fluently bilingual in Greek[11]).

ⲅ	ⲅⲁⲙⲙⲁ	*g*	[k]	*skill* (pronounced the same as ⲕ)
ⲇ	ⲇⲁⲗⲇⲁ	*d*	[t]	*still* (pronounced the same as ⲧ)
ⲍ	ⲍⲏⲧⲁ	*z*	[s]	*see* (pronounced the same as ⲥ)

1.6 **Monograms.** Some letters were optionally used as monograms (a single letter representing two sounds). These were pronounced just like those two letters in succession. For example, ⲑ sounded like the *t* followed by *h* in "*get him*." ⳉⲓ, ⲫⲓ, ⲭⲓ, and ⳁⲓ are also rare in Sahidic except in Greek loanwords.

---

10. In the IPA, aspiration is marked by a superscript *h*: [kʰ] *kill*; [pʰ] *pill*; [tʰ] *till*. In some languages, aspiration (or lack thereof) is sometimes marked in spelling and can even affect meaning.

11. In concurrent Koine Greek, these three letters were pronounced as [ɣ] a soft, purred *g* like Arabic غ; [ð] *then*; and [z] *zoo*, respectively.

ⲑ	ⲑⲏⲧⲁ	*th*	[th][12]	monogram for ⲧϩ
ⲍ	ⲍⲓ	*ks*	[ks]	monogram for ⲕⲥ
ⲫ	ⲫⲓ	*ph*	[ph][13]	monogram for ⲡϩ
ⲭ	ⲭⲓ	*kh*	[kh][14]	monogram for ⲕϩ
ⲯ	ⲯⲓ	*ps*	[ps]	monogram for ⲡⲥ
ϫ	ϫⲁⲛϫⲓⲁ	*č (ch)*	[tʃ]	**ch**ild; also monogram for ⲧϣ
ϯ	ϯ	*ti*	[ti]	monogram for ⲧⲓ

1.7 Vowels and Glides. Sahidic has seven vowel letters, only the first of which needs explanation for English speakers:

ⲁ	ⲁⲗⲫⲁ	*a*	[a]	Spanish g**a**to

This *a* sound is common in many languages, but less used in English. It is close to [æ] c**a**t (especially with a British accent) or [ɑ] f**a**ther (but shorter). The rest of the vowels are common in English:

ⲉ	ⲉⲓ	*e*	[ɛ]	b**e**t[15]
ⲏ	ϩⲏⲧⲁ	*ē*	[e][16]	h**e**y
ⲓ	ⲓⲱⲧⲁ	*i*	[i]	b**ee**t; often spelled as the digram ⲉⲓ
ⲟ	ⲟⲩ	*o*	[o][17]	n**o**te
ⲱ	ⲱ	*ō*	[o]	n**o**te (perhaps drawn out a bit longer)[18]
ⲩ	ϩⲉ	*u*	[u]	b**oo**t; usually spelled as the digram ⲟⲩ[19]

If a vowel is doubled, it generally represents a longer pronunciation of that vowel.[20]

The vowel letters ⲓ and ⲩ can also be spelled with two letters, as the digrams ⲉⲓ (often, especially initially in a word) and ⲟⲩ (almost always). Besides representing the vowels [i] b**ee**t and [u] b**oo**t, they also function as the glides/semivowels [j] and [w].

ⲓ	ⲓⲱⲧⲁ	*y*	[j]	**y**et; often spelled as the digram ⲉⲓ
ⲩ	ϩⲉ	*w*	[w]	**w**et; usually spelled as the digram ⲟⲩ

---

12. In concurrent Koine Greek, this was pronounced as [θ] **th**in.
13. In concurrent Koine Greek, this was pronounced as [f] **ph**one.
14. In concurrent Koine Greek, this was pronounced as [x] Scottish lo**ch**.
15. And likely [ə] t**a**ken, when unstressed.
16. In concurrent Koine Greek, this becomes pronounced as [i] b**ee**t (the same as ⲓ).
17. Conventionally, this is often pronounced like [ɔ] n**o**t, differentiating it from ⲱ. If you have studied Koine Greek, you may be familiar with this difference, especially if you've heard Erasmian or "seminary" pronunciation. However, this Erasmian pronunciation of ⲟ lacks any historical foundation: no native Greek speaker ever made this distinction (and therefore no Sahidic speaker would've either). In fact, ⲱ was originally [ɔː] th**ough**t in Classical (Attic) Greek, but by the time of Koine Greek this was pronounced as [o] n**o**te (the same as ⲟ).
18. This would be my suggestion if you wish to (subtly) distinguish ⲟ and ⲱ.
19. ⲩ occurs frequently on its own in words of Greek origin, where in Koine Greek it originally was pronounced [y] French t**u**, later becoming [i] b**ee**t (the same as ⲓ).
20. Marked by [ː] following the vowel in the IPA. Some scholars consider doubled vowels to be a scribal practice marking the presence of a glottal stop [ʔ], with the second vowel after the glottal stop either pronounced briefly or not at all. See Lambdin, *Introduction*, xiii, and Bentley Layton, *Coptic in 20 Lessons: Introduction to Sahidic Coptic with Exercises and Vocabularies* (Leuven: Peeters, 2007), 8.

1.8 Diphthongs. Diphthongs are a combination of a vowel with a following glide, and they can occur with any of the seven basic vowels or doubled/long vowels (although certain combinations are rare). Some examples:

ⲥⲁⲉⲓⲛ	physician	[sajn]	(the diphthong sounds like "eye" in English)[21]
ⲛⲁⲩ	to see	[naw]	(the diphthong sounds like "ow" in English)
ⲡⲉⲓ̈ⲣⲱⲙⲉ	this person	[pɛj'rɔmɛ]	(the diphthong sounds like "A" [the letter] in English)
ⲉϫⲱⲓ̈	onto me	[ɛ'tʃoj]	(the diphthong sounds like "oy" in English)
ⲙⲁⲁⲩ	mother	[maːw]	(the diphthong sounds like a drawn-out "oww" in English)

Remember that the glides can be spelled either by single letters or by the digrams. Because of the variability in spelling, on occasion it may be ambiguous whether a diphthong is present. For instance, ⲉⲓ could be the simple vowel [i], the glide [j], or the diphthong [ɛj]. Context and grammatical experience will help you to tell the difference. Vocabulary listings will specify proper pronunciation, and I will use a diaeresis (ⲉⲓ̈) to mark potentially ambiguous diphthongs in those cases.[22]

EXERCISE

Copy, transliterate, and sound out the following words. Many are names of people and places you'll encounter frequently in biblical readings. Which ones do you recognize?

1. ⲓⲏⲥⲟⲩ̅ⲥ[23] _____

2. ⲡⲉ́ⲧⲣⲟⲥ _____

---

21. In concurrent Koine Greek, the combinations that had been diphthongs in Classical Greek are no longer actually pronounced that way and have instead shifted to coalesce with other vowel sounds (a process called monophthongization):
- ⲁⲓ sounds like ⲉ [ɛ];
- ⲉⲓ sounds like ⲓ [i];
- ⲟⲓ sounds like ⲩ [y] in early Koine Greek but eventually also sounds like ⲓ [i];
- ⲩⲓ perhaps remained a diphthong in early Koine Greek but eventually also sounds like ⲓ [i];
- ⲁⲩ and ⲉⲩ sound like [aw], [ew] or [aβ], [eβ] in early Koine Greek but eventually like [av], [ev]—and [af], [ef] before ⲡ, ⲧ, ⲕ, ⲫ, ⲑ, ⲭ, ⲯ, and ⲝ—as in Modern Greek.

The question arises, then, of how Copts would pronounce these combinations. Bilingual readers might switch back and forth depending on the origin of the words; readers less fluent in Greek might just pronounce everything the same according to usual Coptic norms. You can choose either way as well, depending on your background with Greek.

22. This is a practice sometimes used by Coptic scribes, but it is the opposite of how Greek scribes employed a diaeresis (to mark that the letters were separate sounds, *not* a diphthong)!

23. The accent marks on words of more than one syllable are to show which syllable receives the main stress. Emphasize that syllable when you pronounce these names. Thus this first one should be pronounced [jɛ'sus]: like "yay-SOOS," not "YAY-soos." Rules for determining Sahidic stress will be discussed in 2.5, although many of these proper names are mediated through Greek, which has its own rules for stress.

LETTERS AND SOUNDS

3. ⲓⲁ́ⲕⲱⲃⲟⲥ[24]

4. ⲓⲱϩⲁ́ⲛⲛⲏⲥ

5. ⲙⲁ́ⲣⲕⲟⲥ

6. ⲡⲁⲩ́ⲗⲟⲥ

7. ⲁⲃⲣⲁϩⲁ́ⲙ

8. ⲙⲱⲩⲥⲏ́ⲥ

9. ⲇⲁⲩⲉⲓ́ⲇ

10. ϣⲉⲛⲟⲩ́ⲧⲉ[25]

11. ⲓⲥⲣⲁⲏ́ⲗ

12. ϩⲓⲉⲣⲟⲩⲥⲁⲗⲏ́ⲙ

13. ⲓⲟⲩⲇⲁⲓ́ⲁ

14. ⲅⲁⲗⲓⲗⲁⲓ́ⲁ

15. ⲕⲏ́ⲙⲉ[26]

16. ⲣⲁⲕⲟ́ⲧⲉ[27]

17. ⲙⲛϥⲉ[28]

18. ϣⲙⲟⲩⲛ[29]

---

24. Through the vagaries of time and language switches, this name somehow becomes "James" in English!
25. The famed writer and leader of the White Monastery in the fourth and fifth centuries.
26. This is the Sahidic name for Egypt ("Egypt" is derived from Greek αἴγυπτος).
27. This is the Sahidic name of the city known in Greek as ἀλεξάνδρεια.
28. μέμφις in Greek.
29. ερμούπολις in Greek.

CHAPTER 2

SCRIBAL MARKS AND SYLLABLES

OVERVIEW

In this chapter, you will learn:

- The usage and pronunciation of the Sahidic overline
- Scribal abbreviations of special words
- How words are divided into syllables and where to place stress
- How Sahidic sentences are divided up
- Certain spelling changes to watch out for

THE SAHIDIC OVERLINE

2.1 **The Overline.** Besides adding additional letters to the adopted Greek alphabet, one other innovation made by Sahidic scribes was the use of a line over certain consonants to show that they are preceded by a shwa, a somewhat indistinct, unstressed vowel sound [ə], like the e in *taken*. This *overline*[1] can theoretically occur over any consonant, but it is most commonly found over the letters ʙ, ʎ, ᴍ, ɴ, and ᴘ. These five are sonorant consonants, meaning that they can be pronounced with a drawn-out, lengthened pronunciation (like vowels and glides but unlike stops). Some examples [with IPA]:

ʙp̄pé[2]	[βər'rɛ]	new, young (adjective)
м̄ᴍᴀʏ	[əm'maw]	there (adverb)
ᴍɴ̄ᴛpé	[mənt'rɛ]	witness, testimony (noun)
ɴ̄ᴋoᴛᴋ̄	[ən'kotək]	to lie down, sleep (verb)

---

1. This is also called the superlinear/supralinear/supraliteral stroke or bar. Similar overlines or tick marks are used by other dialects as well.
2. The accent mark at the end is to show the main stress is on the final syllable -pé (an exception to the usual stress rules of Sahidic). See below, 2.5. This is a modern innovation, which we will use in examples and vocabulary lists.

You will also find that sometimes an expected overline is spelled with an ⲉ, and sometimes this occurs the other way around too. Different scribes (and different dialects and those dialects' influence on them) also utilize the overline with varying styles—including longer overlines bridging to the left of the affected consonant. Due to these fluctuations, modern editions of Sahidic texts, especially online ones,[3] will sometimes choose to omit the overline entirely in their transcriptions.

2.2 **Scribal Abbreviations.** Following the practice of Greek scribes, Coptic scribes utilized a form of abbreviation to mark certain words as special.[4] These were also marked by a long overline over all the letters in the abbreviation. In manuscripts, many important words were regularly treated this way. In our texts, we will usually use the "unpacked," spelled-out forms of these words for clarity. Some are proper names of major biblical people and places:

ⲓⲏⲥⲟⲩⲥ	(abbreviated as ⲓ̅ⲥ̅ or ⲓ̅ⲏ̅ⲥ̅)
ⲇⲁⲩⲉⲓⲇ	(abbreviated as ⲇ̅ⲁ̅ⲇ̅)
ⲑⲓⲉⲣⲟⲩⲥⲁⲗⲏⲙ[5]	(abbreviated as ⲑ̅ⲓ̅ⲗ̅ⲏ̅ⲙ̅ or ⲑ̅ⲓ̅ⲏ̅ⲙ̅)
ⲓⲥⲣⲁⲏⲗ	(abbreviated as ⲓ̅ⲏ̅ⲗ̅)

Other "special" terms and titles were given a similar treatment as well:[6]

ⲡⲛⲉⲩⲙⲁ	spirit (abbreviated as ⲡ̅ⲛ̅ⲁ̅)
ⲥⲧⲁⲩⲣⲟⲥ	execution stake[7] (abbreviated as ⲥ̅ⲣ̅ⲟ̅ⲥ̅)
ⲥⲱⲧⲏⲣ	deliverer (abbreviated as ⲥ̅ⲱ̅ⲣ̅)
ⲭⲣⲓⲥⲧⲟⲥ	anointed one (abbreviated as ⲭ̅ⲥ̅ or ⲭ̅ⲣ̅ⲥ̅)
ϫⲟⲉⲓⲥ	master (abbreviated as ϫ̅ⲥ̅)

RIGHTLY DIVIDING THE WORDS

2.3 **Word and Syllable Divisions.** Take a look at the image of a page from a parchment Sahidic codex (fig. 2). This manuscript, written around 600 CE, contains Paul's letters and the Gospel of John in Sahidic.[8] You'll notice that Coptic scribes (like their Greek counterparts) did not usually separate words within sentences but instead ran them together in a continuous string of letters. Word divisions are therefore modern editorial decisions, usually employing a space or, in certain circumstances, a hyphen to ease

---

3. See, for instance, the texts on the Coptic Scriptorium website (https://data.copticscriptorium.org/index/corpus/).
4. These are referred to as *nomina sacra* ("holy names") in Latin.
5. This spelling with ⲑ is because it is including the definite article, see 3.3.
6. I will be marking Coptic words that are of Greek origin in grey (except for proper names).
7. The Latin terminology for crucifixion is derived from the cross (*crux*) formed by the crossbeam (*patibulum*) joined to the main upright beam (*stipes*)—the Greek terminology is (originally) descriptive of that central stake (ⲥⲧⲁⲩⲣⲟⲥ).
8. This manuscript is housed in Dublin, in the Chester Beatty Library (Copt. Ms. 813). Images of the manuscript can be found online at https://viewer.cbl.ie/viewer/image/Cpt_813/9/LOG_0000/.

modern readers' processing of the sentences. Some small words, such as the definite and indirect articles (see chapters 3 and 4), are typically left prefixed to the beginning of their main words without any intervening spaces or hyphens.

2.4 **Main Stress.** How and why we separate certain words with spaces as opposed to connecting them with hyphens is determined by the important concept of the *bound phrase*. Sahidic sentences often contain multiple words grouped together in phrases. Many smaller words like articles, prepositions, and some particles are "proclitic"—they aren't pronounced with an emphasis of their own and are instead pronounced as part of a phrase with the main stress on a final "main" word. Prepositions

Fig. 2. Dublin, Chester Beatty Library Copt. Ms. 813, 3r: ⲧⲉⲡⲣⲟⲥ-ϩⲣⲱⲙⲁⲓⲟⲩⲥ Romans 1.1–10

and certain parts of verbal conjugations are marked off by hyphens to ease reading analysis, but they should be considered part of the same bound phrase for pronunciation purposes. Spaces separate bound phrases; anything between spaces, including any parts connected by hyphens, is considered part of the same bound phrase, and each bound phrase has a *single* emphasized syllable. As an example, here's a line from Psalm 1.1:

ⲙ̄ⲡⲉϥⲁϩⲉⲣⲁⲧϥ̄ ϩⲓ-ⲧⲉϩⲓⲏ ⲛ̄-ⲛ̄ⲣⲉϥⲣ̄-ⲛⲟⲃⲉ

This line contains three bound phrases (the first is a verbal phrase, and the last two are noun phrases).

Sometimes a bound phrase will contain just a single syllable word, but often lots of syllables are connected together in a single phrase. How do we determine which syllable to emphasize when pronouncing it? If in doubt, follow these rules in order until you've resolved the question:[9]

1. The stress will always be on one of the last two syllables in the phrase.
2. ⲏ, ⲟ, ⲱ, or doubled (long) vowels are always stressed.
3. Final simple -ⲁ and simple -(ⲉ)ⲓ are always stressed.
4. Final -ⲟⲩ is stressed, except

---

9. Modified from Thomas O. Lambdin, *Introduction to Sahidic Coptic* (Macon, GA: Mercer University Press, 1983), xv–xvi. Do keep in mind that these rules only apply to words of Egyptian origin; Greek accentuation patterns frequently do their own thing, and I will mark the stressed syllable of Greek words (including proper nouns) with an accent mark in vocabulary lists *if* these deviate from Coptic norms.

a. the third-person plural personal suffix (see 7.2)
b. with the words ⲡⲁϩⲟⲩ, ⲥⲡⲟⲧⲟⲩ, ⲥⲁϩⲟⲩ, and ⲣⲁⲥⲟⲩ.[10]
5. Final -ⲉ is *un*stressed, except
   a. adjectives like ⲃⲣ̄ⲣⲉ́ and ⲥⲁⲃⲉ́ (see chapter 5)
   b. certain other words: ⲃⲉⲕⲉ́, ⲕⲛ̄ⲧⲉ́, ⲙⲛ̄ⲧⲣⲉ́, ⲛⲁⲙⲉ́.
6. A final syllable marked by an overlined consonant is *un*stressed (unless it's the word's only syllable).

Here's that earlier phrase with the syllables that should be emphasized, along with the rule that determined it:

ⲙ̄ⲡⲉϥⲁϩⲉⲣⲁ́ⲧϥ̄ (rule 6) ϩⲓ-ⲧⲉϩⲓⲏ́ (rule 2) ⲛ̄-ⲛ̄ⲣⲉϥⲣ̄-ⲛⲟ́ⲃⲉ (rule 2)

2.5 **Other Divisions.** By modern standards, Coptic scribes used minimal punctuation. Take a look at fig. 2 again. The ends of major sentences can be marked with a raised dot (·), similar to a period but higher up. Larger section breaks are marked with doubled dots (:), similar in appearance to a colon. A section break can also be signaled in the left margin through the use of *paragraphos* lines and larger, "outdented" initial letters. Poetic texts like the Psalms are often set in a stichometric layout, with the text laid out in poetic line. Special paratextual features like titles and headings are usually offset from the main text through the use of decorative ornamentation, different ink, and/or different script.

Ancient biblical texts, of course, did not have modern chapter or verse numeration. There were earlier systems of section divisions and cross references that were devised, and these are sometimes found in the margins of manuscripts.

Throughout this book—in the examples, exercises, and extended readings found at the end—modern punctuation will be implemented to aid comprehension.

SPELLING CHANGES

2.6 **Letter Changes.** Certain letters or combinations of letters may change spelling depending on their context.

- ⲛ̄ normally assimilates to ⲙ̄ before ⲡ and ⲙ

This is a frequent and consistent change you will find regularly. As you will see, there are lots of ways you can encounter ⲛ̄! Less commonly:

- ⲉ followed by ⲟⲩ can combine into ⲉⲩ
- ⲁ followed by ⲟⲩ can combine into ⲁⲩ

---

10. Exceptions like these will be marked with an accent on the vowel of the stressed syllable in vocabulary lists.

Finally, remember that some letters are used as monograms for two letters in sequence. ⲑ is especially common for ⲧ followed by ϩ.

2.7 **Greek Spellings.** Sahidic has lots of words of Greek origin, but Sahidic scribes sometimes have unique spellings for them, usually (we assume) based on how these words came to be pronounced regionally in Egypt. Keep this in mind if you've already studied Greek; if you haven't, don't worry about it, although you will be learning a bunch of Greek vocabulary as part of your study of Sahidic (you're welcome)! As noted above, throughout our vocabulary lists and examples, words of Greek origin—or those transmitted from other languages through Greek—will be colored grey.

EXERCISE

Below is the text of Psalm 1. Copy and practice sounding out this text, marking where the stress should be placed in the each bound phrase (follow the rules in 2.5—words of Greek origin that would deviate from those rules are already marked with accents). Don't worry about translation yet; we'll revisit this text as you learn more vocabulary.

1 ⲛⲁⲓ̈ⲁⲧϥ̄ ⲙ̄-ⲡⲣⲱⲙⲉ ⲉⲧⲉ-[11]
   ⲙ̄ⲡⲉϥⲃⲱⲕ ϩⲙ̄-ⲡϣⲟϫⲛⲉ ⲛ̄-ⲛ̄ⲁⲥⲉⲃⲏⲥ,
   ⲙ̄ⲡⲉϥⲁϩⲉⲣⲁⲧϥ̄ ϩⲓ-ⲧⲉϩⲓⲏ ⲛ̄-ⲛ̄ⲣⲉϥⲣ̄-ⲛⲟⲃⲉ,
   ⲙ̄ⲡⲉϥϩⲙⲟⲟⲥ ϩⲓ-ⲧⲕⲁⲑⲉ́ⲇⲣⲁ ⲛ̄-ⲛ̄ⲗⲟⲓⲙⲟ́ⲥ.

2 ⲁⲗⲗⲁ ⲉⲣⲉ-ⲡⲉϥⲟⲩⲱϣ ϣⲟⲟⲡ ϩⲙ̄-ⲡⲛⲟ́ⲙⲟⲥ ⲙ̄-ⲡϫⲟⲉⲓⲥ,
   ⲁⲩⲱ ϥⲛⲁⲙⲉⲗⲉⲧⲁ ⲙ̄-ⲡⲉϥⲛⲟ́ⲙⲟⲥ ⲙ̄-ⲡⲉϩⲟⲟⲩ ⲙⲛ̄-ⲧⲉⲩϣⲏ.

3 ϥⲛⲁⲣ̄-ⲑⲉ ⲙ̄-ⲡϣⲏⲛ,
   ⲉⲧⲣⲏⲧ ϩⲓϫⲛ̄-ⲙ̄ⲙⲁ ⲛ̄-ϩⲁⲧⲉ ⲙ̄-ⲙⲟⲟⲩ.
ⲡⲁⲓ̈ ⲉⲧⲛⲁϯ ⲙ̄-ⲡⲉϥⲕⲁⲣⲡⲟⲥ ϩⲙ̄-ⲡⲉϥⲟⲩⲟⲉⲓϣ,
   ⲛ̄-ⲛⲉϥϭⲱⲃⲉ ⲛⲁⲥⲣⲟϥⲣⲉϥ ⲁⲛ,
   ϩⲱⲃ ⲛⲓⲙ ⲉⲧϥ̄ⲛⲁⲁⲁⲩ ⲛⲁⲥⲟⲟⲩⲧⲛ̄.

4 ⲛ̄-ⲧⲁⲓ̈ ⲁⲛ ⲧⲉ ⲑⲉ ⲛ̄-ⲛ̄ⲁⲥⲉⲃⲏⲥ, ⲛ̄-ⲧⲁⲓ̈ ⲁⲛ ⲧⲉ ⲑⲉ!
   ⲁⲗⲗⲁ ⲉⲩⲛⲁⲣ̄-ⲑⲉ ⲙ̄-ⲡϣⲟⲉⲓϣ,
   ⲉ-ϣⲁⲣⲉ-ⲡⲧⲏⲩ ⲑⲗⲟϥ ⲉⲃⲟⲗ ϩⲓϫⲙ̄-ⲡϩⲟ ⲙ̄-ⲡⲕⲁϩ.

5 ⲉⲧⲃⲉ-ⲡⲁⲓ̈ ⲙⲛ̄-ⲁⲥⲉⲃⲏⲥ ⲛⲁⲧⲱⲟⲩⲛ ϩⲛ̄-ⲧⲉⲕⲣⲓ́ⲥⲓⲥ,
   ⲟⲩⲇⲉ́ ⲣⲉϥⲣ̄-ⲛⲟⲃⲉ ϩⲛ̄-ⲧⲥⲩⲛⲁⲅⲱⲅⲏ́ ⲛ̄-ⲛ̄ⲇⲓ́ⲕⲁⲓⲟⲥ.

6 ϫⲉ ⲡϫⲟⲉⲓⲥ ⲥⲟⲟⲩⲛ̄ ⲛ̄-ⲧⲉϩⲓⲏ ⲛ̄-ⲛ̄ⲇⲓ́ⲕⲁⲓⲟⲥ,
   ⲧⲉϩⲓⲏ ⲇⲉ ⲛ̄-ⲛ̄ⲁⲥⲉⲃⲏⲥ ⲛⲁϩⲉ ⲉⲃⲟⲗ.

---

11. This word counts as part of the bound phrase at the start of the next line, but I leave it here with a hyphen because it also connects syntactically with the following two lines after that.

THE SAHIDIC NOUN SYSTEM

CHAPTER 3

NOUNS AND THE DEFINITE ARTICLE

OVERVIEW

In this chapter, you will learn:

- How nouns are categorized by gender and number
- The forms and usage of the definite article
- Your first set of vocabulary words

NOUNS

3.1 **Noun Gender.** Coptic nouns have grammatical gender, either *masculine* or *feminine*. A few words can be either. Learning the correct gender of nouns is an important part of vocabulary, and this information will always be included in the vocabulary lists at the end of chapters from now on (after the definition in parentheses: nm for "noun, masculine"; nf for "noun, feminine"; and nmf for the few words that could be either). Biologically male and female beings, not surprisingly, are typically grammatically male and female respectively, but for the majority of words you will need to learn their seemingly arbitrary gender. In a grammatical sense, Coptic conceives of all things as either "he" or "she"—there's no neuter "it" such as is common in Indo-European languages like Greek, Latin, Sanskrit, or German.

You will find that sometimes masculine and feminine pairs of related words have recognizably similar forms:

masculine		**feminine**	
ⲣ̄ⲣⲟ	king, monarch	ⲣ̄ⲣⲱ	queen
ⲥⲟⲛ	brother, sibling	ⲥⲱⲛⲉ	sister
ϭⲁⲙⲟⲩⲗ	male camel	ϭⲁⲙⲁⲩⲗⲉ	female camel

It is helpful to learn such words in pairs, particularly noting the variation in the vowels. In vocabulary lists and in the lexicon, these are listed under the masculine form, with the feminine form in parentheses after the definition. You'll notice that these examples are people or animals, but not all such potential biological pairings have variant forms—some use a common form, with the specific gender in question being relayed by the gender of the prefixed definite article (see 3.3 below):

| ϩⲙ̄ϩⲁⲗ | male slave or female slave |
| ⲙⲟⲩ(ⲉ)ⲓ | lion or lioness |

As we've already seen, a significant portion of Coptic vocabulary is borrowed from Greek. Masculine and feminine Greek nouns retain their gender, with neuter Greek nouns being treated as masculine in Coptic. For instance, the neuter word ⲡⲛⲉⲩ́ⲙⲁ in Greek is treated as being masculine in Coptic.

3.2 **Noun Number.** Besides gender, nouns also have number, either *singular* or *plural*. Some nouns retain old special forms to denote plurality through internal spelling changes (often with the vowels, like English "t**oo**th/t**ee**th"), through a special plural ending (like English "cat/cat**s**"), or through some combination of the two. However, many nouns do not mark plurality in the form of the noun itself, with this information being signaled only by the plural form of the article prefixed to the word (see 3.3–4 below). A large number of the nouns given in this chapter's vocabulary list have special plural forms, but keep in mind that this is not representative of Sahidic nouns as a whole. Even for these nouns, the use of the special plural form is optional—the standard form can also be used for plurals.

A few words of Greek origin can also be given a distinctly Coptic plural ending (-ⲟⲟⲩⲉ):

singular		**plural**	
ⲅⲣⲁⲫⲏ	writing	ⲅⲣⲁⲫⲟⲟⲩⲉ	writing**s**
ⲉⲡⲓⲥⲧⲟⲗⲏ́	letter	ⲉⲡⲓⲥⲧⲟⲗⲟⲟⲩⲉ	letter**s**
ⲯⲩⲭⲏ	self, (inner) being	ⲯⲩⲭⲟⲟⲩⲉ	sel**ves**, (inner) being**s**

THE DEFINITE ARTICLE

3.3 **Forms of the Definite Article.** Like English and Greek, Coptic has a definite article roughly equivalent to the word "the." The definite article also shows gender (in the singular) and number (singular or plural), taking these forms:

ⲡ-, ⲡⲉ-	*masculine singular*
ⲧ-,[1] ⲧⲉ-	*feminine singular*
ⲛ̄-,[2] ⲛⲉ-	*common plural*

---

1. With words starting with ϩ, ⲧ- frequently combines with it to be spelled ⲑ. With words starting with (ⲉ)ⲓ, it frequently combines as ϯ.

2. Assimilating regularly to ⲙ̄- before ⲡ and ⲙ (see 2.6).

NOUNS AND THE DEFINITE ARTICLE

These are prefixed directly to the front of the noun, without hyphens or spaces:

ⲡⲣ̄ⲣⲟ[3]	**the** king
ⲧⲉⲡⲓⲥⲧⲟⲗⲏ́	**the** letter
ⲛ̄ϫⲓⲥⲟⲟⲩⲉ	**the** masters
ⲙ̄ⲙⲁⲑⲏⲧⲏ́ⲥ	**the** students

Before words beginning with two consonants, the longer forms (ⲡⲉ-, ⲧⲉ-, ⲛⲉ-) are used.[4]

ⲡⲉϣⲃⲏⲣ	**the** friend
ⲧⲉⲅⲣⲁⲫⲏ	**the** writing
ⲛⲉϩⲧⲱⲱⲣ	**the** horses

3.4 Translating the Definite Article. Think of the definite article as the key to the noun's gender and number. Many nouns do not have separate forms for the plural (and for those that do, their use seems to be optional), so in addition to translating the definite article as "the," the form of the definite article will be what tells you if you need to add "-s" to the end of the noun. For example:

singular		**plural**	
ⲡϭⲁⲙⲟⲩⲗ	**the** (male) camel	ⲛ̄ϭⲁⲙⲟⲩⲗ	**the** camel**s**
ⲧⲙⲁⲁⲩ	**the** mother	ⲙ̄ⲙⲁⲁⲩ	**the** mother**s**

The definite article is also attached to nouns used to address someone directly (called the vocative use), but in this case we don't need to include it in our English translations.

VOCABULARY

Each chapter from now on will include a list of important Sahidic words to learn. Many of the ones in this list are very common—commit them to memory!

ⲣ̄ⲣⲟ (pl ⲣ̄ⲣⲱⲟⲩ, ⲉⲣⲱⲟⲩ)	king, monarch (nm; ⲣ̄ⲣⲱ, queen [f])
ⲉⲓⲱⲧ (pl ⲉⲓⲟⲧⲉ)	father; pl: parents, ancestors (nm)
ⲙⲁⲁⲩ	mother (nf)[5]
ⲥⲟⲛ (pl ⲥⲛⲏⲩ)	brother, sibling (nm; ⲥⲱⲛⲉ, sister [f])[6]
ϣⲏⲣⲉ (pl ϣⲣⲏⲩ)	son, child (nm; ϣⲉⲉⲣⲉ, daughter [f])
ϣⲃⲏⲣ (pl ϣⲃⲉⲉⲣ)	friend, companion (nm; ϣⲃⲉⲉⲣⲉ [f])

---

3. Does this word (with its definite article attached) sound familiar? In fact, the ⲡ- was originally part of the word—a phrase meaning "Great House" (*pr ꜥꜣ*) that was used to address the king of Egypt. The ⲡ- was later re-analyzed as being the prefixed article.
4. These longer forms are also used with a few words for time periods (ⲟⲩⲟⲉⲓϣ, ⲣⲟⲙⲡⲉ, ϩⲟⲟⲩ). See 9.3.
5. ⲉⲓⲱⲧ and ⲙⲁⲁⲩ are also used figuratively as titles of respect for leaders of monastic communities.
6. ⲥⲟⲛ and ⲥⲱⲛⲉ are also used by members of monastic communities as titles for fellow members.

THE SAHIDIC NOUN SYSTEM

ⲙⲁⲑⲏⲧⲏⲥ	student, learner[7] (nm)
ϫⲟⲉⲓⲥ (pl ϫⲓⲥⲟⲟⲩⲉ)	master (abbreviated as $\overline{\text{ⲭⲥ}}$) (nmf)
ϩⲙ̄ϩⲁⲗ	slave, servant (nmf)
ϩⲧⲟ (pl ϩⲧⲱⲱⲣ)	horse (nm; ϩⲧⲱⲣⲉ [f])
ϭⲁⲙⲟⲩⲗ	camel (nm; ϭⲁⲙⲁⲩⲗⲉ [f])
ⲟⲩϩⲟⲣ[8] (pl ⲟⲩϩⲟⲟⲣ)	dog (nm; ⲟⲩϩⲱⲣⲉ [f])
ⲉⲙⲟⲩ (pl ⲉⲙⲟⲟⲩⲉ)	cat (nmf)
ⲙⲟⲩ(ⲉ)ⲓ	lion(ess) (nmf)
ⲅⲣⲁⲫⲏ (pl ⲅⲣⲁⲫⲟⲟⲩⲉ)	writing, scripture (nf)
ⲉⲡⲓⲥⲧⲟⲗⲏ (pl ⲉⲡⲓⲥⲧⲟⲗⲟⲟⲩⲉ)	letter (nf)
ⲯⲩⲭⲏ (pl ⲯⲩⲭⲟⲟⲩⲉ)	self, (inner) being (nf)
ⲡⲛⲉⲩⲙⲁ	spirit (abbreviated as $\overline{\text{ⲡⲛⲁ}}$) (nm)

EXERCISE

Copy and translate the following phrases. Pay attention to the form of the definite article!

1. ⲛⲉϣⲣⲏⲩ _____

2. ⲡⲉⲩϩⲟⲣ _____

3. ⲧⲙⲟⲩⲉⲓ _____

4. ⲛ̄ⲣ̄ⲣⲱⲟⲩ _____

5. ⲡⲥⲟⲛ _____

6. ⲛⲉⲯⲩⲭⲟⲟⲩⲉ _____

7. ⲧⲉϣⲃⲉⲉⲣⲉ _____

8. ⲛ̄ϫⲓⲥⲟⲟⲩⲉ _____

9. ⲑⲙ̄ϩⲁⲗ _____

10. ⲙ̄ⲙⲁⲑⲏⲧⲏⲥ _____

11. ⲡⲉⲓⲱⲧ _____

12. ⲛⲉⲡⲛⲉⲩⲙⲁ _____

---

7. The traditional gloss for this—"disciple"— is derived from the Latin word *discipulus*, which also means "student, learner."
8. Note: the initial ⲟⲩ is [w], not [u], so this word begins with a consonant cluster [whor].

CHAPTER 4

THE INDEFINITE ARTICLE AND OWNERSHIP

OVERVIEW

In this chapter, you will learn:

- The forms and usage of the indefinite article
- How to show ownership of one noun by another

THE INDEFINITE ARTICLE

4.1 **Forms of the Indefinite Article.** In addition to the definite article, Coptic also has an indefinite article (like English but unlike Greek). The indefinite article only shows number (singular or plural), not gender.

ⲟⲩ-	*common singular*
ϩⲉⲛ- (ϩⲛ̄-)	*common plural*

The plural form is most often spelled ϩⲉⲛ- (as we will consistently do in our examples and exercises), but in texts it sometimes spelled with the shorter form ϩⲛ̄-, which unfortunately looks like the very common preposition ϩⲛ̄- ("in," see 7.1).

Like definite articles, these are also prefixed directly to the front of the noun:

singular		**plural**	
ⲟⲩⲣⲱⲙⲉ	a person, human	ϩⲉⲛⲣⲱⲙⲉ	(**some**) people, human**s**
ⲟⲩϫⲱⲱⲙⲉ	a scroll	ϩⲉⲛϫⲱⲱⲙⲉ	(**some**) scroll**s**
ⲟⲩⲡⲟⲗⲓⲥ	a city	ϩⲉⲛⲡⲟⲗⲓⲥ	(**some**) cit**ies**

4.2 **Translating the Indefinite Article.** In general, the indefinite article can be translated "a" (for singular) or "some" (for plural). In English, indefinite plurals often have no article—we can just say "houses" instead of "some houses."

Coptic usage of the indefinite (and definite) articles does not always track with how we use these in English. For example, Coptic will regularly use an article with abstract nouns, where we would not in English. The phrase ϨⲚ-ⲞⲨⲘⲈ ("truly") literally means "in a truth." Become familiar with Coptic idioms like these, even if you don't literally express them in translation.

CONNECTING NOUNS

4.3 **Showing Ownership.** To show that one noun belongs to or is closely associated with another, they are connected with the use of ⲚЇ-[1] prefixed to the second noun (the "owner" of the first noun). This genitive particle/preposition can be translated as "of," or you can rephrase it with an apostrophe s (X's) after the "owner" noun.

ⲦϬⲒϪ Ⲛ̄-ⲦⲢ̄ⲢⲰ	the hand **of** the queen *or* the queen**'s** hand
ⲠⲚⲞⲘⲞⲤ Ⲙ̄-ⲠϪⲞⲈⲒⲤ	the law **of** the Master *or* the Master**'s** law
ⲠⲎЇ Ⲛ̄-ⲚⲈⲒⲞⲦⲈ	the house **of** the parents *or* the parents**'** house

This genitive construction is normally used if both nouns are definite. If the first is indefinite, the longer form ⲚⲦⲈ- may be used instead. With this construction, it's better to translate using "of" (rephrasing with apostrophe s [X's] can obscure the indefiniteness of the owned noun).

ⲞⲨϪⲰⲰⲘⲈ Ⲛ̄ⲦⲈ-ⲠⲘⲀⲐⲎⲦⲎⲤ   a scroll **of** the student

4.4 **"The Ⲛ̄-s."** Sahidic is fond of prefixed Ⲛ̄-s. You've seen two already:

Ⲛ̄-   "the"   *common plural definite article*
Ⲛ̄-   "of"   *genitive particle/preposition*

More similar words will be coming, and it will be important to keep these very common, similar looking prefixed words separated in your mind as we proceed. For reference, the five main ways you'll encounter Ⲛ̄- and related forms are summarized in Appendix 1: Survey of "the Ⲛ̄-s."

VOCABULARY

ⲚⲞⲨⲦⲈ (pl Ⲛ̄ⲦⲎⲢ, ⲈⲚⲦⲀⲒⲢ)   god; with definite article: God[2] (nm; Ⲛ̄ⲦⲰⲢⲈ, goddess [f])

---

1. Assimilating regularly to Ⲙ̄- before Π and Ⲙ (see 2.6). This and other simple prepositions are prefixed with a hyphen, showing that they are proclitic (no stress of their own, see 2.4).
2. Like Greek, the use of the definite article signals that it is *the* God—the only true one—that is being discussed. In English, we can signal this emphasis with capitalization.

THE INDEFINITE ARTICLE AND OWNERSHIP

ⲣⲱⲙⲉ	person, human; humanity[3] (nmf)
ϩⲟⲟⲩⲧ	male, man (nm)
ϩⲁⲓ̈	husband (nm)
ⲥϩⲓⲙⲉ (pl ϩⲓⲟⲙⲉ)	female, woman; wife (nf)
ϩⲓⲙⲉ (pl ϩⲓⲟⲙⲉ[4])	wife (nf)
ϣⲁϫⲉ	word, speech; matter (nm)
ϫⲱⲱⲙⲉ	scroll, document[5] (nm)
ⲛⲟⲙⲟⲥ	law, code (nm)
ⲙⲉ(ⲉ)	truth (nf)
ϭⲓϫ	hand (nf)
ⲟⲩⲉⲣⲏⲧⲉ, ⲟⲩⲣⲏⲏⲧⲉ	foot (nf)
ⲃⲁⲗ	eye (nm)
ϩⲓⲏ[6] (pl ϩⲓⲟⲟⲩⲉ)	road, way, path (nf)
ⲏ(ⲉ)ⲓ	house (nm)
ⲁⲅⲟⲣⲁ	marketplace (nf)
ⲣ̄ⲡⲉ[7] (pl ⲣ̄ⲡⲏⲩⲉ)	temple (nm)
ⲡⲟⲗⲓⲥ	city (nf)
ⲕⲁϩ	land, earth, ground (nm)
ⲡⲉ (pl ⲡⲏⲩⲉ)	sky (nf)

EXERCISE

Copy and translate the following phrases.

1. ⲟⲩϭⲁⲙⲟⲩⲗ ⲛ̄ⲧⲉ-ⲡⲥⲟⲛ _____

2. ⲡⲛⲟⲙⲟⲥ ⲛ̄-ⲧⲡⲟⲗⲓⲥ _____

3. ⲧⲉϣⲃⲉⲉⲣⲉ ⲛ̄-ⲧⲥⲱⲛⲉ _____

4. ⲡϣⲁϫⲉ ⲙ̄-ⲡϫⲟⲉⲓⲥ _____

5. ϩⲉⲛϩⲧⲱⲱⲣ ⲛ̄-ⲛ̄ⲣ̄ⲣⲱⲟⲩ _____

6. ⲧⲉⲡⲓⲥⲧⲟⲗⲏ ⲙ̄-ⲡϩⲁⲓ̈ _____

---

3. The singular can be an individual (a human) or collective (humanity), as in the important title ⲡϣⲏⲣⲉ ⲙ̄-ⲡⲣⲱⲙⲉ, the Son of Humanity.

4. While the singular forms are unambiguous, the same plural form is used for "wives" (specifically married women) and "women" (more generally).

5. Scrolls largely give way to the codex—pages bound together in book form—by the sixth century CE.

6. Note: this word begins with a consonant cluster [hje].

7. When definite, the overline can be dropped and the longer form of the article used (ⲡⲉⲣⲡⲉ or ⲡⲣ̄ⲡⲉ).

7. ⲡⲃⲁⲗ ⲛ̄-ⲧⲉⲙⲟⲩ

8. ⲧⲙⲉ ⲛ̄-ⲛ̄ϣⲁϫⲉ

9. ⲡⲉⲓⲱⲧ ⲛ̄-ⲧⲉⲥϩⲓⲙⲉ

10. ⲟⲩⲛⲟⲩⲧⲉ ⲛ̄ⲧⲉ-ⲡⲉⲣⲡⲉ

11. ⲧⲉⲯⲩⲭⲏ ⲙ̄-ⲡⲣⲱⲙⲉ

12. ⲧⲟⲩⲉⲣⲏⲧⲉ ⲙ̄-ⲡⲉⲩϩⲟⲣ

Look back at the text of Psalm 1 at the end of chapter 2. What words and constructions can you now recognize? Write translations of what you know below the Sahidic words. Based on the context, are there other words whose meaning you can now start to guess?

CHAPTER 5

ADJECTIVES AND NOMINAL SENTENCES

OVERVIEW

In this chapter, you will learn:

- How to modify nouns with adjectives
- How to form two kinds of simple nominal sentences (sentences without verbs)

ADJECTIVES

5.1 **Modifying Nouns.** In the last chapter (4.3), we saw how the genitive particle/preposition ⲛ̄- "of" is used to connect two nouns to show ownership. With that construction, the second "owner" noun was definite. Another way this genitive particle/preposition is used is to treat a noun like an adjective. If the second noun in the construction lacks an article, it is acting like an adjective, modifying the noun by adding further description to it. Note the difference:

ⲡϫⲱⲱⲙⲉ ⲛ̄-ⲧⲙⲉ	the scroll of the truth *or* the truth's scroll
ⲡϫⲱⲱⲙⲉ **ⲙ̄-ⲙⲉ**	the **true** scroll
ⲡⲃⲁⲗ ⲙ̄-ⲡⲣⲱⲙⲉ	the eye of the person *or* the person's eye
ⲡⲃⲁⲗ **ⲛ̄-ⲣⲱⲙⲉ**	the **human** eye
ⲟⲩⲙⲟⲩⲉⲓ ⲛ̄ⲧⲉ-ⲡϩⲟⲟⲩⲧ	a lion of the man
ⲟⲩⲙⲟⲩⲉⲓ **ⲛ̄-ϩⲟⲟⲩⲧ**	a **male**[1] lion

These related adjectival meanings are usually easy to determine from the meaning of the noun. This attributive/adjectival construction can be done with almost any noun.

5.2 **Egyptian "Adjectives."** Besides adjectival usage of nouns, there is a small group of common native Egyptian nouns that regularly function as adjectives. Technically, they

---

[1]. This adjectival usage of ϩⲟⲟⲩⲧ can also carry the nuance of "wild, savage."

are "nouns of quality," but due to their frequent usage in this manner I will list these as adjectives ("adj") in vocabulary lists and the lexicon.[2]

These "adjectives" are also linked to the noun they modify by the genitive particle/preposition ⲛ̄- (with only one article at the beginning of the phrase). One special feature they have is that they can be placed either before or after the noun:

ⲡϩⲗⲗⲟ ⲛ̄-ⲣ̄ⲣⲟ *or* ⲡⲣ̄ⲣⲟ ⲛ̄-ϩⲗⲗⲟ	the **old** king
ⲟⲩⲥⲁⲉⲓⲉ ⲙ̄-ⲡⲟⲗⲓⲥ *or* ⲟⲩⲡⲟⲗⲓⲥ ⲛ̄-ⲥⲁⲉⲓⲉ	a **beautiful** city
ⲛ̄ϫⲓϫⲉⲉⲩⲉ ⲛ̄-ϫⲓⲥⲟⲟⲩⲉ *or* ⲛ̄ϫⲓⲥⲟⲟⲩⲉ ⲛ̄-ϫⲓϫⲉⲉⲩⲉ	the **hostile** masters

As in the last example (ϫⲓϫⲉⲉⲩⲉ, plural form of ϫⲁϫⲉ), some have specialized plural or feminine forms that may optionally be used. Despite the general flexibility about placement, certain terms have a preference to be placed either before or after the noun:

| ⲟⲩⲛⲟϭ ⲙ̄-ⲡⲛⲉⲩⲙⲁ | a **great** spirit |
| ⲧϣⲟⲣⲡⲉ ⲛ̄-ⲥϩⲓⲙⲉ | the **first** woman |

And finally, a few can appear after the noun without the linking ⲛ̄-, although these are usually just in older, fixed phrases like ϣⲏⲣⲉ ϣⲏⲙ (**small** child). ⲛⲓⲙ ("every, each") is a special case in that it always follows a singular noun without an article or linking ⲛ̄-:

| ⲥϩⲓⲙⲉ ⲛⲓⲙ | **every** woman |
| ⲡⲟⲗⲓⲥ ⲛⲓⲙ | **every** city |

These special preferences will be noted with given vocabulary. Otherwise, you can assume that either position could be used. The choice of which to place first is likely a matter of emphasis.

5.3   **Greek Adjectives.** In addition, many Greek adjectives are also incorporated into Coptic, and these can also be placed before or after the noun they're modifying. The form they take matches the Greek nominative case,[3] usually in either the Greek masculine (such as ⲁⲅⲁⲑⲟⲥ) or neuter (ⲁⲅⲁⲑⲟⲛ) form. While occasionally you may find a specifically feminine Greek form (ⲁⲅⲁⲑⲏ, for instance) modifying a female person, the same (masculine, ending in -ⲟⲥ) form is often used for either male or female persons.

| ⲡⲁⲅⲁⲑⲟⲥ ⲛ̄-ⲉⲓⲱⲧ *or* ⲡⲉⲓⲱⲧ ⲛ̄-ⲁⲅⲁⲑⲟⲥ | the good father |
| ⲧⲁⲅⲁⲑⲟⲥ ⲙ̄-ⲙⲁⲁⲩ *or* ⲧⲙⲁⲁⲩ ⲛ̄-ⲁⲅⲁⲑⲟⲥ | the good mother |

---

2. See James P. Allen, *Coptic: A Grammar of Its Six Major Dialects*, Languages of the Ancient Near East: Didactica 1 (University Park, PA: Eisenbrauns, 2020), 15–16. Bentley Layton refers to them as "genderless common nouns" (see his *A Coptic Grammar: With Chrestomathy and Glossary. Sahidic Dialect*, 3rd ed., Porta Linguarum Orientalium 2/20 [Wiesbaden: Harrassowitz, 2011]). The Coptic Scriptorium categorizes these modifiers as nouns.

3. And they do not inflect into other cases the way Greek does!

ADJECTIVES AND NOMINAL SENTENCES

The Greek neuter form (ending in -ON) is used for inanimate nouns (anything other than people).

ⲡⲇⲓⲕⲁⲓⲟⲛ ⲛ̄-ϣⲁϫⲉ *or* ⲡϣⲁϫⲉ ⲛ̄-ⲇⲓⲕⲁⲓⲟⲛ	the just word
ⲛ̄ⲇⲓⲕⲁⲓⲟⲛ ⲛ̄-ⲛⲟⲙⲟⲥ *or* ⲛ̄ⲛⲟⲙⲟⲥ ⲛ̄-ⲇⲓⲕⲁⲓⲟⲛ	the just laws

5.4 Adjectives as Nouns. Finally, all adjectives—both native and of Greek origin—can be treated as nouns by prefixing an article to them. Thus nouns can be adjectival (5.1), and adjectives can be substantival (treated as nouns). To translate these substantivized adjectives, you can simply add "one(s)" or "thing(s)" to the adjective. Alternatively, you can use an appropriately synonymous English noun.

ⲡϫⲁϫⲉ	the hostile (one), the enemy
ⲡϩⲗⲗⲟ	the old one, the elder
ϩⲉⲛⲙⲁⲕⲁⲣⲓⲟⲛ	(some) fortunate things

NOMINAL SENTENCES

5.5 Forming Nominal Sentences. In Coptic, it is possible to have sentences that lack verbs (we'll start learning about verbs in chapter 11). These verbless sentences—known as *nominal sentences*—can have nouns and adjectives along with pronouns (chapter 6) and prepositions (chapters 7 and 8). With nominal sentences, we can start to say things in complete statements.

With all sentences, nominal included, there are usually two main components: *subject* and *predicate*. The subject of the sentence is something that is usually already known or has been established by context; the predicate is the new information stated about the subject. With what we've covered so far, we can form predicates with noun phrases and adjectival phrases. We'll be expanding this as we go with further options—and, of course, many sentences will have verbal predicates.

The first type of nominal sentence we can make is the *two-part nominal sentence*. This simplest type of nominal sentences is composed of a predicate followed by ⲡⲉ/ⲧⲉ/ⲛⲉ. This word, which looks like the longer forms of the definite article, is called a *copula*. It works like a pronoun ("he/she/it/they") and stands in for the implied subject of the sentence (with which it shows agreement). There is no explicit verb present for "is/are," but we can supply this for our English translation.[4]

ⲟⲩϣⲃⲏⲣ ⲡⲉ.	**He's** a friend.
ⲧⲙⲉ ⲧⲉ.	**It's** the truth.
ϩⲉⲛⲙⲁⲑⲏⲧⲏⲥ ⲛⲉ.	**They're** (some) students.

---

4. I recommend using contracted forms for this ("he's," etc.), reserving uncontracted forms for when greater emphasis is given through the use of independent personal pronouns (see 6.2), or actual verbal sentences, such as with the Present (chapter 13).

Adjectival predicates will usually take an indefinite article, which we can optionally leave out in translation:

| ⲟⲩⲡⲟⲛⲏⲣⲟⲥ ⲡⲉ. | **He's** (an) evil (one). |
| ϩⲉⲛⲙⲉⲣⲁⲧⲉ ⲛⲉ. | **They're** (some) loved (ones). |

Additional modifiers like genitive phrases ("of") can be placed following their nouns or after the copula:

| ⲡⲏï ⲛ̄-ⲛ̄ⲉⲓⲟⲧⲉ ⲡⲉ. | **It's** the parents' house. = |
| ⲡⲏï ⲡⲉ ⲛ̄-ⲛ̄ⲉⲓⲟⲧⲉ. | **It's** the house of the parents.[5] |

With *three-part nominal sentences*, both the subject and the predicate are fully explicit noun/adjectival phrases that are connected as being equivalent. With these, the copula can agree with the gender/number of either the subject or predicate, but it does not have to do this and can be ⲡⲉ by default. The copula can occur either at the end of the sentence or in the middle. With indefinite predicates, the ⲡⲉ will follow it immediately:

| ⲡϣⲁϫⲉ ⲟⲩⲇⲓ́ⲕⲁⲓⲟⲛ ⲡⲉ. *or* ⲟⲩⲇⲓ́ⲕⲁⲓⲟⲛ ⲡⲉ ⲡϣⲁϫⲉ. | The word**'s** (a) just (one). |
| ⲓⲱϩⲁ́ⲛⲛⲏⲥ ⲟⲩϣⲃⲏⲣ ⲡⲉ. *or* ⲟⲩϣⲃⲏⲣ ⲡⲉ ⲓⲱϩⲁ́ⲛⲛⲏⲥ. | Iōhannēs**'s** a friend. |

If both the subject and predicate are definite, the copula will tend to be in the middle of them, but it can sometimes be unclear technically which is which (especially since the point of the sentence is that they are equivalent). Context will usually help.

| ⲡⲥⲟⲛ ⲡⲉ ⲡϫⲟⲉⲓⲥ. | The brother**'s** the master. *or* The master**'s** the brother. |

5.6 **Negation of Nominal Sentences.** To make a two-part nominal sentence negative, the negative particle ⲁⲛ ("not") is inserted after the predicate and before the copula. An (optional) additional negative particle ⲛ̄-[6] can also be prefixed before the predicate.

| (ⲛ̄-)ⲟⲩϣⲃⲏⲣ ⲁⲛ ⲡⲉ. | He's **not** a friend. |
| (ⲛ̄-)ⲛⲉⲅⲣⲁⲫⲟⲟⲩⲉ ⲁⲛ ⲛⲉ. | They're **not** the writings. |

With three-part nominal sentences, the negative particle bracket ([ⲛ̄-] . . . ⲁⲛ) also surrounds the predicate—or whichever part precedes the copula if it's in the middle.

| ⲓⲱϩⲁ́ⲛⲛⲏⲥ (ⲛ̄-)ⲟⲩϣⲃⲏⲣ ⲁⲛ ⲡⲉ. *or* (ⲛ̄-)ⲟⲩϣⲃⲏⲣ ⲁⲛ ⲡⲉ ⲓⲱϩⲁ́ⲛⲛⲏⲥ. | Iōhannēs's **not** a friend. |
| (ⲙ̄-)ⲡⲥⲟⲛ ⲁⲛ ⲡⲉ ⲡϫⲟⲉⲓⲥ. | The brother's **not** the master. *or* The master's **not** the brother. |

---

5. Again, this is a possible way to express this negligible difference in emphasis in English.
6. Assimilating regularly to ⲙ̄- before ⲡ and ⲙ (see 2.6). And, yes, this is another ⲛ̄-. Keep them sorted!

ADJECTIVES AND NOMINAL SENTENCES

VOCABULARY

ⲃⲣ̄ⲣⲉ́	new, young (adj)
ϩⲗ̄ⲗⲟ (f ϩⲗⲗⲱ; pl ϩⲗⲗⲟⲓ̈)	old[7] (adj)
ⲁⲥ	old[8] (rarely after noun without ⲛ̄-) (adj)
ϣⲏⲙ (f ϣⲏⲙⲉ)	small, little (usually before noun or often after without ⲛ̄-) (adj)
ⲕⲟⲩⲓ̈	small, little; also of quantity: a little; with pl: a few (usually before noun or rarely after without ⲛ̄-) (adj)
ⲛⲟϭ	large, big, great, important (usually before noun or rarely after without ⲛ̄-) (adj)
ϣⲟⲣⲡ̄ (f ϣⲟⲣⲡⲉ)	first (usually before noun) (adj)
ϩⲁⲉ́ (f ϩⲁⲏ; pl ϩⲁⲉⲉⲩ[ⲉ])	last (usually before noun) (adj)
ⲁⲅⲁⲑⲟⲥ	good (adj)
ⲡⲟⲛⲏⲣⲟ́ⲥ	evil, wicked (adj)
ⲇⲓ́ⲕⲁⲓⲟⲥ	just, right (adj)
ⲙⲁⲕⲁ́ⲣⲓⲟⲥ	fortunate (adj)
ⲙⲉⲣⲓⲧ (pl ⲙⲉⲣⲁⲧⲉ)	(be)loved (usually before noun) (adj)
ⲥⲁⲃⲉ́ (f ⲥⲁⲃⲏ; pl ⲥⲁⲃⲉⲉⲩ[ⲉ])	wise (adj)
ⲥⲁⲉⲓⲉ	beautiful (adj)
ϫⲁϫⲉ (pl ϫⲓ[ⲛ]ϫⲉⲉⲩ[ⲉ])	hostile, enemy (adj)
ⲛⲓⲙ	every, each (after singular noun without article or ⲛ̄-) (adj)
ἄγγελος[9]	messenger (nm)
ἐκκλησία[10]	assembly (nf)

EXERCISE

Copy and translate the following phrases.

1. ⲉⲕⲕⲗⲏⲥⲓ́ⲁ ⲛⲓⲙ _____

2. ⲧϭⲓϫ ⲛ̄-ⲛⲟⲩⲧⲉ _____

3. ⲧⲣ̄ⲣⲱ ⲛ̄-ⲥⲁⲉⲓⲉ _____

---

7. As a noun, used as a title for a monk.

8. Usually not used for people (ϩⲗ̄ⲗⲟ instead).

9. In concurrent Koine Greek, the first ɣ of the two was pronounced as [ɲ] *canyon*. "Angel" is derived from this Greek word, but it originally had a broader meaning for messengers in general, whether of human or celestial origin.

10. The traditional English word often used to gloss this—"church"—is actually derived from another Greek word: κυριακη, meaning "belonging to (the) Master."

4. ⲡϣⲟⲣⲡ̄ ⲛ̄-ⲁ́ⲅⲅⲉⲗⲟⲥ

5. ⲙ̄ⲙⲁⲑⲏⲧⲏ́ⲥ ⲛ̄-ⲥⲁⲃⲉⲉⲩⲉ

6. ϩⲉⲛⲕⲟⲩⲓ̈ ⲛ̄-ⲣ̄ⲡⲏⲩⲉ

7. ⲡϣⲏⲣⲉ ⲛ̄-ⲣ̄ⲣⲟ ⲡⲉ.

8. ⲁⲃⲣⲁϩⲁ́ⲙ ⲡⲉ ⲡⲉⲓⲱⲧ.

9. ⲛ̄-ⲟⲩⲙⲁⲕⲁ́ⲣⲓⲟⲥ ⲁⲛ ⲡⲉ ⲡϩⲙ̄ϩⲁⲗ.

10. ⲛⲉϩⲓⲟⲙⲉ ⲛⲉ ⲛ̄-ⲧⲡⲟⲗⲓⲥ.

11. ⲛ̄-ⲟⲩⲁⲅⲁⲑⲟⲛ ⲁⲛ ⲡⲉ ⲧⲁⲅⲟⲣⲁ́ ⲛ̄-ⲃⲣ̄ⲣⲉ.

12. ⲡϫⲟⲉⲓⲥ ⲡⲉ ⲓⲏⲥⲟⲩ́ⲥ.

CHAPTER 6

PRONOUNS AND MORE ARTICLES

OVERVIEW

In this chapter, you will learn:

- The forms of the personal pronouns and how to use them in nominal sentences
- The forms of possessive articles
- The forms of demonstrative articles and pronouns

PERSONAL PRONOUNS

6.1 **Independent Personal Pronouns.** Pronouns take the place of nouns. They describe person (1st, 2nd, or 3rd), number (singular or plural), and (for 2nd and 3rd person singular) gender. Besides completely independent forms (called the *absolute* forms), many also have unstressed, proclitic forms (*construct* forms) that are connected by a hyphen to the following predicate.

	singular			**plural**		
1st	ⲁⲛⲟⲕ	ⲁⲛⲅ̄-	I[1]	ⲁⲛⲟⲛ	ⲁⲛ-	we
2nd	ⲛ̄ⲧⲟⲕ	ⲛ̄ⲧⲕ̄-	you (m)	ⲛ̄ⲧⲱⲧⲛ̄	ⲛ̄ⲧⲉⲧⲛ̄-	you
	ⲛ̄ⲧⲟ	ⲛ̄ⲧⲉ-	you (f)			
3rd	ⲛ̄ⲧⲟϥ	ⲛ̄ⲧϥ̄-	he, it (m)	ⲛ̄ⲧⲟⲟⲩ	they	
	ⲛ̄ⲧⲟⲥ		she, it (f)			

6.2 **Nominal Sentences with Pronouns.** These personal pronouns can also be used in two- and three-part nominal sentences, and they can be either subject or predicate:

ⲁⲛⲟⲕ ⲡⲉ ⲓⲱϩⲁⲛⲛⲏⲥ.	**I** am Iōhannēs.
ⲛ̄ⲧⲟϥ ⲡⲉ ⲡⲉϣⲃⲏⲣ.	**He** is the friend.
ⲁⲛⲟⲕ ⲡⲉ.	It's **me**. (*predicate*)

---

1. These given translations are English subject forms—use object forms (me/him/her/us/them) if used as a predicate (see 6.2).

With indefinite predicates, the construct forms are common for 1st and 2nd persons. No copula is used in these cases:

ⲁⲛⲅ̄-ⲟⲩⲉⲓⲱⲧ.	**I'm** a father.
ⲛ̄ⲧⲉ-ⲟⲩⲙⲁⲁⲩ.	**You're (fsg)** a mother.
ⲛ̄ⲧⲉⲧⲛ̄-ϩⲉⲛⲉⲓⲟⲧⲉ.	**You're (pl)** (some) parents.

Both absolute and construct forms can even be used together for greater emphasis:

ⲁⲛⲟⲕ ⲁⲛⲅ̄-ⲟⲩⲉⲓⲱⲧ.	*Me*, **I'm** a father.

Negation for nominal sentences without copulas is done by placing the negative particle frame ([ⲛ̄-] ... ⲁⲛ) around the hyphenated construct pronoun-predicate unit.

(ⲛ̄-)ⲁⲛⲅ̄-ⲟⲩⲉⲓⲱⲧ ⲁⲛ.	I'm **not** a father.
ⲁⲛⲟⲕ (ⲛ̄-)ⲁⲛⲅ̄-ⲟⲩⲉⲓⲱⲧ ⲁⲛ.	*Me*, I'm **not** a father.

POSSESSIVE ARTICLES AND DEMONSTRATIVES

6.3 **Possessive Articles.** Possessive articles are forms of the definite article that also describe the owner of the possessed noun. They take the following forms, combining ⲡ-, ⲧ-, or ⲛ- with a personal infix for the owner:

	singular			**plural**		
1st	ⲡ/ⲧ/ⲛ-	-ⲁ-	my	ⲡ/ⲧ/ⲛ-	-ⲉⲛ-	our
2nd	ⲡ/ⲧ/ⲛ-	-ⲉⲕ-	your (m)	ⲡ/ⲧ/ⲛ-	-ⲉⲧⲛ̄-	your
	ⲡ/ⲧ/ⲛ-	-ⲟⲩ-	your (f)			
3rd	ⲡ/ⲧ/ⲛ-	-ⲉϥ-	his, its (m)	ⲡ/ⲧ/ⲛ-	-ⲉⲩ-	their
	ⲡ/ⲧ/ⲛ-	-ⲉⲥ-	her, its (f)			

Like other articles, possessive articles are prefixed directly to the front of nouns without spaces or hyphens. Two key pieces of information are encoded in the form of the possessive article. The initial ⲡ/ⲧ/ⲛ- functions like the definite article (3.3) and conveys the same information about the gender and/or number of the *possessed* noun. The personal infix corresponds to the person, number, and (for 2nd and 3rd person singular) gender of the *possessor*. Some examples:

ⲡⲉⲧⲛ̄ϭⲁⲙⲟⲩⲗ   **your (pl)** camel
    (msg noun with **2nd pl possessor**)
ⲧⲉϥϩⲓⲙⲉ   **his** wife
    (fsg noun with **3rd msg possessor**)
ⲛⲉⲩπονηρόν   **their** evil things
    (pl noun with **3rd pl possessor**)

You'll notice that certain letters are similar between corresponding independent personal pronouns and the infixes of the possessive articles. Compare:

I	ⲁⲛⲟⲕ	-ⲁ-	my
you (msg)	ⲛ̄ⲧⲟⲕ	-ⲉⲕ-	your (msg)
you (fsg)	ⲛ̄ⲧⲟ	-ⲟⲩ-	your (fsg)
he, it (m)	ⲛ̄ⲧⲟϥ	-ⲉϥ-	his, its (m)
she, it (f)	ⲛ̄ⲧⲟⲥ	-ⲉⲥ-	her, its (f)
we	ⲁⲛⲟⲛ	-ⲉⲛ-	our
you (pl)	ⲛ̄ⲧⲱⲧⲛ̄	-ⲉⲧⲛ̄-	your (pl)
they	ⲛ̄ⲧⲟⲟⲩ	-ⲉⲩ-	their

Pay attention to diagnostic features like similar letters as you are learning these. You'll see further patterns with other personal prefixes and suffixes attached to prepositions and verbs as well.

6.4 **Demonstrative Articles and Pronouns.** Another specialized variety of article is the demonstrative article—a way of pointing out a specific noun. For nouns nearer the speaker's point of reference, these forms are used:

ⲡⲉⲓ̈-	this (msg)
ⲧⲉⲓ̈-	this (fsg)
ⲛⲉⲓ̈-	these

As with other articles, they are prefixed directly to their nouns:

ⲡⲉⲓ̈ⲣ̄ⲣⲟ	**this** king
ⲧⲉⲓ̈ⲉⲡⲓⲥⲧⲟⲗⲏ	**this** letter
ⲛⲉⲓ̈ϫⲓⲥⲟⲟⲩⲉ	**these** masters

For nouns further away from the speaker's perspective, the relative[2] phrase ⲉⲧ-ⲙ̄ⲙⲁⲩ (literally meaning "who's/which's there") is used after a definite noun to express the concept of "that/those."

| ⲡⲉϣⲃⲏⲣ ⲉⲧ-ⲙ̄ⲙⲁⲩ | **that** friend |
| ⲛⲉϩⲧⲱⲱⲣ ⲉⲧ-ⲙ̄ⲙⲁⲩ | **those** horses |

There are also independent demonstrative pronouns, which are used on their own when no explicit noun is mentioned:

---

2. More fun with relatives coming in 7.5 and chapter 19.

	nearer		**further**
ⲡⲁⲓ̈	this (msg)	ⲡⲏ	that (msg)
ⲧⲁⲓ̈	this (fsg)	ⲧⲏ	that (fsg)
ⲛⲁⲓ̈	these	ⲛⲏ	those

These can be used as subjects in nominal sentences.

ⲛⲁⲓ̈ ⲛⲉ ⲛⲉⲛϣⲁϫⲉ.	**These** are our words.
ⲟⲩⲣ̄ⲣⲱ ⲧⲉ ⲧⲁⲓ̈.	**This** is a queen.

The nearer demonstrative pronouns are common; the further ones are rarer, with the substantivized relative phrase ⲡ-/ⲧ-/ⲛⲉⲧ-ⲙ̄ⲙⲁⲩ often used instead.

VOCABULARY

Learn the forms of the independent personal pronouns (6.1), possessive articles (6.3), and demonstrative articles and pronouns (6.4).

ⲙⲟⲟⲩ (pl ⲙⲟⲩⲉⲓⲟⲟⲩⲉ)	water (nm)
ⲟⲉⲓⲕ	(loaf of) bread (nm)
(ⲉ)ⲓⲣⲏⲛⲏ[3]	peace (nf)
ⲭⲁⲣⲓⲥ	favor (nf)
ⲕⲁⲕⲉ	darkness (nm)
ⲟⲩⲟⲉⲓⲛ	light (nm)
ⲭⲣⲓⲥⲧⲟⲥ	anointed one (abbreviated as x̄c̄ or x̄p̄c̄) (nm)
ⲁⲥⲉⲃⲏⲥ	irreverent, impious (adj)
ⲕⲁⲙⲉ́ (f ⲕⲁⲙⲏ)	black[4] (adj)
ⲟⲩⲱⲃϣ̄	white (rarely after noun without ⲛ̄-) (adj)
ⲡⲓⲥⲧⲟⲥ	trusting, trustworthy (adj)
ⲙ̄ⲙⲁⲩ	there (adv)
ⲉⲧ-ⲙ̄ⲙⲁⲩ	who's/which's there (> further dem: that/those)

EXERCISE

Copy and translate the following phrases.

1. ⲡⲉⲛⲉⲓⲱⲧ _____

2. ⲛⲉⲓ̈ⲣⲱⲙⲉ _____

---

3. With a singular definite article attached, spelled ⲧ̄ⲣⲏⲛⲏ.
4. This word is connected to the native name for Egypt, ⲕⲏⲙⲉ—the black, fertile land of the Nile Valley.

PRONOUNS AND MORE ARTICLES

3. ⲧⲉⲕⲙⲁⲁⲩ

4. ⲟⲩⲡⲓⲥⲧⲟⲥ ⲡⲉ ⲡⲉⲓϣⲁϫⲉ.

5. ⲛ̄ⲧⲟϥ ⲛ̄-ⲡⲉⲭⲣⲓⲥⲧⲟⲥ ⲁⲛ ⲡⲉ.

6. ⲛ̄-ⲧⲁⲓ̈ ⲁⲛ ⲧⲉ ⲧⲙⲉ.

7. ⲡⲏⲓ̈ ⲛ̄-ⲕⲁⲙⲉ́ ⲟⲩⲁⲥ ⲡⲉ.

8. ϩⲉⲛⲉⲡⲓⲥⲧⲟⲗⲟⲟⲩⲉ ⲛ̄ⲧⲉ-ϣⲉⲛⲟⲩⲧⲉ ⲛⲉ ⲛⲁⲓ̈.

9. ⲛ̄ⲧⲕ̄-ⲟⲩⲁⲥⲉⲃⲏⲥ.

10. ⲟⲩⲟⲩⲱⲃϣ̄ ⲡⲉ ⲡⲉⲧⲛ̄ϩⲧⲟ.

11. ⲡϣⲟⲣⲡ̄ ⲛ̄-ⲟⲩⲟⲉⲓⲛ ⲟⲩⲥⲁⲉⲓⲉ ⲡⲉ.

12. ⲡⲣⲱⲙⲉ ⲉⲧ-ⲙ̄ⲙⲁⲩ ⲡⲉ ⲡⲉⲥϫⲁϫⲉ.

CHAPTER 7

PREPOSITIONS, CONJUNCTIONS, AND RELATIVE CLAUSES

OVERVIEW

In this chapter, you will learn:

- The forms of the basic prepositions
- Some ways to say "and" and some other conjunctions
- How to use relative clauses in nominal sentences

SIMPLE PREPOSITIONS

7.1 **Basic Prepositions.** Prepositions describe relationships between nouns and the other parts of the sentence. Coptic really likes prepositions. As you will see, a wide range of simple, compound, and adverbially enhanced prepositions exists, allowing Coptic prepositional phrases to express careful nuance. The basis for all of this is the relatively small list of simple prepositions, about a dozen native ones along with half a dozen borrowed from Greek. Most of these occur frequently, and the more complicated compound prepositions (chapter 8) build off of these. The prepositions in this list usually have two forms. The first is the *prenominal* form, which is prefixed to a noun phrase with a hyphen:

  ⲉ-ⲡⲣ̄ⲣⲟ   **to** the king
  ϩⲛ̄-ⲧⲡⲟⲗⲓⲥ   **in** the city

The second is the *prepersonal*[1] form, to which a personal suffix (7.2) will be attached (the double slash [⸗] is the standard way of marking this form on its own, but this is not included once a suffix has been attached):

  ⲉⲣⲟϥ   **to** him
  ⲛ̄ϩⲏⲧⲥ̄   **in** it (f)

---

1. Also known as *prepronominal*; see Thomas O. Lambdin, *Introduction to Sahidic Coptic* (Macon, GA: Mercer University Press, 1983).

PREPOSITIONS, CONJUNCTIONS, AND RELATIVE CLAUSES

Here's the complete list of these basic prepositions:

ⲁⲛⲧⲓ-		instead of (prep)
ⲉ-	ⲉⲣⲟ⸗	to, for (prep)
ⲕⲁⲧⲁ-	ⲕⲁⲧⲁⲣⲟ⸗	according to (prep)
ⲙⲛ̄-, ⲛⲙ̄-	ⲛⲙ̄ⲙⲁ⸗	with (prep)
ⲛ̄-	ⲙ̄ⲙⲟ⸗	in, with; as adv: -ly[2] (prep)
ⲛ̄-	ⲛⲁ⸗	to, for[3] (prep)
ⲟⲩⲃⲉ-	ⲟⲩⲃⲏ⸗	toward, facing, against (prep)
ⲟⲩⲧⲉ-	ⲟⲩⲧⲱ⸗	between, among (prep)
ⲡⲁⲣⲁ-	ⲡⲁⲣⲁⲣⲟ⸗	beside, beyond, more than (prep)
ⲡⲣⲟⲥ-	ⲡⲣⲟⲥⲣⲟ⸗	according to, for; than (prep)
ⲭⲱⲣⲓ́ⲥ-		without, apart from (prep)
ϣⲁ-	ϣⲁⲣⲟ⸗	to(ward), up to (prep)
ϩⲁ-	ϩⲁⲣⲟ⸗	under; concerning (prep)
ϩⲓ-	ϩⲓⲱ(ⲱ)⸗	on (prep)
ϩⲛ̄-	ⲛ̄ϩⲏⲧ⸗[4]	in, among, within, at (prep)
ϩⲱⲥ-		like, as (prep)
ϫⲓⲛ-, ϫⲛ̄-		from, since (prep)

A prepositional phrase can also be the predicate of a nominal sentence. Definite subjects require no copula, and they are negated by ⲁⲛ after the prepositional phrase:

ⲡⲁⲅⲅⲉⲗⲟⲥ ϩⲛ̄-ⲙ̄ⲡⲏⲩⲉ.	The messenger's **in the skies**.
ⲡⲁⲅⲅⲉⲗⲟⲥ ϩⲛ̄-ⲙ̄ⲡⲏⲩⲉ ⲁⲛ.	The messenger's **not** in the skies.

Indefinite subjects of prepositional phrase predicates are idiomatically required to be preceded by the existential particle ⲟⲩⲛ̄- ("there's/there're") or its negative counterpart (ⲙ̄)ⲙⲛ̄- ("there's no/there're no")[5]:

ⲟⲩⲛ̄-ⲟⲩⲁⲅⲅⲉⲗⲟⲥ ϩⲛ̄-ⲙ̄ⲡⲏⲩⲉ.	**There's** a messenger in the skies.
(ⲙ̄)ⲙⲛ̄-ⲁⲅⲅⲉⲗⲟⲥ ϩⲛ̄-ⲙ̄ⲡⲏⲩⲉ.	**There's no** messenger in the skies.

7.2 **Personal Suffixes.** These are the forms of the endings that are suffixed to the prepersonal forms of prepositions. You will notice many similarities to the personal pronouns and the infixes of the possessive articles you learned in chapter 6. Most of these are very regular across prepositions, but a few (1st person singular, 2nd person feminine singular, and 2nd person plural) have different options depending on the ending of the prepersonal form. This list summarizes the options:

---

2. Adverbial construction is discussed in 8.3. This preposition is also used as a direct object marker and as an equivalence marker with ⲟ†, ϣⲟⲟⲡ†, and suffix pronouns. We'll cover this once we get to verbs (see chapter 12).

3. This preposition is used as an indirect object marker. Again, once we get to verbs, this will be explained.

4. The prepersonal form ⲛ̄ϩⲏⲧ⸗ is derived from ϩⲏ (belly, womb).

5. Note that with this negative existential particle, the indefinite article is not needed. And don't confuse this with the preposition ⲙⲛ̄- "with"!

THE SAHIDIC NOUN SYSTEM

singular
1st	-ï/-т⁶/-()⁷	me
2nd	-к⁸	you (m)
	-є/-тє⁹/-()¹⁰	you (f)
3rd	-ϥ¹¹	him, it (m)
	-с¹²	her, it (f)

plural
1st	-ⲛ¹³	us
2nd	-ⲧⲛ̄¹⁴/-ⲧⲏⲩⲧⲛ̄¹⁵	you
3rd	-(ⲟ)ⲩ	them

It is useful to familiarize yourself with these suffixes when they are actually attached to prepersonal forms of the prepositions, noting the variations. Compare these examples, which cover most of the options you'll encounter with the basic prepositions:

- **ending in o⸗ or ⲱ⸗**

ⲉⲣⲟï	to **me**
ⲉⲣⲟⲕ	to **you (msg)**
ⲉⲣⲟ	to **you (fsg)**
ⲉⲣⲟϥ	to **him, it (m)**
ⲉⲣⲟⲥ	to **her, it (f)**
ⲉⲣⲟⲛ	to **us**
ⲉⲣⲱⲧⲛ̄	to **you (pl)**
ⲉⲣⲟⲟⲩ	to **them**

- **ending in ⲁ⸗**

ⲛⲙ̄ⲙⲁï	with **me**
ⲛⲙ̄ⲙⲁⲕ	with **you (msg)**
ⲛⲙ̄ⲙⲉ	with **you (fsg)**
ⲛⲙ̄ⲙⲁϥ	with **him, it (m)**
ⲛⲙ̄ⲙⲁⲥ	with **her, it (f)**
ⲛⲙ̄ⲙⲁⲛ	with **us**
ⲛⲙ̄ⲙⲏⲧⲛ̄	with **you (pl)**
ⲛⲙ̄ⲙⲁⲩ	with **them**

- **ending in ⲱ(ⲱ)⸗**

ϩⲓⲱⲱⲧ	on **me**
ϩⲓⲱ(ⲱ)ⲕ	on **you (msg)**
ϩⲓⲱⲱⲧⲉ	on **you (fsg)**
ϩⲓⲱ(ⲱ)ϥ	on **him, it (m)**
ϩⲓⲱ(ⲱ)ⲥ	on **her, it (f)**
ϩⲓⲱ(ⲱ)ⲛ	on **us**
ϩⲓ(ⲱⲧ)-ⲧⲏⲩⲧⲛ̄	on **you (pl)**
ϩⲓⲱⲟⲩ	on **them**

- **ending in ⲧ⸗**

ⲛ̄ϩⲏⲧ(ⲧ̄)	in **me**
ⲛ̄ϩⲏⲧⲕ̄	in **you (msg)**
ⲛ̄ϩⲏⲧⲉ	in **you (fsg)**
ⲛ̄ϩⲏⲧϥ̄	in **him, it (m)**
ⲛ̄ϩⲏⲧⲥ̄	in **her, it (f)**
ⲛ̄ϩⲏⲧⲛ̄	in **us**
ⲛ̄ϩⲏⲧ-ⲧⲏⲩⲧⲛ̄	in **you (pl)**
ⲛ̄ϩⲏⲧⲟⲩ	in **them**

---

6. Used after forms ending in double vowels and optionally after forms ending in ⲧ.
7. Meaning no additional suffix, used optionally after forms ending in ⲧ.
8. An overline is added to this suffix if it is preceded by a consonant.
9. Used after forms ending in double vowels.
10. Meaning no additional suffix, used after forms ending in ⲟ or ⲱ.
11. An overline is added to this suffix if it is preceded by a consonant.
12. An overline is added to this suffix if it is preceded by a consonant.
13. An overline is added to this suffix if it is preceded by a consonant.
14. Used after forms ending in single vowels, with a lengthening of any preceding short vowel: ⲁ to ⲏ and ⲟ to ⲱ.
15. Used in other cases, this longer suffix is sometimes attached to the prenominal form (and includes the hyphen).

PREPOSITIONS, CONJUNCTIONS, AND RELATIVE CLAUSES

Don't be dismayed by the (potential) variations, and instead focus on the similar diagnostic features. As you read more and more, recognizing these endings will become second nature. And much of the time, context will help you to know what to expect.

CONJUNCTIONS

7.3 **Saying "And."** Two of the basic prepositions (ⲙⲛ̄- "with" and ϩⲓ- "on") can also be used to link nouns in sequence. With this usage, you can choose to translate them in English with the conjunction "and." Note that ϩⲓ- is only used in this manner to link nouns without articles (even though they have a general, abstract sense, so it may sometimes sound better in English to translate them as plurals).

ⲛ̄ⲉⲓⲟⲧⲉ ⲙⲛ̄-ⲛⲉϣⲏⲣⲩ	the parents **with/and** the children
ϩⲉⲛϩⲧⲱⲱⲣ ⲙⲛ̄-ϩⲉⲛϭⲁⲙⲟⲩⲗ	(some) horses **with/and** (some) camels
ⲭⲁⲣⲓⲥ ϩⲓ-ⲙⲉ	favor **on/and** truth
ϩⲟⲟⲩⲧ ϩⲓ-ⲥϩⲓⲙⲉ	male(s) **on/and** female(s)

In addition to these, the common, general-purpose conjunction ⲁⲩⲱ—more properly "and"—is widely used to join nouns, clauses, and sentences.

ⲧⲉⲭⲁⲣⲓⲥ ⲁⲩⲱ ⲧⲙⲉ	(the) favor **and** (the) truth
ⲡⲉⲧⲛ̄ⲥⲟⲛ ⲁⲩⲱ ⲡⲉⲧⲛ̄ϣⲃⲏⲣ	your (pl) brother **and** your (pl) friend
ⲁⲛⲟⲕ ⲡⲉ ⲓⲱϩⲁⲛⲛⲏⲥ, ⲁⲩⲱ ⲁⲛⲅ̄-ⲟⲩⲉⲓⲱⲧ.	I am Iōhannēs, **and** I'm a father.

7.4 **Other Conjunctions.** In addition to ⲁⲩⲱ ("and"), other conjunctions are used to join clauses and sentences. Some common ones borrowed from Greek include:

ⲁⲗⲗⲁ	but, rather (conj)
ⲏ	or, than (conj)
ⲅⲁⲣ	for (postpositive) (conj)
ⲇⲉ	now, so, yet (postpositive) (conj)

The last two, ⲅⲁⲣ and ⲇⲉ, are *postpositive* (as in Greek usage), meaning that they come after the initial word/phrase of the clause or sentence they are in.

RELATIVE CLAUSES

7.5 **Saying "Who/Which."** The relative pronoun/converter[16] ⲉⲧ- can be prefixed to prepositional phrases to form relative clauses.

---

16. Converters are an important part of the verbal system, but they can also be used with nominal sentences. Full discussion of converters is coming in chapters 19–22.

THE SAHIDIC NOUN SYSTEM

ⲡⲁⲅⲅⲉⲗⲟⲥ ⲉⲧ-ϩⲛ̄-ⲙ̄ⲡⲏⲩⲉ	the messenger **who**'s in the skies
ⲡⲁⲅⲅⲉⲗⲟⲥ ⲉⲧ-ϩⲛ̄-ⲙ̄ⲡⲏⲩⲉ ⲁⲛ	the messenger **who**'s not in the skies
ⲧⲉⲥϩⲓⲙⲉ ⲉⲧ-ϩⲓ-ⲡⲏⲓ̈	the woman **who**'s on the house
ⲛⲉϩⲧⲱⲱⲣ ⲉⲧ-ⲙ̄ⲙⲁⲩ	the horses **which**'re there (= those horses)

Relative clauses add definition to the nouns they are modifying, so they can't be used with indefinite nouns.[17] Note that in English we can often elide the "who/which" of relative clauses (we can just say "the woman on the house" and the "who's" is understood), but they are important syntactical links in Sahidic.

7.6 Relative Clauses as Nouns. Relative clauses can be substantivized (treated as noun phrases) by prefixing a definite article to them:

ⲡⲉⲧ-ϩⲛ̄-ⲙ̄ⲡⲏⲩⲉ	**the one (m) who**'s in the skies
ⲧⲉⲧ-ϩⲓ-ⲡⲏⲓ̈	**the one (f) who**'s on the house
ⲛⲉⲧ-ⲙ̄ⲙⲁⲩ	**the ones which**'re there (= those)

VOCABULARY

Learn the forms of the personal suffixes (7.2).

ⲁⲛⲧⲓ-		instead of (prep)
ⲉ-	ⲉⲣⲟ⸗	to, for (prep)
ⲕⲁⲧⲁ-	ⲕⲁⲧⲁⲣⲟ⸗	according to (prep)
ⲙⲛ̄-, ⲛⲙ̄-	ⲛⲙ̄ⲙⲁ⸗	with; and (prep)
ⲛ̄-	ⲙ̄ⲙⲟ⸗	in, with; as adv: -ly (prep)
ⲛ̄-	ⲛⲁ⸗	to, for (prep)
ⲟⲩⲃⲉ-	ⲟⲩⲃⲏ⸗	toward, facing, against (prep)
ⲟⲩⲧⲉ-	ⲟⲩⲧⲱ⸗	between, among (prep)
ⲡⲁⲣⲁ-	ⲡⲁⲣⲁⲣⲟ⸗	beside, beyond, more than (prep)
ⲡⲣⲟⲥ-	ⲡⲣⲟⲥⲣⲟ⸗	according to, for; than (prep)
ⲭⲱⲣⲓⲥ-		without, apart from (prep)
ϣⲁ-	ϣⲁⲣⲟ⸗	to(ward), up to (prep)
ϩⲁ-	ϩⲁⲣⲟ⸗	under; concerning (prep)
ϩⲓ-	ϩⲓⲱ(ⲱ)⸗	on; and (noun without article only) (prep)
ϩⲛ̄-	ⲛ̄ϩⲏⲧ⸗[18]	in, among, within, at (prep)
ϩⲱⲥ-		like, as (prep)
ϫⲓⲛ-, ϫⲛ̄-		from, since (prep)
ⲁⲩⲱ		and (conj)
ⲁⲗⲗⲁ		but, rather (conj)

---

17. Circumstantial clauses are used when this expression is needed (see 20.2).
18. The prepersonal form ⲛ̄ϩⲏⲧ⸗ is derived from ϩⲏ (belly, womb).

PREPOSITIONS, CONJUNCTIONS, AND RELATIVE CLAUSES

ⲏ	or, than (conj)
ⲅⲁⲣ	for (postpositive) (conj)
ⲇⲉ	now, so, yet (postpositive) (conj)
ⲟⲩⲛ̄-	there's/there're (existential)
(ⲙ̄)ⲙⲛ̄-	there's no/there're no (neg existential)
ⲉⲧ-	who, which (relative converter)

EXERCISE

Copy and translate the following phrases.

1. ⲧⲉⲭⲁ́ⲣⲓⲥ ⲛⲏⲧⲛ̄ ⲙⲛ̄-ϯⲣⲏ́ⲛⲏ

2. ⲡⲉⲛⲉⲓⲱⲧ ⲉⲧ-ϩⲛ̄-ⲙ̄ⲡⲏⲩⲉ

3. ⲟⲩⲛ̄-ⲟⲩⲣⲱⲙⲉ ϩⲓ-ⲧⲉϩⲓⲏ.

4. ⲧⲉⲧ-ϩⲙ̄-ⲡⲏⲓ̈ ⲧⲉ ⲧⲁⲙⲁⲁⲩ.

5. ⲛⲉⲛϣⲃⲉⲉⲣ ⲟⲩⲃⲉ-ⲧⲉⲕⲕⲗⲏⲥⲓ́ⲁ.

6. ⲧⲙⲟⲩⲉⲓ ⲉⲧ-ⲟⲩⲧⲱⲟⲩ

7. ⲡⲕⲁⲕⲉ ⲛ̄-ⲡⲟⲛⲏⲣⲟ́ⲛ ϩⲛ̄-ⲡⲕⲁϩ.

8. ⲡⲛⲟⲩⲧⲉ ⲛⲙ̄ⲙⲁⲛ.

9. ⲧⲉⲕⲕⲗⲏⲥⲓ́ⲁ ⲉⲧ-ϩⲛ̄-ⲣⲁⲕⲟⲧⲉ

CHAPTER 8

COMPOUND PREPOSITIONS AND ADVERBS

OVERVIEW

In this chapter, you will learn:

- How compound prepositions are formed
- How adverbs can also be formed from prepositions and even used to augment other prepositions

COMPOUND PREPOSITIONS

8.1 **Formation of Compound Prepositions.** The simple prepositions we learned last chapter are just the beginning. Sahidic also has *dozens* of compound and adverbially enhanced prepositions (don't worry—you don't have to learn them right away[1]). The basic prepositions from the previous chapter (especially ⲉ-, ⲛ̄-, ϩⲁ-, and ϩⲓ-) are used in the formation of these more complex prepositions. These basic prepositions are combined with certain nouns (often old, abstracted nouns for parts of the body[2]) or verbs to form compound prepositions. Because these combinations are treated as fixed phrases, the hyphen is not retained between the simple preposition and the noun (an exception to our usual practice).

8.2 **Categories of Compound Prepositions.** As mentioned, many compound prepositions are formed from older nouns for parts of the human body. Most of these nouns are otherwise no longer used on their own, especially in a literal sense. Other common words have taken their place: ϭⲓϫ is the usual word for "hand" instead of the older ⲧⲱⲣⲉ, for instance. Because of this, you don't really need to memorize most of these words for parts of the body as vocabulary on their own, although a general sense of their origins can often help with understanding and remembering the meanings of their

---

1. And see Appendix 4 for a conspectus of all simple, compound, and adverbially augmented prepositions.
2. Many of these are a special category of nouns called possessed nouns. They do not take articles and require personal suffixes.

derived prepositions. The following are some of the more common compounds, which have prenominal forms (before nouns) and prepersonal forms (which will take a personal suffix, as discussed in 7.2):

Prepositions Derived from Parts of the Body
- Derived from ⲣⲟ ⲣⲱ⸗ (**mouth**; door, opening [nm]):

  ⲉⲣⲛ̄-   ⲉⲣⲱ⸗   to (the opening of) (prep)
  ϩⲓⲣⲛ̄-   ϩⲓⲣⲱ⸗   at (the opening of) (prep)

- Derived from ⲧⲟⲩⲱ⸗ (**bosom**, lap; embrace [of] [n]):

  ϩⲓⲧⲟⲩⲛ̄-, ϩⲓⲧⲟⲩⲉⲛ-   ϩⲓⲧⲟⲩⲱ⸗   beside, near (prep)

- Derived from ⲧⲱⲣⲉ ⲧⲟⲟⲧ⸗ (**hand**; handle; implement [nf]):

  ⲉⲧⲛ̄-   ⲉⲧⲟⲟⲧ⸗   to (prep)
  ⲛ̄ⲧⲛ̄-   ⲛ̄ⲧⲟⲟⲧ⸗   from, by (prep)
  ϩⲁⲧⲛ̄-   ϩⲁⲧⲟⲟⲧ⸗   beside, near, with (prep)
  ϩⲓⲧⲛ̄-   ϩⲓⲧⲟⲟⲧ⸗   through, by, from (prep)

- Derived from ϩⲏ ϩⲏⲧ⸗ (**front**, fore part; beginning [nf]):

  ϩⲁⲑⲏ   ϩⲁⲧ⸗ϩⲏ   before (prep)

- Derived from ϩⲏⲧ ϩⲧⲏ⸗ (**heart**, mind [nm]):

  ϩⲁ(ϩ)ⲧⲛ̄-   ϩⲁ(ϩ)ⲧⲏ⸗   beside, near, with[3] (prep)

- Derived from ϩⲟ ϩⲣⲁ⸗ (**face**; surface [nm]):

  ⲉϩⲣⲛ̄-   ⲉϩⲣⲁ⸗   toward (prep)
  (ⲛ̄)ⲛⲁϩⲣⲛ̄- (ⲛ̄)ⲛⲁϩⲣⲁ⸗ in front of, facing (prep)

- Derived from ϫⲱ⸗ (**head** [of] [nm]):

  ⲉϫⲛ̄-   ⲉϫⲱ⸗   onto, over (prep)
  ϩⲓϫⲛ̄-   ϩⲓϫⲱ⸗   upon (prep)

Other nouns and certain verbs also contribute to the formation of compound prepositions:

Prepositions Derived from Other Sources
- Derived from ⲁⲧ- (**un-, non-** [negative prefix]) + ϣⲓⲛⲉ (**to seek** [verb]):

  ⲁϫⲛ̄-[4]   ⲁϫⲛ̄ⲧ⸗   without (prep)

- Derived from ⲥⲁ (**side**, part [nm]):

  ⲛ̄ⲥⲁ-   ⲛ̄ⲥⲱ⸗   after, behind; except (prep)
  ⲙⲛ̄ⲛ̄ⲥⲁ-   ⲙⲛ̄ⲛ̄ⲥⲱ⸗   after (of time) (prep)

- Derived from ⲧⲱⲱⲃⲉ (**to repay** [verb]):

  ⲉⲧⲃⲉ-   ⲉⲧⲃⲏⲏⲧ⸗   about, concerning, because of (prep)

ADVERBS

8.3 Nouns as Adverbs. Adverbs modify verbs and prepositions. In combination with certain prepositions, many nouns—including native "adjectives"—form phrases that

---

3. Despite having a different derivation, very similar in form and meaning to ϩⲁⲧⲛ̄- ϩⲁⲧⲟⲟⲧ⸗ above.
4. This is also sometimes spelled as ⲉϫⲛ̄- ⲉϫⲛ̄ⲧ⸗, which can be confused with ⲉϫⲛ̄- ⲉϫⲱ⸗ "onto, over."

can be used in an adverbial sense. When used this way, the prepositional phrase can be translated with a suffixed "-ly." ⲛ̄- (in, with [prep]) is used like this with "adjectives":

ⲛ̄-ⲃⲣ̄ⲣⲉ́	newly, recently
ⲛ̄-ϣⲟⲣⲡ̄	at first, formerly

ϩⲛ̄- (in [prep]) is frequently used this way with an indefinite noun:

ϩⲛ̄-ⲟⲩⲙⲉ	in (a) truth, truly

Nouns without articles combined with ⲁϫⲛ̄- (without [prep]) can also be translated with a suffixed "-lessly."

ⲁϫⲛ̄-ⲛⲟ́ⲙⲟⲥ	without law, lawlessly

8.4 Directional Adverbs. Another very common category of adverbs is directional adverbs. These are also actually prepositional phrases in origin (simple preposition + noun). ⲉ- is the most common simple preposition used to form these, but ⲛ̄-, ϣⲁ-, and ϩⲓ- are also used. Like compound prepositions, these are fixed phrases, so no hyphen is used after the simple prepositions for these as well. Some common ones:

- Derived from ⲃⲟⲗ (outside, outer part [nm]):
    ⲉⲃⲟⲗ   out, away (adv)
- Derived from ϩⲟⲩⲛ[5] (inside, inner part [nm]):
    ⲉϩⲟⲩⲛ   in (adv)
    ⲛ̄ϩⲟⲩⲛ   within, inside (adv)
    ϣⲁϩⲟⲩⲛ   inward (adv)
- Derived from ⲉⲥⲏⲧ (bottom, ground [nm]):
    ⲉⲡⲉⲥⲏⲧ   down (adv)
- Derived from ϩⲣⲁⲓ̈ (top, upper part; bottom, lower part [!][6] [nm]):
    ⲉϩⲣⲁⲓ̈   up; down (!) (adv)
- Derived from ϩⲏ ϩⲏⲧ⸗ (front, fore part; beginning [nf]):
    ⲉⲑⲏ   forward, ahead (adv)
- Derived from ⲡⲁϩⲟⲩ (rear, back part [nm]):
    ⲉⲡⲁϩⲟⲩ   backward, back (adv)

8.5 Adverbially Augmented Prepositions. A final important category to discuss is adverbially augmented prepositions, which combine a directional adverb (8.4) with a following simple (7.1) or compound (8.2) preposition. Dozens of additional combinations are possible with this complex, but fortunately most are fairly straightforward

---

5. The preposition ϩⲛ̄- is also related to this.
6. This potential confusion between "up" and "down" comes from what were originally two similar, but not identical, words that became pronounced and spelled the same in Sahidic (other dialects maintain a more noticeable difference).

combinations of the meanings of the directional adverb and the following preposition. For example, here are some of the combinations that can occur with the simple preposition ⲉ- ⲉⲣⲟ⸗ (to, for):

ⲉⲃⲟⲗ ⲉ-	out to
ⲉϩⲟⲩⲛ ⲉ-	into
ⲉϩⲣⲁⲓ̈ ⲉ-	up/down to
ⲉⲡⲉⲥⲏⲧ ⲉ-	down to
ⲉⲡⲁϩⲟⲩ ⲉ-	back to
ⲉⲑⲏ ⲉ-	forward to
ϣⲁϩⲟⲩⲛ ⲉ-	until

The last one is a bit idiomatic (the components on their own could taken as "inward" and "to"), but you can see how most are regular.

There are some combinations, however, especially with the very common adverb ⲉⲃⲟⲗ, that warrant special attention. These are common, and their combined idiomatic meaning may seem counterintuitive. Be sure to learn these!

ⲉⲃⲟⲗ ⲛ̄-	out of, from (in)
ⲉⲃⲟⲗ ϩⲛ̄-	out of, from (in)
ⲉⲃⲟⲗ ⲛ̄ⲧⲛ̄-	from
ⲉⲃⲟⲗ ϩⲓⲧⲛ̄-	through, by

VOCABULARY

ⲉⲡⲛ̄-	ⲉⲣⲱ⸗	to (the opening of) (prep)
ϩⲓⲡⲛ̄-	ϩⲓⲣⲱ⸗	at (the opening of) (prep)
ϩⲓⲧⲟⲩⲛ̄-, ϩⲓⲧⲟⲩⲉⲛ-	ϩⲓⲧⲟⲩⲱ⸗	beside, near (prep)
ⲉⲧⲛ̄-	ⲉⲧⲟⲟⲧ⸗	to (prep)
ⲛ̄ⲧⲛ̄-	ⲛ̄ⲧⲟⲟⲧ⸗	from, by (prep)
ϩⲁⲧⲛ̄-	ϩⲁⲧⲟⲟⲧ⸗	beside, near, with (prep)
ϩⲓⲧⲛ̄-	ϩⲓⲧⲟⲟⲧ⸗	through, by, from (prep)
ϩⲁⲑⲏ	ϩⲁⲧ⸗ϩⲏ	before (prep)
ϩⲁ(ϩ)ⲧⲛ̄-	ϩⲁ(ϩ)ⲧⲏ⸗	beside, near, with (prep)
ⲉϩⲣⲛ̄-	ⲉϩⲣⲁ⸗	toward (prep)
(ⲛ̄)ⲛⲁϩⲣⲛ̄-	(ⲛ̄)ⲛⲁϩⲣⲁ⸗	in front of, facing (prep)
ⲉϫⲛ̄-	ⲉϫⲱ⸗	onto, over (prep)
ϩⲓϫⲛ̄-	ϩⲓϫⲱ⸗	upon (prep)
ⲁϫⲛ̄-, ⲉϫⲛ̄-	ⲁϫⲛ̄ⲧ⸗, ⲉϫⲛ̄ⲧ⸗	without; as adv: -lessly (prep)
ⲛ̄ⲥⲁ-	ⲛ̄ⲥⲱ⸗	after, behind; except (prep)
ⲙⲛ̄ⲛ̄ⲥⲁ-	ⲙⲛ̄ⲛ̄ⲥⲱ⸗	after (of time) (prep)
ⲉⲧⲃⲉ-	ⲉⲧⲃⲏⲏⲧ⸗	about, concerning, because of (prep)
ⲉⲃⲟⲗ		out, away (adv)

THE SAHIDIC NOUN SYSTEM

ⲉⲃⲟⲗ ⲛ̄-	out of, from (in)
ⲉⲃⲟⲗ ϩⲛ̄-	out of, from (in)
ⲉⲃⲟⲗ ⲛ̄ⲧⲛ̄-	from
ⲉⲃⲟⲗ ϩⲓⲧⲛ̄-	through, by
ⲉϩⲟⲩⲛ	in (adv)
ⲛ̄ϩⲟⲩⲛ	within, inside (adv)
ϣⲁϩⲟⲩⲛ	inward (adv)
ⲉⲡⲉⲥⲏⲧ	down (adv)
ⲉϩⲣⲁⲓ̈	up; down (!) (adv)
ⲉⲑⲏ	forward, ahead (adv)
ⲉⲡⲁϩⲟⲩ	backward, back (adv)

EXERCISE

Copy and translate the following phrases.

1. ϫⲁϫⲉ ⲛⲓⲙ ϩⲁⲧⲟⲟⲧⲛ̄

2. ϩⲛ̄-ⲟⲩ(ⲉ)ⲓⲣⲏ́ⲛⲏ

3. ⲛ̄ⲟⲩⲟⲉⲓⲛ ⲉⲃⲟⲗ ϩⲛ̄-ⲧⲡⲉ

4. ⲡⲉⲧ-ϩⲓⲧⲟⲩⲱⲥ

5. ⲙⲛ̄ⲛ̄ⲥⲁ-ⲛⲁⲓ̈

6. ⲛⲉϩⲓⲟⲟⲩⲉ ⲛ̄ⲛⲁϩⲣⲛ̄-ⲧⲡⲟⲗⲓⲥ.

7. ⲟⲩⲛ̄-ϩⲉⲛⲁ́ⲅⲅⲉⲗⲟⲥ ⲉⲃⲟⲗ ⲛ̄ⲧⲛ̄-ⲡⲣ̄ⲣⲟ.

8. ⲉⲃⲟⲗ ⲙ̄-ⲡⲕⲁϩ ⲛ̄-ⲕⲏⲙⲉ

9. ⲡϣⲏⲣⲉ ⲁϫⲛ̄-ⲧⲉϥⲙⲁⲁⲩ.

10. ⲧⲭⲁ́ⲣⲓⲥ ⲅⲁⲣ ⲉⲃⲟⲗ ϩⲓⲧⲛ̄-ⲡⲛⲟⲩⲧⲉ.

CHAPTER 9

NUMBERS AND TIME

OVERVIEW

In this chapter, you will learn:

- How numbers are formed and used
- Terminology for time and units of time

With this chapter and chapter 10, we are nearing the end of our discussion of nouns and everything that isn't part of the Sahidic verbal system. The material in these chapters is given here for your reference, but not all of it needs to be memorized right away. The vocabulary list at the end specifies what is most important to know.

NUMBERS

9.1 Usage of Numbers. Numbers in Sahidic can be encountered on their own or connected to nouns. If connected to a noun, a numeral is linked with the genitive particle/preposition ⲛ̄-, just as with adjectives (chapter 5). The number precedes the noun, except for ⲥⲛⲁⲩ, ⲥⲛ̄ⲧⲉ ("two"), which follows it without the linking ⲛ̄-. The linking ⲛ̄- is optional after ⲟⲩⲁ, ⲟⲩⲉⲓ ("one").

(ⲡ)ⲟⲩⲁ (ⲛ̄-)ϣⲃⲏⲣ	(the) one friend
(ⲧ)ϭⲓϫ ⲥⲛ̄ⲧⲉ	(the) two hand(s)
(ⲧ)ⲥⲁϣϥⲉ ⲛ̄-ⲉⲕⲕⲗⲏⲥⲓⲁ	(the) seven assembl(ies)

Note that the enumerated noun is treated as singular, even when there are more than one of them. We supply the plural ending in our translations.

As with Greek, the letters of the alphabet are also used as numbers, with an extended overline signifying this usage.

9.2 Forms of Numbers. *Cardinal numbers* are forms used to count and specify quantities (one, two, three, etc.). Depending on the kind of text you're reading, you may encounter numbers rarely, if at all. (It's a different story if you're reading inventories, chronicles, or genealogies!)

THE SAHIDIC NOUN SYSTEM

Below are given the forms of the cardinal numbers: the single digits, the tens, the hundreds, and the special words for thousand and ten thousand, including their feminine variations. Also listed are the forms used when combining single digits with a unit of ten (like ⲙⲛⲧ-ⲁϥⲧⲉ, "ten" + "four," ϣϥⲉⲧ[1]-ⲁⲥⲉ, "seventy" + "six"). Hundreds come before smaller numbers, allowing more complex numbers:

ⲣⲛⲅ̄	ϣⲉ ⲧⲁⲓⲟⲩ-ϣⲟⲙⲧⲉ	one hundred fifty-three
ⲭⲝ̄ⳃ̄	ⲥⲉⲩ-ϣⲉ ⲥⲉⲧ-ⲁⲥⲉ	six hundred sixty-six

Numbers in the thousands and higher will often connect their components with ⲙⲛ̄-:

ⲙⲛ̄ⲧ-ⲁϥⲧⲉ ⲛ̄-ⲧⲃⲁ ⲙⲛ̄-ϥⲧⲟⲟⲩ ⲛ̄-ϣⲟ   fourteen ten thousand(s) **with/and** four thousand
(= one hundred and forty-four thousand)

#		m	f	combined	
ⲁ̄	1	ⲟⲩⲁ	ⲟⲩⲉⲓ	-ⲟⲩⲉ(ⲓ)	one
ⲃ̄	2	ⲥⲛⲁⲩ	ⲥⲛ̄ⲧⲉ	-ⲥⲛⲟⲟⲩⲥ(ⲉ)	two
ⲅ̄	3	ϣⲟⲙⲛ̄ⲧ	ϣⲟⲙⲧⲉ	-ϣⲟⲙⲧⲉ	three
ⲇ̄	4	ϥⲧⲟⲟⲩ	ϥⲧⲟ(ⲉ)	-ⲁϥⲧⲉ	four
ⲉ̄	5	ϯⲟⲩ	ϯ(ⲉ)	-(ⲧ)ⲏ	five
ⳃ̄ [2]	6	ⲥⲟⲟⲩ	ⲥⲟ(ⲉ)	-ⲁⲥⲉ	six
ⲍ̄	7	ⲥⲁϣϥ̄	ⲥⲁϣϥⲉ	-ⲥⲁϣϥ(ⲉ)	seven
ⲏ̄	8	ϣⲙⲟⲩⲛ	ϣⲙⲟⲩⲛⲉ	-ϣⲙⲏⲛ(ⲉ)	eight
ⲑ̄	9	ⲯⲓⲧ, ⲯⲓⲥ	ⲯⲓⲧⲉ, ⲯⲓⲥⲉ		nine
tens					
ⲓ̄	10	ⲙⲏⲧ	ⲙⲏⲧⲉ	ⲙⲛ̄ⲧ-	ten
ⲕ̄	20	ϫⲟⲩⲱⲧ	ϫⲟⲩⲱⲧⲉ	ϫⲟⲩⲧ-	twenty[3]
ⲗ̄	30	ⲙⲁⲁⲃ	ⲙⲁⲁⲃⲉ	ⲙⲁⲃ(ⲧ)-	thirty
ⲙ̄	40	ϩⲙⲉ		ϩⲙⲉ(ⲧ)-	forty
ⲛ̄	50	ⲧⲁ(ⲉ)ⲓⲟⲩ		ⲧⲁⲓⲟⲩ(ⲧ)-	fifty
ⲝ̄	60	ⲥⲉ		ⲥⲉ(ⲧ)-	sixty
ⲟ̄	70	ϣϥⲉ		ϣϥⲉ(ⲧ)-	seventy
ⲡ̄	80	ϩⲙⲉⲛⲉ		ϩⲙⲉⲛⲉ(ⲧ)-	eighty
ϥ̄ [4]	90	ⲡⲥ̄ⲧⲁⲓⲟⲩ		ⲡⲥ̄ⲧⲁⲓⲟⲩ(ⲧ)-	ninety

---

1. This ⲧ, given in parentheses in the list below, is an epenthetic letter added when the suffixed digit begins in a vowel (i.e., -ⲁϥⲧⲉ or -ⲁⲥⲉ).

2. This is the archaic Greek letter *wau/digamma/stigma* (which once had the value of [w]), which is not used in Sahidic except as the symbol for the number six.

3. ϫⲟⲩⲱⲧ is also used as a unit of twenty (a "score"), as in ϥⲧⲟⲟⲩ(ⲛ̄)-ϫⲟⲩⲱⲧ "four score(s)" = eighty.

4. This letter, which looks identical to *fai*, was originally the archaic Greek letter *qoppa* [k], which is not used in Sahidic except as the number ninety.

NUMBERS AND TIME

hundreds

p̄	100	ϣε		(one) hundred
c̄	200	ϣηт	ϣn̄т-сn̄тε	two hundred
т̄	300	ϣ(о)мn̄т-ϣε		three hundred
ȳ	400	ϥтεγ-ϣε, ϥтооγ n̄-ϣε		four hundred
φ̄	500	ϯоγ n̄-ϣε		five hundred
x̄	600	сεγ-ϣε, сооγ n̄-ϣε		six hundred
ψ̄	700	саϣϥ(ε) n̄-ϣε		seven hundred
ω̄	800	ϣмоγn(ε) n̄-ϣε		eight hundred
ϥ̄	900	ϯс(ε) n̄-ϣε		nine hundred
ⲁ̿ [5]	1,000	ϣо		(one) thousand
ⲓ̿	10,000	тва		ten thousand (nm)

Ordinal numbers—numbers used to show sequence (first, second, third, etc.)—are easy. You already know "first"—the "adjective" ϣорп̄ (f ϣорпε). All the rest are formed by prefixing мεϩ(-n̄)- to the cardinal form:

| псаϣϥ n̄-εвот | the seven month(s) (cardinal) |
| пмεϩ-n̄-саϣϥ n̄-εвот | the seven**th** month (ordinal) |

TIME

9.3 Terms. Below are some important terms for periods of time, along with a selection of phrases derived from them. Most of these idioms are pretty easy to understand and can help you to get a sense of these words' usages.

оγоειϣ [6]	time, occasion (nm)
n̄-оγоειϣ ним	every time, always
n̄-оγоγоειϣ	once, on one occasion (in the past)
м̄-πεоγоειϣ	at this/that time
оγноγ [7]	hour, moment (nf)
n̄-тεγноγ	immediately, suddenly
тεноγ	now
ϣа-тεноγ	until now
ϫιn-тεноγ	from now on
ϩооγ [8]	day (nm)
(м̄-)πооγ	today [ϩ drops]
ϣа-πооγ	until today, until now

---

[5]. Starting with one thousand, the letters of the alphabet are reused with a double overline above the letters.
[6]. Note: this word uses the longer form of the definite article (πεоγоειϣ).
[7]. Note: this word begins with a consonant cluster [wnu].
[8]. Note: this word uses the longer form of the definite article (πεϩооγ).

ⲟⲩϣⲏ⁹	night (nf)
ϩⲧⲟⲟⲩⲉ	dawn, morning (nm)
ⲉ/ⲛ̄/ϩⲓ-ϩⲧⲟⲟⲩⲉ	at dawn
ⲣⲟⲩϩⲉ	evening (nm)
ⲉ/ⲛ̄/ϩⲓ-ⲣⲟⲩϩⲉ	in the evening
ϣⲁ-ⲣⲟⲩϩⲉ	until evening
ⲥⲁ́ⲃⲃⲁⲧⲟⲛ	Sabbath; week (sg or pl)¹⁰ (nm)
ⲉⲃⲟⲧ (pl ⲉⲃⲁⲧⲉ, ⲉⲃⲉⲧⲉ)	month (nm)
ⲣⲟⲙⲡⲉ¹¹ (pl ⲣ̄ⲙ̄ⲡⲟⲟⲩⲉ)	year (nf)
(ⲛ̄-)ⲧⲣⲟⲙⲡⲉ	this year
ⲛ̄-ⲟⲩⲣⲟⲙⲡⲉ	for a year
ⲛ̄-ϣⲟⲙⲧⲉ ⲛ̄-ⲣⲟⲙⲡⲉ	for three years

9.4 Days of the Week. Outside of the first and last days of the week, the days of the week do not have special names and are just referred to by the corresponding numeral (literally "the Two," "the Three," etc.). Here are their modern correspondences:

1.	ⲡⲟⲩⲁ, ⲧⲕⲩⲣⲓⲁⲕⲏ¹²	Sunday
2.	ⲡⲉⲥⲛⲁⲩ	Monday
3.	ⲡϣⲟⲙⲛ̄ⲧ	Tuesday
4.	ⲡⲉϥⲧⲟⲟⲩ	Wednesday
5.	ⲡϯⲟⲩ	Thursday
6.	ⲡⲥⲟⲟⲩ	Friday
7.	ⲡⲥⲁ́ⲃⲃⲁⲧⲟⲛ	Saturday

9.5 Months of the Year. The traditional native Egyptian names of the months are retained in the Coptic period for local purposes. They are used in historical and hagiographic writings, but you won't encounter them in biblical translations. They are given here for your reference, along with roughly equivalent months of our current calendar:

1.	ⲑⲟⲟⲩⲧ, ⲑⲱϣ	±September
2.	ⲡⲁⲟⲡⲉ	±October
3.	ϩⲁⲑⲱⲣ	±November
4.	ⲕⲟⲓⲁϩⲕ	±December
5.	ⲧⲱⲃⲉ	±January
6.	ⲙ̄ϣⲓⲣ	±February
7.	ⲡⲁⲣⲙ̄ϩⲟⲧⲡ̄	±March
8.	ⲡⲁⲣⲙⲟⲩⲧⲉ	±April

---

9. Note: this word begins with a consonant cluster [wʃe].

10. Somewhat confusingly, the same word is used for "week" (seven days) and for "Sabbath" (the seventh day of the week). This usage, borrowed from Greek, ultimately goes back to two different (but similar sounding) words in Hebrew/Aramaic, one meaning "cessation" (the Sabbath) and the other meaning "seven" (the week).

11. Note: this word uses the longer form of the definite article (ⲧⲉⲣⲟⲙⲡⲉ).

12. This name, borrowed from Greek, means "the one belonging to (the) Master" (ⲕⲩ́ⲣⲓⲟⲥ).

9.	ⲡⲁϣⲟⲛⲥ̄	±May
10.	ⲡⲁⲱⲛⲉ	±June
11.	ⲉⲡⲏⲡ	±July
12.	ⲙⲉⲥⲟⲣⲏ	±August

Elsewhere (such as in translations of biblical texts), months are often numbered:

ϩⲙ̄-ⲡⲙⲉϩ-ⲛ̄-ⲥⲁϣϥ̄ ⲛ̄-ⲉⲃⲟⲧ   in the seventh month

VOCABULARY

Learn the forms of the numbers up to twenty (9.2).

ⲟⲩⲟⲉⲓϣ	time, occasion (nm)
ⲟⲩⲛⲟⲩ[13]	hour, moment (nf)
ⲧⲉⲛⲟⲩ	now
ϩⲟⲟⲩ	day (nm)
(ⲙ̄-)ⲡⲟⲟⲩ	today [ϩ drops]
ⲟⲩϣⲏ[14]	night (nf)
ϩⲧⲟⲟⲩⲉ	dawn, morning (nm)
ⲣⲟⲩϩⲉ	evening (nm)
ⲥⲁ́ⲃⲃⲁⲧⲟⲛ	Sabbath; week (sg or pl) (nm)
ⲉⲃⲟⲧ (pl ⲉⲃⲁⲧⲉ, ⲉⲃⲉⲧⲉ)	month (nm)
ⲣⲟⲙⲡⲉ (pl ⲣⲙ̄ⲡⲟⲟⲩⲉ)	year (nf)
(ⲛ̄-)ⲧⲣⲟⲙⲡⲉ	this year

EXERCISE

Copy and translate the following phrases.

1. ⲡⲙⲉϩ-ϣⲟⲙⲛ̄ⲧ ⲛ̄-ϩⲟⲟⲩ _____

2. ϣⲙⲛ̄ⲧ-ϣⲉ ⲥⲉ-ⲧⲏ _____

3. ϣⲉ ϩⲙⲉⲛⲉ-ϣⲙⲏⲛⲉ _____

4. ⲙⲛ̄ⲧ-ⲥⲛⲟⲟⲩⲥ ⲛ̄-ϣⲉ ⲙⲛ̄-ⲥⲉ _____

---

13. Note: this word begins with a consonant cluster [wnu].
14. Note: this word begins with a consonant cluster [wʃe].

5. ⲡⲙⲛ̅ⲧ-ⲥⲛⲟⲟⲩⲥ ⲛ̅-ⲙⲁⲑⲏⲧⲏⲥ

6. ϩⲙ̅-ⲡϣⲟⲣⲡ̅ ⲛ̅-ⲉⲃⲟⲧ

7. ϩⲙ̅-ⲡⲙⲉϩ-ⲥⲛⲁⲩ ⲛ̅-ⲉⲃⲟⲧ

8. ⲡⲟⲟⲩ ⲡⲥⲁ́ⲃⲃⲁⲧⲟⲛ ⲡⲉ.

9. ⲧⲉⲛⲟⲩ ⲇⲉ ⲟⲩⲟⲩⲟⲉⲓϣ ⲛ̅-ⲁⲅⲁⲑⲟⲛ ⲡⲉ.

10. ⲡⲉⲓ̈ⲉⲃⲟⲧ ⲡⲁⲣⲙ̅ϩⲟⲧⲡ̅ ⲡⲉ.

11. ⲧⲱⲃⲉ ⲡⲙⲉϩ-ⲛ̅-ϯⲟⲩ ⲛ̅-ⲉⲃⲟⲧ ⲡⲉ.

12. ϫⲓⲛ-ϩⲧⲟⲟⲩⲉ ϣⲁ-ⲣⲟⲩϩⲉ

CHAPTER 10

ODDS AND ENDS

OVERVIEW

In this chapter, you will learn:

- Some further categories of pronouns, including ones used to form questions
- Words for general quantities
- Some elements used to form compound words

This is our final chapter of material before we turn our attention to the Sahidic verbal system.

ASKING QUESTIONS

10.1 Interrogative Pronouns. While Sahidic scribes did not utilize anything equivalent to a question mark[1] (and so many statements could also be read as questions without context), Sahidic does have a set of interrogative pronouns that can be used to form questions.

ⲁϣ	what? (inter pron)
ⲟⲩ[2]	what? (inter pron)
ⲉⲧⲃⲉ-ⲟⲩ	why?
ⲉ-ⲟⲩ	why? for what reason?
ⲛⲓⲙ[3]	who? (inter pron)
ⲟⲩⲏⲣ	how many? how much? (inter pron)
ⲡⲱⲥ	how? (inter pron)
ⲧⲱⲛ	where? (inter pron)
ⲉ-ⲧⲱⲛ	(to) where?
ⲉⲃⲟⲗ ⲧⲱⲛ	(from) where?

---

1. We will be employing question marks in our texts (along with word divisions and other innovations).
2. ⲟⲩ can also have a prefixed indefinite article.
3. To be distinguished from the adjective ⲛⲓⲙ ("every, each").

Typically, these interrogatives are found at the beginning of the sentence, but 1st and 2nd person pronouns may precede them:

ⲚⲒⲘ ⲦⲈ ⲦⲈⲒⲢ̄ⲢⲰ?	**Who**'s this queen?
ⲞⲨⲎⲢ ⲠⲈ ⲠⲀⲒ̈?	**How much**'s this?
Ⲛ̄ⲦⲈⲦⲚ̄-ⲚⲒⲘ?	**Who**'re you?

10.2 Indefinite Pronouns. Unlike the prefixed indefinite article (4.1), these indefinite pronouns stand as independent words on their own.

ⲖⲀⲀⲨ	anyone, anything (neg: nothing); as adj: any (indef pron)
ⲞⲨⲞⲚ	anyone, some(one/thing) (indef pron)
ⲞⲨⲞⲚ ⲚⲒⲘ	everyone
ϨⲞ(Ⲉ)ⲒⲚⲈ	some, certain ones (indef pron)

10.3 Pronouns and Possession. We discussed possessive articles back in 6.3. Remember that those showed both the gender/number of the possessed noun and the person/number/gender of the possessor. There are also *absolute relative pronouns*, which are prefixed to a noun to show possession or connection of something to that noun (with which the pronoun will agree in gender/number). Note that these are not the same as the 1st person possessive article ("my"), a fact that will be emphasized by our use of a hyphen with these!

ⲠⲀ-	(msg)
ⲦⲀ-	(fsg)
ⲚⲀ-	(pl)

These can be translated literally as "(that/those) of/connected to" or other more naturally idiomatic English ways that show possession.

| ⲦⲀ-ⲚⲒⲘ ⲦⲈ ⲦⲈⲒϨⲒⲔⲰⲚ? | **Of** whom's this image? Who**se**'s this image? |
| ⲦⲀ-ⲠⲢ̄ⲢⲞ ⲦⲈ. | It's the king**'s**. |

Finally, there are independent *possessive pronouns*, which stand on their own, agree with the implied noun in gender/number, and have personal suffixes (7.2) that agree with the person/gender/number of the possessor.

ⲠⲰ⸗	(msg)
ⲦⲰ⸗	(fsg)
ⲚⲞⲨ⸗	(pl)

These are translated as "mine," "yours," "his," "hers," etc.

| ⲠⲰϤ ⲠⲈ. | It's **his**. |
| ⲚⲞⲨⲒ̈ ⲚⲈ. | They're **mine**. |

QUANTITIES AND COMPOUNDS

10.4 Quantities. The following are some additional nouns and adjectives that can be used to describe quantities.

ⲟⲩⲱⲧ (f ⲟⲩⲱⲧⲉ)	single, only; very same (usually after noun; rarely without ⲛ̄-) (adj)
ϩⲁϩ	many (usually before singular noun with ⲛ̄-) (adj)
ϩⲟⲩⲟ	greater part, abundance (as adj before noun without ⲛ̄- or after noun with ⲛ̄-: great, much; before adj: more, greater) (nm)
ⲉ-ⲡⲉϩⲟⲩⲟ	greatly, much
ⲛ̄-ϩⲟⲩⲟ ⲉ-, ⲉ-ϩⲟⲩⲟ ⲉ-, ⲉ-ϩⲟⲩⲉ-	more than
ⲕⲉⲧ, ϭⲉ (pl ⲕⲟⲟⲩⲉ) ⲕⲉ-[4]	(an)other; also, even (nm; ⲕⲉⲧⲉ [f])
ⲧⲏⲣ⸗[5]	all, entire, the whole (of) (adj/inflected modifier)
ⲡⲧⲏⲣϥ̄	the entirety, everything
ⲉ-ⲡⲧⲏⲣϥ̄	entirely, completely

10.5 Compounds. These five prefixes are commonly added to other words to form new compounds or abstractions. They are connected directly without hyphens.

ⲁⲧ- un-, non- (neg prefix)
   ⲁⲧ- is used with nouns and verbs to form negative adjectives.

ⲙⲛ̄ⲧ- matter of (-ness, -hood); language of (abstract prefix f)
   ⲙⲛ̄ⲧ- is used with nouns and adjectives to form feminine abstract nouns.

ϭⲓⲛ- + inf (act of) -ing (abstract prefix f)
   ϭⲓⲛ- is used with verbs to form feminine abstract nouns of action.

ⲣⲙ̄(ⲛ̄)- (a contraction of ⲣⲱⲙⲉ ⲛ̄-) person of (nmf)
   ⲣⲙ̄(ⲛ̄)- is used with nouns to form compound nouns.

ⲣⲉϥ- (a contraction of ⲣⲱⲙⲉ ⲉϥ-) person who (does: -ⲣ̄-[6]; something) (nmf)
   ⲣⲉϥ- is used with verbs to form compound nouns.

VOCABULARY

ⲁϣ	what? (inter pron)
ⲟⲩ	what? (inter pron)
ⲉⲧⲃⲉ-ⲟⲩ	why?
ⲉ-ⲟⲩ	why? for what reason?

---

4. Often found in this reduced form and prefixed directly to a noun (like an article).
5. A resumptive suffix (corresponding to the number/person/gender of the noun in question) is required.
6. This is a form of ⲉⲓⲣⲉ, a very common verb you'll encounter in chapter 12. Other verbs are less commonly used as well.

ⲛⲓⲙ	who? (inter pron)
ⲟⲩⲏⲣ	how many? how much? (inter pron)
ⲡⲱⲥ	how? (inter pron)
ⲧⲱⲛ	where? (inter pron)
ⲉ-ⲧⲱⲛ	(to) where?
ⲉⲃⲟⲗ ⲧⲱⲛ	(from) where?
ⲗⲁⲁⲩ	anyone, anything (neg: nothing); as adj: any (indef pron)
ⲟⲩⲟⲛ	anyone, some(one/thing) (indef pron)
ⲟⲩⲟⲛ ⲛⲓⲙ	everyone
ϩⲟ(ⲉ)ⲓⲛⲉ	some, certain ones (indef pron)
ⲡⲁ-	that of, that connected to (absolute rel pron msg)
ⲧⲁ-	that of, that connected to (absolute rel pron fsg)
ⲛⲁ-	those of, those connected to (absolute rel pron pl)
ⲡⲱ⸗	mine, yours, etc. (poss pron msg)
ⲧⲱ⸗	mine, yours, etc. (poss pron fsg)
ⲛⲟⲩ⸗	mine, yours, etc. (poss pron pl)
ⲟⲩⲱⲧ (f ⲟⲩⲱⲧⲉ)	single, only; very same (usually after noun; rarely without ⲛ̄-) (adj)
ϩⲁϩ	many (usually before singular noun with ⲛ̄-) (adj)
ϩⲟⲩⲟ	greater part, abundance (as adj before noun without ⲛ̄- or after noun with ⲛ̄-: great, much; before adj: more, greater) (nm)
ⲉ-ⲡⲉϩⲟⲩⲟ	greatly, much
ⲛ̄-ϩⲟⲩⲟ ⲉ-, ⲉ-ϩⲟⲩⲟ ⲉ-, ⲉ-ϩⲟⲩⲉ-	more than
ⲕⲉⲧ, ϭⲉ (pl ⲕⲟⲟⲩⲉ) ⲕⲉ-	(an)other; also, even (nm; ⲕⲉⲧⲉ [f])
ⲧⲏⲣ⸗	all, entire, the whole (of) (adj/inflected modifier)
ⲡⲧⲏⲣϥ̄	the entirety, everything
ⲉ-ⲡⲧⲏⲣϥ̄	entirely, completely
ⲁⲧ-	un-, non- (neg prefix)
ⲙⲛ̄ⲧ-	matter of (-ness, -hood); language of (abstract prefix f)
ϭⲓⲛ-	+ inf (act of) -ing (abstract prefix f)
ⲣⲙ̄(ⲛ̄)- (a contraction of ⲣⲱⲙⲉ ⲛ̄-)	person of (nmf)
ⲣⲉϥ- (a contraction of ⲣⲱⲙⲉ ⲉϥ-)	person who (does: -ⲡ̄-; something) (nmf)

EXERCISE

Copy and translate the following phrases.

1. ⲟⲩ ⲛⲉ ⲛⲏ? _____

2. ⲉⲧⲃⲉ-ⲟⲩ ⲡⲉⲓ̈ⲡⲟⲛⲏⲣⲟ́ⲛ? _____

ODDS AND ENDS

3. ⲡⲁ-ⲛⲓⲙ ⲡⲉ?

4. ⲡⲁ-ⲡⲁⲉⲓⲱⲧ ⲡⲉ.

5. ⲟⲩϣⲁϫⲉ ⲛ̄-ⲟⲩⲱⲧ

6. ϩⲁϩ ⲛ̄-ⲣⲱⲙⲉ ⲛ̄-ⲇⲓ́ⲕⲁⲓⲟⲥ

7. ϩⲙ̄-ⲡⲕⲁϩ ⲧⲏⲣϥ̄

8. ⲛ̄-ⲙ̄ⲡⲟⲗⲓⲥ ⲧⲏⲣⲟⲩ

9. ⲉⲃⲟⲗ ϩⲓⲧⲛ̄-ⲕⲉϩⲓⲏ

10. ⲙⲛ̄ⲧⲣⲙ̄ⲛ̄ⲕⲏⲙⲉ

THE SAHIDIC
VERB SYSTEM

CHAPTER 11

INTRODUCTION TO SAHIDIC VERBS

OVERVIEW

In this chapter, you will learn:

- Some basics about the form and function of Sahidic verbs
- The main categories of the Sahidic verbal system

SAHIDIC VERBS

11.1 **Verbal Functions.** So far, we've seen how Sahidic can form complete sentences without the use of proper verbs (nominal sentences that employ the copula). Those kinds of sentences can be sufficient to show descriptions, connections, and identifications. But as with other languages, verbs are the engines of most Sahidic sentences. Verbs make things happen—unlike the static portrait of a nominal sentence, a verbal sentence can have *action*.

In this chapter, we'll be doing a quick survey of the entire Sahidic verbal system. Do not feel you need to memorize all these categories and terms right now; we'll be working through them systematically and in much greater detail over the remainder of the chapters. This is just to give you the road map of where we'll be going in our exploration of the Sahidic verbal system.

11.2 **Verbal Forms.** The different forms that verbs take convey many different kinds of information. Many prefixes and suffixes can be attached to a verbal stem (the core, basic, "dictionary" form of the verb). Sahidic verbs have conjugations that can prefix information about the person, number, and (sometimes) gender of the subject doing the action. The conjugation also provides information about the tense (time) and aspect (ongoing, etc.) of the verbal action. At the end of the verbal stem, you may find suffixed information about the object of the action. All of this information may be found within a single Sahidic bound phrase—something we might utilize an entire English sentence to translate.

SURVEY OF THE VERBAL SYSTEM

11.3 **The Two Patterns.** The Sahidic verbal system is comprised of a dozen verbal conjugations. To give you a taste of these, the 1st person singular (common gender) form of each conjugation will be provided along with a basic English translation. The verbal stem for all of these is what will be our model verb ⲥϩⲁⲓ, meaning "to write." In front of that stem is the 1st person singular prefix for that conjugation.

All these conjugations are divided into two major groupings, which we will refer to as *patterns*.

11.4 **The Durative Pattern.** The first of the two patterns is the Durative. As the name implies, verbs in this pattern are characterized by an ongoing, continuous type of action (aspect). The verbal action is usually seen as in process, not a finished or discrete event. Sensibly, this kind of action works for current or impending events in time, and thus the Durative Pattern covers the Present and Future tenses. The ϯ- prefixed to the verbal stem ⲥϩⲁⲓ is the part that supplies the "I am" component. For the future, the infixed -ⲛⲁ- (which comes from a verb of motion) supplies the "going to" part. The verbal stem used in the Durative Pattern can be either the infinitive or the stative (more on those next chapter).

- **Present** (chapter 13)
    ϯⲥϩⲁⲓ   I am writing
- **Future** (chapter 14)
    ϯⲛⲁⲥϩⲁⲓ   I am going to write

11.5 **The Non-Durative Pattern.** The remainder of the Sahidic verbal system's conjugations do not have the Durative pattern's emphasis on ongoing verbal action. Creatively, we refer to this as the Non-Durative pattern. Within the Non-Durative pattern, there are two subgroups of conjugations: *Main Clause* (which can stand on their own in as a full sentence) and *Subordinate Clause* (which are connected to a main clause conjugation and aren't complete sentences on their own). Together, these conjugations cover a wide range of temporal, modal, and syntactical nuances, but they all share the use of a *verbal auxiliary*, a prefixed element that marks the tense. This, in combination with a personal subject prefix, is prefixed to the verbal stem (infinitives only) to form the verbal conjugation. In the 1st person singular Past example below, the ⲁ- is the Past verbal auxiliary, and the -ⲓ- marks the 1st person singular subject ("I").[1]

---

1. Note that these examples are all the *affirmative* versions of these conjugations. Different verbal auxiliaries are used for their *negative* counterparts (but we'll deal with that later).

Main Clause Conjugations
- **Past** (chapter 16)
    - ⲁⲓ̈ⲥϩⲁⲓ̈   I wrote
- **Aorist** (chapter 17)
    - ϣⲁⲓ̈ⲥϩⲁⲓ̈   I write
- **Optative** (chapter 18)
    - ⲉⲓ̈ⲉⲥϩⲁⲓ̈   I will write
- **Jussive** (chapter 18)
    - ⲙⲁⲣⲓⲥϩⲁⲓ̈   let me write!

Subordinate Clause Conjugations
- **Conjunctive** (chapter 24)
    - ⲛ̄ⲧⲁⲥϩⲁⲓ̈   . . . and (I) write
- **Future Conjunctive** (chapter 24)
    - ⲧⲁⲣⲓⲥϩⲁⲓ̈   . . . and I will write
- **Precursive** (chapter 25)
    - ⲛ̄ⲧⲉⲣⲓⲥϩⲁⲓ̈   when/after I had written/wrote
- **Limitative** (chapter 25)
    - ϣⲁⲛϯⲥϩⲁⲓ̈   until I write/wrote/have written/had written
- **Conditional** (chapter 26)
    - ⲉⲓ̈ϣⲁⲛⲥϩⲁⲓ̈   if/when(ever) I write/wrote
- **Causative Infinitive** (chapter 26)
    - ⲧⲣⲁⲥϩⲁⲓ̈   (cause) me to write, me writing

That last one, the Causative Infinitive, is an inflected causative not quite the same as the Subordinate Clause conjugations, but it is convenient to discuss it alongside them. Don't worry about the large number of Non-Durative pattern conjugations—while it is important to be familiar with the less common conjugations, the Past is far and away the most common (attested an order of magnitude more often than the rest on average). Along with the Present and Future of the Durative pattern, these three will be the most frequent verbs you'll usually encounter in your reading.

11.6   **Converters.** In addition to these two patterns, there is a system of prefixed converters. These are used for the Durative (Present and Future) and the primary Non-Durative conjugations (Past and Aorist). We will discuss the conversion system in between the Main Clause and Subordinate Clause conjugations (*Relative* [chapter 19], *Circumstantial* [chapter 20], *Preterite* [chapter 21], and *Focalizing* [chapter 22]). These are not conjugations on their own, but are additional prefixes that give further nuance and emphasis to their verbs.

VOCABULARY

ⲁⲡⲟⲥⲧⲟⲗⲟⲥ   emissary, envoy (nm)

ⲡⲣⲟⲫⲏⲧⲏⲥ   foreteller, spokesperson (nm; ⲡⲣⲟⲫⲏⲧⲓⲥ [f])

caϩ[2]	writer, scribe; teacher, master (nmf)
ⲉⲛⲉϩ	age; eternity; frequently as adv: ever (neg: never) (nm)
ϣⲁ-(ⲛⲓ)ⲉⲛⲉϩ	forever
ⲕⲟⲥⲙⲟⲥ	world, universe (nm)
ⲙⲁ	place (nm)
ⲙ̄-ⲡⲉïⲙⲁ	here, in this place
ⲥⲩⲛⲁⲅⲱⲅⲏ	gathering (place) (nf)
ⲕⲱϩⲧ̄	fire (nm)
ⲱⲛⲉ	stone (nm)
ⲧⲟⲟⲩ (pl ⲧⲟⲩⲉⲓⲏ)	mountain; monastery (nm)
ϩⲁⲗⲁⲥⲥⲁ, θⲁⲗⲁⲥⲥⲁ[3]	sea (nf)
ⲕⲣⲟ (pl ⲕⲣⲱⲟⲩ)	shore, bank, margin (of land) (nm)
ϫⲟï (pl ⲉϫⲏⲩ[4])	ship, boat (nm)
ⲁⲕⲁθⲁⲣⲧⲟⲥ	unclean (adj)
ⲁⲡⲓⲥⲧⲟⲥ[5]	untrusting, untrustworthy (adj)
ⲃⲗ̄ⲗⲉ́ (f ⲃⲗ̄ⲗⲏ; pl ⲃⲗ̄ⲗⲉⲉⲩ[ⲉ])	blind (adj)
ϣⲙ̄ⲙⲟ (f ϣⲙ̄ⲙⲱ; pl ϣⲙ̄ⲙⲟï)	foreign (adj)
ϩⲏⲕⲉ	poor (adj)
ϫⲱⲱⲣⲉ	strong (adj)
ⲉⲓⲥ-(ϩⲏ[ⲏ]ⲧⲉ)	look! see! (interj)

EXERCISE

Copy and translate the following phrases.

1. ⲡⲁⲩ́ⲗⲟⲥ ⲡⲁⲡⲟ́ⲥⲧⲟⲗⲟⲥ ⲛ̄-ⲓⲏⲥⲟⲩ́ⲥ ⲡⲉⲭⲣⲓⲥⲧⲟⲥ _____

2. ⲛⲉϫⲏⲩ ϩⲓϫⲛ̄-θⲁⲗⲁⲥⲥⲁ ⲛⲉ. _____

3. ⲣⲁⲕⲟⲧⲉ ⲧⲡⲟⲗⲓⲥ ⲛ̄-ⲥⲁⲉⲓⲉ _____

4. ⲡⲉⲧⲣⲟⲥ ϩⲛ̄-ⲧⲥⲩⲛⲁⲅⲱⲅⲏ _____

---

2. This noun is related to our model verb ⲥϩⲁï, "to write."
3. The first sound of the Greek word θάλασσα was (usually) re-analyzed as being the prefixed feminine article!
4. With the definite article, the plural is written ⲛⲉϫⲏⲩ.
5. In Greek, the ⲁ- prefix (ⲁⲛ- before a vowel) is used to make a negative adjective, an absence of the base term—similar to our English prefixes "un-," "ir-," "im-," in-," etc.

5. ⲡⲁⲥⲁϩ ⲡⲉ ϣⲉⲛⲟⲩⲧⲉ.

6. ⲉⲓⲥ-ϩⲏⲏⲧⲉ! ⲟⲩⲛ̄-ⲟⲩⲕⲱϩⲧ̄ ϩⲓ-ⲡⲧⲟⲟⲩ!

7. ⲡⲱⲕ ⲡⲉ ⲡⲕόⲥⲙⲟⲥ ϣⲁ-ⲛⲓⲉⲛⲉϩ.

8. ⲛ̄ⲱⲛⲉ ⲛ̄-ϫⲱⲱⲣⲉ ⲙ̄-ⲡⲉⲣⲡⲉ

9. ⲡⲉⲛⲥⲟⲛ ⲟⲩⲁⲕάθⲁⲣⲧⲟⲥ ⲡⲉ.

10. ⲡⲉⲡⲣⲟⲫⲏ́ⲧⲏⲥ ⲛ̄-ⲃⲗ̄ⲗέ ⲟⲩⲃⲉ-ⲡⲉⲕⲣⲟ ⲡⲉ.

CHAPTER 12

FORMS OF THE VERBAL STEM

OVERVIEW

In this chapter, you will learn:

- What kinds of information can be found in a verb's lexical listing
- The three kinds of infinitives, the stative, and the conjunct participle
- How infinitives can be used as imperatives and nouns

INFINITIVES (AND IMPERATIVES)

12.1 Verbal Listings in the Lexicon. Our vocabulary lists will now be including verbs. As an example, here's the full lexical listing for our model verb cϩⲁï:

cϩⲁï   cⲉϩ-   cϩⲁï(c)⸗, cⲁϩ⸗, cⲉϩⲧ⸗[1]   cнϩ†   to write (ⲙ̄ⲙⲟ⸗; on, in: ⲉ[ϫⲛ̄]-, ϩⲓ[ϫⲛ̄]-, ϩⲛ̄-; to: ⲛⲁ⸗, ⲉ-, ϣⲁ-); to register; to draw, paint (vt)
to be written, in writing (vs)
writing, letter (nm)

On the left, the four entries are the three forms of the infinitive and the stative (not all verbs will have forms for all four). After that comes the verb's definition, which can include differences for how the verb is used, including if it takes a direct object or has a stative form. These are listed as their own lines (if present), with the relevant verbal category in parentheses after the definition. Prepositions that the verb regularly uses will be listed in parentheses as well. Many verbal stems are also used as nouns, and this usage is listed if common (or unusual). Finally, special idioms and phrases built off of the verb can be listed. We'll discuss these various options next.

---

1. The multiple forms in this column are variants of the prepersonal form of the infinitive (see below). cϩⲁï is somewhat irregular in this form—most verbs don't demonstrate this kind of variation.

12.2 **The Three Forms of the Infinitive.** In the lexical listings you will see that verbs are categorized (in parentheses, after the definitions) as either *transitive* (vt), *intransitive* (vi), and/or occasionally *reflexive* (vr). Transitive verbs can take direct objects: they are actions that happen to someone or something. "I write the words," would be an example, where "write" is the verb, and "the words" is the direct object. Keep in mind that transitive verbs are not obliged to always have an explicitly stated direct object—"I write" (as a general statement) can be a complete sentence on its own too. Intransitive verbs do not take direct objects: they are simply actions taken by the subject. They have no direct object. "It happens," "they grew," and "we remain" are all intransitive examples. Reflexive verbs are actions taken by the subject that involve or affect the subject. "We got (ourselves) ready," for example. Many Sahidic verbs can be used in multiple categories, so you will see separate line definitions for these different nuances.

Sahidic verbs that are transitive and/or reflexive will have up to three forms of the infinitive listed in their lexical entries:

1. The *absolute* form. This is the base form, and the form under which entries are alphabetized. With the absolute form, direct objects are marked by a prefixed preposition—most commonly ⲛ̄- (prefixed to a noun) / ⲙ̄ⲙⲟⲥ (with a personal suffix, 7.2)—used as the *direct object marker*.[2] In this usage, there is no real sensible translation in English. Think of it as a tag, an arrow pointing to the direct object.

    ⲁⲓ̈ⲥϩⲁⲓ̈[3] ⲛ̄-ⲛ̄ϣⲁϫⲉ.   I wrote > the words.
    ⲁⲓ̈ⲥϩⲁⲓ̈ ⲙ̄ⲙⲟⲟⲩ.   I wrote > them.

2. The *prenominal* form. This is an alternate form directly attached to a suffixed noun that is the direct object of the verb. In our lexical entries, this is marked by a hyphen (-), which is included when the noun is suffixed.

    ⲁⲓ̈ⲥⲉϩ-ⲛ̄ϣⲁϫⲉ.   I wrote the words.

3. The *prepersonal*[4] form. This last alternate form is used with a personal suffix that is the direct object. It is marked by a double slash (⸗) in its lexical form, but this isn't included once a personal object suffix is attached (as with prepositions, see 7.1).

    ⲁⲓ̈ⲥϩⲁⲓ̈ⲥⲟⲩ.   I wrote them.

Now, the question you might be asking is: What's the difference between ⲁⲓ̈ⲥϩⲁⲓ̈ ⲛ̄-ⲛ̄ϣⲁϫⲉ and ⲁⲓ̈ⲥⲉϩ-ⲛ̄ϣⲁϫⲉ if they both mean "I wrote the words"? Or what's the difference between ⲁⲓ̈ⲥϩⲁⲓ̈ ⲙ̄ⲙⲟⲟⲩ and ⲁⲓ̈ⲥϩⲁⲓ̈ⲥⲟⲩ if they both mean "I wrote them"? The short

---

2. In the definitions, this use of ⲛ̄-/ⲙ̄ⲙⲟⲥ as the direct object marker will be regularly marked just by ⲙ̄ⲙⲟⲥ.
3. In these examples, the ⲁⲓ̈- prefixed to the infinitives is for the 1st person singular Past (which we'll get to in chapter 16).
4. Also known as *prepronominal*; see Thomas O. Lambdin, *Introduction to Sahidic Coptic* (Macon, GA: Mercer University Press, 1983).

answer is: nothing, really. It's mostly a stylistic choice of cadence, emphasis, or nuance. One is more distanced, and the other is more directly connected. It's a bit like contractions in English: you can use either "cannot" or "can't," but both mean the same thing. Much of the time, Sahidic verbs have the option of marking direct objects more directly (using the prenominal or prepersonal forms of the infinitive) or in a more distanced manner (using the absolute and ⲛ̄-/ⲙ̄ⲙⲟ⸗). There are a few limitations to this flexibility, as we'll see.[5]

Strictly intransitive verbs will not have prenominal or prepersonal forms listed. As you learn more and more Sahidic verbs, you will start to notice patterns of similar vowel changes in the forms of the infinitives. Most native Sahidic verbs can be grouped by these similarities into morphological categories.[6]

Verbs of Greek origin (whether transitive or not) also do not have these variant forms, with the absolute form being similar to the Greek infinitive without the usual final ending (or the Greek singular imperative).

12.3 **The Imperative.** For the vast majority of verbs, the absolute form of the infinitive can also be used as the imperative—the way to command or tell someone to do something. However, a few common verbs have unique, older forms for the imperative. These will be listed in parentheses after the main verb forms: (impv ⲁⲣⲓⲣⲉ, ⲁⲣⲓ-, ⲁⲣⲓ⸗). Otherwise, you can assume that the absolute infinitive can also be used as an imperative (with the same form used whether addressing a single person or a group).

12.4 **Infinitives as Nouns.** The absolute form of the infinitive can also be used as a masculine noun. This is commonplace and can theoretically be applied to nearly any verb, although certain verbs are more regularly used this way. Commonly attested examples of this—or ones which may have a particularly nuanced usage—will be included in lexical listings after the main verbal definitions and tagged as (nm): noun, masculine.

STATIVES AND CONJUNCT PARTICIPLES

12.5 **The Stative.** The stative is an alternate form of the verbal stem that can *only* be used with the Durative pattern's primary conjugation, the Present—only infinitive forms appear in the Future and the many conjugations of the Non-Durative pattern. In our lexical lists, stative forms are signaled by a dagger mark at the end (†).[7] As its name implies, the stative describes its subject as existing in a certain state. By contrast,

---

5. These limitations are defined as the Stern–Jernstedt Rule(s), which include:
   a. Direct objects that are nouns without articles must use the prenominal form.
   b. The Present conjugation must otherwise use the absolute form and ⲛ̄-/ⲙ̄ⲙⲟ⸗.

A few other exceptions exist, namely, the verb ⲟⲩⲱϣ "to want, wish, desire," which only uses prenominal/prepersonal forms with its direct objects. See Bentley Layton, *Coptic in 20 Lessons: Introduction to Sahidic Coptic with Exercises and Vocabularies* (Leuven: Peeters, 2007), 84 and Layton, *A Coptic Grammar: With Chrestomathy and Glossary. Sahidic Dialect*, 3rd ed., Porta Linguarum Orientalium 2/20 (Wiesbaden: Harrassowitz, 2011), 171.

6. See Appendix 2: Verb Classes.

7. Older works may use the abbreviation Q (for "Qualitative," an older name for this form).

corresponding infinitives would instead focus on the process or action performed (which would lead to being in such a state).

For many verbs, the meaning of a stative form is generally predictable, and they can be translated in English with a passive form of the verb: снϩ† "to be written" as opposed to сϩⲁï "to write." For commonly seen statives (and those with special idiomatic senses), a separate line entry in the verb's definition is marked (vs).

12.6 The Conjunct Participle. Also known as the *construct* participle, this is a relatively rare verbal form attested for only a small percentage of Sahidic verbs. It is prefixed to a noun to form a compound adjective. These will be listed in parentheses after the main verb forms and will be preceded by the abbreviation cp.[8] In general, the conjunct participle can be translated in English as the *-ing* form of the verb and attached by hyphen after the noun, reversing the Sahidic order:[9]

ϫⲁⲧ-ⲙⲉ	truth-**saying**
ⲧⲁï-ⲟⲩⲟⲉⲓⲛ	light-**giving**

VOCABULARY

Chapter vocabulary lists from here on will include verbs. The verbs that have been selected are those that are the most frequently used in the Sahidic New Testament (i.e., verbs that occur more than fifty times).[10] сϩⲁï, which we'll be using as our paradigm verb, shows up more than 200 times, and the other four verbs are each attested more than 1,000 times! In addition to the different verbal forms discussed in this chapter, important idioms using these verbs will also be listed and defined.

ⲉⲓⲣⲉ	ⲣ̄-, ⲉⲣ-[11]	ⲁⲁ⸗	ⲟ†	(impv ⲁⲣⲓⲣⲉ, ⲁⲣⲓ-, ⲁⲣⲓ⸗) to do, make (ⲙ̄ⲙⲟ⸗) (vt)
				to be (ⲛ̄-[12]) (vs)
				doing, making (nm)
сϩⲁï	сⲉϩ-	сϩⲁï(с)⸗, сⲁϩ⸗, сⲉϩⲧ⸗	снϩ†	to write (ⲙ̄ⲙⲟ⸗; on, in: ⲉ[ϫⲛ̄]-, ϩⲓ[ϫⲛ̄]-, ϩⲛ̄-; to: ⲛⲁ⸗, ⲉ-, ϣⲁ-); to register; to draw, paint (vt)
				to be written, in writing (vs)
				writing, letter (nm)

---

8. Older works typically use the abbreviation p.c., from the Latin *participium conjunct(iv)um*.
9. For specifically intransitive/stative verbs, use an adjective instead: ϩⲁⲣϣ̄-ϩⲏⲧ "heart-**heavy**" (an idiom in Sahidic meaning "patient," not "sad").
10. See Bruce Metzger's *List of Words Occur[r]ing Frequently in the Coptic New Testament (Sahidic Dialect)* (Leiden: Brill, 1961).
11. ⲣ̄- is joined with many nouns to form compound verbs with the sense of "to do _" or "to become _" (with the stative form meaning "to be _").
12. The ⲛ̄- here (and with ϣⲟⲟⲡ† below) is the last form of ⲛ̄- you'll encounter: it's an *equivalence marker* used with those two statives. Like the related *direct object marker* use of ⲛ̄-/ⲙ̄ⲙⲟ⸗, there's no real English translation for it. Think of it like an equals sign (=), tagging what the subject is equivalent to.

THE SAHIDIC VERB SYSTEM

ϣⲱⲡⲉ		ϣⲟⲟⲡ†	to become, come into existence; to happen (vi)
			to be, exist[13] (vs)
			being, existence (nm)
ϣⲱⲡⲉ ⲙ̄ⲙⲟ⸗			to happen to (someone)
ⲁⲥϣⲱⲡⲉ			it happened that (followed by main verb)
ⲉϣⲱⲡⲉ			if
ϫⲱ	ϫⲉ-, ϫⲓ-	ϫⲟ(ⲟ)⸗	(cp ϫⲁⲧ-; impv ⲁϫⲓ-, ⲁϫⲓ⸗) to say; to sing (ⲙ̄ⲙⲟ⸗[14]) (vt)
			song (nm)
ⲡⲉϫⲉ-	ⲡⲉϫⲁ⸗		said (ϫⲉ: that " [introducing direct quotation]) (verboid)[15]
†	†-	ⲧⲁⲁ⸗	ⲧⲟ†	(cp ⲧⲁⲓ̈-; impv also ⲙⲁ, ⲙⲁ-, ⲙⲁⲧ⸗) to give (ⲙ̄ⲙⲟ⸗); to entrust (ⲙ̄ⲙⲟ⸗; to: ⲉⲧⲛ̄-) (vt)
			to go, begin (vr)
			to go, move (vi)
			to be given, fated (vs)
			gift (nm)
† ⲉⲃⲟⲗ			to sell (ⲙ̄ⲙⲟ⸗; to: ⲉ-, ⲛⲁ⸗)
† ⲟⲩⲃⲉ-, † ⲙⲛ̄-			to fight with
† ϩⲓ-			to put on (a garment: ⲙ̄ⲙⲟ⸗), to dress
†-ⲧⲟⲟⲧ⸗, † ⲛ̄-ⲧⲟⲟⲧ⸗			to give a hand to, help, assist
†-ϩⲧⲏ⸗			to pay attention, consider (to: ⲉ-, ⲉϫⲛ̄-, ϩⲓ-, ϩⲛ̄-)
ⲁⲡⲉ (pl ⲁⲡⲏ[ⲟ]ⲩⲉ)			head (nf)
ⲁⲥⲡⲉ			language, speech (nf)
ⲙⲁⲁϫⲉ			ear (nm)
ⲥⲙⲏ			voice, sound (nf)
σοφία			wisdom (nf)
ϩⲏⲧ (pl ϩⲉⲧⲉ)	ϩⲧⲏ⸗		heart, mind (nm)
ϩⲁⲣϣ̄-ϩⲏⲧ			heart-heavy (> patient)
ϫⲉ			that, because (conj)

EXERCISE

Copy and translate the following phrases. Even though we haven't gotten into the verbal conjugations yet, remember that our infinitives can be used as imperatives and nouns!

---

13. A predicate adjective is introduced with ⲛ̄- and has no article: ⲛⲉⲛϣⲟⲟⲡ ⲛ̄-δίκαιος (we were [being] just).

14. ϫⲱ will regularly include ⲙ̄ⲙⲟⲥ ("it") as the object before ϫⲉ and the direct quotation (next footnote). Literally "say it that: '[direct quote]'"—but you may leave "it" out of your translation if it feels too wordy in English.

15. This is a special and very common verboid that can be translated as the past tense: ⲡⲉϫⲁϥ "he said." The verb ϫⲱ does have a standard Past conjugation as well (chapter 16). ϫⲉ is a conjunction ("that") which is used, among other things, to introduce direct quotations. Since Sahidic didn't have quotation marks, this was a way to mark the start of the quote. It's similar to saying "quote" to preface aloud a direct quotation in English. You may leave "that" out of your translation if you prefer.

FORMS OF THE VERBAL STEM

1. ⲡⲉϫⲉ-ⲓⲏⲥⲟⲩⲥ ϫⲉ "ⲉⲓⲥ-ϩⲏⲏⲧⲉ!"

2. ⲡⲉⲓⲣⲉ ⲛ̄-ⲛ̄ⲁⲅⲁⲑⲟⲛ

3. ⲙⲁ ⲛⲁⲓ̈ ⲙ̄-ⲡϫⲱⲱⲙⲉ!

4. ϯ ⲙⲛ̄-ⲛⲉⲧⲛ̄ϫⲓϫⲉⲉⲩⲉ!

5. ⲁⲣⲓⲣⲉ ⲛ̄-ⲛ̄ⲁⲅⲁⲑⲟⲛ!

6. ⲁϫⲓ-ⲡϣⲁϫⲉ!

7. ⲥϩⲁⲓ̈ ⲙ̄-ⲡⲁⲅⲅⲉⲗⲟⲥ ⲛ̄-ⲧⲉⲕⲕⲗⲏⲥⲓⲁ!

8. ⲡⲉϫⲁϥ ϫⲉ "ⲧⲥⲟⲫⲓⲁ ϩⲛ̄-ⲡⲁϩⲏⲧ ⲧⲉ."

9. ⲡⲉϫⲁⲥ ϫⲉ "ⲧⲁⲥⲡⲉ ϩⲛ̄-ⲡⲁⲙⲁⲁϫⲉ ⲧⲉ ⲥⲁⲉⲓⲉ."

CHAPTER 13

THE DURATIVE PATTERN: THE PRESENT

OVERVIEW

In this chapter, you will learn:

- How to conjugate the primary Durative pattern conjugation, the Present
- The conjugation of the Negative Present
- How to translate both of these effectively in English

THE PRESENT CONJUGATION

13.1 **Conjugating the Present.** The primary conjugation of the Durative pattern is the Present conjugation. It has just two components: the *personal prefix* (which encodes the person/number/gender of the subject) and the *verbal stem* (which can be an infinitive or a stative). Because of these two parts, the Durative pattern is sometimes called the Bipartite pattern, especially in older works. Speaking of older terminology, the Present conjugation is also sometimes called the "First Present," but we will not be utilizing that nomenclature.[1] The personal prefixes of the Present conjugation are:

	singular		**plural**	
1st	ϯ-	I am	ⲧⲛ̄-	we are
2nd	ⲕ-	you (m) are	ⲧⲉⲧⲛ̄-	you are
	ⲧⲉ-[2]	you (f) are		
3rd	ϥ-	he, it (m) is	ⲥⲉ-	they are
	ⲥ-	she, it (f) is		

Attached to the infinitive ⲥϩⲁⲓ (to write), you get these forms:

---

1. See chapter 22 on the *Focalizing* converter for why.
2. The 2nd person feminine singular prefix is also found in the variant form ⲧⲣ̄-.

THE DURATIVE PATTERN: THE PRESENT

singular
- *1st* ϯⲥϩⲁⲓ — I am writing
- *2nd* ⲕⲥϩⲁⲓ — you (m) are writing
- ⲧⲉⲥϩⲁⲓ[3] — you (f) are writing
- *3rd* ϥⲥϩⲁⲓ — he, it (m) is writing
- ⲥⲥϩⲁⲓ — she, it (f) is writing

plural
- *1st* ⲧⲛ̄ⲥϩⲁⲓ — we are writing
- *2nd* ⲧⲉⲧⲛ̄ⲥϩⲁⲓ — you are writing
- *3rd* ⲥⲉⲥϩⲁⲓ — they are writing

You'll notice similarities between some of these personal prefixes and the independent personal pronouns (6.1), infixes of the possessive articles (6.3), and personal suffixes attached to prepositions (7.2).

If the immediate subject of the verb is a *definite* noun, that noun precedes the verbal stem, separated by a space. No personal prefix required:

ⲡⲣⲱⲙⲉ ⲥϩⲁⲓ.   The person is writing.

Don't be confused if you do also find a personal prefix along with the subject noun. Even though this is redundant, it is not uncommon. You can translate it more literally or smooth it out by simplifying it:

ⲡⲣⲱⲙⲉ, ϥⲥϩⲁⲓ.   The person, **he** is writing. *or* The person is writing.

However, if the subject is an *indefinite* noun, this has to be expressed with the existential particle ⲟⲩⲛ̄-:

ⲟⲩⲛ̄-ⲟⲩⲣⲱⲙⲉ ⲥϩⲁⲓ.   **There's** a person writing. *or* A person is writing.

The personal prefixes of the Durative/Present can also be used without verbs—they can be directly attached to prepositional phrases.

ϥϩⲙ̄-ⲡⲉⲣⲡⲉ.   **He is** in the temple.

13.2 Syntax of the Present. The Present is special in two ways. First, it can use the infinitive or the stative, the only conjugation with this option. Everything else in the Sahidic verbal system only uses forms of the infinitive. There is a small set of five verbs that *exclusively* use the stative with the Present, not the infinitive. These are all verbs of motion, two of which are in this chapter's vocabulary: ⲃⲱⲕ, ⲃⲏⲕ† "to go" and ⲉⲓ, ⲛⲏⲩ† "to come."[4]

---

3. ⲁⲥϩⲁⲓ or ⲁⲣⲉⲥϩⲁⲓ as variant forms.

4. The other three can be remembered as "F-L" verbs: "**fl**ee, run" (ⲡⲱⲧ, chapter 18 vocabulary), "**fa**ll" (ϩⲉ, chapter 19 vocabulary), and "**fl**y" (ϩⲱⲗ).

| ϯⲃⲏⲕ | (stat) | I am going |
| ϯⲛⲏⲩ | (stat) | I am coming |

The second special rule of the Present is that its direct objects with articles may only use the absolute form of the infinitive (with ⲛ̄-/ⲙ̄ⲙⲟ⸗ as the direct object marker).[5] The prenominal and prepersonal forms can be used in all the other conjugations.

| ϯⲥϩⲁⲓ ⲛ̄-ⲛ̄ϣⲁϫⲉ. | I am writing > the words. |
| ϯⲥϩⲁⲓ ⲙ̄ⲙⲟⲟⲩ. | I am writing > them. |

13.3 Translating the Present. The English continuous present ("I am writing") best expresses the durative, ongoing nature of the Sahidic Present in most circumstances, although the English simple present ("I write") can also be used—especially with certain more "cerebral" verbs of perception or thought. To contrast with nominal sentences (5.5), I suggest avoiding contractions of the "to be" part of the phrase.

As we introduced last chapter, the stative describes its subject as existing in a certain state or condition. English passives can often convey this idea:

| ⲥⲉⲥϩⲁⲓ | (inf) | they are writing |
| ⲥⲉⲥⲏϩ | (stat) | they are **written** |

With some verbs, the stative takes on a specific idiom of its own (which you will need to learn):

| ⲥⲉⲉⲓⲣⲉ | (inf) | they are doing |
| ⲥⲉⲟ | (stat) | they are [something] (marked by the equivalence marker ⲛ̄-) |

Vocabulary entries' definitions will regularly supply the nuances in statives' usage as (vs), but most of the time you should be able to see the logical link between the action/process of an infinitive (whether transitive, intransitive, and/or reflexive) and the state/condition of the corresponding stative. With intransitive verbs, you will sometimes find "become/be" in the definition. In these cases, "become" applies to the infinitive (the process), and "be" applies to the stative (the condition). Due to this regularity, the singular definition entry will be marked (vi/vs), covering both.

NEGATION OF THE PRESENT

13.4 The Negative Present. To form a negative sentence with the Present, the negative particle bracket ⲛ̄- ... ⲁⲛ (which we also used to negate nominal sentences, see 5.6) is framed around the Present conjugation form. Note that this causes a slight spelling

---

5. With the exception of the verb ⲟⲩⲱϣ "to want, wish, desire," which only ever uses prenominal/prepersonal forms with its direct objects.

change in the 2nd person feminine singular, along with some potential shifts in the overline for that and the 3rd person singular forms.

singular
1st	ⲛ̄ϯⲥϩⲁⲓ ⲁⲛ	I am **not** writing
2nd	ⲛ̄ⲅⲥϩⲁⲓ ⲁⲛ[6]	you (m) are **not** writing
	ⲛ̄ⲧⲉⲥϩⲁⲓ ⲁⲛ	you (f) are **not** writing
3rd	ⲛ̄ϥⲥϩⲁⲓ ⲁⲛ[7]	he, it (m) is **not** writing
	ⲛ̄ⲥⲥϩⲁⲓ ⲁⲛ[8]	she, it (f) is **not** writing

plural
1st	ⲛ̄ⲧⲛ̄ⲥϩⲁⲓ ⲁⲛ	we are **not** writing
2nd	ⲛ̄ⲧⲉⲧⲛ̄ⲥϩⲁⲓ ⲁⲛ	you are **not** writing
3rd	ⲛ̄ⲥⲉⲥϩⲁⲓ ⲁⲛ	they are **not** writing

With a definite noun as subject, the initial negative ⲛ̄- of the the bracket can be omitted:

(ⲙ̄-)ⲡⲣⲱⲙⲉ ⲥϩⲁⲓ ⲁⲛ   the person is **not** writing

With an indefinite noun, however, the negative existential particle ⲙⲛ̄- is used:

ⲙⲛ̄-(ⲟⲩ)ⲣⲱⲙⲉ ⲥϩⲁⲓ   **there's not** a person writing *or* **no** person is writing

13.5 Translating the Negative Present. The negative forms of the Present don't present any real issues, and the same guidelines for the affirmative Present work with these. Contractions with "not" are possible, of course, but I'd suggest leaving the "to be" part of the verb fuller (to give it more contrast with the supplied "to be" in nominal sentences, as mentioned in 5.5). Thus "you are not/aren't writing" for Present; "you're not the writer" for a nominal sentence.

VOCABULARY

ⲃⲱⲕ		ⲃⲏⲕ†	to go (vi)
			to be going (vs, exclusively with Present)
ⲉⲓ		ⲛⲏⲩ†	(impv ⲁⲙⲟⲩ [msg], ⲁⲙⲏ [fsg], ⲁⲙⲏⲉⲓⲧⲛ̄ [pl]) to come (vi)
			to be coming (vs, exclusively with Present)
ⲉⲓ ⲛ̄ⲥⲁ-			to come after, come to get

---

6. Note that the personal prefix changes spelling from ⲕ- to ⲅ- when the negative particle is attached. This combination is also regularly written with the overline shifted to be above the ⲅ-: ⲛⲅ̄ⲥϩⲁⲓ ⲁⲛ.

7. As with the 2nd person masculine singular, this combination can be written with the overline shifted: ⲛϥ̄ⲥϩⲁⲓ ⲁⲛ.

8. Likewise, this combination can also be written with the overline shifted: ⲛⲥ̄ⲥϩⲁⲓ ⲁⲛ.

ⲕⲱ	ⲕⲁ-	ⲕⲁⲁ⸗	ⲕⲏ†	1. to put, place, set (ⲙ̄ⲙⲟ⸗); 2. to let, allow (someone: ⲙ̄ⲙⲟ⸗) to do (something: ⲉ- + inf); 3. to leave (ⲙ̄ⲙⲟ⸗; behind: ⲛ̄ⲥⲁ-) (vt)
				to be situated, lying; to be, exist (vs)
ⲕⲱ ⲉⲃⲟⲗ				to forgive (someone: ⲛⲁ⸗; something: ⲙ̄ⲙⲟ⸗); to release; to abandon
ⲛⲁⲩ				(impv ⲁⲛⲁⲩ) to see, look (at: ⲉ-) (vt)
				sight (nm)
ϫⲓ	ϫⲓ-	ϫⲓⲧ⸗		(cp ϫⲁⲓ̈-, ϫⲁⲩ-) to take, receive, get (ⲙ̄ⲙⲟ⸗) (vt)
				taking, theft (nm)
ⲙⲏⲧⲉ				middle, midst (nf)
(ϩ)ⲛ̄-ⲧⲙⲏⲧⲉ ⲛ̄-				in the middle/midst of
ⲛ̄ⲕⲁ				thing, stuff, possession (nm)
ⲛ̄ⲕⲁ ⲛⲓⲙ				everything
ϩⲏ(ⲟ)ⲩ				profit, benefit, usefulness (nm)
ⲣ̄-ϩⲏⲩ				to be profitable, useful (to: ⲛⲁ-)
ϯ-ϩⲏⲩ				to give profit, benefit (to: ⲛⲁ-)
ϩⲱⲃ (pl ϩⲃⲏⲩⲉ)				work, deed; thing, matter (nm)
ϩⲱⲃ ⲛ̄-ϭⲓϫ				handiwork, handicraft
ⲟⲩⲛ̄ⲧⲉ-		ⲟⲩⲛ̄ⲧⲁ⸗		has/have (existential verboid)
ⲙⲛ̄ⲧⲉ-		ⲙⲛ̄ⲧⲁ⸗		don't/doesn't have (neg existential verboid)

EXERCISE

Copy and translate the following phrases.

1. ⲕⲱ ⲛⲁⲓ̈ ⲉⲃⲟⲗ ⲛ̄-ⲡⲁϩⲱⲃ ⲛ̄-ϭⲓϫ! _____

2. ⲟⲩⲛ̄ⲧⲉ-ⲡⲣ̄ⲣⲟ ⲛ̄ⲕⲁ ⲛⲓⲙ. _____

3. ⲛ̄ⲧⲉⲛⲁⲩ ⲁⲛ ⲉⲣⲟⲓ̈ ⲉⲛⲉϩ. _____

4. ⲧⲛ̄ⲛⲏⲩ ⲛ̄ⲥⲁ-ⲛ̄ⲥⲁϩ ⲙⲛ̄-ⲛⲉⲡⲣⲟⲫⲏ́ⲧⲏⲥ. _____

5. ϯⲃⲏⲕ ϩⲛ̄-ⲧⲙⲏⲧⲉ ⲛ̄-ⲛⲉⲧⲛ̄ⲥⲩⲛⲁⲅⲱⲅⲏ́. _____

6. ⲧⲉⲥⲙⲏ ϫⲱ ⲙ̄ⲙⲟⲥ ⲛⲁⲛ ϫⲉ "ⲁⲙⲏⲉⲓⲧⲛ̄!" _____

7. ϥⲕⲱ ⲛ̄-ⲛ̄ⲃⲗ̄ⲗⲉⲉⲩⲉ ⲉ-ⲛⲁⲩ. _____

CHAPTER 14

THE FUTURE

OVERVIEW

In this chapter, you will learn:

- The conjugation of the Future conjugation
- The conjugation of the Negative Future
- How to translate both effectively

THE FUTURE CONJUGATION

14.1 Conjugating the Future. The other Durative conjugation is the Future.[1] The Future is really an offshoot of the Present, following its forms with the addition of the infixed *Future auxiliary* -ⲛⲁ- between the personal prefix and the infinitive (*not* the stative).

	singular		**plural**	
1st	ϯⲛⲁ-	I am going to	ⲧⲛ̄ⲛⲁ-	we are going to
2nd	ⲕⲛⲁ-	you (m) are going to	ⲧⲉⲧⲛ̄ⲛⲁ-[2]	you are going to
	ⲧⲉⲛⲁ-[3]	you (f) are going to		
3rd	ϥⲛⲁ-	he, it (m) is going to	ⲥⲉⲛⲁ-	they are going to
	ⲥⲛⲁ-	she, it (f) is going to		

Attached to the infinitive ⲥϩⲁⲓ̈ (to write) produces these forms:

	singular	
1st	ϯⲛⲁⲥϩⲁⲓ̈	I am going to write
2nd	ⲕⲛⲁⲥϩⲁⲓ̈	you (m) are going to write
	ⲧⲉⲛⲁⲥϩⲁⲓ̈[4]	you (f) are going to write

---

1. In older works, this is sometimes called the "First Future." See chapters 18 (the Optative) and 22 (the Focalizing converter).
2. Also found in the variant form ⲧⲉⲧⲛⲁ- (with the ⲛ of -ⲛⲁ- contracting with the ⲛ of the personal prefix).
3. Also found in the variant form ⲧⲉⲣⲁ- (with the ⲛ of -ⲛⲁ- assimilating away entirely).
4. ⲧⲉⲣⲁⲥϩⲁⲓ̈ with the variant prefix.

3rd	ϥⲛⲁⲥϩⲁⲓ	he, it (m) is going to write
	ⲥⲛⲁⲥϩⲁⲓ	she, it (f) is going to write

plural

1st	ⲧⲛ̄ⲛⲁⲥϩⲁⲓ	we are going to write
2nd	ⲧⲉⲧⲛ̄ⲛⲁⲥϩⲁⲓ[5]	you are going to write
3rd	ⲥⲉⲛⲁⲥϩⲁⲓ	they are going to write

With a definite noun as subject:

ⲡⲣⲱⲙⲉ ⲛⲁⲥϩⲁⲓ.   The person is going to write.

And the indefinite noun workaround:

ⲟⲩⲛ̄-ⲟⲩⲣⲱⲙⲉ ⲛⲁⲥϩⲁⲓ.   **There's** a person going to write. *or* A person is going to write.

14.2 Translating the Future. As the Future is based on the Present, it is desirable to show the ongoing nature inherent in the Durative pattern. The Future auxiliary -ⲛⲁ- is in fact derived from a verb of motion in compound with the infinitive. Use of a verb of motion for the future is very similar to how we commonly refer to intended future actions in English (the *"going-to* future"): "I am going to read the book later," "She's going to go to work tomorrow." I suggest reserving the more formal sounding *"will* future" for the Optative conjugation in the Non-Durative pattern (chapter 18).[6]

14.3 The Negative Future. The negative version of the Future is easy to conjugate, with the infixed Future auxiliary -ⲛⲁ- being the only difference from the Negative Present.

singular

1st	ⲛ̄ϯⲛⲁⲥϩⲁⲓ ⲁⲛ	I am **not** going to write
2nd	ⲛ̄ⲅⲛⲁⲥϩⲁⲓ ⲁⲛ[7]	you (m) are **not** going to write
	ⲛ̄ⲧⲉⲛⲁⲥϩⲁⲓ ⲁⲛ	you (f) are **not** going to write
3rd	ⲛ̄ϥⲛⲁⲥϩⲁⲓ ⲁⲛ[8]	he, it (m) is **not** going to write
	ⲛ̄ⲥⲛⲁⲥϩⲁⲓ ⲁⲛ[9]	she, it (f) is **not** going to write

plural

1st	ⲛ̄ⲧⲛ̄ⲛⲁⲥϩⲁⲓ ⲁⲛ	we are **not** going to write
2nd	ⲛ̄ⲧⲉⲧⲛ̄ⲛⲁⲥϩⲁⲓ ⲁⲛ	you are **not** going to write
3rd	ⲛ̄ⲥⲉⲛⲁⲥϩⲁⲓ ⲁⲛ	they are **not** going to write

---

5. ⲧⲉⲧⲛⲁⲥϩⲁⲓ with the variant prefix.
6. And avoiding "shall" entirely.
7. Note that the personal prefix changes spelling from ⲕ- to ⲅ- when the negative particle is attached. This combination is also regularly written with the overline shifted to be above the ⲅ-: ⲛⲅ̄ⲛⲁⲥϩⲁⲓ ⲁⲛ.
8. As with the 2nd person masculine singular, this combination can be written with the overline shifted: ⲛϥ̄ⲛⲁⲥϩⲁⲓ ⲁⲛ.
9. Likewise, this combination can also be written with the overline shifted: ⲛⲥ̄ⲛⲁⲥϩⲁⲓ ⲁⲛ.

With a definite noun as subject:

(ⲙ̄-)ⲡⲣⲱⲙⲉ ⲛⲁⲥϩⲁⲓ ⲁⲛ   the person is **not** going to write

And the indefinite noun workaround:

ⲙⲛ̄-(ⲟⲩ)ⲣⲱⲙⲉ ⲛⲁⲥϩⲁⲓ   **there's not** a person going to write *or* **no** person is going to write

VOCABULARY

ⲙⲟⲩ			ⲙⲟⲟⲩⲧ†	to die, become/be dead (of, from: ⲉⲧⲃⲉ-, ϩⲁ-) (vi/vs)
				death, manner of death (nm)
ⲛⲟⲩϫ(ⲉ)	ⲛⲉϫ-	ⲛⲟϫ⸗	ⲛⲏϫ†	to throw, cast (ⲙ̄ⲙⲟ⸗; at, into: ⲉ-) (vt)
				to be lying, reclining (at table); **to rely** (on: ⲉ-) (vs)
				throw (nm)
ⲟⲩⲟⲡ			ⲟⲩⲁⲁⲃ†	to become/be pure, holy (vi/vs)
				purity, holiness (nm)
ⲟⲩⲱϣ	ⲟⲩⲉϣ-[10]	ⲟⲩⲁϣ⸗		to want, wish, desire (*not* ⲙ̄ⲙⲟ⸗) (vt)
				wish, desire (nm)
ⲙ̄-ⲡⲉϥⲟⲩⲱϣ				as he wished, as he desired
ⲥⲟⲟⲩⲛ̄	ⲥⲟⲩⲛ̄-	ⲥⲟⲩⲱⲛ⸗		to know (ⲙ̄ⲙⲟ⸗; about: ⲉⲧⲃⲉ-; how to: ⲛ̄- + inf; that ϫⲉ); become acquainted with (vt)
				knowledge, acquaintance (nm)
ⲥⲱⲧⲙ̄	ⲥⲉⲧⲙ̄-	ⲥⲟⲧⲙ⸗		to hear, listen to (ⲉ-); to heed, obey (ⲛⲁ⸗, ⲛ̄ⲥⲁ-) (vt)
				hearing, obedience (nm)
ⲁⲣⲭⲓⲉⲣⲉⲩ́ⲥ				primary priest[11] (nm)
ⲁ́ⲣⲭⲱⲛ				ruler (nm)
ⲅⲣⲁⲙⲙⲁⲧⲉⲩ́ⲥ				scholar, scribe (nm)
ⲟⲩⲏⲏⲃ[12]				priest (Christian or otherwise) (nm)
ⲡⲣⲉⲥⲃⲩ́ⲧⲉⲣⲟⲥ				elder, priest (Christian) (nm)
ⲣⲙ̄ⲙⲁⲟ				rich person (nmf)

---

10. ⲟⲩⲉϣ- can be compounded with another inf.
11. Our English word "priest" is actually derived from the Greek word ⲡⲣⲉⲥⲃⲩ́ⲧⲉⲣⲟⲥ (below in the list), which originally meant an older person, especially one who was in the role of leader. The Greek ἱερεύς and the Egyptian ⲟⲩⲏⲏⲃ were originally terms for ritual specialists whose main task was to manage and present sacrifices and offerings in the sacred spaces of the temples.
12. Related to the verb ⲟⲩⲟⲡ, ⲟⲩⲁⲁⲃ† above.

THE SAHIDIC VERB SYSTEM

EXERCISE

Copy and translate the following phrases.

1. ⲥⲱⲧⲙ̄, ⲡⲓⲥⲣⲁⲏⲗ,[13] ⲡϫⲟⲉⲓⲥ ⲡⲉⲛⲛⲟⲩⲧⲉ, ⲡϫⲟⲉⲓⲥ ⲟⲩⲁ ⲡⲉ!

2. ⲡⲉϫⲉ-ⲡⲉⲡⲣⲟⲫⲏ́ⲧⲏⲥ ϫⲉ "ⲥⲛⲁϣⲱⲡⲉ ⲙ̄-ⲡⲟⲩⲟⲩⲱϣ."

3. ⲛⲉⲅⲣⲁⲙⲙⲁⲧⲉⲩ́ⲥ ⲛⲁⲥⲟⲟⲩⲛ̄ ⲉⲧⲃⲉ-ⲡⲛⲟ́ⲙⲟⲥ.

4. ⲉⲓⲥ-ϩⲏⲏⲧⲉ! ⲡⲁⲣⲭⲓⲉⲣⲉⲩ́ⲥ ϩⲙ̄-ⲡⲉϥⲟⲩⲟⲡ!

5. ⲥⲉⲛⲁⲙⲟⲩ ⲛ̄-ⲧⲣⲟⲙⲡⲉ.

6. ⲧⲛ̄ⲛⲏϫ ⲉ-ϯⲣⲏ́ⲛⲏ ⲙ̄-ⲡⲛⲟⲩⲧⲉ.

7. ⲥⲱⲧⲙ̄ ⲉⲣⲟⲓ̈, ⲛⲁϣⲃⲉⲉⲣ!

Look back at the text of Psalm 1 at the end of chapter 2 again. What words and constructions can you now recognize?

---

13. Even though it's a proper name, ⲓⲥⲣⲁⲏⲗ normally appears with the definite article. Similarly, certain place names like ⲅⲁⲗⲓⲗⲁⲓ́ⲁ, ⲓⲟⲩⲇⲁⲓ́ⲁ, and ϩⲓⲉⲣⲟⲩⲥⲁⲗⲏⲙ are given (feminine) definite articles as well.

CHAPTER 15

THE NON-DURATIVE PATTERN: MAIN CLAUSE CONJUGATIONS

OVERVIEW

In this chapter, you will learn:

- The differences between the Durative and the Non-Durative patterns
- How the Non-Durative pattern uses verbal auxiliaries to mark its conjugations

THE NON-DURATIVE PATTERN

15.1 The Two Non-Durative Groups. The Durative pattern is a small category, with the Present and its spinoff, the Future, being the two conjugations that constitute it. As we transition into the Non-Durative pattern, we encounter a much larger number of conjugations. Within it, there are two subgroups of conjugations: *Main Clause* (which can stand on their own in as a full sentence) and *Subordinate Clause* (which are connected to a main clause conjugation and aren't complete sentences on their own). Together, these conjugations cover a wide range of temporal, modal, and syntactical nuances, but they all share the use of a *verbal auxiliary*, a prefixed element that marks the tense. This, in combination with a personal subject prefix/infix, is prefixed to the verbal stem (always a form of the infinitive) to form the verbal conjugation. These three components are why the Non-Durative pattern as also sometimes referred to as the Tripartite pattern. In the next chapters (16–18), we will be exploring the Main Clause conjugations.

15.2 Syntax of the Main Clause Conjugations. Remember, now that we are beyond the Durative/Present, only infinitives are used—no more statives. This limitation, however, comes with a new freedom: all forms of the infinitive can usually be used.[1] Direct objects

---

1. These exceptions are part of the Stern–Jernstedt Rule(s), mentioned in 12.2n:
   a. Direct objects that are nouns without articles must use the prenominal form.
   b. The verb ⲟⲩⲱϣ "to want, wish, desire" only uses prenominal/prepersonal forms with its direct objects.

See Bentley Layton, *Coptic in 20 Lessons: Introduction to Sahidic Coptic with Exercises and Vocabularies* (Leuven: Peeters, 2007), 84 and *A Coptic Grammar: With Chrestomathy and Glossary. Sahidic Dialect*, 3rd ed., Porta Linguarum Orientalium 2/20 (Wiesbaden: Harrassowitz, 2011), 171.

can be linked more directly (with the prenominal or prepersonal forms of the infinitive) or through the use of the absolute infinitive and ⲛ̄-/ⲙ̄ⲙⲟ⸗ as the direct object marker.

ⲁⲓ̈ⲥϩⲁⲓ̈ ⲛ̄-ⲛ̄ϣⲁϫⲉ.	(absolute inf + ⲛ̄-/ⲙ̄ⲙⲟ⸗)
ⲁⲓ̈ⲥⲉϩ-ⲛ̄ϣⲁϫⲉ.	(prenominal inf)

The choice is usually one of style, with both meaning "I wrote the words."

15.3 Negations of the Main Clause Conjugations. Another feature of the Main Clause Non-Durative pattern conjugations is that they utilize unique, alternate verbal auxiliaries to form their negative counterparts. This is unlike the use of the negative particle bracket ⲛ̄- . . . ⲁⲛ that we saw with nominal sentences and the two conjugations of the Durative pattern, Present and Future.

Present

ⲧⲛ̄ⲥϩⲁⲓ̈	we are writing
ⲛ̄ⲧⲛ̄ⲥϩⲁⲓ̈ ⲁⲛ	we are **not** writing

Future

ⲧⲛ̄ⲛⲁⲥϩⲁⲓ̈	we are going to write
ⲛ̄ⲧⲛ̄ⲛⲁⲥϩⲁⲓ̈ ⲁⲛ	we are **not** going to write

Past

ⲁⲛⲥϩⲁⲓ̈	we wrote
ⲙ̄ⲡⲉⲛⲥϩⲁⲓ̈	we did**n't** write

15.4 Survey of the Main Clause Auxiliaries. Here's our roadmap for the next few chapters:

- **Past** (chapter 16) For the Past conjugation, the verbal auxiliary is ⲁ-. The negative verbal auxiliary is ⲙ̄ⲡ(ⲉ)-. The Past also has a "not yet" negative, which uses the auxiliary ⲙ̄ⲡⲁⲧ(ⲉ)-.
- **Aorist** (chapter 17) The Aorist verbal auxiliary is ϣⲁ(ⲣⲉ)- with the negative auxiliary ⲙⲉ(ⲣⲉ)-. The Aorist is a temporally vague conjugation well suited for general, regular, or habitual actions.[2]
- **Optative** (chapter 18) The Optative verbal auxiliary is ⲉ(ⲣ)ⲉ- with the negative auxiliary ⲛ̄ⲛ(ⲉ)-. The Optative is a more formal future ("you will"), and it is also used for potential ("you may/might").
- **Jussive** (chapter 18) The Jussive verbal auxiliary is ⲙⲁⲣ(ⲉ)- with the negative auxiliary ⲙ̄ⲡⲣ̄ⲧⲣ(ⲉ)-. The Jussive is used to give wishes or commands in the 1st or 3rd person ("let us," "let them"). The imperative's 2nd person commands can be used to fill out the paradigm.

---

[2]. If you've studied Greek, be aware that this conjugation *does not* correspond to the Greek Aorist, understood as having an undefined aspect (usually) in past time. The Sahidic Aorist has no inherent, specific time reference.

VOCABULARY

ⲙⲟⲟϣⲉ				to walk, journey (vi)
				walk, journey (nm)
ⲙⲟⲩⲧⲉ				to call, summon (ⲉ-; [by the name of]: ϫⲉ) (vt)
				call, summoning (nm)
ⲟⲩⲱⲙ	ⲟⲩⲉⲙ-	ⲟⲩⲟⲙ⸗		(cp ⲟⲩⲁⲙ-) to eat (ⲙ̄ⲙⲟ⸗; some of: ⲉⲃⲟⲗ ϩⲛ̄-) (vt)
				eating, food (nm)
ⲟⲩⲱⲙ ⲛ̄ⲥⲁ-				to eat away at
ⲟⲩⲱⲛϩ	ⲟⲩⲉⲛϩ-	ⲟⲩⲟⲛϩ⸗	ⲟⲩⲟⲛϩ†	(± ⲉⲃⲟⲗ) to make manifest, show (ⲙ̄ⲙⲟ⸗; to: ⲛⲁ⸗, ⲉ-) (vt)
				to become manifest, appear (vi/vr)
				to be manifest, apparent (vs)
				manifesting, showing, appearance (nm)
ⲟⲩⲱϣⲃ̄	ⲟⲩⲉϣⲃ-	ⲟⲩⲟϣⲃ⸗		to respond to (ⲙ̄ⲙⲟ⸗, ⲛⲁ⸗); to answer (vt)
				response (nm)
ⲟⲩⲱϩ	ⲟⲩⲉϩ-	ⲟⲩⲁϩ⸗	ⲟⲩⲏϩ†	(cp ⲟⲩⲁϩ-) to put, place, set (ⲙ̄ⲙⲟ⸗) (vt)
				to follow, place oneself in the following of (ⲛ̄ⲥⲁ-) (vr)
				to settle, dwell (in: ϩⲛ̄-; with: ⲙⲛ̄-) (vi)
				to be placed, situated, set (vs)
				settlement (nm)
ϭⲱⲗⲡ̄	ϭⲉⲗⲡ̄-	ϭⲟⲗⲡ⸗	ϭⲟⲗⲡ̄†	(cp ϭⲁⲗⲡ̄-) (usually + ⲉⲃⲟⲗ) to uncover, reveal (ⲙ̄ⲙⲟ⸗; to: ⲉ-, ⲛⲁ⸗) (vt)
				to become/be uncovered, revealed (vi/vs)
				uncovering, revelation (nm)
ⲟⲩⲛⲁⲙ				right (hand) (nf)
ⲣⲁⲛ	ⲣⲉⲛ-	ⲣⲓⲛ⸗, ⲣⲛ̄ⲧ⸗		name (nm)
ⲥⲛⲟϥ				blood (nm)
ⲥⲁⲣⲝ̄				flesh (nf)
ⲣ̄-ⲥⲁⲣⲝ̄				(ⲟ† ⲛ̄-) to become/be flesh
ⲥⲱⲙⲁ				body (nm)
ϩⲟ(ⲉ)ⲓⲧⲉ				garment, cloak (nmf)

EXERCISE

Copy and translate the following phrases.

1. ϥⲕⲱ ⲛ̄-ⲧⲉϥⲟⲩⲛⲁⲙ ⲉϩⲣⲁⲓ̈ ⲉϫⲱⲓ̈.

2. ϥϫⲱ ⲙ̄ⲙⲟⲥ ϫⲉ "ⲁⲛⲟⲕ ⲡⲉ ⲡϣⲟⲣⲡ̄ ⲁⲩⲱ ⲡϩⲁⲉ."

3. ⲕⲛⲁⲛⲁⲩ ⲉ-ⲡϣⲏⲣⲉ ⲛ̄-ⲣⲱⲙⲉ.

4. ϯⲛⲁⲟⲩⲱⲙ ⲉⲃⲟⲗ ϩⲛ̄-ⲛ̄ⲟⲉⲓⲕ.

5. ⲥⲁⲣⲝ̄ ϩⲓ-ⲥⲛⲟϥ ⲡⲉ ⲛⲉⲛⲥⲱⲙⲁ.

6. ⲥⲉⲙⲟⲩⲧⲉ ⲉ-ⲡⲉϥⲣⲁⲛ ϫⲉ "ⲓⲱϩⲁ́ⲛⲛⲏⲥ."

CHAPTER 16

THE PAST

OVERVIEW

In this chapter, you will learn:

- How to conjugate the most common Non-Durative pattern conjugation, the Past
- The conjugation of the Negative Past and the "Not Yet" Past
- How to translate these effectively in English

THE PAST CONJUGATION

16.1 Conjugating the Past. The three components of the Past[1] conjugation are the *Past auxiliary* ⲁ-[2] plus a *personal infix* plus an *infinitive* (which can be absolute, prenominal, or prepersonal depending on the situation). The combinations of Past auxiliary and personal infixes are:

	singular		**plural**	
1st	ⲁⲓ̈-	I	ⲁⲛ-	we
2nd	ⲁⲕ-	you (m)	ⲁⲧⲉⲧⲛ̄-	you
	ⲁⲣ-[3]	you (f)		
3rd	ⲁϥ-	he, it (m)	ⲁⲩ-	they
	ⲁⲥ-	she, it (f)		

Attached to the infinitive ⲥϩⲁⲓ, you get these forms:

	singular	
1st	ⲁⲓ̈ⲥϩⲁⲓ̈	I wrote
2nd	ⲁⲕⲥϩⲁⲓ̈	you (m) wrote
	ⲁⲣⲥϩⲁⲓ̈[4]	you (f) wrote

---

1. Called the "First Perfect" in older works.
2. Fun fact: the Past auxiliary is derived from the verb ⲉⲓⲣⲉ ("to do, make").
3. The 2nd person feminine singular prefix is also found in the variant forms ⲁ- and ⲁⲣⲉ-.
4. ⲁⲥϩⲁⲓ or ⲁⲣⲉⲥϩⲁⲓ̈ as variant forms.

3rd	ⲁϥⲥϩⲁⲓ	he, it (m) wrote
	ⲁⲥⲥϩⲁⲓ	she, it (f) wrote
	plural	
1st	ⲁⲛⲥϩⲁⲓ	we wrote
2nd	ⲁⲧⲉⲧⲛ̄ⲥϩⲁⲓ	you wrote
3rd	ⲁⲩⲥϩⲁⲓ	they wrote

With an expressed noun (either definite or indefinite[5]) as subject:

ⲁ-ⲡⲣⲱⲙⲉ ⲥϩⲁⲓ   the person wrote

16.2   Translating the Past. The Past is the most common of all the Main Clause conjugations, and it is used frequently in narratives of past events. Much of the time, the simple English past ("I wrote") will suffice, but sometimes the English perfect ("I have written") might make sense in context.[6] It's also possible to use the simple past emphatic ("I did write")—this makes sense, especially considering the origin of the Past auxiliary and the need for "did(n't)" with the negative (below).

You will find that Sahidic can chain a sequence of two or more Past verbs together without any conjunctions, even though English style may prefer inserting an "and" to link them.

NEGATION(S) OF THE PAST

16.3   The Negative Past. Unlike the Durative Present and Future, where negation was formed by adding the negative particle frame, Non-Durative Main Clause conjugations have unique auxiliaries that are used for their negative counterparts. The Past negative auxiliary is ⲙ̄ⲡ(ⲉ)-. Joining this to the personal infixes produces these prefixes:

	singular		**plural**	
1st	ⲙ̄ⲡⲓ-	I didn't	ⲙ̄ⲡⲉⲛ-	we didn't
2nd	ⲙ̄ⲡⲉⲕ-	you (m) didn't	ⲙ̄ⲡⲉⲧⲛ̄-	you didn't
	ⲙ̄ⲡⲉ-[7]	you (f) didn't		
3rd	ⲙ̄ⲡⲉϥ-	he, it (m) didn't	ⲙ̄ⲡⲟⲩ-	they didn't
	ⲙ̄ⲡⲉⲥ-	she, it (f) didn't		

With our model infinitive:

---

5. The Durative pattern's workaround for indefinite nouns as subjects isn't needed with any of the Non-Durative conjugations. These expressed subjects can be noun phrases, proper names, or even independent demonstrative pronouns.

6. In general, I'd suggest reserving the English perfect for the Sahidic Past with a Preterite conversion (chapter 21).

7. The 2nd person feminine singular prefix is also found in the variant form ⲙ̄ⲡⲣ̄-.

		singular	
1st		ⲙ̄ⲡⲓⲥϩⲁⲓ̈	I didn't write
2nd		ⲙ̄ⲡⲉⲕⲥϩⲁⲓ̈	you (m) didn't write
		ⲙ̄ⲡⲉⲥϩⲁⲓ̈[8]	you (f) didn't write
3rd		ⲙ̄ⲡⲉϥⲥϩⲁⲓ̈	he, it (m) didn't write
		ⲙ̄ⲡⲉⲥⲥϩⲁⲓ̈	she, it (f) didn't write
		plural	
1st		ⲙ̄ⲡⲉⲛⲥϩⲁⲓ̈	we didn't write
2nd		ⲙ̄ⲡⲉⲧⲛ̄ⲥϩⲁⲓ̈	you didn't write
3rd		ⲙ̄ⲡⲟⲩⲥϩⲁⲓ̈	they didn't write

With an expressed noun as subject:

ⲙ̄ⲡⲉ-ⲡⲣⲱⲙⲉ ⲥϩⲁⲓ̈   the person didn't write

As you can see, translating the Negative Past can be done with "didn't," or if context and style requires it, "hasn't/haven't" (English negative perfect).

16.4 The "Not Yet" Past. The Past also has a further conditionally negative conjugation, an expansion of the negative auxiliary with an additional infix -ⲁⲧ-, making the full "Not Yet" auxiliary ⲙ̄ⲡⲁⲧ(ⲉ)-. This "not yet" nuance does imply that eventually the situation could or will change. Joined to the personal infixes produces:

		singular			**plural**	
1st		ⲙ̄ⲡⲁϯ-	I didn't . . . yet		ⲙ̄ⲡⲁⲧⲛ̄-	we didn't . . . yet
2nd		ⲙ̄ⲡⲁⲧⲕ̄-	you (m) didn't . . . yet		ⲙ̄ⲡⲁⲧⲉⲧⲛ̄-	you didn't . . . yet
		ⲙ̄ⲡⲁⲧⲉ-	you (f) didn't . . . yet			
3rd		ⲙ̄ⲡⲁⲧϥ̄-	he, it (m) didn't . . . yet		ⲙ̄ⲡⲁⲧⲟⲩ-	they didn't . . . yet
		ⲙ̄ⲡⲁⲧⲥ̄-	she, it (f) didn't . . . yet			

With our model infinitive:

		singular	
1st		ⲙ̄ⲡⲁϯⲥϩⲁⲓ̈	I didn't write yet
2nd		ⲙ̄ⲡⲁⲧⲕ̄ⲥϩⲁⲓ̈	you (m) didn't write yet
		ⲙ̄ⲡⲁⲧⲉⲥϩⲁⲓ̈	you (f) didn't write yet
3rd		ⲙ̄ⲡⲁⲧϥ̄ⲥϩⲁⲓ̈	he, it (m) didn't write yet
		ⲙ̄ⲡⲁⲧⲥ̄ⲥϩⲁⲓ̈	she, it (f) didn't write yet

---

8. ⲙ̄ⲡⲣ̄ⲥϩⲁⲓ̈ with the variant prefix.

THE SAHIDIC VERB SYSTEM

plural
- *1st* **ⲙ̄ⲡⲁⲧⲛ̄ⲥϩⲁⲓ̈** — we didn't write yet
- *2nd* **ⲙ̄ⲡⲁⲧⲉⲧⲛ̄ⲥϩⲁⲓ̈** — you didn't write yet
- *3rd* **ⲙ̄ⲡⲁⲧⲟⲩⲥϩⲁⲓ̈** — they didn't write yet

With an expressed noun as subject:

ⲙ̄ⲡⲁⲧⲉ-ⲡⲣⲱⲙⲉ ⲥϩⲁⲓ̈ — the person didn't write yet

Like the standard Negative Past, you can translate the "Not Yet" Past with "didn't" or perhaps "hasn't/haven't."

VOCABULARY

ⲡⲓⲥⲧⲉⲩⲉ			to trust, rely on (ⲉ-) (vt)
ⲥⲉⲉⲡⲉ			to remain, be left over (vi)
			remainder, rest (often in plural sense; a redundant ⲕⲉ- appears frequently: ⲡⲕⲉⲥⲉⲉⲡⲉ [the rest]) (nm)
ⲧⲱⲟⲩⲛ	ⲧⲟⲩⲛ-	ⲧⲱⲟⲩⲛ⸗	to raise (ⲙ̄ⲙⲟ⸗) (vt)
			to arise, get up (from: ⲉⲃⲟⲗ ϩⲓ-, ⲉⲃⲟⲗ ϩⲛ̄-); to rise up (against: ⲉ-, ⲉϫⲛ̄-, ⲉϩⲣⲁⲓ̈ ⲉϫⲛ̄-) (vi/vr)
			rising (nm)
ⲱⲛϩ			ⲟⲛϩ† to live, become/be alive (vi/vs)
			life (nm)
ϣⲁϫⲉ			to speak, talk (to, with: ⲉ-, ⲙⲛ̄-; about: ⲉ[ⲧⲃⲉ]-, ϩⲁ-; against: ⲛ̄ⲥⲁ-, ⲟⲩⲃⲉ-) (vt)
			word, speech; matter (nm)
ϥⲓ	ϥⲓ-	ϥⲓⲧ⸗	(cp ϥⲁⲓ̈-) to lift up, take, bear, carry (ⲙ̄ⲙⲟ⸗) (vt)
ϥⲓ ⲙⲛ̄-			to agree with
ϥⲓ ϩⲁ-			to bear, tolerate
ϫⲱⲕ	ϫⲉⲕ-	ϫⲟⲕ⸗	ϫⲏⲕ† (± ⲉⲃⲟⲗ) to finish, complete (ⲙ̄ⲙⲟ⸗) (vt)
			to become finished, completed; to die (vi)
			to be finished, done, perfect (vs)
			end, completion (nm)
ⲗⲁⲟⲥ			people (nm)
ⲙⲏⲏϣⲉ			crowd, multitude (nm)
ϩⲉⲑⲛⲟⲥ			nation, national, native[9] (nm)
ⲉⲣⲏⲩ			companion; each other (nmf)
ⲛ̄ϭⲓ-			that is, namely (apposition marker)[10]

---

9. ϩⲉⲑⲛⲟⲥ is used for both the collective group and an individual within that group.

10. ⲛ̄ϭⲓ- is used to mark postponed subjects (those that come after the verb). It is especially common with texts translated from

EXERCISE

Copy and translate the following phrases.

1. ⲙ̄ⲡⲉ-ⲡⲕⲟⲥⲙⲟⲥ ⲥⲟⲩⲱⲛϥ̄.

2. ⲁⲩⲱ ⲡϣⲁϫⲉ ⲁϥⲣ̄-ⲥⲁⲣⲝ̄, ⲁϥⲟⲩⲱϩ ⲛⲙ̄ⲙⲁⲛ.

3. ⲡⲛⲟⲩⲧⲉ ⲙ̄ⲡⲉ-ⲗⲁⲁⲩ ⲛⲁⲩ ⲉⲣⲟϥ ⲉⲛⲉϩ.

4. ⲁⲩⲱ ⲡⲉϫⲁϥ ϫⲉ "ⲛ̄-ⲁⲛⲟⲕ ⲁⲛ ⲡⲉ."

5. ⲁ-ⲣⲟⲩϩⲉ ϣⲱⲡⲉ, ⲁ-ϩⲧⲟⲟⲩⲉ ϣⲱⲡⲉ, ⲟⲩⲁ ⲛ̄-ϩⲟⲟⲩ.

6. ⲧⲛ̄ⲡⲓⲥⲧⲉⲩⲉ ⲉ-ⲩⲛⲟⲩⲧⲉ ⲛ̄-ⲟⲩⲱⲧ.

7. ⲁⲩⲱ ⲁⲓ̈ⲙⲟⲩ ⲁⲩⲱ ⲉⲓⲥ-ϩⲏⲏⲧⲉ! ϯⲟⲛϩ̄ ϣⲁ-ⲛⲓⲉⲛⲉϩ ⲛ̄-ⲛⲓⲉⲛⲉϩ.

8. ⲁϥⲉⲓ ⲇⲉ ⲉⲃⲟⲗ ϩⲙ̄-ⲡⲙⲁ ⲉⲧ-ⲙ̄ⲙⲁⲩ, ⲁϥⲉⲓ ⲉϩⲣⲁⲓ̈ ⲉ-ⲧⲉϥⲡⲟⲗⲓⲥ.

CHAPTER 17

THE AORIST

OVERVIEW

In this chapter, you will learn:

- The conjugation of the Aorist and the Negative Aorist
- How to translate these effectively in English

THE AORIST CONJUGATION

17.1 Conjugating the Aorist. Our next Main Clause conjugation is the Aorist.[1] It is formed with the *Aorist auxiliary* ϣⲁ- plus a *personal infix* plus an *infinitive*. Before an expressed subject, the auxiliary lengthens to ϣⲁⲣⲉ-.

	singular		**plural**	
1st	ϣⲁⲓ-	I	ϣⲁⲛ-	we
2nd	ϣⲁⲕ-	you (m)	ϣⲁⲧⲉⲧⲛ̄-	you
	ϣⲁⲣ(ⲉ)-	you (f)		
3rd	ϣⲁϥ-	he, it (m)	ϣⲁⲩ-	they
	ϣⲁⲥ-	she, it (f)		

Attached to the infinitive ⲥϩⲁⲓ, you get these forms:

	singular	
1st	ϣⲁⲓⲥϩⲁⲓ	I write
2nd	ϣⲁⲕⲥϩⲁⲓ	you (m) write
	ϣⲁⲣ(ⲉ)ⲥϩⲁⲓ	you (f) write
3rd	ϣⲁϥⲥϩⲁⲓ	he, it (m) writes
	ϣⲁⲥⲥϩⲁⲓ	she, it (f) writes

---

1. Also called the "Habitual" in older works.

	plural	
1st	ϣⲁⲛⲥϩⲁⲓ̈	we write
2nd	ϣⲁⲧⲉⲧⲛ̄ⲥϩⲁⲓ̈	you write
3rd	ϣⲁⲩⲥϩⲁⲓ̈	they write

With an expressed noun as subject (note the longer form of the auxiliary):

ϣⲁⲣⲉ-ⲡⲣⲱⲙⲉ ⲥϩⲁⲓ̈   the person writes

17.2 **Translating the Aorist.** The Aorist is less common than the Past, occurring less than a tenth as often on average, in fact. It is untensed—that is, it has no inherent, specific reference to time.[2] The Aorist is a temporally vague conjugation well suited for general, regular, or habitual actions—things that are done normally and recurrently, not specific or unique occurrences.

ⲛ̄-ⲛⲉⲥⲛⲁⲩ, ϣⲁⲓ̈ⲃⲱⲕ ⲉ-ⲡⲁⲙⲁ ⲛ̄-ϩⲱⲃ.   On Mondays, **I go** to my workplace.

The Aorist's timeless nature also lends itself to timeless statements, making it well suited for gnomic sayings, aphorisms, proverbs, and the like. Because of this, it is much more frequent in texts that are wisdom literature.

ϣⲁⲣⲉ-ⲟⲩϣⲏⲣⲉ ⲛ̄-ⲥⲁⲃⲉ ⲥⲱⲧⲙ̄ ⲛ̄ⲥⲁ-ⲡⲉϥⲉⲓⲱⲧ.   A wise son **heeds** his father. (Prov 13.1a)

Despite the lack of inherent tense in the Aorist, we do need a tense for our English translations. The English simple present ("I write") works much of the time, but context may require other options, so be flexible.

17.3 **The Negative Aorist.** The Aorist negative auxiliary is ⲙⲉ-, ⲙⲉⲣⲉ- before expressed subjects. Joining this to the personal infixes produces these prefixes:

	singular		**plural**	
1st	ⲙⲉⲓ̈-	I don't	ⲙⲉⲛ-	we don't
2nd	ⲙⲉⲕ-	you (m) don't	ⲙⲉⲧⲉⲧⲛ̄-	you don't
	ⲙⲉⲣⲉ-	you (f) don't		
3rd	ⲙⲉϥ-	he, it (m) doesn't	ⲙⲉⲩ-	they don't
	ⲙⲉⲥ-	she, it (f) doesn't		

With our model infinitive:

---

2. If you've studied Greek, keep in mind that this conjugation *does not* correspond to the Greek Aorist, understood as having an undefined aspect (usually) in past time.

singular

1st	ⲙⲉⲓ̈ⲥϩⲁⲓ̈	I don't write
2nd	ⲙⲉⲕⲥϩⲁⲓ̈	you (m) don't write
	ⲙⲉⲣⲉⲥϩⲁⲓ̈	you (f) don't write
3rd	ⲙⲉϥⲥϩⲁⲓ̈	he, it (m) doesn't write
	ⲙⲉⲥⲥϩⲁⲓ̈	she, it (f) doesn't write

plural

1st	ⲙⲉⲛⲥϩⲁⲓ̈	we don't write
2nd	ⲙⲉⲧⲉⲧⲛ̄ⲥϩⲁⲓ̈	you don't write
3rd	ⲙⲉⲩⲥϩⲁⲓ̈	they don't write

With an expressed noun as subject (again note the longer form of the auxiliary):

ⲙⲉⲣⲉ-ⲡⲣⲱⲙⲉ ⲥϩⲁⲓ̈   the person doesn't write

VOCABULARY

ⲉⲓⲙⲉ				to understand (ⲉ-); to know, realize (that: ϫⲉ) (vt)
ⲉⲓⲛⲉ	ⲛ̄-	ⲛ̄ⲧ⸗		(impv ⲁⲛ[ⲉ]ⲓⲛⲉ, ⲁⲛⲓ-, ⲁⲛⲓ⸗) to bring (ⲙ̄ⲙⲟ⸗) (vt)
				reception (nm)
ⲉⲓⲛⲉ ⲉⲃⲟⲗ				to bring out, publish
ⲕⲣⲓⲛⲉ				to judge (ⲙ̄ⲙⲟ⸗) (vt)
ⲕⲱⲧⲉ	ⲕⲉⲧ-	ⲕⲟⲧ⸗	ⲕⲏⲧ†	to turn (ⲙ̄ⲙⲟ⸗; away: ⲉⲃⲟⲗ; back: ⲉⲡⲁϩⲟⲩ) (vt)
				1. to return, go back (to: ⲉⲡⲁϩⲟⲩ ⲉ-, ⲉⲃⲟⲗ ⲉ-, ⲉⲃⲟⲗ ϣⲁ-, ⲉϩⲟⲩⲛ ⲉ-, ⲉϩⲣⲁⲓ̈ ⲉ-); 2. to repeat an action, usually coordinated, as in ⲁϥⲕⲟⲧϥ̄ ⲁϥⲥϩⲁⲓ̈ (he wrote again) or with ⲉ- + inf, as in ⲁϥⲕⲟⲧϥ̄ ⲉ-ⲥϩⲁⲓ̈ (he wrote again) (vr)
				to rotate, circulate; to surround, go around (ⲉ-); to consort (with: ⲙⲛ̄-) (vi)
				to be turned, turning, circulating (vs)
				neighborhood, surroundings (nm)
ⲙⲉ	ⲙⲉⲣⲉ-[3]	ⲙⲉⲣⲓⲧ⸗		(cp ⲙⲁⲓ̈-) to love (ⲙ̄ⲙⲟ⸗) (vt)
				love (nm)
ⲙⲟⲥⲧⲉ	ⲙⲉⲥⲧⲉ-	ⲙⲉⲥⲧⲱ⸗		(cp ⲙⲁⲥⲧ̄-) to hate (ⲙ̄ⲙⲟ⸗) (vt)
				hate, hatred; hated thing (nm)
ⲙⲟⲩⲟⲩⲧ	ⲙⲉⲩⲧ-, ⲙⲟⲩⲧ-	ⲙⲟⲟⲩⲧ⸗		to kill (ⲙ̄ⲙⲟ⸗) (vt)
ⲥⲧⲁⲩⲣⲟⲩ				to (execute by) stake[4] (ⲙ̄ⲙⲟ⸗) (vt)

---

3. ⲙⲉⲣⲉ- can be compounded with another inf.
4. The Latin terminology for crucifixion is derived from the cross (*crux*) formed by the crossbeam (*patibulum*) joined to the main upright beam (*stipes*)—the Greek terminology is (originally) descriptive of that central stake (ⲥⲧⲁⲩⲣⲟⲥ).

THE AORIST

ⲇⲓⲕⲁⲓⲟⲥⲩ́ⲛⲏ	justice, rightness (nf)
ⲙⲛ̄ⲧⲣⲉ́ (pl ⲙⲛ̄ⲧⲣⲉⲉⲩ)	witness, testimony (nm)
ⲙⲛ̄ⲧⲙⲛ̄ⲧⲣⲉ́	testimony (nf)
ⲣ̄-ⲙⲛ̄ⲧⲣⲉ́	to testify, bear witness (to, about: ⲙ̄ⲙⲟ⸗, ⲉⲧⲃⲉ-, ⲉϫⲛ̄-, ⲉ-, ϩⲁ-, ⲙⲛ̄-)
ⲥⲧⲁⲩⲣⲟⲥ	execution stake (abbreviated as ⲥⲣⲟⲥ) (nm)
ϣⲧⲉⲕⲟ (pl ϣⲧⲉⲕⲱⲟⲩ)	prison (nm)
ϩⲁⲡ	judgment (nm)

EXERCISE

Copy and translate the following phrases.

1. ϣⲁⲩϯ ⲛⲁϥ ⲛ̄-ⲟⲩϩⲁⲡ ⲛ̄-ϣⲧⲉⲕⲟ.

2. ϣⲁⲓ̈ϫⲟⲟⲥ ⲙ̄-ⲡⲁⲓ̈ ϫⲉ "ⲃⲱⲕ!" ⲁⲩⲱ ϣⲁϥⲃⲱⲕ.

3. ⲉϣⲱⲡⲉ ϣⲁⲧⲉⲧⲛ̄ⲥⲱⲧⲙ̄ ⲉⲣⲟⲓ̈, ϣⲁⲧⲉⲧⲛ̄ⲉⲓⲙⲉ.

4. ϣⲁⲩⲙⲟⲩⲧⲉ ⲉⲣⲟϥ ϫⲉ ⲙⲱⲩⲥⲏ́ⲥ.

5. ⲁϫⲛ̄-ⲙⲟⲥⲧⲉ ⲇⲉ ⲙⲉⲥⲙⲟⲟⲩⲧϥ̄.

CHAPTER 18

THE OPTATIVE AND THE JUSSIVE

OVERVIEW

In this chapter, you will learn:

- The conjugation of the Optative and the Negative Optative
- The conjugation of the Jussive and the Negative Jussive
- How to translate these effectively in English

THE OPTATIVE CONJUGATION

18.1 Conjugating the Optative. Our last full Main Clause conjugation is the Optative.[1] The Optative describes future events, either determined or potential. The Optative is thus somewhat more formal (and less common) than the Durative Future. It is composed of the *Optative auxiliary* ⲉ[-]ⲉ- (which brackets a *personal infix*) plus an *infinitive*, ⲉⲣⲉ- before an expressed subject.

	singular		**plural**	
1st	ⲉⲓ̈ⲉ-	I will	ⲉⲛⲉ-	we will
2nd	ⲉⲕⲉ-	you (m) will	ⲉⲧⲉⲧⲛⲉ-	you will
	ⲉⲣⲉ-	you (f) will		
3rd	ⲉϥⲉ-	he, it (m) will	ⲉⲩⲉ-	they will
	ⲉⲥⲉ-	she, it (f) will		

Attached to the infinitive ⲥϩⲁⲓ̈, you get these forms:

	singular	
1st	ⲉⲓ̈ⲉⲥϩⲁⲓ̈	I will write
2nd	ⲉⲕⲉⲥϩⲁⲓ̈	you (m) will write

---

1. Also called the "Third Future" in older works.

	ⲉⲣⲉⲥϩⲁⲓ	you (f) will write
3rd	ⲉϥⲥϩⲁⲓ	he, it (m) will write
	ⲉⲥⲥϩⲁⲓ	she, it (f) will write

	plural	
1st	ⲉⲛⲥϩⲁⲓ	we will write
2nd	ⲉⲧⲉⲧⲛⲥϩⲁⲓ	you will write
3rd	ⲉⲩⲥϩⲁⲓ	they will write

With an expressed noun as subject:

ⲉⲣⲉ-ⲡⲣⲱⲙⲉ ⲥϩⲁⲓ	the person will write

18.2 Translating the Optative. By contrast with the Future (chapter 14)—whose ongoing, Present-based nature is best reflected by the common English "*going-to* future"—the Optative can be translated with the "standard" English future auxiliary "will."[2]

The Optative is employed in declarative statements about the future, including those with the force of commands.

ⲥⲟⲟⲩ ⲛ̄-ϩⲟⲟⲩ ⲉⲕⲉⲣ̄-ϩⲱⲃ.	Six days **you will** do work. (Exod 20.9a)
ⲁⲩⲱ ⲉⲕⲉⲙⲉⲣⲉ-ⲡϫⲟⲉⲓⲥ ⲡⲉⲕⲛⲟⲩⲧⲉ.	And **you will** love the Master your God. (Deut 6.5a)

The Optative is also used with potential and causal statements, and "may/might" works in those cases. Note the use of ϫⲉ or ϫⲉⲕⲁ(ⲁ)ⲥ before this usage.

ⲁⲛⲓ-ⲟⲩⲥⲁⲧⲉⲉⲣⲉ ⲛⲁⲓ ϫⲉ ⲉⲓ̈ⲉⲛⲁⲩ ⲉⲣⲟⲥ.	Bring a *sateere*[3] to me that **I may** see it. (Mark 12.15b)

18.3 The Negative Optative. The negative version of the Optative is actually more common than the affirmative. The Optative negative auxiliary is ⲛ̄ⲛ(ⲉ)-. Joining this to the personal infixes produces these prefixes:

	singular		**plural**	
1st	ⲛ̄ⲛⲁ-	I won't	ⲛ̄ⲛⲉⲛ-	we won't
2nd	ⲛ̄ⲛⲉⲕ-	you (m) won't	ⲛ̄ⲛⲉⲧⲛ̄-	you won't
	ⲛ̄ⲛⲉ-	you (f) won't		
3rd	ⲛ̄ⲛⲉϥ-	he, it (m) won't	ⲛ̄ⲛⲉⲩ-	they won't
	ⲛ̄ⲛⲉⲥ-	she, it (f) won't		

---

2. Avoid the really old-fashioned *shall* option, as modern English speakers rarely actually say that (outside of a desire to sound artificially proper and old-timey).

3. A silver coin/weight (derived ultimately from Greek ⲥⲧⲁⲧⲏⲣ).

With our model infinitive:

		singular	
1st		ⲛ̄ⲛⲁⲥϩⲁï	I won't write
2nd		ⲛ̄ⲛⲉⲕⲥϩⲁï	you (m) won't write
		ⲛ̄ⲛⲉⲥϩⲁï	you (f) won't write
3rd		ⲛ̄ⲛⲉϥⲥϩⲁï	he, it (m) won't write
		ⲛ̄ⲛⲉⲥⲥϩⲁï	she, it (f) won't write
		plural	
1st		ⲛ̄ⲛⲉⲛⲥϩⲁï	we won't write
2nd		ⲛ̄ⲛⲉⲧⲛ̄ⲥϩⲁï	you won't write
3rd		ⲛ̄ⲛⲉⲩⲥϩⲁï	they won't write

With an expressed noun as subject:

ⲛ̄ⲛⲉ-ⲡⲣⲱⲙⲉ ⲥϩⲁï   the person won't write

"Won't" works well for many uses, but for more solemn declarations, especially those leaning toward commands, "will not" would be appropriate.

THE JUSSIVE CONJUGATION (AND THE IMPERATIVE)

18.4 Conjugating the Jussive. Our last Main Clause conjugation is the partial conjugation known as the Jussive,[4] which is used to give commands or wishes in the 1st and 3rd person. It is composed of the *Jussive auxiliary* ⲙⲁⲣ(ⲉ)- plus a *personal infix* plus an *infinitive*. The 2nd person imperative (usually the same as the infinitive, a special form with some verbs, see 12.3) can be included alongside the Jussive to round out the paradigm.

	singular		plural	
1st	ⲙⲁⲣⲓ-	let me	ⲙⲁⲣⲛ̄-[5]	let us
{2nd}	{inf}	(you)	{inf}	(you)
3rd	ⲙⲁⲣⲉϥ-	let him, it (m)	ⲙⲁⲣⲟⲩ-	let them
	ⲙⲁⲣⲉⲥ-	let her, it (f)		

Attached to the infinitive ⲥϩⲁï, you get these forms:

	singular	
1st	ⲙⲁⲣⲓⲥϩⲁï	let me write!

---

4. Also called the "Injunctive" or "Optative" (not to be confused with what we described earlier in this chapter!) in older works.

5. A longer form of this prefix (ⲙⲁⲣⲟⲛ) is used on its own as "let's (go)!"

THE OPTATIVE AND THE JUSSIVE

{2nd}	{ⲥϩⲁⲓ̈}	(you) write!
3rd	ⲙⲁⲣⲉϥⲥϩⲁⲓ̈	let him, it (m) write!
	ⲙⲁⲣⲉⲥⲥϩⲁⲓ̈	let her, it (f) write!
	plural	
1st	ⲙⲁⲣⲛ̄ⲥϩⲁⲓ̈	let us write!
{2nd}	{ⲥϩⲁⲓ̈}	(you) write!
3rd	ⲙⲁⲣⲟⲩⲥϩⲁⲓ̈	let them write!

With an expressed noun as subject:

    ⲙⲁⲣⲉ-ⲡⲣⲱⲙⲉ ⲥϩⲁⲓ̈   let the person write!

While the imperative's implied subject ("you") does not need to be stated, the Jussive's subjects[6] are included in the translation, with "let" marking their intended 1st and 3rd person subjects/targets.

    ⲡⲉϫⲁϥ ⲛ̄ϭⲓ ⲡⲛⲟⲩⲧⲉ ϫⲉ "**ⲙⲁⲣⲉ**-ⲟⲩⲟⲉⲓⲛ ϣⲱⲡⲉ!"   God said: "**Let** light happen!" (Gen 1.3a)

18.5 **The Negative Jussive and Imperative.** The Jussive negative auxiliary is ⲙ̄ⲡ̄ⲧⲣ(ⲉ)-. The first bit of this (ⲙ̄ⲡ̄ⲣ-) is prefixed directly to the infinitive (or the specific imperative, see 12.3) to produce our negative imperative forms.

	singular		**plural**	
1st	ⲙ̄ⲡ̄ⲣⲧⲁ-	don't let me	ⲙ̄ⲡ̄ⲣⲧⲉⲛ-	don't let us
{2nd}	{ⲙ̄ⲡ̄ⲣ-}	(you) don't	{ⲙ̄ⲡ̄ⲣ-}	(you) don't
3rd	ⲙ̄ⲡ̄ⲣⲧⲣⲉϥ-	don't let him, it (m)	ⲙ̄ⲡ̄ⲣⲧⲣⲉⲩ-	don't let them
	ⲙ̄ⲡ̄ⲣⲧⲣⲉⲥ-	don't let her, it (f)		

With our model infinitive:

	singular	
1st	ⲙ̄ⲡ̄ⲣⲧⲁⲥϩⲁⲓ̈	don't let me write!
{2nd}	{ⲙ̄ⲡ̄ⲣⲥϩⲁⲓ̈}	(you) don't write!
3rd	ⲙ̄ⲡ̄ⲣⲧⲣⲉϥⲥϩⲁⲓ̈	don't let him, it (m) write!
	ⲙ̄ⲡ̄ⲣⲧⲣⲉⲥⲥϩⲁⲓ̈	don't let her, it (f) write!
	plural	
1st	ⲙ̄ⲡ̄ⲣⲧⲣⲉⲛⲥϩⲁⲓ̈	don't let us write!
{2nd}	{ⲙ̄ⲡ̄ⲣⲥϩⲁⲓ̈}	(you) don't write!
3rd	ⲙ̄ⲡ̄ⲣⲧⲣⲉⲩⲥϩⲁⲓ̈	don't let them write!

---

6. In English, these are worded as objects ("him") of "let" instead of subjects ("he").

With an expressed noun as subject:

ⲙ̄ⲡⲣ̄ⲧⲣⲉ-ⲡⲣⲱⲙⲉ ⲥϩⲁï   don't let the person write!

As you can see, the addition of "don't" is sufficient to mark the negative, "do not" for more emphasis.

ⲙ̄ⲡⲣ̄ⲕⲣⲓⲛⲉ ϫⲉⲕⲁⲥ ⲛ̄ⲛⲉⲩⲕⲣⲓⲛⲉ ⲙ̄ⲙⲱⲧⲛ̄.   Don't judge so that they[7] won't judge you. (Matt 7.1)

VOCABULARY

ⲟⲩϫⲁï		ⲟⲩⲟϫ†		to become/be healthy, delivered (vi/vs)
				health, deliverance (nm)
ⲡⲱⲧ		ⲡⲏⲧ†		to run, flee (vi)
				to be running, fleeing (vs, exclusively with Present)
				flight (nm)
ⲡⲱⲧ ⲛ̄ⲥⲁ-				to run after, pursue
ⲣⲁϣⲉ				to rejoice at, ridicule (ⲙ̄ⲙⲟ⸗) (vt)
				to rejoice (at, over: ⲉ-, ⲉϫⲛ̄-, ⲉϩⲣⲁï ⲉϫⲛ̄-) (vi)
				joy (nm)
ⲥⲱⲟⲩϩ	ⲥⲉⲩϩ-	ⲥⲟⲟⲩϩ⸗	ⲥⲟⲟⲩϩ†	(± ⲉϩⲟⲩⲛ) to gather, collect (ⲙ̄ⲙⲟ⸗; at: ⲉ-, ⲉϫⲛ̄-, ϩⲛ̄-) (vt)
				to gather (vi)
				to be gathered (vs)
				gathering (nm)
ⲧⲁ(ⲟ)ⲩⲟ	ⲧⲁ(ⲟ)ⲩⲉ-	ⲧⲁ(ⲟ)ⲩⲟ⸗		1. (± ⲉⲃⲟⲗ) to send (forth), put out (ⲙ̄ⲙⲟ⸗); 2. to proclaim, tell (ⲙ̄ⲙⲟ⸗) (vt)
				sending, mission; (+ ⲉⲃⲟⲗ) output (nm)
ⲧⲁϫⲣⲟ	ⲧⲁϫⲣⲉ-	ⲧⲁϫⲣⲟ⸗	ⲧⲁϫⲣⲏⲩ†	to strengthen, confirm (ⲙ̄ⲙⲟ⸗) (vt)
				to become/be strengthened, firm (vi/vs)
				strength, firmness (nm)
ϩⲛ̄-ⲟⲩⲧⲁϫⲣⲟ				firmly, certainly
ⲛⲁⲩ, ⲛⲟⲩ				time, hour (nm)
ⲧ(ⲛ̄)ⲛⲁⲩ				when?
ⲥⲟⲡ (pl ⲥⲱ[ⲱ]ⲡ)	ⲥⲉⲡ-, ⲥⲛ̄-			time, occasion (nm)
ⲛ̄-ⲟⲩⲥⲟⲡ				once
ⲛ̄-ⲥ(ⲉ)ⲡ-ⲥⲛⲁⲩ				twice
ⲛ̄-ϣⲙ(ⲛ̄)ⲧ-ⲥⲱ(ⲱ)ⲡ				three times

---

7. A "they" without a clear reference is also a way to express a passive: this phrase could be translated as "so that you won't be judged."

THE OPTATIVE AND THE JUSSIVE

(ⲛ̄-)ⲕⲉⲥⲟⲡ	again
ⲙⲓⲛⲉ	kind, sort, type (nf)
ⲁϣ ⲙ̄-ⲙⲓⲛⲉ	(of) what sort?
ⲛ̄-ⲧⲉïⲙⲓⲛⲉ	of this sort, such
ϩⲉ	way, manner (nf)
ⲛ̄-ⲧⲉïϩⲉ	in this way, thus
ⲛ̄-ⲑⲉ ⲛ̄-, ⲛ̄-ⲧ≠ϩⲉ	like, as, in the manner of
ⲁϣ ⲛ̄-ϩⲉ	(of) what manner?
ⲛ̄-ⲁϣ ⲛ̄-ϩⲉ	in what way? how?
ⲣ̄-ⲑⲉ	(ⲟ† ⲛ̄) to become/be like; to make like
ϩⲱⲥⲧⲉ	so that (conj)
ϫⲉⲕⲁ(ⲁ)ⲥ	so that . . . may/might (+ optative) (conj)

EXERCISE

Below is the text of Matthew 6.9b–13. Copy it. How much can you figure out?

  9b ⲡⲉⲛⲉⲓⲱⲧ ⲉⲧ-ϩⲛ̄-ⲙ̄ⲡⲏⲩⲉ,
      ⲙⲁⲣⲉ-ⲡⲉⲕⲣⲁⲛ ⲟⲩⲟⲡ,
  10   ⲧⲉⲕⲙⲛ̄ⲧⲣ̄ⲣⲟ ⲙⲁⲣⲉⲥⲉⲓ,
      ⲡⲉⲕⲟⲩⲱϣ ⲙⲁⲣⲉϥϣⲱⲡⲉ,
        ⲛ̄-ⲑⲉ ⲉⲧⲉϥϩⲛ̄-ⲧⲡⲉ ⲙⲁⲣⲉϥϣⲱⲡⲉ ⲟⲛ ϩⲓϫⲙ̄-ⲡⲕⲁϩ.
  11 ⲡⲉⲛⲟⲉⲓⲕ ⲉⲧ-ⲛⲏⲩ ⲧⲁⲁϥ ⲛⲁⲛ ⲙ̄-ⲡⲟⲟⲩ.
  12 ⲕⲱ ⲛⲁⲛ ⲉⲃⲟⲗ ⲛ̄-ⲛⲉⲧ-ⲉⲣⲟⲛ,
      ⲛ̄-ⲑⲉ ϩⲱⲱⲛ ⲟⲛ ⲉⲧⲉⲛⲕⲱ ⲉⲃⲟⲗ ⲛ̄-ⲛⲉⲧⲉ-ⲟⲩⲛ̄ⲧⲁⲛ ⲉⲣⲟⲟⲩ.
  13 ⲛ̄ⲅ̄-ⲧⲙ̄ϫⲓⲧⲛ̄ ⲉϩⲟⲩⲛ ⲉ-ⲡⲓⲣⲁⲥⲙⲟⲥ,
      ⲁⲗⲗⲁ ⲛ̄ⲅ̄-ⲛⲁϩⲙⲉⲛ ⲉⲃⲟⲗ ϩⲓⲧⲙ̄-ⲡⲡⲟⲛⲏⲣⲟⲥ.
    ϫⲉ ⲧⲱⲕ ⲧⲉ ⲧϭⲟⲙ ⲙⲛ̄-ⲡⲉⲟⲟⲩ ϣⲁ-ⲛⲓⲉⲛⲉϩ.
    ϩⲁⲙⲏⲛ!

CHAPTER 19

CONVERSIONS: THE RELATIVE CONVERTER

OVERVIEW

In this chapter, you will learn:

- The function and categories of the system of conversions
- How the relative converter works with the Present, Future, Past, and Aorist
- How to translate these conversions effectively in English

CONVERSIONS

19.1 **The Four Conversions.** Sahidic has an additional system of conversions—four converters that can be prefixed to verbs to add additional contextual or temporal information to that already inherent in the conjugated verbal forms to which they are attached:

- **Relative** (this chapter), which turns the following phrase into a dependent relative clause
- **Circumstantial** (chapter 20), which provides context or the circumstances of the main verb
- **Preterite** (chapter 21), which shifts the timing of its verb backward
- **Focalizing** (chapter 22), which emphasizes some part of the sentence other than the subject

19.2 **Conversion Possibilities.** These four converters can be prefixed to the Durative (the Present and the Future) and the primary Non-Durative conjugations (the Past and the Aorist).[1] These four conjugations, along with their negative forms, form a grid of possibilities with the four conversions:

---

1. There are also some attestations of Relative and Circumstantial conversions with the Optative, but only with the somewhat more common Negative Optative.

CONVERSIONS: THE RELATIVE CONVERTER

	Present	Negative Present	Future	Negative Future	Past	Negative Past	"Not Yet" Past	Aorist	Negative Aorist
Relative									
Circumstantial									
Preterite									
Focalizing							---[2]		---[2]

It is also possible to "stack" more than one converter on a verb, combining their nuances. The Relative and Circumstantial conversions are much more common than the Preterite and Focalizing conversions, appearing in biblical texts about seven times more often on average. It is important to know all four and be able to identify their presence in texts. In this chapter, we'll start with the most common, the Relative conversion.

RELATIVE CONVERSION

19.3 The Relative Converter. We encountered the relative converter ⲉⲧ- back in 7.5, where we saw how it could be prefixed to prepositional phrases to form relative clauses. With the verbal conjugations, it will take different forms depending on what it's prefixed to: ⲉⲧ-, ⲉⲧⲉ-, ⲉⲧⲉⲣⲉ-, and ⲉⲛⲧ-.

19.4 Translating the Relative. In general, the relative converter marks the verbal phrase it's attached to as a dependent clause, which we can usually translate as a phrase beginning with an English relative pronoun like "who" or "which." With Sahidic relative clauses, you will frequently find personal markers that, if translated in a strictly literal fashion in English, would sound redundant.

  ⲉⲛⲧⲁϥⲙⲉⲣⲓⲧⲛ̄   who (**he**) loved us

They are part of the usual Sahidic way of expressing these relative relationships, but they can be left out of our translations. Be aware of these and be flexible.

  Relative clauses in the Durative (Present and Future) have some special usages. If the antecedent of the relative clause immediately precedes it, no personal marker is used, and ⲉⲧ- is attached with a hyphen directly to the verbal stem.[3]

---

2. The Focalizing "Not Yet" Past and Focalizing Negative Aorist are extremely rare or unattested.
3. This can also be attached to other things like prepositional and adverbial phrases. We've already seen it with the common ⲉⲧ-ⲙ̄ⲙⲁⲩ "who's/which's there" (used as the further demonstrative "that/those").

ⲠⲢⲰⲘⲈ ⲈⲦ-ⲤϨⲀⲒ (*not* ⲠⲢⲰⲘⲈ ⲈⲦϤ̄ⲤϨⲀⲒ)   the person who's writing

When the verbal stem is a stative that describes a quality (something one can become/be), this kind of relative clause can function like an adjective:

ⲠⲈⲠⲚⲈⲨ́ⲘⲀ ⲈⲦ-ⲞⲨⲀⲀⲂ   the spirit who's holy *or* the holy spirit
ⲦⲈⲤⲘⲎ ⲈⲦ-ⲞⲚϨ̄   the voice which's alive *or* the living voice

As we discussed back in 7.6, all these relative clauses can be substantivized (treated as noun phrases) by prefixing definite articles to them, allowing them to then be used as subjects and objects.

ⲠⲈⲚⲦⲀϤⲘⲈⲢⲒⲦⲚ̄   the one (m) who (he) loved us
ⲦⲈⲦ-ⲤϨⲀⲒ   the one (f) who's writing
ⲚⲈⲦ-ⲞⲨⲀⲀⲂ   the ones who're holy *or* the holy ones

This is a very common way that you'll encounter relative clauses in your readings.

THE RELATIVE CONVERTER WITH THE DURATIVE PATTERN

19.5   **Relative Present.** With the Present conjugation, the relative converter form ⲈⲦ- is attached to the Present personal prefixes (the hyphen isn't included when written[4]). In those cases where the personal prefix begins with Ⲧ, it contracts with the Ⲧ of ⲈⲦ- (*ⲈⲦ-Ⲧ̄Ⲛ- > ⲈⲦⲚ̄-). Note that the 3rd plural personal prefix (-ⲞⲨ-) is different from the ⲤⲈ- of the standard, unconverted Present.

        singular
1st   ⲈϯⲤϨⲀⲒ   who/which I am writing
2nd   ⲈⲦⲔ̄ⲤϨⲀⲒ   who/which you (m) are writing
      ⲈⲦⲈ(Ⲣ)ⲤϨⲀⲒ   who/which you (f) are writing
3rd   ⲈⲦϤ̄ⲤϨⲀⲒ   who/which he, it (m) is writing
      ⲈⲦⲤ̄ⲤϨⲀⲒ   who/which she, it (f) is writing

        plural
1st   ⲈⲦⲚ̄ⲤϨⲀⲒ   who/which we are writing
2nd   ⲈⲦⲈⲦⲚ̄ⲤϨⲀⲒ   who/which you are writing
3rd   ⲈⲦⲞⲨⲤϨⲀⲒ   who/which they are writing

With a definite noun as subject, the longer form ⲈⲦⲈⲢⲈ- (with hyphen included) is used:

---

4. As you'll see, some converters are connected with an included hyphen. While this does feel somewhat inconsistent, it is determined by whether or not the converter combines in spelling/pronunciation with the verbal prefix following it (as with the 1st person singular and plural of the Present here).

CONVERSIONS: THE RELATIVE CONVERTER

| ⲉⲧⲉⲣⲉ-ⲡⲣⲱⲙⲉ ⲥϩⲁⲓ | who/which the person is writing |

The Relative Negative Present is formed throughout by simply putting the relative converter in the longer form ⲉⲧⲉ- before the Negative Present (with the hyphen):[5]

| ⲉⲧⲉ-ⲛ̄ϯⲥϩⲁⲓ ⲁⲛ | who/which I am not writing |
| ⲉⲧⲉ-(ⲙ̄-)ⲡⲣⲱⲙⲉ ⲥϩⲁⲓ ⲁⲛ[6] | who/which the person is not writing |

19.6 Relative Future. The Relative Future is formed the same way as the Relative Present—just with the inclusion of the Future auxiliary -ⲛⲁ- between the personal prefix and the infinitive.

singular
1st	ⲉϯⲛⲁⲥϩⲁⲓ	who/which I am going to write
2nd	ⲉⲧⲕ̄ⲛⲁⲥϩⲁⲓ	who/which you (m) are going to write
	ⲉⲧⲉ(ⲣ)ⲛⲁⲥϩⲁⲓ	who/which you (f) are going to write
3rd	ⲉⲧϥ̄ⲛⲁⲥϩⲁⲓ	who/which he, it (m) is going to write
	ⲉⲧⲥ̄ⲛⲁⲥϩⲁⲓ	who/which she, it (f) is going to write

plural
1st	ⲉⲧⲛ̄ⲛⲁⲥϩⲁⲓ	who/which we are going to write
2nd	ⲉⲧⲉⲧⲛ̄ⲛⲁⲥϩⲁⲓ	who/which you are going to write
3rd	ⲉⲧⲟⲩⲛⲁⲥϩⲁⲓ	who/which they are going to write

With a definite noun as subject:

| ⲉⲧⲉⲣⲉ-ⲡⲣⲱⲙⲉ ⲛⲁⲥϩⲁⲓ | who/which the person is going to write |

The Relative Negative Future is similarly formed throughout by simply putting the relative converter in the longer form ⲉⲧⲉ- before the Negative Future (with the hyphen):

| ⲉⲧⲉ-ⲛ̄ϯⲛⲁⲥϩⲁⲓ ⲁⲛ | who/which I am not going to write |
| ⲉⲧⲉ-(ⲙ̄-)ⲡⲣⲱⲙⲉ ⲛⲁⲥϩⲁⲓ ⲁⲛ | who/which the person is not going to write |

THE RELATIVE CONVERTER WITH THE NON-DURATIVE PATTERN

19.7 Relative Past. For the Past, the relative converter has a spelling change: a ⲛ appears in the middle. This ⲉⲛⲧ-[7] is prefixed to the Past personal prefixes (hyphen not included when written), just like the Present/Future.

---

5. To see the full Relative Negative paradigm, refer to the Appendix 3: Verb Paradigms in the back of the book.
6. ⲉⲧⲉⲣⲉ-ⲡⲣⲱⲙⲉ ⲥϩⲁⲓ ⲁⲛ is also possible with a definite noun as subject.
7. Sometimes this relative converter is spelled ⲛ̄ⲧ-, which can be problematic (it's the usual way that the focalizing converter is spelled with the Past). See 22.5.

THE SAHIDIC VERB SYSTEM

singular
- *1st* ⲉⲛⲧⲁⲓⲥϩⲁⲓ — who/which I wrote
- *2nd* ⲉⲛⲧⲁⲕⲥϩⲁⲓ — who/which you (m) wrote
- ⲉⲛⲧⲁⲣⲉⲥϩⲁⲓ — who/which you (f) wrote
- *3rd* ⲉⲛⲧⲁϥⲥϩⲁⲓ — who/which he, it (m) wrote
- ⲉⲛⲧⲁⲥⲥϩⲁⲓ — who/which she, it (f) wrote

plural
- *1st* ⲉⲛⲧⲁⲛⲥϩⲁⲓ — who/which we wrote
- *2nd* ⲉⲛⲧⲁⲧⲉⲧⲛ̄ⲥϩⲁⲓ — who/which you wrote
- *3rd* ⲉⲛⲧⲁⲩⲥϩⲁⲓ — who/which they wrote

With an expressed noun as subject:

- ⲉⲛⲧⲁ-ⲡⲣⲱⲙⲉ ⲥϩⲁⲓ — who/which the person wrote

The Relative Negative Past is formed throughout by simply putting the relative converter in the longer form ⲉⲧⲉ- before the Negative Past (with the hyphen):

- ⲉⲧⲉ-ⲙ̄ⲡⲓⲥϩⲁⲓ — who/which I didn't write
- ⲉⲧⲉ-ⲙ̄ⲡⲉ-ⲡⲣⲱⲙⲉ ⲥϩⲁⲓ — who/which the person didn't write

Likewise, the Relative "Not Yet" Past is formed throughout by simply putting the relative converter in the longer form ⲉⲧⲉ- before the "Not Yet" Past (with the hyphen):

- ⲉⲧⲉ-ⲙ̄ⲡⲁϯⲥϩⲁⲓ — who/which I didn't write yet
- ⲉⲧⲉ-ⲙ̄ⲡⲁⲧⲉ-ⲡⲣⲱⲙⲉ ⲥϩⲁⲓ — who/which the person didn't write yet

19.8 Relative Aorist. For the Aorist, the longer form of the relative converter ⲉⲧⲉ- is placed before the standard Aorist forms (with the hyphen).[8]

singular
- *1st* ⲉⲧⲉ-ϣⲁⲓⲥϩⲁⲓ — who/which I write
- *2nd* ⲉⲧⲉ-ϣⲁⲕⲥϩⲁⲓ — who/which you (m) write
- ⲉⲧⲉ-ϣⲁⲣ(ⲉ)ⲥϩⲁⲓ — who/which you (f) write
- *3rd* ⲉⲧⲉ-ϣⲁϥⲥϩⲁⲓ — who/which he, it (m) writes
- ⲉⲧⲉ-ϣⲁⲥⲥϩⲁⲓ — who/which she, it (f) writes

plural
- *1st* ⲉⲧⲉ-ϣⲁⲛⲥϩⲁⲓ — who/which we write
- *2nd* ⲉⲧⲉ-ϣⲁⲧⲉⲧⲛ̄ⲥϩⲁⲓ — who/which you write
- *3rd* ⲉⲧⲉ-ϣⲁⲩⲥϩⲁⲓ — who/which they write

---

8. Sometimes this relative converter is spelled ⲉ-, which can be even more problematic (it's the usual way that the circumstantial *and* rocalizing converters are spelled with the Aorist). See 20.6 and 22.6.

CONVERSIONS: THE RELATIVE CONVERTER

With an expressed noun as subject:

    ⲉⲧⲉ-ϣⲁⲣⲉ-ⲡⲣⲱⲙⲉ ⲥϩⲁⲓ   who/which the person writes

The Relative Negative Aorist is also formed throughout by putting the relative converter in the longer form ⲉⲧⲉ- before the Negative Aorist (with the hyphen):

    ⲉⲧⲉ-ⲙⲉⲓ̈ⲥϩⲁⲓ̈   who/which I don't write
    ⲉⲧⲉ-ⲙⲉⲣⲉ-ⲡⲣⲱⲙⲉ ⲥϩⲁⲓ̈   who/which the person doesn't write

VOCABULARY

ⲁⲗⲉ	ⲁⲗⲟ⸗	ⲁⲗⲏⲩ†	(impv ⲁⲗⲱⲧⲛ̄) to go up, climb (onto, up to: ⲉ-); to get on, mount (an animal: ⲉϫⲛ̄-) (vt)
			to be riding, mounted (vs)
ⲱϩⲉ		ⲁϩⲉ†	to stand, stay, wait (vi)
			to be in need (of: ⲛⲁ⸗) (vs)
ⲁϩⲉⲣⲁⲧ⸗[9]			to stand oneself (before: ⲉ-; against: ⲉ-, ⲉϫⲛ̄-, ⲟⲩⲃⲉ-; with: ⲙⲛ̄-)
ϣⲓⲛⲉ	ϣⲛ̄-	ϣⲛ̄ⲧ⸗	to seek, inquire after (ⲛ̄ⲥⲁ-); to visit (ⲉ-); to greet (ⲉ-) (vt)
			search, inquiry; news (nm)
ϣⲱⲡ	ϣⲉⲡ-, ϣⲡ̄-	ϣⲟⲡ⸗ ϣⲏⲡ†	to receive, accept, get; to buy (ⲙ̄ⲙⲟ⸗; from: ⲛ̄ⲧⲛ̄-; for [cost] ϩⲁ-; often with reflexive ⲉⲣⲟ⸗) (vt)
			to be received, acceptable (vs)
			acceptance; purchase (nm)
ϩⲁⲣⲉϩ			to guard, watch (ⲉ-; from: ⲉ-, ⲉⲃⲟⲗ ϩⲛ̄-); to keep, observe, preserve (ⲉ-) (vt)
			guard, watch (nm)
ϩⲉ		ϩⲏⲩ†	to fall (vi)
			to be falling (vs, exclusively with Present)
			fall (nm)
ϩⲉ ⲉ-			to fall to, upon, into; to find, chance upon
ϩⲉ ⲉⲃⲟⲗ			to fall away, perish
ⲙ̄ⲙⲟⲛ			no, not (neg part)
ⲙ̄ⲙⲁⲧⲉ, ⲉⲙⲁⲧⲉ			very much, greatly; only, exclusively (adv)
ⲟⲛ			again, also, additionally (adv)
ϭⲉ			then, thus, any more (postpositive) (adv)
ⲧⲉⲛⲟⲩ ϭⲉ			now then
ⲧⲟⲧⲉ			then, thereupon, next (conj)

---

9. ⲁϩⲉⲣⲁⲧ⸗ requires a reflexive suffix (matching the subject).

EXERCISE

Copy and translate the following phrases.

1. ⲡⲛⲟⲩⲧⲉ ⲡⲉⲛⲧⲁϥⲁⲗⲉ ⲉϩⲣⲁⲓ̈ ⲉϫⲛ̄-ⲧⲡⲉ

2. ⲟⲩⲛ̄-ϩⲟⲉⲓⲛⲉ ⲛ̄-ⲛⲉⲧⲁϩⲉⲣⲁⲧⲟⲩ ⲙ̄-ⲡⲉⲓ̈ⲙⲁ

3. ⲛⲁⲓ̈ ⲅⲁⲣ ⲧⲏⲣⲟⲩ ⲛ̄ϩⲉⲑⲛⲟⲥ ⲛⲉⲧϣⲓⲛⲉ ⲛ̄ⲥⲱⲟⲩ.

4. ⲡⲛⲟⲩⲧⲉ ⲅⲁⲣ ⲡⲉⲛⲧⲁϥϣⲟⲡϥ̄ ⲉⲣⲟϥ.

5. ϩⲁⲙⲏⲛ ϩⲁⲙⲏⲛ ϯϫⲱ ⲙ̄ⲙⲟⲥ ⲛⲏⲧⲛ̄ ϫⲉ ⲡⲉⲧⲛⲁϩⲁⲣⲉϩ ⲉ-ⲡⲁϣⲁϫⲉ, ⲛ̄ϥⲛⲁⲛⲁⲩ ⲁⲛ ⲉ-ⲡⲙⲟⲩ.

6. ⲛ̄-ⲑⲉ ⲉⲧ-ϥ̄ϩⲛ̄-ⲧⲡⲉ ⲙⲁⲣⲉϥϣⲱⲡⲉ ⲟⲛ ϩⲓϫⲙ̄-ⲡⲕⲁϩ.

CHAPTER 20

THE CIRCUMSTANTIAL CONVERTER

OVERVIEW

In this chapter, you will learn:

- How the circumstantial converter works with the Present, Future, Past, and Aorist
- How to translate these conversions effectively in English

CIRCUMSTANTIAL CONVERSION

20.1 **The Circumstantial Converter.** Unlike the more varied forms of the relative converter, the circumstantial converter is regular: it's almost always simply ⲉ-, with the only exception being that it's lengthened to ⲉⲣⲉ- with definite nouns as subjects in the Durative pattern.

20.2 **Translating the Circumstantial.** A verb with a Circumstantial conversion gives context and background for another verb that is the main action of the sentence—it describes the circumstances of that main verb. Frequently, an English participle (the -ing form of the verb) works well to express this.

ⲁ-ⲓⲱϩⲁⲛⲛⲏⲥ ⲟⲩⲱϣⲃ̄, **ⲉϥϫⲱ** ⲙ̄ⲙⲟⲥ   Iōhannēs responded, (**he/him**) **saying** (it)

Information about the person/number/gender of the subject is encoded in these circumstantially converted forms. Sometimes, as in the above example, this can feel redundant or wordy in English, so it may be unnecessary to include everything in your translation.

In addition, the three time-based (Past, Present, Future) circumstantial verbal phrases can be described as having coordinated tenses in relation to that main verb.[1] This relationship can sometimes be clarified by rewording the phrase in English in various ways. The *Circumstantial Past* (20.5) describes a completed action before the main

---

1. The Circumstantial Aorist, being untensed, naturally follows the tense of its main verb.

verb, thus it temporally takes a step back in time from that of the main verb. "When" is another way you can state this sequence in your translation. Sometimes this sequentiality may also suggest causality, which can be expressed with "since" or "because."

- with a Past main verb:
    ⲉ-ⲁϥⲥϩⲁï, ⲁⲛϣⲁϫⲉ   **(he/him)**[2] **having written**, we spoke
    or **when/since/because he had written**, we spoke
- with a Present main verb:
    ⲉ-ⲁϥⲥϩⲁï, ⲧⲛ̄ϣⲁϫⲉ   **(he/him) having written**, we are speaking
    or **since/because he wrote**, we are speaking

The *Circumstantial Present* (20.3) describes an action concurrent with the main verb. "While," "as," or "when" can be used to express this connection.

- with a Past main verb:
    ⲉϥⲥϩⲁï, ⲁⲛϣⲁϫⲉ   **(he/him) writing**, we spoke
    or **while he was writing**, we spoke
- with a Present main verb:
    ⲉϥⲥϩⲁï, ⲧⲛ̄ϣⲁϫⲉ   **(he/him) writing**, we are speaking
    or **as he writes**, we are speaking
- with a Future main verb:
    ⲉϥⲥϩⲁï, ⲧⲛ̄ⲛⲁϣⲁϫⲉ **(he/him) writing**, we are going to speak
    or **when he writes**, we are going to speak

The *Circumstantial Future* (20.4) describes an imminent action taking place after the main verb. "About to" is also an effective way to state this connection.

- with a Past main verb:
    ⲉϥⲛⲁⲥϩⲁï, ⲁⲛϣⲁϫⲉ   **as he was going to write**, we spoke
    or **as he was about to write**, we spoke

Finally, circumstantial clauses are used instead of relative clauses to modify indefinite nouns and pronouns (relative clauses are considered definite, see 7.5). Compare:

ⲡⲣⲱⲙⲉ ⲉⲧ-ⲥϩⲁï   the person who's writing (definite)
ⲟⲩⲣⲱⲙⲉ ⲉϥⲥϩⲁï   a person (he/him) writing *or* a person who's writing (indefinite)

And as with definite relative clauses (19.4), indefinite circumstantial clauses with statives can be adjectival:

---

2. The personal endings (subject or object, depending on how the clause is used in the sentence as a whole) are in parentheses, as you may not want or need to explicitly state this information in translation.

ⲟⲩⲡⲛⲉⲩ́ⲙⲁ ⲉϥⲟⲩⲁⲁⲃ   a spirit (he/him/it) being holy *or* a holy spirit
ⲟⲩϩⲉⲗⲡⲓ́ⲥ ⲉⲥⲟⲛϩ̄   a hope (it) being alive *or* a living hope

THE CIRCUMSTANTIAL CONVERTER WITH THE DURATIVE PATTERN

20.3 Circumstantial Present. With the Present conjugation, the circumstantial converter ⲉ- is prefixed to the Present personal prefixes, ⲉⲣⲉ- with definite nouns as subjects. Conventionally, the hyphen is not included when written, as it would be pronounced in the same syllable as the personal prefix. Note that the 3rd plural personal prefix (-ⲩ- shortened from *-ⲟⲩ-) is again different from the ⲥⲉ- of the standard, unconverted Present.

singular
1st	ⲉⲓ̈ⲥϩⲁⲓ̈	(I/me)[3] writing
2nd	ⲉⲕⲥϩⲁⲓ̈	(you [m]) writing
	ⲉⲣ(ⲉ)ⲥϩⲁⲓ̈	(you [f]) writing
3rd	ⲉϥⲥϩⲁⲓ̈	(he/him, it [m]) writing
	ⲉⲥⲥϩⲁⲓ̈	(she/her, it [f]) writing

plural
1st	ⲉⲛⲥϩⲁⲓ̈	(we/us) writing
2nd	ⲉⲧⲉⲧⲛ̄ⲥϩⲁⲓ̈[4]	(you) writing
3rd	ⲉⲩⲥϩⲁⲓ̈	(they/them) writing

With a definite noun as subject, the longer form ⲉⲣⲉ- (with hyphen included) is used:

ⲉⲣⲉ-ⲡⲣⲱⲙⲉ ⲥϩⲁⲓ̈   the person writing

The Circumstantial Negative Present is formed by prefixing the circumstantial converter ⲉ- before the Negative Present (with the hyphen):

ⲉ-ⲛ̄ϯⲥϩⲁⲓ̈ ⲁⲛ   (I/me) not writing

With a definite noun as subject, the longer form ⲉⲣⲉ- is used:

ⲉⲣⲉ-ⲡⲣⲱⲙⲉ ⲥϩⲁⲓ̈ ⲁⲛ   the person not writing

---

3. The personal endings (subject or object, depending on how the clause is used in the sentence as a whole) are in parentheses, as you may not want or need to explicitly state this information in translation.
4. Note that this is the same as the Relative Present 2nd plural.

THE SAHIDIC VERB SYSTEM

20.4 Circumstantial Future. The Circumstantial Future is formed the same way as the Circumstantial Present—just with the inclusion of the Future auxiliary -ⲛⲁ- between the personal prefix and the infinitive.

singular

1st	ⲉⲓ̈ⲛⲁⲥϩⲁⲓ̈	as I was going to write (as I was about to write)
2nd	ⲉⲕⲛⲁⲥϩⲁⲓ̈	as you (m) were going to write
	ⲉⲣⲉⲛⲁⲥϩⲁⲓ̈	as you (f) were going to write
3rd	ⲉϥⲛⲁⲥϩⲁⲓ̈	as he, it (m) was going to write
	ⲉⲥⲛⲁⲥϩⲁⲓ̈	as she, it (f) was going to write

plural

1st	ⲉⲛⲛⲁⲥϩⲁⲓ̈	as we were going to write
2nd	ⲉⲧⲉⲧⲛ̄ⲛⲁⲥϩⲁⲓ̈⁵	as you were going to write
3rd	ⲉⲩⲛⲁⲥϩⲁⲓ̈	as they were going to write

With a definite noun as subject, the longer form ⲉⲣⲉ- is used:

ⲉⲣⲉ-ⲡⲣⲱⲙⲉ ⲛⲁⲥϩⲁⲓ̈   as the person was going to write

The Circumstantial Negative Future is formed by prefixing the circumstantial converter ⲉ- before the Negative Future (with the hyphen included):

ⲉ-ⲛ̄ϯⲛⲁⲥϩⲁⲓ̈ ⲁⲛ   as I was not going to write

With a definite noun as subject, the longer form ⲉⲣⲉ- is used:

ⲉⲣⲉ-(ⲙ̄)ⲡⲣⲱⲙⲉ ⲛⲁⲥϩⲁⲓ̈ ⲁⲛ   as the person was not going to write

THE CIRCUMSTANTIAL CONVERTER WITH THE NON-DURATIVE PATTERN

20.5 Circumstantial Past. For the Past, ⲉ- is prefixed to the Past forms throughout. The hyphen is conventionally included.

singular

1st	ⲉ-ⲁⲓ̈ⲥϩⲁⲓ̈	(I/me) having written
2nd	ⲉ-ⲁⲕⲥϩⲁⲓ̈	(you [m]) having written
	ⲉ-ⲁⲣⲥϩⲁⲓ̈	(you [f]) having written
3rd	ⲉ-ⲁϥⲥϩⲁⲓ̈	(he/him, it [m]) having written
	ⲉ-ⲁⲥⲥϩⲁⲓ̈	(she/her, it [f]) having written

---

5. Note that this is the same as the Relative Future 2nd plural.

THE CIRCUMSTANTIAL CONVERTER

plural
1st ⲉ-ⲁⲛⲥϩⲁⲓ (we/us) having written
2nd ⲉ-ⲁⲧⲉⲧⲛ̄ⲥϩⲁⲓ (you) having written
3rd ⲉ-ⲁⲩⲥϩⲁⲓ (they/them) having written

With an expressed noun as subject:

ⲉ-ⲁ-ⲡⲣⲱⲙⲉ ⲥϩⲁⲓ   the person having written

The Circumstantial Negative Past and the Circumstantial "Not Yet" Past are also formed throughout by simply putting the circumstantial converter ⲉ- before the Negative and "Not Yet" Past (with the hyphen included):

ⲉ-ⲙ̄ⲡⲓⲥϩⲁⲓ (I/me) not having written
ⲉ-ⲙ̄ⲡⲉ-ⲡⲣⲱⲙⲉ ⲥϩⲁⲓ the person not having written
ⲉ-ⲙ̄ⲡⲁϯⲥϩⲁⲓ (I/me) not having written yet
ⲉ-ⲙ̄ⲡⲁⲧⲉ-ⲡⲣⲱⲙⲉ ⲥϩⲁⲓ the person not having written yet

20.6 Circumstantial Aorist. For the Aorist, ⲉ- is prefixed to the Aorist forms throughout. The hyphen is conventionally included.

singular
1st ⲉ-ϣⲁⲓⲥϩⲁⲓ as I write[6]
2nd ⲉ-ϣⲁⲕⲥϩⲁⲓ as you (m) write
      ⲉ-ϣⲁⲣ(ⲉ)ⲥϩⲁⲓ as you (f) write
3rd ⲉ-ϣⲁϥⲥϩⲁⲓ as he, it (m) writes
      ⲉ-ϣⲁⲥⲥϩⲁⲓ as she, it (f) writes

plural
1st ⲉ-ϣⲁⲛⲥϩⲁⲓ as we write
2nd ⲉ-ϣⲁⲧⲉⲧⲛ̄ⲥϩⲁⲓ as you write
3rd ⲉ-ϣⲁⲩⲥϩⲁⲓ as they write

With an expressed noun as subject:

ⲉ-ϣⲁⲣⲉ-ⲡⲣⲱⲙⲉ ⲥϩⲁⲓ   as the person writes

The Circumstantial Negative Aorist is also formed throughout by putting the circumstantial converter ⲉ- before the Negative Aorist (with the hyphen included):

---

6. Remember, the Aorist is untensed on its own, so be flexible. Since you have to pick something, start with the English simple present.

ⲉ-ⲙⲉⲓⲥϩⲁⲓ				as I don't write
ⲉ-ⲙⲉⲣⲉ-ⲡⲣⲱⲙⲉ ⲥϩⲁⲓ				as the person doesn't write

VOCABULARY

ϩⲙⲟⲟⲥ				to sit down; to dwell (vi)
ϩⲱⲧⲃ̄	ϩⲉⲧⲃ̄-	ϩⲟⲧⲃ⸗	ϩⲟⲧⲃ̄†	(cp ϩⲁⲧⲃ-) to murder, slay (ⲙ̄ⲙⲟ⸗) (vt)
				murder, slaughter; slain (nm)
ϫⲟⲟⲩ	ϫⲉⲩ-	ϫⲟⲟⲩ⸗		to send (ⲙ̄ⲙⲟ⸗; to: ⲉⲣⲁⲧ⸗, ⲛⲁ⸗, ⲉϫⲛ̄-, ϣⲁ-)[7] (vt)
ϫⲟⲟⲩ ⲉⲃⲟⲗ				to send away, out, off
ϫⲟⲟⲩ ϩⲁⲑⲏ				to send ahead
ϫⲡⲟ	ϫⲡⲉ-	ϫⲡⲟ⸗		1. to bring into existence, give birth to (ⲙ̄ⲙⲟ⸗);
				2. to acquire, obtain, get (ⲙ̄ⲙⲟ⸗; often with reflexive ⲛⲁ⸗ [for one's self])[8] (vt)
				birth; acquisition (nm)
ϭⲱ			ϭⲉⲉⲧ†	1. to stay, remain, wait (for: ⲉ-; with ⲙⲛ̄-);
				2. to continue, persist (doing: circum);
				3. to stop, cease (vi)
ϭⲱϣⲧ̄				to watch, look, stare (at: ⲉ-, ⲉϫⲛ̄-, ⲛ̄ⲥⲁ-) (often with ⲉⲃⲟⲗ, ⲉϩⲟⲩⲛ, ⲉϩⲣⲁⲓ, ⲉⲡⲉⲥⲏⲧ) (vi)
				look, stare (nm)
ϭⲱϣⲧ̄ (ⲉⲃⲟⲗ) ϩⲏⲧ⸗				to look forward to, expect, await
ⲁⲅⲁⲡⲏ				love (nf)
ⲡⲓⲥⲧⲓⲥ				trust (nf)
ϩⲉⲗⲡⲓⲥ				hope (nf)
ϩⲟⲧⲉ				fear (nf)
ⲁⲧϩⲟⲧⲉ				fearless
ⲣ̄-ϩⲟⲧⲉ				(ⲟ† ⲛ̄-) to become/be afraid (of: ⲉ-, ⲉϫⲛ̄-, ⲉⲧⲃⲉ-, ϩⲏⲧ⸗)
ⲣⲉϥⲣ̄-ϩⲟⲧⲉ				fearing, respectful
ⲙⲛ̄ⲧⲣⲉϥⲣ̄-ϩⲟⲧⲉ				fear, respect

---

7. ϫⲟⲟⲩ is a causative verb derived from the less common verb ϣⲉ ("to go"), originally meaning "to cause to go." See chapter 23 for more about causative verbs like this.

8. ϫⲡⲟ is a causative of our verb ϣⲱⲡⲉ ("to be[come], happen") from chapter 12.

THE CIRCUMSTANTIAL CONVERTER

EXERCISE

Copy and translate the following phrases.

1. ⲉ-ⲁⲩϩⲙⲟⲟⲥ ϩⲛ̄-ⲧⲡⲟⲗⲓⲥ

2. ⲁⲛⲡⲱⲧ ⲉϥⲛⲁϩⲱⲧⲃ̄ ⲙ̄ⲙⲟⲛ.

3. ⲁϥϭⲱ ⲉⲣⲉ-ⲡⲉϥⲉⲓⲱⲧ ϫⲟⲟⲩ ⲛⲁϥ ⲛ̄-ⲛⲉϥⲟⲩⲱⲙ.

4. ϣⲁⲣⲉ-ⲡⲇⲓⲕⲁⲓⲟⲥ ⲇⲉ ϫⲱ ⲛ̄-ⲟⲩⲡⲓⲥⲧⲓⲥ ⲉⲥⲟⲩⲟⲛϩ̄ ⲉⲃⲟⲗ.

5. ⲡⲁⲓ̈ ⲡⲉ ⲡⲛⲟⲙⲟⲥ ⲛ̄-ⲧⲉⲥϩⲓⲙⲉ ⲉⲥⲛⲁϫⲡⲉ-ⲟⲩϩⲟⲟⲩⲧ ⲏ ⲟⲩⲥϩⲓⲙⲉ.

6. ⲉⲧⲉⲧⲛ̄ϭⲱϣⲧ̄ ϩⲏⲧϥ̄ ⲙ̄-ⲡϭⲱⲗⲡ̄ ⲉⲃⲟⲗ ⲙ̄-ⲡⲉⲛϫⲟⲉⲓⲥ ⲓⲏⲥⲟⲩ̄ⲥ

7. ⲛⲉⲧⲛ̄ϩⲃⲏⲩⲉ ⲧⲏⲣⲟⲩ ⲙⲁⲣⲟⲩϣⲱⲡⲉ ϩⲛ̄-ⲟⲩⲁⲅⲁⲡⲏ.

CHAPTER 21

THE PRETERITE CONVERTER

OVERVIEW

In this chapter, you will learn:

- How the preterite converter works with the Present, Future, Past, and Aorist
- How to translate these conversions effectively in English

PRETERITE CONVERSION

21.1 **The Preterite[1] Converter.** Like the circumstantial converter, the preterite converter is also regular: it's almost always simply ⲛⲉ-, with the only exception being that it's lengthened to ⲛⲉⲣⲉ- with definite nouns as subjects in the Durative pattern. In fact, you'll notice that (with a few exceptions) the Preterite looks just like the Circumstantial with an ⲛ tacked on the front.

21.2 **Translating the Preterite.** In general, the Preterite conversion shifts the timeframe of the verb it's attached to back a step into the past:

- Present   Preterite Present[2]
    I am writing   >   I was writing (I would write)
- Future   Preterite Future
    I am going to write >   I was going to write (I was about to write)
- Past   Preterite Past[3]
    I wrote   >   I had written
- Aorist   Preterite Aorist
    I write   >   I used to write

---

1. Also spelled "Preterit." See Bentley Layton, *Coptic in 20 Lessons: Introduction to Sahidic Coptic with Exercises and Vocabularies* (Leuven: Peeters, 2007) and *A Coptic Grammar: With Chrestomathy and Glossary. Sahidic Dialect*, 3rd ed., Porta Linguarum Orientalium 2/20 (Wiesbaden: Harrassowitz, 2011).
2. The Preterite conversion of the Present is also sometimes referred to as the Imperfect in older works.
3. The Preterite conversion of the Past is also sometimes referred to as the Pluperfect (or Past Perfect) in older works.

THE PRETERITE CONVERTER

Unlike the Relative and Circumstantial, a Preterite converted verb can be a main verb—it can form a complete sentence on its own.

One other thing to be aware of: you may find an extra ⲡⲉ accompanying preterite clauses, looking like a copula in a nominal sentence (5.5). Its presence seems to be optional and somewhat superfluous, so there's no real need to account for it in your translation.

THE PRETERITE CONVERTER WITH THE DURATIVE PATTERN

21.3 Preterite Present. With the Present conjugation, the preterite converter ⲛⲉ- is prefixed to the Present personal prefixes, ⲛⲉⲣⲉ- with definite nouns as subjects. Conventionally, the hyphen is not included when written, as it would be pronounced in the same syllable as the personal prefix. Note that the 3rd plural personal prefix (-ⲩ- shortened from *-ⲟⲩ-) is again different from the ⲥⲉ- of the standard, unconverted Present.

singular
1st	ⲛⲉⲓ̈ⲥϩⲁⲓ̈	I was writing
2nd	ⲛⲉⲕⲥϩⲁⲓ̈	you (m) were writing
	ⲛⲉⲣⲉⲥϩⲁⲓ̈	you (f) were writing
3rd	ⲛⲉϥⲥϩⲁⲓ̈	he, it (m) was writing
	ⲛⲉⲥⲥϩⲁⲓ̈	she, it (f) was writing

plural
1st	ⲛⲉⲛⲥϩⲁⲓ̈	we were writing
2nd	ⲛⲉⲧⲉⲧⲛ̄ⲥϩⲁⲓ̈	you were writing
3rd	ⲛⲉⲩⲥϩⲁⲓ̈	they were writing

With a definite noun as subject, the longer form ⲛⲉⲣⲉ- (with hyphen included) is used:

    ⲛⲉⲣⲉ-ⲡⲣⲱⲙⲉ ⲥϩⲁⲓ̈   the person was writing

The Preterite Negative Present is formed by just adding ⲁⲛ after the Preterite Present forms. You'll notice this is different from the way the Relative Negative Present (ⲉⲧⲉ ⲛ̄ϥⲥϩⲁⲓ̈ ⲁⲛ) and Circumstantial Negative Present (ⲉ-ⲛ̄ϥⲥϩⲁⲓ̈ ⲁⲛ) were formed, both of which had the converter preceding the ⲛ̄- of the full negative bracket ⲛ̄- . . . ⲁⲛ.

    ⲛⲉⲓ̈ⲥϩⲁⲓ̈ ⲁⲛ   I was not writing

With a definite noun as subject, the longer form ⲛⲉⲣⲉ- is used:

    ⲛⲉⲣⲉ-ⲡⲣⲱⲙⲉ ⲥϩⲁⲓ̈ ⲁⲛ   the person was not writing

21.4 Preterite Future. The Preterite Future is formed the same way as the Preterite Present—just with the inclusion of the Future auxiliary **-ⲛⲁ-** between the personal prefix and the infinitive.

singular

1st	ⲛⲉⲓ̈ⲛⲁⲥϩⲁⲓ̈	I was going to write
2nd	ⲛⲉⲕⲛⲁⲥϩⲁⲓ̈	you (m) were going to write
	ⲛⲉⲣⲉⲛⲁⲥϩⲁⲓ̈	you (f) were going to write
3rd	ⲛⲉϥⲛⲁⲥϩⲁⲓ̈	he, it (m) was going to write
	ⲛⲉⲥⲛⲁⲥϩⲁⲓ̈	she, it (f) was going to write

plural

1st	ⲛⲉⲛⲛⲁⲥϩⲁⲓ̈	we were going to write
2nd	ⲛⲉⲧⲉⲧⲛ̄ⲛⲁⲥϩⲁⲓ̈	you were going to write
3rd	ⲛⲉⲩⲛⲁⲥϩⲁⲓ̈	they were going to write

With a definite noun as subject, the longer form **ⲛⲉⲣⲉ-** is used:

ⲛⲉⲣⲉ-ⲡⲣⲱⲙⲉ ⲛⲁⲥϩⲁⲓ̈	the person was going to write

The Preterite Negative Future is also formed by just adding **ⲁⲛ** after the Preterite Future forms:

ⲛⲉⲓ̈ⲛⲁⲥϩⲁⲓ̈ ⲁⲛ	I was not going to write

With a definite noun as subject, the longer form **ⲛⲉⲣⲉ-** is used:

ⲛⲉⲣⲉ-ⲡⲣⲱⲙⲉ ⲛⲁⲥϩⲁⲓ̈ ⲁⲛ	the person was not going to write

THE PRETERITE CONVERTER WITH THE NON-DURATIVE PATTERN

21.5 Preterite Past. For the Past, **ⲛⲉ-** is prefixed to the Past forms throughout. The hyphen is conventionally included.

singular

1st	ⲛⲉ-ⲁⲓ̈ⲥϩⲁⲓ̈	I had written
2nd	ⲛⲉ-ⲁⲕⲥϩⲁⲓ̈	you (m) had written
	ⲛⲉ-ⲁⲣⲥϩⲁⲓ̈	you (f) had written
3rd	ⲛⲉ-ⲁϥⲥϩⲁⲓ̈	he, it (m) had written
	ⲛⲉ-ⲁⲥⲥϩⲁⲓ̈	she, it (f) had written

THE PRETERITE CONVERTER

plural
- *1st* ⲛⲉ-ⲁⲛⲥϩⲁⲓ — we had written
- *2nd* ⲛⲉ-ⲁⲧⲉⲧⲛ̄ⲥϩⲁⲓ — you had written
- *3rd* ⲛⲉ-ⲁⲩⲥϩⲁⲓ — they had written

With an expressed noun as subject:

ⲛⲉ-ⲁ-ⲡⲣⲱⲙⲉ ⲥϩⲁⲓ — the person had written

The Preterite Negative Past and the Preterite "Not Yet" Past are also formed throughout by simply putting the preterite converter ⲛⲉ- before the Negative and "Not Yet" Past (with the hyphen included):

- ⲛⲉ-ⲙ̄ⲡⲓⲥϩⲁⲓ — I had not written
- ⲛⲉ-ⲙ̄ⲡⲉ-ⲡⲣⲱⲙⲉ ⲥϩⲁⲓ — the person had not written
- ⲛⲉ-ⲙ̄ⲡⲁϯⲥϩⲁⲓ — I had not written yet
- ⲛⲉ-ⲙ̄ⲡⲁⲧⲉ-ⲡⲣⲱⲙⲉ ⲥϩⲁⲓ — the person had not written yet

21.6 Preterite Aorist. For the Aorist, ⲛⲉ- is prefixed to the Aorist forms throughout. The hyphen is conventionally included.

singular
- *1st* ⲛⲉ-ϣⲁⲓⲥϩⲁⲓ — I used to write
- *2nd* ⲛⲉ-ϣⲁⲕⲥϩⲁⲓ — you (m) used to write
- ⲛⲉ-ϣⲁⲣ(ⲉ)ⲥϩⲁⲓ — you (f) used to write
- *3rd* ⲛⲉ-ϣⲁϥⲥϩⲁⲓ — he, it (m) used to write
- ⲛⲉ-ϣⲁⲥⲥϩⲁⲓ — she, it (f) used to write

plural
- *1st* ⲛⲉ-ϣⲁⲛⲥϩⲁⲓ — we used to write
- *2nd* ⲛⲉ-ϣⲁⲧⲉⲧⲛ̄ⲥϩⲁⲓ — you used to write
- *3rd* ⲛⲉ-ϣⲁⲩⲥϩⲁⲓ — they used to write

With an expressed noun as subject:

ⲛⲉ-ϣⲁⲣⲉ-ⲡⲣⲱⲙⲉ ⲥϩⲁⲓ — the person used to write

The Preterite Negative Aorist is also formed throughout by putting the preterite converter ⲛⲉ- before the Negative Aorist (with the hyphen included):

- ⲛⲉ-ⲙⲉⲓⲥϩⲁⲓ — I didn't use to write
- ⲛⲉ-ⲙⲉⲣⲉ-ⲡⲣⲱⲙⲉ ⲥϩⲁⲓ — the person didn't use to write

VOCABULARY

ⲁⲙⲁϩⲧⲉ				to grasp, seize, restrain, apprehend (ⲙ̄ⲙⲟ⸗) (vt)
				to get control, rule (over: ⲉϫⲛ̄-, ϩⲓϫⲛ̄-) (vi)
				control, restraint (nm)
ⲁⲣⲭ(ⲉ)ⲓ				to begin (to: ⲛ̄- or ⲉ- + inf); to rule (over: ⲉϫⲛ̄-) (vt)
ⲃⲱⲗ	ⲃⲉⲗ-, ⲃⲗ̄-	ⲃⲟⲗ⸗	ⲃⲏⲗ†	(cp ⲃⲁⲗ-) 1. to release, loosen, undo (ⲙ̄ⲙⲟ⸗); 2. to interpret (ⲙ̄ⲙⲟ⸗) (vt)
				to become released, undone (vi)
				to be released, undone, interpreted (vs)
				interpretation (nm)
ⲃⲱⲗ ⲉⲃⲟⲗ				=1. and also: to dissolve, destroy (ⲙ̄ⲙⲟ⸗)
ⲙⲉⲉⲩⲉ				to think (that: ϫⲉ; about: ⲉ-); to consider (+ ⲉⲃⲟⲗ) (vi)
				thought, mind (nm)
ⲣ̄-ⲡ(⸗)ⲙⲉⲉⲩⲉ				to remember (ⲛ̄-)
ⲙⲟⲩⲣ	ⲙⲉⲣ-, ⲙⲣ̄-	ⲙⲟⲣ⸗	ⲙⲏⲣ†	(cp ⲙⲁⲣ-) to bind, tie (someone: ⲙ̄ⲙⲟ⸗ or suffix; with: ⲙ̄ⲙⲟ⸗, ϩⲛ̄-; to: ⲉ-, ⲉϫⲛ̄-, ⲉϩⲟⲩⲛ ⲉ-) (vt)
				to be bound (vs)
				band, strap (nm)
ⲙⲟⲩϩ	ⲙⲉϩ-[4]	ⲙⲁϩ⸗	ⲙⲏϩ†, ⲙⲉϩ†	(± ⲉⲃⲟⲗ) to fill (something: ⲙ̄ⲙⲟ⸗ or suffix; with: ⲙ̄ⲙⲟ⸗, ϩⲛ̄-, ⲉⲃⲟⲗ ϩⲛ̄-); to fulfill (vt)
				to become filled, full (of, with: ⲙ̄ⲙⲟ⸗ [if indefinite, usually without article]); to become fulfilled (vi)
				to be full (vs)
				fullness (nm)
ϭⲱⲡⲉ	ϭⲉⲡ-	ϭⲟⲡ⸗	ϭⲏⲡ†	to seize, catch, take (ⲙ̄ⲙⲟ⸗) (vt)
βάπτισμα				immersion (nm)
†-βάπτισμα				to give an immersion, immerse
θλίψις				affliction (nf)
ⲛⲟⲃⲉ				wrong, sin (nm)
ⲣ̄-ⲛⲟⲃⲉ				to do wrong, sin
ⲟⲩⲁ				defamation (nm)
ϫⲓ-/ϫⲉ-ⲟⲩⲁ				to defame [cf. ϫⲱ]
ⲟⲩⲟ(ⲉ)ⲓ				woe (nm)

---

4. Used as the ordinal number prefix (9.2).

THE PRETERITE CONVERTER

EXERCISE

Copy and translate the following phrases.

1. ⲡⲣ̅ⲣⲟ ⲛⲉϥⲁⲙⲁϩⲧⲉ ⲉϫⲙ̅-ⲡⲕⲁϩ ⲧⲏⲣϥ̅.

2. ⲁ-ⲙⲁⲣⲕⲟⲥ ⲁⲣⲭⲉⲓ ⲛ̅-ϣⲁϫⲉ ⲛⲙ̅ⲙⲁⲩ.

3. ⲓⲏⲥⲟⲩⲥ ⲁⲛ ⲡⲉ ⲛⲉϥⲃⲁⲡⲧⲓⲍⲉ ⲁⲗⲗⲁ ⲛⲉϥⲙⲁⲑⲏⲧⲏⲥ.

4. ⲕⲥⲟⲟⲩⲛ̅ ⲇⲉ ⲡⲉïⲙⲉⲉⲩⲉ ϣⲁϥⲃⲉⲗ-ϩⲱⲃ ⲛⲓⲙ ⲉⲃⲟⲗ.

5. ⲛⲉϥⲙⲉⲉⲩⲉ ⲇⲉ ⲡⲉ ϫⲉ ⲥⲉⲛⲁⲉⲓⲙⲉ ⲛ̅ϭⲓ-ⲛⲉϥⲥⲛⲏⲩ.

6. ⲁⲩⲱ ⲁϥⲁⲙⲁϩⲧⲉ ⲙ̅ⲙⲟϥ ⲁⲩⲱ ⲁϥⲙⲟⲣϥ̅ ⲛ̅-ϣⲟ ⲛ̅-ⲣⲟⲙⲡⲉ.

7. ⲁ-ⲍⲁⲭⲁⲣⲓⲁⲥ ⲇⲉ ⲡⲉϥⲉⲓⲱⲧ ⲙⲟⲩϩ ⲉⲃⲟⲗ ϩⲙ̅-ⲡⲉⲡⲛⲉⲩⲙⲁ ⲉⲧ-ⲟⲩⲁⲁⲃ.

8. ⲙⲉⲥⲣ̅-ⲡⲙⲉⲉⲩⲉ ϭⲉ ⲛ̅-ⲧⲉⲑⲗⲓⲯⲓⲥ ⲉⲧⲃⲉ-ⲡⲣⲁϣⲉ ϫⲉ ⲁⲥϫⲡⲉ-ⲟⲩⲣⲱⲙⲉ ⲉ-ⲡⲕⲟⲥⲙⲟⲥ.

CHAPTER 22

THE FOCALIZING CONVERTER

OVERVIEW

In this chapter, you will learn:

- How the focalizing converter works with the Present, Future, Past, and Aorist
- How to translate these conversions effectively in English

FOCALIZING CONVERSION

22.1 **The Focalizing Converter.** Our last converter is the focalizing converter. Many older works describe this conversion as being a set of "second tenses" (Second Present, Second Future, etc.) with the corresponding main conjugations referred to as the "first tenses" (First Present, First Future, etc.)—and the Optative as "Third Future"!—but this is an unwieldy way to handle this. We will treat this as another in the system of converters that can be prefixed to verbal conjugations. The focalizing converter, like the relative converter, will take different forms depending on what it's prefixed to: ⲉ-, ⲉⲣⲉ-, and ⲛ̄ⲧ-.[1]

22.2 **Translating the Focalizing Converter.** The focalizing converter marks a shift in the focus of the sentence of which it plays a part. The usual focus of a verbal sentence is naturally on the predicate (the new information about the subject), but with a Focalizing conversion something else becomes the focal point of the sentence. If this explanation feels "fuzzy," it's because it is! Nothing else specifically tells the reader exactly what the new focus is, and so—especially for our English translation needs—some careful and creative analysis of the sentence as whole is needed. If the sentence has a prepositional or adverbial phrase, this is often the intended emphasis. Look at Mark 1.8, which has a Focalizing conversion on the verb in the second half of the sentence:

---

1. Just from those forms, you can probably guess that there can be some confusion with the other converters.

THE FOCALIZING CONVERTER

ⲁⲛⲟⲕ ⲁⲓ†-ⲃⲁⲡⲧⲓⲥⲙⲁ ⲛⲏⲧⲛ̄ ϩⲛ̄-ⲟⲩⲙⲟⲟⲩ,
Me, I gave an immersion to you in (a) water,

ⲛ̄ⲧⲟϥ ⲇⲉ ⲉϥⲛⲁⲃⲁⲡⲧⲓⲍⲉ ⲙ̄ⲙⲱⲧⲛ̄ ϩⲛ̄-ⲟⲩⲡⲛⲉⲩⲙⲁ ⲉϥⲟⲩⲁⲁⲃ.
yet *him*, **it is in (a) holy spirit that** he is going to immerse you.

First of all, you'll notice that this statement has a contrast between *me* and *him*, emphasized by the inclusion of the independent personal pronouns alongside the conjugated verbs (*italics* are used here to highlight this emphasis). But beyond that, the focalizing converter tags the focus in the second half on something else accompanying the verb. In this case, the prepositional phrase ϩⲛ̄-ⲟⲩⲡⲛⲉⲩⲙⲁ ⲉϥⲟⲩⲁⲁⲃ ("in [a] holy spirit") would be the logical choice. As you can see, one common and fairly effective way to signal this in English is through the use of a cleft sentence construction—"it is . . . that"—with the prepositional phrase brought forward into that phrase. The extra wordiness helps to give the extra emphasis to the prepositional phrase. Another way you could do this would be through the use of italics for emphasis ("he is going to immerse you ***in (a) holy spirit***").

Here's another example with a prepositional phrase (ⲉⲧⲃⲏⲏⲧⲟⲩ "about them") as the focus. Compare the two ways of translating it with emphasis:

ⲁⲩⲉⲓⲙⲉ ⲅⲁⲣ ϫⲉ ⲛ̄ⲧⲁϥϫⲉ-ⲧⲉⲓ̈ⲡⲁⲣⲁⲃⲟⲗⲏ ⲉⲧⲃⲏⲏⲧⲟⲩ. (Mark 12.12b)
For they realized that **it is about them that** he said this illustration. (cleft)
or For they realized that he said this illustration ***about them***. (italics)

Either way can work. Things get more complicated if a sentence has multiple possible focal points, in which case you need to pay attention to the context and the flow of thought to deduce what you should emphasize in your translation.

Finally, focalizing converters can show up in questions, especially ones with the interrogative at the end.

ⲉⲣⲉ-ⲛ̄ⲣⲱⲙⲉ ϫⲱ ⲙ̄ⲙⲟⲥ ⲉⲣⲟⲓ̈ ϫⲉ ⲁⲛⲅ̄-ⲛⲓⲙ? (Mark 8.27b)
Who do the people say (it for me) that I am?

In cases like these, the natural extra emphasis of the English simple emphatic ("do") nicely parallels the Focalizing conversion.

Keep in mind that focalizing clauses can be complete sentences on their own, like the Preterite—but unlike the Relative or Circumstantial, which depend on another main verb. This can help you to determine what you're dealing with when you encounter a potentially ambiguous form like ⲉϥⲛⲁⲃⲁⲡⲧⲓⲍⲉ, which without context could be read as a Circumstantial or a Focalizing Future.

With all the forms below, an English cleft construction is given as a gloss, but keep in mind that this is just one way the Focalizing conversion could be translated in context.

THE FOCALIZING CONVERTER WITH THE DURATIVE PATTERN

22.3 Focalizing Present. With the Present conjugation, the focalizing converter ⲉ- prefixed to the Present personal prefixes, ⲉⲣⲉ- with definite nouns as subjects. Conventionally, the hyphen is not included when written, as it would be pronounced in the same syllable as the personal prefix. Note that the 3rd plural personal prefix (-ⲩ- shortened from *-ⲟⲩ-) is again different from the ⲥⲉ- of the standard, unconverted Present. And yes, the Focalizing Present unfortunately looks just like the Circumstantial Present! In actuality, the context you'll have when you're reading texts will (usually) clarify whether you're looking at a Circumstantial or Focalizing conversion. A focalizing clause can be a complete sentence, for instance, but a circumstantial clause needs another main verb.

singular
1st	ⲉⲓⲥϩⲁⲓ̈	it is . . . that I am writing
2nd	ⲉⲕⲥϩⲁⲓ̈	it is . . . that you (m) are writing
	ⲉⲣ(ⲉ)ⲥϩⲁⲓ̈	it is . . . that you (f) are writing
3rd	ⲉϥⲥϩⲁⲓ̈	it is . . . that he, it (m) is writing
	ⲉⲥⲥϩⲁⲓ̈	it is . . . that she, it (f) is writing

plural
1st	ⲉⲛⲥϩⲁⲓ̈	it is . . . that we are writing
2nd	ⲉⲧⲉⲧⲛ̄ⲥϩⲁⲓ̈[2]	it is . . . that you are writing
3rd	ⲉⲩⲥϩⲁⲓ̈	it is . . . that they are writing

With a definite noun as subject, the longer form ⲉⲣⲉ- (with hyphen included) is used:

    ⲉⲣⲉ-ⲡⲣⲱⲙⲉ ⲥϩⲁⲓ̈   it is . . . that the person is writing

The Focalizing Negative Present is formed by adding ⲁⲛ after the Focalizing Present forms (with an optional ⲛ̄- before the converter to complete the full negative bracket). Note that this is different from the Circumstantial Negative Present (ⲉ-ⲛ̄ϯⲥϩⲁⲓ̈ ⲁⲛ), so the ambiguity present in their affirmative forms is no longer a factor to worry about.

    (ⲛ̄-)ⲉⲓⲥϩⲁⲓ̈ ⲁⲛ   it is . . . that I am not writing

With a definite noun as subject, the longer form ⲉⲣⲉ- is used:

    (ⲛ̄-)ⲉⲣⲉ-ⲡⲣⲱⲙⲉ ⲥϩⲁⲓ̈ ⲁⲛ   it is . . . that the person is not writing

---

2. Note that this is the same as the Relative Present 2nd plural (as well as the Circumstantial Present 2nd plural, of course).

22.4 **Focalizing Future.** As you might expect by now, the Focalizing Future is formed the same way as the Focalizing Present—just with the inclusion of the Future auxiliary -ⲛⲁ- between the personal prefix and the infinitive. Again, this looks the same as the Circumstantial Future. Context will be your guide.

singular
- 1st ⲉⲓⲛⲁⲥϩⲁⲓ — it is ... that I going to write
- 2nd ⲉⲕⲛⲁⲥϩⲁⲓ — it is ... that you (m) are going to write
- ⲉⲣⲉⲛⲁⲥϩⲁⲓ — it is ... that you (f) are going to write
- 3rd ⲉϥⲛⲁⲥϩⲁⲓ — it is ... that he, it (m) is going to write
- ⲉⲥⲛⲁⲥϩⲁⲓ — it is ... that she, it (f) is going to write

plural
- 1st ⲉⲛⲛⲁⲥϩⲁⲓ — it is ... that we are going to write
- 2nd ⲉⲧⲉⲧⲛ̄ⲛⲁⲥϩⲁⲓ[3] — it is ... that you are going to write
- 3rd ⲉⲩⲛⲁⲥϩⲁⲓ — it is ... that they are going to write

With a definite noun as subject, the longer form ⲉⲣⲉ- is used:

ⲉⲣⲉ-ⲡⲣⲱⲙⲉ ⲛⲁⲥϩⲁⲓ — it is ... that the person is going to write

As with the Focalizing Negative Present, the Focalizing Negative Future is formed by adding ⲁⲛ after the Focalizing Future forms (with an optional ⲛ̄- before the converter to complete the full negative bracket).

(ⲛ̄-)ⲉⲓⲛⲁⲥϩⲁⲓ ⲁⲛ — it is ... that I am not going to write

With a definite noun as subject, the longer form ⲉⲣⲉ- is used:

(ⲛ̄-)ⲉⲣⲉ-ⲡⲣⲱⲙⲉ ⲛⲁⲥϩⲁⲓ ⲁⲛ — it is ... that the person is not going to write

THE FOCALIZING CONVERTER WITH THE NON-DURATIVE PATTERN

22.5 **Focalizing Past.** For the Past, the focalizing converter is spelled ⲛ̄ⲧ-. This is prefixed to the Past personal prefixes (no hyphen). In manuscripts, this converter is sometimes defectively spelled ⲉⲛⲧ-, which could then cause confusion with the Relative Past.

---

[3]. Note that this is the same as the Relative Future 2nd plural (as well as the Circumstantial Future 2nd plural, of course).

		singular	
1st		ⲛ̄ⲧⲁⲓⲥϩⲁⲓ̈	it is . . . that I wrote
2nd		ⲛ̄ⲧⲁⲕⲥϩⲁⲓ̈	it is . . . that you (m) wrote
		ⲛ̄ⲧⲁⲣⲉⲥϩⲁⲓ̈	it is . . . that you (f) wrote
3rd		ⲛ̄ⲧⲁϥⲥϩⲁⲓ̈	it is . . . that he, it (m) wrote
		ⲛ̄ⲧⲁⲥⲥϩⲁⲓ̈	it is . . . that she, it (f) wrote

		plural	
1st		ⲛ̄ⲧⲁⲛⲥϩⲁⲓ̈	it is . . . that we wrote
2nd		ⲛ̄ⲧⲁⲧⲉⲧⲛ̄ⲥϩⲁⲓ̈	it is . . . that you wrote
3rd		ⲛ̄ⲧⲁⲩⲥϩⲁⲓ̈	it is . . . that they wrote

With an expressed noun as subject:

ⲛ̄ⲧⲁ-ⲡⲣⲱⲙⲉ ⲥϩⲁⲓ̈   it is . . . that the person wrote

The Focalizing Negative Past is anomalous among the Non-Durative conjugations. It is formed simply by adding ⲁⲛ after the forms of the Focalizing Past:

ⲛ̄ⲧⲁⲓⲥϩⲁⲓ̈ ⲁⲛ   it is . . . that I didn't write

The Focalizing "Not Yet" Past and the Focalizing Negative Aorist are extremely rare or unattested.

22.6 Focalizing Aorist. For the Aorist, ⲉ- is prefixed to the Aorist forms throughout. This is very similar to the Circumstantial Aorist. For this reason—unlike the Circumstantial Aorist—the hyphen is conventionally *not* included with the Focalizing Aorist.

		singular	
1st		ⲉϣⲁⲓ̈ⲥϩⲁⲓ̈	it is . . . that I write
2nd		ⲉϣⲁⲕⲥϩⲁⲓ̈	it is . . . that you (m) write
		ⲉϣⲁⲣ(ⲉ)ⲥϩⲁⲓ̈	it is . . . that you (f) write
3rd		ⲉϣⲁϥⲥϩⲁⲓ̈	it is . . . that he, it (m) writes
		ⲉϣⲁⲥⲥϩⲁⲓ̈	it is . . . that she, it (f) writes

		plural	
1st		ⲉϣⲁⲛⲥϩⲁⲓ̈	it is . . . that we write
2nd		ⲉϣⲁⲧⲉⲧⲛ̄ⲥϩⲁⲓ̈	it is . . . that you write
3rd		ⲉϣⲁⲩⲥϩⲁⲓ̈	it is . . . that they write

With an expressed noun as subject:

ⲉϣⲁⲣⲉ-ⲡⲣⲱⲙⲉ ⲥϩⲁⲓ̈   it is . . . that the person writes

VOCABULARY

ⲟⲩⲱⲛ			ⲟⲩⲏⲛ†	(impv ⲁⲩⲱⲛ) to open (ⲙ̄ⲙⲟ⸗, ⲉ-) (vt)
				to become/be open (vi/vs)
				opening (nm)
ⲡⲱϣ	ⲡⲉϣ-	ⲡⲟϣ⸗	ⲡⲏϣ†	to divide (ⲙ̄ⲙⲟ⸗) (vt)
				to become/be divided (vi/vs)
				division (nm)
ⲥⲟⲃⲧⲉ	ⲥⲃ̄ⲧⲉ-	ⲥⲃ̄ⲧⲱⲧ⸗	ⲥⲃ̄ⲧⲱⲧ†	to prepare, make ready (ⲙ̄ⲙⲟ⸗; for: ⲉ-) (vt)
				to become prepared, get ready (vi/vr)
				preparation; equipment (nm)
ⲥⲱ	ⲥⲉ-	ⲥⲟⲟ⸗		(cp ⲥⲁⲩ-) to drink (ⲙ̄ⲙⲟ⸗; some of: ⲉⲃⲟⲗ ϩⲛ̄-) (vt)
				drinking, a drink (nm)
ⲧⲁ(ⲉ)ⲓⲟ	ⲧⲁ(ⲉ)ⲓⲉ-	ⲧⲁ(ⲉ)ⲓⲟ⸗	ⲧⲁ(ⲉ)ⲓⲏⲩ†	to honor, value (ⲙ̄ⲙⲟ⸗) (vt)
				to be honored, valuable (vs)
				honor (nm)
ⲧⲁⲕⲟ	ⲧⲁⲕⲉ-	ⲧⲁⲕⲟ⸗	ⲧⲁⲕⲏⲩ(ⲧ)†	to destroy, ruin (ⲙ̄ⲙⲟ⸗) (vt)
				to become destroyed, ruined (vi)
				destruction, ruin (nm)
ⲧⲁⲙⲓⲟ	ⲧⲁⲙⲓⲉ-	ⲧⲁⲙⲓⲟ⸗	ⲧⲁⲙⲓⲏⲩ†	to create, make; to prepare, make ready (ⲙ̄ⲙⲟ⸗) (vt)
				creation, creature (nm)

δαιμόνιον, δαίμων — supernatural being, daemon (nm)
ⲉⲥⲟⲟⲩ — sheep (nm; ⲉⲥⲱ [f])
θηρίον — beast, wild animal (nm)
ⲟⲩⲟ(ⲉ)ⲓ — approach, advance, rush (nm)
 ϯ-ⲡ(⸗)ⲟⲩⲟ(ⲉ)ⲓ — to (make one's) approach (to: ⲉ-)
παραβολή — illustration, analogy (nf)
ϭⲟⲛⲥ̄ — violence (n)
 ϫⲓ ⲛ̄-ϭⲟⲛⲥ̄ — to treat violently (ⲙ̄ⲙⲟ⸗); violence
 ⲣⲉϥϫⲓ ⲛ̄-ϭⲟⲛⲥ̄ — violent person

EXERCISE

Copy and translate the following phrases.

1. ⲁϥϫⲓ ⲛ̄ϭⲓ-ⲓⲏⲥⲟⲩⲥ ⲛ̄-ⲟⲩⲟⲉⲓⲕ ⲁϥⲡⲟϣϥ̄ ⲁϥϯ ⲙ̄ⲙⲟϥ ⲛ̄-ⲛⲉϥⲙⲁⲑⲏⲧⲏⲥ.

2. ϩⲛ-ⲟⲩⲡⲓ́ⲥⲧⲓⲥ ⲉⲛⲉⲓⲙⲉ ϫⲉ ⲛ̄ⲧⲁⲩⲥⲟⲃⲧⲉ ⲙ̄-ⲡⲕⲟ́ⲥⲙⲟⲥ ϩⲙ̄-ⲡϣⲁϫⲉ ⲙ̄-ⲡⲛⲟⲩⲧⲉ. _____

3. ⲛⲁⲓ̈ ⲇⲉ ⲧⲏⲣⲟⲩ ⲁϥϫⲟⲟⲩ ⲛ̄ϭⲓ-ⲓⲏⲥⲟⲩ́ⲥ ϩⲛ̄-ϩⲉⲛⲡⲁⲣⲁⲃⲟⲗⲏ́ ⲛ̄-ⲙ̄ⲙⲏⲏϣⲉ, _____

4. ⲁⲩⲱ ⲁϫⲛ̄-ⲡⲁⲣⲁⲃⲟⲗⲏ́ ⲙ̄ⲡⲉϥϫⲉ-ⲗⲁⲁⲩ ⲛⲁⲩ. _____

5. ⲁⲗⲗⲁ ϯⲥⲟⲟⲩⲛ ϫⲉ ⲉⲣⲉ-ⲡⲉϥⲧⲁⲉⲓⲟ ϩⲛ̄-ⲙ̄ⲡⲏⲩⲉ ϩⲁϩⲧⲛ̄-ⲡⲛⲟⲩⲧⲉ. _____

6. ⲁ-ⲡⲛⲟⲩⲧⲉ ⲧⲁⲙⲓⲟ ⲛ̄-ⲛⲉⲑⲏⲣⲓ́ⲟⲛ ⲙ̄-ⲡⲕⲁϩ. _____

CHAPTER 23

THE NON-DURATIVE PATTERN: SUBORDINATE CLAUSE CONJUGATIONS

OVERVIEW

In this chapter, you will learn:

- The major categories and features of the Subordinate Clause conjugations
- How many verbs beginning in ⲧ- form a group of causative verbs

OVERVIEW OF THE SUBORDINATE CLAUSE CONJUGATIONS

23.1 Subordinate Clause Conjugations. Having completed our discussion of the four converters, we now return to the Non-Durative pattern's second group, the Subordinate Clause conjugations. With these (and few verbal leftovers in chapter 27), we will complete our survey of the Sahidic verbal system—and Sahidic grammar as a whole!

Remember, as part of the Non-Durative pattern, these Subordinate Clause conjugations are formed by the use of a verbal auxiliary plus a personal subject marker plus an infinitive. They do not take any of the four converters. As subordinate clauses, they aren't complete sentences on their own and require a main verbal clause. These conjugations cover a number of temporal, modal, and syntactical possibilities.

Here's our roadmap for the next few chapters as we work through the Subordinate Clause conjugations:

- **Conjunctive** (chapter 24) The Conjunctive verbal auxiliary is ⲛ̄(ⲧⲉ)-.
  The Conjunctive continues a sequence from the main verb preceding it.
   ⲛ̄ⲧⲁⲥϩⲁⲓ   . . . and (I) write
- **Future Conjunctive** (chapter 24) The Future Conjunctive verbal auxiliary is ⲧⲁⲣ(ⲉ)-. This follows a command, describing what will happen as a result of that being done.
   ⲧⲁⲣⲓⲥϩⲁⲓ   . . . and I will write

- **Precursive** (chapter 25) The Precursive verbal auxiliary is ⲛ̄ⲧⲉⲣ(ⲉ)-.
    This describes something that happened before the main (often Past) verb.
        ⲛ̄ⲧⲉⲣⲓⲥϩⲁⲓ̈   when/after I had written/wrote
- **Limitative** (chapter 25) The Limitative verbal auxiliary is ϣⲁⲛⲧ(ⲉ)-.
    This describes the duration for which the main verb will be in effect.
        ϣⲁⲛϯⲥϩⲁⲓ̈   until I write/wrote/have written/had written
- **Conditional** (chapter 26) The Conditional verbal auxiliary is ⲉ(ⲣ)ϣⲁⲛ-.
    This is used to form "if" clauses, either specific or general.
        ⲉⲓ̈ϣⲁⲛⲥϩⲁⲓ̈   if/when(ever) I write/wrote
- **Causative Infinitive** (chapter 26) The Causative Infinitive auxiliary is ⲧⲣ(ⲉ)-.
    This is combined with another infinitive (sometimes to describe causation) and can be conjugated like one of the primary conjugations.
        ⲧⲣⲁⲥϩⲁⲓ̈   (cause) me to write, me writing

23.2   **Negation of Subordinate Clause Conjugations.** A distinctive feature you'll notice with these conjugations is that they all (apart from the Future Conjunctive, which lacks a negative counterpart) use the negative particle -ⲧⲙ-, usually as an infix before the infinitive.

CAUSATIVE VERBS

23.3   **ⲧ- Causative Verbs.** All of the verbs in this chapter's vocabulary are part of a special category of verbs that are causative forms of other directly active verbs. These verbs come from an older stage of the language and have the distinctive feature of starting with ⲧ-. Later, the Causative Infinitive would take this role in producing causative forms of verbs, but these ⲧ- causative verbs are remnants of that earlier stage. Keep in mind, however, that not all verbs that begin with ⲧ- are causative.

    Sometimes the causative form of a verb is much more common than its directly active form. For instance, the verb ⲧⲁ(ⲉ)ⲓⲟ ("to honor, value"), which you learned in the last chapter, is the fairly common causative of the less common verb ⲁⲓ̈ⲁⲓ̈ ("to increase, grow").

23.4   **ϫ- Causative Verbs.** With verbs starting in ϣ- [ʃ], the ⲧ- [t] combines with it and is spelled as ϫ- [tʃ]. You actually learned two of these verbs back in chapter 20:

ϫⲟⲟⲩ	ϫⲉⲩ-	ϫⲟⲟⲩ⸗	to send (ⲙ̄ⲙⲟ⸗; to: ⲉⲣⲁⲧ⸗, ⲛⲁ⸗, ⲉϫⲛ̄-, ϣⲁ-) (vt) (causative of the uncommon verb ϣⲉ, to go [vi])
ϫⲡⲟ	ϫⲡⲉ-	ϫⲡⲟ⸗	1. to bring into existence, give birth to (ⲙ̄ⲙⲟ⸗); 2. to acquire, obtain, get (ⲙ̄ⲙⲟ⸗; often with reflexive ⲛⲁ⸗ [for one's self]) (vt) (causative of ϣⲱⲡⲉ, chapter 12)

Again, not all verbs that begin with ϫ- are causative.

VOCABULARY

ⲧⲁⲗⲟ, ⲧⲁⲗⲉ	ⲧⲁⲗⲉ-	ⲧⲁⲗⲟ⸗	ⲧⲁⲗⲏⲩ†	(± ⲉϩⲣⲁⲓ) to raise up, offer up; to put on, cause to get on (ⲙ̄ⲙⲟ⸗; to: ⲉ-) (vt)
				to go up, climb, get on, mount (vi)
				(causative of ⲁⲗⲉ, chapter 19)
				raising up, offering (nm)
ⲧⲁⲙⲟ	ⲧⲁⲙⲉ-	ⲧⲁⲙⲟ⸗		to tell, inform (ⲙ̄ⲙⲟ⸗; of, about: ⲉ-, ⲉⲧⲃⲉ-; that: ϫⲉ) (vt)
				(causative of ⲉⲓⲙⲉ, chapter 17)
ⲧⲁϣⲟ	ⲧⲁϣⲉ-	ⲧⲁϣⲟ⸗		to increase (ⲙ̄ⲙⲟ⸗); often prefixed to another inf: to do something more, much (vt)
				(causative of the less common verb ⲁϣⲁⲓ, to become/be many, numerous [vi])
ⲧⲃ̄ⲃⲟ	ⲧⲃ̄ⲃⲉ-	ⲧⲃ̄ⲃⲟ⸗	ⲧⲃ̄ⲃⲏⲩ†	to purify, cleanse (ⲙ̄ⲙⲟ⸗; of, from: ⲉ-, ⲉⲃⲟⲗ ϩⲛ̄-, ϩⲁ-) (vt)
				to become/be pure (vi/vs)
				(causative of ⲟⲩⲟⲡ, chapter 14)
				purity, purification (nm)
ⲧⲛ̄ⲛⲟⲟⲩ	ⲧⲛ̄ⲛⲉⲩ-	ⲧⲛ̄ⲛⲟⲟⲩ⸗		to send (ⲙ̄ⲙⲟ⸗; to a person: ⲛⲁ⸗, ⲉ-; for: ⲛ̄ⲥⲁ-) (vt)
				(causative of ⲉⲓⲛⲉ, chapter 17)
ⲧⲟⲩⲛⲟⲥ	ⲧⲟⲩⲛⲉⲥ-	ⲧⲟⲩⲛⲟⲥ⸗		to awaken, raise up (ⲙ̄ⲙⲟ⸗) (vt)
				(causative of ⲧⲱⲟⲩⲛ, chapter 16)
				raising (nm)
ⲧⲥⲁⲃⲟ	ⲧⲥⲁⲃⲉ-	ⲧⲥⲁⲃⲟ⸗	ⲧⲥⲁⲃⲏⲩ(ⲧ)†	to make wise, teach, instruct (ⲙ̄ⲙⲟ⸗; to: ⲉ-) (vt)
				(causative of the uncommon verb ⲥ[ⲁ]ⲃⲟ, to learn [vt])
				teaching, instruction (nm)
ϫⲛⲟⲩ	ϫⲛⲉ-	ϫⲛⲟⲩ⸗		to ask, question (ⲙ̄ⲙⲟ⸗; for: ⲉ-; about: ⲉⲧⲃⲉ-) (vt)
				(causative of ϣⲓⲛⲉ, chapter 19)
				asking, questioning (nm)
(ⲁ)ϣⲕⲁⲕ				call, shout (nm)
ⲁ(ϣ-)ϣⲕⲁⲕ ⲉⲃⲟⲗ				to call out
ϫⲓ-ϣⲕⲁⲕ ⲉⲃⲟⲗ				to call out (cf. ϫⲱ)
ⲉⲩⲁⲅⲅⲉⲗⲓⲟⲛ				good message[1] (nm)
ⲟⲉⲓϣ				cry (used only in compounds) (n)

---

1. The traditional term "gospel" comes from Old English and means "good message" as well. The Greek term originally refers to an announcement of something good that has happened—and later comes to be used as a genre label.

THE SAHIDIC VERB SYSTEM

ⲧⲁϣⲉ-ⲟⲉⲓϣ			to proclaim (ⲙ̄ⲙⲟ⸗)
ⲣⲟ (pl ⲣⲱⲟⲩ)	ⲣⲛ̄-	ⲣⲱ⸗	mouth; door, opening (nm)
ⲥⲃⲱ (pl ⲥⲃⲟⲟⲩⲉ)			teaching, instruction (nf)
ⲧⲁⲡⲣⲟ			mouth (also figuratively) (nf)

EXERCISE

Copy and translate the following phrases.

1. ⲁϥⲧⲁⲗⲟ ⲇⲉ ⲛ̄-ⲧⲉϥϭⲓϫ ⲉϫⲱⲥ ⲁⲥⲧⲱⲟⲩⲛ ⲛ̄-ⲧⲉⲩⲛⲟⲩ.

2. ⲁ-ⲙ̄ⲙⲁⲑⲏⲧⲏⲥ ⲇⲉ ⲛ̄-ⲓⲱϩⲁⲛⲛⲏⲥ ⲧⲁⲙⲟϥ ⲉⲧⲃⲉ-ⲛⲁⲓ̈ ⲧⲏⲣⲟⲩ.

3. ⲡϫⲟⲉⲓⲥ ⲡⲉⲧⲛ̄ⲛⲟⲩⲧⲉ ⲁϥⲧⲁϣⲉ-ⲑⲏⲩⲧⲛ̄.

4. ⲙⲱⲩⲥⲏⲥ ⲇⲉ ⲁϥⲃⲱⲕ ⲉⲡⲉⲥⲏⲧ ϩⲓϫⲙ̄²-ⲡⲧⲟⲟⲩ ϣⲁ-ⲡⲗⲁⲟⲥ, ⲁϥϫⲟⲟⲥ ⲛⲁⲩ ⲁⲩⲱ ⲁϥⲧⲃ̄ⲃⲟ ⲙ̄ⲙⲟⲟⲩ.

5. ⲡⲉϫⲁϥ ⲛⲁϥ ⲛ̄ϭⲓ-ⲁⲃⲣⲁϩⲁⲙ ϫⲉ "ⲡⲛⲟⲩⲧⲉ ⲛⲁⲧⲛ̄ⲛⲟⲟⲩ ⲛⲁⲛ ⲙ̄-ⲡⲉⲥⲟⲟⲩ ⲉ-ⲡⲧⲁⲗⲟ, ⲡⲁϣⲏⲣⲉ."

6. ⲁⲩϯ-ⲡⲉⲩⲟⲩⲟⲓ ⲉⲣⲟϥ ⲁⲩⲧⲟⲩⲛⲟⲥϥ̄.

7. ⲁⲩⲱ ⲉⲕⲉⲧⲥⲁⲃⲉ-ⲛⲉⲕϣⲏⲣⲉ, ⲉⲣⲟⲟⲩ ⲁⲩⲱ ⲉ-ⲛ̄ϣⲏⲣⲉ ⲛ̄-ⲛⲉⲕϣⲏⲣⲉ.

---

2. With the sense of "(from) upon."

THE NON-DURATIVE PATTERN: SUBORDINATE CLAUSE CONJUGATIONS

8. ϫⲉⲕⲁⲁⲥ ⲉϥⲉϫⲱⲕ ⲉⲃⲟⲗ ⲛ̄ϭⲓ-ⲡⲉⲛⲧⲁⲩϫⲟⲟϥ ϩⲓⲧⲙ̄-ⲡⲉⲡⲣⲟⲫⲏ́ⲧⲏⲥ, _____

_____

9. ⲉϥϫⲱ ⲙ̄ⲙⲟⲥ ϫⲉ "ϯⲛⲁⲟⲩⲱⲛ ⲉ-ⲣⲱⲓ̈ ϩⲛ̄-ϩⲉⲛⲡⲁⲣⲁⲃⲟⲗⲏ́." _____

_____

CHAPTER 24

THE CONJUNCTIVE AND THE FUTURE CONJUNCTIVE

OVERVIEW

In this chapter, you will learn:

- The conjugation and negation of the Conjunctive
- The conjugation of the Future Conjunctive
- How to translate these effectively in English

THE CONJUNCTIVE CONJUGATION

24.1 Conjugating the Conjunctive. The three components of the Conjunctive conjugation are the *Conjunctive auxiliary* ⲛ̄- plus a *personal infix* plus an *infinitive*. Before an expressed subject, the auxiliary lengthens to ⲛ̄ⲧⲉ-.

		singular		plural	
1st		(ⲛ̄)ⲧⲁ-[1]	... and (I)	ⲛ̄ⲧⲛ̄-	... and (we)
2nd		ⲛ̄ⲅ-[2]	... and (you [m])	ⲛ̄ⲧⲉⲧⲛ̄-	... and (you)
		ⲛ̄ⲧⲉ-	... and (you [f])		
3rd		ⲛ̄ϥ-[3]	... and (he, it [m])	ⲛ̄ⲥⲉ-	... and (they)
		ⲛ̄ⲥ-[4]	... and (she, it [f])		

Attached to the infinitive ϭⲣⲁⲓ, you get these forms:

---

1. The 1st person singular form is unusual in that the person infix is -ⲧⲁ- and the initial ⲛ̄- auxiliary can be dropped.
2. Note that the personal prefix regularly changes spelling from ⲕ- to ⲅ- when the negative particle is attached. This combination is also regularly written with the overline shifted to be above the ⲅ-: ⲛ̅ⲅⲥϩⲁⲓ. In addition, a variation without these changes is also attested: ⲛ̄ⲕⲥϩⲁⲓ.
3. This combination can also be written with the overline shifted: ⲛϥ̅ⲥϩⲁⲓ.
4. This combination can also be written with the overline shifted: ⲛⲥ̅ⲥϩⲁⲓ.

THE CONJUNCTIVE AND THE FUTURE CONJUNCTIVE

singular

1st	(ⲛ̄)ⲧⲁⲥϩⲁï	. . . and (I) write
2nd	ⲛ̄ⲅⲥϩⲁï[5]	. . . and (you [m]) write
	ⲛ̄ⲧⲉⲥϩⲁï	. . . and (you [f]) write
3rd	ⲛ̄ϥⲥϩⲁï[6]	. . . and (he, it [m]) writes
	ⲛ̄ⲥⲥϩⲁï[7]	. . . and (she, it [f]) writes

plural

1st	ⲛ̄ⲧⲛ̄ⲥϩⲁï	. . . and (we) write
2nd	ⲛ̄ⲧⲉⲧⲛ̄ⲥϩⲁï	. . . and (you) write
3rd	ⲛ̄ⲥⲉⲥϩⲁï	. . . and (they) write

Except for the 1st person singular, these forms look just like the Negative Present—minus the Negative Present's closing negative particle ⲁⲛ. The presence or absence of a following ⲁⲛ is an important diagnostic to tell the difference between these two options.

With an expressed noun as subject (note the longer form of the auxiliary):

ⲛ̄ⲧⲉ-ⲡⲣⲱⲙⲉ ⲥϩⲁï.   . . . and the person writes

The Negative Conjunctive is formed by infixing the negative particle -ⲧⲙ̄- between the Conjunctive prefix and the infinitive:

(ⲛ̄)ⲧⲁⲧⲙ̄ⲥϩⲁï   . . . and (I) **don't** write
ⲛ̄ⲧⲉⲧⲙ̄-ⲡⲣⲱⲙⲉ ⲥϩⲁï   . . . and the person **doesn't** write

24.2 Translating the Conjunctive. The Conjunctive continues a sequence from the main verb preceding it. Like the Aorist, it doesn't have a defined tense of its own, and so for our English translations we will usually continue the tense of that main verb. The Conjunctive can follow main verbs from the primary conjugations, imperatives, even other Conjunctives in a chain of actions. We include an "and" in our translations, although you may sometimes find an explicit ⲁⲩⲱ preceding a Conjunctive as well.

ⲉⲓⲥ-ϩⲏⲏⲧⲉ! ϯⲛⲁϫⲉⲩ-ⲡⲁⲅⲅⲉⲗⲟⲥ ϩⲓ-ϩⲏ ⲙ̄ⲙⲟⲕ ⲛ̄ϥⲥⲃ̄ⲧⲉ-ⲧⲉⲕϩⲓⲏ. (Mark 1.2b)
See! I am going to send my messenger in front of you **and he is going to prepare** your way.

ϣⲁϥⲃⲱⲕ ⲛ̄ϥϫⲓ ⲛⲙ̄ⲙⲁϥ ⲛ̄-ⲕⲉⲥⲁϣϥ̄ ⲙ̄-ⲡⲛⲉⲩⲙⲁ . . .
He goes **and (he) takes** with him seven other spirits . . .

. . . ⲛ̄ⲥⲉⲃⲱⲕ ⲉϩⲟⲩⲛ ⲛ̄ⲥⲉⲟⲩⲱϩ ϩⲙ̄-ⲡⲙⲁ ⲉⲧ-ⲙ̄ⲙⲁⲩ. (Matt 12.45a)
. . . **and they go** in **and (they) settle** in that place.

---

5. Variants: ⲛ̄ⲅ̄ⲥϩⲁï or ⲛ̄ⲕⲥϩⲁï.
6. Variant: ⲛ̄ϥ̄ⲥϩⲁï.
7. Variant: ⲛ̄ⲥ̄ⲥϩⲁï.

Especially with personal markers that are the same as the previous verb, there's no need to repeat the subject.

THE FUTURE CONJUNCTIVE CONJUGATION

24.3 Conjugating the Future Conjunctive. Our next Subordinate Clause conjugation is the Future Conjunctive.[8] It is composed of the *Future Conjunctive auxiliary* ⲧⲁⲣ(ⲉ)- plus a *personal infix* plus an *infinitive*.

	singular		**plural**	
1st	ⲧⲁⲣⲓ-	… and I will	ⲧⲁⲣⲛ̄-	… and we will
2nd	ⲧⲁⲣⲉⲕ-	… and you (m) will	ⲧⲁⲣ(ⲉⲧ)ⲉⲧⲛ̄-	… and you will
	ⲧⲁⲣⲉ-	… and you (f) will		
3rd	ⲧⲁⲣⲉϥ-	… and he, it (m) will	ⲧⲁⲣⲟⲩ-	… and they will
	ⲧⲁⲣⲉⲥ-	… and she, it (f) will		

With our model infinitive:

	singular	
1st	ⲧⲁⲣⲓⲥϩⲁⲓ	… and I will write
2nd	ⲧⲁⲣⲉⲕⲥϩⲁⲓ	… and you (m) will write
	ⲧⲁⲣⲉⲥϩⲁⲓ	… and you (f) will write
3rd	ⲧⲁⲣⲉϥⲥϩⲁⲓ	… and he, it (m) will write
	ⲧⲁⲣⲉⲥⲥϩⲁⲓ	… and she, it (f) will write

	plural	
1st	ⲧⲁⲣⲛ̄ⲥϩⲁⲓ	… and we will write
2nd	ⲧⲁⲣ(ⲉⲧ)ⲉⲧⲛ̄ⲥϩⲁⲓ	… and you will write
3rd	ⲧⲁⲣⲟⲩⲥϩⲁⲓ	… and they will write

With an expressed noun as subject (note the longer form of the auxiliary):

ⲧⲁⲣⲉ-ⲡⲣⲱⲙⲉ ⲥϩⲁⲓ   … and the person will write

There is no attested Negative Future Conjunctive.

24.4 Translating the Future Conjunctive. Most commonly, the Future Conjunctive follows a command (which could be an Imperative or a Jussive), describing what will happen as a result of that being done. "Will," which we use for the Optative, works here as well. We can supply an "and" in our translations.

---

8. Also known as the Prospective Conjunctive, Future Conjunctive of Result, and Finalis.

THE CONJUNCTIVE AND THE FUTURE CONJUNCTIVE

ⲧⲛ̄ⲛⲟⲟⲩ ⲡⲁⲥⲟⲛ ⲛ̄ⲙⲙⲁⲓ̈ **ⲧⲁⲣⲛ̄ⲃⲱⲕ** ϣⲁ-ⲧⲁⲅⲟⲣά.
Send my brother with me **and we will go** to the marketplace.

On its own, the Future Conjunctive can be used for questions, even rhetorical ones expecting a negative response. "Should" can work in these cases too.

ⲧⲁⲣⲛ̄ϭⲱ ϩⲙ̄-ⲡⲛⲟⲃⲉ ϫⲉ ⲉⲣⲉ-ⲧⲉⲭάⲣⲓⲥ ⲣ̄-ϩⲟⲩⲟ? (Rom 6.1b)
Will/should we remain in the wrong that the favor might become more?

VOCABULARY

ⲁⲓⲧ(ⲉ)ⲓ				to ask (someone); to request (something) (ⲙ̄ⲙⲟ⸗) (vt)
ⲉⲓⲛⲉ				to resemble (ⲙ̄ⲙⲟ⸗) (vt)
				resemblance (nm)
ⲉⲣⲏⲧ				to promise (vt)
(pl ⲉⲣⲁⲧⲉ)				promise (nm)
ⲧⲱϩⲙ̄	ⲧⲉϩⲙ̄-	ⲧⲁϩⲙ⸗	ⲧⲁϩⲙ†	to invite, summon; knock (ⲙ̄ⲙⲟ⸗) (vt)
				invitation, summons (nm)
ϣⲗⲏⲗ				to pray (for something: ⲉ-, ⲉⲧⲃⲉ-, ⲉϫⲛ̄-, ϩⲁ-; for someone: ⲉ-) (vi)
				prayer (nm)
ϣⲙ̄ϣⲉ	ϣⲙ̄ϣⲉ-	ϣⲙ̄ϣⲏⲧ⸗		to serve, worship (ⲛⲁ⸗) (vt)
				service, worship (nm)
ϩⲱⲛ	ϩⲛ̄-	ϩⲟⲛ⸗	ϩⲏⲛ†	to bring near (vt/vr)
				to draw near, approach (someone or something: ⲉ-, ⲉϩⲟⲩⲛ ⲉ-) (vi)
				to be near (vs)
ϩⲱⲛ ⲉⲧⲟⲟⲧ⸗				to command, order someone (to do: ⲉ-, ⲉ-ⲧⲣⲉ-, ϫⲉⲕⲁⲥ)
ϫⲓⲥⲉ	ϫⲉⲥⲧ-	ϫⲁⲥⲧ⸗	ϫⲟⲥⲉ†	(cp ϫⲁⲥⲓ-) (± ⲉϩⲣⲁⲓ̈) to lift up, exalt (ⲙ̄ⲙⲟ⸗; over: ⲉ-, ⲉϫⲛ̄-, ϩⲓϫⲛ̄-) (vt)
				to become lifted up, exalted (vi)
				heights (nm)
ⲡⲉⲧ-ϫⲟⲥⲉ				the Exalted
ϭⲓⲛⲉ	ϭⲛ̄-, ϭⲙ̄-	ϭⲛ̄ⲧ⸗		to find (ⲙ̄ⲙⲟ⸗) (vt)
				finding, found thing (nm)
ⲉϛⲟⲩⲥⲓ́ⲁ				authority (nf)
ⲉⲟⲟⲩ				glory (nm)
θⲣόⲛⲟⲥ				throne (nm)
ⲙⲛ̄ⲧⲣ̄ⲣⲟ, ⲙⲛ̄ⲧⲉⲣⲟ (pl ⲙⲛ̄ⲧⲣ̄ⲣⲱⲟⲩ, ⲙⲛ̄ⲧⲉⲣⲱⲟⲩ)				kingdom, reign (nf)
ϭⲟⲙ				power, force (nf)
(ϣ)ϭⲙ̄-ϭⲟⲙ, ϭⲛ̄-ϭⲟⲙ				to find power, be able (to do: ⲉ- + inf)

THE SAHIDIC VERB SYSTEM

EXERCISE

Copy and translate the following phrases.

1. ⲟⲩⲡⲓⲥⲧⲟⲥ ⲅⲁⲣ ⲡⲉ ⲡⲉⲛⲧⲁϥⲉⲣⲏⲧ.

2. ⲥⲱⲧⲙ̄ ⲉⲣⲟⲓ̈ ⲛ̄ⲧⲁⲧⲁⲙⲟⲕ ⲉ-ϩⲱⲃ ⲛⲓⲙ.

3. ϫⲓ-ϭⲟⲙ ⲛ̄ⲅⲧⲁⲁⲥ ⲙ̄-ⲡⲣ̅ⲣⲟ ⲧⲁⲣⲉϥⲱⲛϩ̄.

4. ⲡⲉϥⲑⲣⲟⲛⲟⲥ ϥⲛⲁϣⲱⲡⲉ ⲉϥⲧⲁϫⲣⲏⲩ ϣⲁ-ⲉⲛⲉϩ.

5. ⲁⲩⲱ ⲁⲛⲛⲁⲩ ⲉ-ⲡⲉϥⲉⲟⲟⲩ, ⲛ̄-ⲑⲉ ⲙ̄-ⲡⲉⲟⲟⲩ ⲛ̄-ⲟⲩϣⲏⲣⲉ ⲛ̄-ⲟⲩⲱⲧ ⲉⲃⲟⲗ ϩⲓⲧⲙ̄-ⲡⲉϥⲉⲓⲱⲧ.

6. ⲕⲱ ⲉⲃⲟⲗ ⲧⲁⲣⲟⲩⲕⲱ ⲛⲏⲧⲛ̄ ⲉⲃⲟⲗ.

7. ⲁⲓⲧⲉⲓ ⲧⲁⲣⲟⲩϯ ⲛⲏⲧⲛ̄, ϣⲓⲛⲉ ⲧⲁⲣⲉⲧⲉⲧⲛ̄ϭⲓⲛⲉ, ⲧⲱϩⲙ̄ ⲧⲁⲣⲟⲩⲟⲩⲱⲛ ⲛⲏⲧⲛ̄.

CHAPTER 25

THE PRECURSIVE AND THE LIMITATIVE

OVERVIEW

In this chapter, you will learn:

- The conjugation and negation of the Precursive
- The conjugation and negation of the Limitative
- How to translate these effectively in English

THE PRECURSIVE CONJUGATION

25.1 Conjugating the Precursive. The two Subordinate Clause conjugations that we'll be discussing in this chapter are both temporal: the Precursive and the Limitative.

The more common of these two is the Precursive. The three components of the Precursive[1] conjugation are the *Precursive auxiliary* ⲛ̄ⲧⲉⲣ(ⲉ)- plus a *personal infix* plus an *infinitive*.

	singular		**plural**	
1st	ⲛ̄ⲧⲉⲣⲓ-	when/after I	ⲛ̄ⲧⲉⲣⲛ̄-[2]	when/after we
2nd	ⲛ̄ⲧⲉⲣⲉⲕ-	when/after you (m)	ⲛ̄ⲧⲉⲣⲉⲧⲛ̄-	when/after you
	ⲛ̄ⲧⲉⲣⲉ(ⲣ)-	when/after you (f)		
3rd	ⲛ̄ⲧⲉⲣⲉϥ-	when/after he, it (m)	ⲛ̄ⲧⲉⲣⲟⲩ-	when/after they
	ⲛ̄ⲧⲉⲣⲉⲥ-	when/after she, it (f)		

Attached to the infinitive ϭⲁⲓ, you get these forms:

---

1. Also known as the Temporal or "When" conjugation.
2. Also spelled ⲛ̄ⲧⲉⲣⲉⲛ-.

		singular	
1st		ⲛ̄ⲧⲉⲣⲓⲥϩⲁⲓ̈	when/after I had written/wrote
2nd		ⲛ̄ⲧⲉⲣⲉⲕⲥϩⲁⲓ̈	when/after you (m) had written/wrote
		ⲛ̄ⲧⲉⲣⲉ(ⲣ)ⲥϩⲁⲓ̈	when/after you (f) had written/wrote
3rd		ⲛ̄ⲧⲉⲣⲉϥⲥϩⲁⲓ̈	when/after he, it (m) had written/wrote
		ⲛ̄ⲧⲉⲣⲉⲥⲥϩⲁⲓ̈	when/after she, it (m) had written/wrote

		plural	
1st		ⲛ̄ⲧⲉⲣⲛ̄ⲥϩⲁⲓ̈³	when/after we had written/wrote
2nd		ⲛ̄ⲧⲉⲣⲉⲧⲛ̄ⲥϩⲁⲓ̈	when/after you had written/wrote
3rd		ⲛ̄ⲧⲉⲣⲟⲩⲥϩⲁⲓ̈	when/after they had written/wrote

With an expressed noun as subject:

    ⲛ̄ⲧⲉⲣⲉ-ⲡⲣⲱⲙⲉ ⲥϩⲁⲓ̈   when/after the person had written/wrote

The Negative Precursive is formed by infixing the negative particle **-ⲧⲙ-** between the Precursive prefix and the infinitive:

    ⲛ̄ⲧⲉⲣⲓⲧⲙ̄ⲥϩⲁⲓ̈   when/after I hadn't written/didn't write
    ⲛ̄ⲧⲉⲣⲉⲧⲙ̄-ⲡⲣⲱⲙⲉ ⲥϩⲁⲓ̈   when/after the person hadn't written/didn't write

25.2 Translating the Precursive. The Precursive describes an event that happened before the main verb of the sentence, and so "when" or "after" is used to show this prior temporal relationship. Most of the time, the main verb in narratives will be a Past conjugation. Naturally, the Precursive will then be translated with an English past tense as well ("when/after I wrote")—or even a past perfect ("when/after I had written").

    ⲛ̄ⲧⲉⲣⲓⲛⲁⲩ ⲇⲉ ⲉⲣⲟϥ, ⲁⲓ̈ϩⲉ ϩⲁ-ⲛⲉϥⲟⲩⲣⲏⲏⲧⲉ ⲛ̄-ⲑⲉ ⲛ̄-ⲛⲉⲧ-ⲙⲟⲟⲩⲧ. (Rev 1.17a)
    Now **when I saw him**, I fell under his feet like the dead ones.

    ⲁⲩⲱ **ⲛ̄ⲧⲉⲣⲛ̄ϭⲱ** ⲙ̄ⲙⲁⲩ ⲛ̄-ϩⲁϩ ⲛ̄-ϩⲟⲟⲩ, ⲁ-ⲩⲡⲣⲟⲫⲏⲧⲏⲥ ⲉⲓ ⲉⲃⲟⲗ ϩⲛ̄-ϯⲟⲩⲇⲁⲓⲁ . . .
(Acts 21.10a)
    And **after we'd stayed** there many days, a foreteller came out of Ioudaia . . .

As you can surmise, Precursives are usually found at the beginnings of sentences. You'll find lots of them in narratives.

---

3. Or **ⲛ̄ⲧⲉⲣⲉⲛⲥϩⲁⲓ̈**.

THE PRECURSIVE AND THE LIMITATIVE

THE LIMITATIVE CONJUGATION

25.3 Conjugating the Limitative. Our next Subordinate Clause conjugation is the Limitative.[4] It is composed of the *Limitative auxiliary* ϣⲁⲛⲧ(ⲉ)- plus a *personal infix* plus an *infinitive*.

	singular		**plural**	
1st	ϣⲁⲛⲧ-[5]	until I	ϣⲁⲛⲧⲛ̄-	until we
2nd	ϣⲁⲛⲧⲕ̄-	until you (m)	ϣⲁⲛⲧⲉⲧⲛ̄-	until you
	ϣⲁⲛⲧⲉ-	until you (f)		
3rd	ϣⲁⲛⲧϥ̄-	until he, it (m)	ϣⲁⲛⲧⲟⲩ-	until they
	ϣⲁⲛⲧⲥ̄-	until she, it (f)		

With our model infinitive:

	singular	
1st	ϣⲁⲛⲧⲥϩⲁⲓ̈[6]	until I write/wrote/have written/had written
2nd	ϣⲁⲛⲧⲕ̄ⲥϩⲁⲓ̈	until you (m) write, etc.
	ϣⲁⲛⲧⲉⲥϩⲁⲓ̈	until you (f) write, etc.
3rd	ϣⲁⲛⲧϥ̄ⲥϩⲁⲓ̈	until he, it (m) writes, etc.
	ϣⲁⲛⲧⲥ̄ⲥϩⲁⲓ̈	until she, it (f) writes, etc.

	plural	
1st	ϣⲁⲛⲧⲛ̄ⲥϩⲁⲓ̈	until we write, etc.
2nd	ϣⲁⲛⲧⲉⲧⲛ̄ⲥϩⲁⲓ̈	until you write, etc.
3rd	ϣⲁⲛⲧⲟⲩⲥϩⲁⲓ̈	until they write, etc.

With an expressed noun as subject:

ϣⲁⲛⲧⲉ-ⲡⲣⲱⲙⲉ ⲥϩⲁⲓ̈.   until the person writes, etc.

The Negative Limitative is formed by infixing the negative particle -ⲧⲙ- between the Limitative prefix and the infinitive:

ϣⲁⲛⲧⲥⲧⲙ̄ⲥϩⲁⲓ̈   until I **don't** write, etc.
ϣⲁⲛⲧⲉⲧⲙ̄-ⲡⲣⲱⲙⲉ ⲥϩⲁⲓ̈   until the person **doesn't** write, etc.

25.4 Translating the Limitative. The Limitative describes the duration for which the main verb will be in effect. Like the Aorist, the Limitative has no inherent tense of its own, so how you'll translate this depends on the surrounding context. The English

---

4. Sometimes just called the "Until" conjugation.
5. Variant form: ϣⲁⲛⲧⲁ-.
6. Or ϣⲁⲛⲧⲁⲥϩⲁⲓ̈.

simple present ("until I write"), simple past ("until I wrote"), present perfect ("until I have written"), or past perfect ("until I had written") could all be options. On occasion, "while" may be fitting.

ⲚⲦⲰⲦⲚ ⲆⲈ ⲤⲘⲞⲞⲤ ϨⲚ-ⲦⲈⲒⲠⲞⲖⲒⲤ **ϢⲀⲚⲦⲈⲦⲚϮ ϨⲒⲰⲦ-ⲐⲨⲦⲚ** Ⲛ-ⲞⲨϬⲞⲘ ⲈⲂⲞⲖ ϨⲚ-ⲦⲠⲈ. (Luke 24.49b)

Yet you—sit in this city **until you've put on yourselves** a power out of the sky.

ⲠⲔⲈⲤⲈⲈⲠⲈ ⲆⲈ Ⲛ-ⲚⲈⲦ-ⲘⲞⲞⲨⲦ ⲘⲠⲞⲨⲰⲚϨ **ϢⲀⲚⲦⲞⲨϪⲰⲔ ⲈⲂⲞⲖ** ⲚϭⲒ-ⲦϢⲞ Ⲛ-ⲢⲞⲘⲠⲈ. (Rev 20.5a)

Yet the rest of the dead ones didn't live **until** the thousand years **had become finished**.

VOCABULARY

ⲔⲦⲞ	ⲔⲦⲈ-	ⲔⲦⲞ⸗	ⲔⲦⲎⲨϮ	to turn[7] (ⲘⲘⲞ⸗) (vt/vr)
				turning, return (nm)
ⲔⲰⲦ	ⲔⲈⲦ-	ⲔⲞⲦ⸗	ⲔⲎⲦϮ	to build (up) (ⲘⲘⲞ⸗) (vt)
				to become/be built up (vi/vs)
				building (the act or the object) (nm)
ⲖⲞ				(impv ⲀⲖⲞⲔ [msg], ⲀⲖⲞ [fsg], ⲀⲖⲰⲦⲚ [pl]) (± ⲘⲘⲀⲨ) 1. to quit, cease, stop (doing: circum); 2. to leave, depart (from: ⲘⲘⲞ⸗, ϨⲚ-, ⲈⲂⲞⲖ ϨⲚ-) (vi)
ⲘⲠϢⲀ				to be worthy, deserving (of: ⲘⲘⲞ⸗; to do: Ⲛ-, Ⲉ- + inf) (vi)
				worth (nm)
ⲞⲨⲰϢⲦ				to greet, bow (to: ⲚⲀ⸗); to revere (ⲘⲘⲞ⸗) (vt)
ⲠⲀⲢⲀⲆⲒⲆⲞⲨ				to betray, give over (ⲘⲘⲞ⸗) (vt)
ⲠⲀⲢⲀⲔⲀⲖⲈⲒ				to encourage (ⲘⲘⲞ⸗) (vt)
ⲠⲰⲰⲚⲈ	ⲠⲈⲈⲚⲈ-	ⲠⲞⲞⲚⲈ⸗	ⲠⲞⲞⲚⲈϮ	to turn, change (ⲘⲘⲞ⸗; to: Ⲉ-); (+ ⲈⲂⲞⲖ) to remove (vt)
				to turn, change (from: ϨⲚ-; to: Ⲉ-); (+ ⲈⲂⲞⲖ) to move out (vi)
				removal, change (nm)
ⲢⲒⲘⲈ				to weep (for someone: Ⲉ-, ⲈϪⲚ-) (vi)
				weeping (nm)
ⲤⲘⲞⲨ			ⲤⲘⲀⲘⲀⲀⲦϮ	to bless (Ⲉ-) (vt)
				to be blessed (vs)
				blessing (nm)
ⲄⲈⲚⲈⲀ				generation (nf)
ⲘⲀⲈⲒⲚ				sign (nm)

---

7. Originally, (Ⲧ)ⲔⲦⲞ was the causative of ⲔⲰⲦⲈ (chapter 17), meaning to cause to turn, but it eventually becomes more or less synonymous with it.

THE PRECURSIVE AND THE LIMITATIVE

ϣⲡⲏⲣⲉ — wonder, amazement (nf)
ϩⲱ(ⲱ)⸗ — own, -self; also, too (intensive pron/inflected modifier)
ϩⲱⲱϥ — however
ⲙⲁⲩⲁⲁ(ⲧ)⸗ — only, alone, -self (intensive pron/inflected modifier)

EXERCISE

Copy and translate the following phrases.

1. ⲛ̄-ⲧⲉⲩⲛⲟⲩ ⲇⲉ ⲛ̄ⲧⲉⲣⲟⲩⲉⲓ ⲉⲃⲟⲗ ϩⲛ̄-ⲧⲥⲩⲛⲁⲅⲱⲅⲏ, ⲁϥⲃⲱⲕ ⲉϩⲟⲩⲛ ⲉⲡⲏⲓ.

2. ϩⲁⲙⲏⲛ ϯϫⲱ ⲙ̄ⲙⲟⲥ ⲛⲏⲧⲛ̄ ϫⲉ ⲛ̄ⲛⲉ-ⲧⲉⲓ̈ⲅⲉⲛⲉⲁ ⲗⲟ ⲙ̄ⲙⲁⲩ ϣⲁⲛⲧⲉ-ⲛⲁⲓ̈ ⲧⲏⲣⲟⲩ ϣⲱⲡⲉ.

3. ⲁⲩⲱ ⲡⲉϫⲁϥ ⲛ̄-ⲛⲉϥⲙⲁⲑⲏⲧⲏⲥ ϫⲉ "ϩⲙⲟⲟⲥ ⲛⲏⲧⲛ̄ ⲙ̄-ⲡⲉⲓ̈ⲙⲁ ϣⲁⲛϯϣⲗⲏⲗ."

4. ⲁⲩⲙⲟⲟϣⲉ ⲇⲉ ⲛ̄-ⲧⲥⲛ̄ⲧⲉ ϣⲁⲛⲧⲟⲩⲉⲓ ⲉϩⲣⲁⲓ̈ ⲉ-ⲃⲏⲑⲗⲉⲉⲙ.

5. ⲛ̄ⲧⲉⲣⲉⲛⲉⲓ ⲉϩⲣⲁⲓ̈ ⲉ-ⲡⲉⲕϩⲙ̄ϩⲁⲗ ⲉⲧⲉ-ⲡⲉⲛⲉⲓⲱⲧ ⲡⲉ, ⲁⲛⲧⲁⲙⲟ ⲙ̄ⲙⲟϥ ⲉ-ⲛ̄ϣⲁϫⲉ ⲙ̄-ⲡⲉⲛϫⲟⲉⲓⲥ.

6. ⲡⲥⲁϩ, ⲧⲛ̄ⲟⲩⲱϣ ⲉⲛⲁⲩ ⲉ-ⲩⲙⲁⲉⲓⲛ ⲉⲃⲟⲗ ϩⲓⲧⲟⲟⲧⲕ̄.

7. ⲛ̄ⲧⲉⲣⲉϥϩⲱⲛ ⲇⲉ ⲉϩⲟⲩⲛ ⲉϥⲛⲁⲩ ⲉ-ⲧⲡⲟⲗⲓⲥ ⲁϥⲣⲓⲙⲉ ⲉϩⲣⲁⲓ̈ ⲉϫⲱⲥ.

CHAPTER 26

THE CONDITIONAL AND THE CAUSATIVE INFINITIVE

OVERVIEW

In this chapter, you will learn:

- The conjugation and negation of the Conditional
- The conjugation and negation of the Causative Infinitive
- How to translate these effectively in English

THE CONDITIONAL CONJUGATION

26.1 **Conjugating the Conditional.** Our last Subordinate Clause conjugation is the Conditional. It is composed of the *Conditional auxiliary* ⲉ[-]ϣⲁⲛ- (which brackets a *personal infix*) plus an *infinitive*, ⲉⲣϣⲁⲛ- before an expressed subject.

	singular		**plural**	
1st	ⲉⲓϣⲁⲛ-	if/when(ever) I	ⲉⲛϣⲁⲛ-	if/when(ever) we
2nd	ⲉⲕϣⲁⲛ-	if/when(ever) you (m)	ⲉⲧⲉⲧⲛϣⲁⲛ-	if/when(ever) you
	ⲉⲣ(ⲉ)ϣⲁⲛ-	if/when(ever) you (f)		
3rd	ⲉϥϣⲁⲛ-	if/when(ever) he, it (m)	ⲉⲩϣⲁⲛ-	if/when(ever) they
	ⲉⲥϣⲁⲛ-	if/when(ever) she, it (f)		

Attached to the infinitive ⲥϩⲁⲓ, you get these forms:

	singular	
1st	ⲉⲓϣⲁⲛⲥϩⲁⲓ	if/when(ever) I write/wrote
2nd	ⲉⲕϣⲁⲛⲥϩⲁⲓ	if/when(ever) you (m) write/wrote
	ⲉⲣ(ⲉ)ϣⲁⲛⲥϩⲁⲓ	if/when(ever) you (f) write/wrote
3rd	ⲉϥϣⲁⲛⲥϩⲁⲓ	if/when(ever) he, it (m) writes/wrote
	ⲉⲥϣⲁⲛⲥϩⲁⲓ	if/when(ever) she, it (m) writes/wrote

THE CONDITIONAL AND THE CAUSATIVE INFINITIVE

plural
1st ⲉⲛϣⲁⲛⲥϩⲁⲓ̈ if/when(ever) we write/wrote
2nd ⲉⲧⲉⲧⲛ̄ϣⲁⲛⲥϩⲁⲓ̈ if/when(ever) you write/wrote
3rd ⲉⲩϣⲁⲛⲥϩⲁⲓ̈ if/when(ever) they write/wrote

With an expressed noun as subject:

ⲉⲣϣⲁⲛ-ⲡⲣⲱⲙⲉ ⲥϩⲁⲓ̈ if/when(ever) the person writes/wrote

The Negative Conditional is formed by infixing the negative particle -ⲧⲙ- between the Conditional prefix and the infinitive. Sometimes the -ϣⲁⲛ- drops in the Negative Conditional, too:

ⲉⲓ̈(ϣⲁⲛ)ⲧⲙ̄ⲥϩⲁⲓ̈ if/when(ever) I don't write/didn't write

With an expressed noun as subject:

ⲉⲣϣⲁⲛⲧⲙ̄-ⲡⲣⲱⲙⲉ ⲥϩⲁⲓ̈[1] if/when(ever) the person doesn't write/didn't write

26.2 Translating the Conditional. The first and most common usage of the Conditional is to form "if" clauses in conditional sentences—the first part (the protasis) of "if . . . then" statements, with the consequence of that condition being supplied by a main verb. When describing more certain occurrences, it can even have the sense of "since." Sometimes words like ⲉϣⲱⲡⲉ ("if") may also precede the Conditional to clarify the situation.

ⲉⲣϣⲁⲛ-ⲟⲩⲁ ⲟⲩⲱⲙ ⲉⲃⲟⲗ ϩⲙ̄-ⲡⲉⲓ̈ⲟⲉⲓⲕ, ϥⲛⲁⲱⲛϩ ϣⲁ-ⲉⲛⲉϩ. (John 6.51b)
If one eats out of this bread, he is going to live forever.

ⲉϣⲱⲡⲉ ⲇⲉ ⲉϥϣⲁⲛⲧⲙ̄ⲥⲱⲧⲙ̄ ⲛ̄ⲥⲱⲟⲩ, ⲁϫⲓⲥ ⲛ̄-ⲧⲉⲕⲕⲗⲏⲥⲓⲁ. (Matt 18.17a)
Yet **if he doesn't heed** them, say it to the assembly.

The second usage of the Conditional is with the temporal meaning of "when" (in a specific sense) or "whenever" (more generally). The conjunction ϩⲟⲧⲁⲛ ("when[ever]") can also be used to make this meaning more explicit.

ⲁⲩⲱ ⲟⲩ ⲡⲉ ⲡⲙⲁⲉⲓⲛ ⲉⲣϣⲁⲛ-ⲛⲁⲓ̈ ⲧⲏⲣⲟⲩ ⲛⲟⲩ[2] ⲉ-ϫⲱⲕ ⲉⲃⲟⲗ? (Mark 13.4b)
And what's the sign **when** all these things are about to be completed?

ϩⲟⲧⲁⲛ ⲇⲉ ⲉⲩϣⲁⲛⲡⲱⲧ ⲛ̄ⲥⲱⲧⲛ̄ ϩⲛ̄-ⲧⲉⲓ̈ⲡⲟⲗⲓⲥ, ⲡⲱⲧ ⲉϩⲣⲁⲓ̈ ⲉ-ⲕⲉⲟⲩⲉⲓ. (Matt 10.23a)
So **when(ever) they run** after you in this city, run down to another one.

---

1. Or without the -ϣⲁⲛ-, ⲉⲣⲉⲧⲙ̄-ⲡⲣⲱⲙⲉ ⲥϩⲁⲓ̈.
2. ⲛⲟⲩ is a verb of motion/futurity (like ⲛⲁ), meaning "going to, about to."

THE SAHIDIC VERB SYSTEM

THE CAUSATIVE INFINITIVE

26.3 Conjugating the Causative Infinitive. Our last conjugation isn't actually a Subordinate Clause conjugation, but it is convenient to discuss it alongside them. The Causative Infinitive[3] is a form of verbal compound that includes the one doing the action and the action they are doing—and *sometimes* this complex is causative (the actor is being made to do the action). The Causative Infinitive complex is composed of the *Causative Infinitive auxiliary* ⲧⲣ(ⲉ)- plus a *personal infix* plus an *infinitive*.

	singular		**plural**	
1st	ⲧⲣⲁ-	(cause) me	ⲧⲣⲉⲛ-	(cause) us
2nd	ⲧⲣⲉⲕ-	(cause) you (m)	ⲧⲣⲉ(ⲧⲉ)ⲧⲛ̄-	(cause) you
	ⲧⲣⲉ-	(cause) you (f)		
3rd	ⲧⲣⲉϥ-	(cause) him, it (m)	ⲧⲣⲉⲩ-	(cause) them
	ⲧⲣⲉⲥ-	(cause) her, it (f)		

With our model infinitive:

	singular	
1st	ⲧⲣⲁⲥϩⲁï	(cause) me to write, me writing
2nd	ⲧⲣⲉⲕⲥϩⲁï	(cause) you (m) to write, you (m) writing
	ⲧⲣⲉⲥϩⲁï	(cause) you (f) to write, you (f) writing
3rd	ⲧⲣⲉϥⲥϩⲁï	(cause) him, it (m) to write, him, it (m) writing
	ⲧⲣⲉⲥⲥϩⲁï	(cause) her, it (m) to write, her, it (m) writing

	plural	
1st	ⲧⲣⲉⲛⲥϩⲁï	(cause) us to write, us writing
2nd	ⲧⲣⲉ(ⲧⲉ)ⲧⲛ̄ⲥϩⲁï	(cause) you to write, you writing
3rd	ⲧⲣⲉⲩⲥϩⲁï	(cause) them to write, them writing

With an expressed noun as subject:

ⲧⲣⲉ-ⲡⲣⲱⲙⲉ ⲥϩⲁï   (cause) the person to write, the person writing

The Negative Causative Infinitive is formed by infixing the negative particle -ⲧⲙ- *either* before the Causative Infinitive prefix *or* between it and the infinitive:

ⲧⲙ̄ⲧⲣⲁⲥϩⲁï *or* ⲧⲣⲁⲧⲙ̄ⲥϩⲁï   (cause) me to not write, me not writing

With an expressed noun as subject:

---

3. In older works, sometimes referred to as the "Inflected Infinitive."

THE CONDITIONAL AND THE CAUSATIVE INFINITIVE

ⲧⲙ̄ⲧⲣⲉ-ⲡⲣⲱⲙⲉ ⲥϩⲁⲓ̈ *or* ⲧⲣⲉⲧⲙ̄-ⲡⲣⲱⲙⲉ ⲥϩⲁⲓ̈   (cause) the person to not write, the person not writing

26.4 Translating the Causative Infinitive. As mentioned, despite the name, the Causative Infinitive is only *sometimes* causative. This does happen if the Causative Infinitive complex is used as the infinitive with one of the main verb conjugations.

ⲁϥϫⲟⲟⲩ ⲇⲉ ⲛ̄ϭⲓ-ⲓⲱⲥⲏⲫ, **ⲁϥⲧⲣⲉⲩⲙⲟⲩⲧⲉ ⲉ-**ⲓⲁⲕⲱⲃ ⲡⲉϥⲉⲓⲱⲧ. (Acts 7.14a)
So Iōsēph sent, **he caused them to call** to Iakōb his father.

ⲁⲩⲱ ϥⲛⲁⲉⲓⲣⲉ ⲛ̄-ϩⲉⲛⲛⲟϭ ⲙ̄-ⲙⲁⲉⲓⲛ, ϩⲱⲥⲧⲉ **ⲛϥ̄ⲧⲣⲉ-ⲡⲕⲱϩⲧ̄ ⲉⲓ** ⲉⲃⲟⲗ ϩⲛ̄-ⲧⲡⲉ. (Rev 13.13a)
And he is going to make great signs, so that **he causes (the) fire to come out** of the sky.

But often the Causative Infinitive complex is used as a (masculine) noun in a prepositional phrase. In these cases, there's no real causative meaning, and we can translate the verb as either an infinitive ("to write") or a participle ("writing").

ⲛ̄ⲧⲟϥ ⲇⲉ ⲡⲉϫⲁϥ ⲛⲁⲩ ϫⲉ "ⲟⲩ ⲡⲉⲧⲉⲧⲛ̄ⲟⲩⲁϣϥ̄ **ⲉ-ⲧⲣⲁⲁⲁϥ** ⲛⲏⲧⲛ̄?" (Mark 10.36)
So he said to them (that) "What's it that you want **for me to do** (it) for you?"

ⲁⲥϣⲱⲡⲉ ⲇⲉ **ϩⲙ̄-ⲡⲧⲣⲉϥⲛⲟϫϥ̄** ⲛⲙ̄ⲙⲁⲩ, ⲁϥϫⲓ ⲛ̄-ⲟⲩⲟⲉⲓⲕ, ⲁϥⲥⲙⲟⲩ ⲉⲣⲟϥ, ⲁϥⲡⲟϣϥ̄, ⲁϥⲧⲁⲁϥ ⲛⲁⲩ. (Luke 24.30)
Now it happened **in him throwing himself**[4] with them, he took a bread, he blessed it, he divided it, he gave it to them.

Phrases with ⲉ- are particularly common ways that you will encounter the Causative Infinitive.

VOCABULARY

ⲥⲁϩⲛⲉ				to supply, provide (vi)
				supply, provisions (nm)
ⲟⲩⲉϩ-ⲥⲁϩⲛⲉ				to (give a) command (something: ⲙ̄ⲙⲟ≠; someone: ⲛⲁ≠, ⲉⲧⲛ̄-; to do: ⲉ-, ⲉ-ⲧⲣⲉ-)
ⲥⲟⲡⲥ̄, ⲥⲟⲡⲥ̄	ⲥⲡ̄ⲥⲛ̄-, ⲥⲉⲡⲥ-	ⲥⲡ̄ⲥⲱⲡ≠	ⲥⲉⲡⲥⲱⲡ†, ⲥⲡ̄ⲥⲱⲡ†	to exhort, implore, encourage (ⲙ̄ⲙⲟ≠) (vt)
				exhortation, encouragement (nm)
ⲥⲱⲧⲡ̄	ⲥⲉⲧⲡ̄-	ⲥⲟⲧⲡ≠	ⲥⲟⲧⲡ̄†	to choose, select (ⲙ̄ⲙⲟ≠) (vt)

---

4. A way of saying he sat down and reclined at the table.

				to be chosen, choice, excellent (vs)
				choice, select one (often as adj) (nm)
ⲧⲁϩⲟ	ⲧⲁϩⲉ-	ⲧⲁϩⲟ⸗	ⲧⲁϩⲏⲩ†	1. to cause to stand, set up (ⲙ̄ⲙⲟ⸗);
				2. to reach, attain, catch, seize
				(ⲙ̄ⲙⲟ⸗) (vt)
				to be able, manage (to do: ⲉ- + inf)
				(vi)
				(causative of ⲱϩⲉ)
				establishment (nm)
ⲧⲁϩⲟ (ⲉ)ⲣⲁⲧ⸗				to make to stand, establish (ⲙ̄ⲙⲟ⸗)
ⲱⲡ	ⲉⲡ-	ⲟⲡ⸗	ⲏⲡ†	to count, calculate (ⲙ̄ⲙⲟ⸗); to consider
				(ⲙ̄ⲙⲟ⸗; as: ⲙ̄ⲙⲟ⸗; as belonging
				to: ⲉ-) (vt)
				to be counted, considered (as
				belonging to: ⲉ-) (vs)
				(ac)count (nm)
ϣⲓⲡⲉ				to be ashamed (about: ⲉⲧⲃⲉ-) (vi)
				shame (nm)
ϣⲓⲡⲉ ϩⲏⲧ⸗ ⲛ̄-				to be ashamed before, revere
ϫⲓ-ϣⲓⲡⲉ				to be put to shame, ashamed
†-ϣⲓⲡⲉ				to (put to) shame
ϣⲧⲟⲣⲧⲣ̄	ϣⲧⲣ̄ⲧⲣ̄-	ϣⲧⲣ̄ⲧⲱⲣ⸗	ϣⲧⲣ̄ⲧⲱⲣ†	to disturb, trouble (ⲙ̄ⲙⲟ⸗) (vt)
				to become disturbed, troubled (vi)
				to be disturbed, upset (vs)
				disturbance, trouble (nm)
ϣⲱⲱⲧ	ϣⲉ(ⲉ)ⲧ-	ϣⲁⲁⲧ⸗	ϣⲁⲁⲧ†	(cp ϣⲁⲧ-) to cut (off), sacrifice (vt)
				to be lacking (for, of, in: ⲉ-, ⲙ̄ⲙⲟ⸗, ϩⲛ̄-)
				(vi/vs)
				cutting off (nm)
ϣⲁ(ⲁ)ⲧⲛ̄-				except, minus, short of (prep)
ⲕⲁⲣⲡⲟⲥ				fruit, crop, profit (nm)
ⲧⲁ(ⲟ)ⲩⲉ-ⲕⲁⲣⲡⲟⲥ				to produce fruit
ⲣⲟⲟⲩϣ				care, concern, anxiety (nm)
ⲣ̄-ⲣⲟⲟⲩϣ				(ⲟ† ⲛ̄-) to become/be a care or
				concern (for: ⲛⲁ⸗)
ⲭⲣ(ⲉ)ⲓⲁ				need, necessity (nf)
ⲣ̄-ⲭⲣ(ⲉ)ⲓⲁ				to need (ⲙ̄ⲙⲟ⸗); to have to (do:
				ⲉ- + inf)
ϩⲙⲟⲧ				favor, gift; gratitude, thanks (nm)
ϣⲡ̄-ϩⲙⲟⲧ ⲛ̄ⲧⲛ̄-				to give thanks to (for: ⲉϫⲛ̄-, ϩⲓ-,
				ϩⲁ-)
ϭⲛ̄-ϩⲙⲟⲧ				to find favor
ϩⲟⲧⲁⲛ				when(ever) (conj)

THE CONDITIONAL AND THE CAUSATIVE INFINITIVE

EXERCISE

Copy and translate the following phrases.

1. ⲉⲣϣⲁⲛ-ⲟⲩⲁ ⲇⲉ ϣⲁϫⲉ ⲛⲙ̄ⲙⲏⲧⲛ̄, ⲁϫⲓⲥ ϫⲉ "ⲡⲉⲩϫⲟⲉⲓⲥ ⲡⲉⲧ-ⲣ̄-ⲭⲣⲉⲓⲁ ⲛⲁⲩ."

2. ⲁϥϩⲱⲛ ⲉⲧⲟⲟⲧⲟⲩ ϫⲉⲕⲁⲁⲥ ⲉ-ⲛ̄ⲛⲉⲩⲧⲁⲩⲉ-ⲛⲉⲛⲧⲁⲩⲛⲁⲩ ⲉⲣⲟⲟⲩ ⲉ-ⲗⲁⲁⲩ.

3. ⲁⲩⲱ ϩⲟⲧⲁⲛ ⲉϥϣⲁⲛϭⲓⲛⲉ ϥⲛⲁϣⲧⲟⲣⲧⲣ̄.

4. ⲛⲁⲓ̈ ⲧⲏⲣⲟⲩ ϯⲛⲁⲧⲁⲁⲩ ⲛⲁⲕ ⲉⲕϣⲁⲛⲟⲩⲱϣⲧ̄ ⲛⲁⲓ̈.

5. ϩⲟⲧⲁⲛ ⲇⲉ ⲉⲩϣⲁⲛⲡⲁⲣⲁⲇⲓⲇⲟⲩ ⲙ̄ⲙⲱⲧⲛ̄, ⲙ̄ⲡⲣ̄ϥⲓ-ⲣⲟⲟⲩϣ ϫⲉ ⲛ̄-ⲁϣ ⲛ̄-ϩⲉ ⲏ ⲉⲧⲉⲧⲛ̄ⲛⲁϫⲟⲟⲥ ϫⲉ ⲟⲩ.

6. ⲉⲣϣⲁⲛ-ⲡⲉⲧ-ⲙ̄ⲙⲁⲩ ⲉⲓ, ϥⲛⲁⲧⲁⲙⲟⲛ ⲉ-ϩⲱⲃ ⲛⲓⲙ.

7. ⲓⲏⲥⲟⲩ̅ⲥ̅ ⲇⲉ ⲡⲉϫⲁϥ ⲛⲁⲩ ϫⲉ "ⲛ̄ⲥⲉⲣ̄-ⲭⲣⲉⲓⲁ ⲁⲛ ⲉ-ⲧⲣⲉⲩⲃⲱⲕ. ⲛ̄ⲧⲱⲧⲛ̄ ϯ ⲛⲁⲩ ⲉ-ⲧⲣⲉⲩⲟⲩⲱⲙ.

8. ⲧⲟⲧⲉ ⲡⲓⲗⲁⲧⲟⲥ ⲁϥⲟⲩⲉϩ-ⲥⲁϩⲛⲉ ⲉ-ⲧⲣⲉⲩⲧⲁⲁϥ ⲛⲁϥ.

CHAPTER 27

VERBOIDS AND IMPERSONAL PREDICATES

OVERVIEW

In this chapter, you will learn:

- How verboids are formed and used
- Some common impersonal predicates and how they are used

The end is near! With this chapter, we've completed our survey of the Sahidic verbal system. Just a few final verb-adjacent leftovers to cover!

VERBOIDS

27.1 **Verboids.** Verboids are a loose category of words that can carry out both verbal and adjectival functions. You've encountered a few of these already:

ⲡⲉϫⲉ-	ⲡⲉϫⲁ⸗	said (verboid, chapter 12)
ⲟⲩⲛ̄ⲧⲉ-	ⲟⲩⲛ̄ⲧⲁ⸗	has/have (existential verboid, chapter 13)
ⲙⲛ̄ⲧⲉ-	ⲙⲛ̄ⲧⲁ⸗	don't/doesn't have (neg existential verboid, chapter 13)

These semi-verbs mark their subjects through suffixes instead of prefixes.

27.2 **ⲛⲁ- Verboids.** A number of verboids begin with ⲛⲁ- or ⲛⲉ-. This important group functions like adjectives, and we can include "is/are" as needed in our English translations. The most common are:

ⲛⲁⲓ̈ⲁⲧ⸗		fortunate
ⲛⲁⲛⲟⲩ-, ⲛⲁⲛⲉ-	ⲛⲁⲛⲟⲩ⸗	good
ⲛⲁϣⲉ-	ⲛⲁϣⲱ⸗	numerous, many, much
ⲛⲉⲥⲉ-	ⲛⲉⲥⲱ⸗	beautiful

VERBOIDS AND IMPERSONAL PREDICATES

These are usually emphasized by being set at the front of their sentences:

ⲛⲁⲓⲁⲧⲟⲩ ⲛ̄-ⲛ̄ϩⲏⲕⲉ, ϫⲉ ⲧⲱⲟⲩ ⲧⲉ ⲧⲙⲛ̄ⲧⲣ̄ⲣⲟ ⲛ̄-ⲙ̄ⲡⲏⲩⲉ! (Luke 6.20b)
Fortunate are the poor, because theirs is the kingdom of the skies!

ⲡϫⲟⲉⲓⲥ, **ⲛⲁⲛⲟⲩⲥ** ⲛⲁⲛ ⲉ-ⲧⲣⲉⲛϭⲱ ⲙ̄-ⲡⲉⲓ̈ⲙⲁ! (Matt 17.4b)
Master, **it's good** to us for us to stay in this place!

Notice, as in the first example, that sometimes there are resumptive/redundant suffixes on the verboid that agree with an expressed subject.[1] These verboids, like other adjectives and verbs, can also be substantivized:

ⲡⲉⲧ-ⲛⲁⲛⲟⲩϥ	the one (m) who's good, that which's good, the good (one)
ⲧⲉⲧ-ⲛⲉⲥⲱⲥ	the one (f) who's beautiful, that which's beautiful, the beautiful (one)

IMPERSONAL PREDICATES

27.3 Impersonal Expressions. We've already seen some examples of impersonal ways of referring to things, such as ⲁⲥϣⲱⲡⲉ, "it happened that," where "it" is just whatever event will be described next. Sahidic has a few common expressions that are used similarly, and we include an "it's" as part of the English translation of these impersonal predicates.

ϣϣⲉ, ⲉϣϣⲉ	it's appropriate, proper, necessary
ϩⲁⲡⲥ̄	it's necessary
ϩⲱ	it's sufficient, enough

Like the verboids in the previous section, these expressions are often fronted in their clauses.

ϩⲁⲡⲥ̄ ⲅⲁⲣ ⲡⲉ ⲉ-ⲧⲣⲉϥⲣ̄-ⲣ̄ⲣⲟ ϣⲁⲛⲧϥ̄ⲕⲱ ⲛ̄-ⲛⲉϥϫⲁϫⲉ ⲧⲏⲣⲟⲩ ϩⲁ-ⲛⲉϥⲟⲩⲉⲣⲏⲧⲉ. (1 Cor 15.25)
For **it's necessary** for him to become king until he's put all his enemies under his feet.

ϩⲱ ⲉⲣⲱⲧⲛ̄ ⲉⲧⲉⲧⲛ̄ⲟⲩⲏϩ ϩⲙ̄-ⲡⲉⲓ̈ⲧⲟⲟⲩ. (Deut 1.6b)
It's enough for you being situated at this mountain.

These can all be negated by the negative particle bracket (ⲛ̄-) . . . ⲁⲛ.[2]

---

1. The suffix (-ⲟⲩ, "they") is linked to the plural noun (ⲛ̄ϩⲏⲕⲉ, "the poor") by the preposition ⲛ̄-, functioning here as an equivalence marker (as with ⲟⲧ̄ and ϣⲟⲟⲡ†).
2. ϣϣⲉ also uses the negative form ⲙⲉϣϣⲉ (cf. the Aorist negative auxiliary [17.3]).

27.4 Greek Impersonals.
Finally, Sahidic uses a few Greek words and phrases in the same impersonal way:

ⲁⲛⲁⲅⲕⲏ	necessity; used impersonally: it's necessary (nf)
ⲅⲉⲛⲟⲓⲧⲟ	may it happen (neg ⲙⲏ ⲅⲉⲛⲟⲓⲧⲟ)
ⲉⲝⲉⲥⲧⲓ	it's authorized (neg ⲟⲩⲕ-ⲉⲝⲉⲥⲧⲓ)

These work similarly to the native expressions, although note the specifically Greek negatives for ⲅⲉⲛⲟⲓⲧⲟ and ⲉⲝⲉⲥⲧⲓ.

> **ⲟⲩⲕ-ⲉⲝⲉⲥⲧⲓ** ⲛⲁⲕ ⲉ-ϫⲓ ⲛ̄-ⲑⲓⲙⲉ ⲙ̄-ⲡⲉⲕⲥⲟⲛ! (Mark 6.18b)
> **It's not authorized** for you to take your brother's wife!

VOCABULARY

ϩⲓⲟⲩⲉ	ϩⲓ-	ϩⲓⲧ⸗		1. to beat, strike (ⲙ̄ⲙⲟ⸗, ⲉ-, ⲉϫⲛ̄-, ϩⲛ̄-, ⲉϩⲟⲩⲛ ⲉ-; with: ⲙ̄ⲙⲟ⸗, ϩⲛ̄-); 2. to cast, throw (ⲙ̄ⲙⲟ⸗; ± ⲉⲃⲟⲗ, ⲉϩⲣⲁⲓ̈) (vt)
ϩⲓ-ⲧⲟⲟⲧ⸗				to begin, undertake (to do: ⲉ- + inf); to place one's hand (on: ⲉ-)
ϩⲓⲥⲉ	ϩⲁⲥⲧ̄-	ϩⲁⲥⲧ⸗	ϩⲟⲥⲉ†	to weary, trouble (ⲙ̄ⲙⲟ⸗) (vt)
				to labor; to become weary, troubled (vi)
				labor, weariness, trouble (nm)
ϩⲟⲟⲩ†³				to be bad, evil (vs)
ϩⲱⲡ	ϩⲉⲡ-	ϩⲟⲡ⸗	ϩⲏⲡ†	to hide, conceal (ⲙ̄ⲙⲟ⸗) (vt)
				to become hidden, hide (oneself) (vi)
				to be hidden (vs)
				hiding (nm)
ϫⲟ	ϫⲉ-	ϫⲟ⸗	ϫⲏⲩ†	to plant, sow (seed: ⲙ̄ⲙⲟ⸗) (vt)
				planting, sowing (nm)
ⲛⲁⲓ̈ⲁⲧ⸗				fortunate⁴ (verboid adj)
ⲛⲁⲛⲟⲩ-, ⲛⲁⲛⲉ-		ⲛⲁⲛⲟⲩ⸗		good (verboid adj)
ⲛⲁϣⲉ-		ⲛⲁϣⲱ⸗		numerous, many, much (verboid adj)
ⲛⲉⲥⲉ-		ⲛⲉⲥⲱ⸗		beautiful (verboid adj)
ⲁⲛⲁⲅⲕⲏ				necessity; used impersonally: it's necessary (nf)
ⲅⲉⲛⲟⲓⲧⲟ				may it happen (neg ⲙⲏ ⲅⲉⲛⲟⲓⲧⲟ) (impersonal predicate)
ⲉⲝⲉⲥⲧⲓ				it's authorized (neg ⲟⲩⲕ-ⲉⲝⲉⲥⲧⲓ) (impersonal predicate)

---

3. This verb is only found in the stative form.
4. ⲛⲁⲓ̈ⲁⲧ⸗ is derived from a combination of another verboid ⲛⲁⲁ- ("great") and the old compound word for eye ⲉⲓⲁ(ⲁ)ⲧ⸗, meaning something like "great are the eyes of…"

VERBOIDS AND IMPERSONAL PREDICATES

ϣϣε, εϣϣε	it's appropriate, proper, necessary (impersonal predicate)
ϩⲁⲡⲥ̄	it's necessary (impersonal predicate)
ϩⲱ	it's sufficient, enough (impersonal predicate)

EXERCISE

Copy and translate the following phrases.

1. ϣϣε ε-ⲥⲱⲧⲙ̄ ⲛ̄ⲥⲁ-ⲡⲛⲟⲩⲧε ε-ϩⲟⲩε-ⲛ̄ⲣⲱⲙε.

2. ⲛ̄ⲧεⲣεϥⲛⲁⲩ ⲇε ε-ⲙ̄ⲙⲏⲏϣε, ⲁϥⲁⲗε εϩⲣⲁⲓ̈ εϫⲙ̄-ⲡⲧⲟⲟⲩ.

3. ⲁⲩⲱ ⲛ̄ⲧεⲣεϥϩⲙⲟⲟⲥ, ⲁⲩϯ-ⲡεⲩⲟⲩⲟⲓ εⲣⲟϥ ⲛ̄ϭⲓ-ⲛεϥⲙⲁⲑⲏⲧⲏⲥ.

4. ⲁϥⲟⲩⲱⲛ ε-ⲣⲱϥ ⲁϥϯ-ⲥⲃⲱ ⲛⲁⲩ, εϥϫⲱ ⲙ̄ⲙⲟⲥ ϫε,

5. ⲛⲁⲓ̈ⲁⲧⲟⲩ ⲛ̄-ⲛ̄ϩⲏⲕε ϩⲙ̄-ⲡεⲡⲛεⲩ́ⲙⲁ, ϫε ⲧⲱⲟⲩ ⲧε ⲧⲙⲛ̄ⲧⲣ̄ⲣⲟ ⲛ̄-ⲙ̄ⲡⲏⲩε!

CHAPTER 28

CONCLUSION AND NEXT STEPS

28.1 **The End and the Beginning.** Congratulations! You've made it to the very end of our survey of Sahidic grammar. We've covered lots of ground, but you should be equipped to begin your exploration of Sahidic literature.

That's the next stage: reading, and lots of it! There's no better way to really ground your understanding of Sahidic grammar and vocabulary than by using it. Whether on your own or in a classroom/seminar setting, this is the way forward. You'll want to read large sections from different kinds of works so you get a feel for the natural flow of the language in extended context. Stories and narratives are probably the easiest place to start before moving into poetry and then on to more complicated readings, like theological and philosophical works. There's a world of Sahidic literature to discover, from the mundane to the (literally) magical![1]

28.2 **Reading Texts.** The following major section of this book contains a number of reading selections, chosen from a variety of canonical and non-canonical sources, both prose and poetry. Most of these are biblical, so if you're familiar at all with that material already, it can help clue you in to what to expect. Reading translations of already familiar texts is a helpful way to build competence and fluency, and you may be able to deduce the meanings of some unknown words just from context. All of these are from texts that were translated to Sahidic from Greek. Three are from the Sahidic Old Testament:

Exodus 1.1–5.21
Psalms 2, 22(23),[2] 90(91), 109(110), and 151
Proverbs 22.17–23.12

Three are from the Sahidic New Testament:

John 1.1–2.12
Matthew 5.1–7.29
Revelation 4.1–8.1

---

1. For an up-to-date overview of Coptic literature, see Paola Buzi, "Literature, Coptic: Update," *Claremont Coptic Encyclopedia*, November 13, 2021, https://ccdl.claremont.edu/digital/collection/ccc/id/2175/rec/10.

2. The double numbers reflect the difference between the Greek/Coptic and the Hebrew (in parentheses) numbering systems for the Psalms.

CONCLUSION AND NEXT STEPS

And the last two are extrabiblical:

The Gospel of Thomas 1–42
The Life of Antony 11–13

All these reading selections have been normalized (given word spacing, overlines, hyphenation, modern punctuation, etc.) according to the practice of this book. Scribal abbreviations are unpacked into the fuller forms.

Unlike Hebrew, Greek, and other biblical languages, no comprehensive critical edition has yet been made for the Sahidic Bible. Many different sections, books, and manuscripts have been edited, but there's no handy single volume you can reach for to see everything.[3] Happily, the Göttingen Sahidic Old Testament project[4] currently underway will remedy this need for the Old Testament. For the New Testament, we do have the editions made by George Horner,[5] but these are now over a century old and are in need of modern updates with our current manuscript evidence and methods. Recently, proper editions of the Psalms,[6] John,[7] and Revelation[8] have been published, and these have been implemented for our readings.

Some of the other base texts for the readings comes from the same digital sources used in the Coptic Scriptorium[9] website's corpora of texts. The Coptic Scriptorium is a fantastic resource with a huge and growing amount of Sahidic texts, and you'll want to turn there for further texts and the tools to help you read and analyze—everything is interlinked to the ANNIS database/search engine[10] and the *Coptic Dictionary Online* (see below)! Just be aware that online texts often lack overlines and punctuation (to ease

---

3. And by "everything," I mean that which has survived: While the New Testament is completely attested in Sahidic, some parts of the Sahidic Old Testament are lacking in our currently available manuscripts, most notably certain historical books like Chronicles and Ezra-Nehemiah. See Hany N. Takla, *An Introduction to the Coptic Old Testament* (Los Angeles: Saint Mark Foundation and Saint Shenouda the Archimandrite Coptic Society, 2007) and Takla, "The Coptic Bible," in *Coptic Civilization: Two Thousand Years of Christianity in Egypt*, ed. Gawdat Gabra (Cairo: American University in Cairo Press, 2014), 105–21, along with Frank Feder, "Old Testament, Coptic Version of the: Update," *Claremont Coptic Encyclopedia*, November 22, 2023, https://ccdl.claremont.edu/digital/collection/cce/id/2188/.

4. See the *Digital Edition of the Coptic Old Testament*, https://coptot.manuscriptroom.com, from the Göttingen Academy of Sciences and Humanities.

5. George William Horner, ed., *The Coptic Version of the New Testament in the Southern Dialect, Otherwise Called Sahidic and Thebaic, with Introduction, Critical Apparatus, and Literal English Translation*, 7 vols (Oxford: Clarendon, 1911–1924).

6. Peter Nagel, ed., *Der sahidische Psalter. Editio Minor nach den Handschriften Ms. Or. 5000 der British Library zu London, Ms. n° 815 der Chester Beatty Library zu Dublin, und Ms. n° 167 der University of Michigan Library zu Ann Arbor*, Texts and Studies on the Coptic Bible 3 (Wiesbaden: Harrassowitz, 2022).

7. Hans Förster, Kerstin Sänger-Böhm, and Matthias H. O. Schulz, eds., *Kritische Edition der sahidischen Version des Johannesevangeliums: Text und Dokumentation*, Arbeiten zur Neutestamentlichen Textforschung 56 (Berlin: de Gruyter, 2021).

8. Christian Askeland, ed. "An Eclectic Edition of the Sahidic Apocalypse of John," in *Studien zum Text der Apokalypse II*, ed. Marcus Sigismund and Darius Müller, Arbeiten zur Neutestamentlichen Textforschung 50 (Berlin: de Gruyter, 2017), 33–79.

9. Caroline T. Schroeder and Amir Zeldes, et al., *Coptic SCRIPTORIUM*, https://copticscriptorium.org. For the New Testament, the Sahidic digital text has a chain of transmission from J. Warren Well's (apparently now defunct) Sahidica project website (2000–2006, www.sahidica.org), which was in turn based on David Brakke's (1991) and the St. Shenouda the Archimandrite Coptic Society's (1998) electronic texts. See https://copticscriptorium.org/download/corpora/Mark/coptic_nt_sahidic.html for full details, including the manuscripts underlying these texts. For the Old Testament, the Sahidic digital text used is also available on the CrossWire Bible Society's Bible Tool website: "Sahidic Bible 2" (based on "Sahidic Bible - Askeland / Schulz"): http://crosswire.org/study/fulllibrary.jsp?show=CopSahBible2. It represents the base working text of the Göttingen Sahidic Old Testament project.

10. ANNIS Database/search engine: https://annis.copticscriptorium.org/annis/scriptorium.

word searches). When you're ready to dive into the numerous lives of saints and other hagiographic texts, the Coptic Scriptorium has what you need.

28.3 **Learning Words.** The vocabulary you've been learning in these past chapters covers all the most common words used in many Sahidic works, but you'll need to look up less common words as they appear in your readings. The Sahidic-English Lexicon after the readings section includes all the chapter vocabulary along with every other word occurring in the readings. Get familiar with it! It's set up the same way as the chapter vocabulary entries have been.

Eventually, you will also want to expand your toolset with a more expansive lexicon. The (g)old standard is Walter Crum's *A Coptic Dictionary*.[11] Crum's comprehensive work with all the material he had available has had a significant and enduring influence on all future dictionaries and lexicons. You may want to acquire a copy at some point. Be warned that besides being rather dated (more recent discoveries like the Nag Hammadi texts aren't included), Crum does have a rather old typeset, and he covers *all* the dialects known at the time, not just Sahidic. Entries are organized by the purported consonantal roots (not a strict alphabetical arrangement) and include voluminous references, so it can be tricky to navigate. Greek vocabulary is not included.

There are also some more recent (and more compact) print Sahidic dictionaries. Azevedo[12] and Smith[13] are both handy, and Azevedo even includes Greek vocabulary. One of my favorites is actually the extensive "Glossary" in Lambdin's grammar.[14]

A modern, digital alternative is the excellent *Coptic Dictionary Online*,[15] which is interlinked with the texts found on the Coptic Scriptorium and the ANNIS database/search engine. Greek vocabulary is included, and the comprehensive *Dictionary* combined with the detailed search capabilities of the ANNIS engine can empower in-depth research (there is a learning curve to make full use of it—follow the tutorials). And it's all free!

Finally, to type in Coptic you need a proper font. The standard Unicode font is Antinoou, available for free online, along with keyboard layouts (I use the "Coptic - English" setup myself).[16] Follow the helpful instructions on the website to get started.

28.4 **Further Studies.** Once you've read a bunch of texts and are ready for further challenges, you can do a deeper dive into Sahidic grammar by getting a copy of the comprehensive reference grammar for Sahidic, Bentley Layton's monumental *A Coptic Grammar*.[17] It's pricey, but priceless for serious grammatical analysis.

---

11. Walter Crum, *A Coptic Dictionary* (Oxford: Oxford University Press, 1939) but reprinted subsequently. A scan of Crum is also available freely online at https://coptot.manuscriptroom.com/crum-coptic-dictionary.

12. Joaquim Azevedo, *A Simplified Coptic Dictionary (Sahidic Dialect)*, 2nd ed. (Lima: Peruvian Union University, 2013).

13. Richard Smith, *A Concise Coptic-English Lexicon*, 2nd ed., Society of Biblical Literature Resources for Biblical Study 35 (Atlanta: Scholars Press, 1999).

14. Thomas O. Lambdin, *Introduction to Sahidic Coptic* (Macon, GA: Mercer University Press, 1983), 209–363.

15. *Coptic Dictionary Online*: https://coptic-dictionary.org. Edited by the Koptische/Coptic Electronic Language and Literature International Alliance (KELLIA).

16. *Antinoou*: A standard font for Coptic: https://www.evertype.com/fonts/coptic/. Unicode Coptic font and keyboard layouts designed by Michael Everson.

17. Bentley Layton, *A Coptic Grammar: With Chrestomathy and Glossary. Sahidic Dialect*, 3rd ed., Porta Linguarum Orientalium 2/20 (Wiesbaden: Harrassowitz, 2011).

CONCLUSION AND NEXT STEPS

The high-water mark for Sahidic literature is the corpus of works by Shenoute, the leader of the White Monastery (Dayr al-Abyad, near Sohāg in Upper Egypt) in the fourth and fifth centuries.[18] Shenoute produced a sizable body of works written in creative, native Sahidic style—without the constraints of being a translation of a Greek original. His high standard of original Sahidic thought and expression is perfect for intermediate and advanced students.

Finally, beyond Sahidic there lie the other dialects—Bohairic, the surviving dialect of the Coptic church through the second millennium, and the other main dialects of the first millennium (Fayyumic, Oxyrhynchite, Lycopolitan, and Akhmimic). Allen's *Coptic: A Grammar of Its Six Major Dialects*[19] treats all these alongside Sahidic. Its concise comparisons of all six together would be daunting for a new student of Coptic, but with a solid grasp of Sahidic under your belt, it's a valuable reference.

Whatever topic you're interested in, the online *Claremont Coptic Encyclopedia*[20] hosts a wealth of articles about all aspects of Coptic language, literature, culture, and history. It's free to use and continues to receive updates.

With many long-awaited projects underway and many excellent and free resources available to students online, there's never been a more exciting time to study Coptic. I wish you well in your continued studies! The past speaks to us still.

ⲛⲉⲧⲉ-ⲟⲩⲛ̄ⲧⲁⲩ ⲙⲁⲁϫⲉ ⲙ̄ⲙⲁⲩ ⲉ-ⲥⲱⲧⲙ̄, ⲙⲁⲣⲉⲩⲥⲱⲧⲙ̄!

---

18. For an overview of Shenoute and his works, see Heike Behlmer, "Shenoute: Update," *Claremont Coptic Encyclopedia*, March 21, 2022, https://ccdl.claremont.edu/digital/collection/cce/id/2178/. His works currently available on the Coptic Scriptorium can be found at https://data.copticscriptorium.org/search?author=Shenoute.

19. James P. Allen, *Coptic: A Grammar of Its Six Major Dialects*, Languages of the Ancient Near East: Didactica 1 (University Park, PA: Eisenbrauns, 2020).

20. Gawdat Gabra et al., eds., *Claremont Coptic Encyclopedia*, 2009–2024, https://ccdl.claremont.edu/digital/collection/cce. Based on *The Coptic Encyclopedia*, ed. Aziz S. Atiya, 8 vols. (New York: Macmillan, 1991).

BIBLIOGRAPHY AND RESOURCES

NOTE: this list primarily includes select materials for an English-speaking audience—there have been many additional resources made available in other languages (especially German).

ONLINE PROJECTS AND RESOURCES

ANNIS Database/search engine: https://annis.copticscriptorium.org/annis/scriptorium.

Antinoou: A standard font for Coptic: https://www.evertype.com/fonts/coptic/. Unicode Coptic font and keyboard layouts designed by Michael Everson.

Claremont Coptic Encyclopedia: https://ccdl.claremont.edu/digital/collection/cce. Gawdat Gabra, et al., eds. Claremont Graduate University, 2009–2024.

Coptic Dictionary Online: https://coptic-dictionary.org. Edited by the Koptische/Coptic Electronic Language and Literature International Alliance (KELLIA).

Coptic SCRIPTORIUM: https://copticscriptorium.org. Caroline T. Schroeder (University of Oklahoma), Amir Zeldes (Georgetown University) et al., 2013–2024.

Digital Edition of the Coptic Old Testament: https://coptot.manuscriptroom.com. Göttingen Academy of Sciences and Humanities.

GRAMMARS (PRINT)

Allen, James P. *Coptic: A Grammar of Its Six Major Dialects*. Languages of the Ancient Near East: Didactica 1. University Park, PA: Eisenbrauns, 2020.

Brankaer, Johanna. *Coptic: A Learning Grammar (Sahidic)*. Subsidia et Instrumenta Linguarum Orientis 1. Wiesbaden: Harrassowitz, 2010.

Lambdin, Thomas O. *Introduction to Sahidic Coptic*. Macon, GA: Mercer University Press, 1983.

Layton, Bentley. *Coptic in 20 Lessons: Introduction to Sahidic Coptic with Exercises and Vocabularies*. Leuven: Peeters, 2007.

———. *A Coptic Grammar: With Chrestomathy and Glossary. Sahidic Dialect*. 3rd ed. Porta Linguarum Orientalium 2/20. Wiesbaden: Harrassowitz, 2011.

Reintges, Chris H. *Coptic Egyptian (Sahidic Dialect): A Learner's Grammar*. Cologne: Köppe, 2004.

Shisha-Halevy, Ariel. *Coptic Grammatical Chrestomathy: A Course for Academic and Private Study.* Orientalia Lovaniensia Analecta 30. Leuven: Peeters, 1988.

Sterling, Gregory E. *Coptic Paradigms: A Summary of Sahidic Coptic Morphology.* Leuven: Peeters, 2008.

Younan, Sameh. *So, You Want to Learn Coptic? A Guide to Bohairic Grammar.* Sydney, Australia: St. Mary, St. Bakhomious, St. Shenouda Coptic Orthodox Church, 2005.

LEXICA/DICTIONARIES/CONCORDANCES (PRINT)

Azevedo, Joaquim. *A Simplified Coptic Dictionary (Sahidic Dialect).* 2nd ed. Lima: Peruvian Union University, 2013.

Crum, Walter Ewing. *A Coptic Dictionary.* Oxford: Oxford University Press, 1939.

Danker, Frederick W., Walter Bauer, William F. Arndt, and F. Wilbur Gingrich. *A Greek-English Lexicon of the New Testament and Other Early Christian Literature.* 3rd ed. Chicago: University of Chicago Press, 2000.

Lefort, Louis-Théophile. *Concordance du Nouveau Testament sahidique I: Let mots d'origine grecque.* Corpus Scriptorum Christianorum Orientalium 124, Subsidia 1. Leuven: Peeters, 1950.

Metzger, Bruce M. *List of Words Occurring Frequently in the Coptic New Testament (Sahidic Dialect).* Leiden: Brill, 1961.

Smith, Richard. *A Concise Coptic-English Lexicon.* 2nd ed. Society of Biblical Literature Resources for Biblical Study 35. Atlanta: Scholars Press, 1999.

Wilmet, Michel. *Concordance du Nouveau Testament sahidique II: Les mots autochtones.* 3 vols. Corpus Scriptorum Christianorum Orientalium 173, Subsidia 11. Leuven: Peeters, 1957.

TEXT EDITIONS (PRINT)

Aranda Pérez, Gonzalo, ed. *El evangelio de San Mateo en copto sahídico (texto de M 569, estudio preliminar y aparato critico).* Textos y Estudios Cardenal Cisneros 35. Madrid: Instituto Arias Montano, 1984.

Askeland, Christian, ed. "An Eclectic Edition of the Sahidic Apocalypse of John." Pages 33–79 in *Studien zum Text der Apokalypse II.* Edited by Marcus Sigismund and Darius Müller. Arbeiten zur Neutestamentlichen Textforschung 50. Berlin: de Gruyter, 2017.

Förster, Hans, Kerstin Sänger-Böhm, and Matthias H. O. Schulz, eds. *Kritische Edition der sahidischen Version des Johannesevangeliums: Text und Dokumentation.* Arbeiten zur Neutestamentlichen Textforschung 56. Berlin: de Gruyter, 2021.

Garitte, Gérard, ed. *S. Antonii vitae: Versio sahidica.* 2 vols. Corpus Scriptorum Christianorum Orientalium 117–118, Scriptores Coptici 13–14. Paris: E Typographeo Reipublicae, 1949.

Gathercole, Simon J. *The Gospel of Thomas: Introduction and Commentary.* Texts and Editions for New Testament Study 11. Leiden: Brill, 2014.

Horner, George William, ed. *The Coptic Version of the New Testament in the Southern Dialect, Otherwise Called Sahidic and Thebaic, with Introduction, Critical Apparatus, and Literal English Translation.* 7 vols. Oxford: Clarendon, 1911–1924.

Kasser, Rodolphe, ed. *Papyrus Bodmer XVI: Exode I–XV, 21 en sahidique*. Cologny-Genéve: Bibliotheca Bodmeriana, 1961.

Layton, Bentley, ed. *Coptic Gnostic Chrestomathy: A Selection of Coptic Texts with Grammatical Analysis and Glossary*. Leuven: Peeters, 2004.

Nagel, Peter, ed. *Das Deuteronomium sahidisch. Nach Ms. BL Or.7594 der British Library mit dem ergänzenden Text und den Textvarianten des Paypyrus Bodmer XVIII und der Hanschrift M 566 der Morgan Library & Museum New York*. Texts and Studies on the Coptic Bible 2. Wiesbaden, Harrassowitz. 2020.

———. *Der sahidische Psalter. Editio Minor nach den Handschriften Ms. Or. 5000 der British Library zu London, Ms. n° 815 der Chester Beatty Library zu Dublin, und Ms. n° 167 der University of Michigan Library zu Ann Arbor*. Texts and Studies on the Coptic Bible 3. Wiesbaden: Harrassowitz, 2022.

Quecke, Hans, ed. *Das Johannesevangelium saïdisch: Text der Handschrift PPalau Rib. Inv.-Nr. 183 mit den Varianten der Handschriften 813 und 814 der Chester Beatty Library und der Handschrift M 569*. Papyrologica Castroctaviana 11. Rome: Pontificia Università Gregoriana, 1984.

———, ed. *Das Lukasevangelium saïdisch: Text der Handschrift PPalau Rib. Inv.-Nr. 181 mit den Varianten der Handschrift M 569*. Papyrologica Castroctaviana 6. Barcelona: Pontificia Università Gregoriana, 1977.

———, ed. *Das Markusevangelium saïdisch: Text der Handschrift PPalau Rib. Inv.-Nr. 182 mit den Varianten der Handschrift M 569*. Papyrologica Castroctaviana 4. Barcelona: Pontificia Università Gregoriana, 1972.

Schüssler, Karlheinz, ed. *Die Katholischen Briefe in der koptischen (sahidischen) Version*. 2 vols. Corpus Scriptorum Christianorum Orientalium 528, Scriptores Coptici 45. Leuven: Peeters, 1991.

Worrell, William Hoyt, ed. *The Proverbs of Solomon in Sahidic Coptic According to the Chicago Manuscript*. The University of Chicago Oriental Institute Publications 12. Chicago: University of Chicago Press, 1931.

OTHER STUDIES

Athanasius of Alexandria. *The Life of Antony: The Coptic Life and the Greek Life*. Translated by Tim Vivian and Apostolos N. Athanassakis. Cistercian Studies 202. Kalamazoo, MI: Cistercian, 2003.

Atiya, Aziz S., ed. *The Coptic Encyclopedia*. 8 vols. New York: Macmillan, 1991.

Behlmer, Heike. "Shenoute: Update." *Claremont Coptic Encyclopedia*. March 21, 2022. https://ccdl.claremont.edu/digital/collection/cce/id/2178/.

Buzi, Paola. "Literature, Coptic: Update." *Claremont Coptic Encyclopedia*. November 13, 2021. https://ccdl.claremont.edu/digital/collection/cce/id/2175/rec/10.

Feder, Frank. "Old Testament, Coptic Version of the: Update." *Claremont Coptic Encyclopedia*. November 22, 2023. https://ccdl.claremont.edu/digital/collection/cce/id/2188/.

Hallo, William W., ed. *Canonical Compositions from the Biblical World*. Vol. 1 of *The Context of Scripture*. Leiden: Brill, 2003.

Layton, Bentley, and David Brakke. *The Gnostic Scriptures*. 2nd ed. Anchor Yale Bible Reference Library. New Haven: Yale University Press, 2021.

"List of Coptic Biblical Manuscripts" [LCBM], Version 1.0, March 31, 2021. Edited by the Göttingen Coptic Old Testament Project, in cooperation with S. Richter and K. Sandmeier, Institute for New Testament Textual Research/Institut für Neutestamentliche Textforschung, Münster. https://coptot.manuscriptroom.com/documents/10231/23535/LCBM_1.0_2021.pdf/dec4f073-dbfa-4af6-9971-3b2bace5b3eb.

Meyer, Marvin, ed. *The Nag Hammadi Scriptures: The International Edition*. New York: HarperOne, 2007.

Takla, Hany N. "The Coptic Bible." Pages 81-95 in *The Oxford Handbook of the Bible in Orthodox Christianity*. Edited by Eugen J. Pentiuc. Oxford: Oxford University Press, 2022.

———. "The Coptic Bible." Pages 105–121 in *Coptic Civilization: Two Thousand Years of Christianity in Egypt*. Edited by Gawdat Gabra. Cairo: American University in Cairo Press, 2014.

———. *An Introduction to the Coptic Old Testament*. Los Angeles: Saint Mark Foundation and Saint Shenouda the Archimandrite Coptic Society, 2007.

READING SELECTIONS

All reading selections have been normalized (given word spacing, overlines,[1] hyphenation, modern punctuation, paragraphing, etc.) according to the practice of this book. Scribal abbreviations are unpacked into the fuller forms.[2]

Biblical
    ⲡϫⲱⲱⲙⲉ ⲛ̄-ⲉ̀ⲝⲟⲇⲟⲥ Exodus 1.1–5.21
    ⲡϫⲱⲱⲙⲉ ⲛ̄-ⲛⲉⲯⲁⲗⲙⲟⲥ Psalms 2, 22(23),[3] 90(91), 109(110), and 151
    ⲙ̄ⲡⲁⲣϩⲟⲓⲙⲓ́ⲁ ⲛ̄-ⲥⲟⲗⲟⲙⲱ́ⲛ Proverbs 22.17–23.12
    ⲡⲉⲩⲁⲅⲅⲉ́ⲗⲓⲟⲛ ⲛ̄-ⲕⲁⲧⲁ-ⲓ̈ⲱϩⲁ́ⲛⲛⲏⲥ John 1.1–2.12
    ⲡⲉⲩⲁⲅⲅⲉ́ⲗⲓⲟⲛ ⲛ̄-ⲕⲁⲧⲁ-ⲙⲁⲑⲑⲁⲓ́ⲟⲥ Matthew 5.1–7.29
    ⲧⲁⲡⲟⲕⲁ́ⲗⲩⲯⲓⲥ ⲛ̄ⲧⲉ-ⲓ̈ⲱϩⲁ́ⲛⲛⲏⲥ Revelation 4.1–8.1
Extrabiblical
    ⲡⲉⲩⲁⲅⲅⲉ́ⲗⲓⲟⲛ ⲡⲕⲁⲧⲁ-ⲑⲱⲙⲁ́ⲥ The Gospel of Thomas 1–42
    ⲡⲃⲓ́ⲟⲥ ⲛ̄-ⲁⲛⲧⲱ́ⲛⲓⲟⲥ The Life of Antony 11–13

ⲡϫⲱⲱⲙⲉ ⲛ̄-ⲉ̀ⲝⲟⲇⲟⲥ EXODUS 1.1–5.21

This selection from Exodus gives the beginning of the story of the Israel's deliverance from bondage in Egypt. It's a good sample of the narrative backbone of the Covenant History (the books of Genesis through Kings), and naturally very Egyptian in its setting!

The text comes from the manuscript known as Papyrus Bodmer XVI (PB 16),[4] containing Exodus 1.1–15.21. Written around the fourth century CE, it was found in 1952 near Dishna, Egypt along with other biblical and nonbiblical texts. Despite being included in the Bodmer

---

1. Some manuscripts and editions use "bridging" overlines (ϩ̄ⲙ), but these have all been adjusted to be over the second letter (ϩⲙ̄), as has been our standard practice thus far.
2. Additional reading selections and resources are available at TextbookPlus for *Basics of Sahidic Coptic*. See https://zondervan academic.com/coptic.
3. The double numbers reflect the difference between the Greek/Coptic and the Hebrew (in parentheses) numbering systems for the Psalms.
4. This manuscript is listed as sa 2000 on the LCBM: "List of Coptic Biblical Manuscripts," Version 1.0, March 31, 2021, edited by the Göttingen Coptic Old Testament Project with S. Richter and K. Sandmeier, Institute for New Testament Textual Research/Institut für Neutestamentliche Textforschung, Münster. https://coptot.manuscriptroom.com/documents/10231/23535/LCBM_1.0_2021.pdf/dec4f073-dbfa-4af6-9971-3b2bace5b3eb.

"Papyri" collection, PB 16 is a *parchment* codex, still bound in its original leather cover. Its text was published in 1961 by Rodolphe Kasser.[5]

Images of the manuscript are available online at the Bodmer Lab website.[6] A few minor, obvious scribal errors have been emended in the normalized text below.

1.1 ⲛⲁⲓ ⲛⲉ ⲛ̄ⲣⲁⲛ ⲛ̄-ⲛ̄ϣⲏⲣⲉ ⲙ̄-ⲡⲓⲥⲣⲁⲏⲗ ⲉⲛⲧⲁⲩⲃⲱⲕ ⲉϩⲣⲁⲓ ⲉ-ⲕⲏⲙⲉ ⲙⲛ̄-ⲓ̈ⲁⲕⲱⲃ ⲡⲉⲩⲓ̈ⲱⲧ. ⲡⲟⲩⲁ ⲡⲟⲩⲁ ⲁϥⲃⲱⲕ ⲉϩⲟⲩⲛ ⲙⲛ̄-ⲡⲉϥⲏⲉⲓ ⲧⲏⲣϥ̄, 2 ϩⲣⲟⲩⲃⲏⲛ, ⲥⲩⲙⲉⲱⲛ, ⲗⲉⲩⲉⲓ, ⲓ̈ⲟⲩⲇⲁⲥ, 3 ⲓ̈ⲥⲥⲁⲭⲁⲣ, ⲍⲁⲃⲟⲩⲗⲱⲛ ⲙⲛ̄-ⲃⲉⲛⲓⲁⲙⲉⲓⲛ, 4 ⲇⲁⲛ ⲙⲛ̄-ⲛⲉⲫⲑⲁⲗⲉⲓⲙ, ⲅⲁⲇ ⲙⲛ̄-ⲁⲥⲏⲣ. 5 ⲓ̈ⲱⲥⲏⲫ ⲇⲉ ⲛⲉϥ-ϩⲛ̄-ⲕⲏⲙⲉ ⲡⲉ. ⲯⲩⲭⲏ ⲇⲉ ⲛⲓⲙ ⲉⲛⲧⲁⲩⲉⲓ ⲉⲃⲟⲗ ϩⲛ̄-ⲓ̈ⲁⲕⲱⲃ ⲉⲩ-ⲙⲉϩ-ϣϥⲉ ⲧⲏ.

6 ⲁϥⲙⲟⲩ ⲛ̄ϭⲓ-ⲓ̈ⲱⲥⲏⲫ ⲙⲛ̄-ⲛⲉϥⲥⲛⲏⲩ ⲧⲏⲣⲟⲩ ⲙⲛ̄-ⲧⲅⲉⲛⲉⲁ ⲧⲏⲣⲥ̄ ⲉⲧ-ⲙ̄ⲙⲁⲩ. 7 ⲛ̄ϣⲏⲣⲉ ⲇⲉ ⲙ̄-ⲡⲓⲥⲣⲁⲏⲗ ⲁⲩⲁⲉⲓⲁⲓ̈ ⲁⲩⲱ ⲁⲩⲁϣⲁⲉⲓ, ⲁⲩⲡⲱⲣϣ̄ ⲉⲃⲟⲗ, ⲁⲩϭⲙ̄-ϭⲟⲙ ⲉⲙⲁⲧⲉ. ⲡⲕⲁϩ ⲇⲉ ⲁϥⲧⲁϣⲟⲟⲩ.

8 ⲁϥⲧⲱⲟⲩⲛ ⲛ̄ϭⲓ-ⲕⲉⲣⲣⲟ ⲉϩⲣⲁⲓ ⲉϫⲛ̄-ⲕⲏⲙⲉ. ⲡⲁⲓ ⲉⲛϥ̄ⲥⲟⲟⲩⲛ ⲁⲛ ⲉ-ⲓ̈ⲱⲥⲏⲫ. 9 ⲡⲉϫⲁϥ ⲙ̄-ⲡⲉϥⲅⲉⲛⲟⲥ ϫⲉ "ⲉⲓⲥ-ϩⲏⲏⲧⲉ! ⲡϩⲉⲑⲛⲟⲥ ⲛ̄-ⲛ̄ϣⲏⲣⲉ ⲙ̄-ⲡⲓⲥⲣⲁⲏⲗ ⲟⲩⲛⲟϭ ⲙ̄-ⲙⲏⲏϣⲉ ⲡⲉ, ⲁⲩⲱ ⲉϥϭⲙ̄-ϭⲟⲙ ⲉ-ϩⲟⲩⲉⲣⲟⲛ. 10 ⲁⲙⲏⲉⲓⲛ ⲛ̄ⲧⲛ̄ⲙⲉⲉⲩⲉ ⲉ-ⲩϩⲱⲃ ⲉⲣⲟⲟⲩ, ⲙⲏⲡⲟⲧⲉ ⲛ̄ⲥⲉⲁϣⲁⲓ ⲛ̄ⲥⲱⲡⲉ ⲛ̄ⲧⲉ-ⲟⲩⲡⲟⲗⲉⲙⲟⲥ ⲧⲱⲟⲩⲛ ⲉϩⲣⲁⲓ ⲉϫⲱⲛ ⲛ̄ⲥⲉϭⲓ ⲙⲛ̄-ⲛⲉⲛϫⲁϫⲉ ⲛ̄ⲥⲉⲙⲓϣⲉ ⲛⲙ̄ⲙⲁⲛ ⲛ̄ⲥⲉⲃⲱⲕ ⲉⲃⲟⲗ ϩⲙ̄-ⲡⲕⲁϩ."

11 ⲁϥⲧⲁϩⲟ ⲉϩⲣⲁⲓ ⲉϫⲱⲟⲩ ⲛ̄-ϩⲉⲛⲥⲁϩ ϩⲛ̄-ⲛⲉϩⲃⲏⲩⲉ ϫⲉⲕⲁⲥ ⲉⲩⲉⲙⲟⲕϩ̄ⲟⲩ ϩⲣⲁⲓ ϩⲛ̄-ⲛⲉϩⲃⲏⲩⲉ. ⲁⲩⲕⲱⲧ ⲛ̄-ϩⲛ̄ⲡⲟⲗⲉⲓⲥ ⲉⲩⲧⲁϫⲣⲏⲩ ⲙ̄-ⲫⲁⲣⲁⲱ, ⲡⲓⲑⲱⲙ ⲙⲛ̄-ϩⲣⲁⲙⲉⲥⲥⲏ[7] ⲙⲛ̄-ⲱⲛ, ⲉⲧⲉ-ⲧⲁⲓ ⲧⲉ ⲧⲡⲟⲗⲓⲥ ⲙ̄-ⲡⲣⲏ. 12 ⲕⲁⲧⲁ-ⲑⲉ ⲇⲉ ⲉⲧⲟⲩⲑⲃⲃⲓⲟ ⲙ̄ⲙⲟⲟⲩ, ⲧⲁⲓ ⲧⲉ ⲑⲉ ⲉⲛⲉⲩⲁϣⲁⲓ ⲛ̄-ϩⲟⲩⲟ, ⲉⲩϭⲙ̄-ϭⲟⲙ ⲉⲙⲁⲧⲉ ⲉⲙⲁⲧⲉ. ⲛ̄ⲣⲙ̄ⲛ̄ⲕⲏⲙⲉ ⲛ̄ⲇⲉ[8] ⲛⲉⲩϫⲓ-ⲃⲟⲧⲉ ⲡⲉ ⲉ-ⲛ̄ϣⲏⲣⲉ ⲙ̄-ⲡⲓⲥⲣⲁⲏⲗ. [13][9] 14 ⲁⲩⲱ ⲛⲉⲩⲙⲟⲩⲕϩ̄[10] ⲙ̄-ⲡⲉⲩⲱⲛϩ̄ ϩⲣⲁⲓ ϩⲛ̄-ⲛⲉϩⲃⲏⲩⲉ ⲉⲧ-ⲛⲁϣⲧ̄, ϩⲙ̄-ⲡⲟⲙⲉ ⲙⲛ̄-ⲧⲙⲛ̄ⲧⲡⲁⲡⲉ-ⲧⲱⲃⲉ, ⲙⲛ̄-ⲛⲉϩⲃⲏⲩⲉ ⲧⲏⲣⲟⲩ ⲛ̄-ⲧⲥⲱϣⲉ, ⲙⲛ̄-ⲛ̄ⲕⲁ ⲛⲓⲙ ⲉⲧⲟⲩⲉⲓⲣⲉ ⲙ̄ⲙⲟⲟⲩ ⲛ̄-ϩⲙ̄ϩⲁⲗ ⲛ̄ϩⲏⲧⲟⲩ ϩⲛ̄-ⲟⲩϫⲓ ⲛ̄-ϭⲟⲛⲥ̄.

15 ⲡⲉϫⲁϥ ⲛ̄ϭⲓ-ⲡⲣ̄ⲣⲟ ⲛ̄-ⲕⲏⲙⲉ ⲛ̄-ⲙ̄ⲙⲉⲥⲓⲟ ⲛ̄-ⲛ̄ϩⲉⲃⲣⲁⲓⲟⲥ, ⲡⲣⲁⲛ ⲛ̄-ⲧⲟⲩⲉⲓ ⲙ̄ⲙⲟⲟⲩ ⲡⲉ ⲥⲉⲫⲫⲱⲣⲁ ⲁⲩⲱ ⲡⲣⲁⲛ ⲛ̄-ⲧⲙⲉϩ-ⲥⲛ̄ⲧⲉ ⲡⲉ ⲫⲟⲩⲁ, 16 ⲉϥϫⲱ ⲙ̄ⲙⲟⲥ ϫⲉ "ⲉⲧⲉⲧⲛ̄ϣⲁⲛⲉⲓ ⲉⲧⲉⲧⲛ̄ⲛⲁⲙⲉⲥⲓⲟ ⲛ̄-ⲛ̄ϩⲉⲃⲣⲁⲓⲁ ⲉⲩⲉⲓ ⲉⲩⲛⲁⲙⲓⲥⲉ, ⲉϣⲱⲡⲉ ⲙⲉⲛ ⲟⲩϩⲟⲟⲩⲧ ⲡⲉ ⲉⲧⲉⲧⲛ̄ⲉⲙⲟⲟⲩⲧϥ̄, ⲉϣⲱⲡⲉ ⲇⲉ ⲟⲩⲥϩⲓⲙⲉ ⲧⲉ ⲉⲧⲉⲧⲛ̄ⲉⲧⲁⲛϩⲟⲥ." 17 ⲁ-ⲙ̄ⲙⲉⲥⲓⲟ ⲇⲉ ⲣ̄-ϩⲟⲧⲉ ϩⲏⲧϥ̄ ⲙ̄-ⲡⲛⲟⲩⲧⲉ, ⲙ̄ⲡⲟⲩⲉⲓⲣⲉ ⲕⲁⲧⲁ-ⲑⲉ ⲉⲛⲧⲁϥϩⲱⲛ ⲉⲧⲟⲟⲧⲟⲩ ⲛ̄ϭⲓ-ⲡⲣ̄ⲣⲟ ⲛ̄-ⲕⲏⲙⲉ, ⲁⲩⲧⲁⲛϩⲟ ⲛ̄-ϩⲟⲟⲩⲧ. 18 ⲁϥⲙⲟⲩⲧⲉ ⲛ̄ϭⲓ-ⲡⲣ̄ⲣⲟ ⲛ̄-ⲕⲏⲙⲉ ⲉ-ⲙ̄ⲙⲉⲥⲓⲟ ⲛ̄-ⲛ̄ϩⲉⲃⲣⲁⲓⲟⲥ, ⲡⲉϫⲁϥ ⲛⲁⲩ ϫⲉ "ⲉⲧⲃⲉ-ⲟⲩ ⲁⲧⲉⲧⲛ̄ⲉⲓⲣⲉ ⲙ̄-ⲡⲉⲓ̈ϩⲱⲃ? ⲁⲧⲉⲧⲛ̄ⲧⲁⲛϩⲟ ⲛ̄-ϩⲟⲟⲩⲧ!"

19 ⲡⲉϫⲁⲩ ⲛ̄ⲇⲉ ⲛ̄ϭⲓ-ⲙ̄ⲙⲉⲥⲓⲟ ⲙ̄-ⲫⲁⲣⲁⲱ ϫⲉ "ⲛⲉⲣⲉ-ⲛ̄ϩⲉⲃⲣⲁⲓⲁ ⲟ ⲁⲛ ⲛ̄-ⲑⲉ ⲛ̄-ⲛⲉϩⲓⲟⲙⲉ ⲛ̄-ⲕⲏⲙⲉ ⲉ-ϣⲁⲩⲙⲓⲥⲉ, ϣⲁⲩⲙⲓⲥⲉ ⲛ̄ⲅⲁⲣ ⲙ̄ⲡⲁⲧⲟⲩⲃⲱⲕ ⲉϩⲟⲩⲛ ϣⲁⲣⲟⲟⲩ ⲛ̄ϭⲓ-ⲙ̄ⲙⲉⲥⲓⲟ ⲁⲩⲱ ⲛⲉⲩⲙⲓⲥⲉ."

20 ⲡⲛⲟⲩⲧⲉ ⲛ̄ⲇⲉ ⲁϥⲣ̄-ⲡⲉⲧ-ⲛⲁⲛⲟⲩϥ ⲛ̄-ⲙ̄ⲙⲉⲥⲓⲟ, ⲁⲩⲱ ⲁ-ⲡⲗⲁⲟⲥ ⲁϣⲁⲉⲓ ⲁϥϭⲙ̄-ϭⲟⲙ ⲉⲙⲁⲧⲉ. 21 ⲉⲃⲟⲗ ⲛ̄ⲇⲉ ϫⲉ ⲁ-ⲙ̄ⲙⲉⲥⲓⲟ ⲣ̄-ϩⲟⲧⲉ ϩⲏⲧϥ̄ ⲙ̄-ⲡⲛⲟⲩⲧⲉ, ⲁⲩⲧⲁⲙⲓⲟ ⲛⲁⲩ ⲛ̄-ϩⲛ̄ⲏⲉⲓ.

22 ⲁ-ⲫⲁⲣⲁⲱ ⲛ̄ⲇⲉ ϩⲱⲛ ⲉⲧⲟⲟⲧϥ̄ ⲙ̄-ⲡⲉϥⲗⲁⲟⲥ ⲧⲏⲣϥ̄, ⲉϥϫⲱ ⲙ̄ⲙⲟⲥ ϫⲉ "ϩⲟⲟⲩⲧ ⲛⲓⲙ ⲉⲧⲟⲩⲛⲁϫⲡⲟⲟⲩ ⲛ̄-ϩⲉⲃⲣⲁⲓⲟⲥ ⲛⲟϫⲟⲩ ⲉ-ⲡⲙⲟⲟⲩ, ⲥϩⲓⲙⲉ ⲛ̄ⲇⲉ ⲛⲓⲙ ⲙⲁ-ⲧⲁⲛϩⲟⲟⲩ."

---

5. Rodolphe Kasser, ed., *Papyrus Bodmer XVI: Exode I–XV, 21 en sahidique* (Cologny-Genéve: Bibliotheca Bodmeriana, 1961).
6. https://bodmerlab.unige.ch/fr/constellations/papyri/barcode/1072205355. The Martin Bodmer Foundation/University of Geneva.
7. Emended from ⲛ̄-ϩⲣⲁⲙⲉⲥⲥⲏ.
8. The scribe of PB 16 frequently uses this anomalous spelling of ⲇⲉ with a prefixed ⲛ̄- with no apparent change in meaning. Similarly, ⲛ̄ⲅⲁⲣ is also found.
9. Verse 13 is skipped in PB 16.
10. Emended from ⲛⲉⲩⲙⲟⲩϫϩ̄.

2.1 ⲛⲉ-ⲩⲛ̄-ⲟⲩⲣⲱⲙⲉ ⲇⲉ ⲉⲃⲟⲗ ϩⲛ̄-ⲧⲉϥⲫⲩⲗⲏ ⲛ̄-ⲗⲉⲩⲉⲓ́, ⲡⲁⲓ̈ ⲁϥϫⲓ ⲛⲁϥ ⲛ̄-ⲟⲩⲥϩⲓⲙⲉ ⲉⲃⲟⲗ ϩⲛ̄-ⲛ̄ϣⲉⲉⲣⲉ ⲛ̄-ⲗⲉⲩⲉⲓ́. ⲁⲥϣⲱⲡⲉ ⲛⲁϥ, 2 ⲁⲥⲱⲱ, ⲁⲥⲭⲡⲟ ⲛ̄-ⲟⲩϣⲏⲣⲉ. ⲁⲩⲛⲁⲩ ⲉⲣⲟϥ ⲇⲉ ⲛⲉⲥⲱϥ ⲁⲩϩⲟⲡϥ̄ ⲛ̄-ϣⲟⲙⲛ̄ⲧ ⲛ̄-ⲉⲃⲟⲧ. 3 ⲉⲃⲟⲗ ⲇⲉ ⲙ̄ⲡⲟⲩϣϭⲙ̄-ϭⲟⲙ ⲉ-ϩⲟⲡϥ̄ ϭⲉ, ⲁ-ⲧⲉϥⲙⲁⲁⲩ ϫⲓ ⲛⲁϥ ⲛ̄-ⲟⲩⲧⲁⲉⲓⲃⲉ, ⲁⲥⲭⲁⲣϭ̄ ⲛ̄-ⲁⲙⲣⲏϩⲉ, ⲁⲥⲛⲟⲩϫⲉ ⲙ̄-ⲡϣⲏⲣⲉ ϣⲏⲙ ⲉⲣⲟⲥ, ⲁⲥⲕⲱ ⲙ̄ⲙⲟⲥ ϩⲛ̄-ⲫⲉ́ⲗⲟⲥ ϩⲁⲧⲛ̄-ⲡⲓⲉⲣⲟ. 4 ⲁ-ⲧⲉϥⲥⲱⲛⲉ ϣⲱⲡⲉ ⲉⲥϭⲱϣⲧ̄ ⲙ̄-ⲡⲟⲩⲉ ⲉ-ⲉⲓⲙⲉ ⲉ-ⲛⲉⲧ-ⲛⲁϣⲱⲡⲉ ⲙ̄ⲙⲟϥ.

5 ⲁ-ⲧϣⲉⲉⲣⲉ ⲇⲉ ⲙ̄-ⲫⲁⲣⲁⲱ ⲉⲓ ⲉⲡⲉⲥⲛ̄ⲧ ⲉϫⲙ̄-ⲡⲓⲉⲣⲟ ⲉ-ϫⲱⲕⲙ̄, ⲁⲩⲱ ⲛⲉⲥϩⲙ̄ϩⲁⲗ ⲛⲉⲩⲙⲟⲟϣⲉ ϩⲁⲧⲛ̄-ⲡⲓⲉⲣⲟ. ⲁⲥⲛⲁⲩ ⲇⲉ ⲉ-ⲧⲧⲁⲉⲓⲃⲉ ϩⲛ̄-ⲫⲉ́ⲗⲟⲥ, ⲁⲥϫⲟⲟⲩ ⲛ̄-ⲧⲉⲥϩⲙ̄ϩⲁⲗ, ⲁⲥⲛ̄ⲧⲥ̄. 6 ⲁⲥⲟⲩⲱⲛ ⲉⲣⲟⲥ, ⲁⲥⲛⲁⲩ ⲉ-ⲡϣⲏⲣⲉ ϣⲏⲙ ⲉϥⲣⲓⲙⲉ ϩⲛ̄-ⲧⲧⲁⲉⲓⲃⲉ. ⲁⲥϯ-ⲥⲟ ⲇⲉ ⲉⲣⲟϥ ⲛ̄ϭⲓ-ⲧϣⲉⲉⲣⲉ ⲙ̄-ⲫⲁⲣⲁⲱ, ⲉⲥϫⲱ ⲙ̄ⲙⲟⲥ ϫⲉ "ⲟⲩ ⲉⲃⲟⲗ ϩⲛ̄-ⲛ̄ϣⲏⲣⲉ ⲛ̄-ⲛ̄ϩⲉⲃⲣⲁⲓ́ⲟⲥ ⲡⲉ ⲡⲁⲓ̈."

7 ⲡⲉϫⲉ-ⲧⲉϥⲥⲱⲛⲉ ⲛ̄-ⲧϣⲉⲉⲣⲉ ⲙ̄-ⲫⲁⲣⲁⲱ ϫⲉ "ⲧⲉⲟⲩⲱϣ ⲉ-ⲧⲣⲁⲙⲟⲩⲧⲉ ⲛⲉ ⲉ-ⲩⲥϩⲓⲙⲉ ⲙ̄ⲙⲟⲛⲉ ⲉⲃⲟⲗ ϩⲛ̄-ⲛ̄ϩⲉⲃⲣⲁⲓ́ⲟⲥ ⲛ̄ⲥⲧⲥⲛ̄ⲕⲟ ⲛⲉ ⲙ̄-ⲡϣⲏⲣⲉ ϣⲏⲙ?"

8 ⲡⲉϫⲁⲥ ⲛⲁⲥ ⲛ̄ϭⲓ-ⲧϣⲉⲉⲣⲉ ⲙⲫⲁⲣⲁⲱ ϫⲉ "ⲃⲱⲕ!" ⲁ-ⲧϣⲉⲉⲣⲉ ⲇⲉ ϣⲏⲙ ⲃⲱⲕ, ⲁⲥⲙⲟⲩⲧⲉ ⲉ-ⲧⲙⲁⲁⲩ ⲙ̄-ⲡϣⲏⲣⲉ ϣⲏⲙ. 9 ⲡⲉϫⲁⲥ ⲛⲁⲥ ⲛ̄ϭⲓ-ⲧϣⲉⲉⲣⲉ ⲙ̄-ⲫⲁⲣⲁⲱ ϫⲉ "ϩⲁⲣⲉϩ ⲉ-ⲡⲉⲓϣⲏⲣⲉ ϣⲏⲙ ⲛ̄ⲧⲉⲥⲛ̄ⲕⲟ ⲙ̄ⲙⲟϥ[11] ⲛⲁⲉⲓ. ⲁⲛⲟⲕ ⲇⲉ ϯⲛⲁϯ ⲛⲉ ⲙ̄-ⲡⲟⲩⲃⲉⲕⲉ́." ⲁ-ⲧⲉⲥϩⲓⲙⲉ ⲛ̄ⲇⲉ ϫⲓ ⲙ̄-ⲡϣⲏⲣⲉ ϣⲏⲙ, ⲁⲥⲧⲥⲛ̄ⲕⲟϥ.

10 ⲛ̄ⲧⲉⲣⲉϥⲣ̄-ⲛⲟϭ ⲛ̄ⲇⲉ ⲛ̄ϭⲓ-ⲡϣⲏⲣⲉ ϣⲏⲙ, ⲁⲥϫⲓ ⲙ̄ⲙⲟϥ ⲉϩⲟⲩⲛ ϣⲁ-ⲧϣⲉⲉⲣⲉ ⲙ̄-ⲫⲁⲣⲁⲱ. ⲁϥϣⲱⲡⲉ ⲛⲁⲥ ⲉ-ⲩϣⲏⲣⲉ, ⲁⲥⲙⲟⲩⲧⲉ ⲉ-ⲡⲉϥⲣⲁⲛ ϫⲉ ⲙⲱⲩ̈ⲥⲏⲥ, ⲉⲥϫⲱ ⲙ̄ⲙⲟⲥ ϫⲉ "ⲛ̄ⲧⲁⲉⲓϥⲓⲧϥ̄ ⲉⲃⲟⲗ ϩⲙ̄-ⲡⲙⲟⲟⲩ."

11 ⲁⲥϣⲱⲡⲉ ⲇⲉ ϩⲛ̄-ⲛⲉϩⲟⲟⲩ ⲉⲧ-ⲛⲁϣⲱⲟⲩ ⲉⲧ-ⲙ̄ⲙⲁⲩ, ⲛ̄ⲧⲉⲣⲉϥⲣ̄-ⲛⲟϭ ⲛ̄ϭⲓ-ⲙⲱⲩ̈ⲥⲏⲥ, ⲁϥⲉⲓ ⲉⲃⲟⲗ ϣⲁ-ⲛⲉϥⲥⲛⲏⲩ, ⲛ̄ϣⲏⲣⲉ ⲙ̄-ⲡⲓⲥⲣⲁⲏⲗ. ⲛ̄ⲧⲉⲣⲉϥϯ-ϩⲧⲏϥ ⲇⲉ ⲉ-ⲡⲉⲩϩⲓⲥⲉ, ⲁϥⲛⲁⲩ ⲉ-ⲩⲣⲱⲙⲉ ⲛ̄-ⲣⲙ̄ⲛ̄ⲕⲏⲙⲉ ⲉϥϩⲓⲟⲩⲉ ⲉ-ⲩϩⲉⲃⲣⲁⲓⲟⲥ ⲉⲃⲟⲗ ϩⲛ̄-ⲛⲉϥⲥⲛⲏⲩ, ⲛ̄ϣⲏⲣⲉ ⲙ̄-ⲡⲓⲥⲣⲁⲏⲗ. 12 ⲁϥϭⲱϣⲧ̄ ⲇⲉ ⲉ-ⲡⲓⲥⲁ ⲙⲛ̄-ⲡⲁⲓ̈, ⲙ̄ⲡϥ̄ⲛⲁⲩ ⲉ-ⲗⲁⲁⲩ, ⲁϥϩⲱⲧⲃ̄ ⲙ̄-ⲡⲣⲙ̄ⲛ̄ⲕⲏⲙⲉ, ⲁϥϩⲟⲡϥ̄ ϩⲙ̄-ⲡϣⲱ.

13 ⲁϥⲉⲓ ⲛ̄ⲇⲉ ⲉⲃⲟⲗ ⲙ̄-ⲡⲉϥⲣⲁⲥⲧⲉ, ⲁϥⲛⲁⲩ ⲉ-ⲣⲱⲙⲉ ⲥⲛⲁⲩ ⲛ̄-ϩⲉⲃⲣⲁⲓⲟⲥ ⲉⲩⲙⲓϣⲉ ⲙⲛ̄-ⲛⲉⲩⲉⲣⲏⲩ. ⲡⲉϫⲁϥ ⲙ̄-ⲡⲉⲧ-ϫⲓ ⲛ̄-ϭⲟⲛⲥ̄ ϫⲉ "ⲉⲧⲃⲉ-ⲟⲩ ⲕϩⲓⲟⲩⲉ ⲉ-ⲡⲉⲧ-ϩⲓⲧⲟⲩⲱⲕ?"

14 ⲛ̄ⲧⲟϥ ⲇⲉ ⲡⲉϫⲁϥ ⲛⲁϥ ϫⲉ "ⲛⲓⲙ ⲡⲉ ⲛ̄ⲧⲁϥⲕⲁⲑⲓⲥⲧⲁ ⲙ̄ⲙⲟⲕ ⲛ̄-ⲁⲣⲭⲱⲛ ⲁⲩⲱ ⲛ̄-ⲣⲉϥϯ-ϩⲁⲡ ⲉϩⲣⲁⲓ̈ ⲉϫⲱⲛ? ⲙⲏ ⲉⲕⲟⲩⲱϣ ⲛ̄ⲧⲟⲕ ⲉ-ϩⲟⲧⲃⲉⲧ ⲛ̄-ⲑⲉ ⲛ̄ⲧⲁⲕϩⲱⲧⲃ̄ ⲙ̄-ⲡⲣⲙ̄ⲛ̄ⲕⲏⲙⲉ ⲛ̄-ⲥⲁϥ?" ⲁϥⲣ̄-ϩⲟⲧⲉ ⲇⲉ ⲛ̄ϭⲓ-ⲙⲱⲩ̈ⲥⲏⲥ, ⲉϥϫⲱ ⲙ̄ⲙⲟⲥ ϫⲉ "ⲉⲉⲓⲉ ⲁ-ⲡϣⲁϫⲉ ⲟⲩⲱⲛϩ ⲉⲃⲟⲗ ⲛ̄-ⲧⲉⲉⲓϩⲉ!"

15 ⲁ-ⲫⲁⲣⲁⲱ ⲥⲱⲧⲙ̄ ⲉ-ⲡⲉⲉⲓϣⲁϫⲉ, ⲁϥϣⲓⲛⲉ ⲛ̄ⲥⲁ-ϩⲱⲧⲃ̄ ⲙ̄-ⲙⲱⲩ̈ⲥⲏⲥ. ⲁϥⲡⲱⲧ ⲛ̄ⲇⲉ ⲛ̄ϭⲓ-ⲙⲱⲩ̈ⲥⲏⲥ ⲛ̄ⲛⲁϩⲣⲛ̄-ϥⲟ ⲙ̄-ⲫⲁⲣⲁⲱ, ⲁϥⲟⲩⲱϩ ⲉϩⲣⲁⲓ̈ ⲉϫⲙ̄-ⲡⲕⲁϩ ⲙ̄-ⲙⲁⲇⲓϩⲁ́ⲙ. ⲛ̄ⲧⲉⲣⲉϥⲉⲓ ⲇⲉ ⲉϩⲣⲁⲓ̈ ⲉ-ⲡⲕⲁϩ ⲙ̄-ⲙⲁⲇⲓϩⲁ́ⲙ,[12] ⲁϥⲙⲟⲟⲥ ⲉϩⲣⲁⲓ̈ ⲉϫⲛ̄-ⲧϣⲱⲧⲉ.

16 ⲡⲟⲩⲏⲏⲃ ⲛ̄ⲇⲉ ⲙ̄-ⲙⲁⲇⲓϩⲁ́ⲙ ⲛⲉ-ⲩⲛ̄ⲧⲁϥ ⲙ̄ⲙⲁⲩ ⲛ̄-ⲥⲁϣϥⲉ ⲛ̄-ϣⲉⲉⲣⲉ, ⲉⲩⲙⲟⲟⲛⲉ ⲛ̄-ⲛⲉⲥⲟⲟⲩ ⲙ̄-ⲡⲉⲩⲉⲓⲱⲧ. ⲁⲩⲉⲓ ⲛ̄ⲇⲉ ⲁⲩⲥⲱⲕ ϣⲁⲛⲧⲟⲩⲙⲟⲩϩ ⲛ̄-ⲧϭⲱⲧ ⲛ̄ⲥⲉⲧⲥⲟ ⲛ̄-ⲛⲉⲥⲟⲟⲩ ⲙ̄-ⲡⲉⲩⲉⲓⲱⲧ ⲓ̈ⲟⲑⲟⲣ. 17 ⲁ-ⲛ̄ϣⲟⲟⲥ ⲛ̄ⲇⲉ ⲉⲓ, ⲁⲩⲛⲟϫⲟⲩ ⲉⲃⲟⲗ. ⲁϥⲧⲱⲟⲩⲛ ⲛ̄ⲇⲉ ⲛ̄ϭⲓ-ⲙⲱⲩ̈ⲥⲏⲥ, ⲁϥⲛⲁϩⲙⲟⲩ ⲙⲛ̄-ⲛⲉⲩⲉⲥⲟⲟⲩ ⲉⲃⲟⲗ ϩⲓⲧⲟⲟⲧⲟⲩ ⲛ̄-ⲛ̄ϣⲟⲟⲥ ⲁϥⲥⲕ̄-ⲙⲟⲟⲩ ⲛⲁⲩ ⲁϥⲧⲥⲟ ⲛ̄-ⲛⲉⲩⲉⲥⲟⲟⲩ.

18 ⲛ̄ⲧⲉⲣⲟⲩⲉⲓ[13] ⲛ̄ⲇⲉ ϣⲁ-ⲓ̈ⲟⲑⲟⲣ ⲡⲉⲩⲉⲓⲱⲧ, ⲡⲉϫⲁϥ ⲛⲁⲩ ϫⲉ "ⲉⲧⲃⲉ-ⲟⲩ ⲁⲧⲉⲧⲛ̄ϭⲉⲡⲏ ⲉ-ⲉⲓ ⲙ̄-ⲡⲟⲟⲩ?"

19 ⲛ̄ⲧⲟⲟⲩ ⲛ̄ⲇⲉ ⲡⲉϫⲁⲩ ϫⲉ "ⲟⲩⲣⲱⲙⲉ ⲛ̄-ⲣⲙ̄ⲛ̄ⲕⲏⲙⲉ ⲡⲉⲛⲧⲁϥⲛⲁϩⲙⲛ̄ ⲉⲃⲟⲗ ϩⲓⲧⲟⲟⲧⲟⲩ ⲛ̄-ⲛ̄ϣⲟⲟⲥ, ⲁϥⲥⲕ̄-ⲙⲟⲟⲩ ⲛⲁⲛ ⲁϥⲧⲥⲟ ⲛ̄-ⲛⲉⲛⲉⲥⲟⲟⲩ."

---

11. Emended from ⲙ̄ⲙⲟϥ.
12. ⲛ̄ⲧⲉⲣⲉϥⲉⲓ ⲇⲉ ⲉϩⲣⲁⲓ̈ ⲉ-ⲡⲕⲁϩ ⲙ̄-ⲙⲁⲇⲓϩⲁ́ⲙ added here as in Greek (perhaps a haplography, an accidental skipping due to similar wording with the previous phrase).
13. Emended from ⲛ̄ⲧⲁⲣⲟⲩⲉⲓ.

20 ⲛ̄ⲧⲟϥ ⲛ̄ⲇⲉ ⲡⲉϫⲁϥ ⲛ̄-ⲛⲉϥϣⲉⲉⲣⲉ ϫⲉ "ⲁⲩⲱ ⲉϥⲧⲱⲛ? ⲉⲧⲃⲉ-ⲟⲩ ⲁⲧⲉⲧⲛ̄ⲕⲁ-ⲡⲣⲱⲙⲉ ⲉⲃⲟⲗ ⲛ̄-ⲧⲉⲉⲓϩⲉ? ⲙⲟⲩⲧⲉ ϭⲉ ⲉⲣⲟϥ ϫⲉ ⲉϥⲉⲟⲩⲱⲙ ⲛ̄-ⲟⲩⲟⲉⲓⲕ!"

21 ⲙⲱⲩ̈ⲥⲏⲥ ⲇⲉ ⲁϥⲟⲩⲱϩ ⲙⲛ̄-ⲡⲣⲱⲙⲉ. ⲁϥϯ ⲛ̄-ⲥⲉⲫⲫⲱⲣⲁ ⲧⲉϥϣⲉⲉⲣⲉ ⲙ̄-ⲙⲱⲩ̈ⲥⲏⲥ ⲛ̄-ⲥϩⲓⲙⲉ. 22 ⲁⲥⲱⲱ, ⲁⲥϫⲡⲟ ⲛ̄-ⲟⲩϣⲏⲣⲉ. ⲁ-ⲙⲱⲩ̈ⲥⲏⲥ ⲙⲟⲩⲧⲉ ⲉ-ⲡⲉϥⲣⲁⲛ ϫⲉ ⲅⲏⲣⲥⲁⲙ, ⲉϥϫⲱ ⲙ̄ⲙⲟⲥ ϫⲉ "ⲁⲛⲅ̄-ⲟⲩⲣⲙ̄ⲛ̄ϭⲟⲉⲓⲗⲉ ϩⲛ̄-ⲟⲩⲕⲁϩ ⲉ-ⲙ̄-ⲡⲱⲓ̈ ⲁⲛ ⲡⲉ."[14]

23 ⲙⲛ̄ⲛ̄ⲥⲁ-ⲛⲉϩⲟⲟⲩ[15] ⲇⲉ ⲉⲧ-ⲛⲁϣⲱⲟⲩ ⲉⲧ-ⲙ̄ⲙⲁⲩ, ⲁϥⲙⲟⲩ ⲛ̄ϭⲓ-ⲡⲣ̄ⲣⲟ ⲛ̄-ⲕⲏⲙⲉ. ⲁ-ⲛ̄ϣⲏⲣⲉ ⲛ̄ⲇⲉ ⲙ̄-ⲡⲓⲥⲣⲁⲏⲗ ⲁϣ-ⲁϩⲟⲙ ⲉⲃⲟⲗ ϩⲛ̄-ⲛⲉϩⲃⲏⲩⲉ ⲉⲧ-ⲛⲁϣⲧ̄, ⲁⲩⲱ ⲉⲃⲟⲗ, ⲁ-ⲡⲉⲩⲁϣⲕⲁⲕ ⲃⲱⲕ ⲉϩⲣⲁⲓ̈ ϣⲁ-ⲡⲛⲟⲩⲧⲉ ⲉⲃⲟⲗ ϩⲛ̄-ⲛⲉϩⲃⲏⲩⲉ. 24 ⲡⲛⲟⲩⲧⲉ ⲛ̄ⲇⲉ ⲁϥⲥⲱⲧⲙ̄ ⲉ-ⲡⲉⲩⲁϣⲕⲁⲕ ⲙⲛ̄-ⲡⲉⲩⲁϣ-ⲁϩⲟⲙ, ⲁⲩⲱ ⲁϥⲣ̄-ⲡⲙⲉⲉⲩⲉ ⲛ̄ϭⲓ-ⲡⲛⲟⲩⲧⲉ ⲛ̄-ⲧⲉϥⲇⲓⲁⲑⲏⲕⲏ, ⲧⲁⲓ̈ ⲛ̄ⲧⲁϥⲥⲙⲛ̄ⲧⲥ̄ ⲙⲛ̄-ⲁⲃⲣⲁϩⲁⲙ ⲁⲩⲱ ⲓ̈ⲥⲁⲁ́ⲕ[16] ⲙⲛ̄-ⲓ̈ⲁⲕⲱⲃ. 25 ⲁ-ⲡⲛⲟⲩⲧⲉ ϭⲱϣⲧ̄ ⲉϫⲛ̄-ⲛ̄ϣⲏⲣⲉ ⲙ̄-ⲡⲓⲥⲣⲁⲏⲗ, ⲁϥⲣ̄-ⲡⲙⲉⲉⲩⲉ.

3.1 ⲙⲱⲩ̈ⲥⲏⲥ ⲇⲉ ⲛⲉϥⲙⲟⲟⲛⲉ ⲛ̄-ⲛⲉⲥⲟⲟⲩ ⲙ̄-ⲡⲉϥϣⲟⲙ, ⲡⲟⲩⲏⲏⲃ ⲙ̄-ⲙⲁⲇⲓϩⲁ́ⲙ. ⲁϥⲉⲓⲛⲉ ⲛ̄-ⲛⲉⲥⲟⲟⲩ ϩⲁⲣⲁⲧⲥ̄ ⲛ̄-ⲧⲉⲣⲏⲙⲟⲥ, ⲁϥⲉⲓ ⲉϩⲣⲁⲓ̈ ⲉ-ⲡⲧⲟⲟⲩ ⲙ̄-ⲡⲛⲟⲩⲧⲉ, ⲭⲱⲣⲏ́ⲃ ⲡⲧⲟⲟⲩ ⲙ̄-ⲡϫⲟⲉⲓⲥ ⲡⲛⲟⲩⲧⲉ. 2 ⲁϥⲟⲩⲱⲛϩ̄ ⲇⲉ ⲛⲁϥ ⲉⲃⲟⲗ ⲛ̄ϭⲓ-ⲡⲁⲅⲅⲉⲗⲟⲥ ⲙ̄-ⲡϫⲟⲉⲓⲥ ϩⲛ̄-ⲟⲩϣⲁϩ ⲛ̄-ⲥⲁⲧⲉ ⲉⲃⲟⲗ ϩⲛ̄-ⲟⲩⲃⲁ́ⲧⲟⲥ. ⲁⲩⲱ ⲁϥⲛⲁⲩ ϫⲉ ⲡϣⲏⲛ ⲙⲉⲛ ⲙⲟⲩϩ ϩⲛ̄-ⲟⲩⲕⲱϩⲧ̄, ⲡϣⲏⲛ ⲛ̄ⲇⲉ ⲛⲉϥⲣⲱⲕϩ̄ ⲁⲛ ⲡⲉ. 3 ⲡⲉϫⲁϥ ⲛ̄ⲇⲉ ⲛ̄ϭⲓ-ⲙⲱⲩ̈ⲥⲏⲥ ϫⲉ "ϯⲛⲁⲃⲱⲕ ⲧⲁⲛⲁⲩ ⲉ-ⲡⲉⲓⲛⲟϭ ⲛ̄-ϩⲟⲣⲁⲙⲁ, ϫⲉ ⲙ̄-ⲡϣⲏⲛ ⲣⲱⲕϩ̄ ⲁⲛ!"

4 ⲛ̄ⲧⲉⲣⲉ-ⲡϫⲟⲉⲓⲥ ⲛ̄ⲇⲉ ⲛⲁⲩ ϫⲉ ϥⲛⲁϩⲱⲛ ⲉϩⲟⲩⲛ, ⲁ-ⲡϫⲟⲉⲓⲥ ⲙⲟⲩⲧⲉ ⲉⲣⲟϥ ⲉⲃⲟⲗ ϩⲛ̄-ⲡϣⲏⲛ, ⲉϥϫⲱ ⲙ̄ⲙⲟⲥ ϫⲉ "ⲙⲱⲩ̈ⲥⲏⲥ! ⲙⲱⲩ̈ⲥⲏⲥ!"

ⲛ̄ⲧⲟϥ ⲇⲉ ⲡⲉϫⲁϥ "ⲟⲩ ⲡⲉⲧ-ϣⲟⲟⲡ?"

5 ⲡⲉϫⲁϥ ⲛ̄ⲇⲉ ⲛⲁϥ ϫⲉ "ⲙ̄ⲡⲣ̄ϩⲱⲛ ⲉϩⲟⲩⲛ ⲉ-ⲡⲉⲉⲓⲙⲁ! ⲃⲱⲗ ⲉⲃⲟⲗ ⲙ̄-ⲡⲧⲟⲟⲩⲉ ⲉⲧ-ϩⲛ̄-ⲛⲉⲕⲟⲩⲉⲣⲏⲧⲉ, ⲡⲙⲁ ⲅⲁⲣ ⲉⲧⲕⲁϩⲉⲣⲁⲧⲕ̄ ⲛ̄ϩⲏⲧϥ̄ ⲟⲩⲕⲁϩ ⲉϥⲟⲩⲁⲁⲃ ⲡⲉ." 6 ⲡⲉϫⲁϥ ⲟⲛ ⲛⲁϥ ϫⲉ "ⲁⲛⲟⲕ ⲡⲉ ⲡⲛⲟⲩⲧⲉ ⲙ̄-ⲡⲉⲕⲉⲓⲱⲧ ⲁⲃⲣⲁϩⲁⲙ, ⲡⲛⲟⲩⲧⲉ ⲛ̄-ⲓ̈ⲥⲁⲁ́ⲕ, ⲡⲛⲟⲩⲧⲉ ⲛ̄-ⲓ̈ⲁⲕⲱⲃ." ⲁϥⲕⲱⲧⲉ ⲇⲉ ⲙ̄-ⲡⲉϥϩⲟ ⲉⲃⲟⲗ ⲛ̄ϭⲓ-ⲙⲱⲩ̈ⲥⲏⲥ, ⲛⲉ-ⲁϥⲣ̄-ϩⲟⲧⲉ ⲅⲁⲣ ⲉ-ϭⲱϣⲧ̄ ⲙ̄-ⲡⲉⲙⲧⲟ ⲉⲃⲟⲗ ⲙ̄-ⲡⲛⲟⲩⲧⲉ.

7 ⲡⲉϫⲁϥ ⲛ̄ⲇⲉ ⲛ̄ϭⲓ-ⲡϫⲟⲉⲓⲥ ⲙ̄-ⲙⲱⲩ̈ⲥⲏⲥ ϫⲉ "ϩⲛ̄-ⲟⲩⲛⲁⲩ ⲁⲓ̈ⲛⲁⲩ ⲉ-ⲡⲉⲧϩⲙ̄ⲕⲟ ⲙ̄-ⲡⲁⲗⲁⲟⲥ, ⲡⲁⲓ̈ ⲉⲧ-ϣⲟⲟⲡ ϩⲛ̄-ⲕⲏⲙⲉ, ⲁⲩⲱ ⲁⲓ̈ⲥⲱⲧⲙ̄ ⲉ-ⲡⲉⲩⲁϣⲕⲁⲕ ⲉⲃⲟⲗ ϩⲛ̄-ⲛ̄ⲉⲣⲅⲟⲇⲓⲱ́ⲕⲧⲏⲥ, ϯⲥⲟⲟⲩⲛ ⲅⲁⲣ ⲙ̄-ⲡⲉⲩϩⲓⲥⲉ. 8 ⲁⲩⲱ ⲁⲓ̈ⲉⲓ ⲉⲡⲉⲥⲛⲧ ⲉ-ⲛⲁϩⲙⲟⲩ ⲉⲃⲟⲗ ϩⲛ̄-ⲧϭⲓϫ ⲛ̄-ⲣ̄ⲣⲙ̄ⲛ̄ⲕⲏⲙⲉ, ⲉ-ⲛ̄ⲧⲟⲩ ⲉⲃⲟⲗ ϩⲛ̄-ⲡⲕⲁϩ ⲛ̄-ⲕⲏⲙⲉ, ⲉ-ϫⲓⲧⲟⲩ ⲉϩⲟⲩⲛ ⲉ-ⲩⲕⲁϩ ⲉ-ⲛⲁⲛⲟⲩϥ ⲁⲩⲱ ⲉ-ⲛⲁϣⲱϥ, ⲉ-ⲩⲕⲁϩ ⲉϥϣⲟⲩⲉ-ⲉⲣⲱⲧⲉ ⲉⲃⲟⲗ ϩⲓ-ⲉⲃⲓⲱ, ⲉϩⲣⲁⲓ̈ ⲉ-ⲡⲙⲁ ⲛ̄-ⲛⲉⲭⲁⲛⲁⲛⲁⲓⲟⲥ ⲙⲛ̄-ⲛⲉⲭⲉⲧⲧⲁⲓⲟⲥ ⲙⲛ̄-ⲛ̄ⲁⲙⲟⲣⲣⲁⲓⲟⲥ ⲙⲛ̄-ⲛⲉⲫⲉⲣⲉⲍⲁⲓⲟⲥ ⲙⲛ̄-ⲛⲉⲩⲁⲓⲟⲥ ⲙⲛ̄-ⲛⲉⲅⲉⲣⲅⲉⲥⲁⲓⲟⲥ ⲙⲛ̄-ⲛ̄ⲓ̈ⲉⲃⲟⲩⲥⲁⲓⲟⲥ. 9 ⲧⲉⲛⲟⲩ ϭⲉ ⲉⲓⲥ! ⲡⲁϣⲕⲁⲕ ⲛ̄-ⲛ̄ϣⲏⲣⲉ ⲙ̄-ⲡⲓⲥⲣⲁⲏⲗ ⲁϥⲉⲓ ⲉϩⲣⲁⲓ̈ ⲉⲣⲟⲓ̈. ⲁⲛⲟⲕ ⲁⲓ̈ⲛⲁⲩ ⲉ-ⲡⲉⲩϩⲟϫϩ̄ϫ̄, ⲛⲁⲓ̈ ⲉⲧⲉⲣⲉ-ⲛ̄ⲣⲙ̄ⲛ̄ⲕⲏⲙⲉ ⲑⲗⲓⲃⲉ ⲙ̄ⲙⲟⲟⲩ ⲛ̄ϩⲏⲧϥ̄. 10 ⲧⲉⲛⲟⲩ ϭⲉ ⲁⲙⲟⲩ! ⲧⲁϫⲟⲟⲩⲕ ϣⲁ-ⲫⲁⲣⲁⲱ ⲡⲣ̄ⲣⲟ ⲛ̄-ⲕⲏⲙⲉ, ⲛ̄ⲅⲉⲓⲛⲉ ⲙ̄-ⲡⲁⲗⲁⲟⲥ ⲉⲃⲟⲗ, ⲛ̄ϣⲏⲣⲉ ⲙ̄-ⲡⲓⲥⲣⲁⲏⲗ, ⲉⲃⲟⲗ ϩⲛ̄-ⲡⲕⲁϩ ⲛ̄-ⲕⲏⲙⲉ."

11 ⲡⲉϫⲁϥ ⲛ̄ⲇⲉ ⲛ̄ϭⲓ-ⲙⲱⲩ̈ⲥⲏⲥ ⲛ̄ⲛⲁϩⲣⲛ̄-ⲡⲛⲟⲩⲧⲉ ϫⲉ "ⲁⲛⲅ̄-ⲛⲓⲙ ⲁⲛⲟⲕ ϫⲉ ⲉⲉⲓⲉⲃⲱⲕ ϣⲁ-ⲫⲁⲣⲁⲱ ⲡⲣ̄ⲣⲟ ⲛ̄-ⲕⲏⲙⲉ ⲁⲩⲱ ϫⲉ ⲉⲉⲓⲉⲉⲓⲛⲉ ⲉⲃⲟⲗ ϩⲛ̄-ⲡⲕⲁϩ ⲛ̄-ⲕⲏⲙⲉ ⲙ̄-ⲡⲗⲁⲟⲥ?"

12 ⲡⲉϫⲁϥ ⲛ̄ⲇⲉ ⲛ̄ϭⲓ-ⲡⲛⲟⲩⲧⲉ ⲙ̄-ⲙⲱⲩ̈ⲥⲏⲥ, ⲉϥϫⲱ ⲙ̄ⲙⲟⲥ ϫⲉ "ϯⲛⲁϣⲱⲡⲉ ⲛⲙ̄ⲙⲁⲕ, ⲁⲩⲱ ⲡⲁⲓ̈ ⲛⲁϣⲱⲡⲉ ⲛⲁⲕ ⲙ̄-ⲙⲁⲉⲓⲛ ϫⲉ ⲁⲛⲟⲕ ⲡⲉⲧ-ⲛⲁϫⲟⲟⲩⲕ, ϩⲙ̄-ⲡⲧⲣⲉⲕⲉⲓⲛⲉ ⲉⲃⲟⲗ ⲙ̄-ⲡⲁⲗⲁⲟⲥ ϩⲙ̄-ⲡⲕⲁϩ ⲛ̄-ⲕⲏⲙⲉ, ⲛ̄ⲧⲉⲧⲛ̄ϣⲙ̄ϣⲉ ⲙ̄-ⲡⲛⲟⲩⲧⲉ ϩⲣⲁⲓ̈ ϩⲙ̄-ⲡⲧⲟⲟⲩ."

---

14. PB 16 has an added marginal note tagged here (cf. Exod 18:4): ⲁⲥϫⲡⲟ ⲇⲉ ⲛ̄-ⲕⲉϣⲏⲣⲉ, ⲁϥⲙⲟⲩⲧⲉ ⲉ-ⲡⲉϥⲣⲁⲛ ϫⲉ ⲉⲗⲓⲉⲍⲉⲣ.
15. Emended from ⲙ̄ⲙⲛ̄ⲛ̄ⲥⲁ-ⲛⲉϩⲟⲟⲩ.
16. Emended from ⲓ̈ⲥⲁⲕ (here and in further occurrences).

13 ⲡⲉϫⲁϥ ⲛ̄ⲇⲉ ⲛ̄ϭⲓ-ⲙⲱⲩ̈ⲥⲏⲥ ⲛ̄ⲛⲁϩⲣⲛ̄-ⲡⲛⲟⲩⲧⲉ ϫⲉ "ⲉⲓⲥ-ϩⲏⲏⲧⲉ! ⲁⲛⲟⲕ ϯⲛⲁⲃⲱⲕ ϣⲁ-ⲛ̄ϣⲏⲣⲉ ⲙ̄-ⲡⲓⲥⲣⲁⲏⲗ ⲧⲁϫⲟⲟⲥ ⲛⲁⲩ ϫⲉ 'ⲡⲛⲟⲩⲧⲉ ⲛ̄-ⲛⲉⲧⲛ̄ⲉⲓⲟⲧⲉ ⲡⲉⲛⲧⲁϥⲧⲛ̄ⲛⲟⲟⲩⲧ ϣⲁⲣⲱⲧⲛ̄,' ⲛ̄ⲥⲉϫⲛⲟⲩⲉⲓ ϫⲉ 'ⲛⲓⲙ ⲡⲉ ⲡⲉϥⲣⲁⲛ?' ⲉⲉⲓⲛⲁϫⲟⲟⲥ ⲛⲁⲩ ϫⲉ ⲟⲩ?"

14 ⲡⲉϫⲁϥ ⲛ̄ϭⲓ-ⲡⲛⲟⲩⲧⲉ ⲙ̄-ⲙⲱⲩ̈ⲥⲏⲥ ϫⲉ "ⲁⲛⲟⲕ ⲡⲉ ⲡⲉⲧ-ϣⲟⲟⲡ. ⲧⲁⲓ̈ ⲧⲉ ⲑⲉ ⲉⲧⲕ̄ⲛⲁϫⲟⲟⲥ ⲛ̄-ⲛ̄ϣⲏⲣⲉ ⲙ̄-ⲡⲓⲥⲣⲁⲏⲗ ϫⲉ 'ⲡⲉⲧ-ϣⲟⲟⲡ ⲡⲉ ⲛ̄ⲧⲁϥⲧⲛ̄ⲛⲟⲟⲩⲧ ϣⲁⲣⲱⲧⲛ̄.'"

15 ⲡⲉϫⲁϥ ⲟⲛ ⲛ̄ϭⲓ-ⲡⲛⲟⲩⲧⲉ ⲙ̄-ⲙⲱⲩ̈ⲥⲏⲥ ϫⲉ "ⲧⲁⲓ̈ ⲧⲉ ⲑⲉ ⲉⲧⲕ̄ⲛⲁϫⲟⲟⲥ ⲛ̄-ⲛ̄ϣⲏⲣⲉ ⲙ̄-ⲡⲓⲥⲣⲁⲏⲗ ϫⲉ 'ⲡϫⲟⲉⲓⲥ ⲡⲛⲟⲩⲧⲉ ⲛ̄-ⲛⲉⲧⲛ̄ⲉⲓⲟⲧⲉ, ⲡⲛⲟⲩⲧⲉ ⲛ̄-ⲁⲃⲣⲁϩⲁⲙ, ⲡⲛⲟⲩⲧⲉ ⲛ̄-ⲓ̈ⲥⲁⲁⲕ, ⲡⲛⲟⲩⲧⲉ ⲛ̄-ⲓ̈ⲁⲕⲱⲃ, ⲡⲉ ⲛ̄ⲧⲁϥⲧⲛ̄ⲛⲟⲟⲩⲧ ϣⲁⲣⲱⲧⲛ̄.

ⲡⲁⲓ̈ ⲡⲉ ⲡⲁⲣⲁⲛ ⲛ̄-ϣⲁ-ⲉⲛⲉϩ,
ⲁⲩⲱ ⲛ̄-ⲣ̄-ⲡⲙⲉⲉⲩⲉ ϫⲓⲛ-ⲛ̄ϫⲱⲙ ϣⲁ-ϫⲱⲙ.

16 "ⲃⲱⲕ ⲉϩⲟⲩⲛ ⲛ̄ⲅⲥⲱⲟⲩϩ ⲛ̄-ⲛ̄ϩⲗ̄ⲗⲟⲉⲓ ⲛ̄-ⲛ̄ϣⲏⲣⲉ ⲙ̄-ⲡⲓⲥⲣⲁⲏⲗ ⲛ̄ⲅϫⲟⲟⲥ ⲛⲁⲩ ϫⲉ 'ⲡϫⲟⲉⲓⲥ ⲡⲛⲟⲩⲧⲉ ⲛ̄-ⲛⲉⲧⲛ̄ⲉⲓⲟⲧⲉ ⲡⲉ ⲛ̄ⲧⲁϥⲟⲩⲱⲛϩ̄ ⲛⲁⲓ̈ ⲉⲃⲟⲗ, ⲡⲛⲟⲩⲧⲉ ⲛ̄-ⲁⲃⲣⲁϩⲁⲙ, ⲡⲛⲟⲩⲧⲉ ⲛ̄-ⲓ̈ⲥⲁⲁⲕ, ⲡⲛⲟⲩⲧⲉ ⲛ̄-ⲓ̈ⲁⲕⲱⲃ, ⲉϥϫⲱ ⲙ̄ⲙⲟⲥ ϫⲉ "ϩⲛ̄-ⲟⲩϭⲙ̄-ⲡϣⲓⲛⲉ ⲁⲓ̈ϭⲛ̄-ⲡⲉⲧⲛ̄ϣⲓⲛⲉ ⲁⲩⲱ ⲛⲉⲛⲧⲁⲩϣⲱⲡⲉ ⲙ̄ⲙⲱⲧⲛ̄ ϩⲣⲁⲓ̈ ϩⲛ̄-ⲡⲕⲁϩ ⲛ̄-ⲕⲏⲙⲉ. 17 ⲁⲓ̈ϫⲟⲟⲥ ϫⲉ ϯⲛⲁⲛ̄-ⲧⲏⲩⲧⲛ̄ ⲉⲃⲟⲗ ϩⲛ̄-ⲡⲉⲧϩⲙ̄ⲕⲟ ⲛ̄-ⲣ̄ⲙⲛ̄ⲕⲏⲙⲉ ⲉϩⲣⲁⲓ̈ ⲉ-ⲡⲕⲁϩ ⲛ̄-ⲛⲉⲭⲁⲛⲁⲛⲁⲓ̈ⲟⲥ ⲙⲛ̄-ⲛⲉⲭⲉⲧⲧⲁⲓ̈ⲟⲥ ⲙⲛ̄-ⲛⲁⲙⲟⲣⲣⲁⲓ̈ⲟⲥ ⲙⲛ̄-ⲛⲉⲫⲉⲣⲉⲍⲁⲓ̈ⲟⲥ ⲙⲛ̄-ⲛ̄ⲅⲉⲣⲅⲉⲥⲁⲓ̈ⲟⲥ ⲙⲛ̄-ⲛ̄ⲓ̈ⲉⲃⲟⲩⲥⲁⲓ̈ⲟⲥ,¹⁷ ⲉ-ⲩⲕⲁϩ ⲉϥϣⲟⲩⲉ ⲉⲣⲱⲧⲉ ⲉⲃⲟⲗ ϩⲓ-ⲉⲃⲓⲱ."'

18 "ⲁⲩⲱ ⲥⲉⲛⲁⲥⲱⲧⲙ̄ ⲉ-ⲡⲉⲕϩⲣⲟⲟⲩ. ⲉⲕⲉⲃⲱⲕ ⲛ̄ⲇⲉ ⲉϩⲟⲩⲛ, ⲛ̄ⲧⲟⲕ ⲙⲛ̄-ⲛ̄ϩⲗ̄ⲗⲟⲉⲓ ⲛ̄-ⲛ̄ϣⲏⲣⲉ ⲙ̄-ⲡⲓⲥⲣⲁⲏⲗ, ϣⲁ-ⲫⲁⲣⲁⲱ ⲡⲣ̄ⲣⲟ ⲛ̄-ⲕⲏⲙⲉ ⲛ̄ⲅϫⲟⲟⲥ ⲛⲁϥ ϫⲉ 'ⲡϫⲟⲉⲓⲥ ⲡⲛⲟⲩⲧⲉ ⲛ̄-ⲛ̄ϩⲉⲃⲣⲁⲓ̈ⲟⲥ ⲡⲉⲛⲧⲁϥⲧⲁϩⲙⲛ̄, ⲧⲛ̄ⲛⲁⲃⲱⲕ ϭⲉ ⲛ̄-ⲟⲩϩⲓⲏ ⲛ̄-ϣⲟⲙⲧ̄ ⲛ̄-ϩⲟⲟⲩ ⲙ̄-ⲙⲟⲟϣⲉ ⲉϩⲣⲁⲓ̈ ⲉ-ⲡϫⲁⲓ̈ⲉ ϫⲉⲕⲁⲁⲥ ⲉⲛⲉϣⲱⲱⲧ ⲛ̄ⲛⲁϩⲣⲛ̄-ⲡϫⲟⲉⲓⲥ ⲡⲉⲛⲛⲟⲩⲧⲉ.'

19 "ⲁⲛⲟⲕ ⲛ̄ⲇⲉ ϯⲥⲟⲟⲩⲛ ϫⲉ ⲛ̄ϥⲛⲁⲕⲁ-ⲧⲏⲩⲧⲛ̄ ⲉⲃⲟⲗ ⲁⲛ ⲛ̄ϭⲓ-ⲫⲁⲣⲁⲱ ⲡⲣ̄ⲣⲟ ⲛ̄-ⲕⲏⲙⲉ ⲉ-ⲃⲱⲕ ⲉⲓⲙⲏⲧⲓ ϩⲛ̄-ⲟⲩϭⲓϫ ⲉⲥϫⲟⲟⲣ. 20 ⲧⲁⲥⲟⲟⲩⲧⲛ̄ ⲉⲃⲟⲗ ⲛ̄-ⲧⲁϭⲓϫ ⲧⲁϣⲁⲁⲣⲉ ⲉ-ⲣ̄ⲙⲛ̄ⲕⲏⲙⲉ¹⁸ ϩⲣⲁⲓ̈ ϩⲛ̄-ⲛⲁϣⲡⲏⲣⲉ ⲧⲏⲣⲟⲩ ⲉⲧⲛⲁⲁⲁⲩ ϩⲣⲁⲓ̈ ⲛ̄ϩⲏⲧⲟⲩ. ⲙⲛ̄ⲛ̄ⲥⲁ-ⲛⲁⲓ̈ ϥⲛⲁⲕⲁ-ⲧⲏⲩⲧⲛ̄ ⲉⲃⲟⲗ.

21 "ⲛ̄ⲧⲁϯ ⲛ̄-ⲟⲩⲭⲁⲣⲓⲥ ⲙ̄-ⲡⲉⲉⲓⲗⲁⲟⲥ ⲙ̄-ⲡⲉⲙⲧⲟ ⲉⲃⲟⲗ ⲛ̄-ⲣ̄ⲙⲛ̄ⲕⲏⲙⲉ. ⲉⲧⲉⲧⲛ̄ⲉⲓ ⲇⲉ ⲉⲧⲉⲧⲛ̄ⲛⲁⲃⲱⲕ ⲉⲃⲟⲗ ⲛ̄ⲛⲉⲧⲛ̄ⲃⲱⲕ ⲉⲧⲉⲧⲛ̄ϣⲟⲩⲉⲓⲧ. 22 ⲉⲥⲉϫⲓ ⲛ̄ϭⲓ-ⲟⲩⲥϩⲓⲙⲉ ⲉⲃⲟⲗ ϩⲓⲧⲟⲟⲧⲥ̄ ⲛ̄-ⲧⲉⲧ-ϩⲓⲧⲟⲩⲱⲥ ⲙⲛ̄-ⲧⲉⲥⲙⲛ̄-ⲛⲉⲓ ⲛ̄-ϩⲛ̄ϩⲛⲁⲁⲩ ⲛ̄-ϩⲁⲧ ⲙⲛ̄-ϩⲛ̄ϩⲛⲁⲁⲩ ⲛ̄-ⲛⲟⲩⲃ ⲙⲛ̄-ϩⲛ̄ϩⲟⲉⲓⲧⲉ. ⲛ̄ⲧⲉⲧⲛ̄ⲧⲁⲗⲟⲟⲩ ⲉϩⲣⲁⲓ̈ ⲉϫⲛ̄-ⲛⲉⲧⲛ̄ϣⲏⲣⲉ ⲙⲛ̄-ⲛⲉⲧⲛ̄ϣⲉⲉⲣⲉ, ⲛ̄ⲧⲉⲧⲛ̄ϣⲱⲗ ⲛ̄-ⲣ̄ⲙⲛ̄ⲕⲏⲙⲉ."

4.1 ⲁϥⲟⲩⲱϣⲃ̄ ⲛ̄ⲇⲉ ⲛ̄ϭⲓ-ⲙⲱⲩ̈ⲥⲏⲥ, ⲉϥϫⲱ ⲙ̄ⲙⲟⲥ ϫⲉ "ⲉϣⲱⲡⲉ ϭⲉ ⲉⲩⲧⲙ̄ⲧⲁⲛϩⲟⲩⲧ ⲣⲉ, ⲁⲩⲱ ⲛ̄ⲥⲉⲧⲙ̄ⲥⲱⲧⲙ̄ ⲉ-ⲡⲁϩⲣⲟⲟⲩ, ⲥⲉⲛⲁϫⲟⲟⲥ ⲅⲁⲣ ϫⲉ 'ⲙ̄ⲡⲉ-ⲡⲛⲟⲩⲧⲉ ⲟⲩⲱⲛϩ ⲛⲁⲕ ⲉⲃⲟⲗ,' ⲟⲩ ⲡⲉ ⲉϯⲛⲁϫⲟⲟϥ ⲛⲁⲩ?"

2 ⲡⲉϫⲁϥ ⲛ̄ⲇⲉ ⲛⲁϥ ⲛ̄ϭⲓ-ⲡϫⲟⲉⲓⲥ ϫⲉ "ⲟⲩ ⲡⲉ ⲡⲁⲓ̈ ⲉⲧ-ϩⲛ̄-ⲧⲉⲕϭⲓϫ?"

ⲛ̄ⲧⲟϥ ⲛ̄ⲇⲉ ⲡⲉϫⲁϥ ϫⲉ "ⲟⲩϭⲉⲣⲱⲃ ⲡⲉ."

3 ⲡⲉϫⲁϥ ⲛⲁϥ ϫⲉ "ⲛⲟⲩϫⲉ ⲙ̄ⲙⲟϥ ⲉϩⲣⲁⲓ̈ ⲉϫⲙ̄-ⲡⲕⲁϩ." ⲁϥⲛⲟⲩϫⲉ ⲙ̄ⲙⲟϥ ⲉϩⲣⲁⲓ̈ ⲉϫⲙ̄-ⲡⲕⲁϩ, ⲁϥϣⲱⲡⲉ ⲛ̄-ⲟⲩϩⲟϥ. ⲁ-ⲙⲱⲩ̈ⲥⲏⲥ ⲡⲱⲧ ϩⲁⲧⲉϥϩⲏ.

4 ⲡⲉϫⲁϥ ⲛⲁϥ ⲛ̄ϭⲓ-ⲡϫⲟⲉⲓⲥ ϫⲉ "ⲥⲟⲟⲩⲧⲛ̄ ⲉⲃⲟⲗ ⲛ̄-ⲧⲉⲕϭⲓϫ ⲛ̄ⲅⲁⲙⲁϩⲧⲉ ⲙ̄-ⲡⲉϥⲥⲛⲧ." ⲁϥⲥⲟⲟⲩⲧⲛ̄ ⲛ̄-ⲧⲉϥϭⲓϫ ⲉⲃⲟⲗ, ⲁϥⲁⲙⲁϩⲧⲉ ⲙ̄-ⲡⲉϥⲥⲁⲧ, ⲁϥϣⲱⲡⲉ ⲛ̄-ⲟⲩϭⲉⲣⲱⲃ ϩⲛ̄-ⲧⲉϥϭⲓϫ. 5 "ϫⲉⲕⲁⲁⲥ ⲉⲩⲉⲧⲁⲛϩⲟⲩⲧⲕ̄ ϫⲉ ⲁ-ⲡϫⲟⲉⲓⲥ ⲡⲛⲟⲩⲧⲉ ⲛ̄-ⲛⲉⲩⲉⲓⲟⲧⲉ ⲟⲩⲱⲛϩ ⲛⲁⲕ ⲉⲃⲟⲗ, ⲡⲛⲟⲩⲧⲉ ⲛ̄-ⲁⲃⲣⲁϩⲁⲙ, ⲡⲛⲟⲩⲧⲉ ⲛ̄-ⲓ̈ⲥⲁⲁⲕ, ⲡⲛⲟⲩⲧⲉ ⲛ̄-ⲓ̈ⲁⲕⲱⲃ."

6 ⲡⲉϫⲁϥ ⲟⲛ ⲛⲁϥ ⲛ̄ϭⲓ-ⲡϫⲟⲉⲓⲥ ϫⲉ "ⲛⲟⲩϫⲉ ⲛ̄-ⲧⲉⲕϭⲓϫ ⲉϩⲟⲩⲛ ϩⲁ-ⲕⲟⲩⲟⲩⲛϥ̄." ⲁϥⲛⲟⲩϫⲉ ⲛ̄-ⲧⲉϥϭⲓϫ ϩⲁ-ⲕⲟⲩⲟⲩⲛϥ̄, ⲁⲩⲱ ⲁϥⲉⲓⲛⲉ ⲛ̄-ⲧⲉϥϭⲓϫ ⲉⲃⲟⲗ ϩⲁ-ⲕⲟⲩⲟⲩⲛϥ̄, ⲁⲥϣⲱⲡⲉ ⲛ̄ϭⲓ-ⲧⲉϥϭⲓϫ ⲛ̄-ⲑⲉ ⲛ̄-ⲟⲩⲭⲓⲱⲛ.

---

17. Emended from ⲙⲛ̄-ⲓ̈ⲉⲃⲟⲩⲥⲁⲓ̈ⲟⲥ.
18. Emended from ⲉ-ⲛ̄ⲣ̄ⲙⲛ̄ⲕⲏⲙⲉ.

7 ⲡⲉϫⲁϥ ⲟⲛ ⲛⲁϥ ϫⲉ "ⲛⲟⲩϫⲉ ⲛ̄-ⲧⲉⲕϭⲓϫ ⲉϩⲟⲩⲛ ϩⲁ-ⲕⲟⲩⲟⲩⲛϥ̄." ⲁϥⲛⲟⲩϫⲉ ⲛ̄-ⲧⲉϥϭⲓϫ ⲉϩⲟⲩⲛ ϩⲁ-ⲕⲟⲩⲟⲩⲛϥ̄, ⲁⲩⲱ ⲁϥⲉⲓⲛⲉ ⲉⲃⲟⲗ ϩⲁ-ⲕⲟⲩⲛϥ̄, ⲁⲥϣⲱⲡⲉ ⲟⲛ ⲛ̄-ⲧⲉⲥϩⲉ ⲛ̄-ⲡⲁϩⲁⲛ ⲛ̄-ⲧⲉϥⲥⲁⲣⲝ̄. 8 "ⲉϣⲱⲡⲉ ⲛ̄ⲇⲉ ⲉⲩⲧⲙ̄ⲧⲁⲛϩⲟⲩⲧⲕ̄ ϩⲙ̄-ⲡⲙⲁⲉⲓⲛ ⲛ̄-ϣⲟⲣⲡ̄, ⲥⲉⲛⲁⲧⲁⲛϩⲟⲩⲧⲕ̄ ϩⲙ̄-ⲡⲙⲁⲉⲓⲛ ⲛ̄-ϩⲁⲉ. 9 ⲉⲩⲧⲙ̄ⲧⲁⲛϩⲟⲩⲧⲕ̄ ϩⲙ̄-ⲡⲉⲓ̈ⲙⲁⲉⲓⲛ ⲥⲛⲁⲩ ⲛ̄ⲥⲉⲧⲙ̄ⲥⲱⲧⲙ̄ ⲉ-ⲧⲉⲕⲥⲙⲏ, ⲉⲕⲉϫⲓ ⲉⲃⲟⲗ ϩⲛ̄-ⲡⲙⲟⲟⲩ ⲙ̄-ⲡⲓⲉⲣⲟ ⲛⲅ̄ⲡⲁϩⲧ̄ ⲙ̄ⲙⲟϥ ⲉϫⲛ̄-ⲡⲉⲧ-ϣⲟⲩⲱⲟⲩ, ⲛϥ̄ϣⲱⲡⲉ ⲛ̄ϭⲓ-ⲡⲙⲟⲟⲩ, ⲡⲁⲓ̈ ⲉⲧⲕ̄ⲛⲁϫⲓⲧϥ̄ ⲉⲃⲟⲗ ϩⲛ̄-ⲡⲓⲉⲣⲟ, ⲉ-ⲩⲥⲛⲟϥ ϩⲣⲁⲓ̈ ϩⲓϫⲛ̄-ⲡⲉⲧ-ϣⲟⲩⲱⲟⲩ."

10 ⲡⲉϫⲁϥ ⲛ̄ⲇⲉ ⲛ̄ϭⲓ-ⲙⲱⲩ̈ⲥⲏⲥ ⲛ̄ⲛⲁϩⲣⲙ̄-ⲡϫⲟⲉⲓⲥ ϫⲉ "†ⲥⲟⲡⲥ̄ ⲙ̄ⲙⲟⲕ, ⲡϫⲟⲉⲓⲥ, ⲁⲛⲅ̄-ⲟⲩⲣⲉϥϣⲁϫⲉ ⲁⲛ ϩⲁⲑⲏ ⲛ̄-ⲥⲁϥ ⲙⲛ̄-ϣⲙ̄ⲧⲉ ⲡⲟⲟⲩ ⲛ̄-ϩⲟⲟⲩ ⲟⲩⲇⲉ ϫⲓⲛ-ⲧⲁⲕⲁⲣⲭⲉⲓ ⲛ̄-ϣⲁϫⲉ ⲙⲛ̄-ⲡⲉⲕϩⲙ̄ϩⲁⲗ, ϫⲉ ⲁⲛⲅ̄-ⲟⲩⲗⲁⲥ-ϣⲓⲣⲉ ⲁⲩⲱ ⲁⲛⲅ̄-ⲟⲩϩⲁⲥⲃ̄-ⲥⲙⲏ."

11 ⲡⲉϫⲁϥ ⲛ̄ⲇⲉ ⲛ̄ϭⲓ-ⲡϫⲟⲉⲓⲥ ⲙ̄-ⲙⲱⲩ̈ⲥⲏⲥ ϫⲉ "ⲛⲓⲙ ⲡⲉ ⲛ̄ⲧⲁϥ-†-ⲧⲁⲡⲣⲟ ⲙ̄-ⲡⲣⲱⲙⲉ, ⲁⲩⲱ ⲛⲓⲙ ⲡⲉⲛⲧⲁϥⲧⲁⲙⲓⲉ-ⲡⲉⲙⲡⲟ ⲙⲛ̄-ⲡⲁⲗ, ⲡⲉⲧ-ⲛⲁⲩ ⲉⲃⲟⲗ ⲙⲛ̄-ⲡⲃⲗ̄ⲗⲉ? ⲙⲏ ⲁⲛⲟⲕ ⲁⲛ ⲡⲉ, ⲡϫⲟⲉⲓⲥ ⲡⲛⲟⲩⲧⲉ? 12 ⲧⲉⲛⲟⲩ ϭⲉ ⲃⲱⲕ! ⲁⲩⲱ ⲁⲛⲟⲕ †ⲛⲁⲟⲩⲱⲛ ⲛ̄-ⲣⲱⲕ ⲛ̄ⲧⲁⲧⲥⲁⲃⲟⲕ ⲉ-ⲡⲉⲧⲕ̄ⲛⲁϫⲟⲟⲥ."

13 ⲡⲉϫⲁϥ ⲛ̄ⲇⲉ ⲛ̄ϭⲓ-ⲙⲱⲩ̈ⲥⲏⲥ ϫⲉ "†ⲥⲟⲡⲥ̄ ⲙ̄ⲙⲟⲕ, ⲡϫⲟⲉⲓⲥ, ⲁⲛⲁⲩ ⲛⲁⲕ ⲉ-ⲕⲉⲩⲁ ⲉ-ⲩⲛ̄-ϭⲟⲙ ⲙ̄ⲙⲟϥ, ⲛⲅ̄ϫⲛⲁϥ!"

14 ⲁ-ⲡϫⲟⲉⲓⲥ ϭⲱⲛⲧ̄ ϩⲛ̄-ⲟⲩⲟⲣⲅⲏ ⲉϫⲛ̄-ⲙⲱⲩ̈ⲥⲏⲥ, ⲉϥϫⲱ ⲙ̄ⲙⲟⲥ ϫⲉ "ⲉⲓⲥ! ⲁⲁⲣⲱⲛ ⲡⲉⲕⲥⲟⲛ ⲡⲗⲉⲩⲉⲓⲧⲏⲥ, †ⲥⲟⲟⲩⲛ ϫⲉ ϩⲛ̄-ⲟⲩϣⲁϫⲉ ϥⲛⲁϣⲁϫⲉ ⲛⲙ̄ⲙⲁⲕ, ⲁⲩⲱ ⲉⲓⲥ-ϩⲏⲧⲉ! ⲛ̄ⲧⲟϥ ϥⲛⲏⲩ ⲉⲃⲟⲗ ⲉ-ⲧⲱⲙⲧ̄ ⲉⲣⲟⲕ, ⲛϥ̄ⲛⲁⲩ ⲉⲣⲟⲕ, ⲛϥ̄ⲣⲁϣⲉ ϩⲣⲁⲓ̈ ⲛ̄ϩⲏⲧϥ̄. 15 ⲛⲅ̄ϫⲟⲟⲥ ⲛⲁϥ ⲁⲩⲱ ⲛⲅ̄†-ⲛⲁϣⲁϫⲉ ⲉϩⲣⲁⲓ̈ ⲉ-ⲧⲉϥⲧⲁⲡⲣⲟ, ⲁⲩⲱ ⲁⲛⲟⲕ †ⲛⲁⲟⲩⲱⲛ ⲛ̄-ⲧⲉϥⲧⲁⲡⲣⲟ ⲙⲛ̄-ⲧⲉⲕⲧⲁⲡⲣⲟ ⲛ̄ⲧⲁⲧⲥⲁⲃⲉ-ⲧⲏⲩⲧⲛ̄ ⲉ-ⲛⲉⲧⲉⲧⲛ̄ⲛⲁⲁⲁⲩ. 16 ⲁⲩⲱ ⲛ̄ⲧⲟϥ ⲡⲉⲧ-ⲛⲁϣⲁϫⲉ ⲛⲙ̄ⲙⲁⲕ ⲛ̄ⲛⲁϩⲣⲙ̄-ⲡⲗⲁⲟⲥ, ⲛϥ̄ϣⲱⲡⲉ ⲛⲁⲕ ⲛ̄-ⲧⲁⲡⲣⲟ. ⲛ̄ⲧⲟⲕ ⲛ̄ⲇⲉ ⲕⲛⲁϣⲱⲡⲉ ⲛⲁϥ ⲛ̄ⲛⲁϩⲣⲙ̄-ⲡⲛⲟⲩⲧⲉ. 17 ⲉⲕⲉϫⲓ ⲇⲉ ⲙ̄-ⲡⲉⲓ̈ϭⲉⲣⲱⲃ ⲉ-ⲛ̄ⲧⲁϥⲕⲧⲟϥ ⲉ-ⲩϩⲟϥ ϩⲣⲁⲓ̈ ϩⲛ̄-ⲧⲉⲕϭⲓϫ, ⲡⲁⲓ̈ ⲉⲧⲕ̄ⲛⲁⲉⲓⲣⲉ ⲛ̄-ⲙ̄ⲙⲁⲉⲓⲛ ϩⲣⲁⲓ̈ ⲛ̄ϩⲏⲧϥ̄."

18 ⲁϥⲃⲱⲕ ⲛ̄ⲇⲉ ⲛ̄ϭⲓ-ⲙⲱⲩ̈ⲥⲏⲥ, ⲁϥⲕⲧⲟϥ ϣⲁ-ⲓ̈ⲟⲑⲟⲣ ⲡⲉϥϣⲟⲙ, ⲉϥϫⲱ ⲙ̄ⲙⲟⲥ ϫⲉ "†ⲛⲁⲃⲱⲕ ⲛ̄ⲧⲁⲕⲧⲟⲉⲓ ϣⲁ-ⲛⲁⲥⲛⲏⲩ, ⲛⲁⲓ̈ ⲉⲧ-ϣⲟⲟⲡ ϩⲛ̄-ⲕⲏⲙⲉ, ⲧⲁⲛⲁⲩ ϫⲉ ⲉⲧⲓ ⲥⲉⲟⲛϩ̄."

ⲡⲉϫⲉ-ⲓ̈ⲟⲑⲟⲣ ⲙ̄-ⲙⲱⲩ̈ⲥⲏⲥ ϫⲉ "ⲃⲱⲕ, ⲉⲕⲟⲩⲟϫ!"

19 ⲙⲛ̄ⲛ̄ⲥⲁ-ⲛⲉϩⲟⲟⲩ ⲛ̄ⲇⲉ ⲉⲧ-ⲙ̄ⲙⲁⲩ ⲉⲧ-ⲛⲁϣⲱⲟⲩ, ⲁϥⲙⲟⲩ ⲛ̄ϭⲓ-ⲡⲣ̄ⲣⲟ ⲛ̄-ⲕⲏⲙⲉ. ⲡⲉϫⲁϥ ⲛ̄ϭⲓ-ⲡϫⲟⲉⲓⲥ ⲙ̄-ⲙⲱⲩ̈ⲥⲏⲥ ϩⲣⲁⲓ̈ ϩⲙ̄-ⲡⲕⲁϩ ⲙ̄-ⲙⲁⲇⲓϩⲁⲙ ϫⲉ "ⲙⲟⲟϣⲉ ⲛⲅ̄ⲃⲱⲕ ⲉϩⲣⲁⲓ̈ ⲉ-ⲕⲏⲙⲉ, ⲁⲩⲙⲟⲩ ⲅⲁⲣ ⲛ̄ϭⲓ-ⲟⲩⲟⲛ ⲛⲓⲙ ⲉⲧ-ϣⲓⲛⲉ ⲛ̄ⲥⲁ-ⲧⲉⲕⲯⲩⲭⲏ." 20 ⲁϥϫⲓ ⲛ̄ⲇⲉ ⲛ̄ϭⲓ-ⲙⲱⲩ̈ⲥⲏⲥ ⲛ̄-ⲧⲉϥⲥϩⲓⲙⲉ ⲙⲛ̄-ⲛⲉϥϣⲏⲣⲉ, ⲁϥⲧⲁⲗⲟ ⲙ̄ⲙⲟⲟⲩ ⲉϩⲣⲁⲓ̈ ⲉϫⲛ̄-ⲛ̄ϥⲁⲓ̈-ⲛⲁϩⲃ̄, ⲁϥⲕⲧⲟϥ ⲉϩⲣⲁⲓ̈ ⲉ-ⲕⲏⲙⲉ. ⲁ-ⲙⲱⲩ̈ⲥⲏⲥ ⲛ̄ⲇⲉ ϫⲓ ⲙ̄-ⲡϭⲉⲣⲱⲃ ⲡⲉⲃⲟⲗ ϩⲓⲧⲟⲟⲧϥ̄ ⲙ̄-ⲡⲛⲟⲩⲧⲉ ϩⲣⲁⲓ̈ ϩⲛ̄-ⲧⲉϥϭⲓϫ.

21 ⲡⲉϫⲁϥ ⲇⲉ ⲛ̄ϭⲓ-ⲡϫⲟⲉⲓⲥ ⲙ̄-ⲙⲱⲩ̈ⲥⲏⲥ ϫⲉ "ⲉⲕⲃⲱⲕ ⲁⲩⲱ ⲉⲕⲕⲱⲧⲉ ⲙ̄ⲙⲟⲕ ⲉϩⲣⲁⲓ̈ ⲉ-ⲕⲏⲙⲉ. †-ϩⲧⲏⲕ ⲉ-ⲣ̄-ⲛⲉϣⲡⲏⲣⲉ ⲧⲏⲣⲟⲩ ⲛ̄ⲧⲁⲓ̈ⲁⲁⲩ ϩⲛ̄-ⲛⲉⲕϭⲓϫ ⲙ̄-ⲡⲉⲙⲧⲟ ⲉⲃⲟⲗ ⲙ̄-ⲫⲁⲣⲁⲱ. ⲁⲛⲟⲕ ⲛ̄ⲇⲉ †ⲛⲁ†-ⲛ̄ϣⲟⲧ ⲙ̄-ⲡⲉϥϩⲏⲧ, ⲛϥ̄ⲧⲙ̄ⲕⲱ ⲉⲃⲟⲗ ⲙ̄-ⲡⲗⲁⲟⲥ. 22 ⲛ̄ⲧⲟⲕ ⲛ̄ⲇⲉ ⲉⲕⲉϫⲟⲟⲥ ⲙ̄-ⲫⲁⲣⲁⲱ ϫⲉ 'ⲛⲁⲓ̈ ⲛⲉⲧⲉⲣⲉ-ⲡϫⲟⲉⲓⲥ ϫⲱ ⲙ̄ⲙⲟⲟⲩ ϫⲉ "ⲡⲁϣⲏⲣⲉ ⲡⲁϣⲣⲡ̄-ⲙ̄-ⲙⲓⲥⲉ ⲡⲉ ⲡⲓⲥⲣⲁⲏⲗ. 23 ⲁⲓ̈ϫⲟⲟⲥ ⲛ̄ⲇⲉ ⲛⲁⲕ ϫⲉ 'ⲕⲱ ⲉⲃⲟⲗ ⲙ̄-ⲡⲁⲗⲁⲟⲥ ϫⲉⲕⲁⲥ ⲉϥⲉϣⲙ̄ϣⲉ ⲛⲁⲓ̈.' ⲉϣⲱⲡⲉ ϭⲉ ⲛ̄ⲅⲟⲩⲱϣ ⲁⲛ ⲉ-ⲕⲱ ⲙ̄ⲙⲟϥ ⲉⲃⲟⲗ, ⲉⲓⲥ-ϩⲏⲏⲧⲉ! ⲁⲛⲟⲕ †ⲛⲁⲙⲟⲩⲟⲩⲧ ⲙ̄-ⲡⲉⲕϣⲣⲡ̄-ⲙ̄-ⲙⲓⲥⲉ!"'"

24 ⲁⲥϣⲱⲡⲉ ⲇⲉ ϩⲣⲁⲓ̈ ϩⲛ̄-ⲧⲉϩⲓⲏ, ⲙ̄-ⲡⲙⲁ ⲛ̄-ⲟⲩⲉϩ-ⲛⲁⲩ, ⲁ-ⲟⲩⲁⲅⲅⲉⲗⲟⲥ ⲧⲱⲙⲧ̄ ⲉⲣⲟϥ ⲛ̄ⲧⲉ-ⲡϫⲟⲉⲓⲥ ⲁϥϣⲓⲛⲉ ⲛ̄ⲥⲁ-ⲙⲟⲩⲟⲩⲧϥ̄. 25 ⲁ-ⲥⲉⲫⲫⲱⲣⲁ ϫⲓ ⲛ̄-ⲟⲩⲱⲛⲉ, ⲁⲥⲥⲃ̄ⲃⲉ ⲛ̄-ⲧⲙⲛ̄ⲧⲁⲧⲥⲃ̄ⲃⲉ ⲙ̄-ⲡⲉⲥϣⲏⲣⲉ. ⲁⲥϩⲉ ϩⲁ-ⲛⲉϥⲟⲩⲉⲣⲏⲧⲉ, ⲡⲉϫⲁⲥ ϫⲉ "ⲁϥⲁϩⲉⲣⲁⲧϥ̄ ⲛ̄ϭⲓ-ⲡⲉⲥⲛⲟϥ ⲙ̄-ⲡⲥⲃ̄ⲃⲉ ⲙ̄-ⲡⲁϣⲏⲣⲉ!" 26 ⲁϥⲥⲁϩⲱϥ ⲉⲃⲟⲗ ⲙ̄ⲙⲟⲥ, ϫⲉ ⲁⲥϫⲟⲟⲥ ϫⲉ "ⲁϥⲁϩⲉⲣⲁⲧϥ̄ ⲛ̄ϭⲓ-ⲡⲉⲥⲛⲟϥ ⲙ̄-ⲡⲥⲃ̄ⲃⲉ ⲙ̄-ⲡⲁϣⲏⲣⲉ!"

27 ⲡⲉϫⲁϥ ⲛ̄ⲇⲉ ⲛ̄ϭⲓ-ⲡϫⲟⲉⲓⲥ ⲛ̄-ⲁⲁⲣⲱⲛ ϫⲉ "ⲃⲱⲕ ⲛ̄ⲕ̄ⲧⲱⲙⲧ̄ ⲉ-ⲙⲱⲩ̈ⲥⲏⲥ ϩⲣⲁⲓ̈ ϩⲛ̄-ⲧⲉⲣⲏⲙⲟⲥ." ⲁϥⲃⲱⲕ ⲛ̄ⲇⲉ ⲉ-ⲧⲱⲙⲧ̄ ⲉⲣⲟϥ ϩⲣⲁⲓ̈ ϩⲙ̄-ⲡⲧⲟⲟⲩ ⲙ̄-ⲡⲛⲟⲩⲧⲉ. ⲁⲩⲁⲥⲡⲁⲍⲉ ⲛ̄-ⲛⲉⲩⲉⲣⲏⲩ. 28 ⲁ-ⲙⲱⲩ̈ⲥⲏⲥ

ⲇⲉ ϫⲱ ⲛ̄-ⲛ̄ϣⲁϫⲉ ⲧⲏⲣⲟⲩ ⲉ-ⲁⲁⲣⲱⲛ ⲡⲉϥⲥⲟⲛ, ⲛⲁⲓ̈ ⲛ̄ⲧⲁϥϫⲟⲟⲩ ⲛ̄ϭⲓ-ⲡϫⲟⲉⲓⲥ, ⲁⲩⲱ ⲙ̄ⲙⲁⲉⲓⲛ ⲧⲏⲣⲟⲩ ⲉⲛⲧⲁϥϩⲟⲛⲟⲩ ⲉⲧⲟⲟⲧϥ̄.

29 ⲁϥⲃⲱⲕ ⲇⲉ ⲛ̄ϭⲓ-ⲙⲱⲩ̈ⲥⲏⲥ ⲙⲛ̄-ⲁⲁⲣⲱⲛ. ⲁⲩⲥⲱⲟⲩϩ ⲉϩⲟⲩⲛ ⲛ̄-ⲛ̄ϩⲗ̄ⲗⲟⲉⲓ ⲛ̄-ⲛ̄ϣⲏⲣⲉ ⲙ̄-ⲡⲓⲥⲣⲁⲏⲗ. 30 ⲁϥϫⲱ ⲛⲁⲩ ⲛ̄ϭⲓ-ⲁⲁⲣⲱⲛ ⲛ̄-ⲛ̄ϣⲁϫⲉ ⲧⲏⲣⲟⲩ ⲛ̄ⲧⲁ-ⲡⲛⲟⲩⲧⲉ ϩⲱⲛ ⲉⲧⲟⲟⲧϥ̄ ⲙ̄-ⲙⲱⲩ̈ⲥⲏⲥ ⲙ̄ⲙⲟⲟⲩ, ⲁⲩⲱ ⲁϥⲉⲓⲣⲉ ⲛ̄-ⲙ̄ⲙⲁⲉⲓⲛ ⲙ̄-ⲡⲉⲙⲧⲟ ⲉⲃⲟⲗ ⲙ̄-ⲡⲗⲁⲟⲥ. 31 ⲁϥⲡⲓⲥⲧⲉⲩⲉ ⲛ̄ϭⲓ-ⲡⲗⲁⲟⲥ, ⲁⲩⲱ ⲁϥⲣⲁϣⲉ ϫⲉ ⲁ-ⲡⲛⲟⲩⲧⲉ ϭⲙ̄-ⲡϣⲓⲛⲉ ⲛ̄-ⲛ̄ϣⲏⲣⲉ ⲙ̄-ⲡⲓⲥⲣⲁⲏⲗ ⲁⲩⲱ ϫⲉ ⲁϥⲛⲁⲩ ⲉ-ⲧⲉⲩⲑⲗⲓⲯⲓⲥ. ⲁϥⲡⲁϩⲧϥ̄ ⲛ̄ⲇⲉ ⲛ̄ϭⲓ-ⲡⲗⲁⲟⲥ, ⲁϥⲟⲩⲱϣⲧ̄ ⲙ̄-ⲡϫⲟⲉⲓⲥ.

5.1 ⲙⲛ̄ⲛ̄ⲥⲁ-ⲛⲁⲓ̈ ⲁϥⲃⲱⲕ ⲉϩⲟⲩⲛ ⲛ̄ϭⲓ-ⲙⲱⲩ̈ⲥⲏⲥ ⲙⲛ̄-ⲁⲁⲣⲱⲛ ϣⲁ-ⲫⲁⲣⲁⲱ. ⲡⲉϫⲁⲩ ⲛⲁϥ ϫⲉ "ⲛⲁⲓ̈ ⲛⲉ ⲉⲧⲉⲣⲉ-ⲡϫⲟⲉⲓⲥ ⲡⲛⲟⲩⲧⲉ ⲙ̄-ⲡⲓⲥⲣⲁⲏⲗ ϫⲱ ⲙ̄ⲙⲟⲟⲩ ϫⲉ 'ⲕⲱ ⲉⲃⲟⲗ ⲙ̄-ⲡⲁⲗⲁⲟⲥ ϫⲉⲕⲁⲁⲥ ⲉⲩⲉⲣ̄-ϣⲁ ⲛⲁⲓ̈ ϩⲣⲁⲓ̈ ϩⲙ̄-ⲡϫⲁⲉⲓⲉ.'"

2 ⲡⲉϫⲁϥ ⲛⲁⲩ ϫⲉ "ⲛⲓⲙ ⲡⲉ ⲡⲁⲓ̈ ⲉϯⲛⲁⲥⲱⲧⲙ̄ ⲉ-ⲡⲉϥϩⲣⲟⲟⲩ, ϩⲱⲥⲧⲉ ⲉ-ⲕⲱ ⲉⲃⲟⲗ ⲛ̄-ⲛ̄ϣⲏⲣⲉ ⲙ̄-ⲡⲓⲥⲣⲁⲏⲗ? ⲛ̄ϯⲥⲟⲟⲩⲛ ⲁⲛ ⲙ̄-ⲡϫⲟⲉⲓⲥ, ⲁⲩⲱ ⲡⲓⲥⲣⲁⲏⲗ ⲛ̄ϯⲛⲁⲕⲁⲁϥ ⲁⲛ ⲉⲃⲟⲗ."

3 ⲡⲉϫⲁⲩ ⲛⲁϥ ϫⲉ "ⲡⲛⲟⲩⲧⲉ ⲛ̄-ⲛ̄ϩⲉⲃⲣⲁⲓⲟⲥ ⲡⲉⲛⲧⲁϥⲧⲁϩⲙ̄ⲛ̄ ⲉⲛⲛⲁⲃⲱⲕ ϭⲉ ⲛ̄-ⲟⲩϩⲓⲏ ⲛ̄-ϣⲟⲙⲧ̄ ⲛ̄-ϩⲟⲟⲩ ⲙ̄-ⲙⲟⲟϣⲉ ϫⲉⲕⲁⲁⲥ ⲉⲛⲉϣⲱⲧ ⲛ̄ⲛⲁϩⲣⲛ̄-ⲡⲉⲛⲛⲟⲩⲧⲉ, ⲙⲏⲡⲟⲧⲉ ⲛ̄ⲧⲉⲩⲙⲟⲩ ⲧⲱⲙⲧ̄ ⲉⲣⲟⲛ ⲙⲛ̄-ⲟⲩϩⲱⲧⲃ̄."

4 ⲡⲉϫⲁϥ ⲛⲁⲩ ⲛ̄ϭⲓ-ⲡⲣ̄ⲣⲟ ⲛ̄-ⲕⲏⲙⲉ ϫⲉ "ⲉⲧⲃⲉ-ⲟⲩ, ⲙⲱⲩ̈ⲥⲏⲥ ⲙⲛ̄-ⲁⲁⲣⲱⲛ, ⲧⲉⲧⲛ̄ⲕⲧⲟ ⲉⲃⲟⲗ ⲙ̄-ⲡⲁⲗⲁⲟⲥ ⲉⲃⲟⲗ ϩⲛ̄-ⲛⲉϥϩⲃⲏⲩⲉ? ⲙⲁⲣⲉ-ⲡⲟⲩⲁ ⲡⲟⲩⲁ ⲙ̄ⲙⲱⲧⲛ̄ ⲃⲱⲕ ϩⲛ̄-ⲛⲉϥϩⲃⲏⲩⲉ!" 5 ⲡⲉϫⲁϥ ⲛ̄ϭⲓ-ⲫⲁⲣⲁⲱ ϫⲉ "ⲉⲓⲥ-ϩⲏⲧⲉ! ⲧⲉⲛⲟⲩ ϥⲟϣ ⲛ̄ϭⲓ-ⲡⲗⲁⲟⲥ ⲙ̄-ⲡⲕⲁϩ. ⲙ̄ⲡⲣ̄ⲧⲣⲉⲛϯ-ⲙ̄ⲧⲟⲛ ϭⲉ ⲛⲁⲩ ⲉⲃⲟⲗ ϩⲛ̄-ⲛⲉϥϩⲃⲏⲩⲉ."

6 ⲁ-ⲫⲁⲣⲁⲱ ϩⲱⲛ ⲉⲧⲟⲟⲧⲟⲩ ⲛ̄-ⲛⲉⲧ-ϩⲓϫⲛ̄-ⲛⲉϩⲃⲏⲩⲉ ⲙ̄-ⲡⲗⲁⲟⲥ ⲙⲛ̄-ⲛⲉⲅⲣⲁⲙⲙⲁⲧⲉⲩⲥ, ⲉϥϫⲱ ⲙ̄ⲙⲟⲥ 7 ϫⲉ "ⲛ̄ⲛⲉⲧⲛ̄ⲟⲩⲱϩ ⲉⲧⲟⲧ-ⲧⲏⲩⲧⲛ̄ ⲉ-ϯ-ⲧⲱϩ ⲙ̄-ⲡⲗⲁⲟⲥ ⲉ-ⲧⲙⲛ̄ⲧⲡⲁⲡⲉ-ⲧⲱⲃⲉ ⲕⲁⲧⲁ-ⲑⲉ ⲛ̄-ⲥⲁϥ ⲙⲛ̄-ϣⲙ̄ⲧⲉ ⲡⲟⲟⲩ ⲛ̄-ϩⲟⲟⲩ. ⲛ̄ⲧⲟⲟⲩ ⲙⲁⲣⲟⲩⲃⲱⲕ ⲛ̄ⲥⲉⲥⲉⲩϩ-ⲧⲱϩ ⲛⲁⲩ ⲉϩⲟⲩⲛ. 8 ⲁⲩⲱ ⲧⲁⲡⲥ̄ ⲛ̄-ⲧⲱⲃⲉ ⲉⲧ-ⲏⲡ, ⲉ-ϣⲁⲩⲧⲁⲙⲓⲟⲥ ⲙ̄-ⲙⲏⲛⲉ, ⲉⲕⲉⲛⲟϫⲥ̄ ⲉϩⲣⲁⲓ̈ ⲉϫⲱⲟⲩ, ⲛ̄ⲛⲉⲕϥⲓ-ⲗⲁⲁⲩ ⲉⲃⲟⲗ ⲛ̄ϩⲏⲧⲟⲩ. ⲥⲉⲥⲣⲟϥⲧ̄ ⲅⲁⲣ! ⲉⲧⲃⲉ-ⲡⲁⲓ̈ ⲥⲉϫⲓ-ϣⲕⲁⲕ ⲉⲃⲟⲗ, ⲉⲩϫⲱ ⲙ̄ⲙⲟⲥ ϫⲉ 'ⲙⲁⲣⲛ̄ⲃⲱⲕ ⲛ̄ⲧⲛ̄ϣⲱⲱⲧ ⲛ̄ⲛⲁϩⲣⲛ̄-ⲡⲉⲛⲛⲟⲩⲧⲉ.' 9 ⲙⲁⲣⲟⲩϩⲣⲟϣ ⲛ̄ϭⲓ-ⲛⲉϩⲃⲏⲩⲉ ⲛ̄-ⲛⲉⲓ̈ⲣⲱⲙⲉ, ⲧⲁⲣⲟⲩϥⲓ-ⲣⲟⲟⲩϣ ⲉ-ⲛⲁⲓ̈, ⲛ̄ⲥⲉⲧⲙ̄ϥⲓ-ⲣⲟⲟⲩϣ ϩⲛ̄-ϩⲉⲛϣⲁϫⲉ ⲉⲩϣⲟⲩⲉⲓⲧ."

10 ⲁⲩϣⲧⲣ̄ⲧⲱⲣⲟⲩ ⲇⲉ ⲛ̄ϭⲓ-ⲛⲉⲧ-ϩⲓϫⲛ̄-ⲛⲉϩⲃⲏⲩⲉ ⲙⲛ̄-ⲛⲉⲅⲣⲁⲙⲙⲁⲧⲉⲩⲥ ⲉⲧ-ϣⲁϫⲉ ⲛ̄ⲛⲁϩⲣⲛ̄-ⲡⲗⲁⲟⲥ, ⲉⲩϫⲱ ⲙ̄ⲙⲟⲥ ϫⲉ "ⲛⲁⲓ̈ ⲛⲉⲧⲉⲣⲉ-ⲫⲁⲣⲁⲱ ϫⲱ ⲙⲙⲟⲟⲩ ϫⲉ 'ϫⲓⲛ ⲧⲉⲛⲟⲩ ⲛ̄ϯⲛⲁϯ-ⲧⲱϩ ⲛⲏⲧⲛ̄ ⲁⲛ. 11 ⲃⲱⲕ ⲛ̄ⲧⲉⲧⲛ̄ⲥⲉⲩϩ-ⲧⲱϩ ⲛⲏⲧⲛ̄ ⲉϩⲟⲩⲛ ⲙ̄-ⲡⲙⲁ ⲉⲧⲉⲧⲛ̄ⲁϩⲉ-ⲉⲩⲟⲛ ⲛ̄ϩⲏⲧϥ̄, ⲛ̄ⲛⲉⲩϥⲓ-ⲗⲁⲁⲩ ⲅⲁⲣ ⲉⲃⲟⲗ ϩⲛ̄-ⲧⲉⲧⲛ̄ⲁⲡⲥ̄ ⲛ̄-ⲧⲱⲃⲉ.'" 12 ⲁⲩϫⲱⲱⲣⲉ ⲛ̄ⲇⲉ ⲉⲃⲟⲗ ⲛ̄ϭⲓ-ⲡⲗⲁⲟⲥ ϩⲣⲁⲓ̈ ϩⲛ̄-ⲕⲏⲙⲉ ⲉ-ⲥⲉⲩϩ-ⲣⲟⲟⲩⲉ[19] ⲛⲁⲩ ⲉϩⲟⲩⲛ ⲉ-ⲩⲧⲱϩ.

13 ⲁⲩϣⲧⲣ̄ⲧⲱⲣⲟⲩ ⲛ̄ⲇⲉ ⲛ̄ϭⲓ-ⲛⲉⲣⲅⲟⲇⲓⲱ́ⲕⲧⲏⲥ, ⲉⲩϫⲱ ⲙ̄ⲙⲟⲥ ϫⲉ "ϫⲱⲕ ⲉⲃⲟⲗ ⲛ̄-ⲛⲉⲧⲛ̄ϩⲃⲏⲩⲉ ⲉⲧ-ⲏⲡ ⲉⲣⲱⲧⲛ̄ ⲙ̄-ⲙⲏⲛⲉ ⲛ̄-ⲑⲉ ⲟⲛ ⲛ̄-ⲛⲉϩⲟⲟⲩ ⲉⲛⲉⲩϯ ⲛⲏⲧⲛ̄ ⲙ̄-ⲡⲧⲱϩ." 14 ⲁⲩϩⲓⲟⲩⲉ ⲉ-ⲛⲉⲅⲣⲁⲙⲙⲁⲧⲉⲩⲥ ⲛ̄-ⲛ̄ϣⲏⲣⲉ ⲙ̄-ⲡⲓⲥⲣⲁⲏⲗ, ⲛⲁⲓ̈ ⲉⲛⲧⲁⲩⲧⲁϩⲟⲟⲩ ⲉⲣⲁⲧⲟⲩ ⲉϩⲣⲁⲓ̈ ⲉϫⲱⲟⲩ ⲉⲃⲟⲗ ϩⲓⲧⲟⲟⲧⲟⲩ ⲛ̄-ⲛ̄ⲥⲁϩ ⲙ̄-ⲫⲁⲣⲁⲱ, ⲉⲩϫⲱ ⲙ̄ⲙⲟⲥ ϫⲉ "ⲉⲧⲃⲉ-ⲟⲩ ⲙ̄ⲡⲉⲧⲛ̄ϫⲱⲕ ⲉⲃⲟⲗ ⲛ̄-ⲧⲉⲧⲛ̄ⲁⲡⲥ̄ ⲛ̄-ⲧⲱⲃⲉ ⲕⲁⲧⲁ-ⲑⲉ ⲛ̄-ⲥⲁϥ ⲙⲛ̄-ϣⲙ̄ⲧⲉ ⲡⲟⲟⲩ ⲛ̄-ϩⲟⲟⲩ?

15 ⲁⲩⲃⲱⲕ ⲇⲉ ⲉϩⲟⲩⲛ ⲛ̄ϭⲓ-ⲛⲉⲅⲣⲁⲙⲙⲁⲧⲉⲩⲥ ⲛ̄-ⲛ̄ϣⲏⲣⲉ ⲙ̄-ⲡⲓⲥⲣⲁⲏⲗ ⲁⲩϫⲓ-ϣⲕⲁⲕ ⲉⲃⲟⲗ ⲛ̄ⲛⲁϩⲣⲛ̄-ⲫⲁⲣⲁⲱ, ⲉⲩϫⲱ ⲙ̄ⲙⲟⲥ ϫⲉ "ⲉⲧⲃⲉ-ⲟⲩ ⲕⲉⲓⲣⲉ ⲛ̄-ⲧⲉⲉⲓϩⲉ ⲛ̄-ⲛⲉⲕϩⲙ̄ϩⲁⲗ? 16 ⲛ̄ⲥⲉϯ-ⲧⲱϩ ⲁⲛ ⲛ̄-ⲛⲉⲕϩⲙ̄ϩⲁⲗ, ⲁⲩⲱ ⲧⲁⲡⲥ̄ ⲛ̄-ⲧⲱⲃⲉ ⲥⲉϫⲱ ⲙ̄ⲙⲟⲥ ⲛⲁⲛ ϫⲉ 'ⲧⲁⲙⲓⲟⲥ!' ⲉⲓⲥ-ϩⲏⲧⲉ! ⲁⲩϩⲓⲟⲩⲉ ⲉ-ⲛⲉⲕϩⲙ̄ϩⲁⲗ. ⲙⲏ ⲉⲕⲛⲁϫⲓ ⲙ̄-ⲡⲉⲕⲗⲁⲟⲥ ⲛ̄-ϭⲟⲛⲥ̄?"

---

19. Emended from ⲉ-ⲥⲟⲟⲩϩ-ⲣⲟⲟⲩⲉ.

17 ⲡⲉϫⲁϥ ⲛⲁⲩ ϫⲉ "ⲧⲉⲧⲛ̄ⲥⲣⲟϥⲧ̄! ⲛ̄ⲧⲉⲧⲛ̄-ϩⲛ̄ⲣⲉϥⲥⲣ̄ϥⲉ, ⲉⲧⲃⲉ-ⲡⲁⲓ̈ ⲧⲉⲧⲛ̄ϫⲱ ⲙ̄ⲙⲟⲥ ϫⲉ
'ⲙⲁⲣⲛ̄ⲃⲱⲕ ⲛ̄ⲧⲉⲧⲛ̄ϣⲱⲧ ⲛ̄ⲛⲁϩⲣⲛ̄-ⲡⲉⲛⲛⲟⲩⲧⲉ.' 18 ⲧⲉⲛⲟⲩ ϭⲉ ⲃⲱⲕ ⲛ̄ⲧⲉⲧⲛ̄ⲣ̄-ϩⲱⲃ! ⲡⲧⲱϩ
ⲛ̄ⲇⲉ ⲛ̄ⲥⲉⲛⲁⲧⲁⲁϥ ⲛⲏⲧⲛ̄ ⲁⲛ, ⲁⲩⲱ ⲧⲁⲡⲥ̄ ⲛ̄-ⲧⲱⲃⲉ ⲧⲉⲧⲛ̄ⲛⲁⲧⲁⲁⲥ."

19 ⲁⲩⲛⲁⲩ ⲇⲉ ⲉⲣⲟⲟⲩ ⲛ̄ϭⲓ-ⲛⲉⲅⲣⲁⲙⲙⲁⲧⲉⲩⲥ ⲛ̄-ⲛ̄ϣⲏⲣⲉ ⲙ̄-ⲡⲓⲥⲣⲁⲏⲗ ϫⲉ ⲥⲉ-ϩⲛ̄-ϩⲉⲛⲡⲉⲑⲟⲟⲩ,
ⲉⲩϫⲱ ⲙ̄ⲙⲟⲥ ϫⲉ "ⲛ̄ⲛⲉⲧⲛ̄ⲥⲱϫⲃ̄ ⲉⲃⲟⲗ ϩⲛ̄-ⲧⲁⲡⲥ̄ ⲛ̄-ⲧⲱⲃⲉ ⲉⲧ-ⲏⲡ ⲉⲣⲱⲧⲛ̄ ⲙ̄-ⲙⲏⲛⲉ." 20 ⲉⲩⲛⲏⲩ
ⲇⲉ ⲉⲃⲟⲗ ϩⲓⲧⲛ̄-ⲫⲁⲣⲁⲱ ⲁⲩⲧⲱⲙⲧ̄ ⲉ-ⲙⲱⲩ̈ⲥⲏⲥ ⲙⲛ̄-ⲁⲁⲣⲱⲛ ⲉⲩⲛⲏⲩ ⲉ-ⲧⲱⲙⲧ̄ ⲉⲣⲟⲟⲩ. 21 ⲡⲉϫⲁⲩ
ⲛⲁⲩ ϫⲉ "ⲉⲣⲉ-ⲡⲛⲟⲩⲧⲉ ⲛⲁⲩ ⲉⲣⲱⲧⲛ̄ ⲛϥ̄ⲕⲣⲓⲛⲉ, ϫⲉ ⲁⲧⲉⲧⲛ̄ⲃⲱⲧⲉ ⲙ̄-ⲡⲉⲛⲥⲧⲟⲓ̈ ⲙ̄-ⲡⲉⲙⲧⲟ ⲉⲃⲟⲗ
ⲙ̄-ⲫⲁⲣⲁⲱ ⲁⲩⲱ ⲙ̄-ⲡⲉⲙⲧⲟ ⲉⲃⲟⲗ ⲛ̄-ⲛⲉϥϩⲙ̄ϩⲁⲗ, ⲉ-† ⲛ̄-ⲟⲩⲥⲏϥⲉ ⲉϩⲣⲁⲓ̈ ⲉ-ⲛⲉϥϭⲓϫ ⲉ-ϩⲱⲧⲃ̄ ⲙ̄ⲙⲟⲛ!"

ⲡϫⲱⲱⲙⲉ ⲛ̄-ⲛⲉⲯⲁⲗⲙⲟⲥ PSALMS 2, 22(23), 90(91), 109(110), AND 151

The Book of Psalms is the best attested major book of the Sahidic Old Testament, with dozens of manuscripts dating from the fourth through the fourteenth centuries CE. Many of these were proper Psalters—manuscripts containing just the Psalms on their own—but the texts of various psalms can also be found within many lectionary, liturgical, and even divinatory manuscripts.

The selection of five psalms below is modified from the recent edition by Peter Nagel.[20] It was edited from three important Psalm manuscripts written in the sixth and seventh centuries CE: British Library, Oriental 5000 ("L"),[21] a papyrus manuscript containing the entire Psalter, along with Chester Beatty Library, Ms. C (Copt. Ms. 815) ("D")[22] and University of Michigan Library, P. Mich. Inv. No. 167 ("M"),[23] two small parchment companion volumes which together contain all the Psalms.

This selection includes Psalm 151, an apocryphal/deuterocanonical Psalm found in the Greek Psalter but not in the Hebrew Masoretic text—although a longer Hebrew version of this Psalm is part of Qumran Psalms Scroll[a] (11QPs[a][11Q5]).

2.1 ⲁϩⲣⲟⲟⲩ ⲛ̄ϩⲉⲑⲛⲟⲥ ⲁⲩϫⲓⲥⲉ ⲛ̄ϩⲏⲧ,
    ⲁ-ⲛ̄ⲗⲁⲟⲥ ⲙⲉⲗⲉⲧⲁ ⲛ̄-ϩⲉⲛⲡⲉⲧ-ϣⲟⲩⲉⲓⲧ?

2 ⲁⲩⲁϩⲉⲣⲁⲧⲟⲩ ⲛ̄ϭⲓ-ⲛⲉⲣⲣⲱⲟⲩ ⲙ̄-ⲡⲕⲁϩ,
    ⲁⲩⲱ ⲁ-ⲛ̄ⲁⲣⲭⲱⲛ ⲥⲱⲟⲩϩ ⲉ-ⲩⲙⲁ ⲛ̄-ⲟⲩⲱⲧ,
    ⲉ-† ⲟⲩⲃⲉ-ⲡϫⲟⲉⲓⲥ ⲙⲛ̄-ⲡⲉϥⲭⲣⲓⲥⲧⲟⲥ.   διάψαλμα

3 "ⲙⲁⲣⲛ̄ⲥⲱⲗⲡ̄ ⲛ̄-ⲛⲉⲩⲙ̄ⲣⲣⲉ,
    ⲛ̄ⲧⲛ̄ⲛⲟⲩϫⲉ ⲙ̄-ⲡⲉⲩⲛⲁϩⲃ̄ ⲉⲃⲟⲗ ϩⲓϫⲱⲛ."

4 ⲡⲉⲧ-ⲟⲩⲏϩ ϩⲛ̄-ⲙ̄ⲡⲏⲩⲉ ⲛⲁⲥⲱⲃⲉ ⲛ̄ⲥⲱⲟⲩ,
    ⲁⲩⲱ ⲡϫⲟⲉⲓⲥ ⲛⲁⲕⲱⲙϣⲟⲩ.

5 ⲧⲟⲧⲉ ϥⲛⲁϣⲁϫⲉ ⲛⲙ̄ⲙⲁⲩ ϩⲛ̄-ⲧⲉϥⲟⲣⲅⲏ,
    ⲛϥ̄ϣⲧⲣ̄ⲧⲱⲣⲟⲩ ϩⲙ̄-ⲡⲉϥϭⲱⲛⲧ̄.

---

20. Peter Nagel, ed., *Der sahidische Psalter. Editio Minor nach den Handschriften Ms. Or. 5000 der British Library zu London, Ms. n° 815 der Chester Beatty Library zu Dublin, und Ms. n° 167 der University of Michigan Library zu Ann Arbor*, Texts and Studies on the Coptic Bible 3 (Wiesbaden: Harrassowitz, 2022).

21. Listed as sa 2031 on the LCBM.

22. Listed as sa 6 on the LCBM.

23. Listed as sa 2010 on the LCBM.

6   ⲁⲛⲟⲕ ⲇⲉ ⲁⲩⲕⲁⲑⲓⲥⲧⲁ ⲙ̄ⲙⲟⲓ̈ ⲛ̄-ⲣ̄ⲣⲟ ⲉⲃⲟⲗ ϩⲓⲧⲟⲟⲧϥ̄,
       ⲉϫⲛ̄-ⲥⲓⲱⲛ ⲡⲉϥⲧⲟⲟⲩ ⲉⲧ-ⲟⲩⲁⲁⲃ.

7   ⲉⲓ̈ϫⲱ ⲙ̄-ⲡⲟⲩⲉϩ-ⲥⲁϩⲛⲉ ⲙ̄-ⲡϫⲟⲉⲓⲥ,
       ⲡⲉϫⲉ-ⲡϫⲟⲉⲓⲥ ⲛⲁⲓ̈ ϫⲉ "ⲛ̄ⲧⲟⲕ ⲡⲉ ⲡⲁϣⲏⲣⲉ,
       ⲁⲛⲟⲕ ⲁⲓ̈ϫⲡⲟⲕ ⲙ̄-ⲡⲟⲟⲩ.

8   ⲁⲓⲧⲓ ⲙ̄ⲙⲟⲓ̈, ⲧⲁϯ ⲛⲁⲕ ⲛ̄-ϩⲉⲛϩⲉⲑⲛⲟⲥ ⲉ-ⲧⲉⲕⲕⲗⲏⲣⲟⲛⲟⲙⲓⲁ,
       ⲁⲩⲱ ⲡⲉⲕⲁⲙⲁϩⲧⲉ ϣⲁ-ⲁⲣⲏϫϥ̄ ⲙ̄-ⲡⲕⲁϩ.

9   ⲕⲛⲁⲙⲟⲟⲛⲉ ⲙ̄ⲙⲟⲟⲩ ϩⲛ̄-ⲟⲩϭⲉⲣⲱⲃ ⲙ̄-ⲡⲉⲛⲓⲡⲉ,[24]
       ⲛ̄ⲅ̄ⲟⲩⲟϣϥⲟⲩ ⲛ̄-ⲑⲉ ⲛ̄-ϩⲉⲛϩⲛⲁⲁⲩ ⲛ̄-ⲕⲉⲣⲁⲙⲉⲩⲥ."

10 ⲧⲉⲛⲟⲩ ϭⲉ ⲛⲉⲣ̄ⲣⲱⲟⲩ, ϯ-ϩⲧⲏⲧⲛ̄,
       ϫⲓ-ⲥⲃⲱ, ⲧⲏⲣⲧⲛ̄ ⲛⲉⲧ-ⲕⲣⲓⲛⲉ ⲙ̄-ⲡⲕⲁϩ.

11 ⲁⲣⲓ-ϩⲙ̄ϩⲁⲗ ⲙ̄-ⲡϫⲟⲉⲓⲥ ϩⲛ̄-ⲟⲩϩⲟⲧⲉ,
       ⲛ̄ⲧⲉⲧⲛ̄ⲧⲉⲗⲏⲗ ⲛⲁϥ ϩⲛ̄-ⲟⲩⲥⲧⲱⲧ.

12 ϭⲁⲗ̄ϫ̄-[25]ⲧⲏⲩⲧⲛ̄ ⲛ̄-ⲧⲉⲥⲃⲱ ⲙⲏⲡⲟⲧⲉ ⲛ̄ⲧⲉ-ⲡϫⲟⲉⲓⲥ ⲛⲟⲩϭⲥ̄,
       ⲛ̄ⲧⲉⲧⲛ̄ϩⲉ ⲉⲃⲟⲗ ϩⲓ-ⲧⲉϩⲓⲏ ⲛ̄-ⲧⲉϥⲙⲛ̄ⲧⲙⲉ.
    ⲉⲣϣⲁⲛ-ⲡⲉϥϭⲱⲛⲧ̄ ⲙⲟⲩϩ ϩⲛ̄-ⲟⲩϭⲉⲡⲏ,
       ⲛⲁⲓ̈ⲁⲧⲟⲩ ⲛ̄-ⲟⲩⲟⲛ ⲛⲓⲙ ⲉⲧ-ⲕⲱ ⲛ̄-ϩⲧⲏⲩ ⲉⲣⲟϥ!

22(23).1[26]   **ⲡⲉⲯⲁⲗⲙⲟⲥ ⲛ̄-ⲇⲁⲩⲉⲓⲇ**

    ⲡϫⲟⲉⲓⲥ ⲡⲉⲧⲙⲟⲟⲛⲉ ⲙ̄ⲙⲟⲓ̈, ⲛ̄ϥ̄ⲛⲁⲧⲣⲁϣⲱⲱⲧ ⲁⲛ ⲛ̄-ⲗⲁⲁⲩ,
2   ⲁϥⲧⲣⲁⲟⲩⲱϩ ϩⲛ̄-ⲟⲩⲙⲁ ⲛ̄ⲟⲩⲟⲧⲟⲩⲉⲧ.
    ⲁϥⲥⲁⲛⲟⲩϣⲧ̄ ϩⲓϫⲛ̄-ⲟⲩⲙⲟⲟⲩ ⲛ̄-ⲙ̄ⲧⲟⲛ,
3   ⲁϥⲕⲧⲉ-ⲧⲁⲯⲩⲭⲏ.
    ⲁϥϫⲓ-ⲙⲟⲉⲓⲧ ϩⲏⲧ ϩⲓ-ⲛⲉϩⲓⲟⲟⲩⲉ ⲛ̄-ⲧⲇⲓⲕⲁⲓⲟⲥⲩⲛⲏ
       ⲉⲧⲃⲉ-ⲡⲉϥⲣⲁⲛ.

4   ⲕⲁⲛ ⲉⲓ̈ϣⲁⲛⲙⲟⲟϣⲉ ⲛ̄-ⲧⲙⲏⲧⲉ ⲛ̄-ⲑⲁⲓ̈ⲃⲉⲥ ⲙ̄-ⲡⲙⲟⲩ,
       ⲛ̄ϯⲛⲁⲣ̄-ϩⲟⲧⲉ ⲁⲛ ϩⲏⲧⲟⲩ ⲛ̄-ⲙ̄ⲡⲉⲧϩⲟⲟⲩ,
       ϫⲉ ⲛ̄ⲧⲟⲕ ⲕ̄ϣⲟⲟⲡ ⲛⲙ̄ⲙⲁⲓ̈,
       ⲡⲉⲕϣ̄ⲗⲉϩ ⲙⲛ̄ ⲡⲉⲕϭⲉⲣⲱⲃ,
       ⲛ̄ⲧⲟⲟⲩ ⲛⲉⲛⲧⲁⲩⲥⲉⲡⲥⲱⲡⲧ̄.

5   ⲁⲕⲥⲟⲃⲧⲉ ⲛ̄-ⲟⲩⲧⲣⲁⲡⲉⲍⲁ ⲙ̄-ⲡⲁⲙ̄ⲧⲟ ⲉⲃⲟⲗ,
       ⲙ̄-ⲡϩⲟⲧ ⲉⲃⲟⲗ ⲛ̄-ⲛⲉⲧ-ⲑⲗⲓⲃⲉ ⲙ̄ⲙⲟⲓ̈.
    ⲁⲕⲧⲉϩⲥ̄-ⲧⲁⲁⲡⲉ ⲛ̄-ⲟⲩⲛⲉϩ,
       ⲁⲩⲱ ⲡⲉⲕϫⲱ ⲉϥⲧⲁϩⲉ ⲛ̄-ⲑⲉ ⲙ̄-ⲡⲉⲧⲁⲙⲁϩⲧⲉ.

6   ⲡⲉⲕⲛⲁ ⲛⲁⲡⲱⲧ ⲛ̄ⲥⲱⲓ̈

---

24. See ⲃⲉⲛⲓⲡⲉ.
25. See ⲕⲗ̄ϫ̄- (ⲕⲱⲗϫ̄).
26. The double numbers reflect the difference between the Greek/Coptic and the Hebrew (in parentheses) numbering systems for the Psalms.

ⲛ̄-ⲛⲉϩⲟⲟⲩ[27] ⲧⲏⲣⲟⲩ ⲙ̄-ⲡⲁⲱⲛϩ̄,
ⲉⲧⲃⲉ-ϫⲉ ⲁⲓ̈ⲟⲩⲱϩ ϩⲙ̄-ⲡⲏⲓ̈ ⲙ̄-ⲡϫⲟⲉⲓⲥ
ⲛ̄-ϩⲉⲛϩⲟⲟⲩ ⲉ-ⲛⲁϣⲱⲟⲩ.

90(91).1   **ⲡⲉⲥⲙⲟⲩ ⲛ̄-ⲧⲱⲇⲏ́ ⲛ̄-ⲇⲁⲩⲉⲓⲇ**

    ⲡⲉⲧⲟⲩⲏϩ ϩⲛ̄-ⲧⲃⲟⲏ́ⲑⲉⲓⲁ ⲙ̄-ⲡⲉⲧ-ϫⲟⲥⲉ,
        ϥⲛⲁϣⲱⲡⲉ ϩⲛ̄-ⲑⲁⲓ̈ⲃⲉⲥ ⲙ̄-ⲡⲛⲟⲩⲧⲉ ⲛ̄-ⲧⲡⲉ.

2   ϥⲛⲁϫⲟⲟⲥ ⲙ̄-ⲡϫⲟⲉⲓⲥ ϫⲉ "ⲛ̄ⲧⲕ̄-ⲡⲁⲣⲉϥϣⲟⲡⲧ̄ ⲉⲣⲟϥ ⲁⲩⲱ ⲡⲁⲙⲁ ⲙ̄-ⲡⲱⲧ,
    ⲡⲁⲛⲟⲩⲧⲉ, ⲉⲓ̈ⲛⲁⲛⲁϩⲧⲉ ⲉⲣⲟϥ."

3   ϫⲉ ⲛ̄ⲧⲟϥ ⲡⲉⲧ-ⲛⲁⲧⲟⲩϫⲟⲓ̈ ⲉ-ⲧϭⲟⲣϭⲥ̄ ⲛ̄-ⲛ̄ϭⲉⲣⲏϭ
    ⲁⲩⲱ ⲉ-ⲩϣⲁϫⲉ ⲉϥⲛⲁϣⲧ̄.
4   ϥⲛⲁⲣ̄-ϩⲁⲓ̈ⲃⲉⲥ ⲉⲣⲟⲕ ϩⲁ-ⲧⲉϥⲙⲉⲥⲧϩⲏⲧ,
    ⲁⲩⲱ ⲕⲛⲁⲛⲁϩⲧⲉ ϩⲁ-ⲛⲉϥⲧⲛϩ̄,
    ⲧⲉϥⲙⲉ ⲛⲁⲕⲱⲧⲉ ⲉⲣⲟⲕ ⲛ̄-ⲑⲉ ⲛ̄-ⲛⲓϩⲟⲡⲗⲟⲛ.
5   ⲛ̄ⲅ̄ⲛⲁⲣ̄-ϩⲟⲧⲉ ⲁⲛ ⲉ-ⲩϩⲟⲧⲉ ⲛ̄-ϭⲱⲣϩ̄,
    ⲁⲩⲱ ϩⲛ̄ⲧϥ̄ ⲛ̄-ⲟⲩⲥⲟⲧⲉ ⲉϥϩⲏⲗ ⲙ̄-ⲡⲉϩⲟⲟⲩ,
6   ϩⲛ̄ⲧϥ̄ ⲛ̄-ⲟⲩϩⲱⲃ ⲉϥⲙⲟⲟϣⲉ ϩⲙ̄-ⲡⲕⲁⲕⲉ,
    ⲉⲃⲟⲗ ϩⲛ̄-ⲟⲩϩⲧⲟⲡ ⲙⲛ̄-ⲟⲩⲇⲁⲓⲙⲟ́ⲛⲓⲟⲛ ⲙ̄-ⲡⲛⲁⲩ ⲙ̄-ⲙⲉⲉⲣⲉ.
7   ⲟⲩⲛ̄-ϣⲟ ⲛⲁϩⲉ ϩⲓ-ϩⲃⲟⲩⲣ ⲙ̄ⲙⲟⲕ
    ⲁⲩⲱ ⲟⲩⲧⲃⲁ ϩⲓ-ⲟⲩⲛⲁⲙ ⲙ̄ⲙⲟⲕ,
    ⲛ̄ⲥⲉⲛⲁϩⲱⲛ ⲇⲉ ⲉⲣⲟⲕ ⲁⲛ.
8   ⲡⲗⲏⲛ ⲕⲛⲁⲙⲉϩ-ⲉⲓⲁⲧⲕ̄ ⲙ̄ⲙⲟⲟⲩ,
    ⲛ̄ⲅ̄ⲛⲁⲩ ⲉ-ⲡⲧⲱⲱⲃⲉ ⲛ̄-ⲛ̄ⲣⲉϥⲣ̄ⲛⲟⲃⲉ.

9   ϫⲉ ⲛ̄ⲧⲟⲕ, ⲡϫⲟⲉⲓⲥ, ⲡⲉ ⲧⲁϩⲉⲗⲡⲓ́ⲥ,
    ⲁⲕⲕⲱ ⲛⲁⲕ ⲙ̄-ⲡⲉⲧ-ϫⲟⲥⲉ ⲙ̄-ⲙⲁ ⲙ̄-ⲡⲱⲧ.
10   ⲙ̄ⲙⲛ̄-ⲡⲉⲑⲟⲟⲩ ⲛⲁϩⲱⲛ ⲉⲣⲟⲕ,
    ⲙ̄ⲙⲛ̄-ⲙⲁ́ⲥⲧⲓⲝ ⲛⲁϩⲱⲛ ⲉϩⲟⲩⲛ ⲉ-ⲡⲉⲕⲙⲁ ⲛ̄-ϣⲱⲡⲉ.
11   ϫⲉ ϥⲛⲁϩⲱⲛ ⲉⲧⲟⲟⲧⲟⲩ ⲛ̄-ⲛⲉϥⲁ́ⲅⲅⲉⲗⲟⲥ ⲉⲧⲃⲏⲏⲧⲕ̄,
    ⲉ-ⲧⲣⲉⲩϩⲁⲣⲉϩ ⲉⲣⲟⲕ ϩⲛ̄-ⲛⲉⲕϩⲓⲟⲟⲩⲉ ⲧⲏⲣⲟⲩ.
12   ⲛ̄ⲥⲉϥⲓⲧⲕ̄ ⲉϫⲛ̄-ⲛⲉⲩϭⲓϫ,
    ⲙⲏ́ⲡⲟⲧⲉ ⲛ̄ⲅ̄ϫⲱⲣⲡ̄ ⲛ̄-ⲧⲉⲕⲟⲩⲉⲣⲏⲧⲉ ⲉ-ⲩⲱⲛⲉ.
13   ⲕⲛⲁⲧⲁⲗⲉ ⲉϩⲣⲁⲓ̈ ⲉϫⲛ̄-ⲟⲩϩⲟϥ ⲙⲛ̄-ⲟⲩⲥⲓⲧ,
    ⲛ̄ⲅ̄ϩⲱⲙ ⲉϫⲛ̄-ⲟⲩⲙⲟⲩⲓ̈ ⲙⲛ̄-ⲟⲩⲇⲣⲁ́ⲕⲱⲛ.

14   "ϫⲉ ⲁϥⲛⲁϩⲧⲉ ⲉⲣⲟⲓ̈, ϯⲛⲁⲧⲟⲩϫⲟϥ
    ϯⲛⲁⲣ̄-ϩⲁⲓ̈ⲃⲉⲥ ⲉⲣⲟϥ, ϫⲉ ⲁϥⲥⲟⲩⲛ̄-ⲡⲁⲣⲁⲛ.
15   ϥⲛⲁⲱϣ ⲉϩⲣⲁⲓ̈ ⲉⲣⲟⲓ̈, ⲁⲩⲱ ⲁⲛⲟⲕ ϯⲛⲁⲥⲱⲧⲙ̄ ⲉⲣⲟϥ,
    ϯ-ⲛⲙ̄ⲙⲁϥ ϩⲛ̄-ⲧⲉϥⲑⲗⲓ́ⲯⲓⲥ,
    ⲁⲩⲱ ϯⲛⲁⲧⲟⲩϫⲟϥ ⲛ̄ⲧⲁϯ-ⲉⲟⲟⲩ ⲛⲁϥ.

---

27. Nagel has a misreading (ⲛⲉϩⲟⲟⲧ). Manuscript L has the correct ⲛⲉϩⲟⲟⲩ.

16 ⲧⲛⲁⲧⲥⲟϥ ⲛ̄-ⲟⲩⲙⲏⲏϣⲉ ⲛ̄-ϩⲟⲟⲩ,
    ⲧⲁⲧⲥⲁⲃⲟϥ ⲉ-ⲡⲁⲟⲩϫⲁⲓ̈."

109(110).1 **ⲡⲉⲯⲁⲗⲙⲟⲥ ⲛ̄-ⲇⲁⲩⲉⲓⲇ**

ⲡⲉϫⲉ-ⲡϫⲟⲉⲓⲥ ⲙ̄-ⲡⲁϫⲟⲉⲓⲥ ϫⲉ
   "ϩⲙⲟⲟⲥ ϩⲓ-ⲟⲩⲛⲁⲙ ⲙ̄ⲙⲟⲓ̈,
ϣⲁⲛϯⲕⲱ ⲛ̄-ⲛⲉⲕϫⲓϫⲉⲉⲩ
   ϩⲁ-ⲡⲉⲥⲏⲧ ⲛ̄-ⲛⲉⲕⲟⲩⲉⲣⲏⲧⲉ."

2 ⲛ̄ⲧⲁ-ⲡϫⲟⲉⲓⲥ ⲧⲛ̄ⲛⲟⲟⲩⲕ ⲛ̄-ϭⲉⲣⲱⲃ ⲛ̄-ϭⲟⲙ ϩⲛ̄-ⲥⲓⲱⲛ,
   ⲁⲩⲱ ⲕⲛⲁⲣ̄-ϫⲟⲉⲓⲥ ⲛ̄-ⲧⲙⲏⲧⲉ ⲛ̄-ⲛⲉⲕϫⲁϫⲉ.
3 ⲧⲉⲕⲁⲣⲭⲏ ⲛⲙ̄ⲙⲁⲕ ⲙ̄-ⲡⲉϩⲟⲟⲩ ⲛ̄-ⲧⲉⲕϭⲟⲙ
   ϩⲛ̄-ⲛ̄ⲟⲩⲟⲉⲓⲛ ⲛ̄-ⲛⲉⲧ-ⲟⲩⲁⲁⲃ.
   ⲉⲃⲟⲗ ϩⲛ̄-ⲑⲏ ⲁⲓ̈ϫⲡⲟⲕ,
   ϩⲁⲑⲏ ⲙ̄-ⲡⲥⲟⲩ-ⲛ̄-ⲧⲟⲟⲩⲉ.

4 ⲁ-ⲡϫⲟⲉⲓⲥ ⲱⲣⲕ̄,
   ⲛϥ̄ⲛⲁⲣ̄-ϩⲧⲏϥ ⲁⲛ ϫⲉ
   "ⲛ̄ⲧⲟⲕ ⲡⲉ ⲡⲟⲩⲏⲏⲃ ϣⲁ-ⲉⲛⲉϩ,
   ⲕⲁⲧⲁ-ⲧ̄ⲧⲁ́ⲝⲓⲥ ⲙ̄-ⲙⲉⲗⲭⲓⲥⲉ́ⲇⲉⲕ."
5 ⲡϫⲟⲉⲓⲥ ⲛⲁⲗⲱϫϩ̄ ⲛ̄-ϩⲉⲛⲉⲣⲱⲟⲩ ϩⲓ-ⲟⲩⲛⲁⲙ ⲙ̄ⲙⲟⲕ
   ⲙ̄-ⲡⲉϩⲟⲟⲩ ⲛ̄-ⲧⲉϥⲟⲣⲅⲏ́.
6 ϥⲛⲁⲕⲣⲓⲛⲉ ⲛ̄-ⲛ̄ϩⲉⲑⲛⲟⲥ, ⲛϥ̄ⲙⲁϩⲟⲩ ⲛ̄-ϩⲱⲧⲃ̄,
   ϥⲛⲁⲗⲱϫϩ̄ ⲛ̄-ⲛⲉⲩⲁⲡⲏⲩⲉ ϩⲓϫⲙ̄-ⲡⲕⲁϩ ⲉⲧ-ⲟϣ.
7 ϥⲛⲁⲥⲉ-ⲙⲟⲟⲩ ϩⲛ̄-ⲟⲩⲙⲟⲩ-ⲛ̄-ⲥⲱⲣⲙ̄ ϩⲓ-ⲧⲉϩⲓⲏ,
   ⲉⲧⲃⲉ-ⲡⲁⲓ̈ ϥⲛⲁϫⲓⲥⲉ ⲛ̄-ⲧⲁⲁⲡⲉ.

151.1 **ⲡⲉⲓ̈ⲯⲁⲗⲙⲟⲥ ⲛ̄ⲧⲁ-ⲇⲁⲩⲉⲓⲇ ⲥⲁϩϥ̄ ⲉⲧⲟⲟⲧϥ̄
ⲉϥ-ⲙ̄-ⲡⲃⲟⲗ ⲛ̄-ⲧⲏⲡⲉ
ⲛ̄ⲧⲉⲣⲉϥⲙⲓϣⲉ ⲙⲛ̄-ⲅⲟⲗⲓⲁⲑ**

ⲛⲉ-ⲁⲛⲅ̄-ⲟⲩⲕⲟⲩⲓ̈ ϩⲛ̄-ⲛⲁⲥⲛⲏⲩ,
   ⲉⲓ̈ⲥⲟⲃⲕ̄ ϩⲙ̄-ⲡⲏⲓ̈ ⲙ̄-ⲡⲁⲉⲓⲱⲧ,
   ⲉⲓ̈ⲙⲟⲟⲛⲉ ⲛ̄-ⲛⲉⲥⲟⲟⲩ ⲙ̄-ⲡⲁⲉⲓⲱⲧ.
2 ⲛⲁϭⲓϫ ⲁⲩⲧⲁⲙⲓⲟ ⲛ̄-ⲟⲩⲟ́ⲣⲅⲁⲛⲟⲛ,
   ⲛⲁⲧⲏⲏⲃⲉ ⲁⲩⲧⲱϣ ⲛ̄-ⲟⲩⲯⲁⲗⲧⲏ́ⲣⲓⲟⲛ.
3 ⲛⲓⲙ ⲡⲉⲧ-ⲛⲁϫⲓ-ⲡⲟⲩⲱ ⲙ̄-ⲡϫⲟⲉⲓⲥ?
   ⲛ̄ⲧⲟϥ ⲡⲉ ⲡϫⲟⲉⲓⲥ, ⲛ̄ⲧⲟϥ ⲉⲧ-ⲥⲱⲧⲙ̄.
4 ⲛ̄ⲧⲟϥ ⲡⲉⲛⲧⲁϥⲧⲛ̄ⲛⲟⲟⲩ ⲙ̄-ⲡⲉϥⲁ́ⲅⲅⲉⲗⲟⲥ,
   ⲁϥϥⲓⲧ ⲏ̄ ϩⲛ̄-ⲛⲉⲥⲟⲟⲩ ⲙ̄-ⲡⲁⲉⲓⲱⲧ,
   ⲁϥⲧⲁϩⲥⲧ ⲙ̄-ⲡⲛⲉϩ ⲙ̄-ⲡⲉϥⲧⲱϩⲥ̄.
5 ⲛⲁⲥⲛⲏⲩ ϩⲉⲛⲛⲟϭ ⲛⲉ ⲉ-ⲛⲉⲥⲱⲟⲩ,
   ⲁⲩⲱ ⲙ̄ⲡⲉ-ⲡϫⲟⲉⲓⲥ ⲟⲩⲁϣⲟⲩ.

6   ⲁⲓ̈ⲉⲓ ⲉⲃⲟⲗ ⲉ-ⲧⲱⲙⲛ̄ⲧ ⲉ-ⲡⲁⲗⲗⲟ́ⲫⲩⲗⲟⲥ,
    ⲁⲩⲱ ⲁϥⲥⲁ́ϩⲟⲩ ⲙ̄ⲙⲟⲓ̈ ϩⲛ̄-ⲛⲉϥⲉⲓ́ⲇⲱⲗⲟⲛ.
7   ⲁⲛⲟⲕ ⲇⲉ ⲁⲓ̈ⲧⲉⲕⲙ̄-ⲧⲉϥⲥⲛϥⲉ,
    ⲛ̄ⲧⲟⲟⲧϥ̄ ⲁⲓ̈ϥⲓ ⲛ̄-ⲧⲉϥⲁⲡⲉ,
    ⲁⲩⲱ ⲁⲓ̈ϥⲓ ⲛ̄-ⲟⲩⲛⲟϭⲛⲉϭ ⲉⲃⲟⲗ ϩⲛ̄-ⲛ̄ϣⲏⲣⲉ ⲙ̄-ⲡⲓⲥⲣⲁⲏⲗ.

ⲙ̄ⲡⲁⲣϩⲟⲓⲙⲓ́ⲁ ⲛ̄-ⲥⲟⲗⲟⲙⲱ́ⲛ PROVERBS 22.17–23.12

This text is a sample of wisdom literature, a form of instruction and education common throughout the ancient Near East. This selection is the first part of a larger section of Proverbs (22.17–24.22) sometimes called the "Thirty Sayings of the Wise" on the basis of the Hebrew text of 22.20.[28] This selection in particular has many parallels to the Egyptian composition known as the *Instruction of Amenemope* (usually dated to around 1200 BCE, during the New Kingdom's Ramesside period).[29] These similarities demonstrate the international nature of wisdom literature during the time of the latter New Kingdom in Egypt and Israel's monarchy, whereby the compilers of Israelite wisdom literature have appropriated and adapted available texts from a range of sources, both from within and without Israel and Judah.

The Sahidic text comes from a sixth-century parchment manuscript held by the Oriental Institute in Chicago (manuscript E 10485),[30] published by William Worrell in 1931.[31]

22.17 ⲣⲓⲕⲉ ⲙ̄-ⲡⲉⲕⲙⲁⲁϫⲉ ⲉ-ⲛ̄ϣⲁϫⲉ ⲛ̄-ⲛ̄ⲥⲟⲫⲟ́ⲥ,
       ⲁⲩⲱ ⲛⲅ̄ⲥⲱⲧⲙ̄ ⲉ-ⲛⲁϣⲁϫⲉ,
       ⲛⲅ̄ⲥⲙⲓⲛⲉ ⲇⲉ ⲙ̄-ⲡⲉⲕϩⲏⲧ,
       ϫⲉ ⲉⲕⲉⲉⲓⲙⲉ ⲉⲣⲟⲟⲩ ϫⲉ ⲛⲁⲛⲟⲩⲟⲩ.
18   ⲁⲩⲱ ⲉⲕϣⲁⲛⲕⲁⲁⲩ ϩⲙ̄-ⲡⲉⲕϩⲏⲧ ⲕⲛⲁϯ-ϩⲏⲩ,
       ⲥⲟⲩⲧⲱⲛⲟⲩ ⲇⲉ ϩⲓ-ⲟⲩⲥⲟⲡ ⲉϫⲛ̄-ⲛⲉⲕⲥⲡⲟ́ⲧⲟⲩ.
19   ϫⲉⲕⲁⲥ ⲉⲣⲉ-ⲟⲩⲧⲱⲕ ⲛ̄-ϩⲏⲧ ϣⲱⲡⲉ ⲛⲁⲕ ⲉϫⲙ̄-ⲡⲛⲟⲩⲧⲉ,
       ⲁⲩⲱ ⲛϥ̄ⲧⲁⲙⲟⲕ ⲉ-ⲧⲉϥϩⲓⲏ.
20   ⲛ̄ⲧⲟⲕ ⲇⲉ ϩⲱⲕ ⲥϩⲁⲓ̈ⲥⲟⲩ ⲛⲁⲕ ⲛ̄-ϣⲙ̄ⲧ-ⲥⲱⲡ,
       ⲉ-ⲩϣⲟϫⲛⲉ ⲙⲛ̄-ⲟⲩⲥⲟⲟⲩⲛ̄.
21   ϯⲧⲥⲁⲃⲟ ⲇⲉ ⲙ̄ⲙⲟⲕ ⲉ-ⲥⲟⲩⲛ̄-ⲧⲙⲉ,
       ⲁⲩⲱ ⲉ-ϫⲱ ⲛ̄-ⲛ̄ϣⲁϫⲉ ⲛ̄-ⲧⲙⲉ ⲛ̄-ⲛⲉⲧ-ⲛⲁϫⲛⲟⲩⲕ.
       ⲡϣⲟϫⲛⲉ ⲛⲁϣⲧ̄ ⲉ-ⲡⲟⲩⲟⲓ̈ ⲛ̄-ⲟⲩⲙⲟⲟⲩ,
       ⲥⲱⲧⲙ̄ ⲉ-ϫⲓ ⲛ̄-ⲟⲩⲱ ⲛ̄-ⲛⲉⲧ-ⲛⲁϫⲛⲟⲩⲕ.[32]

22   ⲙ̄ⲡⲣ̄ϫⲓ-ⲟⲩϩⲛⲕⲉ ⲛ̄-ϭⲟⲛⲥ̄ ϫⲉ ϥⲣ̄-ϭⲣⲱϩ ⲅⲁⲣ,
       ⲁⲩⲱ ⲙ̄ⲡⲣ̄ⲥⲉϣϥ̄-ⲟⲩⲁⲥⲑⲉⲛⲏⲥ ϩⲛ̄-ϩⲉⲛⲡⲩ́ⲗⲏ,

---

28. As you will see, the Sahidic text understands this key phrase in a entirely different way.
29. For this text, see "The Instruction of Amenemope," trans. Miriam Lichtheim (*The Context of Scripture* 1.47:115–22).
30. Listed as sa 2009 on the LCBM.
31. William Hoyt Worrell, ed., *The Proverbs of Solomon in Sahidic Coptic According to the Chicago Manuscript*, The University of Chicago Oriental Institute Publications 12 (Chicago: University of Chicago Press, 1931).
32. Emended from ⲛ̄-ⲛⲉⲧ-ⲛⲁϫⲛⲁⲕ.

23 ⲡϫⲟⲉⲓⲥ ⲅⲁⲣ ⲛⲁⲕⲣⲓⲛⲉ ⲙ̄-ⲡⲉϥϩⲁⲡ,
   ⲁⲩⲱ ⲕⲛⲁⲧⲟⲩϫⲟ ⲛ̄-ⲧⲉⲕⲯⲩⲭⲏ ⲛ̄-ⲁⲧⲁⲣⲓⲕⲉ.

24 ⲙ̄ⲡⲣ̄ⲣ̄-ϣⲃⲏⲣ ⲉ-ⲩⲣⲱⲙⲉ ⲛ̄-ⲣⲉϥϭⲱⲛⲧ̄,
   ⲙ̄ⲡⲣ̄ϣⲱⲡⲉ ⲙⲛ̄-ⲟⲩϣⲃⲏⲣ ⲛ̄-ⲣⲉϥⲛⲟⲩϭⲥ̄,
25 ⲙⲏⲡⲟⲧⲉ ⲛⲅ̄ϫⲓ-ⲥⲃⲱ ⲉ-ⲛⲉϥϩⲓⲟⲟⲩⲉ,
   ⲛⲅ̄ϫⲓ ⲛ̄-ⲟⲩϩⲁϭⲉ ⲉ-ⲧⲉⲕⲯⲩⲭⲏ.

26 ⲙ̄ⲡⲣ̄ⲧⲁⲁⲕ ⲛ̄-ϣⲡ̄-ⲧⲱⲣⲉ ⲉ-ⲁⲕϣⲓⲡⲉ ϩⲏⲧϥ̄ ⲛ̄-ⲟⲩϩⲟ,
27   ⲉϣⲱⲡⲉ ⲅⲁⲣ ⲉ-ⲙⲛ̄ⲧⲁⲕ ⲉ-ⲧⲁⲁⲩ,
   ⲥⲉⲛⲁϥⲓ ⲙ̄-ⲡⲉⲡⲣⲏϣ ⲉⲧ-ϩⲁ-ⲛⲉⲕⲥⲡⲓⲣⲟⲟⲩⲉ.

28 ⲙ̄ⲡⲣ̄ⲡⲉⲉⲛⲉ-ⲛ̄ⲧⲟϣ ⲉⲃⲟⲗ ϣⲁ-ⲉⲛⲉϩ
   ⲛ̄ⲧⲁ-ⲛⲉⲕⲉⲓⲟⲧⲉ ⲥⲙⲛ̄ⲧⲟⲩ.

29 ⲟⲩⲣⲱⲙⲉ ⲛ̄-ⲣⲉϥϯ-ϩⲧⲏϥ ⲛ̄-ⲣⲉϥϭⲉⲡⲏ ϩⲛ̄-ⲛⲉϥϩⲃⲏⲩⲉ,
   ϩⲁⲡⲥ̄ ⲉ-ⲧⲣⲉϥⲁϩⲉⲣⲁⲧϥ̄ ⲉ-ϩⲉⲛⲉⲣⲱⲟⲩ,
   ⲛϥ̄ⲧⲙ̄ⲁϩⲉⲣⲁⲧϥ̄ ⲉ-ϩⲉⲛⲣⲱⲙⲉ ⲛ̄-ϭⲱⲃ.

23.1 ⲉⲕϣⲁⲛϩⲙⲟⲟⲥ ⲉ-ⲟⲩⲱⲙ ϩⲓ-ⲧⲉⲧⲣⲁⲡⲉⲍⲁ ⲛ̄-ⲟⲩϫⲱⲱⲣⲉ,
   ϩⲛ̄-ⲟⲩⲛⲟϊ ⲛⲟϊ ⲛ̄-ⲛⲉⲧⲟⲩⲕⲱ ⲙ̄ⲙⲟⲟⲩ ϩⲁⲣⲱⲕ,
2 ⲛⲅ̄ϩⲓⲧⲟⲟⲧⲕ̄ ⲉⲣⲟⲟⲩ,
   ⲉⲕⲥⲟⲟⲩⲛ ϫⲉ ⲕⲛⲁϫⲡⲓ-ⲥⲟⲃⲧⲉ ⲛ̄-ⲧⲉⲓϩⲉ.
3 ⲉϣⲱⲡⲉ ⲛ̄ⲧⲕ̄-ⲟⲩⲁⲧⲥⲉⲓ, ⲙ̄ⲡⲣ̄ⲉⲡⲓⲑⲩⲙⲓ ⲉ-ⲛⲉϥϭⲓⲛⲟⲩⲱⲙ,[33]
   ⲛⲁϊ ⲅⲁⲣ ϩⲏⲛ ⲉϩⲟⲩⲛ ⲉ-ⲩⲱⲛϩ̄ ⲛ̄-ⲛⲟⲩϫ.

4 ⲙ̄ⲡⲣ̄ⲥⲟⲩⲧⲛ̄-ⲧⲟⲟⲧⲕ̄ ⲉⲃⲟⲗ ⲙⲛ̄-ⲟⲩⲣⲙ̄ⲙⲁⲟ, ⲛ̄ⲧⲕ̄-ⲟⲩϩⲏⲕⲉ,
   ⲥⲁϩⲱⲕ ⲇⲉ ⲉⲃⲟⲗ ⲙ̄ⲙⲟϥ ϩⲙ̄-ⲡⲉⲕϩⲏⲧ.
5 ⲉϣⲱⲡⲉ ⲉⲕϣⲁⲛⲥⲙⲛ̄-ⲉⲓⲁⲧⲕ̄ ⲉϫⲱϥ,
   ⲛ̄ⲛⲉϥⲟⲩⲱⲛϩ̄ ⲉⲃⲟⲗ ϩⲛ̄-ⲗⲁⲁⲩ ⲙ̄-ⲙⲁ.
   ⲁϥⲥⲟⲃⲧⲉ ⲅⲁⲣ ⲛⲁϥ ⲛ̄-ϩⲉⲛⲧⲛ̄ϩ ⲛ̄-ⲑⲉ ⲛ̄-ⲟⲩⲁϩⲱⲙⲉ ⲉⲃⲟⲗ ⲉ-ⲡⲁⲏⲣ,
   ⲁⲩⲱ ϥⲛⲁⲕⲧⲟϥ ⲉ-ⲡⲏϊ ⲙ̄-ⲡⲉⲧ-ϩⲓϫⲱϥ.
   ⲡⲱⲛⲉ ϩⲟⲣϣ̄ ⲁⲩⲱ ⲡϣⲱ ⲙⲟⲕϩ̄ ⲛ̄-ϥⲓ ϩⲁⲣⲟϥ,
   ⲧⲟⲣⲅⲏ ⲇⲉ ⲙ̄-ⲡⲁⲑⲏⲧ ϩⲟⲣϣ̄ ⲉ-ϩⲟⲩⲉⲣⲟⲟⲩ ⲙ̄-ⲡⲉⲥⲛⲁⲩ.

6 ⲙ̄ⲡⲣ̄ⲟⲩⲱⲙ ⲙⲛ̄-ⲟⲩⲣⲱⲙⲉ ⲛ̄-ⲉⲓⲉⲣ-ⲃⲟⲟⲛⲉ,
   ⲁⲩⲱ ⲙ̄ⲡⲣ̄ⲉⲡⲓⲑⲩⲙⲓ ⲉ-ⲛⲉϥϭⲓⲛⲟⲩⲱⲙ.
7 ⲙ̄ⲡⲣ̄ϫⲓⲧϥ̄ ⲉϩⲟⲩⲛ ⲉ-ⲡⲉⲕⲏϊ
   ϫⲉ ⲛ̄ⲛⲉⲕⲟⲩⲱⲙ ⲛ̄-ⲛⲉⲕⲟⲉⲓⲕ ⲛⲙ̄ⲙⲁϥ,
   ⲛ̄-ⲑⲉ ⲅⲁⲣ ⲛ̄-ⲟⲩⲁ ⲉϥⲛⲁⲉⲙⲕ̄-ⲟⲩϣⲱ,
   ⲧⲁϊ ⲧⲉ ⲑⲉ ⲉⲧϥ̄ⲛⲁⲟⲩⲱⲙ ⲁⲩⲱ ⲛϥ̄ⲥⲱ.
8 ϥⲛⲁⲕⲁ-ⲃⲟⲗ ⲅⲁⲣ ⲙ̄ⲙⲟⲟⲩ,

---

[33]. Emended from ⲉ-ⲛⲉϥϭⲓⲛⲟⲩⲟⲙ.

ⲛϥ̄ⲧⲁⲕⲉ-ⲛⲉⲕϣⲁϫⲉ ⲉⲧ-ⲛⲁⲛⲟⲩⲟⲩ.

9 ⲙ̄ⲡⲣ̄ϫⲉ-ⲗⲁⲁⲩ ⲉ-ⲙ̄ⲙⲁⲁϫⲉ ⲙ̄-ⲡⲁⲑⲏⲧ,
ⲙⲏⲡⲟⲧⲉ ⲛϥ̄ⲕⲙ̄ϣ̄-ⲛⲉⲕϣⲁϫⲉ.

10 ⲙ̄ⲡⲣ̄ⲃⲱⲕ ⲉϩⲟⲩⲛ ⲉ-ϭⲱⲙ ⲛ̄-ⲟⲣⲫⲁⲛⲟⲥ,
11 ⲡⲛⲟⲩⲧⲉ ⲅⲁⲣ ⲉⲧ-ϫⲟⲟⲣ ⲡⲉⲧ-ⲥⲱⲧⲉ ⲙ̄ⲙⲟⲟⲩ,
ⲁⲩⲱ ϥⲛⲁϫⲓ-ϩⲁⲡ ⲛⲙ̄ⲙⲁⲕ ϩⲁⲣⲟⲟⲩ.

12 ϯ-ⲡⲉⲕϩⲏⲧ ⲉ-ⲧⲉⲥⲃⲱ,
ⲛⲅ̄ⲥⲃ̄ⲧⲉ-ⲛⲉⲕⲙⲁⲁϫⲉ ⲉ-ⲛ̄ϣⲁϫⲉ ⲛ̄-ⲧⲁⲓⲥⲑⲏⲥⲓⲥ.

ⲡⲉⲩⲁⲅⲅⲉⲗⲓⲟⲛ ⲛ̄-ⲕⲁⲧⲁ-ⲓⲱϩⲁⲛⲛⲏⲥ JOHN 1.1–2.12

The Gospel of John is the best attested book of the Sahidic New Testament, with dozens of known manuscripts. Like the Psalms, these manuscripts span a thousand years of scribal activity.

This text selection, from the beginning of the Gospel, extends from John's cosmic prologue (interweaving a hymn to the Word with the arrival of John the Baptizer) to the first special sign that Jesus performs at a wedding in Kana.

The text is adapted from the recent critical edition,[34] which references ten complete or nearly complete manuscripts, with over 150 more fragmentary manuscripts cited.

1.1 ϩⲛ̄-ⲧⲉϩⲟⲩⲉⲓⲧⲉ ⲛⲉϥϣⲟⲟⲡ ⲛ̄ϭⲓ-ⲡϣⲁϫⲉ,
ⲁⲩⲱ ⲡϣⲁϫⲉ ⲛⲉϥϣⲟⲟⲡ ⲛ̄ⲛⲁϩⲣⲙ̄-ⲡⲛⲟⲩⲧⲉ,
ⲁⲩⲱ ⲛⲉ-ⲩⲛⲟⲩⲧⲉ ⲡⲉ ⲡϣⲁϫⲉ.
2 ⲡⲁⲓ̈ ϩⲛ̄-ⲧⲉϩⲟⲩⲉⲓⲧⲉ ⲛⲉϥϣⲟⲟⲡ ϩⲁⲧⲙ̄-ⲡⲛⲟⲩⲧⲉ.
3 ⲛ̄ⲧⲁ-ⲡⲧⲏⲣϥ̄ ϣⲱⲡⲉ ⲉⲃⲟⲗ ϩⲓⲧⲟⲟⲧϥ̄,
ⲁⲩⲱ ⲁϫⲛ̄ⲧϥ̄ ⲙ̄ⲡⲉ-ⲗⲁⲁⲩ ϣⲱⲡⲉ.
4 ⲡⲉⲛⲧⲁϥϣⲱⲡⲉ ϩⲣⲁⲓ̈ ⲛ̄ϩⲏⲧϥ̄ ⲡⲉ ⲡⲱⲛϩ̄,
ⲁⲩⲱ ⲡⲱⲛϩ̄ ⲡⲉ ⲡⲟⲩⲟⲉⲓⲛ ⲛ̄-ⲛ̄ⲣⲱⲙⲉ.
5 ⲁⲩⲱ ⲡⲟⲩⲟⲉⲓⲛ ϥⲣ̄-ⲟⲩⲟⲉⲓⲛ ϩⲙ̄-ⲡⲕⲁⲕⲉ,
ⲁⲩⲱ ⲙ̄ⲡⲉ-ⲡⲕⲁⲕⲉ ⲧⲁϩⲟϥ.

6 ⲁϥϣⲱⲡⲉ ⲛ̄ϭⲓ-ⲟⲩⲣⲱⲙⲉ ⲉ-ⲁⲩⲧⲛ̄ⲛⲟⲟⲩϥ ⲉⲃⲟⲗ ϩⲓⲧⲙ̄-ⲡⲛⲟⲩⲧⲉ, ⲉ-ⲡⲉϥⲣⲁⲛ ⲡⲉ ⲓ̈ⲱϩⲁⲛⲛⲏⲥ. 7 ⲡⲁⲓ̈ ⲁϥⲉⲓ ⲉ-ⲩⲙⲛ̄ⲧⲙⲛ̄ⲧⲣⲉ, ϫⲉⲕⲁⲥ ⲉϥⲉⲣ̄-ⲙⲛ̄ⲧⲣⲉ ⲉⲧⲃⲉ-ⲡⲟⲩⲟⲉⲓⲛ, ϫⲉⲕⲁⲥ ⲉⲣⲉ-ⲟⲩⲟⲛ ⲛⲓⲙ ⲡⲓⲥⲧⲉⲩⲉ ⲉⲃⲟⲗ ϩⲓⲧⲟⲟⲧϥ̄. 8 ⲛⲉ-ⲡⲉⲧ-ⲙ̄ⲙⲁⲩ ⲁⲛ ⲡⲉ ⲡⲟⲩⲟⲉⲓⲛ, ⲁⲗⲗⲁ ϫⲉⲕⲁⲥ ⲛ̄ⲧⲟϥ ⲉϥⲉⲣ̄-ⲙⲛ̄ⲧⲣⲉ ⲉⲧⲃⲉ-ⲡⲟⲩⲟⲉⲓⲛ.

9 ⲡⲟⲩⲟⲉⲓⲛ ⲙ̄-ⲙⲉ,
ⲉⲧ-ⲣ̄-ⲟⲩⲟⲉⲓⲛ ⲉ-ⲣⲱⲙⲉ ⲛⲓⲙ,

---

34. Hans Förster, Kerstin Sänger-Böhm, and Matthias H. O. Schulz, eds., *Kritische Edition der sahidischen Version des Johannesevangeliums: Text und Dokumentation*, Arbeiten zur Neutestamentlichen Textforschung 56 (Berlin: de Gruyter, 2021).

пе ечину е-пкосмос.

10 нец-ѕм̄-пкосмос пе,
ауω ⲛ̄ⲧⲁ-ⲡⲕⲟⲥⲙⲟⲥ ϣⲱⲡⲉ ⲉⲃⲟⲗ ϩⲓⲧⲟⲟⲧϥ̄,
ⲁⲩⲱ ⲙ̄ⲡⲉ-ⲡⲕⲟⲥⲙⲟⲥ ⲥⲟⲩⲱⲛϥ̄.

11 ⲁϥⲉⲓ ϣⲁ-ⲛⲉⲧⲉ-ⲛⲟⲩϥ ⲛⲉ,
ⲁⲩⲱ ⲙ̄ⲡⲉ-ⲛⲉⲧⲉ-ⲛⲟⲩϥ ⲛⲉ ϫⲓⲧϥ̄.

12 ⲛⲉⲛ̄ⲧⲁⲩϫⲓⲧϥ̄ ⲇⲉ,
ⲁϥϯ ⲛⲁⲩ ⲛ̄-ⲧⲉⲝⲟⲩⲥⲓⲁ ⲉⲧⲣⲉⲩϣⲱⲡⲉ ⲛ̄-ϣⲏⲣⲉ ⲛ̄ⲧⲉ-ⲡⲛⲟⲩⲧⲉ,
ⲛⲉⲧ-ⲡⲓⲥⲧⲉⲩⲉ ⲉ-ⲡⲉϥⲣⲁⲛ.

13 ⲛⲁⲓ̈ ⲛ̄-ϩⲉⲛⲉⲃⲟⲗ ⲁⲛ ⲛⲉ ϩⲛ̄-ⲟⲩⲱϣ ⲛ̄-ⲥⲛⲟϥ ϩⲓ-ⲥⲁⲣⲝ̄,
ⲟⲩⲇⲉ ⲉⲃⲟⲗ ⲁⲛ ϩⲙ̄-ⲡⲟⲩⲱϣ ⲛ̄-ⲣⲱⲙⲉ,
ⲁⲗⲗⲁ ⲛ̄ⲧⲁⲩϫⲡⲟⲟⲩ ⲉⲃⲟⲗ ϩⲙ̄-ⲡⲛⲟⲩⲧⲉ.

14 ⲁⲩⲱ ⲡϣⲁϫⲉ ⲁϥⲣ̄-ⲥⲁⲣⲝ̄,
ⲁϥⲟⲩⲱϩ ⲛⲙ̄ⲙⲁⲛ.
ⲁⲩⲱ ⲁⲛⲛⲁⲩ ⲉ-ⲡⲉϥⲉⲟⲟⲩ,
ⲛ̄-ⲑⲉ ⲙ̄-ⲡⲉⲟⲟⲩ ⲛ̄-ⲟⲩϣⲏⲣⲉ ⲛ̄-ⲟⲩⲱⲧ ⲉⲃⲟⲗ ϩⲓⲧⲙ̄-ⲡⲉϥⲉⲓⲱⲧ,
ⲉϥϫⲏⲕ ⲉⲃⲟⲗ ⲛ̄-ⲭⲁⲣⲓⲥ ϩⲓ-ⲙⲉ.

15 ⲓ̈ⲱϩⲁⲛⲛⲏⲥ ⲣ̄-ⲙⲛ̄ⲧⲣⲉ ⲉⲧⲃⲏⲏⲧϥ̄, ⲁⲩⲱ ϥⲁϣⲕⲁⲕ ⲉⲃⲟⲗ, ⲉϥϫⲱ ⲙ̄ⲙⲟⲥ ϫⲉ "ⲡⲁⲓ̈ ⲡⲉ ⲛ̄ⲧⲁⲓ̈ϫⲟⲟⲥ ⲉⲧⲃⲏⲏⲧϥ̄ ϫⲉ 'ⲡⲉⲧⲛⲏⲩ ⲙⲛ̄ⲛⲥⲱⲓ̈ ⲁϥϣⲱⲡⲉ ϩⲁ-ⲧⲁϩⲏ, ϫⲉ ⲛⲉϥⲟ ⲛ̄ϣⲟⲣⲡ̄ ⲉⲣⲟⲓ̈ ⲡⲉ.'"

16 ϫⲉ ⲉⲃⲟⲗ ϩⲙ̄-ⲡⲉϥϫⲱⲕ ⲁⲛⲟⲛ ⲧⲏⲣⲛ̄ ⲛ̄ⲧⲁⲛϫⲓ ⲛ̄-ⲟⲩⲱⲛϩ̄,
ⲁⲩⲱ ⲟⲩⲭⲁⲣⲓⲥ ⲉ-ⲡⲙⲁ ⲛ̄-ⲟⲩⲭⲁⲣⲓⲥ.

17 ϫⲉ ⲡⲛⲟⲙⲟⲥ ⲛ̄ⲧⲁⲩⲧⲁⲁϥ ⲉⲃⲟⲗ ϩⲓⲧⲙ̄-ⲙⲱⲩ̈ⲥⲏⲥ,
ⲧⲉⲭⲁⲣⲓⲥ ϩⲱⲱⲥ ⲁⲩⲱ ⲧⲙⲉ,
ⲛ̄ⲧⲁⲥϣⲱⲡⲉ ⲉⲃⲟⲗ ϩⲓⲧⲛ̄-ⲓⲏⲥⲟⲩⲥ ⲡⲉⲭⲣⲓⲥⲧⲟⲥ.

18 ⲡⲛⲟⲩⲧⲉ ⲙ̄ⲡⲉ-ⲗⲁⲁⲩ ⲛⲁⲩ ⲉⲣⲟϥ ⲉⲛⲉϩ. ⲡⲛⲟⲩⲧⲉ ⲡϣⲏⲣⲉ ⲛ̄-ⲟⲩⲱⲧ ⲡⲉⲧϣⲟⲟⲡ ϩⲛ̄-ⲕⲟⲩⲛϥ̄ ⲙ̄-ⲡⲉϥⲉⲓⲱⲧ, ⲡⲉⲧ-ⲙ̄ⲙⲁⲩ ⲡⲉ ⲛ̄ⲧⲁϥϣⲁϫⲉ ⲉⲣⲟϥ.

19 ⲁⲩⲱ ⲧⲁⲓ̈ ⲧⲉ ⲧⲙⲛ̄ⲧⲙⲛ̄ⲧⲣⲉ ⲛ̄-ⲓ̈ⲱϩⲁⲛⲛⲏⲥ ⲛ̄ⲧⲉⲣⲉ-ⲛ̄ⲓ̈ⲟⲩⲇⲁⲓ̈ ⲧⲛ̄ⲛⲟⲟⲩ ϣⲁⲣⲟϥ ⲉⲃⲟⲗ ϩⲛ̄-ⲑⲓⲉⲣⲟⲩⲥⲁⲗⲏⲙ ⲛ̄-ϩⲉⲛⲟⲩⲏⲏⲃ ⲙⲛ̄-ϩⲉⲛⲗⲉⲩⲉⲓⲧⲏⲥ ϫⲉⲕⲁⲥ ⲉⲩⲉϫⲛⲟⲩϥ ϫⲉ "ⲛ̄ⲧⲕ̄-ⲛⲓⲙ?"

20 ⲁⲩⲱ ⲁϥϩⲟⲙⲟⲗⲟⲅⲉⲓ ⲁⲩⲱ ⲙ̄ⲡϥ̄ⲁⲣⲛⲁ ϫⲉ "ⲛ̄-ⲁⲛⲟⲕ ⲁⲛ ⲡⲉ ⲡⲉⲭⲣⲓⲥⲧⲟⲥ."

21 ⲁⲩϫⲛⲟⲩϥ ϫⲉ "ⲛ̄ⲧⲟⲕ ⲡⲉ ϩⲏⲗⲓⲁⲥ?"
ⲁⲩⲱ ⲡⲉϫⲁϥ ϫⲉ "ⲛ̄-ⲁⲛⲟⲕ ⲁⲛ ⲡⲉ."
"ⲛ̄ⲧⲟⲕ ⲡⲉ ⲡⲉⲡⲣⲟⲫⲏⲧⲏⲥ?"
ⲁⲩⲱ ⲁϥⲟⲩⲱϣⲃ̄ ϫⲉ "ⲙ̄ⲙⲟⲛ."

22 ⲡⲉϫⲁⲩ ϭⲉ ⲛⲁϥ ϫⲉ "ⲛ̄ⲧⲟⲕ ϭⲉ ⲛ̄ⲧⲕ̄-ⲛⲓⲙ, ϫⲉⲕⲁⲥ ⲉⲛⲉϫⲓ-ⲡⲟⲩⲱ ⲛ̄-ⲛⲉⲛ̄ⲧⲁⲩⲧⲁⲩⲟⲛ? ⲉⲕϫⲱ ⲙ̄ⲙⲟⲥ ϫⲉ ⲟⲩ ⲉⲧⲃⲏⲏⲧⲕ̄?"

23 ⲡⲉϫⲁϥ ϫⲉ "ⲁⲛⲟⲕ ⲡⲉ

ⲧⲉⲥⲙⲏ ⲙ̄-ⲡⲉⲧ-ⲱϣ ⲉⲃⲟⲗ ϩⲓ-ⲡϫⲁⲓ̈ⲉ ϫⲉ
'ⲥⲟⲩⲧⲛ̄ ⲛ̄-ⲧⲉϩⲓⲏ ⲙ̄-ⲡϫⲟⲉⲓⲥ!'

ⲕⲁⲧⲁ-ⲑⲉ ⲛ̄ⲧⲁϥϫⲟⲟⲥ ⲛ̄ϭⲓ-ⲏⲥⲁⲓ̈ⲁⲥ ⲡⲉⲡⲣⲟⲫⲏ́ⲧⲏⲥ.''

24 ⲁⲩⲱ ⲁⲩⲧ̄ⲛ̄ⲛⲉⲩ-ϩⲟⲓ̈ⲛⲉ ϣⲁⲣⲟϥ ⲉⲃⲟⲗ ϩⲛ̄-ⲛⲉⲫⲁⲣⲓⲥⲁⲓ̈ⲟⲥ, 25 ⲁⲩϫⲛⲟⲩϥ ϫⲉ "ⲉⲧⲃⲉ-ⲟⲩ ϭⲉ ⲕⲃⲁⲡⲧⲓⲍⲉ, ⲉϣϫⲉ ⲛ̄ⲧⲟⲕ ⲁⲛ ⲡⲉ ⲡⲉⲭⲣⲓⲥⲧⲟⲥ, ⲟⲩⲇⲉ́ ϩⲏⲗⲓ́ⲁⲥ, ⲟⲩⲇⲉ́ ⲡⲉⲡⲣⲟⲫⲏ́ⲧⲏⲥ?''

26 ⲁ-ⲓ̈ⲱϩⲁ́ⲛⲛⲏⲥ ⲟⲩⲱϣⲃ̄ ⲉϥϫⲱ ⲙ̄ⲙⲟⲥ ⲛⲁⲩ ϫⲉ "ⲁⲛⲟⲕ ⲙⲉⲛ ⲉⲓ̈ⲃⲁⲡⲧⲓⲍⲉ ⲙ̄ⲙⲱⲧⲛ̄ ϩⲛ̄-ⲟⲩⲙⲟⲟⲩ, ϥⲁϩⲉ ⲇⲉ ⲉⲣⲁⲧϥ̄ ϩⲛ̄-ⲧⲉⲧⲛ̄ⲙⲏⲧⲉ ⲡⲁⲓ̈ ⲛ̄ⲧⲱⲧⲛ̄ ⲛ̄ⲧⲉⲧⲛ̄ⲥⲟⲟⲩⲛ ⲙ̄ⲙⲟϥ ⲁⲛ. 27 ⲡⲉⲧ-ⲛⲏⲩ ⲙⲛ̄ⲛ̄ⲥⲱⲓ̈ ⲡⲁⲓ̈ ⲛ̄ϯⲙ̄ⲡϣⲁ ⲁⲛ ⲛ̄-ⲃⲱⲗ ⲉⲃⲟⲗ ⲙ̄-ⲡⲙⲟⲩⲥ ⲙ̄-ⲡⲉϥⲧⲟⲟⲩⲉ.''

28 ⲛⲁⲓ̈ ⲛ̄ⲧⲁⲩϣⲱⲡⲉ ϩⲛ̄-ⲃⲏⲑⲁⲃⲁⲣⲁ́ ⲙ̄-ⲡⲉⲕⲣⲟ ⲙ̄-ⲡⲓ̈ⲟⲣⲇⲁ́ⲛⲏⲥ, ⲡⲙⲁ ⲉⲛⲉⲣⲉ-ⲓ̈ⲱϩⲁ́ⲛⲛⲏⲥ ⲃⲁⲡⲧⲓⲍⲉ ⲛ̄ϩⲏⲧϥ̄.

29 ⲙ̄-ⲡⲉϥⲣⲁⲥⲧⲉ ⲁϥⲛⲁⲩ ⲉ-ⲓⲏⲥⲟⲩ́ⲥ ⲉϥⲛⲏⲩ ϣⲁⲣⲟϥ ⲁⲩⲱ ⲡⲉϫⲁϥ ϫⲉ "ⲉⲓ̈ⲥ! ⲡⲉϩⲓ̈ⲉⲓ̈ⲃ ⲙ̄-ⲡⲛⲟⲩⲧⲉ ⲡⲉⲧ-ⲛⲁϥⲓ ⲙ̄-ⲡⲛⲟⲃⲉ ⲙ̄-ⲡⲕⲟ́ⲥⲙⲟⲥ! 30 ⲡⲁⲓ̈ ⲡⲉ ⲛ̄ⲧⲁⲓ̈ϫⲟⲟⲥ ⲉⲧⲃⲏⲧϥ̄ ϫⲉ 'ⲟⲩⲛ̄-ⲟⲩⲣⲱⲙⲉ ⲛⲏⲩ ϩⲓⲡⲁϩⲟⲩ ⲙ̄ⲙⲟⲓ̈ ⲉⲁϥϣⲱⲡⲉ ϩⲁⲧⲁϩⲏ ϫⲉ ⲛⲉϥⲟ ⲛ̄-ϣⲟⲣⲡ̄ ⲉⲣⲟⲓ̈ ⲡⲉ.' 31 ⲁⲛⲟⲕ ϩⲱ ⲛⲉⲓ̈ⲥⲟⲟⲩⲛ ⲙ̄ⲙⲟϥ ⲁⲛ ⲡⲉ, ⲁⲗⲗⲁ ϫⲉⲕⲁⲥ ⲉϥⲉⲟⲩⲱⲛϩ̄ ⲉⲃⲟⲗ ⲙ̄-ⲡⲓⲥⲣⲁⲏⲗ, ⲉⲧⲃⲉ-ⲡⲁⲓ̈ ⲁⲛⲟⲕ ⲁⲓ̈ⲉⲓ̈ ⲉⲓ̈ⲃⲁⲡⲧⲓⲍⲉ ϩⲛ̄-ⲟⲩⲙⲟⲟⲩ.''

32 ⲁⲩⲱ ⲁϥⲣ̄-ⲙⲛ̄ⲧⲣⲉ ⲛ̄ϭⲓ-ⲓ̈ⲱϩⲁ́ⲛⲛⲏⲥ ⲉϥϫⲱ ⲙ̄ⲙⲟⲥ ϫⲉ "ⲁⲓ̈ⲛⲁⲩ ⲉ-ⲡⲉⲡⲛⲉⲩ́ⲙⲁ ⲉϥⲛⲏⲩ ⲉⲡⲉⲥⲏⲧ ⲉⲃⲟⲗ ϩⲛ̄-ⲧⲡⲉ ⲛ̄-ⲑⲉ ⲛ̄-ⲟⲩϭⲣⲟⲟⲙⲡⲉ, ⲁⲩⲱ ⲁϥⲟⲩⲱϩ ⲉϩⲣⲁⲓ̈ ⲉϫⲱϥ. 33 ⲁⲛⲟⲕ ϩⲱ ⲛⲉⲓ̈ⲥⲟⲟⲩⲛ ⲙ̄ⲙⲟϥ ⲁⲛ ⲡⲉ, ⲁⲗⲗⲁ ⲡⲉⲛⲧⲁϥⲧⲛ̄ⲛⲟⲟⲩⲧ ⲉ-ⲃⲁⲡⲧⲓⲍⲉ ϩⲛ̄-ⲟⲩⲙⲟⲟⲩ, ⲡⲉⲧ-ⲙ̄ⲙⲁⲩ ⲡⲉ ⲛ̄ⲧⲁϥϫⲟⲟⲥ ⲛⲁⲓ̈ ϫⲉ 'ⲡⲉⲧⲕⲛⲁⲛⲁⲩ ⲉ-ⲡⲉⲡⲛⲉⲩ́ⲙⲁ ⲉϥⲛⲏⲩ ⲉⲡⲉⲥⲏⲧ ⲉϥϭⲉⲉⲧ ⲉϩⲣⲁⲓ̈ ⲉϫⲱϥ, ⲡⲁⲓ̈ ⲡⲉⲧ-ⲛⲁⲃⲁⲡⲧⲓⲍⲉ ϩⲛ̄-ⲟⲩⲡⲛⲉⲩ́ⲙⲁ ⲉϥⲟⲩⲁⲁⲃ ⲙⲛ̄-ⲟⲩⲕⲱϩⲧ̄.' 34 ⲁⲩⲱ ⲁⲛⲟⲕ ⲁⲓ̈ⲛⲁⲩ, ⲁⲩⲱ ⲁⲓ̈ⲣ̄-ⲙⲛ̄ⲧⲣⲉ ϫⲉ ⲡⲁⲓ̈ ⲡⲉ, ⲡⲥⲱⲧⲡ̄ ⲛ̄-ϣⲏⲣⲉ ⲛ̄ⲧⲉ-ⲡⲛⲟⲩⲧⲉ.''

35 ⲙ̄-ⲡⲉϥⲣⲁⲥⲧⲉ ⲟⲛ ⲉⲣⲉ-ⲓ̈ⲱϩⲁ́ⲛⲛⲏⲥ ⲁϩⲉⲣⲁⲧϥ̄ ⲁⲩⲱ ⲥⲛⲁⲩ ⲉⲃⲟⲗ ϩⲛ̄-ⲛⲉϥⲙⲁⲑⲏⲧⲏⲥ. 36 ⲁⲩⲱ ⲛ̄ⲧⲉⲣⲉϥϭⲱϣⲧ̄ ⲛ̄ⲥⲁ-ⲓⲏⲥⲟⲩ́ⲥ ⲉϥⲙⲟⲟϣⲉ, ⲡⲉϫⲁϥ ϫⲉ "ⲉⲓ̈ⲥ! ⲡⲉⲭⲣⲓⲥⲧⲟⲥ ⲡⲉϩⲓ̈ⲉⲓ̈ⲃ ⲛ̄ⲧⲉ-ⲡⲛⲟⲩⲧⲉ!''

37 ⲁ-ⲡⲉϥⲙⲁⲑⲏⲧⲏⲥ ⲥⲛⲁⲩ ⲥⲱⲧⲙ̄ ⲉⲣⲟϥ ⲉϥϣⲁϫⲉ, ⲁⲩⲱ ⲁⲩⲟⲩⲁϩⲟⲩ ⲛ̄ⲥⲁ-ⲓⲏⲥⲟⲩ́ⲥ. 38 ⲛ̄ⲧⲉⲣⲉϥⲕⲟⲧϥ̄ ⲇⲉ ⲛ̄ϭⲓ-ⲓⲏⲥⲟⲩ́ⲥ, ⲁϥⲛⲁⲩ ⲉⲣⲟⲟⲩ ⲉⲩⲟⲩⲏϩ ⲛ̄ⲥⲱϥ. ⲡⲉϫⲁϥ ⲛⲁⲩ ϫⲉ "ⲉⲧⲉⲧⲛ̄ϣⲓⲛⲉ ⲛ̄ⲥⲁ-ⲟⲩ?''

ⲡⲉϫⲁⲩ ⲛⲁϥ ϫⲉ "ϩⲣⲁⲃⲃⲉⲓ̈'' (ⲡⲉ-ϣⲁⲩⲟⲩⲁϩⲙⲉϥ ϫⲉ ⲡⲥⲁϩ), "ⲉⲕⲟⲩⲏϩ ⲧⲱⲛ?''

39 ⲡⲉϫⲁϥ ⲛⲁⲩ ϫⲉ "ⲁⲙⲏⲓ̈ⲧⲛ̄ ⲛ̄ⲧⲉⲧⲛ̄ⲛⲁⲩ.[35]''

ⲁⲩⲉⲓ ϭⲉ ⲁⲩⲛⲁⲩ ϫⲉ ⲉϥⲟⲩⲏϩ ⲧⲱⲛ ⲁⲩⲱ ⲁⲩϣⲱⲡⲉ ϩⲁⲧⲛϥ̄[36] ⲙ̄-ⲡⲉϩⲟⲟⲩ ⲉⲧ-ⲙ̄ⲙⲁⲩ, ⲛⲉ-ⲡⲛⲁⲩ ⲅⲁⲣ[37] ⲛ̄-ϫⲡ̄-ⲙⲏⲧⲉ ⲡⲉ.

40 ⲁⲛⲇⲣⲉ́ⲁⲥ ⲡⲥⲟⲛ ⲛ̄-ⲥⲓ́ⲙⲱⲛ ⲡⲉ́ⲧⲣⲟⲥ ⲛⲉ-ⲟⲩⲁ ⲡⲉ ⲉⲃⲟⲗ ϩⲙ̄-ⲡⲉⲥⲛⲁⲩ ⲛ̄ⲧⲁⲩⲥⲱⲧⲙ̄ ⲉⲃⲟⲗ ϩⲓⲧⲛ̄-ⲓ̈ⲱϩⲁ́ⲛⲛⲏⲥ ⲁⲩⲱ ⲁⲩⲟⲩⲁϩⲟⲩ ⲛ̄ⲥⲱϥ. 41 ⲡⲁⲓ̈ ⲁϥϩⲉ ⲉ-ⲡⲉϥⲥⲟⲛ ⲥⲓ́ⲙⲱⲛ ⲛ̄-ϣⲟⲣⲡ̄, ⲁⲩⲱ ⲡⲉϫⲁϥ ⲛⲁϥ ϫⲉ "ⲁⲛϩⲉ ⲉ-ⲙⲉⲥⲥⲓ́ⲁⲥ!'' (ⲡⲉ-ϣⲁⲩⲟⲩⲁϩⲙⲉϥ ϫⲉ ⲡⲉⲭⲣⲓⲥⲧⲟⲥ). 42 ⲁⲩⲱ ⲁϥⲛ̄ⲧϥ̄ ⲉⲣⲁⲧϥ̄ ⲛ̄-ⲓⲏⲥⲟⲩ́ⲥ.

ⲓⲏⲥⲟⲩ́ⲥ ⲇⲉ ⲛ̄ⲧⲉⲣⲉϥϭⲱϣⲧ̄ ⲉϩⲟⲩⲛ ⲉϩⲣⲁϥ, ⲡⲉϫⲁϥ ϫⲉ "ⲛ̄ⲧⲟⲕ ⲡⲉ ⲥⲓ́ⲙⲱⲛ ⲡϣⲏⲣⲉ ⲛ̄-ⲓ̈ⲱϩⲁ́ⲛⲛⲏⲥ. ⲛ̄ⲧⲟⲕ ⲉⲩⲉⲙⲟⲩⲧⲉ ⲉⲣⲟⲕ ϫⲉ ⲕⲏⲫⲁ́'' (ⲡⲉ-ϣⲁⲩⲟⲩⲁϩⲙⲉϥ ϫⲉ ⲡⲉ́ⲧⲣⲟⲥ).

43 ⲙ̄-ⲡⲉϥⲣⲁⲥⲧⲉ ⲇⲉ ⲁϥⲟⲩⲱϣ ⲉ-ⲉⲓ ⲉⲃⲟⲗ ⲉ-ⲧⲅⲁⲗⲓⲗⲁⲓ́ⲁ. ⲁⲩⲱ ⲁϥϩⲉ ⲉ-ⲫⲓ́ⲗⲓⲡⲡⲟⲥ, ⲡⲉϫⲁϥ ⲛⲁϥ ⲛ̄ϭⲓ-ⲓⲏⲥⲟⲩ́ⲥ ϫⲉ "ⲟⲩⲁϩⲕ̄ ⲛ̄ⲥⲱⲓ̈!''

44 ⲫⲓ́ⲗⲓⲡⲡⲟⲥ ⲇⲉ ⲛⲉ-ⲟⲩⲉⲃⲟⲗ ⲡⲉ ϩⲛ̄-ⲃⲏⲇⲥⲁⲓ̈ⲇⲁ́, ⲧⲡⲟⲗⲓⲥ ⲛ̄-ⲁⲛⲇⲣⲉ́ⲁⲥ ⲙⲛ̄-ⲡⲉ́ⲧⲣⲟⲥ. 45 ⲁ-ⲫⲓ́ⲗⲓⲡⲡⲟⲥ ϩⲉ ⲉ-ⲛⲁⲑⲁⲛⲁⲏⲗ, ⲡⲉϫⲁϥ ⲛⲁϥ ϫⲉ "ⲡⲉⲛⲧⲁ-ⲙⲱⲩ̈ⲥⲏⲥ ⲥϩⲁⲓ̈ ⲉⲧⲃⲏⲧϥ̄ ϩⲙ̄-ⲡⲛⲟⲙⲟⲥ ⲁⲩⲱ ⲛⲉⲡⲣⲟⲫⲏ́ⲧⲏⲥ, ⲁⲛϩⲉ ⲉⲣⲟϥ, ⲓⲏⲥⲟⲩⲥ ⲡϣⲏⲣⲉ ⲛ̄-ⲓ̈ⲱⲥⲏⲫ, ⲡⲉⲃⲟⲗ ϩⲛ̄-ⲛⲁⲍⲁⲣⲉⲑ!''

---

35. Variant reading: ⲁⲙⲏⲉⲓ̈ⲧⲛ̄ ⲁⲩⲱ ⲧⲉⲧⲛⲁⲛⲁⲩ.
36. Variant reading: ϩⲁϩⲧⲏϥ.
37. Variant reading: omit ⲅⲁⲣ.

46 ⲡⲉϫⲉ-ⲛⲁⲑⲁⲛⲁⲏⲗ ⲛⲁϥ ϫⲉ "ⲉⲣⲉ-ϣ-ⲟⲩⲁⲅⲁⲑⲟⲛ ϣⲱⲡⲉ ⲉⲃⲟⲗ ϩⲛ̄-ⲛⲁⲍⲁⲣⲉⲑ?"
ⲡⲉϫⲉ-ⲫⲓⲗⲓⲡⲡⲟⲥ ⲛⲁϥ ϫⲉ "ⲁⲙⲟⲩ ⲛⲅ̄ⲛⲁⲩ!"

47 ⲁ-ⲓⲏⲥⲟⲩ́ⲥ ⲛⲁⲩ ⲉⲛⲁⲑⲁⲛⲁⲏⲗ ⲉϥⲛⲏⲩ ϣⲁⲣⲟϥ, ⲁⲩⲱ ⲡⲉϫⲁϥ ⲉⲧⲃⲏⲏⲧϥ̄ ϫⲉ "ⲉⲓⲥ! ⲟⲩⲓ̈ⲥⲣⲁⲏⲗⲓ́ⲧⲏⲥ ⲛⲁⲙⲉ, ⲉ-ⲙⲛ̄-ⲕⲣⲟϥ ⲛ̄ϩⲏⲧϥ̄!"

48 ⲡⲉϫⲉ-ⲛⲁⲑⲁⲛⲁⲏⲗ ⲛⲁϥ ϫⲉ "ⲉⲕⲥⲟⲟⲩⲛ ⲙ̄ⲙⲟⲓ̈ ⲧⲱⲛ?"
ⲁ-ⲓⲏⲥⲟⲩ́ⲥ ⲟⲩⲱϣⲃ̄, ⲉϥϫⲱ ⲙ̄ⲙⲟⲥ ⲛⲁϥ ϫⲉ "ⲙ̄ⲡⲁⲧⲉ-ⲫⲓⲗⲓⲡⲡⲟⲥ ⲙⲟⲩⲧⲉ ⲉⲣⲟⲕ, ⲉⲕ-ⲛ̄ϩⲟⲩⲛ ϩⲁ-ⲧⲃⲱ ⲛ̄-ⲕⲛ̄ⲧⲉ, ⲁⲓ̈ⲛⲁⲩ ⲉⲣⲟⲕ."

49 ⲁ-ⲛⲁⲑⲁⲛⲁⲏⲗ ⲟⲩⲱϣⲃ̄ ⲛⲁϥ ϫⲉ "ϩⲣⲁⲃⲃⲉⲓ̈, ⲛ̄ⲧⲟⲕ ⲡⲉ ⲡϣⲏⲣⲉ ⲙ̄-ⲡⲛⲟⲩⲧⲉ, ⲛ̄ⲧⲟⲕ ⲡⲉ ⲡⲣ̄ⲣⲟ ⲙ̄-ⲡⲓⲥⲣⲁⲏⲗ!"

50 ⲁ-ⲓⲏⲥⲟⲩ́ⲥ ⲟⲩⲱϣⲃ̄, ⲡⲉϫⲁϥ ⲛⲁϥ ϫⲉ "ⲉⲃⲟⲗ ϫⲉ ⲁⲓ̈ϫⲟⲟⲥ ⲛⲁⲕ ϫⲉ 'ⲁⲓ̈ⲛⲁⲩ ⲉⲣⲟⲕ ⲛ̄ϩⲟⲩⲛ ϩⲁ-ⲧⲃⲱ ⲛ̄-ⲕⲛ̄ⲧⲉ,' ⲁⲕⲡⲓⲥⲧⲉⲩⲉ? ⲕⲛⲁⲛⲁⲩ ⲉ-ⲛⲉⲧ-ⲛⲁⲁⲁⲩ ⲉ-ⲛⲁⲓ̈." 51 ⲁⲩⲱ ⲡⲉϫⲁϥ ⲛⲁϥ ϫⲉ "ϩⲁⲙⲏⲛ ϩⲁⲙⲏⲛ ϯϫⲱ ⲙ̄ⲙⲟⲥ ⲛⲏⲧⲛ̄ ϫⲉ ⲧⲉⲧⲛⲁⲛⲁⲩ ⲉ-ⲧⲡⲉ ⲉⲥⲟⲩⲏⲛ, ⲁⲩⲱ ⲛ̄ⲁⲅⲅⲉⲗⲟⲥ ⲙ̄-ⲡⲛⲟⲩⲧⲉ ⲉⲩⲛⲁ ⲉϩⲣⲁⲓ̈ ⲁⲩⲱ ⲉⲩⲛⲏⲩ ⲉⲡⲉⲥⲛ̄ⲧ ⲉϫⲙ̄-ⲡϣⲏⲣⲉ ⲙ̄-ⲡⲣⲱⲙⲉ."

2.1 ⲁⲩⲱ ϩⲙ̄-ⲡⲙⲉϩ-ϣⲟⲙⲛ̄ⲧ ⲛ̄-ϩⲟⲟⲩ, ⲁ-ⲩϣⲉⲗⲉⲉⲧ ϣⲱⲡⲉ ϩⲛ̄-ⲧⲕⲁⲛⲁ́ ⲛ̄-ⲧⲅⲁⲗⲓⲗⲁⲓ́ⲁ, ⲁⲩⲱ ⲛⲉⲣⲉ-ⲧⲙⲁⲁⲩ ⲛ̄-ⲓⲏⲥⲟⲩ́ⲥ ⲙ̄ⲙⲁⲩ. 2 ⲁⲩⲧⲱϩⲙ̄ ⲇⲉ ϩⲱⲱϥ ⲛ̄-ⲓⲏⲥⲟⲩ́ⲥ ⲙⲛ̄-ⲛⲉϥⲙⲁⲑⲏⲧⲏⲥ ⲉ-ⲧϣⲉⲗⲉⲉⲧ. 3 ⲁⲩⲱ ⲛ̄ⲧⲉⲣⲟⲩϣⲱⲱⲧ ⲛ̄-ⲏⲣⲡ̄, ⲡⲉϫⲉ-ⲧⲙⲁⲁⲩ ⲛ̄-ⲓⲏⲥⲟⲩ́ⲥ ⲛⲁϥ ϫⲉ "ⲙⲛ̄ⲧⲟⲩ ⲏⲣⲡ̄ ⲙ̄ⲙⲁⲩ."

4 ⲡⲉϫⲉ-ⲓⲏⲥⲟⲩ́ⲥ ⲛⲁⲥ ϫⲉ "ⲧⲉⲥϩⲓⲙⲉ, ⲉⲣⲉⲟⲩⲉϣ-ⲟⲩ ⲛⲙ̄ⲙⲁⲓ̈? ⲙ̄ⲡⲁⲧⲉ-ⲧⲁⲟⲩⲛⲟⲩ ⲉⲓ̈."

5 ⲡⲉϫⲉ-ⲧⲉϥⲙⲁⲁⲩ ⲛ̄-ⲛⲉⲧⲟⲩⲱⲧϩ̄ ϫⲉ "ⲡⲉⲧϥⲛⲁϫⲟⲟϥ ⲛⲏⲧⲛ̄, ⲁⲣⲓϥ."

6 ⲛⲉ-ⲩⲛ̄-ⲥⲟ ⲇⲉ ⲛ̄-ϩⲩⲇⲣⲓⲁ ⲛ̄-ⲱⲛⲉ ⲕⲏ ⲉϩⲣⲁⲓ̈ ⲙ̄ⲙⲁⲩ ⲕⲁⲧⲁ-ⲡⲧⲃⲃⲟ ⲛ̄-ⲛ̄ⲓ̈ⲟⲩⲇⲁⲓ́, ⲉⲣⲉ-ⲧⲟⲩⲉⲓ̈ ⲧⲟⲩⲉⲓ̈ ϣⲱⲡ ⲙ̄-ⲙⲉⲧⲣⲏⲧⲏⲥ ⲥⲛⲁⲩ ⲏ ϣⲟⲙⲛ̄ⲧ.

7 ⲡⲉϫⲉ-ⲓⲏⲥⲟⲩ́ⲥ ⲛⲁⲩ ϫⲉ "ⲙⲉϩ-ⲛ̄ϩⲩⲇⲣⲓ̈ⲁ ⲙ̄-ⲙⲟⲟⲩ." ⲁⲩⲱ ⲁⲩⲙⲁϩⲟⲩ ⲉϩⲣⲁⲓ̈ ⲉⲣⲱⲟⲩ.

8 ⲡⲉϫⲁϥ ⲛⲁⲩ ϫⲉ "ⲟⲩⲱⲧϩ̄ ⲧⲉⲛⲟⲩ ⲛ̄ⲧⲉⲧⲛ̄ⲉⲓ̈ⲛⲉ ⲙ̄-ⲡⲁⲣⲭⲓⲧⲣⲓ́ⲕⲗⲓⲛⲟⲥ." ⲁⲩⲱ ⲁⲩⲉⲓ̈ⲛⲉ.

9 ⲛ̄ⲧⲉⲣⲉ-ⲡⲁⲣⲭⲓⲧⲣⲓ́ⲕⲗⲓⲛⲟⲥ ⲇⲉ ⲧⲱⲡⲉ ⲙ̄-ⲡⲙⲟⲟⲩ ⲉⲁϥⲣ̄-ⲏⲣⲡ̄, ⲁⲩⲱ ⲛⲉϥⲥⲟⲟⲩⲛ ⲁⲛ ϫⲉ ⲟⲩ ⲉⲃⲟⲗ ⲧⲱⲛ ⲡⲉ. ⲛ̄ⲣⲉϥⲟⲩⲱⲧϩ̄ ⲇⲉ, ⲛ̄ⲧⲟⲟⲩ ⲛ̄ⲧⲁⲩⲙⲉϩ-ⲙ̄ⲙⲟⲟⲩ, ⲛⲉⲩⲥⲟⲟⲩⲛ ⲡⲉ. ⲁ-ⲡⲁⲣⲭⲓⲧⲣⲓ́ⲕⲗⲓⲛⲟⲥ ⲇⲉ ⲙⲟⲩⲧⲉ ⲉ-ⲡⲁ-ⲧϣⲉⲗⲉⲉⲧ, 10 ⲡⲉϫⲁϥ ⲛⲁϥ ϫⲉ "ⲣⲱⲙⲉ ⲛⲓⲙ ⲉ-ϣⲁⲩⲕⲁ-ⲡⲏⲣⲡ̄ ⲉϩⲣⲁⲓ̈ ⲉⲧ-ⲛⲁⲛⲟⲩϥ ⲛ̄-ϣⲟⲣⲡ̄, ⲁⲩⲱ ⲉⲩϣⲁⲛϯϩⲉ ϣⲁⲩⲕⲁ-ⲡⲉⲧ-ϭⲟϣⲃ̄. ⲛ̄ⲧⲟⲕ ⲇⲉ ⲁⲕϩⲁⲣⲉϩ ⲉ-ⲡⲏⲣⲡ̄ ⲉⲧ-ⲛⲁⲛⲟⲩϥ ϣⲁϩⲣⲁⲓ̈ ⲉ-ⲧⲉⲛⲟⲩ!"

11 ⲡⲁⲓ̈ ⲡⲉ ⲡϣⲟⲣⲡ̄ ⲙ̄-ⲙⲁⲉⲓ̈ⲛ ⲛ̄ⲧⲁ-ⲓⲏⲥⲟⲩ́ⲥ ⲁⲁϥ ϩⲛ̄-ⲧⲕⲁⲛⲁ́ ⲛ̄-ⲧⲅⲁⲗⲓⲗⲁⲓ́ⲁ, ⲁⲩⲱ ⲁϥⲟⲩⲱⲛϩ̄ ⲉⲃⲟⲗ ⲙ̄-ⲡⲉϥⲉⲟⲟⲩ, ⲁⲩⲡⲓⲥⲧⲉⲩⲉ ⲉⲣⲟϥ ⲛ̄ϭⲓ-ⲛⲉϥⲙⲁⲑⲏⲧⲏⲥ.

12 ⲙⲛ̄ⲛ̄ⲥⲁ-ⲡⲁⲓ̈ ⲁϥⲉⲓ̈ ⲉϩⲣⲁⲓ̈ ⲉ-ⲕⲁⲫⲁⲣⲛⲁⲟⲩ́ⲙ, ⲛ̄ⲧⲟϥ ⲙⲛ̄-ⲧⲉϥⲙⲁⲁⲩ ⲙⲛ̄-ⲛⲉϥⲥⲛⲏⲩ ⲙⲛ̄-ⲛⲉϥⲙⲁⲑⲏⲧⲏⲥ. ⲁⲩⲱ ⲁⲩϣⲱ ⲙ̄ⲙⲁⲩ ⲛ̄-ϩⲉⲛⲕⲟⲩⲓ̈ ⲛ̄-ϩⲟⲟⲩ.

ⲡⲉⲩⲁⲅⲅⲉ́ⲗⲓⲟⲛ ⲛ̄-ⲕⲁⲧⲁ-ⲙⲁⲑⲑⲁⲓ́ⲟⲥ MATTHEW 5.1–7.29

This selection from the Gospel of Matthew contains the entirety of the Sermon on the Mount, Jesus's instructions on life in God's reign—one of the most famous and quoted sections of biblical literature.

The text is primarily derived from the manuscript Pierpont Morgan Library, MS M.569,[38] fol. 3r–38r. This parchment manuscript of the four gospels was written around the ninth

---

38. Listed as sa 9 on the LCBM. For further information and images of the manuscript, see https://www.themorgan.org/manuscript/77431.

century CE and then found in 1910 at the site of the Monastery of St. Michael (Dayr al-Malāk Mīkhā'īl) near Hamuli, Egypt. This text was published by Gonzalo Aranda Pérez in 1984.[39]

5.1 ⲛ̄ⲧⲉⲣⲉϥⲛⲁⲩ ⲇⲉ ⲉ-ⲙ̄ⲙⲏⲏϣⲉ, ⲁϥⲁⲗⲉ ⲉϩⲣⲁⲓ̈ ⲉϫⲙ̄-ⲡⲧⲟⲟⲩ. ⲁⲩⲱ ⲛ̄ⲧⲉⲣⲉϥϩⲙⲟⲟⲥ, ⲁⲩϯ-ⲡⲉⲩⲟⲩⲟⲓ ⲉⲣⲟϥ ⲛ̄ϭⲓ-ⲛⲉϥⲙⲁⲑⲏⲧⲏⲥ. 2 ⲁϥⲟⲩⲱⲛ ⲉ-ⲣⲱϥ, ⲁϥϯ-ⲥⲃⲱ ⲛⲁⲩ, ⲉϥϫⲱ ⲙ̄ⲙⲟⲥ 3 ϫⲉ

    "ⲛⲁⲓ̈ⲁⲧⲟⲩ ⲛ̄-ⲛ̄ϩⲏⲕⲉ ϩⲙ̄-ⲡⲉⲡⲛⲉⲩⲙⲁ,
        ϫⲉ ⲧⲱⲟⲩ ⲧⲉ ⲧⲙⲛ̄ⲧⲣ̄ⲣⲟ ⲛ̄-ⲙ̄ⲡⲏⲩⲉ!
4   ⲛⲁⲓ̈ⲁⲧⲟⲩ ⲛ̄-ⲛⲉⲧ-ⲣ̄-ϩⲃⲃⲉ,[40]
        ϫⲉ ⲛ̄ⲧⲟⲟⲩ ⲛⲉⲧⲟⲩⲛⲁⲥⲡ̄ⲥⲱⲡⲟⲩ!
5   ⲛⲁⲓ̈ⲁⲧⲟⲩ ⲛ̄-ⲛ̄ⲣⲙ̄ⲣⲁϣ,
        ϫⲉ ⲛ̄ⲧⲟⲟⲩ ⲛⲉⲧ-ⲛⲁⲕⲗⲏⲣⲟⲛⲟⲙⲉⲓ ⲙ̄-ⲡⲕⲁϩ!
6   ⲛⲁⲓ̈ⲁⲧⲟⲩ ⲛ̄-ⲛⲉⲧ-ϩⲕⲁⲉⲓⲧ ⲉⲧ-ⲟⲃⲉ ⲛ̄-ⲧⲇⲓⲕⲁⲓⲟⲥⲩⲛⲏ,
        ϫⲉ ⲛ̄ⲧⲟⲟⲩ ⲛⲉⲧ-ⲛⲁⲥⲉⲓ!
7   ⲛⲁⲓ̈ⲁⲧⲟⲩ ⲛ̄-ⲛ̄ⲛⲁ-ⲏⲧ,
        ϫⲉ ⲛ̄ⲧⲟⲟⲩ ⲛⲉⲧⲟⲩⲛⲁⲛⲁ ⲛⲁⲩ!
8   ⲛⲁⲓ̈ⲁⲧⲟⲩ ⲛ̄-ⲛⲉⲧ-ⲟⲩⲁⲁⲃ ϩⲙ̄-ⲡⲉⲩϩⲏⲧ,
        ϫⲉ ⲛ̄ⲧⲟⲟⲩ ⲛⲉⲧ-ⲛⲁⲛⲁⲩ ⲉ-ⲡⲛⲟⲩⲧⲉ!
9   ⲛⲁⲓ̈ⲁⲧⲟⲩ ⲛ̄-ⲛ̄ⲣⲉϥⲣ̄-ⲉⲓⲣⲏⲛⲏ,
        ϫⲉ ⲛ̄ⲧⲟⲟⲩ ⲛⲉⲧⲟⲩⲛⲁⲙⲟⲩⲧⲉ ⲉⲣⲟⲟⲩ ϫⲉ ⲛ̄ϣⲏⲣⲉ ⲙ̄-ⲡⲛⲟⲩⲧⲉ!
10   ⲛⲁⲓ̈ⲁⲧⲟⲩ ⲛ̄-ⲛ̄ⲧⲁⲩⲡⲱⲧ ⲛ̄ⲥⲱⲟⲩ ⲉⲧⲃⲉ-ⲧⲇⲓⲕⲁⲓⲟⲥⲩⲛⲏ,
        ϫⲉ ⲧⲱⲟⲩ ⲧⲉ ⲧⲙⲛ̄ⲧⲣ̄ⲣⲟ ⲛ̄-ⲙ̄ⲡⲏⲩⲉ!

11 "ⲛⲁⲓ̈ⲁⲧ-ⲧⲏⲩⲧⲛ̄ ⲉⲩϣⲁⲛⲛⲉϭⲛⲉϭ-ⲧⲏⲩⲧⲛ, ⲛ̄ⲥⲉⲡⲱⲧ ⲛ̄ⲥⲱⲧⲛ̄, ⲛ̄ⲥⲉϫⲉ-ϩⲱⲃ ⲛⲓⲙ ⲉⲑⲟⲟⲩ ⲉϩⲟⲩⲛ ⲉⲣⲱⲧⲛ̄ ⲉⲩϫⲓ-ϭⲟⲗ ⲉⲣⲱⲧⲛ̄ ⲉⲧⲃⲏⲏⲧ. 12 ⲣⲁϣⲉ ⲛ̄ⲧⲉⲧⲛ̄ⲧⲉⲗⲏⲗ ϫⲉ ⲡⲉⲧⲛ̄ⲃⲉⲕⲉ ⲛⲁϣⲱϥ ϩⲣⲁⲓ̈ ϩⲛ̄-ⲙ̄ⲡⲏⲩⲉ, ⲧⲁⲓ̈ ⲅⲁⲣ ⲧⲉ ⲑⲉ ⲛ̄ⲧⲁⲩⲡⲱⲧ ⲛ̄ⲥⲁ-ⲛⲉⲡⲣⲟⲫⲏⲧⲏⲥ ⲉⲧ-ϩⲁⲧⲉⲧⲛ̄ϩⲏ!

13 "ⲛ̄ⲧⲱⲧⲛ̄ ⲡⲉ ⲡⲉϩⲙⲟⲩ ⲙ̄-ⲡⲕⲁϩ. ⲉⲣϣⲁⲛ-ⲡⲉϩⲙⲟⲩ ⲇⲉ ⲃⲁⲁⲃⲉ, ⲉⲩⲛⲁⲙⲟⲗϩϥ̄ ⲛ̄-ⲟⲩ? ⲙⲉϥⲣ̄-ϣⲁⲩ ⲛ̄-ⲗⲁⲁⲩ ⲛ̄ⲥⲁ-ⲛⲟϫϥ̄ ⲉⲃⲟⲗ ⲛ̄ⲥⲉϩⲟⲙϥ̄ ϩⲓⲧⲛ̄-ⲛⲉⲣⲱⲙⲉ.

14 "ⲛ̄ⲧⲱⲧⲛ̄ ⲡⲉ ⲡⲟⲩⲟⲉⲓⲛ ⲙ̄-ⲡⲕⲟⲥⲙⲟⲥ. ⲙⲛ̄-ϣϭⲟⲙ ⲛ̄-ⲟⲩⲡⲟⲗⲓⲥ ⲉ-ϩⲱⲡ ⲉⲥⲕⲏ ⲉϩⲣⲁⲓ̈ ϩⲓϫⲛ̄-ⲟⲩⲧⲟⲟⲩ. 15 ⲟⲩⲇⲉ ⲙⲉⲩϫⲉⲣⲉ-ⲟⲩϩⲏⲃⲥ ⲛ̄ⲥⲉⲕⲁⲁϥ ϩⲁ-ⲟⲩϣⲓ, ⲁⲗⲗⲁ ⲛ̄-ϣⲁⲩⲕⲁⲁϥ ϩⲓϫⲛ̄-ⲧⲗⲩⲭⲛⲓⲁ, ⲛϥ̄ⲣ̄-ⲟⲩⲟⲉⲓⲛ ⲉ-ⲛⲉⲧ-ϣⲟⲟⲡ ⲧⲏⲣⲟⲩ ϩⲙ̄-ⲡⲏⲓ̈. 16 ⲧⲁⲓ̈ ⲧⲉ ⲑⲉ ⲙⲁⲣⲉϥⲣ̄-ⲟⲩⲟⲉⲓⲛ ⲛ̄ϭⲓ-ⲡⲉⲧⲛ̄ⲟⲩⲟⲉⲓⲛ ⲙ̄-ⲡⲉⲙ̄ⲧⲟ ⲉⲃⲟⲗ ⲛ̄-ⲛⲉⲣⲱⲙⲉ, ϫⲉⲕⲁⲥ ⲉⲩⲉⲛⲁⲩ ⲉ-ⲛⲉⲧⲛ̄ϩⲃⲏⲩⲉ ⲉⲧ-ⲛⲁⲛⲟⲩⲟⲩ ⲛ̄ⲥⲉϯ-ⲉⲟⲟⲩ ⲙ̄-ⲡⲉⲧⲛ̄ⲉⲓⲱⲧ ⲉⲧ-ϩⲛ̄-ⲙ̄ⲡⲏⲩⲉ.

17 "ⲙ̄ⲡⲣ̄ⲱϣ ϫⲉ ⲛ̄ⲧⲁⲓ̈ⲉⲓ ⲉ-ⲕⲁⲧⲁⲗⲩ ⲙ̄-ⲡⲛⲟⲙⲟⲥ ⲏ ⲛⲉⲡⲣⲟⲫⲏⲧⲏⲥ. ⲛ̄ⲧⲁⲓ̈ⲉⲓ ⲁⲛ ⲉ-ⲕⲁⲧⲁⲗⲩ ⲙ̄ⲙⲟⲟⲩ, ⲁⲗⲗⲁ ⲉϫⲟⲕⲟⲩ ⲉⲃⲟⲗ. 18 ϩⲁⲙⲏⲛ ⲅⲁⲣ ϯϫⲱ ⲙ̄ⲙⲟⲥ ⲛⲏⲧⲛ̄ ϫⲉ ϣⲁⲛⲧⲉ-ⲧⲡⲉ ⲡⲁⲣⲁⲅⲉ ⲙⲛ̄-ⲡⲕⲁϩ, ⲟⲩⲓⲱⲧⲁ ⲛ̄-ⲟⲩⲱⲧ ⲏ ⲟⲩϣⲱⲗϩ̄ ⲛ̄-ⲟⲩⲱⲧ ⲛ̄ⲛⲉⲩⲥⲉⲓⲛⲉ ⲉⲃⲟⲗ ϩⲙ̄-ⲡⲛⲟⲙⲟⲥ ϣⲁⲛⲧⲟⲩϣⲱⲡⲉ ⲧⲏⲣⲟⲩ. 19 ⲡⲉⲧ-ⲛⲁⲃⲱⲗ ϭⲉ ⲉⲃⲟⲗ ⲛ̄-ⲟⲩⲉⲓ ⲛ̄-ⲛⲉⲓ̈ⲉⲛⲧⲟⲗⲏ ⲉⲧ-ⲥⲟⲃⲕ̄ ⲛϥ̄ϯ-ⲥⲃⲱ ⲛ̄-ⲛ̄ⲣⲱⲙⲉ ⲛ̄ⲧⲉⲓ̈ϩⲉ, ⲥⲉⲛⲁⲙⲟⲩⲧⲉ ⲉⲣⲟϥ ϫⲉ ⲡⲉⲗⲁⲭⲓⲥⲧⲟⲥ ϩⲛ̄-ⲧⲙⲛ̄ⲧⲣ̄ⲣⲟ ⲛ̄-ⲙ̄ⲡⲏⲩⲉ. ⲡⲉⲧ-ⲛⲁⲁⲁⲩ ⲇⲉ ⲁⲩⲱ ⲛϥ̄ϯ-ⲥⲃⲱ

---

39. Gonzalo Aranda Pérez, ed., *El evangelio de San Mateo en copto sahídico (texto de M 569, estudio preliminar y aparato crítico)*, Textos y Estudios Cardenal Cisneros 35 (Madrid: Instituto Arias Montano, 1984).

40. See ϩⲏⲃⲉ.

ⲛϩⲏⲧⲟⲩ, ⲡⲁⲓ̈ ⲥⲉⲛⲁⲙⲟⲩⲧⲉ ⲉⲣⲟϥ ϫⲉ ⲡⲛⲟϭ ϩⲛ̄-ⲧⲙⲛ̄ⲧⲣ̄ⲣⲟ ⲙ̄-ⲡⲛⲟⲩⲧⲉ. 20 ϯϫⲱ ⲅⲁⲣ ⲙ̄ⲙⲟⲥ ⲛⲏⲧⲛ̄ ϫⲉ ⲉⲥϣⲁⲛⲧⲙ̄ⲣ̄-ϩⲟⲩⲟ ⲛ̄ϭⲓ-ⲧⲉⲧⲛ̄ⲇⲓⲕⲁⲓⲟⲥⲩⲛⲏ ⲛ̄-ϩⲟⲩⲟ ⲉ-ⲧⲁ-ⲛⲉⲅⲣⲁⲙⲙⲁⲧⲉⲩⲥ ⲙⲛ̄-ⲛⲉⲫⲁⲣⲓⲥⲥⲁⲓⲟⲥ, ⲛ̄ⲛⲉⲧⲛ̄ⲃⲱⲕ ⲉϩⲟⲩⲛ ⲉ-ⲧⲙⲛ̄ⲧⲣ̄ⲣⲟ ⲛ̄-ⲙ̄ⲡⲏⲩⲉ.

21 "ⲁⲧⲉⲧⲛ̄ⲥⲱⲧⲙ̄ ϫⲉ ⲁⲩϫⲟⲟⲥ ⲛ̄-ⲛ̄ⲁⲣⲭⲁⲓⲟⲥ ϫⲉ 'ⲛ̄ⲛⲉⲕϩⲱⲧⲃ̄, ⲡⲉⲧ-ⲛⲁϩⲱⲧⲃ̄ ⲇⲉ ϥⲟ ⲛ̄-ⲉⲛⲟⲭⲟⲥ ⲉ-ⲧⲉⲕⲣⲓⲥⲓⲥ.' 22 ⲁⲛⲟⲕ ⲇⲉ ϯϫⲱ ⲙ̄ⲙⲟⲥ ⲛⲏⲧⲛ̄ ϫⲉ ⲟⲩⲟⲛ ⲛⲓⲙ ⲉⲧ-ⲛⲁⲛⲟⲩϭⲥ ⲉ-ⲡⲉϥⲥⲟⲛ ⲉⲓⲕⲏ ϥⲟ ⲛ̄-ⲉⲛⲟⲭⲟⲥ ⲉ-ⲧⲉⲕⲣⲓⲥⲓⲥ, ⲡⲉⲧ-ⲛⲁϫⲟⲟⲥ ⲙ̄-ⲡⲉϥⲥⲟⲛ ϫⲉ 'ⲕⲱϣⲟⲩⲉⲓⲧ!' ϥⲟ ⲛ̄-ⲉⲛⲟⲭⲟⲥ ⲉ-ⲡⲥⲩⲛϩⲉⲇⲣⲓⲟⲛ, ⲡⲉⲧ-ⲛⲁϫⲟⲟⲥ ϫⲉ 'ⲡⲥⲟϭ!' ϥⲟ ⲛ̄-ⲉⲛⲟⲭⲟⲥ ⲉ-ⲧⲅⲉϩⲉⲛⲛⲁ ⲛ̄-ⲥⲁⲧⲉ.

23 "ⲉϣⲱⲡⲉ ⲇⲉ ⲉⲕϣⲁⲛⲉⲓ ⲉⲕⲛⲁⲧⲁⲗⲟ ⲙ̄-ⲡⲉⲕⲇⲱⲣⲟⲛ ⲉϩⲣⲁⲓ̈ ⲉϫⲙ̄-ⲡⲉⲑⲩⲥⲓⲁⲥⲧⲏⲣⲓⲟⲛ, ⲛⲅ̄ⲣ̄-ⲡⲙⲉⲉⲩⲉ ⲙ̄-ⲡⲙⲁ ⲉⲧ-ⲙ̄ⲙⲁⲩ ϫⲉ ⲟⲩⲛ̄ⲧⲉ-ⲡⲉⲕⲥⲟⲛ ⲟⲩϩⲱⲃ ⲉϩⲟⲩⲛ ⲉⲣⲟⲕ, 24 ⲕⲱ ⲙ̄-ⲡⲙⲁ ⲉⲧ-ⲙ̄ⲙⲁⲩ ⲙ̄-ⲡⲉⲕⲇⲱⲣⲟⲛ ϩⲓ-ⲑⲏ ⲙ̄-ⲡⲉⲑⲩⲥⲓⲁⲥⲧⲏⲣⲓⲟⲛ, ⲛⲅ̄ⲃⲱⲕ ⲛ̄-ϣⲟⲣⲡ̄ ⲛⲅ̄ϩⲱⲧⲡ̄ ⲙⲛ̄-ⲡⲉⲕⲥⲟⲛ. ⲧⲟⲧⲉ ⲛⲅ̄ⲉⲓ ⲛⲅ̄ⲧⲁⲗⲟ ⲉϩⲣⲁⲓ̈ ⲙ̄-ⲡⲉⲕⲇⲱⲣⲟⲛ.

25 "ϣⲱⲡⲉ ⲉⲕⲟⲩⲱⲙⲉ ⲙ̄ⲙⲟⲕ ⲙⲛ̄-ⲡⲉⲧ-ϫⲓ-ϩⲁⲡ ⲛⲙ̄ⲙⲁⲕ ϩⲛ̄-ⲟⲩϭⲉⲡⲏ, ⲉⲛϩⲟⲥⲟⲛ ⲕϣⲟⲟⲡ ⲛⲙ̄ⲙⲁϥ ϩⲓ-ⲧⲉϩⲓⲏ. ⲙⲏⲡⲟⲧⲉ ⲛ̄ⲧⲉ-ⲡⲉⲧ-ϫⲓ-ϩⲁⲡ ⲛⲙ̄ⲙⲁⲕ ⲧⲁⲁⲕ ⲉⲧⲟⲟⲧϥ̄ ⲙ̄-ⲡⲣⲉϥϯ-ϩⲁⲡ, ⲛ̄ⲧⲉ-ⲡⲣⲉϥϯ-ϩⲁⲡ ⲧⲁⲁⲕ ⲉⲧⲟⲟⲧϥ̄ ⲙ̄-ⲡϩⲩⲡⲉⲣⲉⲧⲏⲥ, ⲛ̄ⲥⲉⲛⲟϫⲕ̄ ⲉ-ⲡⲉϣⲧⲉⲕⲟ. 26 ϩⲁⲙⲏⲛ ϯϫⲱ ⲙ̄ⲙⲟⲥ ⲛⲁⲕ ϫⲉ ⲛ̄ⲛⲉⲕⲉⲓ ⲉⲃⲟⲗ ϩⲙ̄-ⲡⲙⲁ ⲉⲧ-ⲙ̄ⲙⲁⲩ ϣⲁⲛⲧⲉⲕϯ ⲙ̄-ⲡϩⲁⲉ ⲛ̄-ⲕⲟⲛⲇⲣⲁⲛⲧⲏⲥ!

27 "ⲁⲧⲉⲧⲛ̄ⲥⲱⲧⲙ̄ ϫⲉ ⲁⲩϫⲟⲟⲥ ϫⲉ 'ⲛ̄ⲛⲉⲕⲣ̄-ⲛⲟⲉⲓⲕ.' 28 ⲁⲛⲟⲕ ⲇⲉ ϯϫⲱ ⲙ̄ⲙⲟⲥ ⲛⲏⲧⲛ̄ ϫⲉ ⲟⲩⲟⲛ ⲛⲓⲙ ⲉⲧ-ⲛⲁϭⲱϣⲧ̄ ⲛ̄ⲥⲁ-ⲟⲩⲥϩⲓⲙⲉ ⲉ-ⲉⲡⲉⲓⲑⲩⲙⲉⲓ ⲉⲣⲟⲥ, ⲁϥⲟⲩⲱ ⲉϥⲣ̄-ⲛⲟⲉⲓⲕ ⲉⲣⲟⲥ ϩⲙ̄-ⲡⲉϥϩⲏⲧ. 29 ⲉϣϫⲉ ⲡⲉⲕⲃⲁⲗ ⲇⲉ ⲛ̄-ⲟⲩⲛⲁⲙ ⲥⲕⲁⲛⲇⲁⲗⲓⲍⲉ ⲙ̄ⲙⲟⲕ, ⲡⲟⲣⲕϥ̄ ⲛⲅ̄ⲛⲟϫϥ̄ ⲛ̄ⲥⲁⲃⲟⲗ ⲙ̄ⲙⲟⲕ. ⲥⲉⲣ̄-ⲛⲟϥⲣⲉ ⲅⲁⲣ ⲛⲁⲕ ϫⲉⲕⲁⲥ ⲉϥⲉϩⲉ ⲉⲃⲟⲗ ⲛ̄ϭⲓ-ⲟⲩⲁ ⲛ̄-ⲛⲉⲕⲙⲉⲗⲟⲥ, ⲛ̄ⲥⲉⲧⲙ̄ⲛⲟⲩϫⲉ ⲙ̄-ⲡⲉⲕⲥⲱⲙⲁ ⲧⲏⲣϥ̄ ⲉ-ⲧⲅⲉϩⲉⲛⲛⲁ ⲛ̄-ⲥⲁⲧⲉ! 30 ⲁⲩⲱ ⲉϣϫⲉ ⲧⲉⲕϭⲓϫ ⲛ̄-ⲟⲩⲛⲁⲙ ⲥⲕⲁⲛⲇⲁⲗⲓⲍⲉ ⲙ̄ⲙⲟⲕ, ⲥⲟⲗⲡⲥ̄ ⲛⲅ̄ⲛⲟϫⲥ̄ ⲥⲁⲃⲟⲗ ⲙ̄ⲙⲟⲕ. ⲥⲉⲣ̄-ⲛⲟϥⲣⲉ ⲅⲁⲣ ⲛⲁⲕ ϫⲉⲕⲁⲥ ⲉϥⲉϩⲉ ⲉⲃⲟⲗ ⲛ̄ϭⲓ-ⲟⲩⲁ ⲛ̄-ⲛⲉⲕⲙⲉⲗⲟⲥ, ⲛ̄ⲥⲉⲧⲙ̄ⲛⲟⲩϫⲉ ⲙ̄-ⲡⲉⲕⲥⲱⲙⲁ ⲧⲏⲣϥ̄ ⲉ-ⲧⲅⲉϩⲉⲛⲛⲁ!

31 "ⲁⲩϫⲟⲟⲥ ⲇⲉ ϫⲉ 'ⲡⲉⲧ-ⲛⲁⲛⲟⲩϫⲉ ⲉⲃⲟⲗ ⲛ̄-ⲧⲉϥⲥϩⲓⲙⲉ, ⲙⲁⲣⲉϥϯ ⲛⲁⲥ ⲛ̄-ⲟⲩϫⲱⲱⲙⲉ ⲛ̄-ⲧⲟⲩⲉⲓⲟ.' 32 ⲁⲛⲟⲕ ⲇⲉ ϯϫⲱ ⲙ̄ⲙⲟⲥ ⲛⲏⲧⲛ̄ ϫⲉ ⲡⲉⲧ-ⲛⲁⲛⲟⲩϫⲉ ⲉⲃⲟⲗ ⲛ̄-ⲧⲉϥⲥϩⲓⲙⲉ, ⲁϫⲛ̄-ϣⲁϫⲉ ⲙ̄-ⲡⲟⲣⲛⲓⲁ, ϥⲛⲁⲧⲣⲉⲩⲣ̄-ⲛⲟⲉⲓⲕ ⲉⲣⲟⲥ, ⲁⲩⲱ ⲡⲉⲧ-ⲛⲁϩⲙⲟⲟⲥ ⲙⲛ̄-ⲟⲩⲉⲓ ⲉⲁ-ⲡⲉⲥϩⲁⲓ̈ ⲛⲟϫⲥ̄ ⲉⲃⲟⲗ ϥⲟ ⲛ̄-ⲛⲟⲉⲓⲕ.

33 "ⲁⲧⲉⲧⲛ̄ⲥⲱⲧⲙ̄ ⲟⲛ ϫⲉ ⲁⲩϫⲟⲟⲥ ϩⲛ̄-ⲛ̄ⲁⲣⲭⲁⲓⲟⲥ ϫⲉ 'ⲛ̄ⲛⲉⲕⲱⲣⲕ̄ ⲛ̄-ⲛⲟⲩϫ, ⲉⲕⲉϯ ⲇⲉ ⲛ̄-ⲛⲉⲕⲁⲛⲁⲩϣ ⲙ̄-ⲡϫⲟⲉⲓⲥ.' 34 ⲁⲛⲟⲕ ⲇⲉ ϯϫⲱ ⲙ̄ⲙⲟⲥ ⲛⲏⲧⲛ̄ ϫⲉ ⲙ̄ⲡⲣ̄ⲱⲣⲕ̄ ⲛ̄-ⲗⲁⲁⲩ. ⲙ̄ⲡⲣ̄ⲱⲣⲕ̄ ⲛ̄-ⲧⲡⲉ, ϫⲉ ⲡⲉⲑⲣⲟⲛⲟⲥ ⲙ̄-ⲡⲛⲟⲩⲧⲉ ⲡⲉ. 35 ⲟⲩⲇⲉ ⲙ̄ⲡⲣ̄ⲱⲣⲕ̄ ⲙ̄-ⲡⲕⲁϩ, ϫⲉ ⲡϩⲩⲡⲟⲡⲟⲇⲓⲟⲛ ⲛ̄-ⲛⲉϥⲟⲩⲉⲣⲏⲧⲉ ⲡⲉ. ⲟⲩⲇⲉ ⲙ̄ⲡⲣ̄ⲱⲣⲕ̄ ⲛ̄-ⲑⲓⲉⲣⲟⲥⲟⲗⲩⲙⲁ, ϫⲉ ⲧⲡⲟⲗⲓⲥ ⲙ̄-ⲡⲛⲟϭ ⲛ̄-ⲣ̄ⲣⲟ ⲧⲉ. 36 ⲟⲩⲇⲉ ⲙ̄ⲡⲣ̄ⲱⲣⲕ̄ ⲛ̄-ⲧⲉⲕⲁⲡⲉ, ϫⲉ ⲙⲛ̄-ϭⲟⲙ ⲙ̄ⲙⲟⲕ ⲉ-ⲧⲣⲉ-ⲟⲩⲃⲱ[41] ⲛ̄-ⲟⲩⲱⲧ ⲟⲩⲃⲁϣ ⲏ ⲛ̄ϥⲕⲙⲟⲙ. 37 ⲙⲁⲣⲉ-ⲡⲉⲧⲛ̄ϣⲁϫⲉ ⲇⲉ ϣⲱⲡⲉ ⲛ̄-'ⲥⲉ' ⲛ̄-'ⲥⲉ' ⲁⲩⲱ 'ⲙ̄ⲙⲟⲛ' ⲛ̄-'ⲙ̄ⲙⲟⲛ.' ⲡⲉϩⲟⲩⲟ ⲇⲉ ⲛ̄-ⲛⲁⲓ ⲟⲩⲉⲃⲟⲗ ϩⲙ̄-ⲡⲡⲟⲛⲏⲣⲟⲥ ⲡⲉ.

38 "ⲁⲧⲉⲧⲛ̄ⲥⲱⲧⲙ̄ ϫⲉ ⲁⲩϫⲟⲟⲥ ϫⲉ 'ⲟⲩⲃⲁⲗ ⲉ-ⲡⲙⲁ ⲛ̄-ⲟⲩⲃⲁⲗ, ⲟⲩⲟϩⲃⲉ[42] ⲉ-ⲡⲙⲁ ⲛ̄-ⲟⲩⲟϩⲃⲉ.' 39 ⲁⲛⲟⲕ ⲇⲉ ϯϫⲱ ⲙ̄ⲙⲟⲥ ⲛⲏⲧⲛ̄ ϫⲉ ⲙ̄ⲡⲣ̄ⲁϩⲉⲣⲁⲧ-ⲧⲏⲩⲧⲛ̄ ⲟⲩⲃⲉ-ⲡⲡⲉⲑⲟⲟⲩ. ⲁⲗⲗⲁ ⲡⲉⲧ-ⲛⲁⲣⲁϩⲧⲕ̄ ⲉ-ⲧⲉⲕⲟⲩⲟϭⲉ ⲛ̄-ⲟⲩⲛⲁⲙ, ⲕⲧⲟ ⲉⲣⲟϥ ⲛ̄-ⲧⲕⲉⲧⲉ. 40 ⲁⲩⲱ ⲡⲉⲧ-ⲟⲩⲱϣ ⲉ-ϫⲓ-ϩⲁⲡ ⲛⲙ̄ⲙⲁⲕ ⲉ-ϥⲓ ⲛ̄-ⲧⲉⲕϣⲧⲏⲛ, ⲕⲱ ⲉⲃⲟⲗ ⲛ̄ⲥⲱϥ ⲙ̄-ⲡⲉⲕⲕⲉϩⲟⲓ̈ⲧⲉ. 41 ⲡⲉⲧ-ⲛⲁⲕⲟⲟⲃⲉⲕ ⲛ̄-ⲟⲩⲕⲟⲧ,

---

41. See ϥⲱ.
42. See ⲟⲃϩⲉ.

ⲃⲱⲕ ⲛⲙ̄ⲙⲁϥ ⲛ̄-ⲥⲛⲁⲩ. 42 ⲡⲉⲧ-ⲁⲓⲧⲉⲓ ⲙ̄ⲙⲟⲕ ϯ ⲛⲁϥ, ⲁⲩⲱ ⲡⲉⲧ-ⲟⲩⲱϣ ⲉ-ϫⲓ ⲛ̄ⲧⲟⲟⲧⲕ̄ ⲙ̄ⲡⲣ̄ⲕⲧⲟϥ
ⲛ̄ⲥⲁⲃⲟⲗ ⲙ̄ⲙⲟⲕ.

43 "ⲁⲧⲉⲧⲛ̄ⲥⲱⲧⲙ̄ ϫⲉ ⲁⲩϫⲟⲟⲥ ϫⲉ 'ⲉⲕⲉⲙⲉⲣⲉ-ⲡⲉⲧ-ϩⲓⲧⲟⲩⲱⲕ, ⲛⲅ̄ⲙⲉⲥⲧⲉ-ⲛⲉⲕϫⲁϫⲉ.' 44 ⲁⲛⲟⲕ
ⲇⲉ ϯϫⲱ ⲙ̄ⲙⲟⲥ ⲛⲏⲧⲛ̄ ϫⲉ ⲙⲉⲣⲉ-ⲛⲉⲧⲛ̄ϫⲓⲛϫⲉⲉⲩⲉ, ⲛ̄ⲧⲉⲧⲛ̄ϣⲗⲏⲗ ⲉϫⲛ̄-ⲛⲉⲧ-ⲡⲏⲧ ⲛ̄ⲥⲁ-
ⲧⲏⲩⲧⲛ̄, 45 ϫⲉⲕⲁⲥ ⲉⲧⲉⲧⲛⲉϣⲱⲡⲉ ⲛ̄-ϣⲏⲣⲉ ⲙ̄-ⲡⲉⲧⲛ̄ⲉⲓⲱⲧ ⲉⲧ-ϩⲛ̄-ⲙ̄ⲡⲏⲩⲉ, ϫⲉ ϥⲧⲣⲉ-ⲡⲉϥⲣⲏ
ϣⲁ ⲉϫⲛ̄-ⲛ̄ⲁⲅⲁⲑⲟⲥ ⲙⲛ̄-ⲙ̄ⲡⲟⲛⲏⲣⲟⲥ, ⲁⲩⲱ ϥϩⲱⲟⲩ ⲉϫⲛ̄-ⲛ̄ⲇⲓⲕⲁⲓⲟⲥ ⲙⲛ̄-ⲛ̄ⲣⲉϥϫⲓ ⲛ̄-ϭⲟⲛⲥ̄.
46 ⲉⲧⲉⲧⲛ̄ϣⲁⲛⲙⲉⲣⲉ-ⲛⲉⲧ-ⲙⲉ ⲅⲁⲣ ⲙ̄ⲙⲱⲧⲛ̄, ⲁϣ ⲡⲉ ⲡⲉⲧⲛ̄ⲃⲉⲕⲉ ⲉⲧⲉ-ⲩⲛ̄ⲧⲏⲧⲛ̄ϥ̄? ⲛ̄ⲧⲉⲗⲱⲛⲏⲥ
ⲛ̄ⲧⲟⲟⲩ ⲉⲓⲣⲉ ⲁⲛ ⲛ̄-ⲧⲉⲓϩⲉ? 47 ⲁⲩⲱ ⲉⲧⲉⲧⲛ̄ϣⲁⲛⲁⲥⲡⲁⲍⲉ ⲛ̄-ⲛⲉⲧⲛ̄ⲉⲣⲏⲩ ⲙ̄ⲙⲁⲧⲉ, ⲟⲩ ⲡⲉ ⲡⲉϩⲟⲩⲟ
ⲉⲧⲉⲧⲛ̄ⲉⲓⲣⲉ ⲙ̄ⲙⲟϥ? ⲛ̄ⲕⲉϩⲉⲑⲛⲟⲥ ⲛ̄ⲧⲟⲟⲩ ⲉⲓⲣⲉ ⲁⲛ ⲙ̄-ⲡⲁⲓ? 48 ϣⲱⲡⲉ ϭⲉ ⲛ̄ⲧⲱⲧⲛ̄ ⲛ̄-ⲧⲉⲗⲓⲟⲥ ⲛ̄-ⲑⲉ
ⲙ̄-ⲡⲉⲧⲛ̄ⲉⲓⲱⲧ ⲉⲧ-ϩⲛ̄-ⲙ̄ⲡⲏⲩⲉ ⲉ-ⲩⲧⲉⲗⲓⲟⲥ ⲡⲉ.

6.1 "ϯ-ϩⲧⲏⲧⲛ̄ ⲉ-ⲡⲉⲧⲛ̄ϯ ⲉ-ⲧⲙⲁⲁϥ ⲙ̄-ⲡⲉⲙⲧⲟ ⲉⲃⲟⲗ ⲛ̄-ⲛⲉⲣⲱⲙⲉ ϫⲉⲕⲁⲥ ⲉⲩⲉⲛⲁⲩ ⲉⲣⲱⲧⲛ̄.
ⲉϣⲱⲡⲉ ⲙ̄ⲙⲟⲛ, ⲙⲛ̄ⲧⲏⲧⲛ̄ ⲃⲉⲕⲉ ⲙ̄ⲙⲁⲩ ⲛⲁϩⲣⲙ̄-ⲡⲉⲧⲛ̄ⲉⲓⲱⲧ ⲉⲧ-ϩⲛ̄-ⲙ̄ⲡⲏⲩⲉ.

2 "ϩⲟⲧⲁⲛ ϭⲉ ⲕϣⲁⲛⲉⲓⲣⲉ ⲛ̄-ⲟⲩⲙⲛ̄ⲧⲛⲁ, ⲙ̄ⲡⲣ̄ⲱϣ ⲉⲃⲟⲗ ϩⲁⲧⲉⲕϩⲏ ⲛ̄-ⲑⲉ ⲉⲧⲉⲣⲉ-ⲛ̄ϩⲩⲡⲟⲕⲣⲓⲧⲏⲥ
ⲉⲓⲣⲉ ⲙ̄ⲙⲟⲥ ϩⲣⲁⲓ ϩⲛ̄-ⲛ̄ⲥⲩⲛⲁⲅⲱⲅⲏ ⲁⲩⲱ ϩⲣⲁⲓ ϩⲛ̄-ⲛ̄ϩⲓⲣ, ϫⲉⲕⲁⲥ ⲉⲩⲉϫⲓ-ⲉⲟⲟⲩ ⲉⲃⲟⲗ ϩⲓⲧⲟⲟⲧⲟⲩ
ⲛ̄-ⲛ̄ⲣⲱⲙⲉ. ϩⲁⲙⲏⲛ ϯϫⲱ ⲙ̄ⲙⲟⲥ ⲛⲏⲧⲛ̄ ϫⲉ ⲁⲩⲟⲩⲱ ⲉⲩϫⲓ ⲙ̄-ⲡⲉⲩⲃⲉⲕⲉ! 3 ⲛ̄ⲧⲟⲕ ⲇⲉ ⲉⲕⲉⲓⲣⲉ ⲛ̄-
ⲟⲩⲙⲛ̄ⲧⲛⲁ, ⲙ̄ⲡⲣ̄ⲧⲣⲉ-ⲧⲉⲕϩⲃⲟⲩⲣ ⲉⲓⲙⲉ ϫⲉ ⲟⲩ ⲡⲉⲧⲉⲣⲉ-ⲧⲉⲕⲟⲩⲛⲁⲙ ⲉⲓⲣⲉ ⲙ̄ⲙⲟϥ, 4 ϫⲉⲕⲁⲥ
ⲉⲣⲉ-ⲧⲉⲕⲙⲛ̄ⲧⲛⲁ ϣⲱⲡⲉ ϩⲛ̄-ⲟⲩⲡⲉⲑⲏⲡ, ⲁⲩⲱ ⲡⲉⲕⲉⲓⲱⲧ ⲉⲧ-ϭⲱϣⲧ̄ ⲉⲣⲟⲕ ϩⲙ̄-ⲡⲡⲉⲑⲏⲡ
ϥⲛⲁⲧⲱⲱⲃⲉ ⲛⲁⲕ.

5 "ⲉⲧⲉⲧⲛ̄ⲉⲓ ⲇⲉ ⲉⲧⲉⲧⲛⲁϣⲗⲏⲗ, ⲛ̄ⲛⲉⲧⲛ̄ϣⲱⲡⲉ ⲛ̄-ⲑⲉ ⲛ̄-ⲛⲓϩⲩⲡⲟⲕⲣⲓⲧⲏⲥ ϫⲉ ⲥⲉⲙⲉ ⲛ̄-ⲁϩⲉⲣⲁⲧⲟⲩ
ϩⲛ̄-ⲛ̄ⲥⲩⲛⲁⲅⲱⲅⲏ ⲙⲛ̄-ⲛ̄ⲕⲗϫⲉ ⲛ̄-ⲛⲉⲡⲗⲁⲧⲓⲁ ⲉϣⲗⲏⲗ, ϫⲉⲕⲁⲥ ⲉⲩⲉⲟⲩⲱⲛϩ ⲉⲃⲟⲗ ⲛ̄-ⲛ̄ⲣⲱⲙⲉ.
ϩⲁⲙⲏⲛ ϯϫⲱ ⲙ̄ⲙⲟⲥ ⲛⲏⲧⲛ̄ ϫⲉ ⲁⲩⲟⲩⲱ ⲉⲩϫⲓ ⲙ̄-ⲡⲉⲩⲃⲉⲕⲉ! 6 ⲛ̄ⲧⲟⲕ ⲇⲉ ⲉⲕⲛⲁϣⲗⲏⲗ, ⲃⲱⲕ
ⲉϩⲟⲩⲛ ⲉ-ⲡⲉⲕⲧⲁⲙⲓⲟⲛ, ⲛⲅ̄ϣⲧⲁⲙ ⲙ̄-ⲡⲉⲕⲣⲟ, ⲛⲅ̄ϣⲗⲏⲗ ⲉ-ⲡⲉⲕⲉⲓⲱⲧ ⲉⲧ-ϩⲙ̄-ⲡⲡⲉⲑⲏⲡ. ⲁⲩⲱ
ⲡⲉⲕⲉⲓⲱⲧ ⲉⲧ-ϭⲱϣⲧ̄ ⲉⲣⲟⲕ ϩⲙ̄-ⲡⲡⲉⲑⲏⲡ ϥⲛⲁⲧⲱⲱⲃⲉ ⲛⲁⲕ. 7 ⲉⲧⲉⲧⲛ̄ϣⲗⲏⲗ ⲇⲉ, ⲙ̄ⲡⲣ̄ⲣ̄-ϩⲁϩ
ⲛ̄-ϣⲁϫⲉ ⲛ̄-ⲑⲉ ⲛ̄-ⲛⲉⲓϩⲉⲑⲛⲓⲕⲟⲥ, ⲉⲩⲙⲉⲉⲩⲉ ⲅⲁⲣ ϫⲉ ϩⲣⲁⲓ ϩⲛ̄-ⲧⲉⲩⲙⲛ̄ⲧϩⲁϩ ⲛ̄-ϣⲁϫⲉ ⲉⲩⲛⲁⲥⲱⲧⲙ̄
ⲉⲣⲟⲟⲩ. 8 ⲙ̄ⲡⲣ̄ⲉⲓⲛⲉ ϭⲉ ⲙ̄ⲙⲟⲩ, ⲡⲛⲟⲩⲧⲉ ⲅⲁⲣ ⲥⲟⲟⲩⲛ, ⲡⲉⲧⲛ̄ⲉⲓⲱⲧ, ⲙ̄-ⲡⲉⲧⲉⲧⲛ̄ⲣ̄-ⲭⲣⲓⲁ ⲙ̄ⲙⲟϥ
ⲙ̄ⲡⲁⲧⲉⲧⲛ̄ⲁⲓⲧⲉⲓ ⲙ̄ⲙⲟϥ.

9 "ⲧⲁⲓ ϭⲉ ⲧⲉ ⲑⲉ ⲛ̄ⲧⲱⲧⲛ̄ ⲉⲧⲉⲧⲛⲁϣⲗⲏⲗ ⲙ̄ⲙⲟⲥ ϫⲉ,

'ⲡⲉⲛⲉⲓⲱⲧ ⲉⲧ-ϩⲛ̄-ⲙ̄ⲡⲏⲩⲉ,
ⲙⲁⲣⲉ-ⲡⲉⲕⲣⲁⲛ ⲟⲩⲟⲡ,
10   ⲧⲉⲕⲙⲛ̄ⲧⲣ̄ⲣⲟ ⲙⲁⲣⲉⲥⲉⲓ,
ⲡⲉⲕⲟⲩⲱϣ ⲙⲁⲣⲉϥϣⲱⲡⲉ,
ⲛ̄-ⲑⲉ ⲉⲧⲉϥϩⲛ̄-ⲧⲡⲉ ⲙⲁⲣⲉϥϣⲱⲡⲉ ⲟⲛ ϩⲓϫⲙ̄-ⲡⲕⲁϩ.
11   ⲡⲉⲛⲟⲉⲓⲕ ⲉⲧ-ⲛⲏⲩ ⲧⲁⲁϥ ⲛⲁⲛ ⲙ̄-ⲡⲟⲟⲩ.
12   ⲕⲱ ⲛⲁⲛ ⲉⲃⲟⲗ ⲛ̄-ⲛⲉⲧ-ⲉⲣⲟⲛ,
ⲛ̄-ⲑⲉ ϩⲱⲱⲛ ⲟⲛ ⲉⲧⲉⲛⲕⲱ ⲉⲃⲟⲗ ⲛ̄-ⲛⲉⲧⲉ-ⲟⲩⲛ̄ⲧⲁⲛ ⲉⲣⲟⲟⲩ.
13   ⲛⲅ̄ⲧⲙ̄ϫⲓⲧⲛ̄ ⲉϩⲟⲩⲛ ⲉ-ⲡⲓⲣⲁⲥⲙⲟⲥ,
ⲁⲗⲗⲁ ⲛⲅ̄ⲛⲁϩⲙⲉⲛ ⲉⲃⲟⲗ ϩⲓⲧⲙ̄-ⲡⲡⲟⲛⲏⲣⲟⲥ.
ϫⲉ ⲧⲱⲕ ⲧⲉ ⲧϭⲟⲙ ⲙⲛ̄-ⲡⲉⲟⲟⲩ ϣⲁ-ⲛⲓⲉⲛⲉϩ.
ϩⲁⲙⲏⲛ!'

14 ⲉⲧⲉⲧⲛ̅ϣⲁⲛⲕⲱ ⲅⲁⲣ ⲉⲃⲟⲗ ⲛ̅-ⲛ̅ⲣⲱⲙⲉ ⲛ̅-ⲛⲉⲩⲛⲟⲃⲉ, ϥⲛⲁⲕⲱ ϩⲱⲱϥ ⲛⲏⲧⲛ̅ ⲉⲃⲟⲗ ⲛ̅ϭⲓ-ⲡⲉⲧⲛ̅ⲉⲓⲱⲧ ⲉⲧ-ϩⲛ̅-ⲙ̅ⲡⲏⲩⲉ ⲛ̅-ⲛⲉⲧⲛ̅ⲛⲟⲃⲉ. 15 ⲉⲧⲉⲧⲛ̅ⲧⲙ̅ⲕⲱ ⲇⲉ ⲉⲃⲟⲗ ⲛ̅-ⲛ̅ⲣⲱⲙⲉ ⲛ̅-ⲛⲉⲩⲛⲟⲃⲉ, ⲛϥ̅ⲛⲁⲕⲱ ⲛⲏⲧⲛ̅ ⲁⲛ ⲉⲃⲟⲗ ⲛ̅ϭⲓ-ⲡⲉⲧⲛ̅ⲉⲓⲱⲧ ⲉⲧ-ϩⲛ̅-ⲙ̅ⲡⲏⲩⲉ ⲛ̅-ⲛⲉⲧⲛ̅ⲛⲟⲃⲉ.

16 "ⲉⲧⲉⲧⲛ̅ⲛⲏⲥⲧⲉⲩⲉ ⲇⲉ, ⲙ̅ⲡⲣ̅ϣⲱⲡⲉ ⲛ̅-ⲑⲉ ⲛ̅-ⲛⲉⲓϩⲩⲡⲟⲕⲣⲓⲧⲏⲥ ⲉⲩⲟⲕⲙ̅. ⲥⲉⲧⲁⲕⲟ ⲅⲁⲣ ⲛ̅-ⲛⲉⲩϩⲟ ϫⲉⲕⲁⲥ ⲉⲩⲉⲟⲩⲱⲛϩ̅ ⲉⲃⲟⲗ ⲛ̅-ⲛ̅ⲣⲱⲙⲉ ⲉⲩⲛⲏⲥⲧⲉⲩⲉ. ϩⲁⲙⲏⲛ ϯϫⲱ ⲙ̅ⲙⲟⲥ ⲛⲏⲧⲛ̅ ϫⲉ ⲁⲩⲟⲩⲱ ⲉⲩϫⲓ ⲙ̅-ⲡⲉⲩⲃⲉⲕⲉ! 17 ⲛ̅ⲧⲟⲕ ⲇⲉ ⲉⲕⲛⲏⲥⲧⲉⲩⲉ, ⲧⲱϩⲥ̅ ⲛ̅-ⲧⲉⲕⲁⲡⲉ ⲛ̅ⲅⲉⲓⲱ ⲙ̅-ⲡⲉⲕϩⲟ, 18 ϫⲉⲕⲁⲥ ⲛ̅ⲛⲉⲕⲟⲩⲱⲛϩ̅ ⲉⲃⲟⲗ ⲛ̅-ⲛ̅ⲣⲱⲙⲉ ⲉⲕⲛⲏⲥⲧⲉⲩⲉ, ⲁⲗⲗⲁ ⲙ̅-ⲡⲉⲕⲉⲓⲱⲧ ⲉⲧ-ϩⲙ̅-ⲡⲡⲉⲑⲏⲡ. ⲁⲩⲱ ⲡⲉⲕⲉⲓⲱⲧ ⲉⲧ-ϭⲱϣⲧ̅ ⲉⲣⲟⲕ ϩⲙ̅-ⲡⲡⲉⲑⲏⲡ ϥⲛⲁⲧⲱⲱⲃⲉ ⲛⲁⲕ.

19 "ⲙ̅ⲡⲣ̅ⲥⲱⲟⲩϩ ⲛⲏⲧⲛ̅ ⲉϩⲟⲩⲛ ⲛ̅-ϩⲛ̅ⲁϩⲟ ϩⲓϫⲙ̅-ⲡⲕⲁϩ, ⲡⲙⲁ ⲛ̅-ϣⲁⲣⲉ-ⲧϫⲟⲟⲗⲉⲥ ⲙⲛ̅-ⲑⲟⲟⲗⲉ ⲧⲁⲕⲟ ⲛ̅ϩⲏⲧϥ̅, ⲁⲩⲱ ⲡⲙⲁ ⲛ̅-ϣⲁⲣⲉ ⲛ̅ⲣⲉϥϫⲓⲟⲩⲉ ϣⲟϫⲧ̅ ⲉⲣⲟϥ ⲛ̅ⲥⲉϫⲓⲟⲩⲉ. 20 ⲥⲱⲟⲩϩ ⲇⲉ ⲛⲏⲧⲛ̅ ⲉϩⲟⲩⲛ ⲛ̅-ϩⲛ̅ⲁϩⲟ ϩⲛ̅-ⲧⲡⲉ, ⲡⲙⲁ ⲉⲧⲉ-ⲙⲉⲣⲉ-ϫⲟⲟⲗⲉⲥ ⲟⲩⲇⲉ ϩⲟⲟⲗⲉ ⲧⲁⲕⲟ ⲛ̅ϩⲏⲧϥ̅, ⲁⲩⲱ ⲡⲙⲁ ⲉⲧⲉ-ⲙⲉⲣⲉ-ⲣⲉϥϫⲓⲟⲩⲉ ϭⲱⲧϩ̅ ⲉⲣⲟϥ ⲛ̅ⲥⲉϫⲓⲟⲩⲉ. 21 ⲡⲙⲁ ⲅⲁⲣ ⲉⲧⲉⲣⲉ-ⲡⲉⲕⲁϩⲟ ⲛⲁϣⲱⲡⲉ ⲛ̅ϩⲏⲧϥ̅, ⲉϥⲛⲁϣⲱⲡⲉ ⲙ̅ⲙⲁⲩ ⲛ̅ϭⲓ-ⲡⲉⲕⲕⲉϩⲏⲧ.

22 "ⲡϩⲏⲃⲥ̅ ⲙ̅-ⲡⲥⲱⲙⲁ ⲡⲉ ⲡⲃⲁⲗ. ⲉϣⲱⲡⲉ ⲇⲉ ⲡⲉⲕⲃⲁⲗ ⲟⲩϩⲁⲡⲗⲟⲩⲥ ⲡⲉ, ⲡⲉⲕⲥⲱⲙⲁ ⲧⲏⲣϥ̅ ⲛⲁϣⲱⲡⲉ ⲉϥⲟ ⲛ̅-ⲟⲩⲟⲉⲓⲛ. 23 ⲉϣⲱⲡⲉ ⲇⲉ ⲡⲉⲕⲃⲁⲗ ⲟⲩⲡⲟⲛⲏⲣⲟⲥ ⲡⲉ, ⲡⲉⲕⲥⲱⲙⲁ ⲧⲏⲣϥ̅ ⲛⲁϣⲱⲡⲉ ⲉϥⲟ ⲛ̅-ⲕⲁⲕⲉ. ⲉϣϫⲉ ⲡⲟⲩⲟⲉⲓⲛ ϭⲉ ⲉⲧ-ⲛ̅ϩⲏⲧⲕ̅ ⲟⲩⲕⲁⲕⲉ ⲡⲉ, ⲡⲕⲁⲕⲉ ⲟⲩⲏⲣ ⲡⲉ!
24 "ⲙⲛ̅-ϭⲟⲙ ⲛ̅-ⲗⲁⲁⲩ ⲉ-ⲣ̅-ϩⲙ̅ϩⲁⲗ ⲛ̅-ϫⲟⲉⲓⲥ ⲥⲛⲁⲩ. ⲏ ⲅⲁⲣ ϥⲛⲁⲙⲉⲥⲧⲉ-ⲟⲩⲁ ⲛϥ̅ⲙⲉⲣⲉ-ⲟⲩⲁ, ⲏ ⲛϥ̅ϭⲟⲗϫϥ̅ ⲛ̅-ⲟⲩⲁ ⲛϥ̅ⲕⲁⲧⲁⲫⲣⲟⲛⲉⲓ ⲙ̅-ⲡⲕⲉⲟⲩⲁ. ⲙⲛ̅-ϭⲟⲙ ⲙ̅ⲙⲱⲧⲛ̅ ⲉ-ⲣ̅-ϩⲙ̅ϩⲁⲗ ⲙ̅-ⲡⲛⲟⲩⲧⲉ ⲙⲛ̅-ⲡⲙⲁⲙⲱⲛⲁⲥ.

25 "ⲉⲧⲃⲉ-ⲡⲁⲓ̈ ϯϫⲱ ⲙ̅ⲙⲟⲥ ⲛⲏⲧⲛ̅ ϫⲉ ⲙ̅ⲡⲣ̅ϥⲓ-ⲣⲟⲟⲩϣ ⲉ-ⲧⲉⲧⲛ̅ⲯⲩⲭⲏ, ϫⲉ ⲟⲩ ⲡⲉⲧⲉⲧⲛⲁⲟⲩⲟⲙϥ̅ ⲏ ⲟⲩ ⲡⲉⲧⲉⲧⲛⲁⲥⲟⲟϥ, ⲟⲩⲧⲉ ⲡⲉⲧⲛ̅ⲥⲱⲙⲁ, ϫⲉ ⲟⲩ ⲡⲉⲧⲉⲧⲛⲁⲧⲁⲁϥ ϩⲓⲱⲧ-ⲧⲏⲩⲧⲛ̅. ⲙⲏ ⲧⲉⲯⲩⲭⲏ ⲟⲩⲟⲟⲧ ⲁⲛ ⲉ-ⲧⲉϩⲣⲉ ⲁⲩⲱ ⲡⲥⲱⲙⲁ ⲉ-ⲑⲃ̅ⲥⲱ? 26 ϭⲱϣⲧ̅ ⲉ-ⲛ̅ϩⲁⲗⲁⲁⲧⲉ ⲛ̅-ⲧⲡⲉ, ϫⲉ ⲛ̅ⲥⲉϫⲟ ⲁⲛ, ⲟⲩⲧⲉ ⲛ̅ⲥⲉⲱϩⲥ̅ ⲁⲛ, ⲟⲩⲧⲉ ⲛ̅ⲥⲉⲥⲱⲟⲩϩ ⲁⲛ ⲉϩⲟⲩⲛ ⲉ-ⲁⲡⲟⲑⲏⲕⲏ, ⲁⲩⲱ ⲡⲉⲧⲛ̅ⲉⲓⲱⲧ ⲉⲧ-ϩⲛ̅-ⲙ̅ⲡⲏⲩⲉ ⲥⲁⲛϣ̅ ⲙ̅ⲙⲟⲟⲩ. ⲛ̅ⲧⲱⲧⲛ̅ ϭⲉ ⲛ̅-ϩⲟⲩⲟ ⲙⲏ ⲛ̅ⲧⲉⲧⲛ̅ϣⲟⲃⲉ ⲁⲛ ⲉⲣⲟⲟⲩ? 27 ⲛⲓⲙ ⲇⲉ ⲉⲃⲟⲗ ⲛ̅ϩⲏⲧ-ⲧⲏⲩⲧⲛ̅ ⲉϥϥⲓ-ⲣⲟⲟⲩϣ, ⲉ-ⲩⲛ̅-ϭⲟⲙ ⲙ̅ⲙⲟϥ ⲉ-ⲟⲩⲉϩ-ⲟⲩⲙⲁϩⲉ ⲉϩⲣⲁⲓ̈ ⲉϫⲛ̅-ⲧⲉϥϣⲓⲏ?

28 "ⲁⲩⲱ ⲁϩⲣⲱⲧⲛ̅ ⲧⲉⲧⲛ̅ϥⲓ-ⲣⲟⲟⲩϣ ϩⲁ-ⲑⲃ̅ⲥⲱ? ϭⲱϣⲧ̅ ⲉ-ⲛⲉⲕⲣⲓⲛⲟⲛ ⲛ̅-ⲧⲥⲱϣⲉ, ⲛ̅-ⲑⲉ ⲉⲧⲟⲩⲁⲩⲝⲁⲛⲉ ⲙ̅ⲙⲟⲥ, ϫⲉ ⲛ̅ⲥⲉϩⲓⲥⲉ ⲁⲛ, ⲟⲩⲇⲉ ⲛ̅ⲥⲉⲣ̅-ⲉⲓⲟⲡⲉ ⲁⲛ. 29 ϯϫⲱ ⲙ̅ⲙⲟⲥ ⲛⲏⲧⲛ̅ ϫⲉ ⲟⲩⲇⲉ ⲥⲟⲗⲟⲙⲱⲛ ϩⲙ̅-ⲡⲉϥⲉⲟⲟⲩ ⲧⲏⲣϥ̅ ⲙ̅ⲡⲉϥϯ ϩⲓⲱⲱϥ ⲛ̅-ⲑⲉ ⲛ̅-ⲟⲩⲁ ⲛ̅-ⲛⲁⲓ̈! 30 ⲉϣϫⲉ ⲡⲉⲭⲟⲣⲧⲟⲥ ⲛ̅-ⲧⲥⲱϣⲉ ⲉϥϣⲟⲟⲡ ⲙ̅-ⲡⲟⲟⲩ, ⲣⲁⲥⲧⲉ ⲉⲩⲛⲁⲛⲟϫϥ̅ ⲉ-ⲧⲉⲧⲣⲓⲣ, ⲡⲛⲟⲩⲧⲉ ϯ ϩⲓⲱⲱϥ ⲛ̅-ⲧⲉⲓ̈ϩⲉ, ⲡⲟⲥⲟ ⲙⲁⲗⲗⲟⲛ ϩⲓⲱⲧ-ⲧⲏⲩⲧⲛ̅, ⲛⲁ-ⲧⲕⲟⲩⲓ̈ ⲙ̅-ⲡⲓⲥⲧⲓⲥ? 31 ⲙ̅ⲡⲣ̅ϥⲓ-ⲣⲟⲟⲩϣ ϭⲉ, ⲉⲧⲉⲧⲛ̅ϫⲱ ⲙ̅ⲙⲟⲥ ϫⲉ 'ⲟⲩ ⲡⲉⲧⲛ̅ⲛⲁⲟⲩⲟⲙϥ̅,' ⲏ 'ⲟⲩ ⲡⲉⲧⲛ̅ⲛⲁⲥⲟⲟϥ?' ⲏ ⲟⲩ ⲡⲉⲧⲉⲧⲛⲁⲧⲁⲁϥ ϩⲓⲱⲧ-ⲧⲏⲩⲧⲛ̅. 32 ⲛⲁⲓ̈ ⲅⲁⲣ ⲧⲏⲣⲟⲩ ⲛ̅ϩⲉⲑⲛⲟⲥ ⲛⲉⲧ-ϣⲓⲛⲉ ⲛ̅ⲥⲱⲟⲩ. ϥⲥⲟⲟⲩⲛ ⲅⲁⲣ ⲛ̅ϭⲓ-ⲡⲉⲧⲛ̅ⲉⲓⲱⲧ ⲉⲧ-ϩⲛ̅-ⲙ̅ⲡⲏⲩⲉ ϫⲉ ⲧⲉⲧⲛ̅ⲣ̅-ⲭⲣⲓⲁ ⲛ̅-ⲛⲁⲓ̈ ⲧⲏⲣⲟⲩ. 33 ϣⲓⲛⲉ ⲇⲉ ⲛ̅-ϣⲟⲣⲡ̅ ⲛ̅ⲥⲁ-ⲧⲉϥⲙⲛ̅ⲧⲣ̅ⲣⲟ ⲙⲛ̅-ⲧⲉϥⲇⲓⲕⲁⲓⲟⲥⲩⲛⲏ, ⲁⲩⲱ ⲛⲁⲓ̈ ⲧⲏⲣⲟⲩ ⲥⲉⲛⲁⲟⲩⲁϩⲟⲩ ⲉⲣⲱⲧⲛ̅. 34 ⲙ̅ⲡⲣ̅ϥⲓ-ⲣⲟⲟⲩϣ ϭⲉ ⲉ-ⲡⲉϥⲣⲁⲥⲧⲉ, ⲣⲁⲥⲧⲉ ⲅⲁⲣ ⲛⲁϥⲓ-ⲣⲟⲟⲩϣ ϩⲁⲣⲟϥ. ϩⲱ ⲉ-ⲡⲉϩⲟⲟⲩ ⲡⲉϩⲟⲟⲩ ⲉ-ⲧⲉϥⲕⲁⲕⲓⲁ.

7.1 "ⲙ̅ⲡⲣ̅ⲕⲣⲓⲛⲉ, ϫⲉⲕⲁⲥ ⲛ̅ⲛⲉⲩⲕⲣⲓⲛⲉ ⲙ̅ⲙⲱⲧⲛ̅. 2 ϩⲙ̅-ⲡϩⲁⲡ ⲅⲁⲣ ⲉⲧⲉⲧⲛⲁϯ-ϩⲁⲡ ⲛ̅ϩⲏⲧϥ̅, ⲉⲩⲛⲁⲕⲣⲓⲛⲉ ⲙ̅ⲙⲱⲧⲛ̅ ⲛ̅ϩⲏⲧϥ̅, ⲁⲩⲱ ϩⲙ̅-ⲡϣⲓ ⲉⲧⲉⲧⲛⲁϣⲓ ⲙ̅ⲙⲟϥ, ⲉⲩⲛⲁϣⲓ ⲛⲏⲧⲛ̅ ⲙ̅ⲙⲟϥ.

3 "ⲁϩⲣⲟⲕ ⲇⲉ ⲕϭⲱϣⲧ̅ ⲉ-ⲡϫⲏ ⲉⲧ-ϩⲙ̅-ⲡⲃⲁⲗ ⲙ̅-ⲡⲉⲕⲥⲟⲛ, ⲡⲥⲟⲓ̈ ⲇⲉ ⲉⲧ-ϩⲙ̅-ⲡⲉⲕⲃⲁⲗ ⲛ̅ⲅ̅ⲛⲁⲩ ⲉⲣⲟϥ ⲁⲛ? 4 ⲏ ⲛ̅-ⲁϣ ⲛ̅-ϩⲉ ⲕⲛⲁϫⲟⲟⲥ ⲙ̅-ⲡⲉⲕⲥⲟⲛ ϫⲉ 'ⲡⲁⲥⲟⲛ, ϭⲱ ⲧⲁⲛⲉϫ-ⲡϫⲏ ⲉⲃⲟⲗ

ϩⲙ̄-ⲡⲉⲕⲃⲁⲗ,' ⲁⲩⲱ ⲉⲓⲥ-ϩⲏⲏⲧⲉ! ⲡⲥⲟⲓ̈ ϩⲙ̄-ⲡⲉⲕⲃⲁⲗ! 5 ⲡϩⲩⲡⲟⲕⲣⲓⲧⲏⲥ, ⲛⲟⲩϫⲉ ⲛ̄-ϣⲟⲣⲡ̄ ⲙ̄-ⲡⲥⲟⲓ̈ ⲉⲃⲟⲗ ϩⲙ̄-ⲡⲉⲕⲃⲁⲗ, ⲁⲩⲱ ⲕⲛⲁⲛⲁⲩ ⲉⲃⲟⲗ ⲉ-ⲛⲉϫ-ⲡϫⲏ ⲉⲃⲟⲗ ϩⲙ̄-ⲡⲃⲁⲗ ⲙ̄-ⲡⲉⲕⲥⲟⲛ.

6 "ⲙ̄ⲡⲣ̄ϯ ⲛ̄-ⲛⲉⲧ-ⲙ̄-ⲡⲉⲧ-ⲟⲩⲁⲁⲃ ⲛ̄-ⲛⲉⲩϩⲟⲟⲣ, ⲟⲩⲇⲉ ⲙ̄ⲡⲣ̄ⲛⲟⲩϫⲉ ⲛ̄-ⲛⲉⲧⲛ̄ⲉⲛⲉ-ⲙ̄-ⲙⲉ ϩⲁⲣⲱⲟⲩ ⲛ̄-ⲛⲉϣⲁⲩ, ⲙⲏⲡⲟⲧⲉ ⲛ̄ⲥⲉϩⲟⲙⲟⲩ ⲛ̄-ⲛⲉⲩⲟⲩⲉⲣⲏⲧⲉ, ⲛ̄ⲥⲉⲕⲟⲧⲟⲩ, ⲛ̄ⲥⲉⲡⲉϩ-ⲧⲏⲩⲧⲛ̄.

7 "ⲁⲓⲧⲉⲓ ⲧⲁⲣⲟⲩϯ ⲛⲏⲧⲛ̄, ϣⲓⲛⲉ ⲧⲁⲣⲉⲧⲉⲧⲛ̄ϭⲓⲛⲉ, ⲧⲱϩⲙ̄ ⲧⲁⲣⲟⲩⲟⲩⲱⲛ ⲛⲏⲧⲛ̄. 8 ⲟⲩⲟⲛ ⲅⲁⲣ ⲛⲓⲙ ⲉⲧ-ⲁⲓⲧⲉⲓ ϥⲛⲁϫⲓ, ⲁⲩⲱ ⲡⲉⲧ-ϣⲓⲛⲉ ϥⲛⲁϩⲉ ⲉ-ⲟⲩⲟⲛ, ⲁⲩⲱ ⲡⲉⲧ-ⲧⲱϩⲙ̄ ⲥⲉⲛⲁⲟⲩⲱⲛ ⲛⲁϥ.

9 "ⲏ ⲛⲓⲙ ⲛ̄-ⲣⲱⲙⲉ ⲉⲃⲟⲗ ⲛ̄ϩⲏⲧ-ⲧⲏⲩⲧⲛ̄, ⲡⲉⲧⲉⲣⲉ-ⲡⲉϥϣⲏⲣⲉ ⲛⲁⲁⲓⲧⲉⲓ ⲙ̄ⲙⲟϥ ⲛ̄-ⲟⲩⲟⲉⲓⲕ, ⲙⲏ ϥⲛⲁϯ ⲛⲁϥ ⲛ̄-ⲟⲩⲱⲛⲉ? 10 ⲏ ⲛϥ̄ⲁⲓⲧⲉⲓ ⲙ̄ⲙⲟϥ ⲛ̄-ⲟⲩⲧⲏⲃⲧ̄, ⲙⲏ ϥⲛⲁϯ ⲛⲁϥ ⲛ̄-ⲟⲩϩⲟϥ? 11 ⲉϣϫⲉ ⲛ̄ⲧⲱⲧⲛ̄ ϭⲉ ⲛ̄ⲧⲉⲧⲛ̄-ϩⲉⲛⲡⲟⲛⲏⲣⲟⲥ, ⲧⲉⲧⲛ̄ⲥⲟⲟⲩⲛ ⲉ-ϯ ⲛ̄-ϩⲉⲛϯ ⲉ-ⲛⲁⲛⲟⲩⲟⲩ ⲛ̄-ⲛⲉⲧⲛ̄ϣⲏⲣⲉ, ⲡⲟⲥⲟ ⲙⲁⲗⲗⲟⲛ ⲡⲉⲧⲛ̄ⲉⲓⲱⲧ ⲉⲧ-ϩⲛ̄-ⲙ̄ⲡⲏⲩⲉ ϥⲛⲁϯ ⲛ̄-ϩⲉⲛⲁⲅⲁⲑⲟⲛ ⲛ̄-ⲛⲉⲧ-ⲁⲓⲧⲉⲓ ⲙ̄ⲙⲟϥ? 12 ϩⲱⲃ ϭⲉ ⲛⲓⲙ ⲉⲧⲉⲧⲛ̄ⲟⲩⲁϣⲟⲩ ϫⲉⲕⲁⲥ ⲉⲣⲉ-ⲛ̄ⲣⲱⲙⲉ ⲁⲁⲩ ⲛⲏⲧⲛ̄, ⲛ̄ⲧⲱⲧⲛ̄ ϩⲱⲧ-ⲧⲏⲩⲧⲛ̄ ⲁⲣⲓⲥⲟⲩ ⲛⲁⲩ ⲛ̄-ⲧⲉⲓ̈ϩⲉ. ⲡⲁⲓ̈ ⲅⲁⲣ ⲡⲉ ⲡⲛⲟⲙⲟⲥ ⲁⲩⲱ ⲛⲉⲡⲣⲟⲫⲏ́ⲧⲏⲥ.

13 "ⲃⲱⲕ ⲉϩⲟⲩⲛ ϩⲓⲧⲛ̄-ⲧⲡⲩⲗⲏ ⲉⲧ-ϭⲏⲩ, ϫⲉ ⲥⲟⲩⲟϣⲥ̄ ⲛ̄ϭⲓ-ⲧⲡⲩⲗⲏ ⲁⲩⲱ ⲥⲟⲩⲉⲥⲧⲱⲛ ⲛ̄ϭⲓ-ⲧⲉϩⲓⲏ ⲉⲧ-ϫⲓ-ⲙⲟⲉⲓⲧ ⲉϩⲟⲩⲛ ⲉ-ⲡⲧⲁⲕⲟ, ⲁⲩⲱ ϩⲁϩ ⲛⲉⲧ-ⲛⲁⲃⲱⲕ ⲉϩⲟⲩⲛ ϩⲓⲧⲟⲟⲧⲥ̄. 14 ϫⲉ ⲥϭⲏⲩ ⲇⲉ ⲛ̄ϭⲓ-ⲧⲡⲩⲗⲏ ⲁⲩⲱ ⲥϩⲉϫϩⲱϫ ⲛ̄ϭⲓ-ⲧⲉϩⲓⲏ ⲉⲧ-ϫⲓ-ⲙⲟⲉⲓⲧ ⲉϩⲟⲩⲛ ⲉ-ⲡⲱⲛϩ, ⲁⲩⲱ ϩⲉⲛⲕⲟⲩⲓ̈ ⲛⲉⲧ-ⲛⲁϩⲉ ⲉⲣⲟⲥ.

15 "ϯ-ϩⲧⲏⲧⲛ̄ ⲇⲉ ⲉⲣⲱⲧⲛ̄ ⲉ-ⲛⲉⲡⲣⲟⲫⲏ́ⲧⲏⲥ ⲛ̄-ⲛⲟⲩϫ, ⲛⲁⲓ̈ ⲉⲧ-ⲛⲏⲩ ϣⲁⲣⲱⲧⲛ̄ ϩⲛ̄-ϩⲉⲛϩⲃⲥⲱ ⲛ̄-ⲉⲥⲟⲟⲩ, ⲡⲉⲩϩⲟⲩⲛ ⲇⲉ ϩⲉⲛⲟⲩⲱⲛϣ̄ ⲛ̄-ⲣⲉϥⲧⲱⲣⲡ ⲛⲉ. 16 ⲉⲃⲟⲗ ϩⲛ̄-ⲛⲉⲩⲕⲁⲣⲡⲟⲥ ⲉⲧⲉⲧⲛⲁⲥⲟⲩⲱⲛⲟⲩ. ⲙⲏⲧⲉⲓ ϣⲁⲩϫⲉⲉⲗⲉ-ⲉⲗⲟⲟⲗⲉ ⲉⲃⲟⲗ ϩⲛ̄-ϣⲟⲛⲧⲉ, ⲏ ϣⲁⲩⲕⲉⲧϥ̄-ⲕⲛ̄ⲧⲉ ⲉⲃⲟⲗ ϩⲛ̄-ⲁⲣⲟⲟⲩⲉ? 17 ⲧⲁⲓ̈ ⲧⲉ ⲑⲉ ⲛ̄-ϣⲏⲛ ⲛⲓⲙ ⲉ-ⲛⲁⲛⲟⲩϥ ⲉ-ϣⲁϥⲧⲁⲩⲉ-ⲕⲁⲣⲡⲟⲥ ⲉⲃⲟⲗ ⲉ-ⲛⲁⲛⲟⲩϥ. ⲡϣⲏⲛ ⲇⲉ ⲉⲑⲟⲟⲩ ⲛ̄-ϣⲁϥⲧⲁⲩⲉ-ⲕⲁⲣⲡⲟⲥ ⲉⲃⲟⲗ ⲉϥϩⲟⲟⲩ. 18 ⲙⲛ̄-ϣϭⲟⲙ ⲛ̄-ⲟⲩϣⲏⲛ ⲉ-ⲛⲁⲛⲟⲩϥ ⲉ-ⲧⲁⲩⲉ-ⲕⲁⲣⲡⲟⲥ ⲉⲃⲟⲗ ⲉϥϩⲟⲟⲩ, ⲟⲩⲇⲉ ϣⲏⲛ ⲉϥϩⲟⲟⲩ ⲉ-ⲧⲁⲩⲉ-ⲕⲁⲣⲡⲟⲥ ⲉⲃⲟⲗ ⲉ-ⲛⲁⲛⲟⲩϥ. 19 ϣⲏⲛ ϭⲉ ⲛⲓⲙ ⲉⲧⲉ-ⲛϥ̄ⲛⲁⲧⲁⲩⲉ-ⲕⲁⲣⲡⲟⲥ ⲁⲛ ⲉ-ⲛⲁⲛⲟⲩϥ, ⲥⲉⲛⲁⲕⲟⲟⲣⲉϥ ⲛ̄ⲥⲉⲛⲟϫϥ̄ ⲉ-ⲧⲥⲁⲧⲉ. 20 ⲁⲣⲁ ϭⲉ ⲉⲃⲟⲗ ϩⲛ̄-ⲛⲉⲩⲕⲁⲣⲡⲟⲥ ⲉⲧⲉⲧⲛⲁⲥⲟⲩⲱⲛⲟⲩ.

21 "ⲟⲩⲟⲛ ⲛⲓⲙ ⲁⲛ ⲉⲧ-ϫⲱ ⲙ̄ⲙⲟⲥ ⲛⲁⲓ̈ ϫⲉ 'ⲡϫⲟⲉⲓⲥ, ⲡϫⲟⲉⲓⲥ,' ⲡⲉⲧⲛⲁⲃⲱⲕ ⲉϩⲟⲩⲛ ⲉ-ⲧⲙⲛ̄ⲧⲣ̄ⲣⲟ ⲛ̄-ⲙ̄ⲡⲏⲩⲉ, ⲁⲗⲗⲁ ⲡⲉⲧ-ⲉⲓⲣⲉ ⲡⲉ ⲙ̄-ⲡⲟⲩⲱϣ ⲙ̄-ⲡⲁⲉⲓⲱⲧ ⲉⲧ-ϩⲛ̄-ⲙ̄ⲡⲏⲩⲉ. 22 ⲟⲩⲛ̄-ϩⲁϩ ⲅⲁⲣ ⲛⲁϫⲟⲟⲥ ⲛⲁⲓ̈ ϩⲙ̄-ⲡⲉϩⲟⲟⲩ ⲉⲧ-ⲙ̄ⲙⲁⲩ ϫⲉ 'ⲡϫⲟⲉⲓⲥ, ⲡϫⲟⲉⲓⲥ, ⲙⲏ ϩⲣⲁⲓ̈ ⲁⲛ ϩⲙ̄-ⲡⲉⲕⲣⲁⲛ ⲁⲛⲡⲣⲟⲫⲏⲧⲉⲩⲉ, ⲁⲩⲱ ϩⲣⲁⲓ̈ ϩⲙ̄-ⲡⲉⲕⲣⲁⲛ ⲁⲛⲛⲉϫ-ⲇⲁⲓⲙⲱ́ⲛⲓⲟⲛ ⲉⲃⲟⲗ, ⲙⲏ ϩⲣⲁⲓ̈ ⲁⲛ ϩⲙ̄-ⲡⲉⲕⲣⲁⲛ ⲁⲛⲣ̄-ϩⲁϩ ⲛ̄-ϭⲟⲙ?' 23 ⲁⲩⲱ ⲧⲟⲧⲉ ϯⲛⲁϩⲟⲙⲟⲗⲟⲅⲉⲓ ⲛⲁⲩ ϫⲉ 'ⲙ̄ⲡⲉⲓ̈ⲥⲟⲩⲛ̄-ⲧⲏⲩⲧⲛ̄ ⲉⲛⲉϩ. ⲥⲁϩⲉ-ⲧⲏⲩⲧⲛ̄ ⲉⲃⲟⲗ ⲙ̄ⲙⲟⲓ̈, ⲛⲉⲧ-ⲣ̄-ϩⲱⲃ ⲉ-ⲧⲁⲛⲟⲙⲓ́ⲁ!'

24 "ⲟⲩⲟⲛ ϭⲉ ⲛⲓⲙ ⲉⲧ-ⲥⲱⲧⲙ̄ ⲉ-ⲛⲁϣⲁϫⲉ ⲉⲧⲉ-ⲛⲁⲓ̈ ⲛⲉ, ⲉϥⲉⲓⲣⲉ ⲙ̄ⲙⲟⲟⲩ, ⲉϥⲛⲁⲉⲓⲛⲉ ⲛ̄-ⲟⲩⲣⲱⲙⲉ ⲛ̄-ⲥⲁⲃⲉ, ⲡⲁⲓ̈ ⲛ̄ⲧⲁϥⲕⲱⲧ ⲙ̄-ⲡⲉϥⲏⲓ̈ ⲉϩⲣⲁⲓ̈ ⲉϫⲛ̄-ⲧⲡⲉ́ⲧⲣⲁ. 25 ⲁϥⲉⲓ ⲉⲡⲉⲥⲏⲧ ⲛ̄ϭⲓ-ⲡϩⲱⲟⲩ, ⲁⲩⲉⲓ ⲛ̄ϭⲓ-ⲛⲉⲓ̈ⲉⲣⲱⲟⲩ, ⲁⲩⲛⲓϥⲉ ⲛ̄ϭⲓ-ⲛ̄ⲧⲏⲩ, ⲁⲩϩⲓⲟⲩⲉ ⲉϩⲟⲩⲛ ϩⲙ̄-ⲡⲏⲓ̈ ⲉⲧ-ⲙ̄ⲙⲁⲩ, ⲁⲩⲱ ⲙ̄ⲡⲉϥϩⲉ, ϫⲉ ⲛⲉϥⲧⲁϫⲣⲏⲩ ⲅⲁⲣ ⲉϩⲣⲁⲓ̈ ⲉϫⲛ̄-ⲧⲡⲉ́ⲧⲣⲁ.

26 "ⲁⲩⲱ ⲟⲩⲟⲛ ⲛⲓⲙ ⲉⲧ-ⲥⲱⲧⲙ̄ ⲉ-ⲛⲁϣⲁϫⲉ ⲉⲧⲉ-ⲛⲁⲓ̈ ⲛⲉ, ⲛ̄ϥⲉⲓⲣⲉ ⲙ̄ⲙⲟⲟⲩ ⲁⲛ, ⲉϥⲛⲁⲉⲓⲛⲉ ⲛ̄-ⲟⲩⲣⲱⲙⲉ ⲛ̄-ⲥⲟϭ, ⲡⲁⲓ̈ ⲛ̄ⲧⲁϥⲕⲱⲧ ⲙ̄-ⲡⲉϥⲏⲓ̈ ϩⲓϫⲙ̄-ⲡϣⲱ. 27 ⲁϥⲉⲓ ⲉⲡⲉⲥⲏⲧ ⲛ̄ϭⲓ-ⲡϩⲱⲟⲩ, ⲁⲩⲉⲓ ⲛ̄ϭⲓ-ⲛⲉⲓ̈ⲉⲣⲱⲟⲩ, ⲁⲩⲛⲓϥⲉ ⲛ̄ϭⲓ-ⲛ̄ⲧⲏⲩ, ⲁⲩϩⲓⲟⲩⲉ ⲉϩⲟⲩⲛ ϩⲙ̄-ⲡⲏⲓ̈ ⲉⲧ-ⲙ̄ⲙⲁⲩ, ⲁϥϩⲉ, ⲁⲩⲱ ⲡⲉϥϩⲉ ⲛⲉϥⲟ ⲛ̄-ⲟⲩⲛⲟϭ!"

28 ⲁⲥϣⲱⲡⲉ ⲇⲉ ⲛ̄ⲧⲉⲣⲉ-ⲓⲏⲥⲟⲩⲥ ⲟⲩⲱ ⲛ̄-ⲛⲉⲓ̈ϣⲁϫⲉ, ⲁⲩⲣ̄-ϣⲡⲏⲣⲉ ⲛ̄ϭⲓ-ⲙ̄ⲙⲏⲏϣⲉ ⲉϩⲣⲁⲓ̈ ⲉϫⲛ̄-ⲧⲉϥⲥⲃⲱ, 29 ⲛⲉϥϯ-ⲥⲃⲱ ⲅⲁⲣ ⲛⲁⲩ ⲡⲉ ϩⲱⲥ ⲉ-ⲩⲛ̄ⲧϥ̄ ⲉϫⲟⲩⲥⲓ́ⲁ ⲙ̄ⲙⲁⲩ, ⲁⲩⲱ ⲛ̄-ⲑⲉ ⲁⲛ ⲛ̄-ⲛⲉⲩⲅⲣⲁⲙⲙⲁⲧⲉⲩⲥ.

READING SELECTIONS

ⲦⲀⲠⲞⲔⲀⲖⲨⲮⲒⲤ ⲚⲦⲈ-ⲒⲰⲎⲀⲚⲚⲎⲤ REVELATION 4.1–8.1

This text selection comes from John's first vision of the divine throne room and the Lamb with a seven-sealed scroll. It is a dramatic and symbolic narrative of John's experience as he witnesses God's plan for his people's future going into effect. Despite the riddles and mysteries inherent in Revelation, it has played a formative and enduring role in liturgy, with the depictions of the worship above being models for the worship below.

The text is taken from the recent edition by Christian Askeland and is based off the evidence of two nearly complete manuscripts and an additional twenty-four fragmentary manuscripts.[43]

4.1 ⲘⲚⲚⲤⲀ-ⲚⲀⲒ ⲀⲒⲚⲀⲨ Ⲉ-ⲨⲢⲞ ⲈϤⲞⲨⲎⲚ ⲈⲢⲀⲒ ⲈⲚ-ⲦⲠⲈ, ⲀⲨⲰ ⲦϢⲞⲢⲠ Ⲛ-ⲤⲘⲎ ⲈⲚⲦⲀⲒⲤⲰⲦⲘ ⲈⲢⲞⲤ Ⲛ-ⲐⲈ Ⲛ-ⲞⲨⲤⲀⲖⲠⲒⲄⲜ ⲈⲤϢⲀϪⲈ ⲚⲘⲘⲀⲒ, ⲈⲤϪⲰ ⲘⲘⲞⲤ ϪⲈ "ⲀⲘⲞⲨ ⲈⲢⲀⲒ Ⲉ-ⲠⲈⲒⲘⲀ, ⲈⲚⲦⲀⲦⲤⲀⲂⲞⲔ Ⲉ-ⲚⲈⲦ-ⲚⲀϢⲰⲠⲈ ⲘⲚⲚⲤⲀ-ⲚⲀⲒ."

2 Ⲛ-ⲦⲈⲨⲚⲞⲨ ⲀⲒϢⲰⲠⲈ ⲈⲚ-ⲠⲈⲠⲚⲈⲨⲘⲀ ⲀⲨⲰ ⲈⲒⲤ-ⲈⲎⲎⲦⲈ! ⲚⲈ-ⲨⲚ-ⲞⲨⲐⲢⲞⲚⲞⲤ ⲔⲎ ⲈⲢⲀⲒ ⲈⲚ-ⲦⲠⲈ, ⲈⲢⲈ-ⲨⲀ ⲤⲘⲞⲞⲤ ⲈⲒ-ⲠⲈⲐⲢⲞⲚⲞⲤ. 3 ⲀⲨⲰ ⲠⲈⲦ-ⲤⲘⲞⲞⲤ ⲈϤⲈⲒⲚⲈ Ⲛ-ⲐⲞⲢⲀⲤⲒⲤ Ⲛ-ⲞⲨⲰⲚⲈ Ⲛ-ⲒⲀⲤⲠⲒⲤ ⲀⲨⲰ Ⲛ-ⲤⲀⲢⲆⲒⲚⲞⲤ. ⲈⲢⲈ-ⲨⲞⲈⲒⲚ ⲔⲰⲦⲈ Ⲉ-ⲠⲈⲐⲢⲞⲚⲞⲤ ⲈϤⲞ Ⲛ-ⲐⲈ Ⲙ-ⲠⲈⲒⲚⲈ Ⲛ-ⲞⲨⲤⲘⲀⲢⲀⲄⲦⲞⲤ.

4 ⲀⲨⲰ ⲈⲢⲈ-ϪⲞⲨⲦ-ⲀϤⲦⲈ Ⲛ-ⲐⲢⲞⲚⲞⲤ Ⲙ-ⲠⲔⲰⲦⲈ Ⲙ-ⲠⲈⲐⲢⲞⲚⲞⲤ. ⲈⲢⲈ-ϪⲞⲨⲦ-ⲀϤⲦⲈ Ⲙ-ⲠⲢⲈⲤⲂⲨⲦⲈⲢⲞⲤ ⲤⲘⲞⲞⲤ ⲈⲒⲦⲚ-ⲚⲐⲢⲞⲚⲞⲤ, ⲈⲨϬⲞⲞⲖⲈ Ⲛ-ⲈⲚⲈⲞⲈⲒⲦⲈ Ⲛ-ⲞⲨⲰⲂϢ, ⲈⲢⲈ-ⲈⲚⲔⲖⲞⲘ Ⲛ-ⲚⲞⲨⲂ ⲈⲒϪⲚ-ⲚⲈⲨⲀⲠⲎⲨⲈ.

5 ⲀⲨⲰ ⲚⲈⲨⲚⲎⲨ ⲈⲂⲞⲖ ⲈⲚ-ⲠⲈⲐⲢⲞⲚⲞⲤ ⲚϬⲒ-ⲈⲚⲈⲂⲢⲎϬⲈ ⲘⲚ-ⲈⲚⲤⲘⲎ ⲘⲚ-ⲈⲚⲢⲞⲨ-Ⲃ̄-ⲂⲀⲒ. ⲈⲢⲈ-ⲤⲀϢϤⲈ Ⲛ-ⲖⲀⲘⲠⲀⲤ Ⲛ-ⲔⲰⲈⲦ ⲘⲞⲨⲈ Ⲙ-ⲠⲈⲘⲦⲞ ⲈⲂⲞⲖ Ⲙ-ⲠⲈⲐⲢⲞⲚⲞⲤ, ⲈⲦⲈ-ⲚⲀⲒ ⲚⲈ ⲚⲈⲠⲚⲈⲨⲘⲀ Ⲙ-ⲠⲚⲞⲨⲦⲈ. 6 ⲀⲨⲰ Ⲙ-ⲠⲈⲘⲦⲞ ⲈⲂⲞⲖ Ⲙ-ⲠⲈⲐⲢⲞⲚⲞⲤ ⲚⲈ-ⲨⲚ-ⲞⲨⲐⲀⲖⲀⲤⲤⲀ Ⲛ-ⲀⲂⲀϬⲈⲒⲚ ⲈⲤⲈⲒⲚⲈ Ⲛ-ⲞⲨⲔⲢⲨⲤⲦⲀⲖⲞⲤ.

ⲀⲨⲰ Ⲛ-ⲦⲘⲎⲦⲈ Ⲙ-ⲠⲈⲐⲢⲞⲚⲞⲤ ⲘⲚ-ⲠⲈϤⲔⲰⲦⲈ ⲚⲈ-ⲨⲚ-ϤⲦⲞⲨ Ⲛ-ⲌⲰⲞⲚ, ⲈⲨⲘⲈⲈ Ⲛ-ⲂⲀⲖ ⲈⲒⲐⲎ ⲀⲨⲰ ⲈⲒⲠⲀⲈⲞⲨ. 7 ⲠϢⲞⲢⲠ Ⲛ-ⲌⲰⲞⲚ ⲈϤⲈⲒⲚⲈ Ⲛ-ⲞⲨⲘⲞⲨⲒ, ⲠⲘⲈⲈ-ⲤⲚⲀⲨ Ⲛ-ⲌⲰⲞⲚ ⲈϤⲈⲒⲚⲈ Ⲛ-ⲞⲨⲘⲀⲤⲈ, ⲠⲘⲈⲈ-ϢⲞⲘⲚⲦ Ⲛ-ⲌⲰⲞⲚ ⲈϤⲞ Ⲛ-ⲈⲞ Ⲛ-ⲢⲰⲘⲈ, ⲠⲘⲈⲈ-ϤⲦⲞⲞⲨⲈ Ⲛ-ⲌⲰⲞⲚ ⲈϤⲈⲒⲚⲈ Ⲛ-ⲞⲨⲀⲈⲦⲞⲤ ⲈϤⲈⲢⲀⲖ. 8 ⲀⲨⲰ ⲠⲈϤⲦⲞⲞⲨ Ⲛ-ⲌⲰⲞⲚ ⲚⲈ-ⲨⲚⲦⲈ-ⲠⲞⲨⲀ ⲠⲞⲨⲀ ⲘⲘⲞⲞⲨ ⲤⲞⲞⲨ Ⲛ-ⲦⲚⲈ ϪⲒⲚ-ⲚⲈⲨⲈⲒⲈⲒⲂ Ⲙ-ⲠⲈⲨⲔⲰⲦⲈ, ⲈⲨⲘⲈⲈ Ⲛ-ⲂⲀⲖ Ⲙ-ⲠⲈⲨⲈⲞⲨⲚ. ⲀⲨⲰ ⲘⲈⲨⲔⲀ-ⲦⲞⲞⲦⲞⲨ ⲈⲂⲞⲖ Ⲙ-ⲠⲈⲈⲞⲞⲨ ⲘⲚ-ⲦⲈⲨϢⲎ, ⲈⲨϪⲰ ⲘⲘⲞⲤ ϪⲈ

> "ϤⲞⲨⲀⲀⲂ, ϤⲞⲨⲀⲀⲂ, ϤⲞⲨⲀⲀⲂ,
> ⲚϬⲒ-ⲠϪⲞⲈⲒⲤ ⲠⲚⲞⲨⲦⲈ ⲠⲠⲀⲚⲦⲞⲔⲢⲀⲦⲰⲢ,
> ⲠⲈⲦ-ϢⲞⲞⲠ ⲀⲨⲰ ⲠⲈⲦⲈ-ⲚⲈϤϢⲞⲞⲠ ⲀⲨⲰ ⲠⲈⲦ-ⲚⲎⲨ!"

9 ⲀⲨⲰ ⲈⲢϢⲀⲚ-Ⲛ-ⲌⲰⲞⲚ ϯ Ⲙ-ⲠⲈⲞⲞⲨ ⲘⲚ-ⲠⲦⲀⲈⲒⲞ ⲘⲚ-ⲦⲈⲨⲬⲀⲢⲒⲤϮⲀ Ⲙ-ⲠⲈⲦ-ⲤⲘⲞⲞⲤ ⲈϪⲘ-ⲠⲈⲐⲢⲞⲚⲞⲤ, ⲈⲦ-ⲞⲚⲈ ϢⲀ-ⲚⲒⲈⲚⲈⲈ Ⲛ-ⲚⲒⲈⲚⲈⲈ, 10 ϢⲀⲨⲠⲀⲈⲦⲞⲨ ⲚϬⲒ-ⲠϪⲞⲨⲦ-ⲀϤⲦⲈ Ⲙ-ⲠⲢⲈⲤⲂⲨⲦⲈⲢⲞⲤ Ⲙ-ⲠⲈⲘⲦⲞ ⲈⲂⲞⲖ Ⲙ-ⲠⲈⲦ-ⲤⲘⲞⲞⲤ ⲈⲒϪⲘ-ⲠⲈⲐⲢⲞⲚⲞⲤ ⲚⲤⲈⲞⲨⲰϢⲦ Ⲙ-ⲠⲈⲦ-ⲞⲚⲈ ϢⲀ-ⲚⲒⲈⲚⲈⲈ Ⲛ-ⲚⲒⲈⲚⲈⲈ ⲀⲨⲰ ⲚⲤⲈⲚⲞⲨϪⲈ Ⲛ-ⲚⲈⲨⲔⲖⲞⲘ Ⲙ-ⲠⲈⲘⲦⲞ ⲈⲂⲞⲖ Ⲙ-ⲠⲈⲐⲢⲞⲚⲞⲤ, ⲈⲨϪⲰ ⲘⲘⲞⲤ 11 ϪⲈ

---

43. Christian Askeland, ed., "An Eclectic Edition of the Sahidic Apocalypse of John," in *Studien zum Text der Apokalypse II*, ed. Marcus Sigismund and Darius Müller, Arbeiten zur Neutestamentlichen Textforschung 50 (Berlin: de Gruyter, 2017), 33–79. A few corrections to this edition have been footnoted.

"ⲕⲙ̄ⲡϣⲁ, ⲡϫⲟⲉⲓⲥ ⲡⲛⲟⲩⲧⲉ,
ⲉ-ϫⲓ ⲙ̄-ⲡⲉⲟⲟⲩ ⲙⲛ̄-ⲡⲧⲁⲉⲓⲟ ⲙⲛ̄-ⲧϭⲟⲙ,
ϫⲉ ⲛ̄ⲧⲟⲕ ⲁⲕⲥⲛ̄ⲧ-ⲛ̄ⲕⲁ ⲛⲓⲙ,
ⲁⲩⲱ ⲉⲩϣⲟⲟⲡ ⲁⲩⲱ ⲛ̄ⲧⲁⲩϣⲱⲡⲉ ⲉⲧⲃⲉ-ⲡⲉⲕⲟⲩⲱϣ!"

5.1 ⲁⲩⲱ ⲁⲓ̈ⲛⲁⲩ ⲉ-ⲩϫⲱⲱⲙⲉ ϩⲛ̄-ⲧⲟⲩⲛⲁⲙ ⲙ̄-ⲡⲉⲧ-ϩⲙⲟⲟⲥ ϩⲓ-ⲡⲉⲑⲣⲟⲛⲟⲥ, ⲉϥⲥⲏϩ ϩⲓⲑⲏ ⲁⲩⲱ ϩⲓⲡⲁϩⲟⲩ, ⲉϥⲧⲟⲟⲃⲉ ⲛ̄-ⲥⲁϣϥⲉ ⲛ̄-ⲥⲫⲣⲁⲅⲓⲥ. 2 ⲁⲩⲱ ⲁⲓ̈ⲛⲁⲩ ⲉ-ⲩⲁⲅⲅⲉⲗⲟⲥ ⲉϥϭⲙ̄-ϭⲟⲙ ⲉϥⲕⲏⲣⲩⲥⲥⲉ ϩⲛ̄-ⲟⲩⲛⲟϭ ⲛ̄-ⲥⲙⲏ ϫⲉ "ⲛⲓⲙ ⲡⲉⲧ-ⲙ̄ⲡϣⲁ ⲛ̄-ⲟⲩⲱⲛ ⲙ̄-ⲡϫⲱⲱⲙⲉ ⲁⲩⲱ ⲉ-ⲃⲱⲗ ⲉⲃⲟⲗ ⲛ̄-ⲛⲉϥⲥⲫⲣⲁⲅⲓⲥ?" 3 ⲁⲩⲱ ⲙ̄ⲡⲉ-ⲗⲁⲁⲩ ⲉϣϭⲙ̄-ϭⲟⲙ ⲟⲩⲇⲉ ϩⲛ̄-ⲧⲡⲉ ⲟⲩⲇⲉ ϩⲓϫⲙ̄-ⲡⲕⲁϩ ⲟⲩⲇⲉ ϩⲁⲡⲉⲥⲏⲧ ⲙ̄-ⲡⲕⲁϩ ⲉ-ⲩⲱⲛ ⲙ̄-ⲡϫⲱⲱⲙⲉ ⲏ ⲉ-ⲛⲁⲩ ⲉⲣⲟϥ.

4 ⲁⲩⲱ ⲁⲓ̈ⲣⲓⲙⲉ ⲉⲙⲁⲧⲉ ϫⲉ ⲙ̄ⲡⲟⲩϩⲉ ⲉ-ⲗⲁⲁⲩ ⲉϥⲙ̄ⲡϣⲁ ⲛ-ⲟⲩⲱⲛ ⲙ̄-ⲡϫⲱⲱⲙⲉ ⲏ ⲉ-ⲛⲁⲩ ⲉⲣⲟϥ. 5 ⲡⲉϫⲉ-ⲟⲩⲁ ⲛⲁⲓ̈ ⲉⲃⲟⲗ ϩⲛ̄-ⲛⲉⲡⲣⲉⲥⲃⲩⲧⲉⲣⲟⲥ ϫⲉ "ⲙ̄ⲡⲣ̄ⲣⲓⲙⲉ! ⲉⲓⲥ-ϩⲏⲏⲧⲉ! ⲁϥϭⲣⲟ ⲛ̄ϭⲓ-ⲡⲙⲟⲩⲉⲓ ⲉⲃⲟⲗ ϩⲛ̄-ⲧⲉⲫⲩⲗⲏ ⲛ̄-ⲓⲟⲩⲇⲁ, ⲧⲛⲟⲩⲛⲉ ⲛ̄-ⲇⲁⲩⲉⲓⲇ, ⲉ-ⲧⲣⲉϥⲟⲩⲱⲛ ⲙ̄-ⲡϫⲱⲱⲙⲉ ⲙⲛ̄-ⲧⲉϥⲥⲁϣϥⲉ ⲛ̄-ⲥⲫⲣⲁⲅⲓⲥ!"

6 ⲁⲩⲱ ⲁⲓ̈ⲛⲁⲩ ⲛ̄-ⲧⲙⲏⲧⲉ ⲙ̄-ⲡⲉⲑⲣⲟⲛⲟⲥ ⲙⲛ̄-ⲡⲉϥⲧⲟⲟⲩ ⲛ̄-ⲍⲱⲟⲛ ⲁⲩⲱ ⲛ̄-ⲧⲙⲏⲧⲉ ⲛ̄-ⲛⲉⲡⲣⲉⲥⲃⲩⲧⲉⲣⲟⲥ ⲉ-ⲩϩⲓⲉⲓⲃ ⲉϥⲁϩⲉⲣⲁⲧϥ̄ ⲉ-ⲁⲩⲕⲟⲛⲥϥ̄, ⲉ-ⲩⲛ̄-ⲥⲁϣϥ̄ ⲛ̄-ⲧⲁⲡ ⲙ̄ⲙⲟϥ ⲁⲩⲱ ⲥⲁϣϥ̄ ⲛ̄-ⲃⲁⲗ, ⲉⲧⲉ-ⲛⲁⲓ̈ ⲛⲉ ⲡⲥⲁϣϥ̄ ⲙ̄-ⲡⲛⲉⲩⲙⲁ ⲙ̄-ⲡⲛⲟⲩⲧⲉ ⲉⲧⲟⲩϫⲟⲟⲩ ⲙ̄ⲙⲟⲟⲩ ⲉⲃⲟⲗ ⲉϫⲙ̄-ⲡⲕⲁϩ ⲧⲏⲣϥ̄. 7 ⲁⲩⲱ ⲁϥⲉⲓ ⲁϥϫⲓ ⲙ̄-ⲡϫⲱⲱⲙⲉ ⲉⲃⲟⲗ ϩⲛ̄-ⲧⲟⲩⲛⲁⲙ ⲙ̄-ⲡⲉⲧ-ϩⲙⲟⲟⲥ ϩⲓ-ⲡⲉⲑⲣⲟⲛⲟⲥ.

8 ⲁⲩⲱ ⲛ̄ⲧⲉⲣⲉϥϫⲓⲧϥ̄, ⲁⲩⲡⲁϩⲧⲟⲩ ⲛ̄ϭⲓ-ⲡⲉϥⲧⲟⲟⲩ ⲛ̄-ⲍⲱⲟⲛ ⲙⲛ̄-ⲡϫⲟⲩⲧ-ⲁϥⲧⲉ ⲙ̄-ⲡⲣⲉⲥⲃⲩⲧⲉⲣⲟⲥ ⲙ̄-ⲡⲉⲙⲧⲟ ⲉⲃⲟⲗ ⲙ̄-ⲡⲉϩⲓⲉⲓⲃ, ⲉ-ⲩⲛ̄-ⲟⲩⲕⲓⲑⲁⲣⲁ ⲛ̄ⲧⲙ̄-ⲡⲟⲩⲁ ⲡⲟⲩⲁ ⲙⲛ̄-ϩⲉⲛⲫⲓⲁⲗⲏ ⲛ̄-ⲛⲟⲩⲃ ⲉⲩⲙⲉϩ ⲛ̄-ϣⲟⲩϩⲏⲛⲉ, ⲉⲧⲉ-ⲛⲁⲓ̈ ⲛⲉ ⲛⲉϣⲗⲏⲗ ⲛ̄-ⲛⲉⲧⲟⲩⲁⲁⲃ. 9 ⲁⲩⲱ ⲁⲩϫⲱ ⲛ̄-ⲟⲩϫⲱ ⲛ̄-ⲃⲣ̄ⲣⲉ, ⲉⲩϫⲱ ⲙ̄ⲙⲟⲥ ϫⲉ

"ⲕⲙ̄ⲡϣⲁ ⲛ̄-ϫⲓ ⲙ̄-ⲡϫⲱⲱⲙⲉ
ⲁⲩⲱ ⲉ-ⲩⲱⲛ ⲛ̄-ⲛⲉϥⲥⲫⲣⲁⲅⲓⲥ,
ϫⲉ ⲁⲩⲕⲟⲛⲥⲕ̄,
ⲁⲩⲱ ⲁⲕϣⲟⲡⲛ̄ ⲙ̄-ⲡⲉⲛⲛⲟⲩⲧⲉ[44] ϩⲣⲁⲓ̈ ϩⲙ̄-ⲡⲉⲕⲥⲛⲟϥ
ⲉⲃⲟⲗ ϩⲛ̄-ⲫⲩⲗⲏ ⲛⲓⲙ ϩⲓ-ⲁⲥⲡⲉ ϩⲓ-ⲗⲁⲟⲥ ϩⲓ-ϩⲉⲑⲛⲟⲥ.
10   ⲁⲩⲱ ⲁⲕⲉⲓⲣⲉ ⲙ̄ⲙⲟⲛ ⲛ̄-ⲟⲩⲙⲛ̄ⲧⲉⲣⲟ ⲙ̄-ⲡⲉⲛⲛⲟⲩⲧⲉ ⲁⲩⲱ ⲛ̄ⲟⲩⲏⲏⲃ,
ⲁⲩⲱ ⲥⲉⲛⲁⲣ̄-ⲣ̄ⲣⲟ ⲉϩⲣⲁⲓ̈ ⲉϫⲙ̄-ⲡⲕⲁϩ!"

11 ⲁⲓ̈ⲛⲁⲩ ⲁⲩⲱ ⲁⲓ̈ⲥⲱⲧⲙ̄ ⲛ̄-ⲑⲉ ⲛ̄-ⲧⲉⲥⲙⲏ ⲛ̄-ϩⲉⲛⲁⲅⲅⲉⲗⲟⲥ ⲉ-ⲛⲁϣⲱⲟⲩ ⲙ̄-ⲡⲕⲱⲧⲉ ⲙ̄-ⲡⲉⲑⲣⲟⲛⲟⲥ ⲙⲛ̄-ⲛⲉⲡⲣⲉⲥⲃⲩⲧⲉⲣⲟⲥ ⲙⲛ̄-ⲛ̄ⲍⲱⲟⲛ ⲉⲣⲉ-ⲧⲉⲩⲏⲡⲉ ⲉⲓⲣⲉ ⲛ̄-ϩⲉⲛⲧⲃⲁ ⲛ̄-ⲧⲃⲁ ⲙⲛ̄-ϩⲉⲛϣⲟ ⲛ̄-ϣⲟ, 12 ⲉⲩϫⲱ ⲙ̄ⲙⲟⲥ ϩⲛ̄-ⲟⲩⲛⲟϭ ⲛ̄-ⲥⲙⲏ ϫⲉ

"ϥⲙ̄ⲡϣⲁ ⲛ̄ϭⲓ-ⲡⲉϩⲓⲉⲓⲃ ⲉⲛⲧⲁⲩⲕⲟⲛⲥϥ̄
ⲉ-ϫⲓ ⲛ̄-ⲧⲙⲛ̄ⲧⲛⲟϭ ⲙⲛ̄-ⲧⲙⲛ̄ⲧⲣⲙ̄ⲙⲁⲟ ⲙⲛ̄-ⲧⲥⲟⲫⲓⲁ
ⲁⲩⲱ ⲡⲁⲙⲁϩⲧⲉ ⲙⲛ̄-ⲡⲧⲁⲉⲓⲟ ⲙⲛ̄-ⲡⲉⲟⲟⲩ ⲙⲛ̄-ⲡⲉⲥⲙⲟⲩ!"

13 ⲁⲩⲱ ⲥⲱⲛⲧ̄ ⲛⲓⲙ ⲉⲧ-ϩⲛ̄-ⲧⲡⲉ ⲁⲩⲱ ϩⲓϫⲙ̄-ⲡⲕⲁϩ ⲁⲩⲱ ϩⲁⲡⲉⲥⲏⲧ ⲙ̄-ⲡⲕⲁϩ ⲁⲩⲱ ⲑⲁⲗⲁⲥⲥⲁ ⲙⲛ̄-ⲛⲉⲧ-ⲛ̄ϩⲏⲧⲟⲩ ⲧⲏⲣⲟⲩ, ⲁⲓ̈ⲥⲱⲧⲙ̄ ⲉⲣⲟⲟⲩ ⲉⲩϫⲱ ⲙ̄ⲙⲟⲥ ϫⲉ

---

44. Corrected from ⲁⲕϣⲟⲡ ⲙ̄ⲡⲉⲛⲛⲟⲩⲧⲉ.

"ⲡⲉⲥⲙⲟⲩ ⲙ̄-ⲡⲉⲧ-ϩⲙⲟⲟⲥ ϩⲓ-ⲡⲉⲑⲣⲟⲛⲟⲥ ⲙⲛ̄-ⲡⲉϩⲓⲉⲓⲃ,
ⲁⲩⲱ ⲡⲧⲁⲉⲓⲟ ⲙⲛ̄-ⲡⲉⲟⲟⲩ ⲙⲛ̄-ⲡⲁⲙⲁϩⲧⲉ
ϣⲁ-ⲛⲓⲉⲛⲉϩ ⲛ̄-ⲛⲓⲉⲛⲉϩ!"

14 ⲁⲩⲱ ⲡⲉϥⲧⲟⲟⲩ ⲛ̄-ⲍⲱⲟⲛ ⲛⲉⲩϫⲱ ⲙ̄ⲙⲟⲥ ϫⲉ "ϩⲁⲙⲏⲛ!" ⲁⲩⲱ ⲛⲉⲡⲣⲉⲥⲃⲩⲧⲉⲣⲟⲥ ⲁⲩⲡⲁϩⲧⲟⲩ ⲁⲩⲟⲩⲱϣⲧ̄.

6.1 ⲁⲩⲱ ⲁⲓ̈ⲛⲁⲩ ⲛ̄ⲧⲉⲣⲉϥⲟⲩⲱⲛ ⲛ̄ϭⲓ-ⲡⲉϩⲓⲉⲓⲃ ⲛ̄-ⲟⲩⲉⲓ ⲛ̄-ⲛⲉⲥⲫⲣⲁⲅⲓ́ⲥ, ⲁⲓ̈ⲥⲱⲧⲙ̄ ⲉ-ⲩⲁ ⲙ̄-ⲡⲉϥⲧⲟⲟⲩ ⲛ̄-ⲍⲱⲟⲛ ⲛ̄-ⲑⲉ ⲛ̄-ⲟⲩⲥⲙⲏ ⲛ̄-ϩⲣⲟⲩ-ⲙ̄-ⲡⲉ, ⲉϥϫⲱ ⲙ̄ⲙⲟⲥ ϫⲉ "ⲁⲙⲟⲩ!" 2 ⲁⲓ̈ⲛⲁⲩ ⲁⲩⲱ ⲉⲓⲥ! ⲟⲩϩⲧⲟ ⲉϥⲟⲩⲟⲃϣ̄, ⲉⲣⲉ-ⲩⲡⲓⲧⲉ ⲛ̄ⲧⲟⲟⲧϥ̄ ⲙ̄-ⲡⲉⲧ-ⲁⲗⲉ ⲉⲣⲟϥ, ⲁⲩⲱ ⲁⲩϯ ⲛⲁϥ ⲛ̄-ⲟⲩⲕⲗⲟⲙ. ⲁϥⲉⲓ ⲉⲃⲟⲗ ⲉϥϫⲣⲁⲉⲓⲧ ⲁⲩⲱ ⲁϥϫⲣⲟ.

3 ⲛ̄ⲧⲉⲣⲉϥⲟⲩⲱⲛ ⲇⲉ ⲛ̄-ⲧⲙⲉϩ-ⲥⲛ̄ⲧⲉ ⲛ̄-ⲥⲫⲣⲁⲅⲓ́ⲥ, ⲁⲓ̈ⲥⲱⲧⲙ̄ ⲉ-ⲡⲙⲉϩ-ⲥⲛⲁⲩ ⲛ̄-ⲍⲱⲟⲛ ⲉϥϫⲱ ⲙ̄ⲙⲟⲥ ϫⲉ "ⲁⲙⲟⲩ!" 4 ⲁⲩⲱ ⲁϥⲉⲓ ⲉⲃⲟⲗ ⲛ̄ϭⲓ-ⲟⲩϩⲧⲟ ⲉϥⲧⲣⲉϣⲣⲱϣ, ⲁⲩⲱ ⲡⲉⲧ-ⲁⲗⲉ ⲉⲣⲟϥ ⲁⲩϯ ⲛⲁϥ ⲉ-ⲧⲣⲉϥϥⲓ ⲛ̄-ϯⲣⲏⲛⲏ ⲉⲃⲟⲗ ϩⲓϫⲙ̄-ⲡⲕⲁϩ ϫⲉⲕⲁⲥ ⲉⲩⲉϩⲱⲧⲃ̄ ⲛ̄-ⲛⲉⲩⲉⲣⲏⲩ, ⲁⲩⲱ ⲁⲩϯ ⲛⲁϥ ⲛ̄-ⲟⲩⲛⲟϭ ⲛ̄-ⲥⲏϥⲉ.

5 ⲛ̄ⲧⲉⲣⲉϥⲟⲩⲱⲛ ⲇⲉ ⲛ̄-ⲧⲙⲉϩ-ϣⲟⲙⲧⲉ ⲛ̄-ⲥⲫⲣⲁⲅⲓ́ⲥ, ⲁⲓ̈ⲥⲱⲧⲙ̄ ⲉ-ⲡⲙⲉϩ-ϣⲟⲙⲛ̄ⲧ ⲛ̄-ⲍⲱⲟⲛ ⲉϥϫⲱ ⲙ̄ⲙⲟⲥ ϫⲉ "ⲁⲙⲟⲩ!" ⲁⲩⲱ ⲉⲓⲥ! ⲟⲩϩⲧⲟ ⲛ̄-ⲕⲁⲙⲏ, ⲁⲩⲱ ⲡⲉⲧ-ⲁⲗⲉ ⲉⲣⲟϥ ⲉ-ⲩⲛ̄-ⲟⲩⲙⲁϣⲉ ϩⲛ̄-ⲧⲉϥϭⲓϫ.

6 ⲁⲓ̈ⲥⲱⲧⲙ̄ ⲉ-ⲩⲥⲙⲏ ⲛ̄-ⲧⲙⲏⲧⲉ ⲙ̄-ⲡⲉϥⲧⲟⲟⲩ ⲛ̄-ⲍⲱⲟⲛ ⲉⲥϫⲱ ⲙ̄ⲙⲟⲥ ϫⲉ "ⲟⲩϭⲁⲡⲓϫⲉ ⲛ̄-ⲥⲟⲩⲟ ϩⲁ-ⲟⲩⲥⲁⲧⲉⲉⲣⲉ ⲁⲩⲱ ϣⲟⲙⲧⲉ ⲛ̄-ϭⲁⲡⲓϫⲉ ⲛ̄-ⲉⲓⲱⲧ ϩⲁ-ⲟⲩⲥⲁⲧⲉⲉⲣⲉ. ⲡⲛⲉϩ ⲇⲉ ⲛ̄ⲧⲟϥ ⲙⲛ̄-ⲡⲏⲣⲡ̄ ⲙ̄ⲡⲣ̄ⲧⲁⲕⲟⲟⲩ."

7 ⲛ̄ⲧⲉⲣⲉϥⲟⲩⲱⲛ ⲇⲉ ⲛ̄-ⲧⲙⲉϩ-ϥⲧⲟ ⲛ̄-ⲥⲫⲣⲁⲅⲓ́ⲥ, ⲁⲓ̈ⲥⲱⲧⲙ̄ ⲉ-ⲧⲉⲥⲙⲏ ⲙ̄-ⲡⲙⲉϩ-ϥⲧⲟⲟⲩ ⲛ̄-ⲍⲱⲟⲛ ⲉϥϫⲱ ⲙ̄ⲙⲟⲥ ϫⲉ "ⲁⲙⲟⲩ!" 8 ⲁⲓ̈ⲛⲁⲩ ⲁⲩⲱ ⲉⲓⲥ! ⲟⲩϩⲧⲟ ⲉϥⲟⲩⲉⲧⲟⲩⲱⲧ, ⲁⲩⲱ ⲡⲉⲧ-ⲁⲗⲉ ⲉⲣⲟϥ ⲉ-ⲡⲉϥⲣⲁⲛ ⲡⲉ ⲡⲙⲟⲩ, ⲉⲣⲉ-ⲁⲙⲛ̄ⲧⲉ ⲟⲩⲏϩ ⲛ̄ⲥⲱϥ, ⲁⲩϯ ⲛⲁϥ ⲛ̄-ⲟⲩⲉⲝⲟⲩⲥⲓ́ⲁ ⲉϫⲙ̄-ⲡⲟⲩⲛ̄-ϥⲧⲟⲟⲩ ⲙ̄-ⲡⲕⲁϩ, ⲉ-ⲙⲟⲟⲩⲧⲟⲩ ϩⲛ̄-ⲧⲥⲏϥⲉ ⲙⲛ̄-ⲡϩⲉⲃⲱⲛ ⲙⲛ̄-ⲡⲙⲟⲩ ⲙⲛ̄-ⲛⲉⲑⲏⲣⲓ́ⲟⲛ ⲙ̄-ⲡⲕⲁϩ.

9 ⲛ̄ⲧⲉⲣⲉϥⲟⲩⲱⲛ ⲇⲉ ⲛ̄-ⲧⲙⲉϩ-ϯⲉ ⲛ̄-ⲥⲫⲣⲁⲅⲓ́ⲥ, ⲁⲓ̈ⲛⲁⲩ ϩⲁⲡⲉⲥⲛ̄ⲧ ⲙ̄-ⲡⲉⲑⲩⲥⲓⲁⲥⲧⲏ́ⲣⲓⲟⲛ ⲉ-ⲛⲉⲯⲩⲭⲏ ⲛ̄-ⲛ̄ⲣⲱⲙⲉ ⲉⲛⲧⲁⲩϩⲟⲧⲃⲟⲩ ⲉⲧⲃⲉ-ⲡϣⲁϫⲉ ⲙ̄-ⲡⲛⲟⲩⲧⲉ ⲙⲛ̄-ⲧⲙⲛ̄ⲧⲙⲛ̄ⲧⲣⲉ ⲉ-ⲛⲉ-ⲩⲛ̄ⲧⲁⲩⲥ. 10 ⲁⲩⲱ ⲁⲩⲁϣⲕⲁⲕ ⲉⲃⲟⲗ ϩⲛ̄-ⲟⲩⲛⲟϭ ⲛ̄-ⲥⲙⲏ, ⲉⲩϫⲱ ⲙ̄ⲙⲟⲥ ϫⲉ "ϣⲁⲛⲧⲉ-ⲩ ϣⲱⲡⲉ, ⲡϫⲟⲉⲓⲥ ⲡⲉⲧ-ⲟⲩⲁⲁⲃ ⲙ̄-ⲙⲉ, ⲛ̄ⲅⲕⲣⲓⲛⲉ ⲁⲛ ⲁⲩⲱ ⲛ̄ⲅϫⲓ ⲁⲛ ⲙ̄-ⲡⲉⲕⲃⲁ ⲙ̄-ⲡⲉⲛⲥⲛⲟϥ ⲉⲃⲟⲗ ϩⲛ̄-ⲛⲉⲧ-ⲟⲩⲏϩ ϩⲓϫⲙ̄-ⲡⲕⲁϩ?" 11 ⲁⲩⲱ ⲁⲩϯ ⲛⲁⲩ ⲡⲟⲩⲁ ⲡⲟⲩⲁ ⲛ̄-ⲟⲩⲥⲧⲟⲗⲏ́ ⲛ̄-ⲟⲩⲱⲃϣ̄, ⲁⲩⲱ ⲁⲩϫⲟⲟⲥ ⲛⲁⲩ ϫⲉⲕⲁⲥ ⲉⲩⲉⲙⲧⲟⲛ ⲙ̄ⲙⲟⲟⲩ ⲛ̄-ⲕⲉⲕⲟⲩⲓ̈ ⲛ̄-ⲟⲩⲟⲉⲓϣ ϣⲁⲛⲧⲟⲩϫⲱⲕ ⲉⲃⲟⲗ ⲛ̄ϭⲓ-ⲛⲉⲩⲕⲉⲥⲛⲏⲩ ⲛⲉⲩϣⲃⲣ̄-ϩⲙ̄ϩⲁⲗ, ⲛⲁⲓ̈ ⲉⲧⲟⲩⲛⲁⲙⲟⲟⲩⲧⲟⲩ ϩⲱⲟⲩ ⲛ̄-ⲧⲉⲩϩⲉ.

12 ⲁⲩⲱ ⲁⲓ̈ⲛⲁⲩ ⲛ̄ⲧⲉⲣⲉϥⲟⲩⲱⲛ ⲛ̄-ⲧⲙⲉϩ-ⲥⲟ ⲛ̄-ⲥⲫⲣⲁⲅⲓ́ⲥ, ⲁⲩⲛⲟϭ ⲛ̄-ⲕⲙ̄ⲧⲟ ϣⲱⲡⲉ, ⲡⲣⲏ ⲁϥⲕⲙⲟⲙ ⲛ̄-ⲑⲉ ⲛ̄-ⲟⲩϭⲟⲟⲩⲛⲉ, ⲁⲩⲱ ⲡⲟⲟϩ ⲁϥⲣ̄-ⲥⲛⲟϥ. 13 ⲛ̄ⲥⲓⲟⲩ ⲛ̄-ⲧⲡⲉ ⲁⲩϩⲉ ⲉϩⲣⲁⲓ̈ ⲉϫⲙ̄-ⲡⲕⲁϩ ⲛ̄-ⲑⲉ ⲛ̄-ⲟⲩⲃⲱ ⲛ̄-ⲕⲛ̄ⲧⲉ ⲉⲥⲛⲟⲩϫⲉ ⲉⲃⲟⲗ ⲛ̄-ⲛⲉⲥϣⲱⲃⲉ ⲉⲣⲉ-ⲟⲩⲛⲟϭ ⲛ̄-ⲧⲏⲩ ⲕⲓⲙ ⲉⲣⲟⲥ. 14 ⲧⲡⲉ ⲁⲥϭⲱⲗ ⲛ̄-ⲑⲉ ⲛ̄-ⲟⲩϫⲱⲱⲙⲉ ⲉϥⲥⲏⲗ. ⲧⲟⲟⲩ ⲛⲓⲙ ϩⲓ-ⲛⲏⲥⲟⲥ ⲛⲓⲙ ⲁⲩⲕⲓⲙ ⲉⲃⲟⲗ ϩⲛ̄-ⲛⲉⲩⲙⲁ.

15 ⲁⲩⲱ ⲛ̄ⲣ̄ⲣⲱⲟⲩ ⲙ̄-ⲡⲕⲁϩ ⲙⲛ̄-ⲛ̄ⲛⲟϭ ⲙⲛ̄-ⲛ̄ⲭⲓⲗⲓⲁⲣⲭⲟⲥ ⲙⲛ̄-ⲛ̄ⲣⲙ̄ⲙⲁⲟ ⲙⲛ̄-ⲛ̄ϫⲱⲱⲣⲉ ⲁⲩⲱ ϩⲙ̄ϩⲁⲗ ⲛⲓⲙ ϩⲓ-ⲣⲙ̄ϩⲉ ⲁⲩϩⲟⲡⲟⲩ ϩⲛ̄-ⲛⲉⲥⲡⲏ́ⲗⲁⲓⲟⲛ ⲙⲛ̄-ⲛ̄ⲥⲓⲃⲧ̄ ⲛ̄-ⲛ̄ⲧⲟⲩⲉⲓⲏ, 16 ⲉⲩϫⲱ ⲙ̄ⲙⲟⲥ ⲛ̄-ⲛ̄ⲧⲟⲟⲩ ⲙⲛ̄-ⲛ̄ⲥⲓⲃⲧ̄ ϫⲉ "ϩⲉ ⲉϩⲣⲁⲓ̈ ⲉϫⲱⲛ ⲛ̄ⲧⲉⲧⲛ̄ϩⲟⲡⲛ̄ ⲙ̄-ⲡⲉⲙⲧⲟ ⲉⲃⲟⲗ ⲙ̄-ⲡⲉⲧ-ϩⲙⲟⲟⲥ

ϩι-πεθρόνος ⲁⲩⲱ ⲉⲃⲟⲗ ϩⲛ̄-ⲧⲟⲣⲅⲏ́ ⲙ̄-ⲡⲉϩⲓⲉⲓⲃ, 17 ϫⲉ ⲁϥⲉⲓ ⲛ̄ϭⲓ-ⲡⲛⲟϭ ⲛ̄-ϩⲟⲟⲩ ⲛ̄-ⲧⲉϥⲟⲣⲅⲏ́! ⲛⲓⲙ ⲡⲉⲧ-ⲛⲁϣⲁϩⲉⲣⲁⲧϥ̄?"

7.1 ⲙⲛ̄ⲛ̄ⲥⲁ-ⲛⲁⲓ̈ ⲁⲓ̈ⲛⲁⲩ ⲉ-ϥⲧⲟⲟⲩ ⲛ̄-ⲁ́ⲅⲅⲉⲗⲟⲥ ⲉⲩⲁϩⲉⲣⲁⲧⲟⲩ ⲉ-ⲡⲉϥⲧⲟⲟⲩ ⲛ̄-ⲕⲟⲟϩ ⲙ̄-ⲡⲕⲁϩ, ⲉⲩⲁⲙⲁϩⲧⲉ ⲙ̄-ⲡⲉϥⲧⲟⲟⲩ ⲛ̄-ⲧⲏⲩ ⲙ̄-ⲡⲕⲁϩ ϫⲉ ⲛ̄ⲛⲉ-ⲧⲏⲩ ⲛⲓϥⲉ ⲉϫⲙ̄-ⲡⲕⲁϩ ⲏ̄ ⲉϫⲛ̄-ⲑⲁ́ⲗⲁⲥⲥⲁ ⲏ̄ ⲉϫⲛ̄-ⲗⲁⲁⲩ ⲛ̄-ϣⲏⲛ.

2 ⲁⲩⲱ ⲁⲓ̈ⲛⲁⲩ ⲉ-ⲕⲉⲁ́ⲅⲅⲉⲗⲟⲥ ⲉϥⲛⲏⲩ ⲉⲃⲟⲗ ϩⲛ̄-ⲙ̄ⲙⲁ ⲛ̄-ϣⲁ ⲙ̄-ⲡⲣⲏ, ⲉ-ⲟⲩⲛ̄-ⲟⲩⲥⲫⲣⲁⲅⲓ́ⲥ ⲛ̄ⲧⲟⲟⲧϥ̄ ⲛ̄ⲧⲉ-ⲡⲛⲟⲩⲧⲉ ⲉⲧ-ⲟⲛϩ̄. ⲁϥϫⲓ-ϣⲕⲁⲕ ⲉⲃⲟⲗ ϩⲛ̄-ⲟⲩⲛⲟϭ ⲛ̄-ⲥⲙⲏ ⲉ-ⲡⲉϥⲧⲟⲟⲩ ⲛ̄-ⲁ́ⲅⲅⲉⲗⲟⲥ ⲛⲉⲛⲧⲁⲩⲧⲁⲁⲥ ⲛⲁⲩ ⲉ-ⲧⲁⲕⲉ-ⲡⲕⲁϩ ⲙⲛ̄-ⲑⲁ́ⲗⲁⲥⲥⲁ, 3 ⲉϥϫⲱ ⲙ̄ⲙⲟⲥ ϫⲉ "ⲙ̄ⲡⲣ̄ⲧⲁⲕⲉ-ⲡⲕⲁϩ ⲙⲛ̄-ⲑⲁ́ⲗⲁⲥⲥⲁ ⲙⲛ̄-ⲛ̄ϣⲏⲛ ϣⲁⲛⲧⲛ̄ⲧⲱϣⲃⲉ⁴⁵ ⲛ̄-ⲛ̄ϩⲙ̄ϩⲁⲗ ⲙ̄-ⲡⲛⲟⲩⲧⲉ ⲉϩⲣⲁⲓ̈ ⲉϫⲛ̄-ⲧⲉⲩⲧⲉϩⲛⲉ!"

4 ⲁⲩⲱ ⲁⲓ̈ⲥⲱⲧⲙ̄ ⲉ-ⲧⲏⲡⲉ ⲛ̄-ⲛⲉⲛⲧⲁⲩⲥⲫⲣⲁⲅⲓⲍⲉ ⲙ̄ⲙⲟⲟⲩ, ⲙⲛ̄ⲧ-ⲁϥⲧⲉ ⲛ̄-ⲧⲃⲁ ⲙⲛ̄-ϥⲧⲟⲟⲩ ⲛ̄-ϣⲟ ⲉⲃⲟⲗ ϩⲛ̄-ⲫⲩⲗⲏ ⲛⲓⲙ ⲛ̄-ⲛ̄ϣⲏⲣⲉ ⲙ̄-ⲡⲓⲥⲣⲁⲏⲗ.

5 ⲉⲃⲟⲗ ϩⲛ̄-ⲧⲉⲫⲩⲗⲏ ⲛ̄-ⲓⲟⲩ́ⲇⲁ ⲙⲛ̄ⲧ-ⲥⲛⲟⲟⲩⲥ ⲛ̄-ϣⲟ ⲉⲩⲧⲟⲟⲃⲉ,
ⲉⲃⲟⲗ ϩⲛ̄-ⲧⲉⲫⲩⲗⲏ ⲛ̄-ϩⲣⲟⲩⲃⲏⲛ ⲙⲛ̄ⲧ-ⲥⲛⲟⲟⲩⲥ ⲛ̄-ϣⲟ,
ⲉⲃⲟⲗ ϩⲛ̄-ⲧⲉⲫⲩⲗⲏ ⲛ̄-ⲅⲁⲇ ⲙⲛ̄ⲧ-ⲥⲛⲟⲟⲩⲥ ⲛ̄-ϣⲟ,

6 ⲉⲃⲟⲗ ϩⲛ̄-ⲧⲉⲫⲩⲗⲏ ⲛ̄-ⲁⲥⲏⲣ ⲙⲛ̄ⲧ-ⲥⲛⲟⲟⲩⲥ ⲛ̄-ϣⲟ,
ⲉⲃⲟⲗ ϩⲛ̄-ⲧⲉⲫⲩⲗⲏ ⲛ̄-ⲛⲉⲫⲑⲁⲗⲉⲓⲙ́⁴⁶ ⲙⲛ̄ⲧ-ⲥⲛⲟⲟⲩⲥ ⲛ̄-ϣⲟ,
ⲉⲃⲟⲗ ϩⲛ̄-ⲧⲉⲫⲩⲗⲏ ⲙ̄-ⲙⲁⲛⲁⲥⲥⲏ ⲙⲛ̄ⲧ-ⲥⲛⲟⲟⲩⲥ ⲛ̄-ϣⲟ,

7 ⲉⲃⲟⲗ ϩⲛ̄-ⲧⲉⲫⲩⲗⲏ ⲛ̄-ⲥⲩⲙⲉⲱⲛ ⲙⲛ̄ⲧ-ⲥⲛⲟⲟⲩⲥ ⲛ̄-ϣⲟ,
ⲉⲃⲟⲗ ϩⲛ̄-ⲧⲉⲫⲩⲗⲏ ⲛ̄-ⲗⲉⲩⲉⲓ́ ⲙⲛ̄ⲧ-ⲥⲛⲟⲟⲩⲥ ⲛ̄-ϣⲟ,
ⲉⲃⲟⲗ ϩⲛ̄-ⲧⲉⲫⲩⲗⲏ ⲛ̄-ⲓⲥⲥⲁⲭⲁ́ⲣ ⲙⲛ̄ⲧ-ⲥⲛⲟⲟⲩⲥ ⲛ̄-ϣⲟ,

8 ⲉⲃⲟⲗ ϩⲛ̄-ⲧⲉⲫⲩⲗⲏ ⲛ̄-ⲍⲁⲃⲟⲩⲗⲱⲛ ⲙⲛ̄ⲧ-ⲥⲛⲟⲟⲩⲥ ⲛ̄-ϣⲟ,
ⲉⲃⲟⲗ ϩⲛ̄-ⲧⲉⲫⲩⲗⲏ ⲛ̄-ⲓⲱⲥⲏⲫ ⲙⲛ̄ⲧ-ⲥⲛⲟⲟⲩⲥ ⲛ̄-ϣⲟ,
ⲉⲃⲟⲗ ϩⲛ̄-ⲧⲉⲫⲩⲗⲏ ⲛ̄-ⲃⲉⲛⲓⲁⲙⲓ́ⲛ ⲙⲛ̄ⲧ-ⲥⲛⲟⲟⲩⲥ ⲛ̄-ϣⲟ ⲉⲩⲧⲟⲟⲃⲉ.

9 ⲙⲛ̄ⲛ̄ⲥⲁ-ⲛⲁⲓ̈ ⲁⲓⲛⲁⲩ ⲉ-ⲩⲙⲏⲏϣⲉ ⲉ-ⲛⲁϣⲱϥ ⲉ-ⲙⲛ̄-ⲗⲁⲁⲩ ⲛⲁϣϭⲙ̄-ϭⲟⲙ ⲉ-ⲟⲡϥ̄, ⲉⲃⲟⲗ ϩⲛ̄-ϩⲉⲑⲛⲟⲥ ⲛⲓⲙ ϩⲓ-ⲫⲩⲗⲏ ϩⲓ-ⲁⲥⲡⲉ, ⲉⲩⲁϩⲉⲣⲁⲧⲟⲩ ⲙ̄ⲡⲉⲙⲧⲟ ⲉⲃⲟⲗ ⲙ̄-ⲡⲉⲑⲣⲟ́ⲛⲟⲥ ⲙⲛ̄-ⲙ̄ⲡⲉⲙⲧⲟ ⲉⲃⲟⲗ ⲙ̄-ⲡⲉϩⲓⲉⲓⲃ, ⲉⲩϭⲟⲟⲗⲉ ⲛ̄-ϩⲉⲛⲥⲧⲟⲗⲏ́ ⲛ̄-ⲟⲩⲱⲃϣ̄, ⲉⲣⲉ-ϩⲉⲛⲃⲁ⁴⁷ ϩⲛ̄-ⲛⲉⲩϭⲓϫ, 10 ⲉⲩϣⲕⲁⲕ ⲉⲃⲟⲗ ϩⲛ̄-ⲟⲩⲛⲟϭ ⲛ̄-ⲥⲙⲏ, ⲉⲩϫⲱ ⲙ̄ⲙⲟⲥ ϫⲉ

"ⲡⲟⲩϫⲁⲓ̈ ⲙ̄-ⲡⲉⲛⲛⲟⲩⲧⲉ ⲉⲧ-ϩⲙⲟⲟⲥ ϩⲓ-ⲡⲉⲑⲣⲟ́ⲛⲟⲥ
ⲙⲛ̄-ⲡⲉϩⲓⲉⲓⲃ!"

11 ⲁⲩⲱ ⲛ̄ⲁ́ⲅⲅⲉⲗⲟⲥ ⲧⲏⲣⲟⲩ ⲛⲉⲩⲁϩⲉⲣⲁⲧⲟⲩ ⲙ̄-ⲡⲕⲱⲧⲉ ⲙ̄-ⲡⲉⲑⲣⲟ́ⲛⲟⲥ ⲙⲛ̄-ⲛⲉⲡⲣⲉⲥⲃⲩ́ⲧⲉⲣⲟⲥ ⲙⲛ̄-ⲡⲉϥⲧⲟⲟⲩ ⲛ̄-ⲍⲱ̂ⲟⲛ ⲁⲩⲱ ⲁⲩⲡⲁϩⲧⲟⲩ ⲉϫⲙ̄-ⲛⲉⲩϩⲟ ⲙ̄ⲡⲉⲙⲧⲟ ⲉⲃⲟⲗ ⲙ̄-ⲡⲉⲑⲣⲟ́ⲛⲟⲥ ⲁⲩⲟⲩⲱϣⲧ̄ ⲙ̄-ⲡⲛⲟⲩⲧⲉ, 12 ⲉⲩϫⲱ ⲙ̄ⲙⲟⲥ ϫⲉ

"ϩⲁⲙⲏⲛ!
ⲡⲉⲥⲙⲟⲩ ⲙⲛ̄-ⲡⲉⲟⲟⲩ ⲙⲛ̄-ⲧⲥⲟⲫⲓ́ⲁ

---

45. Corrected from ϣⲁⲛⲧⲉⲛ̄ⲧⲱϣⲃⲉ.
46. Corrected from ⲛ̄ⲉⲫⲑⲁⲗⲉⲓⲙ.
47. Corrected from ⲉⲣⲉϩⲉⲛⲃⲁϩ (!)

ⲁⲩⲱ ⲧⲉⲩⲭⲁⲣⲓⲥⲧⲉⲓⲁ ⲙⲛ̄-ⲡⲧⲁⲉⲓⲟ ⲙⲛ̄-ⲧϭⲟⲙ ⲙⲛ̄-ⲡⲁⲙⲁϩⲧⲉ
ⲙ̄-ⲡⲉⲛⲛⲟⲩⲧⲉ ϣⲁ-ⲛⲓⲉⲛⲉϩ ⲛ̄-ⲛⲓⲉⲛⲉϩ!
ϩⲁⲙⲏⲛ!"

13 ⲁϥⲟⲩⲱϣⲃ̄ ⲛ̄ϭⲓ-ⲟⲩⲁ ⲉⲃⲟⲗ ϩⲛ̄-ⲛⲉⲡⲣⲉⲥⲃⲩⲧⲉⲣⲟⲥ, ⲉϥϫⲱ ⲙ̄ⲙⲟⲥ ⲛⲁⲓ̈ ϫⲉ "ⲛⲓⲙ ⲛⲉ ⲛⲁⲓ̈ ⲉⲧϭⲟⲟⲗⲉ ⲛ̄-ⲛⲉⲓ̈ⲥⲧⲟⲗⲏ ⲛ̄-ⲟⲩⲱⲃϣ̄, ⲁⲩⲱ ⲛ̄ⲧⲁⲩⲉⲓ ⲉⲃⲟⲗ ⲧⲱⲛ?"
14 ⲡⲉϫⲁⲓ̈ ϫⲉ "ⲡϫⲟⲉⲓⲥ, ⲛ̄ⲧⲟⲕ ⲉⲧⲥⲟⲟⲩⲛ."
ⲡⲉϫⲁϥ ⲛⲁⲓ̈ ϫⲉ

"ⲛⲁⲓ̈ ⲛⲉ ⲛⲉⲧ-ⲛⲏⲩ ⲉⲃⲟⲗ ϩⲛ̄-ⲧⲛⲟϭ ⲛ̄-ⲑⲗⲓⲯⲓⲥ,
 ⲉ-ⲁⲩⲉⲓⲱ ⲛ̄-ⲛⲉⲩⲥⲧⲟⲗⲏ,
 ⲁⲩⲧⲃ̄ⲃⲟⲟⲩ ϩⲙ̄-ⲡⲉⲥⲛⲟϥ ⲙ̄-ⲡⲉϩⲓⲉⲓⲃ.
15 ⲉⲧⲃⲉ-ⲡⲁⲓ̈ ⲥⲉⲙ̄-ⲡⲉⲙⲧⲟ ⲉⲃⲟⲗ ⲙ̄-ⲡⲉⲑⲣⲟⲛⲟⲥ ⲙ̄-ⲡⲛⲟⲩⲧⲉ,
 ⲉⲩϣⲙ̄ϣⲉ ⲛⲁϥ ⲙ̄-ⲡⲉϩⲟⲟⲩ ⲙⲛ̄-ⲧⲉⲩϣⲏ ϩⲙ̄-ⲡⲉϥⲣ̄ⲡⲉ.
 ⲁⲩⲱ ⲡⲉⲧ-ϩⲙⲟⲟⲥ ϩⲓ-ⲡⲉϥⲑⲣⲟⲛⲟⲥ
 ϥⲛⲁⲣ̄-ϩⲁⲓ̈ⲃⲉⲥ ⲉⲣⲟⲟⲩ.
16 ⲛ̄ⲥⲉⲛⲁϩⲕⲟ ⲁⲛ ⲛ̄ⲥⲉⲛⲁⲉⲓⲃⲉ ⲁⲛ ϫⲓⲛ-ⲧⲉⲛⲟⲩ,
 ⲁⲩⲱ ⲡⲣⲏ ⲙⲛ̄-ⲕⲁⲩⲙⲁ ⲛⲓⲙ ⲛⲁϩⲉ ⲁⲛ ⲉϩⲣⲁⲓ̈ ⲉϫⲱⲟⲩ.
17 ϫⲉ ⲡⲉϩⲓⲉⲓⲃ ⲉⲧ-ⲛ̄-ⲧⲙⲏⲧⲉ ⲙ̄-ⲡⲉⲑⲣⲟⲛⲟⲥ
 ⲛⲁⲙⲟⲟⲛⲉ ⲙ̄ⲙⲟⲟⲩ,
 ⲛⲉϥϫⲓ-ⲙⲟⲉⲓⲧ ϩⲏⲧⲟⲩ ⲉϩⲣⲁⲓ̈ ⲉϫⲛ̄-ⲙ̄ⲡⲏⲅⲏ ⲙ̄-ⲙⲟⲟⲩ ⲛ̄-ⲱⲛϩ,
 ⲛ̄ⲧⲉ-ⲡⲛⲟⲩⲧⲉ ϥⲱⲧⲉ ⲛ̄-ⲣⲙ̄ⲉⲓⲏ ⲛⲓⲙ ⲉⲃⲟⲗ ϩⲛ̄-ⲛⲉⲩⲃⲁⲗ."

8.1 ⲛ̄ⲧⲉⲣⲉϥⲟⲩⲱⲛ ⲛ̄-ⲧⲙⲉϩ-ⲥⲁϣϥⲉ ⲛ̄-ⲥⲫⲣⲁⲅⲓⲥ, ⲁⲩⲕⲁ-ⲣⲱⲟⲩ ϩⲣⲁⲓ̈ ϩⲛ̄-ⲧⲡⲉ ⲛⲁ ⲟⲩϭⲓⲥ-ⲟⲩⲛⲟⲩ.

ⲡⲉⲩⲁⲅⲅⲉⲗⲓⲟⲛ ⲡⲕⲁⲧⲁ-ⲑⲱⲙⲁⲥ THE GOSPEL OF THOMAS 1–42

Of all of the texts discovered in the cache of thirteen papyrus codices near Nag Hammadi in 1945, none has captivated scholarly (and broader public) attention as much as the Gospel of Thomas—a "gospel" with almost no narrative, composed of 144 sayings attributed to Jesus. It was likely composed in Greek sometime in the second century CE and then subsequently translated into Coptic in the third century CE. Previously known from a few Greek fragments and the references made about it by early Christian authors, this discovery allowed us to read a version of the Gospel of Thomas in its entirety.

The second tractate in Nag Hammadi Codex 2 (NHC II 2) was copied and bound in a manuscript along with six other works probably in the fourth or fifth century CE.[48] All of the Nag Hammadi codices now reside in the Coptic Museum in Cairo.

---

48. The complete Coptic text can be found in Bentley Layton, ed., *Coptic Gnostic Chrestomathy: A Selection of Coptic Texts with Grammatical Analysis and Glossary*. (Leuven: Peeters, 2004), 189–205. For the text with translation and commentary, see Simon J. Gathercole, *The Gospel of Thomas: Introduction and Commentary*, Texts and Editions for New Testament Study 11 (Leiden: Brill, 2014). For additional translations, see Marvin Meyer, ed., *The Nag Hammadi Scriptures: The International Edition* (New York: HarperOne, 2007), 133–56, and Bentley Layton and David Brakke, *The Gnostic Scriptures*, 2nd ed., Anchor Yale Bible Reference Library (New Haven: Yale University Press, 2021), 555–88.

BASICS OF SAHIDIC COPTIC

The text generally aligns with standard Sahidic, but it does show some influence from the local Lycopolitan dialect, including some frequent interchanges in vowels (especially between ⲉ and ⲁ, ⲟ and ⲁ) and regular use of ⲣ̄- before Greek verbs. Other than adjusting all overlines to the right and ignoring some additional tick marks, the spelling of the manuscript has been retained (outside of a few noted emendations of more obvious scribal errors).

ⲛⲁⲉⲓ ⲛⲉ ⲛ̄ϣⲁϫⲉ ⲉⲑⲏⲡ ⲉⲛⲧⲁ-ⲓⲏⲥⲟⲩⲥ ⲉⲧ-ⲟⲛϩ ϫⲟⲟⲩ ⲁⲩⲱ ⲁϥⲥϩⲁⲓ̈ⲥⲟⲩ ⲛ̄ϭⲓ-ⲇⲓⲇⲩⲙⲟⲥ ⲓ̈ⲟⲩⲇⲁⲥ ⲑⲱⲙⲁⲥ.

1 ⲁⲩⲱ ⲡⲉϫⲁϥ ϫⲉ "ⲡⲉⲧⲁϩⲉ[49] ⲉ-ⲑⲉⲣⲙⲏⲛⲉⲓⲁ ⲛ̄-ⲛⲉⲉⲓϣⲁϫⲉ ϥⲛⲁϫⲓ-ϯⲡⲉ ⲁⲛ ⲙ̄-ⲡⲙⲟⲩ."

2 ⲡⲉϫⲉ-ⲓⲏⲥⲟⲩⲥ "ⲙⲛ̄ⲧⲣⲉϥⲗⲟ[50] ⲛ̄ϭⲓ-ⲡⲉⲧ-ϣⲓⲛⲉ ⲉϥϣⲓⲛⲉ ϣⲁⲛⲧⲉϥϭⲓⲛⲉ, ⲁⲩⲱ ϩⲟⲧⲁⲛ ⲉϥϣⲁⲛϭⲓⲛⲉ ϥⲛⲁϣⲧⲣ̄ⲧⲣ̄, ⲁⲩⲱ ⲉϥϣⲁⲛϣⲧⲟⲣⲧⲣ̄ ϥⲛⲁⲣ̄-ϣⲡⲏⲣⲉ, ⲁⲩⲱ ϥⲛⲁⲣ̄-ⲣ̄ⲣⲟ ⲉϫⲙ̄-ⲡⲧⲏⲣϥ̄."

3 ⲡⲉϫⲉ-ⲓⲏⲥⲟⲩⲥ ϫⲉ "ⲉⲩϣⲁϫⲟⲟⲥ ⲛⲏⲧⲛ̄ ⲛ̄ϭⲓ-ⲛⲉⲧⲥⲱⲕ ϩⲏⲧ-ⲑⲏⲩⲧⲛ̄ ϫⲉ 'ⲉⲓⲥ-ϩⲏⲏⲧⲉ! ⲉ-ⲧⲙⲛ̄ⲧⲉⲣⲟ ϩⲛ̄-ⲧⲡⲉ,' ⲉⲉⲓⲉ ⲛ̄ϩⲁⲗⲏⲧ ⲛⲁⲣ̄-ϣⲟⲣⲡ ⲉⲣⲱⲧⲛ̄ ⲛ̄ⲧⲉ-ⲧⲡⲉ! ⲉⲩϣⲁⲛϫⲟⲟⲥ ⲛⲏⲧⲛ̄ ϫⲉ 'ⲥϩⲛ̄ ⲑⲁⲗⲁⲥⲥⲁ,' ⲉⲉⲓⲉ ⲛ̄ⲧⲃⲧ ⲛⲁⲣ̄ ϣⲟⲣⲡ ⲉⲣⲱⲧⲛ̄! ⲁⲗⲗⲁ ⲧⲙⲛ̄ⲧⲉⲣⲟ ⲥⲙ̄-ⲡⲉⲧⲛ̄ϩⲟⲩⲛ ⲁⲩⲱ ⲥⲙ̄-ⲡⲉⲧⲛ̄ⲃⲁⲗ. ϩⲟⲧⲁⲛ ⲉⲧⲉⲧⲛ̄ϣⲁⲛⲥⲟⲩⲱⲛ-ⲑⲏⲩⲧⲛ̄, ⲧⲟⲧⲉ ⲥⲉⲛⲁⲥⲟⲩⲱⲛ-ⲧⲏⲛⲉ, ⲁⲩⲱ ⲧⲉⲧⲛⲁⲉⲓⲙⲉ ϫⲉ ⲛ̄ⲧⲱⲧⲛ̄ ⲡⲉ ⲛ̄ϣⲏⲣⲉ ⲙ̄-ⲡⲉⲓⲱⲧ ⲉⲧ-ⲟⲛϩ. ⲉϣⲱⲡⲉ ⲇⲉ ⲧⲉⲧⲛⲁⲥⲟⲩⲱⲛ-ⲑⲏⲩⲧⲛ̄ ⲁⲛ, ⲉⲉⲓⲉ ⲧⲉⲧⲛ̄ϣⲟⲟⲡ ϩⲛ̄-ⲟⲩⲙⲛ̄ⲧϩⲏⲕⲉ, ⲁⲩⲱ ⲛ̄ⲧⲱⲧⲛ̄ ⲡⲉ ⲧⲙⲛ̄ⲧϩⲏⲕⲉ."

4 ⲡⲉϫⲉ-ⲓⲏⲥⲟⲩⲥ "ϥⲛⲁϫⲛⲁⲩ ⲁⲛ ⲛ̄ϭⲓ-ⲡⲣⲱⲙⲉ ⲛ̄-ϩⲗⲗⲟ ϩⲛ̄-ⲛⲉϥϩⲟⲟⲩ ⲉ-ϫⲛⲉ-ⲟⲩⲕⲟⲩⲉⲓ ⲛ̄-ϣⲏⲣⲉ ϣⲏⲙ ⲉϥϩⲛ̄-ⲥⲁϣϥ̄ ⲛ̄-ϩⲟⲟⲩ ⲉⲧⲃⲉ-ⲡⲧⲟⲡⲟⲥ ⲙ̄-ⲡⲱⲛϩ, ⲁⲩⲱ ϥⲛⲁⲱⲛϩ. ϫⲉ ⲟⲩⲛ̄-ϩⲁϩ ⲛ̄-ϣⲟⲣⲡ ⲛⲁⲣ̄-ϩⲁⲉ, ⲁⲩⲱ ⲛ̄ⲥⲉϣⲱⲡⲉ ⲟⲩⲁ ⲟⲩⲱⲧ."

5 ⲡⲉϫⲉ-ⲓⲏⲥⲟⲩⲥ "ⲥⲟⲩⲱⲛ-ⲡⲉⲧ-ⲙ̄-ⲡⲙ̄ⲧⲟ ⲙ̄-ⲡⲉⲕϩⲟ ⲉⲃⲟⲗ, ⲁⲩⲱ ⲡⲉⲑⲏⲡ ⲉⲣⲟⲕ ϥⲛⲁϭⲱⲗⲡ ⲉⲃⲟⲗ ⲛⲁⲕ. ⲙⲛ̄-ⲗⲁⲁⲩ ⲅⲁⲣ ⲉϥϩⲏⲡ ⲉϥⲛⲁⲟⲩⲱⲛϩ ⲉⲃⲟⲗ ⲁⲛ."

6 ⲁⲩϫⲛⲟⲩϥ ⲛ̄ϭⲓ-ⲛⲉϥⲙⲁⲑⲏⲧⲏⲥ, ⲡⲉϫⲁⲩ ⲛⲁϥ ϫⲉ "ⲕⲟⲩⲱϣ ⲉ-ⲧⲣⲛ̄ⲣ̄-ⲛⲏⲥⲧⲉⲩⲉ? ⲁⲩⲱ ⲉϣ ⲧⲉ ⲑⲉ ⲉⲛⲁϣⲗⲏⲗ? ⲉⲛⲁϯ-ⲉⲗⲉⲏⲙⲟⲥⲩⲛⲏ? ⲁⲩⲱ ⲉⲛⲁⲣ̄-ⲡⲁⲣⲁⲧⲏⲣⲉⲓ ⲉ-ⲟⲩ ⲛ̄-ϭⲓⲟⲩⲱⲙ[51]?"

ⲡⲉϫⲉ-ⲓⲏⲥⲟⲩⲥ ϫⲉ "ⲙ̄ⲡⲣ̄ϫⲉ-ϭⲟⲗ, ⲁⲩⲱ ⲡⲉⲧⲉⲧⲙ̄ⲙⲟⲥⲧⲉ ⲙ̄ⲙⲟϥ ⲙ̄ⲡⲣⲁⲁϥ, ϫⲉ ⲥⲉϭⲟⲗⲡ ⲧⲏⲣⲟⲩ ⲉⲃⲟⲗ ⲙ̄-ⲡⲉⲙⲧⲟ ⲉⲃⲟⲗ ⲛ̄-ⲧⲙⲉ.[52] ⲙⲛ̄-ⲗⲁⲁⲩ ⲅⲁⲣ ⲉϥϩⲏⲡ ⲉϥⲛⲁⲟⲩⲱⲛϩ ⲉⲃⲟⲗ ⲁⲛ, ⲁⲩⲱ ⲙⲛ̄-ⲗⲁⲁⲩ ⲉϥϩⲟⲃⲥ̄ ⲉⲩⲛⲁϭⲱ ⲟⲩⲉϣⲛ̄-ϭⲟⲗⲡϥ̄."

7 ⲡⲉϫⲉ-ⲓⲏⲥⲟⲩⲥ "ⲟⲩⲙⲁⲕⲁⲣⲓⲟⲥ ⲡⲉ ⲡⲙⲟⲩⲉⲓ ⲡⲁⲉⲓ ⲉⲧⲉ-ⲡⲣⲱⲙⲉ ⲛⲁⲟⲩⲟⲙϥ, ⲁⲩⲱ ⲛ̄ⲧⲉ-ⲡⲙⲟⲩⲉⲓ ϣⲱⲡⲉ ⲣ̄-ⲣⲱⲙⲉ. ⲁⲩⲱ ϥⲃⲏⲧ ⲛ̄ϭⲓ-ⲡⲣⲱⲙⲉ ⲡⲁⲉⲓ ⲉⲧⲉ-ⲡⲙⲟⲩⲉⲓ ⲛⲁⲟⲩⲟⲙϥ, ⲁⲩⲱ ⲡⲣⲱⲙⲉ ⲛⲁϣⲱⲡⲉ ⲙ̄-ⲙⲟⲩⲉⲓ.[53]"

8 ⲁⲩⲱ ⲡⲉϫⲁϥ ϫⲉ "ⲉ-ⲡⲣⲱⲙⲉ ⲧⲛ̄ⲧⲱⲛ ⲁ-ⲩⲟⲩⲱϩⲉ ⲣ̄-ⲣⲙ̄ⲛ̄ϩⲏⲧ, ⲡⲁⲉⲓ ⲛ̄ⲧⲁϩⲛⲟⲩϫⲉ ⲛ̄-ⲧⲉϥⲁⲃⲱ ⲉ-ⲑⲁⲗⲁⲥⲥⲁ. ⲁϥⲥⲱⲕ ⲙ̄ⲙⲟⲥ ⲉϩⲣⲁⲓ̈ ϩⲛ̄-ⲑⲁⲗⲁⲥⲥⲁ ⲉⲥⲙⲉϩ ⲛ̄-ⲧⲃⲧ ⲛ̄-ⲕⲟⲩⲉⲓ. ⲛ̄ϩⲣⲁⲓ̈ ⲛ̄ϩⲏⲧⲟⲩ ⲁϥϩⲉ ⲁ-ⲩⲛⲟϭ ⲛ̄-ⲧⲃⲧ ⲉ-ⲛⲁⲛⲟⲩϥ ⲛ̄ϭⲓ-ⲡⲟⲩⲱϩⲉ ⲣ̄-ⲣⲙ̄ⲛ̄ϩⲏⲧ. ⲁϥⲛⲟⲩϫⲉ ⲛ̄-ⲛ̄ⲕⲟⲩⲉⲓ ⲧⲏⲣⲟⲩ ⲛ̄-ⲧⲃⲧ ⲉⲃⲟⲗ ⲉⲡⲉⲥⲏⲧ ⲉ-ⲑⲁⲗⲁⲥⲥⲁ, ⲁϥⲥⲱⲧⲡ̄ ⲙ̄-ⲡⲛⲟϭ ⲛ̄-ⲧⲃⲧ ⲭⲱⲣⲓⲥ-ϩⲓⲥⲉ. ⲡⲉⲧⲉ-ⲟⲩⲛ̄-ⲙⲁⲁϫⲉ ⲙ̄ⲙⲟϥ ⲉ-ⲥⲱⲧⲙ̄, ⲙⲁⲣⲉϥⲥⲱⲧⲙ̄!"

9 ⲡⲉϫⲉ-ⲓⲏⲥⲟⲩⲥ ϫⲉ "ⲉⲓⲥ-ϩⲏⲏⲧⲉ! ⲁϥⲉⲓ ⲉⲃⲟⲗ ⲛ̄ϭⲓ-ⲡⲉⲧ-ⲥⲓⲧⲉ, ⲁϥⲙⲉϩ-ⲧⲟⲟⲧϥ̄, ⲁϥⲛⲟⲩϫⲉ. ⲁ-ϩⲟⲉⲓⲛⲉ ⲙⲉⲛ ϩⲉ ⲉϫⲛ̄-ⲧⲉϩⲓⲏ, ⲁⲩⲉⲓ ⲛ̄ϭⲓ-ⲛ̄ϩⲁⲗⲁⲧⲉ, ⲁⲩⲕⲁⲧϥⲟⲩ. ϩⲛ̄ⲕⲟⲟⲩⲉ ⲁⲩϩⲉ ⲉϫⲛ̄-ⲧⲡⲉⲧⲣⲁ, ⲁⲩⲱ ⲙ̄ⲡⲟⲩϫⲉ-ⲛⲟⲩⲛⲉ ⲉⲡⲉⲥⲏⲧ ⲉ-ⲡⲕⲁϩ ⲁⲩⲱ ⲙ̄ⲡⲟⲩⲧⲉⲩⲉ-ϩⲙ̄ⲥ̄ ⲉϩⲣⲁⲓ̈ ⲉⲧⲡⲉ. ⲁⲩⲱ ϩⲛ̄ⲕⲟⲟⲩⲉ ⲁⲩϩⲉ ⲉϫⲛ̄-ⲛ̄ϣⲟⲛⲧⲉ, ⲁⲩⲱϭⲧ ⲙ̄-ⲡⲉϭⲣⲟϭ, ⲁⲩⲱ ⲁ-ⲡϥⲛ̄ⲧ ⲟⲩⲟⲙⲟⲩ. ⲁⲩⲱ ⲁ-ϩⲛ̄ⲕⲟⲟⲩⲉ ϩⲉ ⲉϫⲛ̄-ⲡⲕⲁϩ

---

49. Read as Sahidic ⲡⲉⲧ-ⲛⲁϩⲉ.
50. The ⲙⲛ̄ⲧⲣⲉ- prefixed here is an alternate negative jussive form (equivalent to Sahidic ⲙ̄ⲡⲣ̄ⲧⲣⲉ-).
51. ϭⲓ(ⲛ)ⲟⲩⲱⲙ
52. Emended (based on the Greek text) from ⲛ̄-ⲧⲡⲉ (although that could work as well).
53. Emended from ⲡⲙⲟⲩⲉⲓ ⲛⲁϣⲱⲡⲉ ⲣ̄-ⲣⲱⲙⲉ.

ετ-ναΝογϥ, αγω αϥϯ-καρπος εϩραϊ ετπε εΝαΝογϥ. αϥϥι⁵⁴ Ν̄-cε ε-cοτε αγω ϣε ϫογωτ
ε-cοτε."

10 πεϫε-ιηcογc ϫε "αειΝογϫε Ν̄-ογκωϩτ εϫΝ̄-πκόcμοc, αγω ειcϩηητε! ϯαρεϩ εροϥ
ϣαντεϥϫερο."

11 πεϫε-ιηcογc ϫε "τεειπε Ναρ̄-παραγε, αγω τετ-Ν̄-τπε μ̄μοc Ναρ̄-παραγε. αγω
Νετ-μοογτ cεονϩ αν, αγω Νετ-ονϩ cεναμογ αν. Ν̄ϩοογ Νετετν̄ογωμ μ̄-πετ-μοογτ,
Νετετν̄ειρε μ̄μοϥ μ̄-πετ-ονϩ. ϩοταν ετετν̄ϣανϣωπε ϩμ̄-πογοειν, ογ πετετναα϶?
ϩμ̄-ϥοογ ετετν̄ο Ν̄-ογα, ατετν̄ειρε μ̄-πcναγ. ϩοταν δε ετετν̄ϣαϣωπε Ν̄-cναγ, ογ πε
ετετν̄Νααϥ?"

12 πεϫε-μ̄μαθητηc Ν̄-ιηcογc ϫε "τν̄cοογν ϫε κναβωκ Ν̄τοοτν̄. ΝΙΜ πε ετ-Ναρ̄-νοϭ
εϩραϊ εϫων?"

πεϫε-ιηcογc ναγ ϫε "πμα Ν̄τατετν̄ει μ̄μαγ, ετετναβωκ ϣα-ϊάκωβοc πδίκαιοc,
παει Ν̄τα-τπε μν̄-πκαϩ ϣωπε ετβητϥ̄."

13 πεϫε-ιηcογc Ν̄-νεϥμαθητηc ϫε "τν̄τωντ Ν̄τετν̄ϫοοc ναει ϫε εειΝε Ν̄-ΝΙΜ."

πεϫαϥ ναϥ Ν̄ϭι-cίμων πέτροc ϫε "εκειΝε Ν̄-ογάγγελοc Ν̄-δίκαιοc."

πεϫαϥ ναϥ Ν̄ϭι-μαθθαίοc ϫε "εκειΝε Ν̄-ογρωμε μ̄-ϥιλόcοϥοc Ν̄-ρμ̄Ν̄ϩητ."

πεϫαϥ ναϥ Ν̄ϭι-θωμάc ϫε "πcαϩ, ϩόλωc ταταπρο ναϣ-ϣαπϥ⁵⁵ αν ε-τραϫοοc ϫε
εκειΝε Ν̄-ΝΙΜ."

πεϫε-ιηcογc ϫε "αΝΟΚ πεκcαϩ αν. επεί ακcω, ακϯϩε εβολ ϩΝ̄-τπηγη ετ-βρ̄βρε ταει
αΝΟΚ Ν̄ταειϣιτc̄.⁵⁶" αγω αϥϫιτϥ̄, αϥαναχωρει, αϥϫω ναϥ Ν̄-ϣομτ Ν̄-ϣαϫε.

Ν̄ταρε-θωμάc δε ει ϣα-νεϥϣβεερ, αγϫνογϥ ϫε "Ν̄τα-ιηcογc ϫοοc ϫε ογ νακ?"

πεϫαϥ ναγ Ν̄ϭι-θωμάc ϫε "ειϣανϫω Ν̄ητν̄ ογα ϩΝ̄-Ν̄ϣαϫε Ν̄ταϥϫοογ ναει,
τετΝαϥι-ωνε Ν̄τετν̄νογϫε εροει. αγω Ν̄τε-ογκωϩτ ει εβολ ϩΝ̄-Ν̄ωνε Ν̄ϥρωκϩ⁵⁷ μ̄μωτν̄."

14 πεϫε-ιηcογc ναγ ϫε "ετετν̄ϣανρ̄-νηcτεγε, τετναχπο Ν̄ητν̄ Ν̄Ν⁵⁸-ογνοβε.
αγω ετετν̄ϣανϣληλ, cεναρ̄-κατακρινε μ̄μωτν̄. αγω ετετν̄ϣανϯ-ελεημοcγνη,
ετετναειρε Ν̄-ογκακον Ν̄-νετμ̄πνεγμα. αγω ετετν̄ϣανβωκ εϩογν ε-καϩ νιμ αγω
Ν̄τετν̄μοοϣε ϩν̄-Ν̄χώρα, εγϣαρ̄-παραδεχε μ̄μωτν̄, πετογνακααϥ ϩαρωτν̄ ογομϥ.
νετ-ϣωνε Ν̄ϩητογ ερι-θεραπεγε μ̄μοογ. πετ-ναβωκ γαρ εϩογν ϩΝ̄-τετν̄ταπρο
ϥναϫωϩμ̄-θητν̄ αν. αλλα πετ-Ν̄νηγ εβολ ϩΝ̄-τετν̄ταπρο, Ν̄τοϥ πετ-ναϫαϩμ̄-θητν̄."

15 πεϫε-ιηcογc ϫε "ϩοταν ετετν̄ϣανναγ ε-πετε-μ̄πογϫποϥ εβολ ϩΝ̄-τcϩιμε, πεϩτ-
θητν̄ εϫμ̄-πετν̄ϩο Ν̄τετν̄ογωϣτ ναϥ. πετ-μ̄μαγ πε πετν̄ειωτ."

16 πεϫε-ιηcογc ϫε "τάχα εγμεεγε Ν̄ϭι-ρ̄ρωμε ϫε Ν̄ταειει ε-ΝογϫΕ Ν̄-ογειρηνη
εϫμ̄-πκόcμοc. αγω cεcοογν αν ϫε Ν̄ταειει α-ΝογϫΕ Ν̄-ϩμ̄πωρϫ εϫν̄-πκαϩ, ογκωϩτ,
ογcηϥε, ογπόλεμοc. ογν̄-ϯογ γαρ ναϣωπε ϩν̄-ογηει, ογν̄-ϣομτ ναϣωπε εϫν̄-cναγ
αγω cναγ εϫν̄-ϣομτ, πειωτ εϫμ̄-πϣηρε αγω πϣηρε εϫμ̄-πειωτ. αγω cεναωϩε ερατογ
εγο μ̄-μοναχοc."

17 πεϫε-ιηcογc ϫε "ϯναϯ Ν̄ητν̄ μ̄-πετε-μ̄πε-βαλ ναγ εροϥ, αγω πετε-μ̄πε-μααϫε
cοτμεϥ, αγω πετε-μ̄πε-ϭιϫ ϭμ̄ϭωμϥ, αγω μ̄πεϥει εϩραϊ ϩι-ϥητ ρ̄-ρωμε."

---

54. Emended from αϥει.
55. Emended from ναϣαπϥ.
56. See perhaps ϣικε, ϣιτε (ϣι[κ]τ⸗).
57. Emended from Ν̄cρωϩκ. See ρωκϩ.
58. The Ν̄- sometimes appears in this reduplicated form (Ν̄Ν-) before vowels (such as the singular indefinite article), both here and in the Life of Antony.

18 ⲡⲉϫⲉ-ⲙ̄ⲙⲁⲑⲏⲧⲏⲥ ⲛ̄-ⲓⲏⲥⲟⲩⲥ ϫⲉ "ϫⲟⲟⲥ ⲉⲣⲟⲛ ϫⲉ ⲧⲛ̄ϩⲁⲏ ⲉⲥⲛⲁϣⲱⲡⲉ ⲛ̄-ⲁϣ ⲛ̄-ϩⲉ."

ⲡⲉϫⲉ-ⲓⲏⲥⲟⲩⲥ "ⲁⲧⲉⲧⲛ̄ϭⲱⲗⲡ ⲅⲁⲣ ⲉⲃⲟⲗ ⲛ̄-ⲧⲁⲣⲭⲏ, ϫⲉⲕⲁⲁⲥ ⲉⲧⲉⲧⲛⲁϣⲓⲛⲉ ⲛ̄ⲥⲁ-ⲑⲁϩⲏ? ϫⲉ ϩⲙ̄-ⲡⲙⲁ ⲉⲧⲉ-ⲧⲁⲣⲭⲏ ⲙ̄ⲙⲁⲩ, ⲉ-ⲑⲁϩⲏ ⲛⲁϣⲱⲡⲉ ⲙ̄ⲙⲁⲩ. ⲟⲩⲙⲁⲕⲁⲣⲓⲟⲥ ⲡⲉⲧ-ⲛⲁⲱϩⲉ ⲉⲣⲁⲧϥ ϩⲛ̄-ⲧⲁⲣⲭⲏ, ⲁⲩⲱ ϥⲛⲁⲥⲟⲩⲛ-ⲑϩⲁⲏ ⲁⲩⲱ ϥⲛⲁϫⲓ-†ⲡⲉ ⲁⲛ ⲙ̄-ⲙⲟⲩ."

19 ⲡⲉϫⲉ-ⲓⲏⲥⲟⲩⲥ ϫⲉ "ⲟⲩⲙⲁⲕⲁⲣⲓⲟⲥ ⲡⲉⲛⲧⲁϩϣⲱⲡⲉ ϩⲁⲧⲉϩⲏ ⲉ-ⲙⲡⲁⲧⲉϥϣⲱⲡⲉ. ⲉⲧⲉⲧⲛ̄ϣⲁⲛϣⲱⲡⲉ ⲛⲁⲉⲓ ⲙ̄-ⲙⲁⲑⲏⲧⲏⲥ ⲛ̄ⲧⲉⲧⲛ̄ⲥⲱⲧⲙ̄ ⲁ-ⲛⲁϣⲁϫⲉ, ⲛⲉⲉⲓⲱⲛⲉ ⲛⲁⲣ̄-ⲇⲓⲁⲕⲟⲛⲉⲓ ⲛⲏⲧⲛ̄. ⲟⲩⲛ̄ⲧⲏⲧⲛ̄ ⲅⲁⲣ ⲙ̄ⲙⲁⲩ ⲛ̄-†ⲟⲩ ⲛ̄-ϣⲏⲛ ϩⲙ̄-ⲡⲁⲣⲁⲇⲓⲥⲟⲥ, ⲉ-ⲥⲉⲕⲓⲙ ⲁⲛ ⲛ̄ϣⲱⲙ ⲙ̄ⲡⲣⲱ, ⲁⲩⲱ ⲙⲁⲣⲉ-ⲛⲟⲩϭⲱⲃⲉ ϩⲉ ⲉⲃⲟⲗ. ⲡⲉⲧ-ⲛⲁⲥⲟⲩⲱⲛⲟⲩ ϥⲛⲁϫⲓ-†ⲡⲉ ⲁⲛ ⲙ̄-ⲙⲟⲩ."

20 ⲡⲉϫⲉ-ⲙ̄ⲙⲁⲑⲏⲧⲏⲥ ⲛ̄-ⲓⲏⲥⲟⲩⲥ ϫⲉ "ϫⲟⲟⲥ ⲉⲣⲟⲛ ϫⲉ ⲧⲙⲛ̄ⲧⲉⲣⲟ ⲛ̄-ⲙ̄ⲡⲏⲩⲉ ⲉⲥⲧⲛ̄ⲧⲱⲛ ⲉ-ⲛⲓⲙ."

ⲡⲉϫⲁϥ ⲛⲁⲩ ϫⲉ "ⲉⲥⲧⲛ̄ⲧⲱⲛ ⲁ-ⲩⲃⲁⲃⲓⲗⲉ ⲛ̄-ϣⲗ̄ⲧⲁⲙ. ⲥⲥⲟⲃⲕ̄[59] ⲡⲁⲣⲁ-ⲛ̄ϭⲣⲟϭ ⲧⲏⲣⲟⲩ. ϩⲟⲧⲁⲛ ⲇⲉ ⲉⲥϣⲁⲛϩⲉ ⲉϫⲙ̄-ⲡⲕⲁϩ ⲉⲧⲟⲩⲣ̄-ϩⲱⲃ ⲉⲣⲟϥ, ϣⲁϥⲧⲉⲩⲟ ⲉⲃⲟⲗ ⲛ̄ⲛ-ⲟⲩⲛⲟϭ ⲛ̄-ⲧⲁⲣ ⲛϥϣⲱⲡⲉ ⲛ̄-ⲥⲕⲉⲡⲏ ⲛ̄-ϩⲁⲗⲁⲧⲉ ⲛ̄-ⲧⲡⲉ."

21 ⲡⲉϫⲉ-ⲙⲁⲣⲓϩⲁⲙ ⲛ̄-ⲓⲏⲥⲟⲩⲥ ϫⲉ "ⲉ-ⲛⲉⲕⲙⲁⲑⲏⲧⲏⲥ ⲉⲓⲛⲉ ⲛ̄-ⲛⲓⲙ?"

ⲡⲉϫⲁϥ ϫⲉ "ⲉⲩⲉⲓⲛⲉ ⲛ̄-ϩⲛ̄ϣⲏⲣⲉ ϣⲏⲙ ⲉⲩϭⲉⲗⲓⲧ[60] ⲁ-ⲩⲥⲱϣⲉ ⲉ-ⲧⲱⲟⲩ ⲁⲛ ⲧⲉ. ϩⲟⲧⲁⲛ ⲉⲩϣⲁⲉⲓ ⲛ̄ϭⲓ-ⲛ̄ϫⲟⲉⲓⲥ ⲛ̄-ⲧⲥⲱϣⲉ, ⲥⲉⲛⲁϫⲟⲟⲥ ϫⲉ 'ⲕⲉ-ⲧⲛ̄ⲥⲱϣⲉ ⲉⲃⲟⲗ ⲛⲁⲛ.' ⲛ̄ⲧⲟⲟⲩ ⲥⲉⲕⲁⲕ ⲁϩⲏⲩ ⲙ̄-ⲡⲟⲩⲙ̄ⲧⲟ ⲉⲃⲟⲗ, ⲉ-ⲧⲣⲟⲩⲕⲁⲁⲥ ⲉⲃⲟⲗ ⲛⲁⲩ, ⲛ̄ⲥⲉ†-ⲧⲟⲩⲥⲱϣⲉ ⲛⲁⲩ. ⲇⲓⲁ-ⲧⲟⲩⲧⲟ †ϫⲱ ⲙ̄ⲙⲟⲥ ϫⲉ ⲉϥϣⲁⲉⲓⲙⲉ ⲛ̄ϭⲓ-ⲡϫⲉⲥ-ϩⲛ̄-ϩⲉⲓ ϫⲉ ϥⲛⲏⲩ ⲛ̄ϭⲓ-ⲡⲣⲉϥϫⲓⲟⲩⲉ, ϥⲛⲁⲣⲟⲉⲓⲥ ⲉ-ⲙⲡⲁⲧⲉϥⲉⲓ, ⲛ̄ϥⲧⲙ̄ⲕⲁⲁϥ ⲉ-ϣⲟϫⲧ ⲉϩⲟⲩⲛ ⲉ-ⲡⲉϥⲏⲉⲓ ⲛ̄ⲧⲉ-ⲧⲉϥⲙⲛ̄ⲧⲉⲣⲟ ⲉ-ⲧⲣⲉϥϥⲓ ⲛ̄-ⲛⲉϥⲥⲕⲉⲩⲟⲥ. ⲛ̄ⲧⲱⲧⲛ̄ ⲇⲉ ⲣⲟⲉⲓⲥ ϩⲁⲧⲉϩⲏ ⲙ̄-ⲡⲕⲟⲥⲙⲟⲥ. ⲙⲟⲩⲣ ⲙ̄ⲙⲱⲧⲛ̄ ⲉϫⲛ̄-ⲛⲉⲧⲛ̄†ⲡⲉ ϩⲛ̄-ⲟⲩⲛⲟϭ ⲛ̄-ⲇⲩⲛⲁⲙⲓⲥ ϣⲓⲛⲁ ϫⲉ ⲛⲉ-ⲛⲗⲏⲥⲧⲏⲥ ϩⲉ ⲉ-ϩⲓⲏ ⲉ-ⲉⲓ ϣⲁⲣⲱⲧⲛ̄, ⲉⲡⲉⲓ ⲧⲉⲭⲣⲉⲓⲁ ⲉⲧⲉⲧⲛ̄ϭⲱϣⲧ ⲉⲃⲟⲗ ϩⲏⲧⲥ̄ ⲥⲉⲛⲁϩⲉ ⲉⲣⲟⲥ. ⲙⲁⲣⲉϥϣⲱⲡⲉ ϩⲛ̄-ⲧⲉⲧⲛ̄ⲙⲏⲧⲉ ⲛ̄ϭⲓ-ⲟⲩⲣⲱⲙⲉ ⲛ̄-ⲉⲡⲓⲥⲧⲏⲙⲱⲛ. ⲛ̄ⲧⲁⲣⲉ-ⲡⲕⲁⲣⲡⲟⲥ ⲡⲱϩ, ⲁϥⲉⲓ ϩⲛ̄-ⲟⲩϭⲉⲡⲏ ⲉ-ⲉⲡⲉϥⲁⲥϩ ϩⲛ̄-ⲧⲉϥϭⲓϫ ⲁϥϩⲁⲥϥ.[61] ⲡⲉⲧⲉ-ⲟⲩⲛ̄-ⲙⲁⲁϫⲉ ⲙ̄ⲙⲟϥ ⲉ-ⲥⲱⲧⲙ̄, ⲙⲁⲣⲉϥⲥⲱⲧⲙ̄!"

22 ⲁ-ⲓⲏⲥⲟⲩⲥ ⲛⲁⲩ ⲁ-ϩⲛ̄ⲕⲟⲩⲉⲓ ⲉⲩϫⲓ-ⲉⲣⲱⲧⲉ. ⲡⲉϫⲁϥ ⲛ̄-ⲛⲉϥⲙⲁⲑⲏⲧⲏⲥ ϫⲉ "ⲛⲉⲉⲓⲕⲟⲩⲉⲓ ⲉⲧ-ϫⲓ-ⲉⲣⲱⲧⲉ ⲉⲩⲧⲛ̄ⲧⲱⲛ ⲁ-ⲛⲉⲧ-ⲃⲏⲕ ⲉϩⲟⲩⲛ ⲁ-ⲧⲙⲛ̄ⲧⲉⲣⲟ."

ⲡⲉϫⲁⲩ ⲛⲁϥ ϫⲉ "ⲉⲉⲓⲉ ⲉⲛⲟ[62] ⲛ̄-ⲕⲟⲩⲉⲓ ⲧⲛ̄ⲛⲁⲃⲱⲕ ⲉϩⲟⲩⲛ ⲉ-ⲧⲙⲛ̄ⲧⲉⲣⲟ?"

ⲡⲉϫⲉ-ⲓⲏⲥⲟⲩⲥ ⲛⲁⲩ ϫⲉ "ϩⲟⲧⲁⲛ ⲉⲧⲉⲧⲛ̄ϣⲁⲣ̄-ⲡⲥⲛⲁⲩ ⲟⲩⲁ, ⲁⲩⲱ ⲉⲧⲉⲧⲛ̄ϣⲁⲣ̄-ⲡⲥⲁ ⲛϩⲟⲩⲛ ⲛ̄-ⲑⲉ ⲙ̄-ⲡⲥⲁ ⲛⲃⲟⲗ, ⲁⲩⲱ ⲡⲥⲁ ⲛⲃⲟⲗ ⲛ̄-ⲑⲉ ⲙ̄-ⲡⲥⲁ ⲛϩⲟⲩⲛ, ⲁⲩⲱ ⲡⲥⲁ ⲛ-ⲧⲡⲉ ⲛ̄-ⲑⲉ ⲙ̄-ⲡⲥⲁ ⲙ-ⲡⲓⲧⲛ̄, ⲁⲩⲱ ϣⲓⲛⲁ ⲉⲧⲉⲧⲛⲁⲉⲓⲣⲉ ⲙ̄-ⲫⲟⲟⲩⲧ ⲙⲛ̄-ⲧⲥϩⲓⲙⲉ ⲙ̄-ⲡⲟⲩⲁ ⲟⲩⲱⲧ, ϫⲉⲕⲁⲁⲥ ⲛⲉ-ⲫⲟⲟⲩⲧ ⲣ̄-ϩⲟⲟⲩⲧ ⲛ̄ⲧⲉ-ⲧⲥϩⲓⲙⲉ ⲣ̄-ⲥϩⲓⲙⲉ. ϩⲟⲧⲁⲛ ⲉⲧⲉⲧⲛ̄ϣⲁⲉⲓⲣⲉ ⲛ̄-ϩⲛ̄ⲃⲁⲗ ⲉ-ⲡⲙⲁ ⲛ̄-ⲟⲩⲃⲁⲗ, ⲁⲩⲱ ⲟⲩϭⲓϫ ⲉ-ⲡⲙⲁ ⲛ̄ⲛ-ⲟⲩϭⲓϫ, ⲁⲩⲱ ⲟⲩⲉⲣⲏⲧⲉ ⲉ-ⲡⲙⲁ ⲛ̄-ⲟⲩⲉⲣⲏⲧⲉ, ⲟⲩϩⲓⲕⲱⲛ ⲉ-ⲡⲙⲁ ⲛ̄-ⲟⲩϩⲓⲕⲱⲛ, ⲧⲟⲧⲉ ⲧⲉⲧⲛⲁⲃⲱⲕ ⲉϩⲟⲩⲛ ⲉ-ⲧⲙⲛ̄ⲧⲉⲣⲟ."

23 ⲡⲉϫⲉ-ⲓⲏⲥⲟⲩⲥ ϫⲉ "†ⲛⲁⲥⲉⲧⲡ-ⲧⲏⲛⲉ, ⲟⲩⲁ ⲉⲃⲟⲗ ϩⲛ̄-ϣⲟ, ⲁⲩⲱ ⲥⲛⲁⲩ ⲉⲃⲟⲗ ϩⲛ̄-ⲧⲃⲁ. ⲁⲩⲱ ⲥⲉⲛⲁⲱϩⲉ ⲉⲣⲁⲧⲟⲩ ⲉⲩⲟ ⲟⲩⲁ ⲟⲩⲱⲧ."

24 ⲡⲉϫⲉ-ⲛⲉϥⲙⲁⲑⲏⲧⲏⲥ ϫⲉ "ⲙⲁ-ⲧⲥⲉⲃⲟⲛ ⲉ-ⲡⲧⲟⲡⲟⲥ ⲉⲧⲕ̄ⲙ̄ⲙⲁⲩ, ⲉⲡⲉⲓ ⲧⲁⲛⲁⲅⲕⲏ ⲉⲣⲟⲛ ⲧⲉ ⲉ-ⲧⲣⲛ̄ϣⲓⲛⲉ ⲛ̄ⲥⲱϥ."

ⲡⲉϫⲁϥ ⲛⲁⲩ ϫⲉ "ⲡⲉⲧⲉ-ⲩⲛ̄-ⲙⲁⲁϫⲉ ⲙ̄ⲙⲟϥ, ⲙⲁⲣⲉϥⲥⲱⲧⲙ̄! ⲟⲩⲛ̄-ⲟⲩⲟⲉⲓⲛ ϣⲟⲟⲡ ⲙ̄-ⲫⲟⲩⲛ ⲛ̄ⲛ-ⲟⲩⲣⲙ̄-ⲟⲩⲟⲉⲓⲛ, ⲁⲩⲱ ϥⲣ̄-ⲟⲩⲟⲉⲓⲛ ⲉ-ⲡⲕⲟⲥⲙⲟⲥ ⲧⲏⲣϥ. ⲉϥⲧⲙ̄ⲣ̄-ⲟⲩⲟⲉⲓⲛ, ⲟⲩⲕⲁⲕⲉ ⲡⲉ."

25 ⲡⲉϫⲉ-ⲓⲏⲥⲟⲩⲥ ϫⲉ "ⲙⲉⲣⲉ-ⲡⲉⲕⲥⲟⲛ ⲛ̄-ⲑⲉ ⲛ̄-ⲧⲉⲕⲯⲩⲭⲏ. ⲉⲣⲓ-ⲧⲏⲣⲉⲓ ⲙ̄ⲙⲟϥ ⲛ̄-ⲑⲉ ⲛ̄-ⲧⲉⲗⲟⲩ ⲙ̄-ⲡⲉⲕⲃⲁⲗ."

---

59. Emended from ⲥⲟⲃⲕ̄.
60. See ϭⲟ(ⲉ)ⲓⲗⲉ.
61. See ⲱϩⲥ̄, ⲱⲥϩ̄.
62. Emended from ⲛⲟ.

26 ⲡⲉϫⲉ-ⲓⲏⲥⲟⲩⲥ ϫⲉ "ⲡϫⲏ ⲉⲧ-ϩⲙ̄-ⲡⲃⲁⲗ ⲙ̄-ⲡⲉⲕⲥⲟⲛ ⲕⲛⲁⲩ ⲉⲣⲟϥ, ⲡⲥⲟⲉⲓ ⲇⲉ ⲉⲧ-ϩⲙ̄-ⲡⲉⲕⲃⲁⲗ ⲕⲛⲁⲩ ⲁⲛ ⲉⲣⲟϥ! ϩⲟⲧⲁⲛ ⲉⲕϣⲁⲛⲛⲟⲩϫⲉ ⲙ̄-ⲡⲥⲟⲉⲓ ⲉⲃⲟⲗ ϩⲙ̄-ⲡⲉⲕⲃⲁⲗ, ⲧⲟⲧⲉ ⲕⲛⲁⲛⲁⲩ ⲉⲃⲟⲗ ⲉ-ⲛⲟⲩϫⲉ ⲙ̄-ⲡϫⲏ ⲉⲃⲟⲗ ϩⲙ̄-ⲡⲃⲁⲗ ⲙ̄-ⲡⲉⲕⲥⲟⲛ."

27 "ⲉⲧⲉⲧⲛ̄ⲧⲙ̄ⲣ̄-ⲛⲏⲥⲧⲉⲩⲉ[63] ⲉ-ⲡⲕⲟⲥⲙⲟⲥ, ⲧⲉⲧⲛⲁϩⲉ ⲁⲛ ⲉ-ⲧⲙⲛ̄ⲧⲉⲣⲟ. ⲉⲧⲉⲧⲛ̄ⲧⲙ̄ⲉⲓⲣⲉ ⲙ̄-ⲡⲥⲁⲙⲃⲁⲧⲟⲛ ⲛ̄-ⲥⲁⲃⲃⲁⲧⲟⲛ, ⲛ̄ⲧⲉⲧⲛⲁⲩ ⲁⲛ ⲉ-ⲡⲉⲓⲱⲧ."

28 ⲡⲉϫⲉ-ⲓⲏⲥⲟⲩⲥ ϫⲉ "ⲁⲉⲓⲱϩⲉ ⲉⲣⲁⲧ ϩⲛ̄-ⲧⲙⲏⲧⲉ ⲙ̄-ⲡⲕⲟⲥⲙⲟⲥ ⲁⲩⲱ ⲁⲉⲓⲟⲩⲱⲛϩ ⲉⲃⲟⲗ ⲛⲁⲩ ϩⲛ̄-ⲥⲁⲣⲝ. ⲁⲉⲓϩⲉ ⲉⲣⲟⲟⲩ ⲧⲏⲣⲟⲩ ⲉⲩⲧⲁϩⲉ, ⲙ̄ⲡⲓϩⲉ ⲉ-ⲗⲁⲁⲩ ⲛ̄ϩⲏⲧⲟⲩ ⲉϥⲟⲃⲉ. ⲁⲩⲱ ⲁ-ⲧⲁⲯⲩⲭⲏ ϯ-ⲧⲕⲁⲥ ⲉϫⲛ̄-ⲛ̄ϣⲏⲣⲉ ⲛ̄-ⲣ̄ⲣⲱⲙⲉ, ϫⲉ ϩⲛ̄ⲃⲗⲗⲉⲉⲩⲉ ⲛⲉ ϩⲙ̄-ⲡⲟⲩϩⲏⲧ ⲁⲩⲱ ⲥⲉⲛⲁⲩ ⲉⲃⲟⲗ ⲁⲛ, ϫⲉ ⲛ̄ⲧⲁⲩⲉⲓ ⲉ-ⲡⲕⲟⲥⲙⲟⲥ ⲉⲩϣⲟⲩⲉⲓⲧ, ⲉⲩϣⲓⲛⲉ ⲟⲛ ⲉ-ⲧⲣⲟⲩⲉⲓ ⲉⲃⲟⲗ ϩⲙ̄-ⲡⲕⲟⲥⲙⲟⲥ ⲉⲩϣⲟⲩⲉⲓⲧ. ⲡⲗⲏⲛ ⲧⲉⲛⲟⲩ ⲥⲉⲧⲟϩⲉ, ϩⲟⲧⲁⲛ ⲉⲩϣⲁⲛⲛⲉϩ-ⲡⲟⲩⲏⲣⲡ, ⲧⲟⲧⲉ ⲥⲉⲛⲁⲣ̄-ⲙⲉⲧⲁⲛⲟⲉⲓ."

29 ⲡⲉϫⲉ-ⲓⲏⲥⲟⲩⲥ "ⲉϣϫⲉ ⲛ̄ⲧⲁ-ⲧⲥⲁⲣⲝ ϣⲱⲡⲉ ⲉⲧⲃⲉ-ⲡⲛⲉⲩⲙⲁ, ⲟⲩϣⲡⲏⲣⲉ ⲧⲉ! ⲉϣϫⲉ ⲡⲛⲉⲩⲙⲁ ⲇⲉ ⲉⲧⲃⲉ-ⲡⲥⲱⲙⲁ, ⲟⲩϣⲡⲏⲣⲉ ⲛ̄-ϣⲡⲏⲣⲉ ⲡⲉ! ⲁⲗⲗⲁ ⲁⲛⲟⲕ ϯⲣ̄-ϣⲡⲏⲣⲉ ⲙ̄-ⲡⲁⲉⲓ, ϫⲉ ⲡⲱⲥ ⲁ-ⲧⲉⲉⲓⲛⲟϭ ⲙ̄-ⲙⲛ̄ⲧⲣⲙ̄ⲙⲁⲟ ⲁⲥⲟⲩⲱϩ ϩⲛ̄-ⲧⲉⲉⲓⲙⲛ̄ⲧϩⲏⲕⲉ!"

30 ⲡⲉϫⲉ-ⲓⲏⲥⲟⲩⲥ ϫⲉ "ⲡⲙⲁ ⲉ-ⲩⲛ̄-ϣⲟⲙⲧ ⲛ̄-ⲛⲟⲩⲧⲉ ⲙ̄ⲙⲁⲩ, ϩⲛ̄ⲛⲟⲩⲧⲉ ⲛⲉ. ⲡⲙⲁ ⲉ-ⲩⲛ̄-ⲥⲛⲁⲩ ⲏ ⲟⲩⲁ, ⲁⲛⲟⲕ ϯϣⲟⲟⲡ ⲛⲙⲙⲁϥ."[64]

31 ⲡⲉϫⲉ-ⲓⲏⲥⲟⲩⲥ "ⲙⲛ̄-ⲡⲣⲟⲫⲏⲧⲏⲥ ϣⲏⲡ ϩⲙ̄-ⲡⲉϥϯⲙⲉ. ⲙⲁⲣⲉ-ⲥⲟⲉⲓⲛ ⲣ̄-ⲑⲉⲣⲁⲡⲉⲩⲉ ⲛ̄-ⲛⲉⲧ-ⲥⲟⲟⲩⲛ ⲙ̄ⲙⲟϥ."

32 ⲡⲉϫⲉ-ⲓⲏⲥⲟⲩⲥ ϫⲉ "ⲟⲩⲡⲟⲗⲓⲥ ⲉⲩⲕⲱⲧ ⲙ̄ⲙⲟⲥ ϩⲓϫⲛ̄-ⲟⲩⲧⲟⲟⲩ ⲉϥϫⲟⲥⲉ, ⲉⲥⲧⲁϫⲣⲏⲩ, ⲙⲛ̄-ϭⲟⲙ ⲛ̄ⲥϩⲉ, ⲟⲩⲇⲉ ⲥⲛⲁϣ-ϩⲱⲡ ⲁⲛ."

33 ⲡⲉϫⲉ-ⲓⲏⲥⲟⲩⲥ "ⲡⲉⲧⲕⲛⲁⲥⲱⲧⲙ̄ ⲉⲣⲟϥ ϩⲙ̄-ⲡⲉⲕⲙⲁⲁϫⲉ, ϩⲙ̄-ⲡⲕⲉⲙⲁⲁϫⲉ[65] ⲧⲁϣⲉ-ⲟⲉⲓϣ ⲙ̄ⲙⲟϥ ϩⲓϫⲛ̄-ⲛⲉⲧⲛ̄ϫⲉⲛⲉⲡⲱⲣ. ⲙⲁⲣⲉ-ⲗⲁⲁⲩ ⲅⲁⲣ ϫⲉⲣⲉ-ϩⲏⲃⲥ ⲛ̄ϥⲕⲁⲁϥ ϩⲁ-ⲙⲁⲁϫⲉ, ⲟⲩⲇⲉ ⲙⲁϥⲕⲁⲁϥ ϩⲙ̄-ⲙⲁ ⲉϥϩⲏⲡ. ⲁⲗⲗⲁ ⲉϣⲁⲣⲉϥⲕⲁⲁϥ ϩⲓϫⲛ̄-ⲧⲗⲩⲭⲛⲓⲁ ϫⲉⲕⲁⲁⲥ ⲟⲩⲟⲛ ⲛⲓⲙ ⲉⲧ-ⲃⲏⲕ ⲉϩⲟⲩⲛ ⲁⲩⲱ ⲉⲧ-ⲛ̄ⲛⲏⲩ ⲉⲃⲟⲗ ⲉⲩⲛⲁⲛⲁⲩ ⲁ-ⲡⲉϥⲟⲩⲟⲉⲓⲛ."

34 ⲡⲉϫⲉ-ⲓⲏⲥⲟⲩⲥ ϫⲉ "ⲟⲩⲃⲗ̄ⲗⲉ ⲉϥϣⲁⲛⲥⲱⲕ ϩⲏⲧϥ ⲛ̄ⲛ-ⲟⲩⲃⲗ̄ⲗⲉ, ϣⲁⲩϩⲉ ⲙ̄-ⲡⲉⲥⲛⲁⲩ ⲉⲡⲉⲥⲏⲧ ⲉ-ⲩϩⲓⲉⲓⲧ."

35 ⲡⲉϫⲉ-ⲓⲏⲥⲟⲩⲥ ϫⲉ "ⲙⲛ̄-ϭⲟⲙ ⲛ̄ⲧⲉ-ⲟⲩⲁ ⲃⲱⲕ ⲉϩⲟⲩⲛ ⲉ-ⲡⲏⲉⲓ ⲙ̄-ⲡϫⲱⲱⲣⲉ ⲛ̄ϥϫⲓⲧϥ ⲛ̄-ϫⲛⲁϩ, ⲉⲓⲙⲏⲧⲓ ⲛ̄ϥⲙⲟⲩⲣ ⲛ̄-ⲛⲉϥϭⲓϫ. ⲧⲟⲧⲉ ϥⲛⲁⲡⲱⲱⲛⲉ ⲉⲃⲟⲗ ⲙ̄-ⲡⲉϥⲏⲉⲓ."

36 ⲡⲉϫⲉ-ⲓⲏⲥⲟⲩⲥ ϫⲉ "ⲙⲛ̄ϥⲓ-ⲣⲟⲟⲩϣ ϫⲓⲛ-ϩⲧⲟⲟⲩⲉ ϣⲁ-ⲣⲟⲩϩⲉ ⲁⲩⲱ ϫⲓⲛ-ϩⲓⲣⲟⲩϩⲉ ϣⲁ-ϩⲧⲟⲟⲩⲉ ϫⲉ ⲟⲩ ⲡⲉⲧⲉⲧⲛⲁⲧⲁⲁϥ[66] ϩⲓⲱⲧ-ⲧⲏⲩⲧⲛ̄."

37 ⲡⲉϫⲉ-ⲛⲉϥⲙⲁⲑⲏⲧⲏⲥ ϫⲉ "ⲁϣ ⲛ̄-ϩⲟⲟⲩ ⲉⲕⲛⲁⲟⲩⲱⲛϩ ⲉⲃⲟⲗ ⲛⲁⲛ, ⲁⲩⲱ ⲁϣ ⲛ̄-ϩⲟⲟⲩ ⲉⲛⲁⲛⲁⲩ ⲉⲣⲟⲕ?"

ⲡⲉϫⲉ-ⲓⲏⲥⲟⲩⲥ ϫⲉ "ϩⲟⲧⲁⲛ ⲉⲧⲉⲧⲛ̄ϣⲁⲕⲉⲕ-ⲧⲏⲩⲧⲛ̄ ⲉϩⲛⲩ ⲙ̄ⲡⲉⲧⲛ̄ϣⲓⲡⲉ, ⲁⲩⲱ ⲛ̄ⲧⲉⲧⲛ̄ϥⲓ ⲛ̄-ⲛⲉⲧⲛ̄ϣⲧⲏⲛ ⲛ̄ⲧⲉⲧⲛ̄ⲕⲁⲁⲩ ϩⲁⲡⲉⲥⲏⲧ ⲛ̄-ⲛⲉⲧⲛ̄ⲟⲩⲉⲣⲏⲧⲉ ⲛ̄-ⲑⲉ ⲛ̄-ⲛⲓⲕⲟⲩⲉⲓ ⲛ̄-ϣⲏⲣⲉ ϣⲏⲙ ⲛ̄ⲧⲉⲧⲛ̄ϫⲟⲡϫⲡ̄[67] ⲙ̄ⲙⲟⲟⲩ, ⲧⲟⲧⲉ ⲧⲉⲧⲛⲁⲩ ⲉ-ⲡϣⲏⲣⲉ ⲙ̄-ⲡⲉⲧ-ⲟⲛϩ ⲁⲩⲱ ⲧⲉⲧⲛⲁⲣ̄-ϩⲟⲧⲉ ⲁⲛ."

38 ⲡⲉϫⲉ-ⲓⲏⲥⲟⲩⲥ ϫⲉ "ϩⲁϩ ⲛ̄-ⲥⲟⲡ ⲁⲧⲉⲧⲛ̄ⲣ̄-ⲉⲡⲓⲑⲩⲙⲉⲓ ⲉ-ⲥⲱⲧⲙ̄ ⲁ-ⲛⲉⲉⲓϣⲁϫⲉ ⲛⲁⲉⲓ ⲉϯϫⲱ ⲙ̄ⲙⲟⲟⲩ ⲛⲏⲧⲛ̄, ⲁⲩⲱ ⲙⲛ̄ⲧⲏⲧⲛ̄ ⲕⲉⲟⲩⲁ ⲉ-ⲥⲟⲧⲙⲟⲩ ⲛ̄ⲧⲟⲟⲧϥ̄. ⲟⲩⲛ̄-ϩⲛ̄ϩⲟⲟⲩ ⲛⲁϣⲱⲡⲉ ⲛ̄ⲧⲉⲧⲛ̄ϣⲓⲛⲉ ⲛ̄ⲥⲱⲉⲓ, ⲧⲉⲧⲛⲁϩⲉ ⲁⲛ ⲉⲣⲟⲉⲓ."

---

63. Emended from ⲉⲧⲉⲧⲙ̄ⲣ̄-ⲛⲏⲥⲧⲉⲩⲉ. Perhaps also missing a preceding ⲡⲉϫⲉ-ⲓⲏⲥⲟⲩⲥ ϫⲉ (as in the Greek).

64. The Greek text of this saying contains further material, which in Sahidic form is found later as part of saying 77: ⲡⲱϩ ⲛ̄ⲛ-ⲟⲩϣⲉ, ⲁⲛⲟⲕ ϯⲙ̄ⲙⲁⲩ. ϥⲓ ⲙ̄-ⲡⲱⲛⲉ ⲉϩⲣⲁⲓ̈, ⲁⲩⲱ ⲧⲉⲧⲛⲁϩⲉ ⲉⲣⲟⲉⲓ ⲙ̄ⲙⲁⲩ.

65. ϩⲙ̄-ⲡⲕⲉⲙⲁⲁϫⲉ is confusing. It's perhaps a dittography (an accidental near-duplication of the previous ϩⲙ̄-ⲡⲉⲕⲙⲁⲁϫⲉ).

66. Emended from ⲡⲉⲉⲧⲛⲁⲧⲁⲁϥ.

67. See (ϩ)ϫⲟⲡϫⲡ̄.

39 ⲡⲉϫⲉ-ⲓⲏⲥⲟⲩⲥ ϫⲉ "ⲙ̄ⲫⲁⲣⲓⲥⲁⲓⲟⲥ ⲙⲛ̄-ⲛ̄ⲅⲣⲁⲙⲙⲁⲧⲉⲩⲥ ⲁⲩϫⲓ-ⲛ̄ϣⲁϣⲧ ⲛ̄-ⲧⲅⲛⲱⲥⲓⲥ ⲁⲩϩⲟⲡⲟⲩ. ⲟⲩⲧⲉ ⲙ̄ⲡⲟⲩⲃⲱⲕ ⲉϩⲟⲩⲛ, ⲁⲩⲱ ⲛⲉⲧⲟⲩⲱϣ ⲉ-ⲃⲱⲕ ⲉϩⲟⲩⲛ ⲙ̄ⲡⲟⲩⲕⲁⲁⲩ. ⲛ̄ⲧⲱⲧⲛ̄ ⲇⲉ ϣⲱⲡⲉ ⲙ̄-ⲫⲣⲟ́ⲛⲓⲙⲟⲥ ⲛ̄-ⲑⲉ ⲛ̄-ⲛ̄ϩⲟϥ ⲁⲩⲱ ⲛ̄-ⲁⲕⲉ́ⲣⲁⲓⲟⲥ ⲛ̄-ⲑⲉ ⲛ̄-ⲛ̄ϭⲣⲟⲙⲡⲉ."

40 ⲡⲉϫⲉ-ⲓⲏⲥⲟⲩⲥ "ⲟⲩⲃⲉ-ⲛ-ⲉⲗⲟⲟⲗⲉ ⲁⲩⲧⲟϭⲥ ⲙ̄-ⲡⲥⲁ ⲛⲃⲟⲗ ⲙ̄-ⲡⲉⲓⲱⲧ, ⲁⲩⲱ ⲉⲥⲧⲁϫⲣⲏⲩ ⲁⲛ. ⲥⲉⲛⲁⲡⲟⲣⲕⲥ̄ ϩⲁ-ⲧⲉⲥⲛⲟⲩⲛⲉ ⲛ̄ⲥⲧⲁⲕⲟ."

41 ⲡⲉϫⲉ-ⲓⲏⲥⲟⲩⲥ ϫⲉ "ⲡⲉⲧⲉ-ⲩⲛ̄ⲧⲁϥ ϩⲛ̄-ⲧⲉϥϭⲓϫ, ⲥⲉⲛⲁϯ ⲛⲁϥ. ⲁⲩⲱ ⲡⲉⲧⲉ-ⲙⲛ̄ⲧⲁϥ, ⲡⲕⲉϣⲏⲙ ⲉⲧ-ⲟⲩⲛ̄ⲧⲁϥ ⲥⲉⲛⲁϥⲓⲧϥ̄ ⲛ̄ⲧⲟⲟⲧϥ̄."

42 ⲡⲉϫⲉ-ⲓⲏⲥⲟⲩⲥ ϫⲉ "ϣⲱⲡⲉ ⲉⲧⲉⲧⲛ̄ⲣ̄-ⲡⲁⲣⲁⲅⲉ!"

ⲡⲃⲓ́ⲟⲥ ⲛ̄-ⲁⲛⲧⲱ́ⲛⲓⲟⲥ THE LIFE OF ANTONY 11–13

Written in Greek by Athanasius of Alexandria (c. 297–373), archbishop of Alexandria, the Life of Antōnios/Antony the Great (251–356) inspired monastic ideals throughout the Christian world for centuries to come, both in the East and the West (in Latin translation).

This text selection describes how Antony, around the age of thirty-five, withdraws into the desert to an abandoned fort at a mountain (Pispir, modern Dayr al-Maymūn), where he would dwell in isolation for nearly twenty years. Eventually he would yield to the requests of would-be followers and emerge to guide them (after they tore down his door).

The primary source for the text is Pierpont Morgan Library, MS M.579, fol. 16v–73r.[68] This parchment manuscript was written 822/823 CE and then found in 1910 at the site of the Monastery of St. Michael (Dayr al-Malāk Mīkhā'il) near Hamuli, Egypt. This text, combined with a few other fragmentary manuscripts, was edited by Gérard Garitte in 1949.[69]

11 ⲙ̄-ⲡⲉϥⲣⲁⲥⲧⲉ ⲁϥⲉⲓ ⲉⲃⲟⲗ, ⲉϥⲣⲟⲟⲩⲧ ⲉϥϣⲙ̄ϣⲉ ⲙ̄-ⲡⲛⲟⲩⲧⲉ. ⲁϥⲃⲱⲕ ϣⲁ-ⲡϩⲗⲗⲟ ⲛ̄-ϣⲟⲣⲡ̄ ⲙ̄-ⲙⲟⲛⲁⲭⲟⲥ, ⲁϥⲁϩⲓⲟⲩ ⲙ̄ⲙⲟϥ ⲉ-ⲧⲣⲉϥⲃⲱⲕ ⲛⲙ̄ⲙⲁϥ ⲛ̄ⲥⲉϣⲙ̄ϣⲉ ⲙ̄-ⲡⲭⲟⲉⲓⲥ ϩⲓ-ⲡϫⲁⲓⲉ.

ⲡⲏ ⲇⲉ ⲁϥⲡⲁⲣⲁⲓⲧⲉⲓ,[70] ⲉϥϫⲱ ⲙ̄ⲙⲟⲥ ⲉⲧⲃⲉ-ⲧⲉϥϩⲗⲏⲕⲓ́ⲁ, ⲁⲩⲱ ⲟⲛ ϫⲉ ⲙ̄ⲡⲉ-ⲥⲩⲛⲏ́ⲑⲓⲁ ⲛ̄-ⲧⲉⲓ̈ⲙⲓⲛⲉ ϣⲱⲡⲉ ⲛⲁϥ ⲉⲛⲉϩ. ⲛ̄ⲧⲟϥ ⲇⲉ ⲟⲛ ⲛ̄-ⲧⲉⲩⲛⲟⲩ ⲁϥϯ ⲙ̄-ⲡⲉϥⲟⲩⲟⲓ ⲉ-ⲡⲧⲟⲟⲩ.

ⲡϫⲁϫⲉ ⲇⲉ ⲟⲛ ⲁϥⲛⲁⲩ ⲉ-ⲧϥ̄ⲥⲡⲟⲩⲇⲏ, ⲁϥⲟⲩⲱϣ ⲉ-ϯ-ϫⲣⲟⲡ ⲛⲁϥ ϩⲓ-ⲧⲉϩⲓⲏ, ⲁⲩⲱ ⲁϥⲛⲟⲩϫⲉ ⲛ̄-ⲟⲩⲛⲟϭ ⲛ̄-ⲇⲓ́ⲥⲕⲟⲥ ⲛ̄-ϩⲁⲧ ϩⲓ-ⲧⲉϩⲓⲏ ϩⲛ̄-ⲟⲩⲫⲁⲛⲧⲁⲥⲓ́ⲁ.

ⲁⲛⲧⲱ́ⲛⲓⲟⲥ ⲇⲉ[71] ⲁϥⲉⲓⲙⲉ ⲉ-ⲛ̄ⲕⲟⲧⲥ̄ ⲙ̄-ⲡⲙⲁⲥⲧⲉ-ⲡⲉⲧ-ⲛⲁⲛⲟⲩϥ, ⲁϥⲁϩⲉⲣⲁⲧϥ̄, ⲁϥϭⲱϣⲧ̄ ⲉ-ⲡⲇⲓ́ⲥⲕⲟⲥ. ⲁϥⲉⲓⲙⲉ ϫⲉ ⲟⲩϩⲱⲃ ⲛ̄ⲧⲉ-ⲡⲇⲓⲁ́ⲃⲟⲗⲟⲥ ⲡⲉⲧ-ⲛ̄ϩⲏⲧϥ̄, ⲁⲩⲱ ⲡⲉϫⲁϥ ϫⲉ "ⲛ̄ⲧⲁ-ⲡⲉⲓ̈ⲇⲓ́ⲥⲕⲟⲥ ⲉⲓ ⲧⲱⲛ[72] ϩⲙ̄-ⲡⲉⲓ̈ϫⲁⲓⲉ? ⲛ̄ⲛ-ⲟⲩϩⲓⲏ ⲁⲛ ⲧⲉ ⲧⲁⲓ̈ ⲉⲥⲕⲉϩⲕⲱϩ, ⲙⲛ̄-ⲧⲁϭⲥⲉ ⲛ̄-ⲣⲱⲙⲉ ⲛ̄ϩⲏⲧⲥ̄ ⲉϥⲙⲟⲟϣⲉ. ϩⲙ̄-ⲡⲧⲣⲉϥϩⲉ ⲇⲉ, ⲛⲉ-ⲙⲛ̄-ϭⲟⲙ ⲉ-ⲧⲙ̄ⲧⲣⲉⲩⲉⲓⲙⲉ[73] ⲉⲣⲟϥ, ϫⲉ ⲟⲩⲛⲟϭ ⲅⲁⲣ ⲡⲉ. ⲁⲩⲱ ⲡⲉⲛⲧⲁϥⲥⲟⲣⲙⲉϥ, ϥⲛⲁⲕⲟⲧϥ̄, ⲛ̄ϥϣⲓⲛⲉ ⲛ̄ⲥⲱϥ, ⲛ̄ϥϩⲉ ⲉⲣⲟϥ, ⲉⲃⲟⲗ ϫⲉ ⲟⲩϫⲁⲓ̈ⲉ ⲡⲉ ⲡⲉⲓ̈ⲙⲁ. ⲟⲩⲧⲉ́ⲭⲛⲏ

---

68. For further information and images of the manuscript, see https://www.themorgan.org/manuscript/77281.

69. Gérard Garitte, ed., *S. Antonii vitae: Versio sahidica*, 2 vols., Corpus Scriptorum Christianorum Orientalium 117–118, Scriptores Coptici 13–14 (Paris: E Typographeo Reipublicae, 1949). Most of Garitte's emendations have been followed and noted. For a translation and introduction, see Athanasius of Alexandria, *The Life of Antony: The Coptic Life and the Greek Life*, trans. Tim Vivian and Apostolos N. Athanassakis, Cistercian Studies 202 (Kalamazoo, MI: Cistercian, 2003).

70. Emended from ⲁϥⲡⲁⲣⲁⲧⲉⲓ.

71. ⲁⲛⲧⲱ́ⲛⲓⲟⲥ ⲇⲉ added (as in the Greek text).

72. Emended from ⲉ-ⲧⲱⲛ.

73. Emended from ⲉ-ⲧⲣⲉⲩⲉⲓⲙⲉ.

те таї ⲛ̄ⲧⲉ-ⲡⲇⲓⲁ́ⲃⲟⲗⲟⲥ ⲛ̄ⲧⲁⲥϣⲱⲡⲉ! ⲛⲅ̄ⲛⲁⲉϣ-ϯ-ϫⲣⲟⲡ ⲛⲁⲓ̈ ⲁⲛ, ⲱ ⲡⲇⲓⲁ́ⲃⲟⲗⲟⲥ, ϩⲙ̄-ⲡⲁⲓ̈, ⲁⲗⲗⲁ ⲡⲁⲓ̈ ⲛⲁϣⲱⲡⲉ ⲛⲁⲕ ⲉ-ⲩⲧⲁⲕⲟ!"

ⲛⲁⲓ̈ ⲇⲉ ⲉϥϫⲱ ⲙ̄ⲙⲟⲟⲩ ⲛ̄ϭⲓ-ⲁⲛⲧⲱ́ⲛⲓⲟⲥ, ⲁϥⲱϫⲛ ⲛ̄ϭⲓ-ⲡⲉⲧ-ⲙ̄ⲙⲁⲩ ⲛ̄-ⲑⲉ ⲛ̄ⲛ-ⲟⲩⲕⲁⲡⲛⲟⲥ.

12 ⲙⲛ̄ⲛ̄ⲥⲱⲥ ⲟⲛ ⲉϥⲙⲟⲟϣⲉ ϩⲓ-ⲧⲉϩⲓⲏ, ⲁϥⲛⲁⲩ ⲉ-ⲩⲛⲟⲩⲃ ϩⲙ̄-ⲟⲩⲫⲁⲛⲧⲁⲥⲓⲁ ⲁⲛ, ⲁⲗⲗⲁ ϩⲙ̄-ⲟⲩⲙⲉ, ⲉⲓⲧⲉ ⲡϫⲁϫⲉ ⲡⲉⲛⲧⲁϥⲧⲥⲁⲃⲟϥ ⲉⲣⲟϥ, ⲉⲓⲧⲉ ⲟⲩⲇⲩ́ⲛⲁⲙⲓⲥ ⲉⲥϫⲟⲥⲉ ⲉⲥⲅⲩⲙⲛⲁⲍⲉ[74] ⲙ̄-ⲡϣⲟⲉⲓϫ[75] ⲁⲩⲱ ⲉϥⲧⲥⲁⲃⲟ ⲙ̄-ⲡⲇⲓⲁⲃⲟⲗⲟⲥ ϫⲉ ⲛ̄ϥ̄ϩⲏϣ ⲁⲛ ϩⲁ-ⲭⲣⲏⲙⲁ, ⲟⲩⲇⲉ́ ⲙ̄ⲡⲉϥϫⲟⲟⲥ ⲛⲁⲛ ⲟⲩⲇⲉ́ ⲁⲛⲟⲛ ⲙ̄ⲡⲉⲛⲉⲓⲙⲉ, ⲡⲗⲏⲛ ⲟⲩⲛⲟⲩⲃ ⲡⲉⲛⲧⲁϥⲛⲁⲩ ⲉⲣⲟϥ ϩⲛ̄-ⲟⲩⲙⲉ.

ⲁⲛⲧⲱ́ⲛⲓⲟⲥ ⲇⲉ ⲁϥⲣ̄-ϣⲡⲏⲣⲉ ⲙ̄-ⲡⲁϣⲁⲓ̈ ⲙ̄-ⲡⲛⲟⲩⲃ, ⲁϥⲥⲁⲁⲧϥ̄ ⲇⲉ, ⲁϥⲡⲱⲧ ⲛ̄-ⲑⲉ ⲛ̄-ⲟⲩⲁ ⲉϥⲛⲁⲡⲱⲧ ϩⲛ̄ⲧϥ̄ ⲛ̄ⲛ-ⲟⲩⲕⲱϩⲧ̄, ϩⲱⲥⲧⲉ ⲛ̄ϥ̄ⲧⲙ̄ϩⲱⲛ ⲉⲣⲟϥ ⲉ-ⲡⲧⲏⲣϥ̄.

ⲛ̄-ϩⲟⲩⲟ ⲇⲉ ⲛ̄-ϩⲟⲩⲟ ⲁϥϯ ⲙ̄-ⲡⲉϥⲟⲩⲟⲓ ⲉ-ⲡⲧⲟⲟⲩ. ⲁϥⲛⲁⲩ ⲉ-ⲩⲡⲁⲣⲉⲙⲃⲟⲗⲏ́[76] ⲉⲥⲟ ⲛ̄-ϫⲁⲓ̈ⲉ, ⲁⲩⲱ ⲉⲧⲃⲉ-ⲡⲉⲭⲣⲟ́ⲛⲟⲥ ⲉ-ⲛⲉⲥⲙⲉϩ ⲛ̄-ϫⲁⲧϥⲉ, ϩⲓ-ⲡⲉⲕⲣⲟ ⲙ̄-ⲡⲓⲉⲣⲟ, ⲁⲩⲱ ⲁϥⲟⲩⲱϩ ϩⲙ̄-ⲡⲙⲁ ⲉⲧ-ⲙ̄ⲙⲁⲩ. ⲛ̄ϫⲁⲧϥⲉ ⲇⲉ ⲉⲧ-ⲙ̄ⲙⲁⲩ ⲁⲩⲡⲱⲧ ⲛ̄-ⲑⲉ ⲉϣϫⲉ ⲉⲩⲡⲏⲧ ⲛ̄ⲥⲱⲟⲩ, ⲁⲩⲁⲛⲁⲭⲱⲣⲉⲓ ⲛⲁⲩ. ⲛ̄ⲧⲟϥ ⲇⲉ ⲁϥⲧⲱⲙ ⲙ̄-ⲡⲣⲟ ⲁⲩⲱ ⲁϥⲕⲱ ⲛⲁϥ ⲛ̄-ϩⲉⲛⲟⲉⲓⲕ ⲉ-ⲧⲣⲉⲩⲣⲱϣⲉ ⲉⲣⲟϥ ⲛ̄-ⲥⲟⲟⲩ ⲛ̄-ⲛ̄ⲉⲃⲟⲧ. (ⲡⲁⲓ̈ ⲇⲉ ⲥⲉⲉⲓⲣⲉ ⲙ̄ⲙⲟϥ ϩⲱⲟⲩ ⲛ̄ϭⲓ-ⲛⲉⲣⲙ̄ⲛⲕⲏⲙⲉ ⲉ-ϣⲁⲩϭⲱ ⲛ̄-ⲧⲉⲣⲟⲙⲡⲉ ⲧⲏⲣⲥ̄ ⲉ-ⲩⲛ̄ⲧⲟⲩ-ⲟⲉⲓⲕ, ⲁⲩⲱ ⲙⲉⲩϥⲗⲁⲡⲧⲉⲓ[77] ⲛ̄-ⲗⲁⲁⲩ.) ⲛ̄ⲧⲟϥ ⲇⲉ ⲁϥϣⲟⲧϥ̄ ⲉϩⲟⲩⲛ, ⲁⲩⲱ ⲛⲉ-ⲩⲛ̄ⲧⲁϥ ⲙ̄ⲙⲁⲩ ⲙ̄-ⲡⲙⲟⲟⲩ, ⲁϥϭⲱ ⲛ̄ϩⲟⲩⲛ ⲙ̄-ⲡⲙⲁ ⲉⲧ-ⲙ̄ⲙⲁⲩ ⲙⲁⲩⲁⲁϥ, ⲉ-ⲛϥ̄ⲛⲏⲩ ⲉⲃⲟⲗ ⲁⲛ ⲟⲩⲇⲉ ⲉ-ⲛϥ̄ⲛⲁⲩ ⲁⲛ ⲉ-ⲛⲉⲧ-ⲛⲏⲩ ϣⲁⲣⲟϥ. ⲛ̄ⲧⲟϥ ⲇⲉ ⲁϥⲣ̄-ⲟⲩⲛⲟϭ ⲛ̄ⲛ-ⲟⲩⲟⲉⲓϣ ⲉϥⲁⲥⲕⲉⲓ ⲛ̄-ⲧⲉⲓ̈ϩⲉ, ⲉϥⲥⲱⲕ ⲛⲁϥ ⲉϩⲣⲁⲓ̈ ⲛ̄-ⲛⲉϥⲟⲉⲓⲕ ϩⲓ-ⲧⲭⲉⲛⲉⲡⲱⲣ ⲛ̄-ⲥⲉⲡ-ⲥⲛⲁⲩ ⲉ-ⲧⲉⲣⲟⲙⲡⲉ.

13 ⲛⲉⲧ-ⲃⲏⲕ ⲇⲉ ϣⲁⲣⲟϥ, ϩⲛ̄-ⲛⲉⲧⲥⲟⲟⲩⲛ ⲙ̄ⲙⲟϥ ⲉⲧⲃⲉ-ϫⲉ ⲛⲉϥⲕⲱ ⲙ̄ⲙⲟⲟⲩ ⲁⲛ ⲉ-ⲃⲱⲕ ⲉϩⲟⲩⲛ ⲡⲉ, ϣⲁⲩϭⲱ ϩⲓⲃⲟⲗ ⲛ̄-ϩⲁϩ ⲛ̄-ⲥⲟⲡ,[78] ⲛ̄ⲥⲉⲣ̄-ϩⲉⲛϩⲟⲟⲩ ⲙⲛ̄-ϩⲉⲛⲟⲩϣⲏ ϩⲓⲣⲙ̄-ⲡⲣⲟ. ⲉ-ⲛⲉ-ϣⲁⲩⲥⲱⲧⲙ̄ ⲉϣϫⲉ ⲉⲣⲉ-ϩⲉⲛⲙⲏⲏϣⲉ ϩⲓϩⲟⲩⲛ ⲛⲉⲩϣⲧⲣ̄ⲧⲱⲣ ⲁⲩⲱ ⲉⲩϯ-ϩⲣⲟⲟⲩ, ⲉⲩⲧⲁⲩⲟ ⲛ̄-ϩⲉⲛⲥⲙⲏ[79] ⲙ̄-ⲙⲛ̄ⲧϭⲱⲃ, ⲉⲩⲱϣ ⲉⲃⲟⲗ, ⲉⲩϫⲱ ⲙ̄ⲙⲟⲥ ϫⲉ "ⲥⲁϩⲱⲕ ⲉⲃⲟⲗ ⲛ̄-ⲛⲉⲧⲉ-ⲛⲟⲩⲛ ⲛⲉ! ⲟⲩ ⲉⲣⲟⲕ ⲡⲉ ⲡⲉⲓ̈ϫⲁⲓ̈ⲉ ⲉ-ⲟⲩⲱϩ ⲛ̄ϩⲏⲧϥ̄? ⲛⲅ̄ⲛⲁⲉϣϥⲉⲓ ⲉⲣⲟⲕ ⲁⲛ ϩⲁ-ⲧⲉⲛⲉⲡⲉⲓⲃⲟⲩⲗⲏ!"

ⲛ̄ⲣⲱⲙⲉ ⲇⲉ ⲉⲧ-ϩⲓⲃⲟⲗ ⲉ-ⲛⲉⲩⲙⲉⲉⲩⲉ ⲛ̄-ϣⲟⲣⲡ̄ ϫⲉ ϩⲉⲛⲣⲱⲙⲉ ⲛⲉⲧ-ϩⲓϩⲟⲩⲛ ⲛ̄ⲧⲁⲩⲃⲱⲕ ⲉϩⲟⲩⲛ ϣⲁⲣⲟϥ ϩⲓϫⲛ̄-ϩⲉⲛϭⲗⲟⲟϭⲉ. ⲁⲩϭⲱϣⲧ̄ ϭⲉ ⲉϩⲟⲩⲛ ϩⲓⲧⲛ̄-ϩⲉⲛϣⲕⲟⲗ, ⲙ̄ⲡⲟⲩⲛⲁⲩ ⲉ-ⲗⲁⲁⲩ. ⲧⲟⲧⲉ ⲁⲩⲉⲓⲙⲉ ⲛⲁⲙⲉ ϫⲉ ϩⲉⲛⲇⲁⲓⲙⲱⲛ ⲛⲉ ⲛⲉⲧ-ⲙ̄ⲙⲁⲩ.[80]

ⲛ̄ⲧⲟϥ ⲇⲉ ⲛⲉϥⲥⲱⲧⲙ̄ ⲉⲣⲟⲟⲩ ⲁⲩⲱ ⲙ̄-ⲡⲉϥⲣⲟⲟⲩϣ ⲁⲛ ⲡⲉ ϩⲁⲣⲟⲟⲩ. ⲁϥⲉⲓ ⲇⲉ ϩⲁⲧⲙ̄-ⲡⲣⲟ ⲛ̄ϭⲓ-ⲁⲛⲧⲱⲛⲓⲟⲥ, ⲁϥⲡⲁⲣⲁⲕⲁⲗⲉⲓ ⲛ̄-ⲛ̄ⲣⲱⲙⲉ ⲉ-ⲧⲣⲉⲩⲁⲛⲁⲭⲱⲣⲉⲓ ⲛⲁⲩ ⲁⲩⲱ ⲉ-ⲧⲙ̄ⲣ̄-ϩⲟⲧⲉ, ⲉϥϫⲱ ⲙ̄ⲙⲟⲥ ϫⲉ "ⲧⲁⲓ̈ ⲧⲉ ⲑⲉ ⲉ-ϣⲁⲣⲉ-ⲛ̄ⲇⲁⲓⲙⲱ́ⲛⲓⲟⲛ ⲉⲓⲣⲉ ⲛ̄-ⲛⲉⲓ̈ⲥⲙⲟⲧ ⲙ̄-ⲫⲁⲛⲧⲁⲥⲓⲁ ⲉϩⲟⲩⲛ ⲉ-ⲛⲉⲧ-ⲣ̄-ϩⲟⲧⲉ. ⲛ̄ⲧⲱⲧⲛ̄ ⲇⲉ ⲥⲫⲣⲁⲅⲓⲍⲉ ⲙ̄ⲙⲱⲧⲛ̄, ⲛ̄ⲧⲉⲧⲛ̄ⲃⲱⲕ ⲉⲧⲉⲧⲛ̄ⲧⲏⲕ ⲛ̄-ϩⲏⲧ, ⲁⲩⲱ ⲛ̄ⲧⲉⲧⲛ̄ⲗⲟ ϩⲁ-ⲛⲁⲓ̈ ⲉⲩⲥⲱⲃⲉ ⲛ̄ⲥⲱⲟⲩ ⲙⲁⲩⲁⲁⲩ."

ⲛⲁⲓ̈ ⲙⲉⲛ ⲁⲩⲃⲱⲕ, ⲉⲣⲉ-ⲡⲙⲁⲉⲓⲛ ⲙ̄-ⲡⲉⲥⲧⲁⲩⲣⲟⲥ ⲕⲧⲏⲩ ⲉⲣⲟⲟⲩ, ⲛ̄ⲧⲟϥ ⲇⲉ ⲉⲛⲉϥϭⲉⲉⲧ ⲙ̄-ⲙⲁⲩⲁⲁϥ. ⲁⲩⲱ ⲙ̄ⲡⲟⲩⲉϣϭⲙ̄-ϭⲟⲙ ⲉ-ϥⲗⲁⲡⲧⲉⲓ ⲙ̄ⲙⲟϥ ⲛ̄-ⲗⲁⲁⲩ. ⲁⲩⲱ ⲛⲉϥⲁⲅⲱⲛⲓⲍⲉ ⲉ-ⲡⲉϩⲟⲩⲟ,

---

74. See ⲅⲩⲙⲛⲁⲍⲉ.
75. Emended from ⲙ̄-ⲡϣⲟϫⲛⲉ.
76. Emended from ⲉ-ⲩⲡⲁⲣⲁⲃⲟⲗⲏ́.
77. See ⲃⲗⲁⲡⲧⲉⲓ.
78. Emended from ⲛ̄-ϩⲟⲟⲩ.
79. Emended from ⲛ̄-ϩⲉⲛⲙⲏⲏϣⲉ.
80. The manuscript seems to be missing a phrase here. Based on the Greek, it was probably something like: ⲉⲩⲣ̄-ϩⲟⲧⲉ, ⲁⲩⲙⲟⲩⲧⲉ ⲉ-ⲁⲛⲧⲱ́ⲛⲓⲟⲥ.

ⲉⲧⲃⲉ-ϫⲉ ⲛⲉⲑⲉⲱⲣⲏⲙⲁ ⲉⲧ-ⲟⲩⲱϩ[81] ⲉⲧⲟⲟⲧⲟⲩ ⲙ̄-ⲙⲏⲛⲉ ⲉ-ϣⲱⲡⲉ ϩⲙ̄-ⲡⲉϥⲛⲟⲩⲥ ⲁⲩⲱ ⲧⲙⲛ̄ⲧϭⲱⲃ ⲙ̄-ⲡϫⲁϫⲉ ⲉⲧ-ϯ ⲟⲩⲃⲏϥ, ϣⲁⲩϯ ⲛⲁϥ ⲛ̄ⲛ-ⲟⲩⲛⲟϭ ⲛ̄-ⲙ̄ⲧⲟⲛ ϩⲛ̄-ⲛⲉϥϩⲓⲥⲉ ⲁⲩⲱ ⲛ̄ⲥⲉⲉⲓⲣⲉ ⲛ̄ϩⲏⲧϥ̄ ⲛ̄-ⲟⲩⲛⲟϭ ⲛ̄ⲛ-ⲟⲩⲣⲟⲧ ⲉ-ⲡⲉϩⲟⲩⲟ.

ⲕⲁⲓ ⲅⲁⲣ ⲛⲉⲧ-ⲥⲟⲟⲩⲛ ⲙ̄ⲙⲟϥ, ⲉⲩⲃⲏⲕ ⲉ-ⲡⲙⲁ ⲉⲧ-ⲙ̄ⲙⲁⲩ ⲛ̄-ϩⲁϩ ⲛ̄-ⲥⲟⲡ, ⲉⲩⲙⲉⲉⲩⲉ ϫⲉ ⲥⲉⲛⲁϩⲉ ⲉⲣⲟϥ ⲉϥⲙⲟⲟⲩⲧ, ⲁⲩⲱ ϣⲁⲩⲥⲱⲧⲙ̄ ⲉⲣⲟϥ ⲉϥⲯⲁⲗⲗⲉⲓ ϫⲉ

"ⲙⲁⲣⲉ-ⲡⲛⲟⲩⲧⲉ ⲧⲱⲟⲩⲛ, ⲛ̄ⲧⲉ-ⲛⲉϥϫⲁϫⲉ ϫⲱⲱⲣⲉ ⲉⲃⲟⲗ,
    ⲛ̄ⲥⲉⲡⲱⲧ ⲛ̄ϭⲓ-ⲛⲉⲧ-ⲙⲟⲥⲧⲉ ⲙ̄ⲙⲟϥ ⲙ̄-ⲡⲉϥⲙ̄ⲧⲟ ⲉⲃⲟⲗ.
ⲙⲁⲣⲟⲩⲱϫⲛ̄ ⲛ̄-ⲑⲉ ⲉ-ϣⲁⲣⲉ-ⲟⲩⲕⲁⲡⲛⲟⲥ ⲱϫⲛ̄,
    ⲛ̄-ⲑⲉ ⲛ̄ⲛ-ⲟⲩⲙⲟⲩⲗϩ̄ ⲉ-ϣⲁϥⲃⲱⲗ ⲉⲃⲟⲗ ⲛ̄ⲛⲁϩⲣⲙ̄-ⲡⲕⲱϩ̄ⲧ,
ⲛ̄-ⲧⲉⲓ̈ϩⲉ ⲙⲁⲣⲟⲩⲧⲁⲕⲟ ⲛ̄ϭⲓ-ⲛ̄ⲣⲉϥⲣ̄-ⲛⲟⲃⲉ ⲙ̄-ⲡⲙ̄ⲧⲟ ⲉⲃⲟⲗ ⲙ̄-ⲡϩⲟ ⲙ̄-ⲡⲛⲟⲩⲧⲉ."[82]

ⲁⲩⲱ ϫⲉ

"ⲁ-ⲛ̄ϩⲉⲑⲛⲟⲥ ⲧⲏⲣⲟⲩ ⲕⲱⲧⲉ ⲉⲣⲟⲓ̈,
    ⲁⲓ̈ⲃⲟⲟⲣⲟⲩ ϩⲙ̄-ⲡⲣⲁⲛ ⲙ̄-ⲡϫⲟⲉⲓⲥ."[83]

---

81. Emended from ⲛⲉⲑⲉⲱⲣⲓⲁ ⲙⲉⲩⲟⲩⲱϩ.
82. Psalm 67.2–3(68.1–2).
83. Psalm 117(118).10.

SAHIDIC-ENGLISH LEXICON

This lexicon includes all the words covered in the chapter vocabulary lists plus all the additional words found in the Reading Selections. It includes both words of native Egyptian origin and words of Greek origin—*all* organized in a strictly Greco-Coptic alphabetical order. Proper names of people, places, and months (see 9.5 for these) are not included.

The entries match the format of the chapter vocabulary lists. Construct, prenominal, and prepersonal forms of nouns, pronouns, prepositions, etc., follow the main entry's (absolute) form. Noun gender is listed after the definition in parentheses (nm/nf/nmf). Verbs have up to four entries in columns for absolute, prenominal (-), prepersonal (⸗), and stative (†) forms. Special imperative (impv) and conjunct participle (cp) forms precede the definition in parentheses, if attested. Separate line definitions are given for transitive (vt), reflexive (vr), intransitive (vi), stative (vs), and masculine noun (nm) usage.

ⲁ   ἄλφα

ⲁ		about, approximately (with ⲛ̄-: ⲛⲁ) (adv)
ⲁⲃⲁϭⲏⲉⲓⲛ		glass (nmf)
ⲁⲃⲱ (pl ⲁⲃⲟⲟⲩⲉ)		net (nf)
ⲁⲅⲁⲑⲟⲥ		good (adj)
ⲁⲅⲁⲡⲏ		love (nf)
ⲁⲅⲅⲉⲗⲟⲥ		messenger (nm)
ἀγορά		marketplace (nf)
ⲁⲅⲱⲛⲓⲍⲉ		to fight, struggle (ⲙ̄ⲙⲟ⸗) (vt)
ⲁⲉⲧⲟⲥ		eagle, vulture (nm)
ⲁⲏⲣ		air (nm)
ⲁⲓⲁⲓ	ⲟⲓ̈†	to increase, grow (in age, size, quantity) (vi)
		to be great, honored (vs)
ⲁⲓ̈ⲥⲑⲏⲥⲓⲥ		sense, sensation (nf)
ⲁⲓⲧ(ⲉ)ⲓ		to ask (someone); to request (something) (ⲙ̄ⲙⲟ⸗) (vt)
ⲁⲓ̈ⲧⲏⲙⲁ		request (nm)
ⲁⲓ̈ⲱⲛ		age (nm)
ἀκάθαρτος		unclean (adj)
ἀκέραιος		pure, innocent (adj)

ⲁⲗ			deaf (adj)
ⲁⲗ			stone, pebble (nm)
ⲁⲗⲁ́ⲃⲁⲥⲧⲣⲟⲛ			alabaster (vase) (nf)
ⲁⲗⲉ	ⲁⲗⲟ⸗	ⲁⲗⲏⲩ†	(impv ⲁⲗⲱⲧⲛ̄) to go up, climb (onto, up to: ⲉ-); to get on, mount (an animal: ⲉϫⲛ̄-) (vt)
			to be riding, mounted (vs)
ⲁⲗⲗⲁ			but, rather (conj)
ⲁⲗⲗⲏⲗⲟⲩ́-ⲓ̈ⲁ			praise Yah! (ultimately from Hebrew) (impv)
ⲁⲗⲗⲟ́ⲫⲩⲗⲟⲥ			from another tribe, foreign (adj)
ⲁⲗⲟⲩ			child (nmf)
ⲁⲗⲱ, ⲁⲗⲟⲩ (pl ⲁⲗⲟⲟⲩⲉ)			pupil (of eye) (nf)
ⲁⲙⲁ			"mother" (title of respect, ultimately from Aramaic) (nf)
ⲁⲙⲁϩⲧⲉ			to grasp, seize, restrain, apprehend (ⲙ̄ⲙⲟ⸗) (vt)
			to get control, rule (over: ⲉϫⲛ̄-, ϩⲓϫⲛ̄-) (vi)
			control, restraint (nm)
ⲁⲙⲛ̄ⲧⲉ			the netherworld (= Greek ᾅδης) (nm)
ⲁⲙⲣⲏϩⲉ			bitumen, pitch (nm)
ⲁⲛ			not (often preceded by ⲛ̄- . . .) (neg part)
ⲁⲛⲁ́ⲥⲧⲁⲥⲓⲥ			standing up (again), raising (nf)
ⲁⲛⲁ́ⲅⲕⲏ			necessity; used impersonally: it's necessary (nf)
ⲁⲛⲁⲭⲱⲣⲉⲓ			to withdraw, go away (vi)
ⲁⲛⲁϣ (pl ⲁⲛⲁⲩϣ)			oath (nm)
ⲁⲛⲟⲕ	ⲁⲛⲅ̄-		I (ind pers pron)
ⲁⲛⲟⲙⲓ́ⲁ			lawlessness (nf)
ⲁ́ⲛⲟⲙⲟⲥ			lawless (adj)
ⲁⲛⲟⲛ	ⲁⲛ-		we (ind pers pron)
ⲁⲛⲟⲩⲣ̄ϣⲉ			watcher (nm)
ⲁⲛⲧⲓ-			instead of (prep)
ⲁⲝⲓⲟⲩ			to ask (ⲙ̄ⲙⲟ⸗) (vt)
ⲁⲡⲁ			"father" (title of respect, ultimately from Aramaic) (nm)
ⲁⲡⲉ (pl ⲁⲡⲏ[ⲟ]ⲩⲉ)			head (nf)
ⲁ́ⲡⲓⲥⲧⲟⲥ			untrusting, untrustworthy (adj)
ⲁⲡⲟⲑⲏ́ⲕⲏ			storehouse, barn (nf)
ⲁⲡⲟⲕⲁ́ⲗⲩⲯⲓⲥ			uncovering, unveiling (nf)
ⲁⲡⲟ́ⲥⲧⲟⲗⲟⲥ			emissary, envoy (nm)
ⲁⲡⲟⲧ (pl ⲁⲡⲏⲧ)			cup (nm)
ⲁⲡⲥ̄			number (of), amount (nf)
ⲁ́ⲣⲁ			then, so (part)
ⲁⲣⲓⲕⲉ			fault, blame (nm)
ϭⲛ̄-ⲁⲣⲓⲕⲉ			to find fault with, blame (ⲉ-)

ⲁⲣⲏϫ⸗		end of, limit of (requires anticipatory suffix) (n)
ⲁⲣⲛⲁ		to deny (ⲙ̄ⲙⲟ⸗) (vt)
ⲁⲣⲟⲟⲩⲉ		thistle(s) (n)
ⲁⲣⲟϣ		to become cold (vi)
		cold, chill (nm)
ⲁⲣⲭⲁⲓⲟⲥ		ancient, old (adj)
ⲁⲣⲭ(ⲉ)ⲓ		to begin (to: ⲛ̄- or ⲉ- + inf); to rule (over: ⲉϫⲛ̄-) (vt)
ⲁⲣⲭⲏ		beginning; rule (nf)
ⲁⲣⲭⲓⲉⲡⲓ́ⲥⲕⲟⲡⲟⲥ		primary overseer, top supervisor (nm)
ⲁⲣⲭⲓⲉⲣⲉⲩ́ⲥ		primary priest (nm)
ⲁⲣⲭⲓⲧⲣⲓ́ⲕⲗⲓⲛⲟⲥ		primary banquet waiter (nm)
ⲁ́ⲣⲭⲱⲛ		ruler (nm)
ⲁⲥ		old (usually not used for people; rarely after noun without ⲛ̄-) (adj)
ⲁⲥⲉⲃⲏⲥ		irreverent, impious (adj)
ⲁⲥⲑⲉⲛⲏⲥ		weak (adj)
ⲁⲥⲕⲉⲓ		to practice (ⲙ̄ⲙⲟ⸗) (vt)
ⲁⲥⲡⲁⲍⲉ		to greet (ⲙ̄ⲙⲟ⸗) (vt)
ⲁⲥⲡⲁⲥⲙⲟⲥ		greeting (nm)
ⲁⲥⲡⲉ		language, speech (nf)
ⲁⲧ-		un-, non- (neg prefix)
ⲁⲩⲁⲛ		color, complexion (nm)
ⲁⲩⲝⲁⲛⲉ		to grow, increase (vt/vi)
ⲁⲩⲱ		and (conj)
ⲁϣ		what? (inter pron)
ⲁϣⲁⲓ̈	ⲟϣ†	to become/be many, numerous (vi/vs)
		multitude, amount (nm)
ⲁϣ-ⲁϩⲟⲙ		to groan (at: [ⲉϩⲣⲁⲓ̈] ⲉ[ϫⲛ̄]-) (vi)
		groaning (nm)
ⲁϣⲏ		abundance, multitude (nf)
(ⲁ)ϣⲕⲁⲕ		call, shout (nm)
ⲁ(ϣ-)ϣⲕⲁⲕ ⲉⲃⲟⲗ		to call out (cf. ⲱϣ)
ϫⲓ-ϣⲕⲁⲕ ⲉⲃⲟⲗ		to call out (cf. ϫⲱ)
ⲁϥ (pl ⲁϥⲟⲩⲓ)		flesh, (piece of) meat (nm)
ⲁϩⲉ		lifetime (nm)
ⲁϩⲟ (pl ⲁϩⲱⲱⲣ)		treasure, treasury (nm)
ⲁϩⲣⲟ⸗		why? what's with? (requires anticipatory suffix agreeing with following subject) (inter adv)
ⲁϩⲱⲙ(ⲉ)		eagle, falcon (nm)
ⲁϫⲛ̄-, ⲉϫⲛ̄-	ⲁϫⲛ̄ⲧ⸗, ⲉϫⲛ̄ⲧ⸗	without; as adv: -lessly (ⲁⲧ + ϣⲓⲛⲉ) (prep)

Ⲃ ⲂⲎⲦⲀ

ⲃⲁ			date-palm branch (nm)
ⲃⲁⲁⲃⲉ	ⲃⲁⲃⲱ(ⲱ)⸗	ⲃⲁⲃⲟⲧ†	(cp ⲃⲁⲃⲉ-) to despise (ⲙ̄ⲙⲟ⸗) (vt)
			to be despicable (vi)
ⲃⲁⲗ			eye; shame (nm)
ⲃⲁⲡⲧⲓⲍⲉ			to immerse (ⲙ̄ⲙⲟ⸗) (vt)
ⲃⲁⲡⲧⲓⲥⲙⲁ			immersion (nm)
† -ⲃⲁⲡⲧⲓⲥⲙⲁ			to give an immersion, immerse
ⲃⲁⲣⲱⲧ			bronze, brass (nm)
ⲃⲁⲧⲟⲥ			bramble, thorn-bush (nm)
ⲃⲉ(ⲉ)ⲃⲉ			to pour out (ⲙ̄ⲙⲟ⸗) (vt)
			to bubble, be poured out (vi)
ⲃⲉⲕⲉ́ (pl ⲃⲉⲕⲏⲩⲉ, ⲃⲉⲕⲉ[ⲉ]ⲩⲉ)			wage (nm)
ⲃⲉⲛⲓⲡⲉ, ⲡⲉⲛⲓⲡⲉ			iron (nm)
ⲃⲏⲙⲁ			platform, dais, judgment seat (nm)
ⲃⲓⲟⲥ			life (nm)
ⲃⲗⲁⲡⲧⲉⲓ, ϥⲗⲁⲡⲧⲉⲓ			to harm (ⲙ̄ⲙⲟ⸗) (vt)
ⲃⲗ̄ⲃⲓⲗⲉ			kernel, grain, piece (nf)
ⲃⲗ̄ⲗⲉ́ (f ⲃⲗ̄ⲗⲏ; pl ⲃⲗ̄ⲗⲉⲉⲩ[ⲉ])			blind (adj)
ⲃⲟⲏⲑⲉⲓ			to be helpful (to: ⲉ-) (vt)
ⲃⲟⲏⲑ(ⲉ)ⲓⲁ			help (nf)
ⲃⲟⲏⲑⲟⲥ			helpful (adj)
ⲃⲟⲗ			outside, outer part (< ⲃⲱⲗ) (nm)
ⲉⲃⲟⲗ			out, away (adv)
ⲛ̄ⲃⲟⲗ			outside (adv)
(ⲛ̄)ⲥⲁⲃⲟⲗ			outside (adv)
ϣⲁⲃⲟⲗ			outward (adv)
ϩⲓⲃⲟⲗ			outside (adv)
ⲃⲟⲗⲃⲗ̄	ⲃⲁⲗⲃⲗ̄⸗		(cp ⲃⲁⲗⲃⲗ̄-) to dig (up) (ⲙ̄ⲙⲟ⸗) (vt)
			to be undermined (vi)
ⲃⲟⲟⲛⲉ			evil, misfortune (nf)
ⲃⲟⲧⲉ			disgusting, loathsome thing (nf)
ⲣ̄-ⲃⲟⲧⲉ			(ⲟ† ⲛ̄-) to become/be disgusting
ϫⲓ-ⲃⲟⲧⲉ			to get disgusted (by: ⲉ-)
ⲃⲣ̄ⲃⲣ̄			to boil, bubble (vi)
			boiling (nm)
ⲃⲣ̄ⲣⲉ́			new, young (adj)
ⲛ̄-ⲃⲣ̄ⲣⲉ́			newly, recently
ⲃⲱ	ⲃⲉ-		tree, vine (when a specific kind is mentioned; ϣⲏⲛ otherwise) (nf)
ⲃⲱⲕ		ⲃⲏⲕ†	to go (vi)
			to be going (vs, exclusively with Present)

ⲃⲱⲗ	ⲃⲉⲗ-, ⲃⲗ̄-	ⲃⲟⲗ⸗	ⲃⲏⲗ†	(cp ⲃⲁⲗ-) 1. to release, loosen, undo (ⲙ̄ⲙⲟ⸗); 2. to interpret (ⲙ̄ⲙⲟ⸗) (vt)
				to become released, undone (vi)
				to be released, undone, interpreted (vs)
				interpretation (nm)
ⲃⲱⲗ ⲉⲃⲟⲗ				and also: to dissolve, destroy (ⲙ̄ⲙⲟ⸗)
ⲃⲱⲧⲉ	ⲃⲉⲧ-, ⲃⲟ(ⲟ)ⲧ-		ⲃⲏⲧ†	to make disgusting, loathsome (ⲙ̄ⲙⲟ⸗) (vt)
ⲃⲱⲱⲛ				bad, evil (adj)
ⲃⲱⲱⲣⲉ	ⲃⲉⲉⲣⲉ-	ⲃⲟⲟⲣ⸗	ⲃⲟⲟⲣⲉ†	to push, drive (ⲙ̄ⲙⲟ⸗) (vt)
				(+ ⲉⲃⲟⲗ) to push out, protrude (vi)

Γ ΓΆΜΜΑ

ⲅⲁⲣ	for (postpositive) (conj)
ⲅⲉⲛⲉⲁ	generation (nf)
ⲅⲉ́ⲛⲟⲓⲧⲟ	may it happen (neg ⲙⲏ́ ⲅⲉ́ⲛⲟⲓⲧⲟ) (impersonal predicate)
ⲅⲉ́ⲛⲟⲥ	kind, ancestry (nm)
ⲅⲉ́ⲉⲛⲛⲁ	Gehenna ("Valley of Hinnom," ultimately from Hebrew/Aramaic) (nf)
ⲅⲛⲱⲥⲓⲥ	knowledge, acquaintance (nf)
ⲅⲣⲁⲙⲙⲁⲧⲉⲩ́ⲥ	scholar, scribe (nm)
ⲅⲣⲁⲫⲏ (pl ⲅⲣⲁⲫⲟⲟⲩⲉ)	writing, scripture (nf)
ⲅⲩⲙⲛⲁⲍⲉ, ⲕⲩⲙⲛⲁⲍⲉ	to train (ⲙ̄ⲙⲟ⸗) (vt)

Δ ΔΆΛΔΑ

ⲇⲁⲓⲙⲟ́ⲛⲓⲟⲛ, ⲇⲁⲓ́ⲙⲱⲛ	supernatural being, daemon (nm)
ⲇⲉ	now, so, yet (postpositive) (conj)
ⲇⲓⲁ́ⲃⲟⲗⲟⲥ	slanderer (nm)
ⲇⲓⲁⲑⲏ́ⲕⲏ	covenant (nf)
ⲇⲓⲁⲕⲟⲛⲉⲓ	to serve (ⲙ̄ⲙⲟ⸗) (vt)
ⲇⲓⲁⲕⲟⲛⲓ́ⲁ	service (nf)
ⲇⲓⲁ-ⲧⲟⲩ́ⲧⲟ	because of this, therefore
ⲇⲓⲁ́ⲯⲁⲗⲙⲁ	(musical) interlude (nm)
ⲇⲓ́ⲕⲁⲓⲟⲥ	just, right (adj)
ⲇⲓⲕⲁⲓⲟⲥⲩ́ⲛⲏ	justice, rightness (nf)
ⲇⲓ́ⲥⲕⲟⲥ	dish, disk (nm)
ⲇⲣⲁ́ⲕⲱⲛ	dragon, serpent (nm)
ⲇⲩ́ⲛⲁⲙⲓⲥ	power, act of power (nf)
ⲇⲱ́ⲣⲟⲛ	gift (nm)

ⲉ   ⲉⲓ

ⲉ-		ⲉⲣⲟ=	to, for (prep)
ⲉⲃⲟⲗ ⲉ-			out to
ⲉϩⲟⲩⲛ ⲉ-			into
ⲉϩⲣⲁⲓ̈ ⲉ-			up/down to
ⲉⲡⲉⲥⲏⲧ ⲉ-			down to
ⲉⲡⲁϩⲟⲩ ⲉ-			back to
ⲉⲑⲏ ⲉ-			forward to
ϣⲁϩⲟⲩⲛ ⲉ-			until
ⲉⲃⲓⲏⲛ			miserable, pitiful (adj)
ⲉⲃⲓⲱ	ⲉⲃⲓⲉ-		honey (nm)
ⲉⲃⲟⲧ (pl ⲉⲃⲁⲧⲉ, ⲉⲃⲉⲧⲉ)			month (nm)
ⲉⲃⲣⲏϭⲉ			lightning (nf)
ⲉⲓ		ⲛⲏⲩ†	(impv ⲁⲙⲟⲩ [msg], ⲁⲙⲏ [fsg], ⲁⲙⲏⲉⲓⲧⲛ̄ [pl]) to come (vi)
			to be coming (vs, exclusively with Present)
ⲉⲓ ⲛ̄ⲥⲁ-			to come after, come to get
ⲉⲓⲁ	ⲉⲓⲉⲣ-	ⲉⲓⲁ(ⲁ)ⲧ=	eye (usually in compounds) (nf)
ⲉⲓⲃⲉ		ⲟⲃⲉ†	to become/be thirsty (vi/vs)
ⲉⲓⲇⲱⲗⲟⲛ			image (deity) (nm)
ⲉⲓⲉ			then (with if . . . then sentences) (conj)
ⲉⲓ(ⲉⲓ)ⲃ (pl ⲉⲓⲉⲃⲏ)			hoof, claw, sting (nm)
(ⲉ)ⲓⲉⲣⲟ (pl [ⲉ]ⲓⲉⲣⲱⲟⲩ)			river (nm)
ⲉⲓⲕⲏ			without cause, pointlessly (adv)
ⲉⲓⲙⲉ			to understand (ⲉ-); to know, realize (that: ϫⲉ) (vt)
ⲉⲓⲙⲏⲧⲓ(ⲉ)ⲓ			if not, unless, except (conj)
ⲉⲓⲛⲉ	ⲛ̄-	ⲛ̄ⲧ=	(impv ⲁⲛ[ⲉ]ⲓⲛⲉ, ⲁⲛⲓ-, ⲁⲛⲓ=) to bring (ⲙ̄ⲙⲟ=) (vt)
			reception (nm)
ⲉⲓⲛⲉ ⲉⲃⲟⲗ			to bring out, publish
ⲉⲓⲛⲉ			to resemble (ⲙ̄ⲙⲟ=) (vt)
			resemblance (nm)
ⲉⲓⲟⲟⲣ(ⲉ)			canal (nm)
ⲉⲓⲟⲡⲉ			craft, trade (nf)
ⲉⲓⲣⲉ	ⲣ̄-[1], ⲉⲣ-	ⲁⲁ=	ⲟ†	(impv ⲁⲣⲓⲡⲉ, ⲁⲣⲓ-, ⲁⲣⲓ=) to do, make (ⲙ̄ⲙⲟ=) (vt)
			to be (ⲛ̄-) (vs)
			doing, making (nm)
(ⲉ)ⲓⲣⲏⲛⲏ			peace (nf)
ⲉⲓⲥ-(ϩⲏ[ⲏ]ⲧⲉ)			look! see! (interj)
ⲉⲓⲧⲉ			either, or (conj)

---

1. ⲣ̄- is joined with many nouns to form compound verbs with the sense of "to do _" or "to become _" (with the stative form meaning "to be _").

(ⲉ)ⲓⲧⲛ̄				ground, dirt (nm)
ⲉⲡⲓⲧⲛ̄				down (adv)
ⲉⲓⲱ (pl ⲉⲟⲟⲩ)				donkey (nm)
ⲉⲓⲱ	ⲉⲓⲁ-	ⲉⲓⲁⲁ⸗	ⲉⲓⲏ†	(± ⲉⲃⲟⲗ) to wash (ⲙ̄ⲙⲟ⸗) (vt)
ⲉⲓⲱⲧ (pl ⲉⲓⲟⲧⲉ)	ⲉⲓⲧ-			father; pl: parents, ancestors (nm)
ⲉⲓⲱⲧ				barley (nm)
ⲉⲓϣⲉ	ⲉϣⲧ̄-, ⲁϣⲧ̄-	ⲁϣ(ⲧ)⸗	ⲁϣⲉ†	to hang up, suspend (vt)
(ⲉ)ⲕⲓⲃⲉ				nipple, breast (nf)
ⲉⲕⲕⲗⲏⲥⲓ́ⲁ				assembly (nf)
ⲉⲗⲁ́ⲭⲓⲥⲧⲟⲥ				least, insignificant (adj)
ⲉⲗⲉⲏⲙⲟⲥⲩ́ⲛⲏ				alms, charitable giving (nf)
ⲉⲗⲟⲟⲗⲉ				grape (nm)
ⲃⲱ ⲛ̄-ⲉⲗⲟⲟⲗⲉ				grapevine (nf)
ⲙⲁ ⲛ̄-ⲉⲗⲟⲟⲗⲉ				vineyard (nm)
ⲉⲙⲁⲧⲉ, ⲙ̄ⲙⲁⲧⲉ				very much, greatly (adv)
ⲉⲙⲟⲩ (pl ⲉⲙⲟⲟⲩⲉ)				cat (nmf)
ⲉⲛⲉ				(whether)? (inter part)
ⲉⲛⲉϩ				age; eternity; frequently as adv: ever (neg: never) (nm)
ϣⲁ-(ⲛⲓ)ⲉⲛⲉϩ				forever
ⲉ́ⲛⲟⲭⲟⲥ				liable, guilty, deserving (adj)
ⲉⲛⲧⲟⲗⲏ́				command (nf)
ⲉ́ⲝⲉⲥⲧⲓ				it's authorized (neg ⲟⲩⲕ-ⲉ́ⲝⲉⲥⲧⲓ) (impersonal predicate)
ⲉ́ⲝⲟⲇⲟⲥ				going out, way out (nf)
ⲉⲝⲟⲩⲥⲓ́ⲁ				authority (nf)
ⲉⲟⲟⲩ				glory (nm)
ⲉⲡⲉⲓ́				because, since (conj)
ⲉⲡⲉⲓⲃⲟⲩⲗⲏ				plot (nf)
ⲉⲡⲉⲓⲇⲏ				since, when (conj)
ⲉⲡⲉⲓⲇⲏⲡⲉⲣ				inasmuch as, since (conj)
ⲉⲡ(ⲉ)ⲓⲑⲩⲙ(ⲉ)ⲓ				to desire (ⲉ-) (vt)
ⲉⲡⲓ́ⲥⲕⲟⲡⲟⲥ				overseer, supervisor (nm)
ⲉⲡⲓⲥⲧⲏ́ⲙⲱⲛ				understanding (adj)
ⲉⲡⲓⲥⲧⲟⲗⲏ́ (pl ⲉⲡⲓⲥⲧⲟⲗⲟⲟⲩⲉ)				letter (nf)
ⲉⲡⲓⲧⲓⲙⲁ				to warn, rebuke (ⲛⲁ⸗) (vt)
ⲉⲣⲅⲟⲇⲓⲱ́ⲕⲧⲏⲥ				taskmaster, slave-driver (nm)
ⲉⲣⲏ́ⲙⲟⲥ				desert (nf)
ⲉⲣⲏⲧ				to promise (vt)
(pl ⲉⲣⲁⲧⲉ)				promise (nm)
ⲉⲣⲏⲩ				companion; each other (nmf)
ⲉⲣⲱⲧⲉ				milk (nmf)
ⲉⲥⲏⲧ				bottom, ground (nm)
ⲉⲡⲉⲥⲏⲧ				down (adv)

ϩⲁⲡⲉⲥⲏⲧ				under (adv)
ϩⲓⲡⲉⲥⲏⲧ				below (adv)
ⲉⲥⲟⲟⲩ				sheep (nm; ⲉⲥⲱ [f])
ⲉⲧ-, ⲉⲧⲉ-				who, which (rel converter/pron)
ⲉ́ⲧⲓ				still, yet (adv)
ⲉⲩⲁⲅⲅⲉⲗⲓⲍⲉ				to tell a good message (vi)
ⲉⲩⲁⲅⲅⲉ́ⲗⲓⲟⲛ				good message (nm)
ⲉⲩ́ⲅⲉ				well, good (adv)
ⲉⲩⲫⲣⲁⲛⲉ				to make glad, cheer (vt)
				to be glad, rejoice, celebrate (vi)
ⲉⲩⲭⲁⲣⲓⲥⲧ(ⲉ)ⲓ́ⲁ				thankfulness, thanksgiving (nf)
ⲉϣϫⲉ				(as) if (conj)

Ⲍ ⲌⲎⲦⲀ

ⲍⲓⲍⲁ́ⲛⲓⲟⲛ	darnel (a weed resembling wheat) (nm)
ⲍⲱ́ⲟⲛ	living thing, creature (nm)

Ⲏ ϨⲎⲦⲀ

ⲏ	or, than (conj)
ⲏ(ⲉ)ⲓ	house (nm)
ⲏⲡⲉ	number (nf)
ⲏⲣⲡ̄	wine (nm)

Ⲑ ⲐⲎⲦⲀ

ⲑⲁⲃ				leaven (nm)
ⲑⲃ̄ⲃⲓⲟ	ⲑⲃ̄ⲃⲓⲉ-	ⲑⲃ̄ⲃⲓⲟ⸗	ⲑⲃ̄ⲃⲓⲏⲩ†	to humble, humiliate (ⲙ̄ⲙⲟ⸗) (vt)
				to become humble (vi/vr)
				humility (often + ⲛ̄-ϩⲏⲧ), humiliation (nm)
ⲑⲉⲣⲁⲡⲉⲩⲉ				to heal (ⲙ̄ⲙⲟ⸗) (vt)
ⲑⲉⲱ́ⲣⲏⲙⲁ				vision (nm)
ⲑⲉⲱⲣⲓ́ⲁ				viewing (nf)
ⲑⲏⲣⲓ́ⲟⲛ				beast, wild animal (nm)
ⲑⲗⲓⲃⲉ				to afflict (ⲙ̄ⲙⲟ⸗) (vt)
ⲑⲗⲓ́ⲯⲓⲥ				affliction (nf)
ⲑⲗⲟ			ⲑⲗⲟ⸗	to cause to fly, chase away (vt)
ⲑⲙ̄ⲕⲟ	ⲑⲙ̄ⲕⲉ-	ⲑⲙ̄ⲕⲟ⸗	ⲑⲙ̄ⲕⲏⲩ†	to afflict (ⲙ̄ⲙⲟ⸗) (vt)
				(causative of ⲙ̄ⲕⲁϩ)
				affliction (nm)

ⲑⲣόⲛⲟⲥ	throne (nm)
ⲑⲩⲣⲱⲛ	large shield ("door") (nf)
ⲑⲩⲥίⲁ	offering, sacrifice (nf)
ⲑⲩⲥⲓⲁⲥⲧήⲣⲓⲟⲛ	altar (nm)

ⲓ   ⲓⲱⲧⲁ

ἴⲁⲥⲡⲓⲥ	jasper (nf)

ⲕ   ⲕάⲡⲡⲁ

ⲕⲁⲑέⲇⲣⲁ	seat (nf)
ⲕⲁⲑⲓⲥⲧⲁ	to seat, install (ⲙ̄ⲙⲟ⸗; as: ⲛ̄-) (vt)
ⲕⲁⲓ	and, even, also (conj)
ⲕⲁⲕⲉ	darkness (nm)
ⲣ̄-ⲕⲁⲕⲉ	(ⲟ† ⲛ̄-) to become/be dark
ⲕⲁⲕίⲁ	bad(ness) (nf)
ⲕⲁⲕⲟⲥ	bad (adj)
ⲕⲁⲕⲱⲥ	badly (adv)
ⲕⲁⲗⲱⲥ	well (adv)
ⲕⲁⲙⲉ́ (f ⲕⲁⲙⲏ)	black (adj)
ⲕⲁⲡⲛⲟⲥ	smoke (nm)
ⲕⲁⲣⲡⲟⲥ	fruit, crop, profit (nm)
ⲧⲁ(ⲟ)ⲩⲉ-ⲕⲁⲣⲡⲟⲥ	to produce fruit
ⲕⲁⲥⲕⲥ̄	to whisper (vi)
	whisper (nm)
ⲕⲁⲧⲁ- ⲕⲁⲧⲁⲣⲟ⸗	according to (prep)
ⲕⲁⲧⲁⲕⲣⲓⲛⲉ	to condemn, sentence (ⲙ̄ⲙⲟ⸗) (vt)
ⲕⲁⲧⲁⲗⲩ	to destroy, abolish (ⲙ̄ⲙⲟ⸗) (vt)
ⲕⲁⲧⲁⲫⲣⲟⲛⲉⲓ	to despise, disregard (ⲙ̄ⲙⲟ⸗) (vt)
ⲕⲁⲩ́ⲙⲁ	burning, heat (nm)
ⲕⲁϩ	land, earth, ground (nm)
(ⲕ)ⲁϩⲏⲩ	(cf. ⲕⲱⲕ ⲁϩⲏⲩ)
ⲕⲁϩⲕⲥ̄ ⲕⲉϩⲕⲉϩ- ⲕⲉϩⲕⲱϩ⸗ ⲕⲉϩⲕⲱϩ†	to smooth, carve out; to cause to heal (ⲙ̄ⲙⲟ⸗) (vt)
	to heal (vi)
ⲕⲃⲁ	vengeance, revenge (nm)
ⲕⲃⲁ	forced labor, compulsion (nm)
ⲕέⲇⲣⲟⲥ	cedar (nf)
ⲕⲉⲣⲁⲙⲉⲩ́ⲥ	potter (nm)
ⲕⲉⲧ, ϭⲉ (pl ⲕⲟⲟⲩⲉ) ⲕⲉ-	(an)other; also, even (nm; ⲕⲉⲧⲉ [f])
ⲕⲏⲣⲩⲥⲥⲉ	to proclaim (ⲙ̄ⲙⲟ⸗) (vt)

ⲕⲓⲑⲁ́ⲣⲁ				harp (nf)
ⲕⲓⲙ	ⲕⲉⲙⲧ̄-	ⲕⲉⲙⲧ⸗		to touch (ⲉ-; with: ⲉ-); to move, shift, stir (ⲙ̄ⲙⲟ⸗, ⲉ-) (vt)
				to move, stir, be moved (vi)
ⲕⲗⲏⲣⲟⲛⲟⲙⲉⲓ				to inherit (ⲙ̄ⲙⲟ⸗) (vt)
ⲕⲗⲏⲣⲟⲛⲟⲙⲓ́ⲁ				inheritance (nf)
ⲕⲗⲏⲣⲟⲛⲟ́ⲙⲟⲥ				heir (nm)
ⲕⲗⲏ́ⲣⲟⲥ				allotment, lot, share (nm)
ⲕⲗⲟⲙ				crown, wreath (nm)
ϯ-ⲕⲗⲟⲙ ⲉϫⲛ̄-				to crown
ϫⲓ-ⲕⲗⲟⲙ				to receive a crown (> to become a martyr)
ⲕⲗⲟⲟⲗⲉ				cloud (nf)
ⲕⲗ̄ϫⲉ				corner (nf)
ⲕⲙⲟⲙ			ⲕⲏⲙ†	to become/be black (vi/vs)
ⲕⲙ̄ⲧⲟ				shaking, earthquake (nm)
ⲕⲛ̄ⲛⲉ́				to be fat, sweet (vi)
ⲕⲛ̄ⲧⲉ́				fig (nm)
ⲃⲱ ⲛ̄-ⲕⲛ̄ⲧⲉ́				fig tree (nf)
ⲕⲟⲓⲛⲟⲛⲓ́ⲁ				community, commonness (nf)
ⲕⲟⲓⲛⲱⲛⲟ́ⲥ				companion, partner (nmf)
ⲕⲟⲛⲇⲣⲁ́ⲛⲧⲏⲥ				quarter (a small bronze coin, worth 1/64th of a *denarius*) (ultimately from Latin *quadrans*) (nm)
ⲕⲟⲟϩ, ⲕⲱϩ				corner, angle, point (nm)
ⲕⲟ́ⲥⲙⲟⲥ				world, universe (nm)
ⲕⲟⲧ				wheel (nm)
ⲕⲟⲧⲥ̄				turning, circuit; trick (nf)
ⲕⲟⲩⲓ̈	ⲕⲟⲩ-			small, little; also of quantity: a little; with pl: a few (usually before noun or rarely after without ⲛ̄-) (adj)
ⲕⲟⲩⲛ(ⲧ)⸗, ⲕⲟⲩⲟⲩⲛ⸗				bosom, lap (of); embrace (n)
ⲕⲣⲓⲛⲉ				to judge (ⲙ̄ⲙⲟ⸗) (vt)
ⲕⲣⲓ́ⲛⲟⲛ				lily (nm)
ⲕⲣⲓ́ⲥⲓⲥ				judgment (nf)
ⲕⲣⲙ̄ⲣⲙ̄				to grumble (vi)
				grumbling (nm)
ⲕⲣⲟ (pl ⲕⲣⲱⲟⲩ)				shore, bank, margin (of land) (nm)
ⲕⲣⲟϥ				deception (nm)
ⲕⲣⲩ́ⲥⲧⲁⲗⲟⲥ				crystal (nm)
ⲕⲧⲟ	ⲕⲧⲉ-	ⲕⲧⲟ⸗	ⲕⲧⲏⲩ†	to turn (originally [ⲧ]ⲕⲧⲟ meant to cause to turn, but has become =ⲕⲱⲧⲉ) (ⲙ̄ⲙⲟ⸗) (vt/vr)
				[causative of ⲕⲱⲧⲉ]
				turning, return (nm)

ⲕⲩⲣⲓⲁⲕⲏ				"(the one) belonging to (the) Master," Sunday (nf)
ⲕⲱ	ⲕⲁ-	ⲕⲁⲁ⸗	ⲕⲏ†	1. to put, place, set (ⲙ̄ⲙⲟ⸗); 2. to let, allow (someone: ⲙ̄ⲙⲟ⸗) to do (something: ⲉ- + inf); 3. to leave (ⲙ̄ⲙⲟ⸗; behind: ⲛ̄ⲥⲁ-) (vt)
				to be situated, lying; to be, exist (vs)
ⲕⲱ ⲉⲃⲟⲗ				to forgive (someone: ⲛⲁ⸗; something: ⲙ̄ⲙⲟ⸗); to release; to abandon
ⲕⲁ-ⲃⲟⲗ				to vomit (ⲙ̄ⲙⲟ⸗)
ⲕⲱⲕ	ⲕⲉⲕ-	ⲕⲟⲕ⸗	ⲕⲏⲕ†	(± ⲉⲃⲟⲗ) to strip, make bare (ⲙ̄ⲙⲟ⸗) (vt)
				to strip, become bare (vi)
				stripping, bareness (nm)
ⲕⲱⲕ ⲁϩⲏⲩ				to strip naked (also reanalyzed as ⲕⲱ ⲕⲁϩⲏⲩ)
				nakedness (nm)
ⲕⲱⲗⲩ				to restrain, prevent (ⲙ̄ⲙⲟ⸗) (vt)
ⲕⲱⲗϫ̄	ⲕⲗ̄ϫ-, ϭⲗ̄ϫ-	ⲕⲟⲗϫ⸗	ⲕⲟⲗϫ̄†	to bend (ⲙ̄ⲙⲟ⸗) (vt)
				to bow (vr)
				to bend, become bent (vi)
ⲕⲱⲙϣ̄	ⲕⲙ̄ϣ-	ⲕⲟⲙϣ⸗		to mock (ⲛ̄ⲥⲁ-) (vt)
				mockery (nm)
ⲕⲱⲛⲥ̄	ⲕⲉⲛⲥ-	ⲕⲟⲛⲥ⸗	ⲕⲟⲛⲥ̄†	to slay, pierce (ⲙ̄ⲙⲟ⸗) (vt)
				slaughter (nm)
ⲕⲱⲧ	ⲕⲉⲧ-	ⲕⲟⲧ⸗	ⲕⲏⲧ†	to build (up) (ⲙ̄ⲙⲟ⸗) (vt)
				to become/be built up (vi/vs)
				building (the act or the object) (nm)
ⲕⲱⲧⲉ	ⲕⲉⲧ-	ⲕⲟⲧ⸗	ⲕⲏⲧ†	to turn (ⲙ̄ⲙⲟ⸗; away: ⲉⲃⲟⲗ; back: ⲉⲡⲁϩⲟⲩ) (vt)
				1. to return, go back (to: ⲉⲡⲁϩⲟⲩ ⲉ-, ⲉⲃⲟⲗ ⲉ-, ⲉⲃⲟⲗ ϣⲁ-, ⲉϩⲟⲩⲛ ⲉ-, ⲉϩⲣⲁⲓ̈ ⲉ-); 2. to repeat an action, usually coordinated, as in ⲁϥⲕⲟⲧϥ̄ ⲁϥⲥϩⲁⲓ̈ (he wrote again) or with ⲉ- + inf, as in ⲁϥⲕⲟⲧϥ̄ ⲉ-ⲥϩⲁⲓ̈ (he wrote again) (vr)
				to rotate, circulate; to surround, go around (ⲉ-); to consort (with: ⲙⲛ̄-) (vi)
				to be turned, turning, circulating (vs)
				neighborhood, surroundings (nm)
ⲕⲱⲧϥ̄	ⲕⲉⲧϥ̄-	ⲕⲟⲧϥ⸗	ⲕⲟⲧϥ̄†	to collect, gather (ⲙ̄ⲙⲟ⸗) (vt)
ⲕⲱⲱⲃⲉ	ⲕⲉⲉⲃⲉ-	ⲕⲟⲟⲃ⸗		to force, compel (ⲙ̄ⲙⲟ⸗) (vt)
ⲕⲱⲱⲣⲉ	ⲕⲉ(ⲉ)ⲣⲉ-	ⲕⲟⲟⲣⲉ⸗		to cut down (ⲙ̄ⲙⲟ⸗) (vt)
				to be cut down (vi)
ⲕⲱϩ			ⲕⲏϩ†	to become/be zealous, jealous (vi/vs)
				zeal, jealousy (nm)
ⲕⲱϩⲧ̄				fire (nm)

ⲗ   ⲗⲁⲩ́ⲇⲁ

ⲗⲁⲁⲩ			anyone, anything (neg: nothing); as adj: any (indef pron)
ⲗⲁⲕⲙ̄			piece (nf)
ⲗⲁⲙⲡⲁ́ⲥ			torch, lamp (nf)
ⲗⲁⲟⲥ			people (nm)
ⲗⲁⲥ			tongue; language (nm)
ⲗⲉ́ⲥⲭⲏ			lounge; gossip (nf)
ⲗⲏⲥⲧⲏ́ⲥ			bandit, robber (nm)
ⲗⲓⲃⲉ	ⲗⲉⲃⲧ⸗	ⲗⲟⲃⲉ†	(cp ⲗⲁⲃ-) to be crazy (vi)
ⲗⲟ			(impv ⲁⲗⲟⲕ [msg], ⲁⲗⲟ [fsg], ⲁⲗⲱⲧⲛ̄ [pl]) (± ⲙ̄ⲙⲁⲩ) 1. to quit, cease, stop (doing: circum); 2. to leave, depart (from: ⲙ̄ⲙⲟ⸗, ϩⲛ̄-, ⲉⲃⲟⲗ ϩⲛ̄-) (vi)
ⲗⲟ́ⲅⲟⲥ			word (nm)
ⲗⲟ(ⲉ)ⲓϩⲉ			mire, filth (nmf)
ⲗⲟⲓⲙⲟ́ⲥ			troublesome; diseased (adj)
ⲗⲩⲭⲛⲓ́ⲁ			lampstand (nf)
ⲗⲱϫϩ̄	ⲗⲉϫϩ̄-	ⲗⲟϫϩ⸗	ⲗⲟϫϩ̄†	to crush (ⲙ̄ⲙⲟ⸗); to lick / to be crushed (vi) / crushing (nm)

ⲙ   ⲙⲏ

ⲙⲁ			place (nm)
ⲙ̄-ⲡⲉⲓ̈ⲙⲁ			here, in this place
ⲙⲁ	ⲙⲁ-	ⲙⲁⲧ⸗, ⲙⲏⲉⲓ⸗	(used as optional impv of ϯ)
ⲙⲁⲁⲃ (f ⲙⲁⲁⲃⲉ)	ⲙⲁⲃ-		thirty (num)
ⲙⲁⲁⲩ			mother (nf)
ⲙⲁⲁϫⲉ			ear (nm)
ⲙⲁⲁϫⲉ			bushel, grain measure (nf)
ⲙⲁⲉⲓⲛ			sign (nm)
ⲙⲁⲑⲏⲧⲏ́ⲥ			student, learner (nm)
ⲙⲁⲕⲁ́ⲣⲓⲟⲥ			fortunate (adj)
ⲙⲁ́ⲗⲗⲟⲛ			more (adv)
ⲙⲁⲙⲱⲛⲁ́ⲥ			Wealth (personified) (ultimately from Aramaic) (nm)
ⲙⲁⲛⲓ́ⲁ			insanity, craziness (nf)
ⲙⲁ́ⲛⲛⲁ			manna (ultimately from Hebrew for "what?") (nm)
ⲙⲁⲥ(ⲉ)			calf, young animal (nm)
ⲙⲁ́ⲥⲧⲓⲝ			whip, scourge (nf)

SAHIDIC-ENGLISH LEXICON

ⲙⲁⲧⲟⲓ̈			soldier (nm)
ⲙⲁⲩⲁⲁ(ⲧ)⸗			only, alone, -self (intensive pron/inflected modifier)
ⲙⲁϣⲉ			balance, scales (nf)
ⲙⲁϩⲉ			cubit (length of a forearm) (nm)
ⲙⲉ	ⲙⲉⲣⲉ-[2]	ⲙⲉⲣⲓⲧ⸗	(cp ⲙⲁⲓ̈-) to love (ⲙ̄ⲙⲟ⸗) (vt)
			love (nm)
ⲙⲉ(ⲉ)			truth; as adj: true (nf)
ⲙⲛ̄ⲧⲙⲉ́			truthfulness (nf)
ⲛⲁⲙⲉ́			truly (adv)
ϩⲛ̄-ⲟⲩⲙⲉ			truly
ⲙⲉⲉⲣⲉ			noon, midday (nf)
ⲙⲉⲉⲩⲉ			to think (that: ϫⲉ; about: ⲉ-); to consider (+ ⲉⲃⲟⲗ) (vi)
			thought, mind (nm)
ⲣ̄-ⲡ(⸗)ⲙⲉⲉⲩⲉ			to remember (ⲛ̄-)
ⲙⲉⲗⲉⲧⲁ			to meditate, study (ⲙ̄ⲙⲟ⸗) (vt)
ⲙⲉ́ⲗⲟⲥ			member, part (nm)
ⲙⲉⲛ			now, indeed (postpositive) (conj)
ⲙⲉⲣⲓⲧ (pl ⲙⲉⲣⲁⲧⲉ)			(be)loved (usually before noun) (adj)
ⲙⲉ́ⲣⲟⲥ			part (nm)
ⲙⲉⲥⲓⲟ		ⲙⲉⲥⲓⲟ⸗	to midwife (ⲙ̄ⲙⲟ⸗) (vt)
ⲙⲉⲥⲓⲱ, ⲙⲉⲥ(ⲉ)ⲓⲟ			midwife (nf)
ⲙⲉⲥⲥⲓ̈ⲁⲥ			"anointed one" (title, ultimately from Aramaic) (nm)
ⲙⲉⲥⲧⲉ			hated one (nm; ⲙⲉⲥⲧⲏ [f])
ⲙⲉⲥⲧϩ̄ⲧ, ⲙⲉⲥⲧⲛ̄ϩⲧ			chest, torso (nf)
ⲙⲉⲧⲁⲛⲟⲉⲓ			to change one's thinking (vi)
ⲙⲉⲧⲁ́ⲛⲟⲓⲁ			change of thinking (nf)
ⲙⲉⲧⲣⲏⲧⲏ́ⲥ			liquid measure (about 40 liters/9 gallons) (nm)
ⲙⲉϣⲉ-		ⲙⲉϣⲁ⸗	not know (verboid)
ⲙⲉϣⲁⲕ			maybe, perhaps ("you don't know")
ⲙⲏ			not; isn't? (introducing rhetorical question) (neg part)
ⲙⲏⲏϣⲉ			crowd, multitude (nm)
ⲙⲏⲛⲉ			period of a day, only in: (n)
ⲙ̄-ⲙⲏⲛⲉ			daily
ⲙⲏ́ⲡⲟⲧⲉ			that ... not (+ conjunctive) (neg part)
ⲙⲏⲧ (f ⲙⲏⲧⲉ)	ⲙⲛ̄ⲧ-		ten (num)
ⲙⲏⲧⲉ			middle, midst (nf)
(ϩ)ⲛ̄-ⲧⲙⲏⲧⲉ ⲛ̄-			in the middle/midst of

---

2. ⲙⲉⲣⲉ- can be compounded with another inf.

ⲘⲎⲦⲈⲒ   not; isn't? (introducing rhetorical question, somewhat more emphatic than ⲘⲎ) (neg part)

ⲘⲒⲚⲈ   kind, sort, type (nf)
    ⲀϢ Ⲙ̄-ⲘⲒⲚⲈ   (of) what sort?
    Ⲛ̄-ⲦⲈⲒⲘⲒⲚⲈ   of this sort, such

ⲘⲒⲤⲈ   ⲘⲈⲤ(Ⲧ̄)-   ⲘⲀⲤⲦ⸗   ⲘⲞⲤⲈ†   (cp ⲘⲀⲤ-, ⲘⲈⲤ-) to bear, birth (a child: Ⲙ̄ⲘⲞ⸗) (vt)
    to be born (vs)
    giving birth; offspring, progeny, one born (nm)

ⲘⲒϢⲈ   to fight, battle (with, against: ⲘⲚ̄-, ⲞⲨⲂⲈ-, Ⲉ-) (vi)
    fight, battle (nm)

Ⲙ̄ⲔⲀϨ   ⲘⲞⲔϨ̄†   to become/be painful, difficult (vi/vs)
    to be difficult, used impersonally: ⲤⲘⲞⲔϨ̄ (it's difficult; to do: Ⲉ-, Ⲉ-ⲦⲢⲈ-) (vs)
    (pl ⲘⲔⲞⲞϨ)   pain, difficulty, grief (nm)

Ⲙ̄ⲘⲀⲦⲈ, ⲈⲘⲀⲦⲈ   very much, greatly; only, exclusively (adv)

Ⲙ̄ⲘⲀⲨ   there (adv)
    ⲈⲦ-Ⲙ̄ⲘⲀⲨ   who's/which's there (> further dem: that/those)

Ⲙ̄ⲘⲀϨ-   in the presence of (a deity) (prep)

Ⲙ̄ⲘⲒⲚ Ⲙ̄ⲘⲞ⸗   own, -self (intensive pron/inflected modifier)

(Ⲙ̄)ⲘⲚ̄-   there's no/there're no (neg existential)

Ⲙ̄ⲘⲞⲚ   no, not (neg part)

ⲘⲚ̄-, ⲚⲘ̄-   ⲚⲘ̄ⲘⲀ⸗   with; and (prep)

ⲘⲚ̄Ⲧ-   matter of (-ness, -hood); language of (abstract prefix f)

ⲘⲚ̄ⲦⲈ-   ⲘⲚ̄ⲦⲀ⸗   don't/doesn't have (neg existential verboid)

ⲘⲚ̄ⲦⲢⲈ́ (pl ⲘⲚ̄ⲦⲢⲈⲈⲨ)   witness, testimony (nm)
    ⲘⲚ̄ⲦⲘⲚ̄ⲦⲢⲈ́   testimony (nf)
    Ⲣ̄-ⲘⲚ̄ⲦⲢⲈ́   to testify, bear witness (to, about: Ⲙ̄ⲘⲞ⸗, ⲈⲦⲂⲈ-, ⲈϪⲚ̄-, Ⲉ-, ϨⲀ-, ⲘⲚ̄-)

ⲘⲞⲈⲒⲦ   road, path (nm)
    ϪⲒ-ⲘⲞⲈⲒⲦ   to guide, lead (before: ϨⲎⲦ⸗)

ⲘⲞⲔⲘⲈⲔ   ⲘⲈⲔⲘⲞⲨⲔ⸗   to consider, ponder, meditate (vi/vr)
    consideration (nm)

ⲘⲞⲚⲀⲬⲞⲤ   solitary (adj)

ⲘⲞⲞⲚⲈ   ⲘⲈⲚⲈ-   ⲘⲀⲚⲞⲨ(ⲞⲨ)⸗   (cp ⲘⲀⲚ[Ⲉ]-) to tend, herd (Ⲙ̄ⲘⲞ⸗) (vt)

ⲘⲞⲞⲨ (pl ⲘⲞⲨⲈⲒⲞⲞⲨⲈ)   ⲘⲞⲨ-   water (nm)

ⲘⲞⲞϢⲈ   to walk, journey (vi)
    walk, journey (nm)

ⲘⲞⲢⲤ̄   binding (nf)

ⲙⲟⲥⲧⲉ	ⲙⲉⲥⲧⲉ-	ⲙⲉⲥⲧⲱ⸗		(cp ⲙⲁⲥⲧ̄-) to hate (ⲙ̄ⲙⲟ⸗) (vt)
				hate, hatred; hated thing (nm)
ⲙⲟⲩ			ⲙⲟⲟⲩⲧ†	to die, become/be dead (of, from: ⲉⲧⲃⲉ-, ϩⲁ-) (vi/vs)
				death, manner of death (nm)
ⲙⲟⲩ(ⲉ)ⲓ				lion(ess) (nmf)
ⲙⲟⲩⲕϩ	ⲙⲉⲕϩ-	ⲙⲟⲕϩ⸗		to afflict, oppress (ⲙ̄ⲙⲟ⸗) (vt)
ⲙⲟⲩⲗϩ	ⲙⲉⲗϩ-	ⲙⲟⲗϩ⸗	ⲙⲟⲗϩ†	to make salt(y) (ⲙ̄ⲙⲟ⸗) (vt)
				to become/be salty (vi/vs)
ⲙⲟⲩⲗϩ				wax (nm)
ⲙⲟⲩⲛ			ⲙⲏⲛ†	(± ⲉⲃⲟⲗ) to remain, last, endure; (+ ⲉⲃⲟⲗ) to continue (doing: circum) (vi)
				to be enduring, lasting, continual (vs)
				perseverance, continuing (nm)
ϩⲛ̄-ⲟⲩⲙⲟⲩⲛ ⲉⲃⲟⲗ				continuously
ⲙⲟⲩ-ⲛ̄-ⲥⲗϩⲟ				lukewarm water (nm)
ⲙⲟⲩⲟⲩⲧ	ⲙⲉⲩⲧ-, ⲙⲟⲩⲧ-	ⲙⲟⲟⲩⲧ⸗		to kill (ⲙ̄ⲙⲟ⸗) (vt)
ⲙⲟⲩⲣ	ⲙⲉⲣ-, ⲙⲣ̄-	ⲙⲟⲣ⸗	ⲙⲏⲣ†	(cp ⲙⲁⲣ-) to bind, tie (someone: ⲙ̄ⲙⲟ⸗ or suffix; with: ⲙ̄ⲙⲟ⸗, ϩⲛ̄-; to: ⲉ-, ⲉϫⲛ̄-, ⲉϩⲟⲩⲛ ⲉ-) (vt)
				to be bound (vs)
				band, strap (nm)
ⲙⲟⲩⲥ				strap (nm)
ⲙⲟⲩⲧⲉ				to call, summon (ⲉ-; [by the name of]: ϫⲉ) (vt)
				call, summoning (nm)
ⲙⲟⲩϣⲧ̄	ⲙⲉϣⲧ-	ⲙⲟϣⲧ⸗	ⲙⲟϣⲧ†	(cp ⲙⲁϣⲧ̄-) to consider, examine (ⲙ̄ⲙⲟ⸗) (vt)
ⲙⲟⲩϩ	ⲙⲉϩ-	ⲙⲁϩ⸗	ⲙⲏϩ†, ⲙⲉϩ†	(± ⲉⲃⲟⲗ) to fill (something: ⲙ̄ⲙⲟ⸗ or suffix; with: ⲙ̄ⲙⲟ⸗, ϩⲛ̄-, ⲉⲃⲟⲗ ϩⲛ̄-); to fulfill (vt)
				to become filled, full (of, with: ⲙ̄ⲙⲟ⸗ [if indefinite, usually without article]); to become fulfilled (vi)
				to be full (vs)
				fullness (nm)
ⲙⲉϩ-				(ordinal number prefix)
ⲙⲟⲩϩ				to burn (with: ⲙ̄ⲙⲟ⸗) (vi)
ⲙⲟϫϩ				belt, girdle, sash (nm)
ⲙ̄ⲡⲟ, ⲉⲙⲡⲟ (f ⲛⲙⲡⲱ)				mute (adj)
ⲙ̄ⲡⲱⲣ	ⲙ̄ⲡⲣ̄-			don't (impv) (neg part)
ⲙ̄ⲡϣⲁ				to be worthy, deserving (of: ⲙ̄ⲙⲟ⸗; to do: ⲛ̄-, ⲉ- + inf) (vi)
				worth (nm)
ⲙ̄ⲣ̄ⲣⲉ				bond (nf)
ⲙ̄ⲣⲱ (pl ⲙ̄ⲣⲟⲟⲩⲉ)				harbor (nf)
ⲙ̄ⲧⲟ ⲉⲃⲟⲗ				presence (nm)
ⲙ̄-ⲡⲉⲙⲧⲟ ⲉⲃⲟⲗ ⲛ̄-				in the presence of

ⲙ̄ⲧⲟⲛ	ⲙⲟⲧⲛ̄†	to become/be at ease, at rest, relieved (vi)
		to rest (self: ⲙ̄ⲙⲟ⸗) (vr)
		to be easy, often used impersonally: ⲥⲙⲟⲧⲛ̄ (it's easy; to do: ⲉ-, ⲉ-ⲧⲣⲉ-) (vs)
		rest, relief (nm)
ⲙⲩⲥⲧⲏⲣⲓⲟⲛ		secret (nm)

Ⲛ   ⲛⲉ

ⲛ̄-	ⲙ̄ⲙⲟ⸗	in, with; as adv.: -ly; [direct object marker; equivalence marker with ⲟ†, ϣⲟⲟⲡ†, and suffix pronouns] (prep)
ⲉⲃⲟⲗ ⲛ̄-		out of, from (in)
ⲛ̄-	ⲛⲁ⸗	to, for [indirect object marker] (prep)
ⲛ̄- . . . ⲁⲛ		not (neg part)
ⲛ̄-, ⲛ̄ⲧⲉ-		of; [attribution/adjectival without article] (genitive part/prep)
ⲛ̄-, ⲛⲉ-		the (def art pl)
ⲛⲁ-		those of, those connected to (absolute rel pron pl)
ⲛⲁ		to have pity, mercy (on: ⲛⲁ⸗, ϩⲁ-); to pity (vi)
		mercy, pity, charity (nm)
ⲙⲛ̄ⲧⲛⲁ		pity, charity (nf)
ⲛⲁ-(ϩ)ⲏⲧ		merciful, compassionate (adj)
ⲛⲁ		to be going (to: ⲉ-) [Future auxiliary] (vi)
ⲛⲁⲁ-, ⲛⲁⲉ-	ⲛⲁⲁ(ⲁ)⸗	great (verboid adj)
ⲛⲁⲓ̈		these (nearer dem pron)
ϩⲓ-ⲛⲁⲓ̈		thus
ⲛⲁⲓ̈ⲁⲧ⸗		fortunate (<ⲛⲁⲁ-ⲉⲓⲁ[ⲁ]ⲧ⸗) (verboid adj)
ⲛⲁⲛⲟⲩ-, ⲛⲁⲛⲉ-	ⲛⲁⲛⲟⲩ⸗	good (verboid adj)
ⲡⲉⲧ-ⲛⲁⲛⲟⲩϥ		the one who's good, the good (one)
ⲛⲁⲣⲇⲟⲥ		(spike) nard (nf)
ⲛⲁⲩ (ⲛⲟⲩ)		time, hour (nm)
ⲧ(ⲛ̄)ⲛⲁⲩ		when?
ⲛⲁⲩ		(impv ⲁⲛⲁⲩ) to see, look (at: ⲉ-) (vt)
		sight (nm)
ⲁⲧⲛⲁⲩ ⲉⲣⲟ⸗		unseen, unseeable
ⲛⲁϣⲉ-	ⲛⲁϣⲱ⸗	numerous, many, much (verboid adj)
ⲛⲁϣⲧⲉ		protection, strength (nf)
ⲛⲁϩⲃ̄, ⲛⲁϩⲃⲉϥ		yoke (nm)
ⲛⲁϩⲗⲱϭ⸗, ⲛⲁϩⲗⲟϭ⸗		pleasant (verboid adj)
ⲛⲁϩⲧⲉ ⲛ̄ϩⲉⲧ-	ⲛ̄ϩⲟ(ⲩ)ⲧ†	to trust, rely on (ⲉ[ⲭⲛ̄]-, ϩⲛ̄-) (vt/vi)
		to be trustworthy (vs)
		trust (nm)

ⲛⲉ				are (copula pl)
ⲛⲉⲓ-				these (nearer dem pl)
ⲛⲉⲥⲃⲱⲱ⸗				intelligent (verboid adj)
ⲛⲉⲥⲉ-		ⲛⲉⲥⲱ⸗		beautiful (verboid adj)
ⲛⲉϥⲣ̄-				good, profitable (verboid adj)
ⲛⲉϩ, ⲛⲏϩ				oil (nm)
ⲛⲉϩⲡⲉ				to mourn (for: ⲉ[ϫⲛ̄]-) (vi)
				mourning (nm)
ⲛⲉϭⲱ(ⲱ)⸗				ugly (verboid adj)
ⲛⲏ				those (further dem pron pl)
ⲛⲏⲥⲟⲥ				island (nf)
ⲛⲏⲥⲧⲉⲩⲉ				to fast (vi)
ⲛⲓⲙ				every, each (after singular noun without article or ⲛ̄-) (adj)
ⲛⲓⲙ				who? (inter pron)
ⲛⲓϥⲉ		ⲛⲁϥⲧ⸗, ⲛⲉϥⲧ⸗		to blow (ⲙ̄ⲙⲟ⸗) (vt)
				to blow, breathe (vi)
				breath (nm)
ⲛ̄ⲕⲁ				thing, stuff, possession (nm)
ⲛ̄ⲕⲁ ⲛⲓⲙ				everything
ⲛ̄ⲕⲟⲧⲕ̄				to lie down, sleep (> to die) (vi)
ⲛⲟⲃⲉ				wrong, sin (nm)
ⲣ̄-ⲛⲟⲃⲉ				to do wrong, sin
ⲛⲟ(ⲉ)ⲓ				to consider, understand (ⲙ̄ⲙⲟ⸗) (vt)
ⲛⲟⲉⲓⲕ				adulterer (nm)
ⲣ̄-ⲛⲟⲉⲓⲕ				to commit adultery (with: ⲉ-, ⲙⲛ̄-)
ⲛⲟⲙⲟⲥ				law, code (nm)
ⲛⲟⲩ		ⲛⲁ†		to be going to, be about to (ⲉ- + inf) (v)
ⲛⲟⲩ⸗				mine, yours, etc. (poss pron pl)
ⲛⲟⲩⲃ				gold (nm)
ⲛⲟⲩⲛ				abyss, deep, depth (nm)
ⲛⲟⲩⲛⲉ				root (nf)
ⲛⲟⲩⲥ				mind (nm)
ⲛⲟⲩⲧⲉ (pl ⲛ̄ⲧⲏⲣ, ⲉⲛⲧⲁⲓⲣ)				god; with definite article: God (nm; ⲛ̄ⲧⲱⲣⲉ, goddess [f])
ⲛⲟⲩϥⲉ				good (adj)
ⲛⲟⲩϥⲣ̄		ⲛⲟⲩϥⲣ̄†		to become/be good (vi/vs)
ⲛⲟⲩϩ				rope (nm)
ⲛⲟⲩϩⲃ̄	ⲛⲁϩⲃ-	ⲛⲁϩⲃ⸗	ⲛⲁϩⲃ†	to yoke (ⲙ̄ⲙⲟ⸗; to: ⲉϩⲟⲩⲛ ⲉ-) (vt)
ⲛⲟⲩϩⲉ	ⲛⲉϩ-	ⲛⲁϩ⸗	ⲛⲏϩ†, ⲛⲉϩ†	(± ⲉⲃⲟⲗ) 1. to shake off, cast off (ⲙ̄ⲙⲟ⸗); 2. to separate, set apart (ⲙ̄ⲙⲟ⸗) (vt)
				to separate oneself; to (re)turn (vr)
				to come apart, loose (vi)
ⲛⲟⲩϩⲙ̄	ⲛⲉϩⲙ-	ⲛⲁϩⲙ⸗		to rescue, save (ⲙ̄ⲙⲟ⸗) (vt)

				to be rescued, saved (vi)
				to be safe (vs)
				safety (nm)
ⲛⲟⲩϫ				lying, false (adj)
ⲛⲟⲩϫ(ⲉ)	ⲛⲉϫ-	ⲛⲟϫ⸗	ⲛⲏϫ†	to throw, cast (ⲙ̄ⲙⲟ⸗; at, into: ⲉ-) (vt)
				to be lying, reclining (at table); **to rely** (on: ⲉ-) (vs)
				throw (nm)
ⲛⲟⲩϭⲥ	ⲛⲉϭⲥ-		ⲛⲟϭⲥ†	to become/be indignant, wrathful (at: ⲉ-, ⲉϫⲛ̄-) (vi/vs)
				indignation, wrath (nm)
ⲛⲟⲩϥⲉ				good, profit (nf)
ⲛⲟϭ				large, big, great, important (usually before noun or rarely after without ⲛ̄-) (adj)
ⲛⲟϭⲛⲉϭ	ⲛⲉϭⲛⲉϭ-	ⲛⲉϭⲛⲟⲩϭ⸗		to reproach, mock (vt)
				reproach, mockery (nm)
ⲛ̄ⲧⲟ	ⲛ̄ⲧⲉ-			you (fsg) (ind pers pron)
ⲛ̄ⲧⲟⲕ	ⲛ̄ⲧⲕ̄-			you (msg) (ind pers pron)
ⲛ̄ⲧⲟⲟⲩ				they (ind pers pron)
ⲛ̄ⲧⲟⲥ				she, it (f) (ind pers pron)
ⲛ̄ⲧⲟϥ	ⲛ̄ⲧϥ̄-			he, it (m) (ind pers pron)
ⲛ̄ⲧⲱⲧⲛ̄	ⲛ̄ⲧⲉⲧⲛ̄-			you (pl) (ind pers pron)
ⲛ̄ϣⲟⲧ			ⲛⲁϣⲧ̄†	to become/be hard, strong, difficult (vi/vs)
				hardness (nm)
ⲛ̄ϭⲓ-				that is, namely (apposition marker)

ϩ   ϩⲓ

ⲟ   ⲟⲩ

ⲟⲃϩⲉ, ⲟϩⲃⲉ	tooth (nm)
ⲟⲉⲓⲕ	(loaf of) bread (nm)
ⲟⲉⲓϣ	cry (used only in compounds) (n)
ⲧⲁϣⲉ-ⲟⲉⲓϣ	to proclaim (ⲙ̄ⲙⲟ⸗)
οἰκουμένη	inhabited world (nf)
ⲟⲙⲉ	clay, mud (nmf)
ⲟⲛ	again, also, additionally (adv)
ⲟⲟϩ	moon (nm)
ὄργανον	instrument (nm)
ὀργή	indignation, wrath (nf)
ὀρινή	mountain region, hill country (nf)

ορφανος		orphan (nm)
ⲟⲩ- (-ⲩ-)		a (-ⲩ- after ⲉ- or ⲁ-) (< ⲟⲩⲁ) (indef art sg)
ⲟⲩ		what? (inter pron)
ⲉⲧⲃⲉ-ⲟⲩ		why?
ⲉ-ⲟⲩ		why? for what reason?
ⲟⲩⲁ		defamation (nm)
ϫⲓ-/ϫⲉ-ⲟⲩⲁ		to defame (cf. ϫⲱ)
ⲟⲩⲁ (f ⲟⲩⲉⲓ) -ⲟⲩⲉ(ⲓ)		one (num)
ⲟⲩⲁⲁ(ⲧ)⸗		only, alone, -self (intensive pron/inflected modifier)
ⲟⲩⲁϩⲉ		oasis (our English word is ultimately from Egyptian) (n)
ⲟⲩⲃⲁϣ	ⲟⲩⲟⲃϣ̄†	to become/be white (vi/vs)
ⲟⲩⲃⲉ-	ⲟⲩⲃⲏ⸗	toward, facing, against (prep)
ουδέ, οὔτε		neither, nor, yet not (conj)
ⲟⲩⲉ	ⲟⲩⲏⲩ†	to become/be distant, far (from: ⲉ-, ⲙ̄ⲙⲟ⸗, ⲉⲃⲟⲗ ⲙ̄ⲙⲟ⸗) (vi/vs)
		distance (nm)
ⲉ-ⲡⲟⲩⲉ		away, to a distance
ⲙ̄-ⲡⲟⲩⲉ		at a distance
ⲟⲩⲉⲓⲛⲉ		to pass (subj. usually a period of time) (vi)
ⲟⲩⲉⲣⲏⲧⲉ, ⲟⲩⲣⲏⲏⲧⲉ		foot (nf)
ⲟⲩⲉⲧ-		distinct, different (verboid adj)
ⲟⲩⲏⲏⲃ		priest (Christian or otherwise) (nm)
ⲟⲩⲏⲣ		how many? how much? (inter pron)
ⲟⲩⲛ̄-		there's/there're (existential)
ⲟⲩⲛⲁⲙ		right (hand) (nf)
ⲟⲩⲛⲟⲩ		hour, moment (nf)
ⲛ̄-ⲧⲉⲩⲛⲟⲩ		immediately, suddenly
ⲧⲉⲛⲟⲩ		now
ϣⲁ-ⲧⲉⲛⲟⲩ		until now
ϫⲓⲛ-ⲧⲉⲛⲟⲩ		from now on
ⲟⲩⲛⲟϥ		to be glad (for: ⲉϫⲛ̄-, ϩⲓϫⲛ̄-) (vi/vr)
		gladness (nm)
ⲟⲩⲛ̄ⲧⲉ-	ⲟⲩⲛ̄ⲧⲁ⸗	has/have (existential verboid)
ⲟⲩⲟ(ⲉ)ⲓ		approach, advance, rush (nm)
ϯ-ⲡ(⸗)ⲟⲩⲟ(ⲉ)ⲓ		to (make one's) approach (to: ⲉ-)
ⲟⲩⲟ(ⲉ)ⲓ		woe (nm)
ⲟⲩⲟⲉⲓⲛ		light (nm)
ⲣ̄-ⲟⲩⲟⲉⲓⲛ		to shine, make light
ⲟⲩⲟⲉⲓϣ		time, occasion (nm)
ⲛ̄-ⲟⲩⲟⲉⲓϣ ⲛⲓⲙ		every time, always
ⲛ̄-ⲟⲩⲟⲩⲟⲉⲓϣ		once, on one occasion (in the past)
ⲙ̄-ⲡⲉⲟⲩⲟⲉⲓϣ		at this/that time

ϩⲛ̄-ⲁϣ ⲛ̄-ⲟⲩⲟⲉⲓϣ				at what time?
ⲟⲩⲟⲛ				anyone, some(one/thing) (indef pron)
ⲟⲩⲟⲛ ⲛⲓⲙ				everyone
ⲟⲩⲟ(ⲟ)ϭⲉ				cheek, jaw (nf)
ⲟⲩⲟⲡ			ⲟⲩⲁⲁⲃ†	to become/be pure, holy (vi/vs)
				purity, holiness (nm)
ⲟⲩⲟⲥⲧⲛ̄			ⲟⲩⲉⲥⲧⲱⲛ†	to make broad, wide (ⲙ̄ⲙⲟ⸗) (vt)
				to become/be broad, wide (vi/vs)
				breadth (nm)
ⲟⲩⲟⲧⲟⲩⲉⲧ			ⲟⲩⲉⲧⲟⲩⲱⲧ†	to become/be green (vi/vs)
				greenness; herbs (nm)
ⲟⲩⲣⲟⲧ			ⲣⲟⲟⲩⲧ†	to become glad, eager (vi)
				to be glad, eager; to be flourishing (vs)
				gladness, eagerness (nm)
ⲟⲩⲣ̄ϣⲉ				watch; watchtower (nf)
ⲟⲩⲧⲉ-		ⲟⲩⲧⲱ⸗		between, among (prep)
ⲟⲩⲱ				report, announcement (nm)
ⲟⲩⲱ				sprout, blossom (n)
ⲟⲩⲱ				to cease, stop; to finish doing, to have already done (doing: circum) (vi)
ⲟⲩⲱⲃϣ̄				white (rarely after noun without ⲛ̄-) (adj)
ⲟⲩⲱⲗϭ	ⲟⲩⲉⲗϭ-	ⲟⲩⲟⲗϭ⸗	ⲟⲩⲟⲗϭ†	to bend, humiliate (ⲙ̄ⲙⲟ⸗) (vt)
				to bend down (vi)
				humiliation (nm)
ⲟⲩⲱⲙ	ⲟⲩⲉⲙ-	ⲟⲩⲟⲙ⸗		(cp ⲟⲩⲁⲙ-) to eat (ⲙ̄ⲙⲟ⸗; some of: ⲉⲃⲟⲗ ϩⲛ̄-) (vt)
				eating, food (nm)
ⲟⲩⲱⲙ ⲛ̄ⲥⲁ-				to eat away at
ⲟⲩⲱⲛ			ⲟⲩⲏⲛ†	(impv ⲁⲩⲱⲛ) to open (ⲙ̄ⲙⲟ⸗, ⲉ-) (vt)
				to become/be open (vi/vs)
				opening (nm)
ⲟⲩⲱⲛ	ⲟⲩⲛ̄-			part, portion (followed by a number for a fractional) (nm)
ⲟⲩⲱⲛϣ̄				wolf (nm)
ⲟⲩⲱⲛϩ	ⲟⲩⲉⲛϩ-	ⲟⲩⲟⲛϩ⸗	ⲟⲩⲟⲛϩ†	(± ⲉⲃⲟⲗ) to make manifest, show (ⲙ̄ⲙⲟ⸗; to: ⲛⲁ⸗, ⲉ-) (vt)
				to become manifest, appear (vi/vr)
				to be manifest, apparent (vs)
				manifesting, showing, appearance (nm)
ⲟⲩⲱⲧ	ⲟⲩⲉⲧ-	ⲟⲩⲉⲧ⸗		to make green, tender (vt)
				to become/be green, tender (vi)
(pl ⲟⲩⲟ[ⲟ]ⲧⲉ)				greens, herbs (nm)
ⲟⲩⲱⲧ (f ⲟⲩⲱⲧⲉ)				single, only; very same (usually after noun; rarely without ⲛ̄-) (adj)
ⲟⲩⲱⲧϩ	ⲟⲩⲉⲧϩ-	ⲟⲩⲟⲧϩ⸗		to pour, draw (liquid) (ⲙ̄ⲙⲟ⸗) (vt)

SAHIDIC-ENGLISH LEXICON

				poured (cast metal) thing (nm)
ⲟⲩⲱ(ⲱ)ⲙⲉ		ⲟⲩⲟ(ⲟ)ⲙ⸗		to accommodate (ⲙ̄ⲙⲟ⸗; someone: ⲙⲛ̄-) (vr)
ⲟⲩⲱ(ⲱ)ⲧⲉ		ⲟⲩⲟ(ⲟ)ⲧ⸗	ⲟⲩⲟⲟⲧ(ⲉ)†	to send, separate (ⲙ̄ⲙⲟ⸗; out: ⲉⲃⲟⲗ); to differentiate (ⲙ̄ⲙⲟ⸗; from: ⲉ-) (vt)
				to become/be different (vi/vs)
ⲟⲩⲱϣ	ⲟⲩⲉϣ-[3]	ⲟⲩⲁϣ⸗		to want, wish, desire (*not* ⲙ̄ⲙⲟ⸗) (vt)
				wish, desire (nm)
ⲙ̄-ⲡⲉϥⲟⲩⲱϣ				as he wished, as he desired
ⲟⲩⲱϣ				gap, interval, pause (nm)
(ⲛ̄)ⲟⲩⲉϣⲛ̄-				without (prep)
ⲟⲩⲱϣⲃ̄	ⲟⲩⲉϣⲃ̄-	ⲟⲩⲱϣⲃ⸗		to respond to (ⲙ̄ⲙⲟ⸗, ⲛⲁ⸗); to answer (vt)
				response (nm)
ⲟⲩⲱϣⲥ̄	ⲟⲩⲉϣⲥ̄-	ⲟⲩⲱϣⲥ⸗	ⲟⲩⲟϣⲥ̄†	to make broad, relaxed (ⲙ̄ⲙⲟ⸗) (vt)
				to become/be broad, relaxed (vi/vs)
				breadth (nm)
ⲟⲩⲱϣⲥ̄ ⲉⲃⲟⲗ				to spread out, extend
ⲟⲩⲱϣⲧ̄				to greet, bow (to: ⲛⲁ⸗); to revere (ⲙ̄ⲙⲟ⸗) (vt)
ⲟⲩⲱϣϥ̄	ⲟⲩⲉϣϥ̄-	ⲟⲩⲱϣϥ⸗	ⲟⲩⲟϣϥ̄†	to break down, crush (ⲙ̄ⲙⲟ⸗) (vt)
				to be broken, crushed (vi)
				breakage (nm)
ⲟⲩⲱϩ	ⲟⲩⲉϩ-	ⲟⲩⲁϩ⸗	ⲟⲩⲏϩ†	(cp ⲟⲩⲁϩ-) to put, place, set (ⲙ̄ⲙⲟ⸗) (vt)
				to follow, place oneself in the following of (ⲛ̄ⲥⲁ-) (vr)
				to settle, dwell (in: ϩⲛ̄-; with: ⲙⲛ̄-) (vi)
				to be placed, situated, set (vs)
				settlement (nm)
ⲟⲩⲱϩ ⲉⲧⲟⲟⲧ⸗				to continue, repeat, add (to do: circum, ⲉ- + inf)
ⲟⲩⲱϩⲉ				fisherman (nm)
ⲟⲩⲱϩⲙ̄	ⲟⲩⲉϩⲙ̄-	ⲟⲩⲁϩⲙ⸗	ⲟⲩⲟϩⲙ̄†	to repeat, interpret (vt/vi)
				response, interpretation (nm)
ⲟⲩⲱϭⲡ̄	ⲟⲩⲉϭⲡ̄-	ⲟⲩⲟϭⲡ⸗	ⲟⲩⲟϭⲡ̄†	to break, destroy (ⲙ̄ⲙⲟ⸗) (vt)
				to be broken, destroyed (vi)
				breakage, destruction (nm)
ⲟⲩϣⲏ				night (nf)
ⲟⲩϩⲟⲣ (pl ⲟⲩϩⲟⲟⲣ)				dog (nm; ⲟⲩϩⲱⲣⲉ [f])
ⲟⲩϫⲁⲓ̈			ⲟⲩⲟϫ†	to become/be healthy, delivered (vi/vs)
				health, deliverance (nm)
ⲟϩⲥ̄, ⲟⲥϩ̄				sickle (nm)

---

3. ⲟⲩⲉϣ- can be compounded with another inf.

ⲡ   ⲡⲓ

ⲡ-, ⲡⲉ-		the (def art msg)
ⲡⲁ-		that of, that connected to (absolute rel pron msg)
ⲡⲁⲓ̈		this (nearer dem pron msg)
ⲉⲧⲃⲉ-ⲡⲁⲓ̈		therefore
ⲉⲧⲉ-ⲡⲁⲓ̈ ⲡⲉ		which is this, namely, i.e., that is to say
ⲡⲁⲛⲧⲟⲕⲣⲁ́ⲧⲱⲣ		All-controller (nm)
ⲡⲁⲣⲁ-	ⲡⲁⲣⲁⲣⲟ⸗	beside, beyond, more than (prep)
ⲡⲁⲣⲁⲃⲟⲗⲏ́		illustration, analogy (nf)
ⲡⲁⲣⲁⲅⲉ		to pass away/by (vi)
ⲡⲁⲣⲁ́ⲇ(ⲉ)ⲓⲥⲟⲥ		paradise (ultimately Persian for an enclosed garden) (nm)
ⲡⲁⲣⲁⲇⲉⲭⲉ		to receive, accept (ⲙ̄ⲙⲟ⸗) (vt)
ⲡⲁⲣⲁⲇⲓⲇⲟⲩ		to betray, give over (ⲙ̄ⲙⲟ⸗) (vt)
ⲡⲁⲣⲁⲓⲧⲉⲓ		to decline, refuse (vt)
ⲡⲁⲣⲁⲕⲁⲗⲉⲓ		to encourage (ⲙ̄ⲙⲟ⸗) (vt)
ⲡⲁⲣⲁⲛⲟⲙⲓ́ⲁ		lawbreaking (nf)
ⲡⲁⲣⲁ́ⲛⲟⲙⲟⲥ		lawbreaker (nm)
ⲡⲁⲣⲁⲧⲏⲣⲉⲓ		to keep, observe (ⲉ-) (vt)
ⲡⲁⲣⲉⲙⲃⲟⲗⲏ́		fortification, barracks (nf)
ⲡⲁⲣⲑⲉ́ⲛⲟⲥ		virgin (nf)
ⲡⲁⲣⲣⲏⲥⲓ́ⲁ		boldness (nf)
ⲡⲁⲣϩⲟⲓⲙⲓ́ⲁ		proverb (nf)
ⲡⲁ́ⲥⲭⲁ		Passover (ultimately from Hebrew/Aramaic) (nm)
ⲡⲁϣⲉ	ⲡⲁϣ-	half (nf)
ⲡⲁ́ϩⲟⲩ		rear, back part (nm)
ⲉⲡⲁ́ϩⲟⲩ		backward, back (adv)
ϩⲓⲡⲁ́ϩⲟⲩ		behind (adv)
ⲡⲁϩⲣⲉ		medicine; dye (nm)
ⲡⲉ		is (copula msg)
ⲡⲉ (pl ⲡⲏⲩⲉ)		sky (nf)
ⲉⲧⲡⲉ		skyward, upward (adv)
ϩⲣⲟⲩ-ⲙ̄-ⲡⲉ		sky-voice, thunder (nm)
ⲡⲉⲓ̈-		this (nearer dem msg)
ⲡ(ⲉ)ⲓⲣⲁⲥⲙⲟⲥ		testing, tempting (nm)
ⲡ(ⲉ)ⲓⲣⲁⲍⲉ		to test, tempt (ⲙ̄ⲙⲟ⸗) (vt)
ⲡ(ⲉ)ⲓⲣⲉ́ (ⲡⲣ̄ⲣⲉ́)	ⲡⲟⲣⲉ†	to emerge, come forth (vi)
		emergence, coming forth (nm)
ⲙⲁ ⲙ̄-ⲡⲉⲓⲣⲉ́		sunrise, east (nm)
ⲡⲉⲣⲓ́ⲭⲱⲣⲟⲥ		surrounding countryside (nf)
ⲡⲉ́ⲧⲣⲁ		rock (nf)

ⲡⲉϫⲉ-		ⲡⲉϫⲁ⸗		said (ϫⲉ: that " [introducing direct quotation]) (verboid)
ⲡⲏ				that (further dem pron msg)
ⲡⲏⲅⲏ́				spring, fountain (nf)
ⲡⲓⲥⲉ	ⲡⲉⲥ(ⲧ̄)-	ⲡⲁⲥⲧ⸗	ⲡⲟⲥⲉ†	(cp ⲡⲁⲥ-) to cook, melt (ⲙ̄ⲙⲟ⸗) (vt)
ⲡⲓⲥⲧⲉⲩⲉ				to trust, rely on (ⲉ-) (vt)
ⲡⲓ́ⲥⲧⲓⲥ				trust (nf)
ⲡⲓⲥⲧⲟⲥ				trusting, trustworthy (adj)
ⲡⲓⲧⲉ				bow (nf)
ⲡⲗⲁⲛⲁ				to mislead, deceive (ⲙ̄ⲙⲟ⸗) (vt)
ⲡⲗⲁⲥⲥⲉ				to form, mold (ⲙ̄ⲙⲟ⸗) (vt)
ⲡⲗⲁⲧ(ⲉ)ⲓ́ⲁ				broad street (nf)
ⲡⲗⲏⲛ				nevertheless, only, except (adv/conj)
ⲡⲛⲉⲩ́ⲙⲁ				spirit (abbreviated as ⲡ̄ⲛ̄ⲁ̄) (nm)
ⲡⲟ́ⲗⲉⲙⲟⲥ				war (nm)
ⲡⲟⲗⲓⲥ				city (nf)
ⲡⲟⲛⲏⲣⲟ́ⲥ				evil, wicked (adj)
ⲡⲟⲣⲛⲉⲩⲉ				to prostitute (oneself) (vi)
ⲡⲟⲣⲛⲉⲓ́ⲁ				prostitution (nf)
ⲡⲟ́ⲥⲟ				how much? (inter pron)
ⲡⲣⲉⲥⲃⲩ́ⲧⲉⲣⲟⲥ				elder, priest (Christian) (nm)
ⲡⲣⲏϣ				spread, mat, cloak (nm)
ⲡⲣⲟⲥ-		ⲡⲣⲟⲥⲣⲟ⸗		according to, for; than (prep)
ⲡⲣⲟⲫⲏⲧ(ⲉ)ⲓ́ⲁ				foretelling (nf)
ⲡⲣⲟⲫⲏⲧⲉⲩⲉ				to foretell (vi)
ⲡⲣⲟⲫⲏ́ⲧⲏⲥ				foreteller, spokesperson (nm; ⲡⲣⲟⲫⲏ́ⲧⲓⲥ [f])
ⲡⲣⲱ				winter (nf)
ⲡⲥ̄ⲧⲁⲓⲟⲩ				ninety (num)
ⲡⲩ́ⲗⲏ				gate (nf)
ⲡⲱ⸗				mine, yours, etc. (poss pron msg)
ⲡⲱⲣⲕ̄	ⲡⲣ̄ⲕ-	ⲡⲟⲣⲕ⸗		(± ⲉⲃⲟⲗ) to pluck out, uproot (ⲙ̄ⲙⲟ⸗) (vt)
				to be plucked out, uprooted (vi)
				plucking out, uprooting (nm)
ⲡⲱⲣϣ̄	ⲡⲣ̄ϣ-	ⲡⲟⲣϣ⸗	ⲡⲟⲣϣ†	to spread (ⲙ̄ⲙⲟ⸗; out ± ⲉⲃⲟⲗ) (vt)
				to be spread (vi)
				spread, mat (nm)
ⲡⲱⲣϫ̄	ⲡⲣ̄ϫ-	ⲡⲟⲣϫ⸗	ⲡⲟⲣϫ̄†	(± ⲉⲃⲟⲗ) to divide, separate (ⲙ̄ⲙⲟ⸗) (vt)
				to become/be divided, separated; to (de)part (vi/vs)
				division, separation (nm)
ⲡⲱⲥ				how? (inter pron)
ⲡⲱⲧ			ⲡⲏⲧ†	to run, flee (vi)
				to be running, fleeing (vs, exclusively with Present)

				flight (nm)
ⲡⲱⲧ ⲛ̄ⲥⲁ-				to run after, pursue
ⲡⲱⲱⲛⲉ	ⲡⲉⲉⲛⲉ-	ⲡⲟⲟⲛⲉ⸗	ⲡⲟⲟⲛⲉ†	to turn, change (ⲙ̄ⲙⲟ⸗; to: ⲉ-); (+ ⲉⲃⲟⲗ) to remove (vt)
				to turn, change (from: ϩⲛ̄-; to: ⲉ-); (+ ⲉⲃⲟⲗ) to move out (vi)
				removal, change (nm)
ⲡⲱⲱⲡⲉ	ⲡⲁⲡⲉ-	ⲡⲁⲡⲱ⸗		to make (bricks: ⲧⲱⲃⲉ) (vt)
ⲡⲱϣ	ⲡⲉϣ-	ⲡⲟϣ⸗	ⲡⲏϣ†	to divide (ⲙ̄ⲙⲟ⸗) (vt)
				to become/be divided (vi/vs)
				division (nm)
ⲡⲱϩ	ⲡⲉϩ-, ⲡⲁϩ-	ⲡⲟϩ⸗	ⲡⲏϩ†, ⲡⲉϩ†	to break, split (ⲙ̄ⲙⲟ⸗) (vt/vi)
				break, piece (nm)
ⲡⲱϩ	ⲡⲉϩ-		ⲡⲏϩ†	to reach, attain (ⲉ-, ϣⲁ-) (vt/vi)
ⲡⲱϩⲧ̄	ⲡⲉϩⲧ̄-	ⲡⲁϩⲧ⸗	ⲡⲁϩⲧ̄†	1. to bend, bow (ⲙ̄ⲙⲟ⸗); 2. (± ⲉⲃⲟⲗ) to pour (out), shed (ⲙ̄ⲙⲟ⸗) (vt)
				to bow, prostrate self (vi/vr)
				to pour, flow (vi)
				to be bowing, prostrated (vs)
				pouring, shedding (nm)

ⲣ   ⲣⲱ

ⲣⲁⲛ	ⲣⲉⲛ-	ⲣⲓⲛ⸗, ⲣⲛ̄ⲧ⸗	name (nm)
ⲣⲁⲥⲧⲉ			tomorrow (nm)
ⲡⲣⲁⲥⲧⲉ, ⲛ̄-ⲣⲁⲥⲧⲉ, ⲉ-ⲣⲁⲥⲧⲉ, ⲙ̄-ⲡⲉϥⲣⲁⲥⲧⲉ			tomorrow
ⲣⲁ́ⲥⲟⲩ			dream (nf)
ⲣⲁⲧ⸗			foot (of) (usually in compounds) (nm)
ⲉⲣⲁⲧ⸗			to the foot of (prep)
ϩⲁⲣⲁⲧ⸗			under (prep)
ϩⲓⲣⲁⲧ⸗			toward (prep)
ⲣⲁϣⲉ			to rejoice at, ridicule (ⲙ̄ⲙⲟ⸗) (vt)
			to rejoice (at, over: ⲉ-, ⲉϫⲛ̄-, ⲉϩⲣⲁⲓ̈ ⲉϫⲛ̄-) (vi)
			joy (nm)
ⲣⲉ			(so/then) what? (inter part)
ⲣ(ⲉ)ⲕⲣⲓⲕⲉ			slumbering, nodding off (nf)
ⲣⲏ			sun (nm)
ⲣⲓ			cell, room (nf)
ⲣⲓⲕⲉ	ⲣⲉⲕ(ⲧ̄)-	ⲣⲉⲕⲧ⸗	ⲣⲟⲕⲉ†	to bend, turn, incline (ⲙ̄ⲙⲟ⸗) (vt)
			to become/be bent, turnt (vi/vr/vs)
			turning, inclination (nm)
ⲣⲓⲙⲉ			to weep (for someone: ⲉ-, ⲉϫⲛ̄-) (vi)

SAHIDIC-ENGLISH LEXICON

ⲣⲙ̄ⲉⲓⲏ (pl ⲣⲙ̄ⲉⲓⲟⲟⲩⲉ)   weeping (nm); tear(s) (nf)

ⲣⲙ̄ⲙⲁⲟ   rich person (nmf)

ⲣⲙ̄ⲣⲁϣ   gentle person (nmf)

ⲣⲙ̄ϩⲉ (pl ⲣⲙ̄ϩⲉⲉⲩⲉ)   free person (nm; ⲣⲙ̄ϩⲏ [f])

ⲣⲟ (pl ⲣⲱⲟⲩ)   ⲣⲛ̄-   ⲣⲱ⸗   mouth; door, opening (usually in compounds) (nm)

   ⲉⲣⲛ̄-   ⲉⲣⲱ⸗   to (the opening of) (prep)

   ϩⲁⲣⲛ̄-   ϩⲁⲣⲱ⸗   before (setting food) (prep)

   ϩⲓⲣⲛ̄-   ϩⲓⲣⲱ⸗   at (the opening of) (prep)

   ⲕⲱ ⲛ̄-ⲣⲱ⸗   ⲕⲁ-ⲣⲱ⸗   ⲕⲁⲣⲁⲉⲓⲧ†   to remain silent

     ⲕⲁ-ⲣⲱϥ   silence (nm)

ⲣⲟⲉⲓⲥ   ⲣⲏⲥ†   to watch (over: ⲉ-) (vi); watch (nm)

ⲣⲟⲙⲡⲉ (pl ⲣⲙ̄ⲡⲟⲟⲩⲉ)   ⲣⲙ̄ⲡⲉ-   year (nf)

   (ⲛ̄-)ⲧⲣⲟⲙⲡⲉ   this year

   ⲛ̄-ⲟⲩⲣⲟⲙⲡⲉ   for a year

   ⲛ̄-ϣⲟⲙⲧⲉ ⲛ̄-ⲣⲟⲙⲡⲉ   for three years

ⲣⲟⲟⲩⲉ   stubble, straw (nm)

ⲣⲟⲟⲩϣ   care, concern, anxiety (nm)

   ⲣ̄-ⲣⲟⲟⲩϣ   (ⲟ† ⲛ̄-) to become/be a care or concern (for: ⲛⲁ⸗); to become/be anxious (with reflexive ⲛⲁ⸗)

   ϥⲓ-ⲣⲟⲟⲩϣ   to take care (to, for: ⲉ[ⲧⲃⲉ], ϩⲁ, ⲛⲁ⸗)

ⲣⲟⲩϩⲉ   evening (nm)

   ⲉ/ⲛ̄/ϩⲓ-ⲣⲟⲩϩⲉ   in the evening

   ϣⲁ-ⲣⲟⲩϩⲉ   until evening

ⲣ̄ⲡⲉ (pl ⲣ̄ⲡⲏⲩⲉ)   temple (nm)

ⲣ̄ⲣⲟ (pl ⲣ̄ⲣⲱⲟⲩ, ⲉⲣⲱⲟⲩ)   king, monarch (nm; ⲣ̄ⲣⲱ, queen [f])

   ⲙⲛ̄ⲧⲣ̄ⲣⲟ, ⲙⲛ̄ⲧⲉⲣⲟ (pl ⲙⲛ̄ⲧⲣ̄ⲣⲱⲟⲩ, ⲙⲛ̄ⲧⲉⲣⲱⲟⲩ)   kingdom, reign (nf)

ⲣⲱⲕϩ̄   ⲣⲉⲕϩ-   ⲣⲟⲕϩ⸗   ⲣⲟⲕϩ̄†   to burn (ⲙ̄ⲙⲟ⸗) (vt); to burn (vi); to be burned, destroyed by fire (vs)

ⲣⲱⲙⲉ   ⲣⲙ̄(ⲛ̄)-   person, human; humanity (nmf)

   ⲣⲉϥ-   person who (does: -ⲣ̄-; something) (nmf)

ⲣⲱⲧ   ⲣⲉⲧ-   ⲣⲏⲧ†   (cp ⲣⲁⲧ-) to sprout, grow; to become overgrown (with: ⲙ̄ⲙⲟ⸗) (vi)

   (pl ⲣⲁⲧⲉ)   growth, vegetation (nm)

ⲣⲱϣⲉ   ⲣⲉϣ̄-   ⲣⲁϣ⸗   to satisfy (ⲙ̄ⲙⲟ⸗) (vt); to be enough, suffice (vi); enough, sufficiency (nm)

ⲣⲱϩⲧ̄   ⲣⲉϩⲧ-   ⲣⲁϩⲧ⸗   ⲣⲁϩⲧ†   to strike, kill (ⲙ̄ⲙⲟ⸗); to strike down, cast down (vt)

С   СНММА

са				side, part, direction (nm)
	ⲛ̄са-		ⲛ̄сѡ⸗	after, behind; except (prep)
	ⲙⲛ̄ⲛ̄са-		ⲙⲛ̄ⲛ̄сѡ⸗	after (of time) (prep)
	ⲙⲛ̄ⲛ̄сѡс			afterwards (adv)
са(а)ⲛϣ̄	са(а)ⲛϣ̄-	саⲛоуϣ⸗	саⲛаϣ̄†	to nourish, maintain (ⲙ̄ⲙо⸗) (vt)
				to be alive (vi)
				to be nourished (vs)
				nourishment (nm)
са́ⲃⲃатоⲛ				Sabbath; week (sg or pl) (nm)
саⲃⲉ́ (f саⲃⲏ; pl саⲃⲉⲉу[ⲉ])				wise (adj)
с(а)ⲃо		саⲃо⸗		to learn (to: ⲉ-) (vt)
саⲉⲓⲉ				beautiful (adj)
саⲉⲓⲛ				physician (nm)
са́ⲗⲡⲓⲅⲝ̄				trumpet (nf)
са́ⲣⲇⲓⲛоⲥ				carnelian (nm)
саⲣⲕⲓⲕоⲥ				fleshly (adj)
саⲣⲝ̄				flesh (nf)
	ⲣ̄-саⲣⲝ̄			(о† ⲛ̄-) to become/be flesh
сат, сⲏⲧ				tail (nm)
сатаⲛа́ⲥ				adversary (ultimately from Hebrew/Aramaic) (nm)
сатⲃⲉ				to ruminate, chew (vi)
сатⲉ				fire (nf)
сатⲉⲉⲣⲉ				stater (a silver coin/weight) (from Greek ⲥⲧⲁⲧⲏⲣ) (nf)
саϣϥ̄ (f саϣϥⲉ)	-саϣϥⲉ			seven (num)
сау				yesterday (nm)
	ⲛ̄-сау			yesterday
саϩ				writer, scribe; teacher, master (nmf)
саϩⲛⲉ				to supply, provide (vi)
				supply, provisions (nm)
	оуⲉϩ-саϩⲛⲉ			to (give a) command (something: ⲙ̄ⲙо⸗; someone: ⲛа⸗, ⲉⲧⲛ̄-; to do: ⲉ-, ⲉ-ⲧⲣⲉ-)
са́ϩоу(ⲉ)	сϩоуⲣ̄-	сϩоуѡⲣ⸗	сϩоуоⲣⲧ̄†	to curse (ⲙ̄ⲙо⸗) (vt)
				curse (nm)
сⲃ̄ⲃⲉ	сⲃ̄ⲃⲉ-	сⲃ̄ⲃⲏⲧ⸗	сⲃ̄ⲃⲏу(ⲧ)†	to circumcise (ⲙ̄ⲙо⸗) (vt)
				circumcision (nm)
сⲃок			соⲃⲕ̄†	to become/be few, small (vi/vs)
				fewness, smallness (nm)
сⲃѡ (pl сⲃооуⲉ)				teaching, instruction (nf)
сⲉ				yes (affirmative part)
сⲉ	сⲉ(т)-			sixty (num)

ⲥⲉⲉⲡⲉ				to remain, be left over (vi)
				remainder, rest (often in plural sense; a redundant ⲕⲉ- appears frequently: ⲡⲕⲉⲥⲉⲉⲡⲉ [the rest]) (nm)
ⲥ(ⲉ)ⲓ			ⲥⲏⲩ†	to become sated, filled (with: ⲙ̄ⲙⲟ⸗) (vi)
				to be sated, full (vs)
ⲥ(ⲉ)ⲓⲛⲉ	ⲥⲛ̄-	ⲥⲁⲁⲧ⸗		to pass (through: ϩⲛ̄-; out of: ⲉⲃⲟⲗ) (vt/vi)
ⲥⲏϥⲉ				sword (nf)
ⲥⲓⲃⲧ̄				hill (nf)
ⲥⲓⲟⲩ	ⲥⲟⲩ-			star (nm)
ⲥⲟⲩ-ⲛ̄-(ϩ)ⲧⲟⲟⲩⲉ				morning star
ⲥⲟⲩ-ⲛ̄-ⲣⲟⲩϩⲉ				evening star
ⲥⲓⲧ				serpent, cobra (nm)
ⲥⲓⲧⲉ	ⲥⲉⲧ-	ⲥⲁⲧ⸗	ⲥⲏⲧ†	to throw, cast, sow (ⲙ̄ⲙⲟ⸗) (vt)
ⲥⲕⲁⲛⲇⲁⲗⲓⲍⲉ				to obstruct (ⲙ̄ⲙⲟ⸗) (vt)
				to be obstructed (vi)
ⲥⲕⲁⲛⲇⲁⲗⲟⲛ				obstruction (nm)
ⲥⲕⲉⲡⲏ				shelter, shade (nf)
ⲥⲕⲉⲩⲏ				implement, object (nf)
ⲥⲕⲉⲩⲟⲥ				thing, object, implement, vessel (nm)
ⲥⲗⲁⲁⲧⲉ				to stumble, slip (vi)
				stumbling (nm)
ⲥⲗϩⲟ				(cf. ⲙⲟⲩ-ⲛ̄-ⲥⲗϩⲟ)
ⲥⲙⲁⲣⲁⲅⲧⲟⲥ				emerald (nm)
ⲥⲙⲏ				voice, sound (nf)
ⲥⲙⲓⲛⲉ	ⲥⲙⲛ̄-	ⲥⲙⲛ̄ⲧ⸗	ⲥⲙⲟⲛⲧ̄†	to establish, set up (ⲙ̄ⲙⲟ⸗) (vt)
				to be established, set up (vi)
				to exist; to be correct (vs)
				establishing (nm)
ⲥⲙⲟⲧ				form, likeness, appearance; character, behavior (nm)
ⲥⲙⲟⲩ			ⲥⲙⲁⲙⲁⲁⲧ†	to bless (ⲉ-) (vt)
				to be blessed (vs)
				blessing (nm)
ⲥⲛⲁⲩ (f ⲥⲛ̄ⲧⲉ)	-ⲥⲛⲟⲟⲩⲥ(ⲉ)			two (num)
ⲙ̄-ⲡⲉⲥⲛⲁⲩ				(they) both, both (of them)
ⲥⲛⲁⲩϩ				bond, fetter (nm)
ⲥⲛⲟϥ				blood (nm)
ⲥⲛ̄ⲧⲉ				foundation (nf)
ⲥⲟ				(cf. †-ⲥⲟ)
ⲥⲟⲃⲧⲉ	ⲥⲃ̄ⲧⲉ-	ⲥⲃ̄ⲧⲱⲧ⸗	ⲥⲃ̄ⲧⲱⲧ†	to prepare, make ready (ⲙ̄ⲙⲟ⸗; for: ⲉ-) (vt)
				to become prepared, get ready (vi/vr)
				preparation; equipment (nm)
ⲁⲧⲥⲃ̄ⲧⲱⲧ⸗				unprepared, unequipped

со(є)ı				beam (of wood) (nmf)
солсл̄	сл̄сл̄-	сл̄сωλ⸗	сл̄сωλ†	to console, comfort (ⲙ̄ⲙⲟ⸗) (vt)
				to be comforted (vi)
				to be consoled (vs)
				consolation (nm)
сон (pl снну)	сн̄-, сен-			brother, sibling (> fellow monk) (nm; сωне, sister [f])
сооу (f сo[є])	-асе			six (num)
сооун̄	соун̄-	соуωн⸗		to know (ⲙ̄ⲙⲟ⸗; about: етве-; how to: н̄- + inf; that xe); become acquainted with (vt)
				knowledge, acquaintance (nm)
соотн̄	соутн̄-	соутωн⸗	соутωн†	1. to straighten (ⲙ̄ⲙⲟ⸗); 2. (± евол) to stretch out (ⲙ̄ⲙⲟ⸗; to: е-, ϣа-, еϩоун е-) (vt)
				to become straight, (up)right; to stretch (vi)
				uprightness (nm)
со(о)ϩе	саϩе-	саϩω⸗		to set (up)right; to correct (ⲙ̄ⲙⲟ⸗) (vt)
				to be set (up)right; to be corrected (vi)
сооϩе	саϩе-	саϩω(ω)⸗	саϩну†	to remove (ⲙ̄ⲙⲟ⸗) (vt)
				(+ евол) to withdraw, remove oneself (from: ⲙ̄ⲙⲟ⸗) (vr)
				withdrawal, removal (nm)
соп (pl сω[ω]п)	сеп-, сп̄-			time, occasion (nm)
н̄-оусоп				once
н̄-с(е)п-снау				twice
н̄-ϣм(н̄)т-сω(ω)п				three times
(н̄-)кесоп				again
ϩı-оусоп				all at once, altogether
соп нім				always, on every occasion
(н̄-)ϩаϩ н̄-соп				many times, often
ката-соп н̄- (+ inf)				on every occasion of
сопсп̄, сопс̄	сп̄сп̄-, сепс̄-, сп̄с̄-	сп̄сωп⸗	сепсωп†, сп̄сωп†	to exhort, implore, encourage (ⲙ̄ⲙⲟ⸗) (vt)
				exhortation, encouragement (nm)
сорт̄				wool (nmf)
соте (pl сооте)				arrow, dart; measure (nmf)
соуо				wheat, grain (nm)
σοφία				wisdom (nf)
σοφός				wise (adj)
соϭ				fool (nm)
соϭн̄				ointment (nm)
σπέρμα				seed, offspring (nm)
σπήλαιον				cave, hideout (nm)
спıр (pl спıрооуе)				rib, side (nm)
σπότου				lips; shore (nm)
σπουδή				haste (nf)

сроүреч		среүрωч⸗		to dissipate (ⲙ̄ⲙⲟ⸗) (vt)
				to wither (vi)
				withering (nm)
ср̄ϥⲉ		сроϥⲧ̄†		to become/be at leisure, relaxed (vi/vs)
				leisure, relaxation (nm)
ⲥⲧⲁⲩⲣⲟⲥ				execution stake (abbreviated as ⲥ̄ⲣ̄ⲟ̄ⲥ̄) (nm)
ⲥⲧⲁⲩⲣⲟⲩ				to (execute by) stake (ⲙ̄ⲙⲟ⸗) (vt)
ⲥⲧⲉⲣⲉⲱⲙⲁ				firmness, solidity (nm)
ⲥⲧⲟ(ⲉ)ⲓ	ⲥϯ-			smell (nm)
ⲥⲧⲟⲗⲏ́				robe (nf)
ⲥⲧⲩ́ⲗ(ⲗ)ⲟⲥ				pillar, column (nm)
ⲥⲧⲱⲧ				to tremble (at: ϩⲏⲧ⸗, ϩⲁ-) (vi)
				trembling (nm)
ⲥⲩⲅⲅⲉⲛⲏⲥ				relative (nm)
ⲥⲩⲛⲁⲅⲱⲅⲏ́				gathering (place) (nf)
ⲥⲩⲛⲏ́ⲑ(ⲉ)ⲓⲁ				custom, habit (nf)
ⲥⲩⲛϩⲉ́ⲇⲣⲓⲟⲛ				council (nm)
ⲥⲫⲣⲁⲅⲓⲍⲉ				to seal (ⲙ̄ⲙⲟ⸗) (vt)
ⲥⲫⲣⲁⲅⲓ́ⲥ				seal (nf)
ⲥⲭⲏ́ⲙⲁ				fashion of clothing; monk's habit (nm)
ⲙⲟⲩⲣ ⲙ̄ⲙⲟ⸗ ⲙ̄-ⲡⲉⲥⲭⲏ́ⲙⲁ				to garb someone in a monk's habit, induct into monkhood
ⲥⲱ	ⲥⲉ-	ⲥⲟⲟ⸗		(cp ⲥⲁⲩ-) to drink (ⲙ̄ⲙⲟ⸗; some of: ⲉⲃⲟⲗ ϩⲛ̄-) (vt)
				drinking, a drink (nm)
ⲥⲱⲃⲉ				to mock (ⲙ̄ⲙⲟ⸗) (vt)
				to laugh (at: ⲉϫⲛ̄-, ⲛ̄ⲥⲁ-) (vi)
				laughter, mocking (nm)
ⲥⲱⲕ	ⲥⲉⲕ-	ⲥⲟⲕ⸗	ⲥⲏⲕ†	to pull, draw; to lead (ⲙ̄ⲙⲟ⸗) (vt)
				to glide, flow (vi/vr)
				drawing; (± ⲉⲃⲟⲗ) gliding away (dying) (nm)
ⲥⲱⲗⲡ̄	ⲥⲗ̄ⲡ-	ⲥⲟⲗⲡ⸗	ⲥⲟⲗⲡ̄†	(± ⲉⲃⲟⲗ) to break off, cut off (ⲙ̄ⲙⲟ⸗) (vt)
				to be broken off, cut off (vi)
				breaking off, separation (nm)
ⲥⲱ́ⲙⲁ				body (nm)
ⲥⲱⲙ(ⲛ̄)ⲧ		ⲥⲟⲙ(ⲛ̄)ⲧ⸗	ⲥⲟⲙ(ⲛ̄)ⲧ†	to stretch, extend (ⲙ̄ⲙⲟ⸗) (vt)
				to be stretched; to wait (vi)
ⲥⲱⲛⲕ̄				to suck (ⲙ̄ⲙⲟ⸗) (vt)
ⲥⲱⲛⲧ̄	ⲥⲛ̄ⲧ-	ⲥⲟⲛⲧ⸗	ⲥⲟⲛⲧ̄†	to create (ⲙ̄ⲙⲟ⸗) (vt)
				to be created (vi)
				creation, creature (nm)
ⲥⲱⲟⲩϩ	ⲥⲉⲩϩ-	ⲥⲟⲟⲩϩ⸗	ⲥⲟⲟⲩϩ†	(± ⲉϩⲟⲩⲛ) to gather, collect (ⲙ̄ⲙⲟ⸗; at: ⲉ-, ⲉϫⲛ̄-, ϩⲛ̄-) (vt)
				to gather (vi)

				to be gathered (vs)
				gathering (nm)
cⲱⲣ	cⲡ̄-, ⲥⲉⲣ-	ⲥⲟⲣ⸗	ⲥⲏⲣ†	(cp ⲥⲁⲣ-) (± ⲉⲃⲟⲗ) to scatter, spread (ⲙ̄ⲙⲟ⸗) (vt/vi)
				spreading, distribution (nm)
ⲥⲱⲣⲙ̄	ⲥⲉⲣⲙ̄-	ⲥⲟⲣⲙ⸗	ⲥⲟⲣⲙ̄†	to mislead; to lose (ⲙ̄ⲙⲟ⸗) (vt)
				to be misled, err; to get lost (vi)
				error (nm)
ⲙⲟⲩ-ⲛ̄-ⲥⲱⲣⲙ̄				seasonal stream, wadi
ⲥⲱⲧⲏ́ⲣ				deliverer (abbreviated as c̄ⲱ̄ⲣ̄) (nm)
ⲥⲱⲧⲉ	ⲥⲉⲧ-	ⲥⲟ(ⲟ)ⲧ⸗		to redeem, ransom (ⲙ̄ⲙⲟ⸗) (vt)
				redemption, ransom (nm)
ⲥⲱⲧⲙ̄	ⲥⲉⲧⲙ̄-	ⲥⲟⲧⲙ⸗		to hear, listen to (ⲉ-); to heed, obey (ⲛⲁ⸗, ⲛ̄ⲥⲁ-) (vt)
				hearing, obedience (nm)
ⲥⲱⲧⲡ̄	ⲥⲉⲧⲡ̄-	ⲥⲟⲧⲡ⸗	ⲥⲟⲧⲡ̄†	to choose, select (ⲙ̄ⲙⲟ⸗) (vt)
				to be chosen, choice, excellent (vs)
				choice, select one (often as adj) (nm)
ⲥⲱϣⲉ				field, open country (nf)
ⲥⲱϣⲧ̄	ⲥⲉϣⲧ̄-	ⲥⲟϣⲧ⸗	ⲥⲟϣⲧ̄†	to block, stop (ⲙ̄ⲙⲟ⸗, from: ⲉ- + [neg] inf) (vt)
				to be blocked, stopped (from: ⲉ- + inf) (vi)
ⲥⲱϣ(ϥ̄)	ⲥⲉϣ(ϥ̄)-	ⲥⲟϣ(ϥ)⸗	ⲥⲏϣ†, ⲥⲟϣϥ̄†	to scorn, despise (ⲙ̄ⲙⲟ⸗) (vt)
				to be scorned, despised (vs)
				scorn, contempt (nm)
ⲥⲱϭ	ⲥⲉϭ-	ⲥⲟϭ⸗	ⲥⲏϭ†	to paralyze (ⲙ̄ⲙⲟ⸗) (vt)
				to become/be paralyzed (vi/vs)
ⲥϩⲁⲓ̈	ⲥⲉϩ-	ⲥϩⲁⲓ̈(ⲥ)⸗, ⲥⲁϩ⸗, ⲥⲉϩⲧ⸗	ⲥⲏϩ†	to write (ⲙ̄ⲙⲟ⸗; on, in: ⲉ[ϫⲛ̄]-, ϩⲓ[ϫⲛ̄]-, ϩⲛ̄-; to: ⲛⲁ⸗, ⲉ-, ϣⲁ-); to register; to draw, paint (vt)
				to be written, in writing (vs)
				writing, letter (nm)
ⲥϩⲓⲙⲉ (pl ϩⲓⲟⲙⲉ)				female, woman; wife (nf)
ϩⲓⲙⲉ (pl ϩⲓⲟⲙⲉ)				wife (nf)

Ⲧ   ⲧⲁⲩ

ⲧ-, ⲧⲉ-				the (def art fsg)
ⲧⲁ-				that of, that connected to (absolute rel pron fsg)
ⲧⲁ(ⲉ)ⲓⲃⲉ				casket, coffer (nf)
ⲧⲁ(ⲉ)ⲓⲟ	ⲧⲁ(ⲉ)ⲓⲉ-	ⲧⲁ(ⲉ)ⲓⲟ⸗	ⲧⲁ(ⲉ)ⲓⲏⲩ†	to honor, value (ⲙ̄ⲙⲟ⸗) (vt)
				to be honored, valuable (vs)
				(causative of ⲁⲓ̈ⲁⲓ̈)
				honor (nm)
ⲧⲁ(ⲉ)ⲓⲟⲩ				fifty (num)

ⲧⲁⲓ̈				this (nearer dem pron fsg)
ⲧⲁⲕⲟ	ⲧⲁⲕⲉ-	ⲧⲁⲕⲟ⸗	ⲧⲁⲕⲏⲩ(ⲧ)†	to destroy, ruin (ⲙ̄ⲙⲟ⸗) (vt)
				to become destroyed, ruined (vi)
				destruction, ruin (nm)
ταλαιπωρία				misery, distress (nf)
ταλαίπωρος				miserable, distressed (adj)
ⲧⲁⲗⲟ, ⲧⲁⲗⲉ	ⲧⲁⲗⲉ-	ⲧⲁⲗⲟ⸗	ⲧⲁⲗⲏⲩ†	(± ⲉϩⲣⲁⲓ̈) to raise up, offer up; to put on, cause to get on (ⲙ̄ⲙⲟ⸗; to: ⲉ-) (vt)
				to go up, climb, get on, mount (vi)
				(causative of ⲁⲗⲉ)
				raising up, offering (nm)
ⲧⲁⲗϭⲟ	ⲧⲁⲗϭⲉ-	ⲧⲁⲗϭⲟ⸗	ⲧⲁⲗϭⲏⲩ†	to heal, cure (ⲙ̄ⲙⲟ⸗; of, from: [ⲉⲃⲟⲗ] ϩⲛ̄-) (vt)
				to become/be healed (vi/vs)
				healing, curing (nm)
ⲧⲁⲙⲓⲟ	ⲧⲁⲙⲓⲉ-	ⲧⲁⲙⲓⲟ⸗	ⲧⲁⲙⲓⲏⲩ†	to create, make; to prepare, make ready (ⲙ̄ⲙⲟ⸗) (vt)
				creation, creature (nm)
ταμίον				storeroom, inner room (nm)
ⲧⲁⲙⲟ	ⲧⲁⲙⲉ-	ⲧⲁⲙⲟ⸗		to tell, inform (ⲙ̄ⲙⲟ⸗; of, about: ⲉ-, ⲉⲧⲃⲉ-; that: ϫⲉ) (vt)
				(causative of ⲉⲓⲙⲉ)
ⲧⲁⲛϩⲟ	ⲧⲁⲛϩⲉ-	ⲧⲁⲛϩⲟ⸗	ⲧⲁⲛϩⲏⲩ†	to bring (back) to life, let live, keep alive (ⲙ̄ⲙⲟ⸗) (vt)
				to become/be alive (vi/vs)
				(causative of ⲱⲛϩ̄)
				life preserving (nm)
ⲧⲁⲛϩⲟⲩⲧ	ⲧⲁⲛϩⲉⲧ-	ⲧⲁⲛϩⲟⲩⲧ⸗	ⲧⲁⲛϩⲏⲩⲧ†	to trust, entrust (ⲙ̄ⲙⲟ⸗; to: ⲉ[ϫⲛ̄]-) (vt/vr)
				(causative of ⲛⲁϩⲧⲉ)
τάξις				order (nf)
ⲧⲁ(ⲟ)ⲩⲟ	ⲧⲁ(ⲟ)ⲩⲉ-	ⲧⲁ(ⲟ)ⲩⲟ⸗		1. (± ⲉⲃⲟⲗ) to send (forth), put out (ⲙ̄ⲙⲟ⸗); 2. to proclaim, tell (ⲙ̄ⲙⲟ⸗) (vt)
				sending, mission; (+ ⲉⲃⲟⲗ) output (nm)
ⲧⲁⲡ				horn (nm)
ⲧⲁⲡⲣⲟ				mouth (also figuratively) (nf)
ⲧⲁⲣ				branch (nm)
τάφος				tomb (nm)
τάχα				perhaps (adv)
ταχύ				quickly (adv)
ⲧⲁϣⲟ	ⲧⲁϣⲉ-	ⲧⲁϣⲟ⸗		to increase (ⲙ̄ⲙⲟ⸗); often prefixed to another inf: to do something more, much (vt)
				(causative of ⲁϣⲁⲓ)
ⲧⲁϩⲟ	ⲧⲁϩⲉ-	ⲧⲁϩⲟ⸗	ⲧⲁϩⲏⲩ†	1. to cause to stand, set up (ⲙ̄ⲙⲟ⸗); 2. to reach, attain, catch, seize (ⲙ̄ⲙⲟ⸗) (vt)
				to be able, manage (to do: ⲉ- + inf) (vi)

				(causative of ⲱϩⲉ)
				establishment (nm)
ⲧⲁϩⲟ (ⲉ)ⲣⲁⲧ⸗				to make to stand, establish (ⲙ̄ⲙⲟ⸗)
ⲧⲁϫⲣⲟ	ⲧⲁϫⲣⲉ-	ⲧⲁϫⲣⲟ⸗	ⲧⲁϫⲣⲏⲩ†	to strengthen, confirm (ⲙ̄ⲙⲟ⸗) (vt)
				to become/be strengthened, firm (vi/vs)
				strength, firmness (nm)
ϩⲛ̄-ⲟⲩⲧⲁϫⲣⲟ				firmly, certainly
ⲧⲁϭⲥⲉ				sole of foot, footprint (nf)
ⲧⲃⲁ				ten thousand (nm)
ⲧⲃ̄ⲃⲟ	ⲧⲃ̄ⲃⲉ-	ⲧⲃ̄ⲃⲟ⸗	ⲧⲃ̄ⲃⲏⲩ†	to purify, cleanse (ⲙ̄ⲙⲟ⸗; of, from: ⲉ-, ⲉⲃⲟⲗ ϩⲛ̄-, ϩⲁ-) (vt)
				to become/be pure (vi/vs)
				(causative of ⲟⲩⲟⲡ)
				purity, purification (nm)
ⲧⲃⲛⲏ (pl ⲧⲃ̄ⲛⲟⲟⲩⲉ)				cattle, domestic animal (nm)
ⲧⲃ̄ⲧ, ⲑⲏⲃⲧ̄				fish (nm)
ⲧⲉ				is (copula fsg)
ⲧⲉⲓ-				this (nearer dem fsg)
τέλ(ε)ιος				perfect, complete (adv)
ⲧⲉⲗⲏⲗ				to rejoice (over: ⲉϫⲛ̄-) (vi)
				joy (nm)
τελώνης				tax collector (nm)
τέχνη				craft, skill, trade (nf)
ⲧⲉϩⲛⲉ				forehead (nf)
ⲧⲏ				that (further dem pron fsg)
ⲧⲏⲏⲃⲉ				finger (nm)
ⲧⲏⲣ⸗[4]				all, entire, the whole (of) (adj/inflected modifier)
ⲡⲧⲏⲣϥ̄				the entirety, everything
ⲉ-ⲡⲧⲏⲣϥ̄				entirely, completely
ⲧⲏⲣⲉⲓ				to guard (ⲙ̄ⲙⲟ⸗) (vt)
ⲧⲏⲩ	ⲧⲟⲩ-			wind, breath (nm)
(ⲧ)ⲕⲁⲥ				pain (nm)
ⲧⲙ̄-				don't (inf) (neg part)
ⲧⲛ̄ⲛⲟⲟⲩ	ⲧⲛ̄ⲛⲉⲩ-	ⲧⲛ̄ⲛⲟⲟⲩ⸗		to send (ⲙ̄ⲙⲟ⸗; to a person: ⲛⲁ⸗, ⲉ-; for: ⲛ̄ⲥⲁ-) (vt)
				(causative of ⲉⲓⲛⲉ)
ⲧⲛ̄ϩ, ⲧⲛ̄ϩ̄				wing (nm)
ⲧⲟⲛⲧⲛ̄	ⲧⲛ̄ⲧⲛ̄-	ⲧⲛ̄ⲧⲱⲛ⸗	ⲧⲛ̄ⲧⲱⲛ†	to liken, compare (ⲙ̄ⲙⲟ⸗; to ⲉ-, ⲙⲛ̄-, ⲉϫⲛ̄-) (vt)
				likeness, comparison (nm)
ⲧⲟⲟⲩ (pl ⲧⲟⲩⲉⲓⲏ)				mountain; monastery (nm)
ⲧⲟⲟⲩⲉ				sandal, shoe (nm)

---

4. A resumptive suffix (corresponding to the number/person/gender of the noun in question) is required.

τόπος				place (nm)
τότε				then, thereupon, next (conj)
ⲧⲟⲩⲉⲓⲟ		ⲧⲟⲩⲓⲟ⸗		to repay, return (ⲙ̄ⲙⲟ⸗) (vt)
				repayment, return (nm)
ⲧⲟⲩⲛⲟⲥ	ⲧⲟⲩⲛⲉⲥ-	ⲧⲟⲩⲛⲟⲥ⸗		to awaken, raise up (ⲙ̄ⲙⲟ⸗) (vt)
				(causative of ⲧⲱⲟⲩⲛ)
				raising (nm)
ⲧⲟⲩⲱ⸗				bosom, lap; embrace (of) (n)
ⲉⲧⲟⲩⲛ̄-, ⲉⲧⲟⲩⲉⲛ-		ⲉⲧⲟⲩⲱ⸗		beside, near (prep)
ϩⲓⲧⲟⲩⲛ̄-, ϩⲓⲧⲟⲩⲉⲛ-		ϩⲓⲧⲟⲩⲱ⸗		beside, near (prep)
ⲡⲉⲧ-ϩⲓⲧⲟⲩⲱ⸗				neighbor
ⲧⲟⲩϫⲟ	ⲧⲟⲩϫⲉ-	ⲧⲟⲩϫⲟ⸗	ⲧⲟⲩϫⲏⲩ†	to deliver, make safe (ⲙ̄ⲙⲟ⸗; from: ⲉ-, ⲉⲃⲟⲗ ϩ[ⲓⲧ]ⲛ̄-) (vt)
				to become/be delivered, safe (vi/vs)
				(causative of ⲟⲩϫⲁⲓ̈)
				deliverance, safety (nm)
ⲧⲟϣ				limit, border, district (nm)
τράπεζα				table (nf)
ⲧⲣⲓⲣ				oven (nf)
ⲧⲣⲟϣⲣⲉϣ			ⲧⲣⲉϣⲣⲱϣ†	to become/be red (vi/vs)
				redness (nm)
ⲧⲥⲁⲃⲟ	ⲧⲥⲁⲃⲉ-	ⲧⲥⲁⲃⲟ⸗	ⲧⲥⲁⲃⲏⲩ(ⲧ)†	to make wise, teach, instruct (ⲙ̄ⲙⲟ⸗; to: ⲉ-) (vt)
				(causative of ⲥ[ⲁ]ⲃⲟ)
				teaching, instruction (nm)
ⲧⲥⲛ̄ⲕⲟ, ⲧⲥⲉⲛⲕⲟ		ⲧⲥⲛ̄ⲕⲟ⸗		to breastfeed, nurse (ⲙ̄ⲙⲟ⸗) (vt)
				(causative of ⲥⲱⲛⲕ̄)
ⲧⲥⲟ	ⲧⲥⲉ-	ⲧⲥⲟ⸗	ⲧⲥⲏⲩ†	to give to drink, water (ⲙ̄ⲙⲟ⸗; with: ⲙ̄ⲙⲟ⸗) (vt)
				(causative of ⲥⲱ)
				watering (nm)
ⲧⲱ⸗				mine, yours, etc. (poss pron fsg)
ⲧⲱⲕ	ⲧⲉⲕ-	ⲧⲟⲕ⸗	ⲧⲏⲕ†	to strengthen, fortify, thicken (ⲙ̄ⲙⲟ⸗) (vt)
				to strengthen oneself (vr)
				to become strong, fortified, thick (vi)
ⲧⲱⲕ ⲛ̄-ϩⲏⲧ				to become courageous, confident
				confidence (nm)
ⲧⲱⲕⲙ̄	ⲧⲉⲕⲙ̄-	ⲧⲟⲕⲙ⸗	ⲧⲟⲕⲙ̄†	to pluck, pull (ⲙ̄ⲙⲟ⸗) (vt)
ⲧⲱⲗⲙ̄		ⲧⲟⲗⲙ⸗	ⲧⲟⲗⲙ̄†	to stain, defile (ⲙ̄ⲙⲟ⸗) (vt)
				to become stained, defiled (with, by: ϩⲛ̄-, ⲙ̄ⲙⲟ⸗) (vi)
				stain, defilement (nm)
ⲧⲱⲙ	ⲧⲉⲙ-	ⲧⲟⲙ⸗	ⲧⲏⲙ†	to close, shut (ⲙ̄ⲙⲟ⸗) (vt)
				to shut, close (subject: door, eyes, mouth, etc.) (vi)
				to be shut (vs)

ⲧⲱⲙ		ⲧⲏⲙ†	to sharpen (ⲙ̄ⲙⲟ⸗) (vt)
			to become sharp (vi)
ⲧⲱⲙⲧ̄, ⲧⲱⲙⲛ̄ⲧ		ⲧⲟⲙⲛ̄ⲧ†	to meet (someone: [ⲉϩⲟⲩⲛ] ⲉ-) (vi)
			meeting (nm)
ⲧⲱⲛ			where? (inter pron)
ⲉ-ⲧⲱⲛ			(to) where?
ⲉⲃⲟⲗ ⲧⲱⲛ			(from) where?
ⲧⲱⲟⲩⲛ	ⲧⲟⲩⲛ-	ⲧⲱⲟⲩⲛ⸗	to raise (ⲙ̄ⲙⲟ⸗) (vt)
			to arise, get up (from: ⲉⲃⲟⲗ ϩⲓ-, ⲉⲃⲟⲗ ϩⲛ̄-); to rise up (against: ⲉ-, ⲉϫⲛ̄-, ⲉϩⲣⲁⲓ̈ ⲉϫⲛ̄-) (vi/vr)
			rising (nm)
ⲧⲱⲡⲉ	ⲧⲉⲡ-	ⲧⲟⲡ⸗, ⲧⲱⲡ⸗	to taste (ⲙ̄ⲙⲟ⸗) (vt)
			tasting (nm)
ⲧⲱⲣⲉ	ⲧⲛ̄-	ⲧⲟⲟⲧ⸗	hand; handle; implement (usually in compounds) (nf)
ⲉⲧⲛ̄-		ⲉⲧⲟⲟⲧ⸗	to (prep)
ⲛ̄ⲧⲛ̄-		ⲛ̄ⲧⲟⲟⲧ⸗	from, by (prep)
ⲉⲃⲟⲗ ⲛ̄ⲧⲛ̄-			from
ⲛ̄ⲧⲉ- = ⲛ̄ⲧⲛ̄-			
ϩⲁⲧⲛ̄-		ϩⲁⲧⲟⲟⲧ⸗	beside, near, with (prep)
ϩⲓⲧⲛ̄-		ϩⲓⲧⲟⲟⲧ⸗	through, by, from (prep)
ⲉⲃⲟⲗ ϩⲓⲧⲛ̄-			through, by
ϣⲛ̄-ⲧⲱⲣⲉ			to shake hands, guarantee
			guarantee, assurance (nm)
ⲧⲱⲣⲡ̄	ⲧⲉⲣⲡ̄-	ⲧⲟⲣⲡ⸗	to plunder (ⲙ̄ⲙⲟ⸗) (vt)
			plunder (nm)
ⲧⲱⲣⲧ̄			staircase (nm)
ⲧⲱ(ⲣ)ⲧⲣ̄			step, degree (nm)
ⲧⲱⲣϣ̄, ⲧⲣⲟϣ		ⲧⲟⲣϣ̄†	to become/be red (vi/vs)
ⲧⲱ(ⲱ)ⲃⲉ			brick ("adobe" is ultimately derived from this word) (nmf)
ⲧⲱⲱⲃⲉ	ⲧⲉⲃⲉ-	ⲧⲟⲟⲃ⸗	to repay (ⲙ̄ⲙⲟ⸗) (vt)
			repayment (nm)
ⲉⲧⲃⲉ-		ⲉⲧⲃⲏⲏⲧ⸗	about, concerning, because of (prep)
ⲧⲱⲱⲃⲉ		ⲧⲟⲟⲃ⸗ ⲧⲟ(ⲟ)ⲃⲉ†	to seal (ⲙ̄ⲙⲟ⸗) (vt)
			seal (nm)
ⲧⲱϭⲉ	ⲧⲉϭ-	ⲧⲟ(ⲟ)ϭ⸗ ⲧⲏϭ†	1. to join, attach (ⲙ̄ⲙⲟ⸗; to: ⲉ-); 2. to plant (ⲙ̄ⲙⲟ⸗) (vt)
			to join, cling (to: ⲉ-) (vi)
			planting (nm)
ⲧⲱϭⲉ ⲉⲃⲟⲗ			to publish
ⲧⲱϣ	ⲧⲉϣ-	ⲧⲟϣ⸗ ⲧⲏϣ†	to limit, determine (ⲙ̄ⲙⲟ⸗) (vt)
			to become limited, determined (vi)

				determination, destiny (nm)
ⲧⲱϩ				chaff (nm)
ⲧⲱϩⲃ̄		ⲧⲁϩⲃ⸗	ⲧⲁϩⲃ†	to moisten, soak (ⲙ̄ⲙⲟ⸗) (vt)
ⲧⲱϩⲙ̄	ⲧⲉϩⲙ̄-	ⲧⲁϩⲙ⸗	ⲧⲁϩⲙ̄†	to invite, summon; knock (ⲙ̄ⲙⲟ⸗) (vt)
				invitation, summons (nm)
ⲧⲱϩⲥ̄	ⲧⲉϩⲥ̄-	ⲧⲁϩⲥ⸗	ⲧⲁϩⲥ̄†	to anoint (ⲙ̄ⲙⲟ⸗) (vt)
				anointing (nm)
ⲧϭⲁ(ⲉ)ⲓⲟ	ⲧϭⲁ(ⲉ)ⲓⲉ-	ⲧϭⲁ(ⲉ)ⲓⲟ⸗	ⲧϭⲁ(ⲉ)ⲓⲏⲩ†	to make ugly, disgrace, condemn (ⲙ̄ⲙⲟ⸗) (vt)
				to be ugly, disgraced, condemned (vi)
				ugliness, disgrace, condemnation (nm)

Ⲩ ϩⲉ

Ⲫ ⲫⲓ

ⲫⲁⲛⲧⲁⲥⲓⲁ	appearance (nf)
ⲫⲓⲁⲗⲏ	bowl (nf)
ⲫⲓⲗⲟⲥⲟⲫⲟⲥ	philosopher, one who is "fond of wisdom" (nm)
ⲫⲣⲟⲛⲓⲙⲟⲥ	thoughtful, clever, shrewd (adj)
ⲫⲩⲗⲏ	tribe (nf)

Ⲭ ⲭⲓ

ⲭⲁⲓⲣⲉ (pl ⲭⲁⲓⲣⲉⲧⲉ)	rejoice! (an impv used as a greeting)
ⲭⲁⲣⲓⲥ	favor (nf)
ⲭⲏⲣⲁ	widow (nf)
ⲭⲓⲗⲓⲁⲣⲭⲟⲥ	commander (of a cohort, originally a "thousand") (nm)
ⲭⲓⲱⲛ	snow (nf)
ⲭⲟⲣⲧⲟⲥ	grass (nm)
ⲭⲣ(ⲉ)ⲓⲁ	need, necessity (nf)
ⲣ̄-ⲭⲣ(ⲉ)ⲓⲁ	to need (ⲙ̄ⲙⲟ⸗); to have to (do: ⲉ- + inf)
ⲭⲣⲏⲙⲁ	money, wealth (nm)
ⲭⲣⲏⲥⲧⲟⲥ	useful, helpful (adj)
ⲭⲣⲓⲥⲧⲟⲥ	anointed one (abbreviated as x̄c̄ or x̄p̄c̄) (nm)
ⲭⲣⲟⲛⲟⲥ	time (nm)
ⲭⲱⲣⲁ	region, country(side) (nf)
ⲭⲱⲣⲓⲥ-	without, apart from (prep)

ⲯ   ⲯⲓ

ⲯⲁⲗⲗⲉⲓ	to sing, chant; to play (an instrument) (to: ⲉ-) (vi)
ⲯⲁⲗⲙⲟⲥ	musical composition (originally with instrumental accompaniment) (nm)
ⲯⲁⲗⲧⲏⲣⲓⲟⲛ	harp (nm)
ⲯⲓⲧ, ⲯⲓⲥ (f ⲯⲓⲧⲉ, ⲯⲓⲥⲉ)	nine (num)
ⲯⲩⲫⲟⲥ	pebble, stone (nf)
ⲯⲩⲭⲏ (pl ⲯⲩⲭⲟⲟⲩⲉ)	self, (inner) being (nf)

ⲱ   ⲱ

ⲱ				oh! (interj)
ⲱ(-ⲙⲉⲅⲁ)				ō(-mega) (last letter of Greek alphabet) (nm)
ⲱⲃϣ̄	ⲉⲃϣ̄-	ⲟⲃϣ⸗	ⲟⲃϣ†	to forget, overlook, neglect (ⲙ̄ⲙⲟ⸗) (vt)
				to sleep, fall asleep (vi)
				forgetting; sleep (nm)
	ⲣ̄-ⲡ(⸗)ⲱⲃϣ̄			to forget (ⲛ̄-)
ⲱⲇⲏ				song (nf)
ⲱⲕⲙ̄	ⲉⲕⲙ̄-		ⲟⲕⲙ̄†	to become/be gloomy, dark (vi/vs)
				gloom (nm)
ⲱⲙⲕ̄	ⲉⲙⲕ̄-	ⲟⲙⲕ⸗		to swallow (ⲙ̄ⲙⲟ⸗) (vt)
				to be swallowed (vi)
ⲱⲙⲥ̄	ⲉⲙⲥ̄-	ⲟⲙⲥ⸗	ⲟⲙⲥ†	to sink, dip, immerse (ⲙ̄ⲙⲟ⸗) (vt)
				to sink (into: ϩⲛ̄-, ⲉ-, ⲉϩⲟⲩⲛ ⲉ-) (vi)
ⲱⲛⲉ	ⲉⲛⲉ-			stone (nm)
	ⲉⲛⲉ-ⲙ̄-ⲙⲉ			precious stone, jewel (nm)
ⲱⲛϩ̄			ⲟⲛϩ†	to live, become/be alive (vi/vs)
				life (nm)
ⲱⲡ	ⲉⲡ-	ⲟⲡ⸗	ⲏⲡ†	to count, calculate (ⲙ̄ⲙⲟ⸗); to consider (ⲙ̄ⲙⲟ⸗; as: ⲙ̄ⲙⲟ⸗; as belonging to: ⲉ-) (vt)
				to be counted, considered (as belonging to: ⲉ-) (vs)
				(ac)count (nm)
ⲱⲣⲕ̄		ⲟⲣⲕ⸗		to swear (ⲙ̄ⲙⲟ⸗) (vt)
				swearing, oath (nm)
ⲱⲣϣ̄			ⲟⲣϣ†	to become/be cold (vi/vs)
ⲱⲣⲭ̄	ⲉⲣⲭ̄-, ⲣⲭ-	ⲟⲣⲭ⸗	ⲟⲣⲭ̄†	to fasten, bind, imprison; to close (ⲙ̄ⲙⲟ⸗; against: ⲉ-) (vt)
				to be firm, secure (vi)
				firmness, assurance; deed of security (nm)
	ϩⲛ̄-ⲟⲩⲱⲣⲭ̄			firmly, surely, certainly, diligently

ⲱⲥⲕ̄			ⲟⲥⲕ̄†	to delay, tarry; to be prolonged; to continue (doing: circum) (vi)
ⲱⲧⲡ̄	ⲉⲧⲡ̄-	ⲟⲧⲡ⸗	ⲟⲧⲡ̄†	(± ⲉϩⲟⲩⲛ) to imprison, shut in (ⲙ̄ⲙⲟ⸗) (vt)
ⲱ(ⲱ)			ⲉⲉⲧ†	to become/be pregnant, conceive (vi/vs)
ⲱϣ	ⲉϣ-	ⲟϣ⸗		to utter, read (aloud) (ⲙ̄ⲙⲟ⸗) (vt)
ⲱϣ ⲉⲃⲟⲗ				to cry out
ⲱϩⲉ			ⲁϩⲉ†	to stand, stay, wait (vi)
				to be in need (of: ⲛⲁ⸗) (vs)
ⲁϩⲉⲣⲁⲧ⸗				to stand oneself (before: ⲉ-; against: ⲉ-, ⲉϫⲛ̄-, ⲟⲩⲃⲉ-; with: ⲙⲛ̄-)
ⲱϩⲥ̄, ⲱⲥϩ̄	ⲉϩⲥ̄-	ⲟϩⲥ⸗, ⲟⲥϩ⸗		to reap, harvest (ⲙ̄ⲙⲟ⸗) (vt)
				reaping (nm)
ⲱϫⲛ̄	ⲉϫⲛ̄-	ⲟϫⲛ⸗		to make cease (ⲙ̄ⲙⲟ⸗) (vt)
				to cease (vi)
				ceasing (nm)
ⲱϭⲧ̄	ⲉϭⲧ̄-	ⲟϭⲧ⸗		to choke, strangle (ⲙ̄ⲙⲟ⸗) (vt)

ϣ ϣⲁⲓ

ϣ-, ⲉϣ-			originally a full verb "to know (how to)," may be prefixed to any inf to express "can, be able" ⲙ̄ⲡⲉϥϣ-ⲃⲱⲕ (he was not able to go) (v)
ϣⲁ			festival, feast day (nm)
ϣⲁ-	ϣⲁⲣⲟ⸗		to(ward), up to (prep)
ϣⲁ			to rise (of sun, etc.) (vi)
			rising (nm)
ϣⲁ	ϣⲁⲛⲧ⸗		nose (nm)
ϣⲁⲁⲣⲉ	ϣⲁⲣ⸗	ϣⲁⲣ†	to strike (ⲉ-) (vt)
			strike (nm)
ϣⲁⲩ	ϣⲟⲩ-		use, worth, value (nm)
ϣⲁϩ			flame (nm)
ϣⲁϫⲉ			to speak, talk (to, with: ⲉ-, ⲙⲛ̄-; about: ⲉ[ⲧⲃⲉ]-, ϩⲁ-; against: ⲛ̄ⲥⲁ-, ⲟⲩⲃⲉ-) (vt)
			word, speech; matter (nm)
ϣⲃⲏⲣ (pl ϣⲃⲉⲉⲣ) ϣⲃⲣ̄-			friend, companion (nm; ϣⲃⲉⲉⲣⲉ [f])
ϣⲉ (pl ⲉϣⲁⲩ)			pig (nm; ⲉϣⲱ, sow [f])
ϣⲉ			wood (nm)
ϣⲉ			(one) hundred (num)
ϣⲉ			to go (vi)
ϣⲉⲗⲉⲉⲧ			bride; wedding, marriage (nf)
ⲡⲁ-ⲧϣⲉⲗⲉⲉⲧ			bridegroom
ϣⲏⲓ			pit, cistern (nm)

ϣнм (f ϣнмє) — small, little (usually before noun or often after without ⲛ̄-) (adj)

ϣнⲛ — tree (nm)

ϣнⲣє (pl ϣⲣⲏⲩ) ϣⲣ̄-, ϣⲛ̄-, ϣє- — son, child (nm; ϣєєⲣє, daughter [f])
   ϣнⲣє ϣнм — little child, baby

ϣнⲧ — two hundred (num)

ϣⲓ   ϣⲓ-   ϣⲓⲧ⸗ — to measure (ⲙ̄ⲙⲟ⸗); to measure out (vt)
measure, weight, extent; measuring basket; moderation (nm)

ϣⲓⲃє   ϣⲃ̄(ⲧ)-   ϣⲃ̄ⲧ⸗   ϣⲟⲃє† — to change, alter (ⲙ̄ⲙⲟ⸗) (vt)
to change, be altered (to: є-; into: ϩⲛ̄-; in form ⲛ̄-ⲥⲙⲟⲧ) (vi/vr)
to be different, various (vs)
change, difference (nm)

ϣїн — length (nf)

ϣⲓⲕє, ϣⲓⲧє   ϣєⲕⲧ̄-   ϣⲁⲕⲧ⸗, ϣⲓ(ⲕ)ⲧ⸗   ϣⲟⲕє† — to dig (vt/vi)
depth (nm)

ϣⲓⲛⲁ — so that (conj)

ϣⲓⲛє   ϣⲛ̄-   ϣⲛ̄ⲧ⸗ — to seek, inquire after (ⲛ̄ⲥⲁ-); to visit (є-); to greet (є-) (vt)
search, inquiry; news (nm)
   ϭⲙ̄-ⲡϣⲓⲛє ⲛ̄-, ϭⲙ̄-ⲡ⸗ϣⲓⲛє — to search out, visit

ϣⲓⲡє — to be ashamed (about: єⲧⲃє-) (vi)
shame (nm)
   ϣⲓⲡє ϩⲏⲧ⸗ ⲛ̄- — to be ashamed before, revere
   ϫⲓ-ϣⲓⲡє — to be put to shame, ashamed
   ϯ-ϣⲓⲡє — to (put to) shame

ϣⲓⲣє, ϣⲏⲣє (f ϣєєⲣє) — small (adj)

ϣⲕⲟⲗ — hole (nm)

ϣⲗⲏⲗ — to pray (for something: є-, єⲧⲃє-, єϫⲛ̄-, ϩⲁ-; for someone: є-) (vi)
prayer (nm)

ϣⲗϭⲟⲙ, ϣⲗ̄ⲧⲁⲙ — mustard (nmf)

ϣⲙ̄ⲙⲟ (f ϣⲙ̄ⲙⲱ; pl ϣⲙ̄ⲙⲟï) — foreign (adj)

ϣⲙⲟⲩⲛ (f ϣⲙⲟⲩⲛє) -ϣⲙⲏⲛ(є) — eight (num)

ϣⲙ̄ϣє   ϣⲙ̄ϣє-   ϣⲙ̄ϣⲏⲧ⸗ — to serve, worship (ⲛⲁ⸗) (vt)
service, worship (nm)

ϣⲛ̄ⲧⲟ, ϣⲛ̄ⲧⲱ — linen robe, sheet (nf)

ϣⲟ — (one) thousand (num)

ϣⲟєⲓϣ — dust (nm)

ϣⲟєⲓϫ — contender, athlete (nmf)

ϣⲟⲙⲛ̄ⲧ (f ϣⲟⲙⲧє) -ϣⲟⲙⲧє — three (num)

ϣⲟⲛⲧє — thorn bush/tree (acacia) (nf)

SAHIDIC-ENGLISH LEXICON

ϣo(o)м (pl ϣмoүı)				father/son-in-law (nm; ϣωмε, mother/daughter-in-law [f])
ϣooүε			ϣoүωoү†	to become/be dry (vi/vs)
ϣoрπ̄ (f ϣoрπε)				first (usually before noun) (adj)
ⲛ̄-ϣoрπ̄				at first, formerly
ϣoтϣ̄т, ϣoxт̄	ϣeтϣωт-		ϣeтϣωт†	to carve, hollow (ⲙ̄мoϵ; into: ϵ-) (vt)
ϣoүo	ϣoү(ε)-	ϣoүω=	ϣoүϵıт†	to empty, pour out, discharge (ⲙ̄мoϵ; from: ⲙ̄мoϵ, ϵвoλ ⲙ̄мoϵ, ϵвoλ ϩⲛ̄-; into: ϩⲛ̄-) (vt)
				to flow, pour out (vi)
				to be empty, vain (vs)
ϣoϣт̄				block, lock; key [cf. cωϣт̄] (nm)
ϣoxⲛε				to consider (ⲙ̄мoϵ); to take counsel (concerning: ϵ-, ϵxⲛ̄-; with: мⲛ̄-) (vt)
				consideration, counsel (nm)
ϣπнрε				wonder, amazement (nf)
ϣčⲛε				sudden (moment) (n)
ϩⲛ̄-oүϣčⲛε				suddenly
ϣтoм			ϣтaм†	to close, shut (ⲙ̄мoϵ; against: ϵрⲛ̄-) (vt)
				to be closed, shut (vi)
				gate, what is shut (nm)
ϣтεкo (pl ϣтεкωoү)				prison (nm)
ϣтнⲛ				garment, tunic (nf)
ϣтoртр̄	ϣтр̄тр̄-	ϣтр̄тωр=	ϣтр̄тωр†	to disturb, trouble (ⲙ̄мoϵ) (vt)
				to become disturbed, troubled (vi)
				to be disturbed, upset (vs)
				disturbance, trouble (nm)
ϣω				sand (nm)
ϣωвϩ̄, ϣωϩв		ϣoвϩ=, ϣoϩв=	ϣoвϩ̄†	to scorch, wither (ⲙ̄мoϵ) (vt)
				to become scorched, withered (vi)
ϣωı				height, (what is) above (< ϣ[ı]aı) (nm)
ϵπϣωı				upward (adv)
ϣωλ	ϣϵλ-	ϣoλ=		(cp ϣaλ-) to plunder (ⲙ̄мoϵ) (vt)
ϣωλϩ̄		ϣoλϩ=	ϣoλϩ̄†	to mark (ⲙ̄мoϵ) (vt)
				mark, marker (nm)
ϣωм				summer (nm)
ϣωⲛε			ϣooⲛε†	(cp ϣaⲛ-, ϣⲛ̄-) to become/be sick (vi/vs)
				sickness (nm)
ϣωπ	ϣεπ-, ϣπ̄-	ϣoπ=	ϣнπ†	to receive, accept, get; to buy (ⲙ̄мoϵ; from: ⲛ̄тⲛ̄-; for [cost] ϩa-; often with reflexive ϵрoϵ) (vt)
				to be received, acceptable (vs)
				acceptance; purchase (nm)

ϣⲱⲡⲉ			ϣⲟⲟⲡ†	to become, come into existence; to happen (vi)
				to be, exist[5] (vs)
				being, existence (nm)
ϣⲱⲡⲉ ⲙ̄ⲙⲟ⸗				to happen to (someone)
ⲁⲥϣⲱⲡⲉ				it happened that (followed by main verb)
ⲉϣⲱⲡⲉ				if
ϣⲱⲣⲡ̄	ϣⲣ̄ⲡ-	ϣⲟⲣⲡ⸗	ϣⲟⲣⲡ̄†	to be early, first (vi)
				morning (nm)
ϣⲱⲥ (pl ϣⲟⲟⲥ)				shepherd (nm)
ϣⲱⲧⲉ				well, cistern (nf)
ϣⲱⲧⲙ̄	ϣⲉⲧⲙ̄-, ϣⲧⲙ̄-		ϣⲟⲧⲙ̄†	to close, seal (ⲙ̄ⲙⲟ⸗; against: ⲉⲣⲛ̄-) (vt)
				to be closed, sealed (vi)
ϣⲱⲱⲧ	ϣⲉ(ⲉ)ⲧ-	ϣⲁⲁⲧ⸗	ϣⲁⲁⲧ†	(cp ϣⲁⲧ-) to cut (off), sacrifice (vt)
				to be lacking (for, of, in: ⲉ-, ⲙ̄ⲙⲟ⸗, ϩⲛ̄-) (vi/vs)
				cutting off (nm)
ϣⲁ(ⲁ)ⲧⲛ̄-				except, minus, short of (prep)
ϣⲱⲱϭⲉ	ϣⲉⲉϭⲉ-	ϣⲟⲟϭ⸗		to strike, wound (vt)
ϣⲱϫⲉ				to contend (vi)
				contest (nm)
ϣⲱϫⲛ̄	ϣⲉϫⲛ̄-	ϣⲟϫⲛ⸗	ϣⲟϫⲛ̄†	to allow to remain, leave (ⲙ̄ⲙⲟ⸗) (vt)
				to remain, be left over (vi)
				remainder (nm)
ϣϣⲉ, ⲉϣϣⲉ				it's appropriate, proper, necessary (impersonal predicate)
ϣϥⲉ				seventy (num)

ϥ   ϥⲁⲓ

ϥⲓ	ϥⲓ-	ϥⲓⲧ⸗		(cp ϥⲁï-) to lift up, take, bear, carry (ⲙ̄ⲙⲟ⸗) (vt)
ϥⲓ ⲙⲛ̄-				to agree with
ϥⲓ ϩⲁ-				to bear, tolerate
ϥⲛ̄ⲧ, ϥⲛ̄ⲧ̄				worm (nmf)
ϥⲧⲟⲟⲩ (f ϥⲧⲟ[ⲉ])	-ⲁϥⲧⲉ			four (num)
ϥⲱ, ⲃⲱ				hair (nm)
ϥⲱⲧⲉ	ϥⲉⲧ-	ϥⲟⲧ⸗		(± ⲉⲃⲟⲗ) to wipe away/out (ⲙ̄ⲙⲟ⸗) (vt)

ϩ   ϩⲟⲡⲓ

| ϩⲁ- | | ϩⲁⲣⲟ⸗ | | under; concerning (prep) |
| ϩⲁⲣⲓϩⲁⲣⲟ⸗ | | | | alone, -self |

---

5. A predicate adjective is introduced with ⲛ̄- and has no article: ⲛⲉⲛϣⲟⲟⲡ ⲛ̄-δίκαιος (we were [being] just).

ϩⲁⲉ (f ϩⲁⲏ; pl ϩⲁⲉⲉⲩ[ⲉ]) — last (usually before noun) (adj)
ϩⲁ(ⲉ)ⲓⲃⲉⲥ — shade, shadow (nf)
    ⲣ̄-ϩⲁ(ⲉ)ⲓⲃⲉⲥ — to make shade (for: ⲉ-, ⲉϫⲛ̄-)
ϩⲁⲓ̈ — husband (nm)
ϩⲁⲕ — sober, prudent (adj)
ϩάλασσα, θάλασσα — sea (nf)
ϩⲁⲗⲏⲧ (pl ϩⲁⲗⲁ[ⲁ]ⲧⲉ) — bird, flying animal (nm)
ϩⲁⲗⲟⲩⲥ — spiderweb (nm)
ϩⲁⲙⲏⲛ — (it's) trustworthy! so be it! (ultimately from Hebrew) (interj)
ϩⲁⲙϣⲉ (pl ϩⲁⲙϣⲏⲩⲉ) — carpenter (nm)
ϩⲁⲡ — judgment (nm)
ϩⲁⲡⲗⲟⲩⲥ — single, simple, sincere (adj)
ϩⲁⲡⲥ̄ — it's necessary (impersonal predicate)
ϩⲁⲣⲉϩ — to guard, watch (ⲉ-; from: ⲉ-, ⲉⲃⲟⲗ ϩⲛ̄-); to keep, observe, preserve (ⲉ-) (vt)
     — guard, watch (nm)
ϩάρμα — chariot (nm)
ϩⲁⲧ — silver; coins, money (nm)
ϩⲁⲧⲉ — (± ⲉⲃⲟⲗ) to pour (ⲙ̄ⲙⲟ⸗) (vt)
     — to flow (vi)
     — flow (nm)
    ⲙⲁ ⲛ̄-ϩⲁⲧⲉ — channel (nm)
ϩⲁϩ — many (usually before singular noun with ⲛ̄-) (adj)
ϩⲁϭⲉ — snare (nm)
ϩⲃⲟ(ⲟ)ⲥ (pl ϩⲃⲱ[ⲱ]ⲥ) — covering, garment; linen (nmf)
ϩⲃⲟⲩⲣ — left (hand) (nf)
ϩⲃⲥⲱ (pl ϩⲃⲥⲟⲟⲩⲉ) — covering, garment (nf)
ϩⲉ — way, manner (nf)
    ⲧⲁⲓ̈ ⲧⲉ ⲑⲉ — this is the way
    ⲛ̄-ⲧⲉⲓ̈ϩⲉ — in this way, thus
    ⲛ̄-ⲑⲉ ⲛ̄-, ⲛ̄-ⲧ⸗ϩⲉ — like, as, in the manner of
    ⲁϣ ⲛ̄-ϩⲉ — (of) what manner?
    ⲛ̄-ⲁϣ ⲛ̄-ϩⲉ — in what way? how?
    ⲣ̄-ⲑⲉ — (ⲟ† ⲛ̄) to become/be like; to make like
ϩⲉ-   ϩ- — season (nm)
ϩⲉ   ϩⲏⲩ† — to fall (vi)
     — to be falling (vs, exclusively with Present)
     — fall (nm)
    ϩⲉ ⲉ- — to fall to, upon, into; to find, chance upon
    ϩⲉ ⲉⲃⲟⲗ — to fall away, perish
ϩⲉⲑⲛⲓⲕⲟⲥ — national, native (adj)
ϩⲉⲑⲛⲟⲥ — nation, national, native (nm)

ϩέλος		marsh (nm)
ϩελπιζε		to hope (in, for: ⲉ-) (vt)
ϩελπίς		hope (nf)
ϩⲉⲛ-, ϩⲛ̄-		some, certain (< ϩⲟⲉⲓⲛⲉ) (indef art)
ϩⲉⲛⲉⲉⲧⲉ		monastery, convent (nf)
ϩερμηнεία		interpretation (nf)
ϩⲏ, ⲉϩⲏ, ϩⲓⲏ	ϩⲏⲧ⸗	front, fore part; beginning (nf)
ⲉⲑⲏ		forward, ahead (adv)
(ⲉ)ϩⲏⲧ⸗		before (of place) (prep)
ϩⲁⲑⲏ	ϩⲁⲧ⸗ϩⲏ	before (prep)
ϩⲓ-ⲑⲏ ⲛ̄-		in front of
ϩⲏ	ϩⲏⲧ⸗	belly, womb (nf)
ⲛ̄ϩⲏⲧ⸗		in, among, within, at (see ϩⲛ̄-) (prep)
ϩⲏⲃⲉ, ϩⲃ̄ⲃⲉ		mourning, grief (nmf)
ϩⲏⲃⲥ̄		lamp (nm)
ϩⲏⲅⲉⲙⲱⲛ		governor (nm)
ϩⲏⲕⲉ		poor (adj)
ϩηλικία		maturity, (old) age (nf)
ϩⲏⲛⲉ		(usually pl) spice, incense (nm)
ϣⲟⲩ-ϩⲏⲛⲉ		incense (nm)
ϩⲏ(ⲟ)ⲩ		profit, benefit, usefulness (nm)
ⲣ̄-ϩⲏⲩ		to be profitable, useful (to: ⲛⲁ-)
ϯ-ϩⲏⲩ		to give profit, benefit (to: ⲛⲁ-)
ϩⲏⲧ (pl ϩⲉⲧⲉ)	ϩⲧⲏ⸗	heart, mind (nm)
ϩⲏⲧ ϣⲏⲙ		little heart (> impatience)
ⲣ̄-ϩⲧⲏ⸗		to change one's mind (about: ⲉ-, ⲉϫⲛ̄-, ⲛ̄ⲥⲁ-)
ϣⲁⲛ-/ϣⲛ̄-ϩⲧⲏ⸗		to have compassion, pity (on: ⲉϫⲛ̄-, ⲉϩⲣⲁⲓ̈ ⲉϫⲛ̄-)
ϯ-ϩⲧⲏ⸗		to pay attention, consider (to: ⲉ-, ⲉϫⲛ̄-, ϩⲓ-, ϩⲛ̄-)
ⲃⲁⲗ-ϩⲏⲧ		heart-loose (> simple, innocent)
ϩⲁⲣϣ̄-ϩⲏⲧ		heart-heavy (> patient)
ϫⲁⲥⲓ-ϩⲏⲧ		heart-exalting (> arrogant)
ϭⲁⲃ-ϩⲏⲧ		heart-weak (> scared)
ϩⲁ(ϩ)ⲧⲛ̄-	ϩⲁ(ϩ)ⲧⲏ⸗	beside, near, with (prep)
ϩⲏⲧ (pl ϩⲧⲉⲉⲩ)	ϩⲧⲏ⸗	tip, edge (nm)
ϩⲓ-	ϩⲓⲱ(ⲱ)⸗	on; and (noun without article only) (prep)
ϩⲓ-ⲛⲁⲓ̈		thus
ⲉⲃⲟⲗ ϩⲓ-		from on
ⲉϩⲟⲩⲛ ϩⲓ-		in on
ⲉϩⲣⲁⲓ̈ ϩⲓ-		up/down on
ⲉⲡⲉⲥⲏⲧ ϩⲓ-		down on
ϩⲓⲉⲓⲃ		lamb (nmf; also ϩⲓⲁ[ⲓ]ⲃⲉ [f])
ϩⲓⲉⲓⲧ		pit, ditch (nm)

ϩⲓⲏ (pl ϩⲓⲟⲟⲩⲉ)				road, way, path (nf)
ϩⲓⲕ				magic, ritual power (nm)
ϩⲓⲕⲱⲛ				image (nf)
ϩⲓⲟⲩⲉ	ϩⲓ-	ϩⲓⲧ⸗		1. to beat, strike (ⲙ̄ⲙⲟ⸗, ⲉ-, ⲉϫⲛ̄-, ϩⲛ̄-, ⲉϩⲟⲩⲛ ⲉ-; with: ⲙ̄ⲙⲟ⸗, ϩⲛ̄-); 2. to cast, throw (ⲙ̄ⲙⲟ⸗; ± ⲉⲃⲟⲗ, ⲉϩⲣⲁⲓ̈) (vt)
	ϩⲓ-ⲧⲟⲟⲧ⸗			to begin, undertake (to do: ⲉ- + inf); to place one's hand (on: ⲉ-)
ϩⲓⲣ				street (nm)
ϩⲓⲥⲉ	ϩⲁⲥⲧ̄-	ϩⲁⲥⲧ⸗	ϩⲟⲥⲉ†	to weary, trouble (ⲙ̄ⲙⲟ⸗) (vt) to labor; to become weary, troubled (vi) labor, weariness, trouble (nm)
ϩⲕⲟ			ϩⲕⲁⲉⲓⲧ†	to become/be hungry (vi/vs) hunger, famine (nm)
ϩⲗⲗⲟ (f ϩⲗⲗⲱ; pl ϩⲗⲗⲟⲓ̈)				old (as nm > monk) (adj)
ϩⲗⲟⲟⲗⲉ				to nurse (a child: ⲙ̄ⲙⲟ⸗) (vt)
ϩⲗⲟϭ			ϩⲟⲗϭ̄†	(cp ϩⲁⲗϭ̄-) to become/be sweet (vi/vs) sweetness (nm)
ϩⲙⲉ	ϩⲙⲉ(ⲧ)-			forty (num)
ϩⲙⲉⲛⲉ	ϩⲙⲉⲛⲉ(ⲧ)-			eighty (num)
ϩⲙⲟⲙ			ϩⲏⲙ†	to become/be hot (vi/vs) heat, fever (nm)
ϩⲙⲟⲟⲥ				to sit down; to dwell (vi)
ϩⲙⲟⲧ				favor, gift; gratitude, thanks (nm)
ϣⲡ̄-ϩⲙⲟⲧ ⲛ̄ⲧⲛ̄-				to give thanks to (for: ⲉϫⲛ̄-, ϩⲓ-, ϩⲁ-)
ϭⲛ̄-ϩⲙⲟⲧ				to find favor
ϩⲙⲟⲩ				salt (nm)
ϩⲙ̄ⲥ, ϩⲙ̄ⲥ̄				ear of grain (nm)
ϩⲙ̄ϩⲁⲗ				slave, servant (nmf)
ϩⲛ̄-		ⲛ̄ϩⲏⲧ⸗		in, among, within, at (ⲛ̄ϩⲏⲧ⸗ from ϩⲏ belly, womb) (prep)
ⲉⲃⲟⲗ ϩⲛ̄-				out of, from (in)
ⲉϩⲟⲩⲛ ϩⲛ̄-				into, within
ⲛ̄ϩⲟⲩⲛ ϩⲛ̄-				within
ϩⲣⲁⲓ̈ ϩⲛ̄-				in
ϩⲛ̄-ⲟⲩ-				often adv: -ly
ϩⲛⲁ(ⲁ)ⲩ				vessel, object (nm)
ϩⲛⲉ-		ϩⲛⲁ⸗		pleased, willing (to: ⲉ- + inf) (verboid)
ⲣ̄-ϩⲛⲁ⸗				to be pleased, willing (to: ⲉ-[ⲧⲣⲉ-])
ϩⲛ̄ⲕⲉ				beer (nm)
ϩⲟ		ϩⲣⲁ⸗		face; surface (nm)
ⲉϩⲣⲛ̄-		ⲉϩⲣⲁ⸗		toward (prep)
ⲉⲃⲟⲗ ⲉϩⲣⲛ̄-				out toward
ⲉϩⲟⲩⲛ ⲉϩⲣⲛ̄-				in toward

ϩⲓϩⲣⲁ⸗				on the face of (prep)
(ⲛ̄)ⲛⲁϩⲣⲛ̄-	(ⲛ̄)ⲛⲁϩⲣⲁ⸗			in front of, facing (prep)
ϩⲟ(ⲉ)ⲓⲛⲉ				some, certain ones (indef pron)
ϩⲟ(ⲉ)ⲓⲧⲉ				garment, cloak (nmf)
ϩⲟⲗⲱⲥ				wholly, entirely (adv)
ϩⲟⲙⲛ̄ⲧ, ϩⲟⲙⲧ̄				copper, bronze; coin (nm)
ϩⲟⲙⲟⲗⲟⲅⲉⲓ				to acknowledge (ⲙ̄ⲙⲟ⸗) (vt)
ϩⲟⲟⲗⲉ				moth (nf)
ϩⲟⲟⲩ				day (nm)
(ⲙ̄-)ⲡⲟⲟⲩ				today (ϩ drops)
ϣⲁ-ⲡⲟⲟⲩ				until today, until now
ϩⲟⲟⲩ†				to be bad, evil (vs)
ⲡⲉⲑⲟⲟⲩ				the one who's evil, the evil (one)
ϩⲟⲟⲩⲧ				male, man; as adj: male, wild, savage (nm)
ϩⲟⲡⲗⲟⲛ				armament, weapon (nm)
ϩⲟⲣⲁⲙⲁ				sight, vision (nm)
ϩⲟⲣⲁⲥⲓⲥ				appearance, sight (nf)
ϩⲟⲥⲟⲛ				as long as, as much as (+ circum) (adj/conj)
ⲉ-ⲡϩⲟⲥⲟⲛ				inasmuch as
ⲉⲛϩⲟⲥⲟⲛ				as long as, while
ϩⲟⲧⲁⲛ				when(ever) (conj)
ϩⲟⲧⲉ				fear (nf)
ⲁⲧϩⲟⲧⲉ				fearless
ⲣ̄-ϩⲟⲧⲉ				(ⲟ† ⲛ̄-) to become/be afraid (of: ⲉ-, ⲉϫⲛ̄-, ⲉⲧⲃⲉ-, ϩⲏⲧ⸗)
ⲣⲉϥⲣ̄-ϩⲟⲧⲉ				fearing, respectful
ⲙⲛ̄ⲧⲣⲉϥⲣ̄-ϩⲟⲧⲉ				fear, respect
ϩⲟⲧϩ̄ⲧ	ϩⲉⲧϩ̄-	ϩⲉⲧϩⲱⲧ⸗	ϩⲉⲧϩⲱⲧ†	to inquire, examine (vt)
				inquiry, question (nm)
ϩⲟⲩⲉⲓⲧ (f ϩⲟⲩⲉⲓⲧⲉ; pl ϩⲟⲩⲁⲧⲉ)				first, original (adj)
ϩⲟⲩⲛ				inside, inner part (cf. ϩⲛ̄-) (nm)
ⲉϩⲟⲩⲛ				in (adv)
ⲛ̄ϩⲟⲩⲛ				within, inside (adv)
ϣⲁϩⲟⲩⲛ				inward (adv)
ϩⲓϩⲟⲩⲛ				within (adv)
ϩⲟⲩⲟ				greater part, abundance (as adj before noun without ⲛ̄- or after noun with ⲛ̄-: great, much; before adj: more, greater) (nm)
ⲉ-ⲡⲉϩⲟⲩⲟ				greatly, much
ⲛ̄-ϩⲟⲩⲟ ⲉ-, ⲉ-ϩⲟⲩⲟ ⲉ-, ⲉ-ϩⲟⲩⲉ-				more than
ϩⲟϥ, ϩⲟⲃ (pl ϩⲃⲟⲩⲓ)				snake, serpent, asp (nm; ϩϥⲱ, ϩⲃⲱ [f])
ϩⲟϫϩ̄ϫ	ϩⲉϫϩ̄ϫ-	ϩⲉϫϩⲱϫ⸗	ϩⲉϫϩⲱϫ†	to distress, restrict (ⲙ̄ⲙⲟ⸗) (vt)
				to become/be distressed, restricted (vi/vs)
				distress (nm)

ϩραββεϊ				"my great one" (title of respect for a teacher, ultimately from Hebrew/Aramaic) (nm)
ϩραϊ				top, upper part; bottom, lower part (!) (nm)
ⲉϩραϊ				up; down (!) (adv)
ⲛ̄ϩραϊ				above; below (!) (adv)
ϣⲁϩραϊ				upward; downward (!) (adv)
ϩιϩραϊ				upward (adv)
ϩⲣⲉ (pl ϩⲣⲏⲩⲉ)				food (nmf)
ϩⲣⲏϣⲉ				weight (nf)
ϩⲣⲟⲟⲩ	ϩⲣⲟⲩ-	ϩⲣⲁ=		sound, voice (nm)
ϥⲓ-ϩⲣⲟⲟⲩ				to raise one's voice, utter (± ⲉⲃⲟⲗ, ⲉϩⲣⲁϊ)
ϩⲣⲟⲩ-(ⲛ̄-)ⲃⲁϊ				sky-voice, thunder (nf)
ϩⲣⲟⲩ-ⲙ̄-ⲡⲉ				sky-voice, thunder (nm)
ϩⲣⲟϣ	ϩⲣ̄ϣ-, ϩⲉⲣϣ-		ϩⲟⲣϣ†	(cp ϩⲁⲣϣ-) to make heavy, slow (vt)
				to become heavy, slow (vi)
				heaviness, weight (nm)
ϩⲣⲟϫⲣ(ⲉ)ϫ				to grind, gnash (ⲙ̄ⲙⲟ=) (vt)
				grinding (nm)
ϩⲣⲱ				oven, furnace (nf)
ϩⲧⲟ (pl ϩⲧⲱⲱⲣ)				horse (nm; ϩⲧⲱⲣⲉ [f])
ϩⲧⲟⲟⲩⲉ				dawn, morning (nm)
ⲉ/ⲛ̄/ϩⲓ-ϩⲧⲟⲟⲩⲉ				at dawn
ϩⲧⲟⲡ				mishap, accident, downfall (nm)
ϩⲩⲇρία				water jar (nf)
ϩⲩⲡⲉⲣέⲧⲏⲥ				assistant, attendant (nm)
ϩⲩⲡⲟⲕⲣⲓⲧⲏⲥ				pretender, playactor (nm)
ϩⲩⲡⲟⲙ(ⲉ)ⲓⲛⲉ				to endure (vi)
ϩⲩⲡⲟⲙⲟⲛή				endurance (nf)
ϩⲩⲡⲟ́ⲡⲟⲇⲓⲟⲛ				footrest (nm)
ϩⲩⲡⲟⲧⲁⲥⲥⲉ				to subject, submit (oneself) (to: ⲛⲁ=) (vt)
ϩⲱ				it's sufficient, enough (impersonal predicate)
ϩⲱⲃ (pl ϩⲃⲏⲩⲉ)				work, deed; thing, matter (nm)
ϩⲱⲃ ⲛ̄-ϭⲓϫ				handiwork, handicraft
ϩⲱⲃⲥ̄	ϩⲉⲃⲥ-	ϩⲟⲃⲥ=	ϩⲟⲃⲥ†	to cover (ⲙ̄ⲙⲟ=) (vt)
				to become covered (vi)
				covering (nm)
(ϩ)ⲱⲇή				song (nf)
ϩⲱⲗ			ϩⲏⲗ†	to fly (vi)
				to be flying (vs, exclusively with Present)
ϩⲱⲙ	ϩⲉⲙ-	ϩⲟⲙ=	ϩⲏⲙ†	to trample, tread (ⲙ̄ⲙⲟ=) (vt)
				trampling, treading (nm)
ϩⲱⲛ	ϩⲛ̄-	ϩⲟⲛ=	ϩⲏⲛ†	to bring near (vt/vr)
				to draw near, approach (someone or something: ⲉ-, ⲉϩⲟⲩⲛ ⲉ-) (vi)

				to be near (vs)
ϩⲱⲛ ⲉⲧⲟⲟⲧ⸗				to command, order someone (to do: ⲉ-, ⲉ-ⲧⲣⲉ-, ϫⲉⲕⲁⲥ)
ϩⲱⲟⲩ	ϩⲟⲩ-			to rain (ⲙ̄ⲙⲟ⸗) (vt/vi)
				rain (nm)
ϩⲱⲡ	ϩⲉⲡ-	ϩⲟⲡ⸗	ϩⲏⲡ†	to hide, conceal (ⲙ̄ⲙⲟ⸗) (vt)
				to become hidden, hide (oneself) (vi)
				to be hidden (vs)
				hiding (nm)
ϩⲱⲣⲃ̄, ϩⲱⲣϥ̄		ϩⲟⲣⲃ⸗	ϩⲟⲣ(ⲉ)ϥ†	to break (ⲙ̄ⲙⲟ⸗) (vt)
				to be broken (vi)
ϩⲱⲥ-				like, as (prep)
ϩⲱⲥⲧⲉ				so that (conj)
ϩⲱⲧⲃ̄	ϩⲉⲧⲃ̄-	ϩⲟⲧⲃ⸗	ϩⲟⲧⲃ̄†	(cp ϩⲁⲧⲃ̄-) to murder, slay (ⲙ̄ⲙⲟ⸗) (vt)
				murder, slaughter; slain (nm)
ϩⲱⲧⲡ̄	ϩⲉⲧⲡ̄-	ϩⲟⲧⲡ⸗	ϩⲟⲧⲡ̄†	to settle, reconcile (ⲙ̄ⲙⲟ⸗) (vt)
				to set (sun, etc.); to become/be reconciled (vi/vs)
				reconciliation; (sun)set (nm)
ϩⲱ(ⲱ)⸗				own, -self; also, too (intensive pron/inflected modifier)
ϩⲱⲱϥ				however
ϩⲱϣ	ϩⲉϣ-	ϩⲟϣ⸗	ϩⲏϣ†	to distress (ⲙ̄ⲙⲟ⸗) (vt)
				to become/be distressed (vi/vs)
				distress (nm)
ϩⲱϭⲃ̄	ϩⲉϭⲃ̄-	ϩⲟϭⲃ⸗	ϩⲟϭⲃ̄†	(cp ϩⲁϭⲃ̄-) to (cause to) wither (ⲙ̄ⲙⲟ⸗) (vt)
				to wither (vi)
				withering (nm)
(ϩ)ϫⲟⲛϫⲛ̄				to trample, tread (ⲙ̄ⲙⲟ⸗) (vt)
				to feel, grope (for: [ⲉϩⲟⲩⲛ] ⲉ-)

ϫ   ϫⲁⲛϫⲓⲁ

ϫⲁ(ⲉ)ⲓⲉ	desert (nm)
ϫⲁⲧϥⲉ	reptile (nm)
ϫⲁϫⲉ (pl ϫⲓ[ⲛ]ϫⲉⲉⲩ[ⲉ])	hostile, enemy (adj)
ϫⲉ	1. " (introducing direct quotation), that (introducing noun clauses after verbs of speaking, perceiving); 2. introduces name or epithet in naming constructions; 3. (so) that . . . may/might (+ optative); 4. that is, namely; 5. because, since (conj)
ⲉⲃⲟⲗ ϫⲉ, ⲉⲧⲃⲉ-ϫⲉ	because
ⲛ̄ⲥⲁⲃⲏⲗ ϫⲉ	except that, unless, if not

ϫⲉⲕⲁ(ⲁ)ⲥ				so that . . . may/might (+ optative) (conj)
ϫⲉⲛⲉⲡⲱⲣ				roof (nf)
ϫⲉⲣⲟ	ϫⲉⲣⲉ-	ϫⲉⲣⲟ⸗		to set on fire, ignite, kindle (ⲙ̄ⲙⲟ⸗) (vt)
				to be on fire, burn (vi)
ϫⲏ				speck (nm)
ϫⲓ	ϫⲓ-	ϫⲓⲧ⸗		(cp ϫⲁⲓ̈-, ϫⲁⲩ-) to take, receive, get (ⲙ̄ⲙⲟ⸗) (vt)
				taking, theft (nm)
ϫⲓ (ⲙ̄ⲙⲟ⸗) ⲉϫⲱ⸗				to borrow (ⲉϫⲱ⸗ is reflexive)
ϫⲓⲛ-, ϫⲛ̄-				from, since (prep)
ϫⲓⲥⲉ	ϫⲉⲥⲧ̄-	ϫⲁⲥⲧ⸗	ϫⲟⲥⲉ†	(cp ϫⲁⲥⲓ-) (± ⲉϩⲣⲁⲓ̈) to lift up, exalt (ⲙ̄ⲙⲟ⸗; over: ⲉ-, ⲉϫⲛ̄-, ϩⲓϫⲛ̄-) (vt)
				to become lifted up, exalted (vi)
				heights (nm)
ⲡⲉⲧ-ϫⲟⲥⲉ				the Exalted
ϫⲓⲟⲩⲉ				to steal (ⲙ̄ⲙⲟ⸗; from: ϩⲛ̄-, ⲉⲃⲟⲗ ϩⲛ̄-) (vt)
				stealing, theft (nm)
ⲛ̄-ϫⲓⲟⲩⲉ				stealthily, secretly
ϫⲛ̄, ϫⲉⲛ, ϫⲉ				or (conj)
ϫⲛⲁ⸗				to send (away) (vt)
ϫⲛⲁⲩ				to delay, hesitate (to: ⲉ-) (vi)
ϫⲛⲁϩ (pl ϫⲛⲁⲩϩ)				forearm; force (nm)
ϫⲓ ⲛ̄-ϫⲛⲁϩ				to treat forcibly (ⲙ̄ⲙⲟ⸗)
ϫⲛⲟⲩ	ϫⲛⲉ-	ϫⲛⲟⲩ⸗		to ask, question (ⲙ̄ⲙⲟ⸗; for: ⲉ-; about: ⲉⲧⲃⲉ-) (vt)
				(causative of ϣⲓⲛⲉ)
				asking, questioning (nm)
ϫⲟ	ϫⲉ-	ϫⲟ⸗	ϫⲏⲩ†	to plant, sow (seed: ⲙ̄ⲙⲟ⸗) (vt)
				planting, sowing (nm)
ϫⲟⲉⲓⲥ (pl ϫⲓⲥⲟⲟⲩⲉ) ϫⲉⲥ-				master (abbreviated as $\overline{\text{ⲭⲥ}}$) (nmf)
ϫⲟⲓ̈ (pl ⲉϫⲏⲩ)				ship, boat (nm)
ϫⲟⲟⲗⲉⲥ				moth (nf)
ϫⲟⲟⲩ	ϫⲉⲩ-	ϫⲟⲟⲩ⸗		to send (ⲙ̄ⲙⲟ⸗; to: ⲉⲣⲁⲧ⸗, ⲛⲁ⸗, ⲉϫⲛ̄-, ϣⲁ-) (vt)
				(causative of ϣⲉ)
ϫⲟⲟⲩ ⲉⲃⲟⲗ				to send away, out, off
ϫⲟⲟⲩ ϩⲁⲑⲏ				to send ahead
ϫⲟⲩⲱⲧ (f ϫⲟⲩⲱⲧⲉ) ϫⲟⲩⲧ-				twenty (num)
ϫⲡ̄-				hour (usually prefixed to number) (nmf)
ϫⲡⲓ-, ϫⲡⲉ-				to need to, have to (+ inf) (v)
ϫⲡⲓⲟ	ϫⲡⲓⲉ-	ϫⲡⲓⲟ⸗	ϫⲡⲓⲏⲧ†	to put to shame; to blame, scold, reproach (ⲙ̄ⲙⲟ⸗; for: ⲉⲧⲃⲉ-, ⲉϫⲛ̄-, ϩⲁ-) (vt)
				(causative of ϣⲓⲡⲉ)
ϫⲡⲟ	ϫⲡⲉ-	ϫⲡⲟ⸗		1. to bring into existence, give birth to (ⲙ̄ⲙⲟ⸗); 2. to acquire, obtain, get (ⲙ̄ⲙⲟ⸗; often with reflexive ⲛⲁ⸗ [for one's self]) (vt)
				(causative of ϣⲱⲡⲉ)

				birth; acquisition (nm)
ϫⲣⲟ		ϫⲣⲁⲉⲓⲧ†		(cp ϫⲁⲣ-) to make strong (ⲙ̄ⲙⲟ⸗) (vt)
				to become strong, victorious (over: ⲉ-, ⲉϫⲛ̄-) (vi)
		(ϫⲟⲟⲣ†)		to be strong (vs)
				strength, victory (nm)
ϫⲣⲟⲡ				impediment (nm)
ϫⲱ⸗				head (of) (usually in compounds) (nm)
ⲉϫⲛ̄-	ⲉϫⲱ⸗			onto, over (prep)
ⲉⲃⲟⲗ ⲉϫⲛ̄-				out onto
ⲉϩⲟⲩⲛ ⲉϫⲛ̄-				in onto
ⲉϩⲣⲁⲓ̈ ⲉϫⲛ̄-				up/down onto
ⲉⲡⲉⲥⲏⲧ ⲉϫⲛ̄-				down onto
ϩⲁϫⲛ̄-	ϩⲁϫⲱ⸗			before (prep)
ϩⲓϫⲛ̄-	ϩⲓϫⲱ⸗			upon (prep)
ϩⲣⲁⲓ̈ ϩⲓϫⲛ̄-				upon
ⲡⲉⲧ-ϩⲓϫⲛ̄-				the one in command of
ϫⲱ	ϫⲉ-, ϫⲓ-	ϫⲟ(ⲟ)⸗		(cp ϫⲁⲧ-; impv ⲁϫⲓ-, ⲁϫⲓ⸗) to say; to sing (ⲙ̄ⲙⲟ⸗) (vt)
				song (nm)
ϫⲱⲕ	ϫⲉⲕ-	ϫⲟⲕ⸗	ϫⲏⲕ†	(± ⲉⲃⲟⲗ) to finish, complete (ⲙ̄ⲙⲟ⸗) (vt)
				to become finished, completed; to die (vi)
				to be finished, done, perfect (vs)
				end, completion (nm)
ϫⲱⲕⲙ̄	ϫⲉⲕⲙ̄-	ϫⲟⲕⲙ⸗	ϫⲟⲕⲙ̄†	to wash (ⲙ̄ⲙⲟ⸗; in, with: [ⲉⲃⲟⲗ] ϩⲛ̄-) (vt)
				washing (nm)
ϫⲱⲙ				generation (nm)
ϫⲱⲣⲡ̄				to trip, be impeded (vi)
				impediment (nm)
ϫⲱ(ⲱ)ⲗⲉ	ϫⲉ(ⲉ)ⲗⲉ-	ϫⲟ(ⲟ)ⲗ⸗		to harvest (ⲙ̄ⲙⲟ⸗) (vt)
				harvest (nm)
ϫⲱⲱⲙⲉ				scroll, document (nm)
ϫⲱⲱⲣⲉ				strong (adj)
ϫⲱⲱⲣⲉ	ϫⲉⲉⲣⲉ-	ϫⲟⲟⲣ⸗	ϫⲟⲟⲣⲉ†	(± ⲉⲃⲟⲗ) to scatter, disperse (ⲙ̄ⲙⲟ⸗) (vt)
				scattering, dispersion (nm)
ϫⲱϩ	ϫⲉϩ-	ϫⲁϩ⸗	ϫⲏϩ†	to smear (ⲙ̄ⲙⲟ⸗, ⲉ-; with: ⲙ̄ⲙⲟ⸗, [ϩ]ⲛ̄-) (vt)
ϫⲱϩⲙ̄	ϫⲉϩⲙ̄-	ϫⲁϩⲙ⸗	ϫⲁϩⲙ̄†	to defile, pollute (ⲙ̄ⲙⲟ⸗) (vt)
				to become/be defiled, polluted (with, by: [ⲉⲃⲟⲗ] ϩⲛ̄-) (vi/vs)
				defilement, pollution (nm)

ϭ   ϭⲓⲙⲁ

ϭⲁ	ugliness (nm)

ϭⲁ(ⲉ)ⲓⲉ			ugly (adj)
ϭⲁⲗⲉ́ (pl ϭⲁⲗⲉⲉⲩ[ⲉ])			lame (adj)
ϭⲁⲙⲟⲩⲗ			camel (nm; ϭⲁⲙⲁⲩⲗⲉ [f])
ϭⲁⲡⲓϫⲉ			measure (dry, approximately 1 liter/quart) (nmf)
ϭⲃⲃⲉ		ϭⲟⲟⲃ†	(cp ϭⲁⲃ-) to become/be weak (vi/vs)
			weakness (nm)
ϭⲃⲟⲓ			arm, limb (nm)
ϭⲉ			then, thus, any more (postpositive) (adv)
ⲧⲉⲛⲟⲩ ϭⲉ			now then
ϭⲉⲡⲏ			to hurry, hasten (to: ⲉ-, ⲉⲣⲁⲧ≠; to do: ⲉ- + inf) (vi)
ϩⲛ̄-ⲟⲩϭⲉⲡⲏ			quickly, hurriedly
ϭⲉⲣⲏϭ (pl ϭⲉⲣⲁϭⲉ)			hunter, trapper (nm)
ϭⲉⲣⲱⲃ (pl ϭⲉⲣⲟⲟⲃ)			rod, staff (nm)
ϭⲓⲛ-			+ inf (act of) -ing (abstract prefix f)
ϭⲓⲛⲉ	ϭⲛ̄-, ϭⲙ̄-	ϭⲛ̄ⲧ≠	to find (ⲙ̄ⲙⲟ≠) (vt)
			finding, found thing (nm)
ϭⲓϫ			hand (nf)
ϭⲗⲟⲟϭⲉ			ladder (nf)
ϭⲗⲟϭ			bed (nm)
ϭⲱⲧ (pl ϭⲗⲟⲟⲧⲉ)			kidney (pl also used for entrails in general) (nmf)
ϭⲟ(ⲉ)ⲓⲗⲉ	ϭⲁⲗⲉ- ϭⲁⲗⲱ(ⲱ)≠	ϭⲁⲗⲱⲟⲩ†, ϭⲁⲗⲏⲩ(ⲧ)†	to deposit, entrust (ⲙ̄ⲙⲟ≠; with: ⲉ-) (vt)
			to dwell, sojourn (at, in: ⲉ-) (vi)
			dwelling, sojourn; deposit (nm)
ϭⲟⲗ			lie; liar (nm)
ϭⲟⲙ			power, force (nf)
(ϣ)ϭⲙ̄-ϭⲟⲙ, ϭⲛ̄-ϭⲟⲙ			to find power, be able (to do: ⲉ- + inf)
ϭⲟⲙϭⲙ̄		ϭⲙ̄ϭⲱⲙ≠	to touch, grope for (ⲉ-) (vt)
			sense of touch (nm)
ϭⲟⲛⲥ̄			violence (n)
ϫⲓ ⲛ̄-ϭⲟⲛⲥ̄			to treat violently (ⲙ̄ⲙⲟ≠); violence
ⲣⲉϥϫⲓ ⲛ̄-ϭⲟⲛⲥ̄			violent person
ϭⲟⲟⲩⲛⲉ			sackcloth, haircloth (nf)
ϭⲟⲣϭⲥ̄			trap, snare (nf)
ϭⲟⲥ	ϭⲓⲥ-		half (nm)
ϭⲣⲟ(ⲟ)ⲙⲡⲉ			dove (nmf)
ϭⲣⲟ(ⲟ)ϭ (pl ϭⲣⲱ[ⲱ]ϭ)			seed (nm)
ϭⲣⲱϩ			need (nm)
ϭⲱ		ϭⲉⲉⲧ†	1. to stay, remain, wait (for: ⲉ-; with ⲙⲛ̄-); 2. to continue, persist (doing: circum); 3. to stop, cease (vi)
ϭⲱⲃ			weak (adj)

243

ϭⲱⲗ	ϭⲗ̄-	ϭⲟⲗ⸗	ϭⲏⲗ†	to roll up (ⲙ̄ⲙⲟ⸗) (vt)
				to roll up/back (vi)
ϭⲱⲗ ⲉⲃⲟⲗ				to turn back, return (ⲙ̄ⲙⲟ⸗)
ϭⲱⲗⲡ̄	ϭⲉⲗⲡ̄-	ϭⲟⲗⲡ⸗	ϭⲟⲗⲡ̄†	(cp ϭⲁⲗⲡ̄-) (usually + ⲉⲃⲟⲗ) to uncover, reveal (ⲙ̄ⲙⲟ⸗; to: ⲉ-, ⲛⲁ⸗) (vt)
				to become/be uncovered, revealed (vi/vs)
				uncovering, revelation (nm)
ϭⲱⲗϫ̄	ϭⲗ̄ϫ-	ϭⲟⲗϫ⸗	ϭⲟⲗϫ̄†	to entangle, ensnare (ⲙ̄ⲙⲟ⸗) (vt)
				to become entangled; to adhere, cling (vi/vr)
				entanglement (nm)
ϭⲱⲙ (pl ϭⲟⲟⲙ)				yard, property (nm)
ϭⲱⲛⲧ̄			ϭⲟⲛⲧ̄†	to become/be angry, furious (at: ⲉ-, ⲉϫⲛ̄-) (vi/vs)
				anger, fury (nm)
ϭⲱⲟⲩ		ϭⲟⲟⲩ⸗	ϭⲏⲩ†	to make narrow, constrained (ⲙ̄ⲙⲟ⸗) (vt)
				to become/be narrow, constrained (vi/vs)
				narrowness (nm)
ϭⲱⲡⲉ	ϭⲉⲡ-	ϭⲟⲡ⸗	ϭⲏⲡ†	to seize, catch, take (ⲙ̄ⲙⲟ⸗) (vt)
ϭⲱⲣϩ̄				night (nm)
ϭⲱⲣϭ			ϭⲟⲣϭ†	to hunt, trap (ⲙ̄ⲙⲟ⸗) (vt)
				trap, snare (nm)
ϭⲱⲧ				drinking trough (nf)
ϭⲱⲧϩ̄		ϭⲟⲧϩ⸗	ϭⲟⲧϩ̄†	to pierce, make a hole in (ⲙ̄ⲙⲟ⸗) (vt)
				hole (nm)
ϭⲱ(ⲱ)ⲃⲉ	ϭⲃ̄-			leaf (nf)
ϭⲱ(ⲱ)ⲗⲉ	ϭⲉ(ⲉ)ⲗⲉ-	ϭⲟⲟⲗ⸗	ϭⲟⲟⲗⲉ†	to cover, clothe (ⲉ-; with: ⲙ̄ⲙⲟ⸗, ϩⲛ̄-) (vt)
				covering, cloak (nm)
ϭⲱϣⲧ̄				to watch, look, stare (at: ⲉ-, ⲉϫⲛ̄-, ⲛ̄ⲥⲁ) (often with ⲉⲃⲟⲗ, ⲉϩⲟⲩⲛ, ⲉϩⲣⲁⲓ, ⲉⲡⲉⲥⲏⲧ) (vi)
				look, stare (nm)
ϭⲱϣⲧ̄ (ⲉⲃⲟⲗ) ϩⲏⲧ⸗				to look forward to, expect, await
ϭⲱϫⲃ̄	ϭⲉϫⲃ̄-	ϭⲟϫⲃ⸗	ϭⲟϫⲃ̄†	to make small, less (ⲙ̄ⲙⲟ⸗) (vt)
				to become small, less (vi)
				to be small, lesser (vs)
				smallness, inferiority (nm)

† †

ϯ	ϯ-	ⲧⲁⲁ⸗	ⲧⲟ†	(cp ⲧⲁⲓ-; impv also ⲙⲁ, ⲙⲁ-, ⲙⲁⲧ⸗) to give (ⲙ̄ⲙⲟ⸗); to entrust (ⲙ̄ⲙⲟ⸗; to: ⲉⲧⲛ̄-) (vt)
				to go, begin (vr)
				to go, move (vi)
				to be given, fated (vs)
				gift (nm)

SAHIDIC-ENGLISH LEXICON

ϯ ⲉⲃⲟⲗ		to sell (ⲙ̄ⲙⲟ⸗; to: ⲉ-, ⲛⲁ⸗)
ϯ ⲟⲩⲃⲉ-, ϯ ⲙⲛ̄-		to fight with
ϯ ϩⲓ-		to put on (a garment: ⲙ̄ⲙⲟ⸗), to dress
ϯ-ⲥⲟ		to spare, give mercy (to: ⲉ-)
ϯ-ⲧⲟⲟⲧ⸗, ϯ ⲛ̄-ⲧⲟⲟⲧ⸗		to give a hand to, help, assist
ϯⲙⲉ (pl ⲧⲙⲉ)		town, village (nm)
ϯⲟⲩ (f ϯ[ⲉ]) -(ⲧ)ⲏ		five (num)
ϯⲡⲉ		taste (nf)
ϫⲓ-ϯⲡⲉ		to (get a) taste
ϯϩⲉ	ⲧⲁϩⲉϯ	to become/be drunk (with: ϩⲁ-, ⲙ̄ⲙⲟ⸗, ϩⲛ̄-) (vi/vs)
		drunkenness (nm)

APPENDIX 1

SURVEY OF "THE Ⲛ̄-S"

	(related)	translation	grammatical category/function
• Ⲛ̄-	(Ⲛⲉ-)	"the"	common plural definite article
• Ⲛ̄-	(. . . ⲁⲛ)	"not"	negative particle
• Ⲛ̄-	(Ⲛ̄ⲧⲉ-)	"of"	genitive particle/preposition
		[—]	attribution/adjectival marker (without article)
• Ⲛ̄-	(Ⲙ̄ⲙⲟ⸗)	"in, with"	preposition
		"-ly"	adverbial construction
		[>]	direct object marker
		[=]	equivalence marker (with ⲟ†, ϣⲟⲟⲡ†, and suffix pronouns)
• Ⲛ̄-	(ⲛⲁ⸗)	"to, for"	preposition (indirect object marker)

APPENDIX 2

VERB CLASSES

Organized by number of consonants and vowel patterns ("v" within these class designations stands for a variable vowel), these are the native Sahidic verb classes, with representative examples.[1]

ONE CONSONANT

- **1v [Allen (a)]**

	ϫⲱ	ϫⲉ-	ϫⲟⲟ⸗		cp ϫⲁⲧ-
	ϯ	ϯ-	ⲧⲁⲁ⸗	ⲧⲟ†	cp ⲧⲁï-
	ϥⲓ	ϥⲓ-	ϥⲓⲧ⸗		cp ϥⲁï-
[(1)v]	ⲉⲓ			ⲛⲏⲩ†	

TWO CONSONANTS

- **1v2 [Allen (b), Layton II]**

	ⲃⲱⲗ	ⲃⲉⲗ-, ⲃⲗ̄-	ⲃⲟⲗ⸗	ⲃⲏⲗ†	cp ⲃⲁⲗ-
	ⲕⲱⲧ	ⲕⲉⲧ-	ⲕⲟⲧ⸗	ⲕⲏⲧ†	
	ϣⲱⲡ	ϣⲉⲡ-, ϣⲡ̄-	ϣⲟⲡ⸗	ϣⲏⲡ†	
	ⲙⲟⲩⲛ			ⲙⲏⲛ†	
[(1)v2]	ⲱⲡ	ⲉⲡ-	ⲟⲡ⸗	ⲏⲡ†	

- **1v2v, some with unstable third consonant ⲧ [Allen (c), Layton VII]**

[1v2(ⲧ)]	ϫⲓⲥⲉ	ϫⲉⲥⲧ̄-	ϫⲁⲥⲧ⸗	ϫⲟⲥⲉ†	cp ϫⲁⲥⲓ-
[1v2(ⲧ)]	ⲣⲓⲕⲉ	ⲣⲉⲕ(ⲧ̄)-	ⲣⲉⲕⲧ⸗	ⲣⲟⲕⲉ†	
	ⲕⲱⲧⲉ	ⲕⲉⲧ-	ⲕⲟⲧ⸗	ⲕⲏⲧ†	
	ϣⲟⲟⲩⲉ			ϣⲟⲩⲱⲟⲩ†	

---

1. Categories are referenced to the discussions in James P. Allen, *Coptic: A Grammar of Its Six Major Dialects*, Languages of the Ancient Near East: Didactica 1 (University Park, PA: Eisenbrauns, 2020), 43–48, and Bentley Layton, *A Coptic Grammar: With Chrestomathy and Glossary. Sahidic Dialect*, 3rd ed., Porta Linguarum Orientalium 2/20 (Wiesbaden: Harrassowitz, 2011), 151–57.

VERB CLASSES

- **12v2 [Allen (d)]**

  | ϩⲙⲟⲙ | | | ϩⲏⲙ† |
  | ⲕⲙⲟⲙ | | | ⲕⲏⲙ† |

- **122é [Allen (e)]**

  | ⲡ(ⲉ)ⲓⲣé, ⲡⲣ̄ⲣé | | | ⲡⲟⲣⲉ† |
  | ⲕⲛ̄ⲛé | | | |

THREE CONSONANTS

- **1v23 [Allen (f), Layton I and III]**

	ⲥⲱⲧⲡ̄	ⲥⲉⲧⲡ-	ⲥⲟⲧⲡ⸗	ⲥⲟⲧⲡ̄†	
	ϩⲱⲧⲃ̄	ϩⲉⲧⲃ-	ϩⲟⲧⲃ⸗	ϩⲟⲧⲃ̄†	ср ϩⲁⲧⲃ̄-
[1v(2)3]	ϣⲱⲱⲧ	ϣⲉ(ⲉ)ⲧ-	ϣⲁⲁⲧ⸗	ϣⲁⲁⲧ†	ср ϣⲁⲧ-

- **12v3 (mostly intransitive) [Allen (g), Layton VI]**

	ϩⲣⲟϣ	ϩⲣ̄ϣ-, ϩⲉⲣϣ̄-		ϩⲟⲣϣ̄†	ср ϩⲁⲣϣ̄-
	ϩⲗⲟϭ			ϩⲟⲗϭ̄†	ср ϩⲁⲗϭ̄-
	ⲙ̄ⲧⲟⲛ			ⲙⲟⲧⲛ̄†	

- **1v23v [Allen (h), Layton III]**

	ⲥⲟⲃⲧⲉ	ⲥⲃ̄ⲧⲉ-	ⲥⲃ̄ⲧⲱⲧ⸗	ⲥⲃ̄ⲧⲱⲧ†
	ϣⲙ̄ϣⲉ	ϣⲙ̄ϣⲉ-	ϣⲙ̄ϣⲏⲧ⸗	
[1v(2)3v]	ⲡⲱⲱⲛⲉ	ⲡⲉⲉⲛⲉ-	ⲡⲟⲟⲛⲉ⸗	ⲡⲟⲟⲛⲉ†

REDUPLICATED PAIRS

- **1v21v2/12v32v3 [Allen (i), Layton IV]**

	ⲥⲟⲗⲥⲗ̄	ⲥⲗ̄ⲥⲗ-	ⲥⲗ̄ⲥⲱⲗ⸗	ⲥⲗ̄ⲥⲱⲗ†	
	ϩⲟⲧϩⲧ̄	ϩⲉⲧϩⲧ̄-	ϩⲉⲧϩⲱⲧ⸗	ϩⲉⲧϩⲱⲧ†	
	ϣⲧⲟⲣⲧⲣ̄	ϣⲧⲣ̄ⲧⲣ̄-	ϣⲧⲣ̄ⲧⲱⲣ⸗	ϣⲧⲣ̄ⲧⲱⲣ†	
[1v(2)1v(2)]	ⲃⲁⲁⲃⲉ		ⲃⲁⲃⲱ(ⲱ)⸗	ⲃⲁⲃⲟⲧ†	ср ⲃⲁⲃⲉ-
	ⲕⲁⲥⲕⲥ̄				
	ⲕⲣⲙ̄ⲣⲙ̄				

FOUR CONSONANTS

- **1v234 [Allen (j)]**

	ⲥⲟⲟⲩⲧⲛ̄	ⲥⲟⲩⲧⲛ̄-	ⲥⲟⲩⲧⲱⲛ⸗	ⲥⲟⲩⲧⲱⲛ†
	ⲥⲁⲁⲛϣ̄	ⲥⲁⲁⲛϣ̄-	ⲥⲁⲛⲟⲩϣ⸗	ⲥⲁⲛⲁϣⲧ̄†
[12v(3)4]	ϩⲗⲟⲟⲗⲉ			

T-CAUSATIVES

- ⲧ- . . . -ⲟ **[Allen (k), Layton V]**

ⲧⲁⲗⲟ	ⲧⲁⲗⲉ-	ⲧⲁⲗⲟ⸗	ⲧⲁⲗⲏⲩ†
ⲧⲁⲕⲟ	ⲧⲁⲕⲉ-	ⲧⲁⲕⲟ⸗	ⲧⲁⲕⲏⲩ(ⲧ)†

APPENDIX 3

VERB PARADIGMS

In the following paradigms, the bullet (•) shows the placement of the verbal stem.

DURATIVE PATTERN

Present   \<negative\>
I am writing (I write)   I am not writing
ϯ•   ⲛ̄ϯ• ⲁⲛ
ⲕ•   ⲛ̄ⲅ• ⲁⲛ [ⲛⲅ̄• ⲁⲛ]
ⲧⲉ• [ⲧⲣ̄•]   ⲛ̄ⲧⲉ• ⲁⲛ
ϥ•   ⲛ̄ϥ• ⲁⲛ [ⲛϥ̄• ⲁⲛ]
ⲥ•   ⲛ̄ⲥ• ⲁⲛ [ⲛⲥ̄• ⲁⲛ]
ⲧⲛ̄•   ⲛ̄ⲧⲛ̄• ⲁⲛ
ⲧⲉⲧⲛ̄•   ⲛ̄ⲧⲉⲧⲛ̄• ⲁⲛ
ⲥⲉ•   ⲛ̄ⲥⲉ• ⲁⲛ
ⲡⲣⲱⲙⲉ •   (ⲙ̄-)ⲡⲣⲱⲙⲉ • ⲁⲛ
ⲟⲩⲛ̄-(ⲟⲩ)ⲣⲱⲙⲉ •   ⲙⲛ̄-(ⲟⲩ)ⲣⲱⲙⲉ •

Relative Present   \<negative\>
who/which I am writing   who/which I am not writing
ⲉϯ•   ⲉⲧⲉ-ⲛ̄ϯ• ⲁⲛ
ⲉⲧⲕ̄•   ⲉⲧⲉ-ⲛ̄ⲅ• ⲁⲛ [ⲉⲧⲉ-ⲛⲅ̄• ⲁⲛ]
ⲉⲧⲉ(ⲣ)•   ⲉⲧⲉ-ⲛ̄ⲧⲉ• ⲁⲛ
ⲉⲧϥ̄•   ⲉⲧⲉ-ⲛ̄ϥ• ⲁⲛ [ⲉⲧⲉ-ⲛϥ̄• ⲁⲛ]
ⲉⲧⲥ̄•   ⲉⲧⲉ-ⲛ̄ⲥ• ⲁⲛ [ⲉⲧⲉ-ⲛⲥ̄• ⲁⲛ]
ⲉⲧⲛ̄•   ⲉⲧⲉ-ⲛ̄ⲧⲛ̄• ⲁⲛ
ⲉⲧⲉⲧⲛ̄•   ⲉⲧⲉ-ⲛ̄ⲧⲉⲧⲛ̄• ⲁⲛ
ⲉⲧⲟⲩ•   ⲉⲧⲉ-ⲛ̄ⲥⲉ• ⲁⲛ
ⲉⲧⲉⲣⲉ-ⲡⲣⲱⲙⲉ •   ⲉⲧⲉ-(ⲙ̄-)ⲡⲣⲱⲙⲉ • ⲁⲛ [ⲉⲧⲉⲣⲉ-ⲡⲣⲱⲙⲉ • ⲁⲛ]

Circumstantial Present   \<negative\>
(I/me) writing   (I/me) not writing
ⲉⲓ̈•   ⲉ-ⲛ̄ϯ• ⲁⲛ

ⲉⲕ•	ⲉ-ⲛⲅ̄• ⲁⲛ [ⲉ-ⲛⲅ̄• ⲁⲛ]
ⲉⲣ(ⲉ)•	ⲉ-ⲛ̄ⲧⲉ• ⲁⲛ
ⲉϥ•	ⲉ-ⲛ̄ϥ• ⲁⲛ [ⲉ-ⲛϥ̄• ⲁⲛ]
ⲉⲥ•	ⲉ-ⲛ̄ⲥ• ⲁⲛ [ⲉ-ⲛⲥ̄• ⲁⲛ]
ⲉⲛ•	ⲉ-ⲛ̄ⲧⲛ̄• ⲁⲛ
ⲉⲧⲉⲧⲛ̄•	ⲉ-ⲛ̄ⲧⲉⲧⲛ̄• ⲁⲛ
ⲉⲩ•	ⲉ-ⲛ̄ⲥⲉ• ⲁⲛ
ⲉⲣⲉ-ⲡⲣⲱⲙⲉ •	ⲉⲣⲉ-ⲡⲣⲱⲙⲉ • ⲁⲛ

Preterite Present — <negative>
I was writing (I would write) — I was not writing

ⲛⲉⲓ̈•	ⲛⲉⲓ̈• ⲁⲛ
ⲛⲉⲕ•	ⲛⲉⲕ• ⲁⲛ
ⲛⲉⲣⲉ•	ⲛⲉⲣⲉ• ⲁⲛ
ⲛⲉϥ•	ⲛⲉϥ• ⲁⲛ
ⲛⲉⲥ•	ⲛⲉⲥ• ⲁⲛ
ⲛⲉⲛ•	ⲛⲉⲛ• ⲁⲛ
ⲛⲉⲧⲉⲧⲛ̄•	ⲛⲉⲧⲉⲧⲛ̄• ⲁⲛ
ⲛⲉⲩ•	ⲛⲉⲩ• ⲁⲛ
ⲛⲉⲣⲉ-ⲡⲣⲱⲙⲉ •	ⲛⲉⲣⲉ-ⲡⲣⲱⲙⲉ • ⲁⲛ

Focalizing Present — <negative>
it is . . . that I am writing — it is . . . that I am not writing

ⲉⲓ̈•	(ⲛ̄-)ⲉⲓ̈• ⲁⲛ
ⲉⲕ•	(ⲛ̄-)ⲉⲕ• ⲁⲛ
ⲉⲣ(ⲉ)•	(ⲛ̄-)ⲉⲣ(ⲉ)• ⲁⲛ
ⲉϥ•	(ⲛ̄-)ⲉϥ• ⲁⲛ
ⲉⲥ•	(ⲛ̄-)ⲉⲥ• ⲁⲛ
ⲉⲛ•	(ⲛ̄-)ⲉⲛ• ⲁⲛ
ⲉⲧⲉⲧⲛ̄•	(ⲛ̄-)ⲉⲧⲉⲧⲛ̄• ⲁⲛ
ⲉⲩ•	(ⲛ̄-)ⲉⲩ• ⲁⲛ
ⲉⲣⲉ-ⲡⲣⲱⲙⲉ •	(ⲛ̄-)ⲉⲣⲉ-ⲡⲣⲱⲙⲉ • ⲁⲛ

Future — <negative>
I am going to write — I am not going to write

ϯⲛⲁ•	ⲛ̄ϯⲛⲁ• ⲁⲛ
ⲕⲛⲁ•	ⲛ̄ⲅⲛⲁ• ⲁⲛ [ⲛⲅ̄ⲛⲁ• ⲁⲛ]
ⲧⲉⲛⲁ• [ⲧⲉⲣⲁ•]	ⲛ̄ⲧⲉⲛⲁ• ⲁⲛ
ϥⲛⲁ•	ⲛ̄ϥⲛⲁ• ⲁⲛ [ⲛϥ̄ⲛⲁ• ⲁⲛ]
ⲥⲛⲁ•	ⲛ̄ⲥⲛⲁ• ⲁⲛ [ⲛⲥ̄ⲛⲁ• ⲁⲛ]
ⲧⲛ̄ⲛⲁ•	ⲛ̄ⲧⲛ̄ⲛⲁ• ⲁⲛ
ⲧⲉⲧⲛ̄ⲛⲁ• [ⲧⲉⲧⲛⲁ•]	ⲛ̄ⲧⲉⲧⲛ̄ⲛⲁ• ⲁⲛ
ⲥⲉⲛⲁ•	ⲛ̄ⲥⲉⲛⲁ• ⲁⲛ
ⲡⲣⲱⲙⲉ ⲛⲁ•	(ⲙ̄-)ⲡⲣⲱⲙⲉ ⲛⲁ• ⲁⲛ

ⲟⲩⲛ̄-(ⲟⲩ)ⲣⲱⲙⲉ ⲛⲁ•   ⲙⲛ̄-(ⲟⲩ)ⲣⲱⲙⲉ ⲛⲁ•

Relative Future   \<negative\>
who/which I am going to write   who/which I am not going to write

ⲉϯⲛⲁ•   ⲉⲧⲉ-ⲛ̄ϯⲛⲁ• ⲁⲛ
ⲉⲧⲕ̄ⲛⲁ•   ⲉⲧⲉ-ⲛ̄ⲅⲛⲁ• ⲁⲛ [ⲉⲧⲉ-ⲛⲅ̄ⲛⲁ• ⲁⲛ]
ⲉⲧⲉ(ⲣ)ⲛⲁ•   ⲉⲧⲉ-ⲛ̄ⲧⲉⲛⲁ• ⲁⲛ
ⲉⲧϥ̄ⲛⲁ•   ⲉⲧⲉ-ⲛ̄ϥⲛⲁ• ⲁⲛ [ⲉⲧⲉ-ⲛϥ̄ⲛⲁ• ⲁⲛ]
ⲉⲧⲥ̄ⲛⲁ•   ⲉⲧⲉ-ⲛ̄ⲥⲛⲁ• ⲁⲛ [ⲉⲧⲉ-ⲛⲥ̄ⲛⲁ• ⲁⲛ]
ⲉⲧⲛ̄ⲛⲁ•   ⲉⲧⲉ-ⲛ̄ⲧⲛ̄ⲛⲁ• ⲁⲛ
ⲉⲧⲉⲧⲛ̄ⲛⲁ•   ⲉⲧⲉ-ⲛ̄ⲧⲉⲧⲛ̄ⲛⲁ• ⲁⲛ
ⲉⲧⲟⲩⲛⲁ•   ⲉⲧⲉ-ⲛ̄ⲥⲉⲛⲁ• ⲁⲛ
ⲉⲧⲉⲣⲉ-ⲡⲣⲱⲙⲉ ⲛⲁ•   ⲉⲧⲉ-(ⲙ̄-)ⲡⲣⲱⲙⲉ ⲛⲁ• ⲁⲛ

Circumstantial Future   \<negative\>
as I was going to write (about to)   as I was not going to write

ⲉⲓ̈ⲛⲁ•   ⲉ-ⲛ̄ϯⲛⲁ• ⲁⲛ
ⲉⲕⲛⲁ•   ⲉ-ⲛ̄ⲅⲛⲁ• ⲁⲛ [ⲉ-ⲛⲅ̄ⲛⲁ• ⲁⲛ]
ⲉⲣⲉⲛⲁ•   ⲉ-ⲛ̄ⲧⲉⲛⲁ• ⲁⲛ
ⲉϥⲛⲁ•   ⲉ-ⲛ̄ϥⲛⲁ• ⲁⲛ [ⲉ-ⲛϥ̄ⲛⲁ• ⲁⲛ]
ⲉⲥⲛⲁ•   ⲉ-ⲛ̄ⲥⲛⲁ• ⲁⲛ [ⲉ-ⲛⲥ̄ⲛⲁ• ⲁⲛ]
ⲉⲛⲛⲁ•   ⲉ-ⲛ̄ⲧⲛ̄ⲛⲁ• ⲁⲛ
ⲉⲧⲉⲧⲛ̄ⲛⲁ•   ⲉ-ⲛ̄ⲧⲉⲧⲛ̄ⲛⲁ• ⲁⲛ
ⲉⲩⲛⲁ•   ⲉ-ⲛ̄ⲥⲉⲛⲁ• ⲁⲛ
ⲉⲣⲉ-ⲡⲣⲱⲙⲉ ⲛⲁ•   ⲉⲣⲉ-(ⲙ̄-)ⲡⲣⲱⲙⲉ ⲛⲁ• ⲁⲛ

Preterite Future   \<negative\>
I was going to write (about to)   I was not going to write

ⲛⲉⲓ̈ⲛⲁ•   ⲛⲉⲓ̈ⲛⲁ• ⲁⲛ
ⲛⲉⲕⲛⲁ•   ⲛⲉⲕⲛⲁ• ⲁⲛ
ⲛⲉⲣⲉⲛⲁ•   ⲛⲉⲣⲉⲛⲁ• ⲁⲛ
ⲛⲉϥⲛⲁ•   ⲛⲉϥⲛⲁ• ⲁⲛ
ⲛⲉⲥⲛⲁ•   ⲛⲉⲥⲛⲁ• ⲁⲛ
ⲛⲉⲛⲛⲁ•   ⲛⲉⲛⲛⲁ• ⲁⲛ
ⲛⲉⲧⲉⲧⲛ̄ⲛⲁ•   ⲛⲉⲧⲉⲧⲛ̄ⲛⲁ• ⲁⲛ
ⲛⲉⲩⲛⲁ•   ⲛⲉⲩⲛⲁ• ⲁⲛ
ⲛⲉⲣⲉ-ⲡⲣⲱⲙⲉ ⲛⲁ•   ⲛⲉⲣⲉ-ⲡⲣⲱⲙⲉ ⲛⲁ• ⲁⲛ

Focalizing Future   \<negative\>
it is . . . that I going to write   it is . . . that I am not going to write

ⲉⲓ̈ⲛⲁ•   (ⲛ̄-)ⲉⲓ̈ⲛⲁ• ⲁⲛ
ⲉⲕⲛⲁ•   (ⲛ̄-)ⲉⲕⲛⲁ• ⲁⲛ
ⲉⲣⲉⲛⲁ•   (ⲛ̄-)ⲉⲣⲉⲛⲁ• ⲁⲛ
ⲉϥⲛⲁ•   (ⲛ̄-)ⲉϥⲛⲁ• ⲁⲛ

ⲉⲥⲛⲁ•	(ⲛ̄-)ⲉⲥⲛⲁ• ⲁⲛ
ⲉⲛⲛⲁ•	(ⲛ̄-)ⲉⲛⲛⲁ• ⲁⲛ
ⲉⲧⲉⲧⲛ̄ⲛⲁ•	(ⲛ̄-)ⲉⲧⲉⲧⲛ̄ⲛⲁ• ⲁⲛ
ⲉⲩⲛⲁ•	(ⲛ̄-)ⲉⲩⲛⲁ• ⲁⲛ
ⲉⲣⲉ-ⲡⲣⲱⲙⲉ ⲛⲁ•	(ⲛ̄-)ⲉⲣⲉ-ⲡⲣⲱⲙⲉ ⲛⲁ• ⲁⲛ

NON-DURATIVE PATTERN: MAIN CLAUSE CONJUGATIONS

Past	<negative>	<not yet>
I wrote (I did write)	I didn't write	I didn't write yet
ⲁⲓ̈•	ⲙ̄ⲡⲓ•	ⲙ̄ⲡⲁϯ•
ⲁⲕ•	ⲙ̄ⲡⲉⲕ•	ⲙ̄ⲡⲁⲧⲕ̄•
ⲁⲣ• [ⲁ•] [ⲁⲣⲉ•]	ⲙ̄ⲡⲉ• [ⲙ̄ⲡⲣ̄•]	ⲙ̄ⲡⲁⲧⲉ•
ⲁϥ•	ⲙ̄ⲡⲉϥ•	ⲙ̄ⲡⲁⲧϥ̄•
ⲁⲥ•	ⲙ̄ⲡⲉⲥ•	ⲙ̄ⲡⲁⲧⲥ̄•
ⲁⲛ•	ⲙ̄ⲡⲉⲛ•	ⲙ̄ⲡⲁⲧⲛ̄•
ⲁⲧⲉⲧⲛ̄•	ⲙ̄ⲡⲉⲧⲛ̄•	ⲙ̄ⲡⲁⲧⲉⲧⲛ̄•
ⲁⲩ•	ⲙ̄ⲡⲟⲩ•	ⲙ̄ⲡⲁⲧⲟⲩ•
ⲁ-ⲡⲣⲱⲙⲉ •	ⲙ̄ⲡⲉ-ⲡⲣⲱⲙⲉ •	ⲙ̄ⲡⲁⲧⲉ-ⲡⲣⲱⲙⲉ •

Relative **Past**	<negative>	<not yet>
who/which I wrote	who/which I didn't write	who/which I didn't write yet
ⲉⲛⲧⲁⲓ̈• [ⲛ̄ⲧⲁⲓ̈• (etc.)]	ⲉⲧⲉ-ⲙ̄ⲡⲓ•	ⲉⲧⲉ-ⲙ̄ⲡⲁϯ•
ⲉⲛⲧⲁⲕ•	ⲉⲧⲉ-ⲙ̄ⲡⲉⲕ•	ⲉⲧⲉ-ⲙ̄ⲡⲁⲧⲕ̄•
ⲉⲛⲧⲁⲣⲉ•	ⲉⲧⲉ-ⲙ̄ⲡⲉ•	ⲉⲧⲉ-ⲙ̄ⲡⲁⲧⲉ•
ⲉⲛⲧⲁϥ•	ⲉⲧⲉ-ⲙ̄ⲡⲉϥ•	ⲉⲧⲉ-ⲙ̄ⲡⲁⲧϥ̄•
ⲉⲛⲧⲁⲥ•	ⲉⲧⲉ-ⲙ̄ⲡⲉⲥ•	ⲉⲧⲉ-ⲙ̄ⲡⲁⲧⲥ̄•
ⲉⲛⲧⲁⲛ•	ⲉⲧⲉ-ⲙ̄ⲡⲉⲛ•	ⲉⲧⲉ-ⲙ̄ⲡⲁⲧⲛ̄•
ⲉⲛⲧⲁⲧⲉⲧⲛ̄•	ⲉⲧⲉ-ⲙ̄ⲡⲉⲧⲛ̄•	ⲉⲧⲉ-ⲙ̄ⲡⲁⲧⲉⲧⲛ̄•
ⲉⲛⲧⲁⲩ•	ⲉⲧⲉ-ⲙ̄ⲡⲟⲩ•	ⲉⲧⲉ-ⲙ̄ⲡⲁⲧⲟⲩ•
ⲉⲛⲧⲁ-ⲡⲣⲱⲙⲉ •	ⲉⲧⲉ-ⲙ̄ⲡⲉ-ⲡⲣⲱⲙⲉ •	ⲉⲧⲉ-ⲙ̄ⲡⲁⲧⲉ-ⲡⲣⲱⲙⲉ •

Circumstantial **Past**	<negative>	<not yet>
(I/me) having written	(I/me) not having written	(I/me) not having written yet
ⲉ-ⲁⲓ̈•	ⲉ-ⲙ̄ⲡⲓ•	ⲉ-ⲙ̄ⲡⲁϯ•
ⲉ-ⲁⲕ•	ⲉ-ⲙ̄ⲡⲉⲕ•	ⲉ-ⲙ̄ⲡⲁⲧⲕ̄•
ⲉ-ⲁⲣ•	ⲉ-ⲙ̄ⲡⲉ•	ⲉ-ⲙ̄ⲡⲁⲧⲉ•
ⲉ-ⲁϥ•	ⲉ-ⲙ̄ⲡⲉϥ•	ⲉ-ⲙ̄ⲡⲁⲧϥ̄•
ⲉ-ⲁⲥ•	ⲉ-ⲙ̄ⲡⲉⲥ•	ⲉ-ⲙ̄ⲡⲁⲧⲥ̄•
ⲉ-ⲁⲛ•	ⲉ-ⲙ̄ⲡⲉⲛ•	ⲉ-ⲙ̄ⲡⲁⲧⲛ̄•
ⲉ-ⲁⲧⲉⲧⲛ̄•	ⲉ-ⲙ̄ⲡⲉⲧⲛ̄•	ⲉ-ⲙ̄ⲡⲁⲧⲉⲧⲛ̄•
ⲉ-ⲁⲩ•	ⲉ-ⲙ̄ⲡⲟⲩ•	ⲉ-ⲙ̄ⲡⲁⲧⲟⲩ•
ⲉ-ⲁ-ⲡⲣⲱⲙⲉ •	ⲉ-ⲙ̄ⲡⲉ-ⲡⲣⲱⲙⲉ •	ⲉ-ⲙ̄ⲡⲁⲧⲉ-ⲡⲣⲱⲙⲉ •

VERB PARADIGMS

Preterite Past	**\<negative\>**	**\<not yet\>**
I had written	I had not written	I had not written yet
ⲛⲉ-ⲁⲓ•	ⲛⲉ-ⲙ̄ⲡⲓ•	ⲛⲉ-ⲙ̄ⲡⲁϯ•
ⲛⲉ-ⲁⲕ•	ⲛⲉ-ⲙ̄ⲡⲉⲕ•	ⲛⲉ-ⲙ̄ⲡⲁⲧⲕ̄•
ⲛⲉ-ⲁⲣ•	ⲛⲉ-ⲙ̄ⲡⲉ•	ⲛⲉ-ⲙ̄ⲡⲁⲧⲉ•
ⲛⲉ-ⲁϥ•	ⲛⲉ-ⲙ̄ⲡⲉϥ•	ⲛⲉ-ⲙ̄ⲡⲁⲧϥ̄•
ⲛⲉ-ⲁⲥ•	ⲛⲉ-ⲙ̄ⲡⲉⲥ•	ⲛⲉ-ⲙ̄ⲡⲁⲧⲥ̄•
ⲛⲉ-ⲁⲛ•	ⲛⲉ-ⲙ̄ⲡⲉⲛ•	ⲛⲉ-ⲙ̄ⲡⲁⲧⲛ̄•
ⲛⲉ-ⲁⲧⲉⲧⲛ̄•	ⲛⲉ-ⲙ̄ⲡⲉⲧⲛ̄•	ⲛⲉ-ⲙ̄ⲡⲁⲧⲉⲧⲛ̄•
ⲛⲉ-ⲁⲩ•	ⲛⲉ-ⲙ̄ⲡⲟⲩ•	ⲛⲉ-ⲙ̄ⲡⲁⲧⲟⲩ•
ⲛⲉ-ⲁ-ⲡⲣⲱⲙⲉ •	ⲛⲉ-ⲙ̄ⲡⲉ-ⲡⲣⲱⲙⲉ •	ⲛⲉ-ⲙ̄ⲡⲁⲧⲉ-ⲡⲣⲱⲙⲉ •

Focalizing Past	**\<negative\>**
it is . . . that I wrote	it is . . . that I didn't write
ⲛ̄ⲧⲁⲓ• [ⲉⲛⲧⲁⲓ• (etc.)]	ⲛ̄ⲧⲁⲓ• ⲁⲛ
ⲛ̄ⲧⲁⲕ•	ⲛ̄ⲧⲁⲕ• ⲁⲛ
ⲛ̄ⲧⲁⲣⲉ•	ⲛ̄ⲧⲁⲣⲉ• ⲁⲛ
ⲛ̄ⲧⲁϥ•	ⲛ̄ⲧⲁϥ• ⲁⲛ
ⲛ̄ⲧⲁⲥ•	ⲛ̄ⲧⲁⲥ• ⲁⲛ
ⲛ̄ⲧⲁⲛ•	ⲛ̄ⲧⲁⲛ• ⲁⲛ
ⲛ̄ⲧⲁⲧⲉⲧⲛ̄•	ⲛ̄ⲧⲁⲧⲉⲧⲛ̄• ⲁⲛ
ⲛ̄ⲧⲁⲩ•	ⲛ̄ⲧⲁⲩ• ⲁⲛ
ⲛ̄ⲧⲁ-ⲡⲣⲱⲙⲉ •	ⲛ̄ⲧⲁ-ⲡⲣⲱⲙⲉ • ⲁⲛ

Aorist	**\<negative\>**
I write	I don't write
ϣⲁⲓ•	ⲙⲉⲓ•
ϣⲁⲕ•	ⲙⲉⲕ•
ϣⲁⲣ(ⲉ)•	ⲙⲉⲣⲉ•
ϣⲁϥ•	ⲙⲉϥ•
ϣⲁⲥ•	ⲙⲉⲥ•
ϣⲁⲛ•	ⲙⲉⲛ•
ϣⲁⲧⲉⲧⲛ̄•	ⲙⲉⲧⲉⲧⲛ̄•
ϣⲁⲩ•	ⲙⲉⲩ•
ϣⲁⲣⲉ-ⲡⲣⲱⲙⲉ •	ⲙⲉⲣⲉ-ⲡⲣⲱⲙⲉ •

Relative Aorist	**\<negative\>**
who/which I write	who/which I don't write
ⲉⲧⲉ-ϣⲁⲓ• [ⲉ-ϣⲁⲓ• (etc.)]	ⲉⲧⲉ-ⲙⲉⲓ•
ⲉⲧⲉ-ϣⲁⲕ•	ⲉⲧⲉ-ⲙⲉⲕ•
ⲉⲧⲉ-ϣⲁⲣ(ⲉ)•	ⲉⲧⲉ-ⲙⲉⲣⲉ•
ⲉⲧⲉ-ϣⲁϥ•	ⲉⲧⲉ-ⲙⲉϥ•
ⲉⲧⲉ-ϣⲁⲥ•	ⲉⲧⲉ-ⲙⲉⲥ•
ⲉⲧⲉ-ϣⲁⲛ•	ⲉⲧⲉ-ⲙⲉⲛ•

ⲉⲧⲉ-ϣⲁⲧⲉⲧⲛ̄•   ⲉⲧⲉ-ⲙⲉⲧⲉⲧⲛ̄•
ⲉⲧⲉ-ϣⲁⲩ•   ⲉⲧⲉ-ⲙⲉⲩ•
ⲉⲧⲉ-ϣⲁⲣⲉ-ⲡⲣⲱⲙⲉ •   ⲉⲧⲉ-ⲙⲉⲣⲉ-ⲡⲣⲱⲙⲉ •

Circumstantial Aorist   \<negative\>
as I write   as I don't write

ⲉ-ϣⲁⲓ̈•   ⲉ-ⲙⲉⲓ̈•
ⲉ-ϣⲁⲕ•   ⲉ-ⲙⲉⲕ•
ⲉ-ϣⲁⲣ(ⲉ)•   ⲉ-ⲙⲉⲣⲉ•
ⲉ-ϣⲁϥ•   ⲉ-ⲙⲉϥ•
ⲉ-ϣⲁⲥ•   ⲉ-ⲙⲉⲥ•
ⲉ-ϣⲁⲛ•   ⲉ-ⲙⲉⲛ•
ⲉ-ϣⲁⲧⲉⲧⲛ̄•   ⲉ-ⲙⲉⲧⲉⲧⲛ̄•
ⲉ-ϣⲁⲩ•   ⲉ-ⲙⲉⲩ•
ⲉ-ϣⲁⲣⲉ-ⲡⲣⲱⲙⲉ •   ⲉ-ⲙⲉⲣⲉ-ⲡⲣⲱⲙⲉ •

Preterite Aorist   \<negative\>
I used to write   I didn't use to write

ⲛⲉ-ϣⲁⲓ̈•   ⲛⲉ-ⲙⲉⲓ̈•
ⲛⲉ-ϣⲁⲕ•   ⲛⲉ-ⲙⲉⲕ•
ⲛⲉ-ϣⲁⲣ(ⲉ)•   ⲛⲉ-ⲙⲉⲣⲉ•
ⲛⲉ-ϣⲁϥ•   ⲛⲉ-ⲙⲉϥ•
ⲛⲉ-ϣⲁⲥ•   ⲛⲉ-ⲙⲉⲥ•
ⲛⲉ-ϣⲁⲛ•   ⲛⲉ-ⲙⲉⲛ•
ⲛⲉ-ϣⲁⲧⲉⲧⲛ̄•   ⲛⲉ-ⲙⲉⲧⲉⲧⲛ̄•
ⲛⲉ-ϣⲁⲩ•   ⲛⲉ-ⲙⲉⲩ•
ⲛⲉ-ϣⲁⲣⲉ-ⲡⲣⲱⲙⲉ •   ⲛⲉ-ⲙⲉⲣⲉ-ⲡⲣⲱⲙⲉ •

Focalizing Aorist
it is . . . that I write

ⲉϣⲁⲓ̈•
ⲉϣⲁⲕ•
ⲉϣⲁⲣ(ⲉ)•
ⲉϣⲁϥ•
ⲉϣⲁⲥ•
ⲉϣⲁⲛ•
ⲉϣⲁⲧⲉⲧⲛ̄•
ⲉϣⲁⲩ•
ⲉϣⲁⲣⲉ-ⲡⲣⲱⲙⲉ •

Optative   \<negative\>
I will write (I may/might write)   I won't write

ⲉⲓ̈ⲉ•   ⲛ̄ⲛⲁ•
ⲉⲕⲉ•   ⲛ̄ⲛⲉⲕ•

ⲉⲣⲉ•   ⲛ̄ⲛⲉ•
ⲉϥⲉ•   ⲛ̄ⲛⲉϥ•
ⲉⲥⲉ•   ⲛ̄ⲛⲉⲥ•
ⲉⲛⲉ•   ⲛ̄ⲛⲉⲛ•
ⲉⲧⲉⲧⲛⲉ•   ⲛ̄ⲛⲉⲧⲛ̄•
ⲉⲩⲉ•   ⲛ̄ⲛⲉⲩ•
ⲉⲣⲉ-ⲡⲣⲱⲙⲉ •   ⲛ̄ⲛⲉ-ⲡⲣⲱⲙⲉ •

Relative Optative   **\<negative\>**

who/which I won't write

ⲉⲧⲉ-ⲛ̄ⲛⲁ• [ⲉⲧⲉ-ⲛⲁ• (etc.)]
ⲉⲧⲉ-ⲛ̄ⲛⲉⲕ•
ⲉⲧⲉ-ⲛ̄ⲛⲉ•
ⲉⲧⲉ-ⲛ̄ⲛⲉϥ•
ⲉⲧⲉ-ⲛ̄ⲛⲉⲥ•
ⲉⲧⲉ-ⲛ̄ⲛⲉⲛ•
ⲉⲧⲉ-ⲛ̄ⲛⲉⲧⲛ̄•
ⲉⲧⲉ-ⲛ̄ⲛⲉⲩ•
ⲉⲧⲉ-ⲛ̄ⲛⲉ-ⲡⲣⲱⲙⲉ •

Circumstantial Optative   **\<negative\>**

as I won't write

ⲉ-ⲛ̄ⲛⲁ•
ⲉ-ⲛ̄ⲛⲉⲕ•
ⲉ-ⲛ̄ⲛⲉ•
ⲉ-ⲛ̄ⲛⲉϥ•
ⲉ-ⲛ̄ⲛⲉⲥ•
ⲉ-ⲛ̄ⲛⲉⲛ•
ⲉ-ⲛ̄ⲛⲉⲧⲛ̄•
ⲉ-ⲛ̄ⲛⲉⲩ•
ⲉ-ⲛ̄ⲛⲉ-ⲡⲣⲱⲙⲉ •

Jussive {+imperative}   **\<negative\>**

let me write!   don't let me write!

ⲙⲁⲣⲓ•   ⲙ̄ⲡⲣ̄ⲧⲣⲁ•
{•}   {ⲙ̄ⲡⲣ̄•}
{•}   {ⲙ̄ⲡⲣ̄•}
ⲙⲁⲣⲉϥ•   ⲙ̄ⲡⲣ̄ⲧⲣⲉϥ•
ⲙⲁⲣⲉⲥ•   ⲙ̄ⲡⲣ̄ⲧⲣⲉⲥ•
ⲙⲁⲣⲛ̄•   ⲙ̄ⲡⲣ̄ⲧⲣⲉⲛ•
{•}   {ⲙ̄ⲡⲣ̄•}
ⲙⲁⲣⲟⲩ•   ⲙ̄ⲡⲣ̄ⲧⲣⲉⲩ•
ⲙⲁⲣⲉ-ⲡⲣⲱⲙⲉ •   ⲙ̄ⲡⲣ̄ⲧⲣⲉ-ⲡⲣⲱⲙⲉ •

NON-DURATIVE PATTERN: SUBORDINATE CLAUSE CONJUGATIONS

Conjunctive　　　　　　　　　**<negative>**
… and (I) write　　　　　　　　… and (I) don't write
(ⲛ̄)ⲧⲁ•　　　　　　　　　　　　(ⲛ̄)ⲧⲁⲧⲙ̄•
ⲛ̄ⲅ• [ⲛ̄ⲅ̄•] [ⲛ̄ⲕ•]　　　　　　　ⲛ̄ⲅⲧⲙ̄• [ⲛ̄ⲅ̄ⲧⲙ̄•] [ⲛ̄ⲕⲧⲙ̄•]
ⲛ̄ⲧⲉ•　　　　　　　　　　　　　ⲛ̄ⲧⲉⲧⲙ̄•
ⲛ̄ϥ• [ⲛ̄ϥ̄•]　　　　　　　　　　ⲛ̄ϥⲧⲙ̄• [ⲛ̄ϥ̄ⲧⲙ̄•]
ⲛ̄ⲥ• [ⲛ̄ⲥ̄•]　　　　　　　　　　ⲛ̄ⲥⲧⲙ̄• [ⲛ̄ⲥ̄ⲧⲙ̄•]
ⲛ̄ⲧⲛ̄•　　　　　　　　　　　　　ⲛ̄ⲧⲛ̄ⲧⲙ̄•
ⲛ̄ⲧⲉⲧⲛ̄•　　　　　　　　　　　ⲛ̄ⲧⲉⲧⲛ̄ⲧⲙ̄•
ⲛ̄ⲥⲉ•　　　　　　　　　　　　　ⲛ̄ⲥⲉⲧⲙ̄•
ⲛ̄ⲧⲉ-ⲡⲣⲱⲙⲉ •　　　　　　　　ⲛ̄ⲧⲉⲧⲙ̄-ⲡⲣⲱⲙⲉ •

Future Conjunctive
… and I will write
ⲧⲁⲣⲓ•
ⲧⲁⲣⲉⲕ•
ⲧⲁⲣⲉ•
ⲧⲁⲣⲉϥ•
ⲧⲁⲣⲉⲥ•
ⲧⲁⲣⲛ̄•
ⲧⲁⲣ(ⲉⲧ)ⲉⲧⲛ̄•
ⲧⲁⲣⲟⲩ•
ⲧⲁⲣⲉ-ⲡⲣⲱⲙⲉ •

Precursive　　　　　　　　　**<negative>**
when/after I had written/wrote　when/after I hadn't written/didn't write
ⲛ̄ⲧⲉⲣⲓ•　　　　　　　　　　　　ⲛ̄ⲧⲉⲣⲓⲧⲙ̄•
ⲛ̄ⲧⲉⲣⲉⲕ•　　　　　　　　　　　ⲛ̄ⲧⲉⲣⲉⲕⲧⲙ̄•
ⲛ̄ⲧⲉⲣⲉ(ⲣ)•　　　　　　　　　　ⲛ̄ⲧⲉⲣⲉⲧⲙ̄•
ⲛ̄ⲧⲉⲣⲉϥ•　　　　　　　　　　　ⲛ̄ⲧⲉⲣⲉϥⲧⲙ̄•
ⲛ̄ⲧⲉⲣⲉⲥ•　　　　　　　　　　　ⲛ̄ⲧⲉⲣⲉⲥⲧⲙ̄•
ⲛ̄ⲧⲉⲣⲛ̄• [ⲛ̄ⲧⲉⲣⲉⲛ•]　　　　　ⲛ̄ⲧⲉⲣⲛ̄ⲧⲙ̄•
ⲛ̄ⲧⲉⲣⲉⲧⲛ̄•　　　　　　　　　　ⲛ̄ⲧⲉⲣⲉⲧⲛ̄ⲧⲙ̄•
ⲛ̄ⲧⲉⲣⲟⲩ•　　　　　　　　　　　ⲛ̄ⲧⲉⲣⲟⲩⲧⲙ̄•
ⲛ̄ⲧⲉⲣⲉ-ⲡⲣⲱⲙⲉ •　　　　　　　ⲛ̄ⲧⲉⲣⲉⲧⲙ̄-ⲡⲣⲱⲙⲉ •

Limitative　　　　　　　　　**<negative>**
until I write (etc.)　　　　　　until I don't write (etc.)
ϣⲁⲛϯ• [ϣⲁⲛⲧⲁ•]　　　　　　　ϣⲁⲛϯⲧⲙ̄•
ϣⲁⲛⲧⲕ̄•　　　　　　　　　　　ϣⲁⲛⲧⲕ̄ⲧⲙ̄•
ϣⲁⲛⲧⲉ•　　　　　　　　　　　ϣⲁⲛⲧⲉⲧⲙ̄•
ϣⲁⲛⲧϥ̄•　　　　　　　　　　　ϣⲁⲛⲧϥ̄ⲧⲙ̄•

ϣⲁⲛⲧⲥ̄•   ϣⲁⲛⲧⲥ̄ⲧⲛ̄•
ϣⲁⲛⲧⲛ̄•   ϣⲁⲛⲧⲛ̄ⲧⲛ̄•
ϣⲁⲛⲧⲉⲧⲛ̄•   ϣⲁⲛⲧⲉⲧⲛ̄ⲧⲛ̄•
ϣⲁⲛⲧⲟⲩ•   ϣⲁⲛⲧⲟⲩⲧⲛ̄•
ϣⲁⲛⲧⲉ-ⲡⲣⲱⲙⲉ •   ϣⲁⲛⲧⲉⲧⲛ̄-ⲡⲣⲱⲙⲉ •

Conditional   **\<negative\>**
if/when(ever) I write/wrote   if/when(ever) I don't write/didn't write
ⲉⲓϣⲁⲛ•   ⲉⲓ(ϣⲁⲛ)ⲧⲙ̄•
ⲉⲕϣⲁⲛ•   ⲉⲕ(ϣⲁⲛ)ⲧⲙ̄•
ⲉⲣ(ⲉ)ϣⲁⲛ•   ⲉⲣⲉ(ϣⲁⲛ)ⲧⲙ̄•
ⲉϥϣⲁⲛ•   ⲉϥ(ϣⲁⲛ)ⲧⲙ̄•
ⲉⲥϣⲁⲛ•   ⲉⲥ(ϣⲁⲛ)ⲧⲙ̄•
ⲉⲛϣⲁⲛ•   ⲉⲛ(ϣⲁⲛ)ⲧⲙ̄•
ⲉⲧⲉⲧⲛ̄ϣⲁⲛ•   ⲉⲧⲉⲧⲛ̄(ϣⲁⲛ)ⲧⲙ̄•
ⲉⲩϣⲁⲛ•   ⲉⲩ(ϣⲁⲛ)ⲧⲙ̄•
ⲉⲣϣⲁⲛ-ⲡⲣⲱⲙⲉ •   ⲉⲣϣⲁⲛⲧⲙ̄-ⲡⲣⲱⲙⲉ • [ⲉⲣⲉⲧⲙ̄-ⲡⲣⲱⲙⲉ •]

Causative Infinitive   **\<negative\>**
(cause) me to write, me writing   (cause) me to not write, me not writing
ⲧⲣⲁ•   (ⲧⲙ̄)ⲧⲣⲁ(ⲧⲙ̄)•
ⲧⲣⲉⲕ•   (ⲧⲙ̄)ⲧⲣⲉⲕ(ⲧⲙ̄)•
ⲧⲣⲉ•   (ⲧⲙ̄)ⲧⲣⲉ(ⲧⲙ̄)•
ⲧⲣⲉϥ•   (ⲧⲙ̄)ⲧⲣⲉϥ(ⲧⲙ̄)•
ⲧⲣⲉⲥ•   (ⲧⲙ̄)ⲧⲣⲉⲥ(ⲧⲙ̄)•
ⲧⲣⲉⲛ•   (ⲧⲙ̄)ⲧⲣⲉⲛ(ⲧⲙ̄)•
ⲧⲣⲉ(ⲧⲉ)ⲧⲛ̄•   (ⲧⲙ̄)ⲧⲣⲉⲧⲉⲧⲛ̄(ⲧⲙ̄)•
ⲧⲣⲉⲩ•   (ⲧⲙ̄)ⲧⲣⲉⲩ(ⲧⲙ̄)•
ⲧⲣⲉ-ⲡⲣⲱⲙⲉ •   (ⲧⲙ̄)ⲧⲣⲉ(ⲧⲙ̄)-ⲡⲣⲱⲙⲉ •

APPENDIX 4

PREPOSITIONS AND DIRECTIONAL ADVERBS

PREPOSITIONS

ⲁⲛⲧⲓ-		instead of (prep)
ⲁϫⲛ̄-, ⲉϫⲛ̄-	ⲁϫⲛ̄ⲧ⸗, ⲉϫⲛ̄ⲧ⸗	without; as adv: -lessly (ⲁⲧ + ϣⲓⲛⲉ) (prep)
ⲉ-	ⲉⲣⲟ⸗	to, for (prep)
ⲉⲃⲟⲗ ⲉ-		out to
ⲉϩⲟⲩⲛ ⲉ-		into
ⲉϩⲣⲁⲓ̈ ⲉ-		up/down to
ⲉⲡⲉⲥⲏⲧ ⲉ-		down to
ⲉⲡⲁϩⲟⲩ ⲉ-		back to
ⲉⲑⲏ ⲉ-		forward to
ϣⲁϩⲟⲩⲛ ⲉ-		until
ⲕⲁⲧⲁ-	ⲕⲁⲧⲁⲣⲟ⸗	according to (prep)
ⲙ̄ⲙⲁϩ-		in the presence of (a deity) (prep)
ⲙⲛ̄-, ⲛⲙ̄-	ⲛⲙ̄ⲙⲁ⸗	with; and (prep)
ⲛ̄-	ⲙ̄ⲙⲟ⸗	in, with; as adv: -ly (direct object marker; equivalence marker with ⲟ†, ϣⲟⲟⲡ†, and suffix pronouns) (prep)
ⲉⲃⲟⲗ ⲛ̄-		out of, from (in)
ⲛ̄-	ⲛⲁ⸗	to, for (indirect object marker) (prep)
ⲛ̄-, ⲛ̄ⲧⲉ-		of (attribution/adjectival without article) (genitive part/prep)
ⲟⲩⲃⲉ-	ⲟⲩⲃⲏ⸗	toward, facing, against (prep)
ⲟⲩⲧⲉ-	ⲟⲩⲧⲱ⸗	between, among (prep)
ⲟⲩⲱϣ		gap, interval, pause (nm)
(ⲛ̄)ⲟⲩⲉϣⲛ̄-		without (prep)
ⲡⲁⲣⲁ-	ⲡⲁⲣⲁⲣⲟ⸗	beside, beyond, more than (prep)
ⲡⲣⲟⲥ-	ⲡⲣⲟⲥⲣⲟ⸗	according to, for; than (prep)
ⲣⲁⲧ⸗		foot (of) (usually in compounds) (nm)

PREPOSITIONS AND DIRECTIONAL ADVERBS

ⲉⲣⲁⲧ⸗			to the foot of (prep)
ϩⲁⲣⲁⲧ⸗			under (prep)
ϩⲓⲣⲁⲧ⸗			toward (prep)
ⲣⲟ (pl ⲣⲱⲟⲩ)	ⲣⲛ̄-	ⲣⲱ⸗	mouth; door, opening (usually in compounds) (nm)
ⲉⲣⲛ̄-		ⲉⲣⲱ⸗	to (the opening of) (prep)
ϩⲁⲣⲛ̄-		ϩⲁⲣⲱ⸗	before (setting food) (prep)
ϩⲓⲣⲛ̄-		ϩⲓⲣⲱ⸗	at (the opening of) (prep)
ⲥⲁ			side, part, direction (nm)
ⲛ̄ⲥⲁ-		ⲛ̄ⲥⲱ⸗	after, behind; except (prep)
ⲙⲛ̄ⲛ̄ⲥⲁ-		ⲙⲛ̄ⲛ̄ⲥⲱ⸗	after (of time) (prep)
ⲙⲛ̄ⲛ̄ⲥⲱⲥ			afterwards (adv)
ⲧⲟⲩⲱ⸗			bosom, lap; embrace (of) (n)
ⲉⲧⲟⲩⲛ̄-, ⲉⲧⲟⲩⲉⲛ-		ⲉⲧⲟⲩⲱ⸗	beside, near (prep)
ϩⲓⲧⲟⲩⲛ̄-, ϩⲓⲧⲟⲩⲉⲛ-		ϩⲓⲧⲟⲩⲱ⸗	beside, near (prep)
ⲡⲉⲧ-ϩⲓⲧⲟⲩⲱ⸗			neighbor
ⲧⲱⲣⲉ	ⲧⲛ̄-	ⲧⲟⲟⲧ⸗	hand; handle; implement (usually in compounds) (nf)
ⲉⲧⲛ̄-		ⲉⲧⲟⲟⲧ⸗	to (prep)
ⲛ̄ⲧⲛ̄-		ⲛ̄ⲧⲟⲟⲧ⸗	from, by (prep)
ⲉⲃⲟⲗ ⲛ̄ⲧⲛ̄-			from
ⲛ̄ⲧⲉ- = ⲛ̄ⲧⲛ̄-			
ϩⲁⲧⲛ̄-		ϩⲁⲧⲟⲟⲧ⸗	beside, near, with (prep)
ϩⲓⲧⲛ̄-		ϩⲓⲧⲟⲟⲧ⸗	through, by, from (prep)
ⲉⲃⲟⲗ ϩⲓⲧⲛ̄-			through, by
ⲧⲱⲱⲃⲉ	ⲧⲉⲃⲉ-	ⲧⲟⲟⲃ⸗	to repay (ⲙ̄ⲙⲟ⸗) (vt)
ⲉⲧⲃⲉ-		ⲉⲧⲃⲏⲏⲧ⸗	about, concerning, because of (prep)
χωρίϲ-			without, apart from (prep)
ϣⲁ-		ϣⲁⲣⲟ⸗	to(ward), up to (prep)
ϣⲱⲱⲧ	ϣⲉ(ⲉ)ⲧ-	ϣⲁⲁⲧ⸗ ϣⲁⲁⲧ†	(cp ϣⲁⲧ-) to cut (off), sacrifice (vt) to be lacking (for, of, in: ⲉ-, ⲙ̄ⲙⲟ⸗, ϩⲛ̄-) (vi/vs)
ϣⲁ(ⲁ)ⲧⲛ̄-			except, minus, short of (prep)
ϩⲁ-		ϩⲁⲣⲟ⸗	under; concerning (prep)
ϩⲁⲣⲓϩⲁⲣⲟ⸗			alone, -self
ϩⲏ, ⲉϩⲏ, ϩⲓⲏ		ϩⲏⲧ⸗	front, fore part; beginning (nf)
ⲉⲑⲏ			forward, ahead (adv)
(ⲉ)ϩⲏⲧ⸗			before (of place) (prep)
ϩⲁⲑⲏ		ϩⲁⲧ⸗ϩⲏ	before (prep)
ϩⲓ-ⲑⲏ ⲛ̄-			in front of
ϩⲏ		ϩⲏⲧ⸗	belly, womb (nf)
ⲛ̄ϩⲏⲧ⸗			in, among, within, at (see ϩⲛ̄-) (prep)

ϩⲏⲧ (pl ϩⲉⲧⲉ)	ϩⲧⲏ⸗	heart, mind (nm)
ϩⲁ(ϩ)ⲧⲛ̄-	ϩⲁ(ϩ)ⲧⲏ⸗	beside, near, with (prep)
ϩⲓ-	ϩⲓⲱ(ⲱ)⸗	on; and (noun without article only) (prep)
ⲉⲃⲟⲗ ϩⲓ-		from on
ⲉϩⲟⲩⲛ ϩⲓ-		in on
ⲉϩⲣⲁⲓ̈ ϩⲓ-		up/down on
ⲉⲡⲉⲥⲏⲧ ϩⲓ-		down on
ϩⲛ̄-	ⲛ̄ϩⲏⲧ⸗	in, among, within, at (ⲛ̄ϩⲏⲧ⸗ from ϩⲏ belly, womb) (prep)
ⲉⲃⲟⲗ ϩⲛ̄-		out of, from (in)
ⲉϩⲟⲩⲛ ϩⲛ̄-		into, within
ⲛ̄ϩⲟⲩⲛ ϩⲛ̄-		within
ϩⲣⲁⲓ̈ ϩⲛ̄-		in
ϩⲛ̄-ⲟⲩ-		often adv: -ly
ϩⲟ	ϩⲣⲁ⸗	face; surface (nm)
ⲉϩⲣⲛ̄-	ⲉϩⲣⲁ⸗	toward (prep)
ⲉⲃⲟⲗ ⲉϩⲣⲛ̄-		out toward
ⲉϩⲟⲩⲛ ⲉϩⲣⲛ̄-		in toward
ϩⲓϩⲣⲁ⸗		on the face of (prep)
(ⲛ̄)ⲛⲁϩⲣⲛ̄-	(ⲛ̄)ⲛⲁϩⲣⲁ⸗	in front of, facing (prep)
ϩⲱⲥ-		like, as (prep)
ϫⲓⲛ-, ϫⲛ̄-		from, since (prep)
ϫⲱ⸗		head (of) (usually in compounds) (nm)
ⲉϫⲛ̄-	ⲉϫⲱ⸗	onto, over (prep)
ⲉⲃⲟⲗ ⲉϫⲛ̄-		out onto
ⲉϩⲟⲩⲛ ⲉϫⲛ̄-		in onto
ⲉϩⲣⲁⲓ̈ ⲉϫⲛ̄-		up/down onto
ⲉⲡⲉⲥⲏⲧ ⲉϫⲛ̄-		down onto
ϩⲁϫⲛ̄-	ϩⲁϫⲱ⸗	before (prep)
ϩⲓϫⲛ̄-	ϩⲓϫⲱ⸗	upon (prep)
ϩⲣⲁⲓ̈ ϩⲓϫⲛ̄-		upon
ⲡⲉⲧ-ϩⲓϫⲛ̄-		the one in command of

DIRECTIONAL ADVERBS

ⲃⲟⲗ	outside, outer part (< ⲃⲱⲗ) (nm)
ⲉⲃⲟⲗ	out, away (adv)
ⲛ̄ⲃⲟⲗ	outside (adv)
(ⲛ̄)ⲥⲁⲃⲟⲗ	outside (adv)
ϣⲁⲃⲟⲗ	outward (adv)
ϩⲓⲃⲟⲗ	outside (adv)
(ⲉ)ⲓⲧⲛ̄	ground, dirt (nm)

PREPOSITIONS AND DIRECTIONAL ADVERBS

ⲉⲡⲓⲧⲛ̄		down (adv)
ⲉⲥⲏⲧ		bottom, ground (nm)
ⲉⲡⲉⲥⲏⲧ		down (adv)
ϩⲁⲡⲉⲥⲏⲧ		under (adv)
ϩⲓⲡⲉⲥⲏⲧ		below (adv)
ⲡⲁϩⲟⲩ		rear, back part (nm)
ⲉⲡⲁϩⲟⲩ		backward, back (adv)
ϩⲓⲡⲁϩⲟⲩ		behind (adv)
ⲡⲉ (pl ⲡⲏⲩⲉ)		sky (nf)
ⲉⲧⲡⲉ		skyward, upward (adv)
ϣⲱⲓ		height, (what is) above (< ϣ[ⲓ]ⲁⲓ) (nm)
ⲉⲡϣⲱⲓ		upward (adv)
ϩⲏ, ⲉϩⲏ, ϩⲓⲏ	ϩⲏⲧ⸗	front, fore part; beginning (nf)
ⲉⲑⲏ		forward, ahead (adv)
ϩⲟⲩⲛ		inside, inner part (cf. ϩⲛ̄-) (nm)
ⲉϩⲟⲩⲛ		in (adv)
ⲛ̄ϩⲟⲩⲛ		within, inside (adv)
ϣⲁϩⲟⲩⲛ		inward (adv)
ϩⲓϩⲟⲩⲛ		within (adv)
ϩⲣⲁⲓ̈		top, upper part; bottom, lower part (!) (nm)
ⲉϩⲣⲁⲓ̈		up; down (!) (adv)
ⲛ̄ϩⲣⲁⲓ̈		above; below (!) (adv)
ϣⲁϩⲣⲁⲓ̈		upward; downward (!) (adv)
ϩⲓϩⲣⲁⲓ̈		upward (adv)

INDEX OF VERBAL FORMS

This list is designed to help you determine the main lexicon entry for less predictable (non-absolute) verbal forms—including prenominal (-), prepersonal (⸗), stative (†), imperative (impv) and conjunct participle (cp) forms. Not all non-absolute verbal forms are listed; ones that follow more easily predictable patterns (for instance: just replace the vowel with ⲱ, and check that) are not listed below.

Form:	See entry:		
		ⲉⲉⲧ†	ⲱ(ⲱ)
		ⲉⲣ-	ⲉⲓⲣⲉ
ⲁⲁ⸗	ⲉⲓⲣⲉ	ⲉϣⲧ̄-	ⲉⲓϣⲉ
ⲁⲗⲏⲩ†	ⲁⲗⲉ		
ⲁⲗⲟ⸗	ⲁⲗⲉ	ⲕⲉⲙⲧ̄-, ⲕⲉⲙⲧ⸗	ⲕⲓⲙ
ⲁⲗⲟ (impv fsg)	ⲗⲟ	ⲕⲉϩⲕⲉϩ-	ⲕⲁϩⲕ︤ϩ︥
ⲁⲗⲟⲕ (impv msg)	ⲗⲟ	ⲕⲉϩⲕⲱϩ⸗, ⲕⲉϩⲕⲱϩ†	ⲕⲁϩⲕ︤ϩ︥
ⲁⲗⲱⲧⲛ̄ (impv)	ⲁⲗⲉ	ⲕⲏⲙ†	ⲕⲙⲟⲙ
ⲁⲗⲱⲧⲛ̄ (impv pl)	ⲗⲟ		
ⲁⲙⲏ (impv fsg)	ⲉⲓ	ⲗⲁⲃ- (cp)	ⲗⲓⲃⲉ
ⲁⲙⲏⲉⲓⲧⲛ̄ (impv pl)	ⲉⲓ	ⲗⲉⲃⲧ⸗	ⲗⲓⲃⲉ
ⲁⲙⲟⲩ (impv msg)	ⲉⲓ	ⲗⲟⲃⲉ†	ⲗⲓⲃⲉ
ⲁⲛ(ⲉ)ⲓⲛⲉ (impv)	ⲉⲓⲛⲉ		
ⲁⲛⲓ-, ⲁⲛⲓ⸗ (impv)	ⲉⲓⲛⲉ	ⲙⲁ- (impv)	†
ⲁⲣⲓ-, ⲁⲣⲓ⸗ (impv)	ⲉⲓⲣⲉ	ⲙⲁⲓ̈- (cp)	ⲙⲉ
ⲁⲣⲓⲣⲉ (impv)	ⲉⲓⲣⲉ	ⲙⲁⲛ(ⲉ)- (cp)	ⲙⲟⲟⲛⲉ
ⲁⲩⲱⲛ (impv)	ⲟⲩⲱⲛ	ⲙⲁⲛⲟⲩ(ⲟⲩ)⸗	ⲙⲟⲟⲛⲉ
ⲁϣⲉ†	ⲉⲓϣⲉ	ⲙⲁⲣ- (cp)	ⲙⲟⲩⲣ
ⲁϣⲧ̄-, ⲁϣ(ⲧ)⸗	ⲉⲓϣⲉ	ⲙⲁⲥ- (cp)	ⲙⲓⲥⲉ
ⲁϩⲉ†	ⲱϩⲉ	ⲙⲁⲥⲧ⸗	ⲙⲓⲥⲉ
ⲁϫⲓ-, ⲁϫⲓ⸗ (impv)	ϫⲱ	ⲙⲁⲥⲧ̄- (cp)	ⲙⲟⲥⲧⲉ
		ⲙⲁⲧ⸗ (impv)	†
ⲃⲁⲃⲉ- (cp)	ⲃⲁⲁⲃⲉ	ⲙⲁϣⲧ̄- (cp)	ⲙⲟⲩϣⲧ̄
ⲃⲁⲃⲟⲧ†	ⲃⲁⲁⲃⲉ	ⲙⲁϩ⸗	ⲙⲟⲩϩ
ⲃⲁⲃⲱ(ⲱ)⸗	ⲃⲁⲁⲃⲉ	ⲙⲉⲕⲙⲟⲩⲕ⸗	ⲙⲟⲕⲙⲉⲕ
ⲃⲁⲗⲃ︤ⲗ︥- (cp)	ⲃⲟⲗⲃ︤ⲗ︥	ⲙⲉⲕ︤ϩ︥-	ⲙⲟⲩⲕ︤ϩ︥
ⲃ︤ⲗ︥ⲃⲱⲗ⸗	ⲃⲟⲗⲃ︤ⲗ︥	ⲙⲉⲗ︤ϩ︥-	ⲙⲟⲩⲗ︤ϩ︥

ⲙⲉⲛⲉ-	ⲙⲟⲟⲛⲉ	ⲛⲟⲭ⸗	ⲛⲟⲩⲭ(ⲉ)
ⲙⲉⲣ-	ⲙⲟⲩⲣ	ⲛⲟϭⲥ̄†	ⲛⲟⲩϭⲥ̄
ⲙⲉⲣⲉ-	ⲙⲉ	ⲛ̄ⲧ⸗	ⲉⲓⲛⲉ
ⲙⲉⲣⲓⲧ⸗	ⲙⲉ	ⲛ̄ϩⲉⲧ-	ⲛⲁϩⲧⲉ
ⲙⲉⲥ- (cp)	ⲙⲓⲥⲉ	ⲛ̄ϩⲟ(ⲩ)ⲧ†	ⲛⲁϩⲧⲉ
ⲙⲉⲥ(ⲧ̄)-	ⲙⲓⲥⲉ		
ⲙⲉⲥⲧⲉ-	ⲙⲟⲥⲧⲉ	ⲟ†	ⲉⲓⲣⲉ
ⲙⲉⲥⲧⲱ⸗	ⲙⲟⲥⲧⲉ	ⲟⲃⲉ†	ⲉⲓⲃⲉ
ⲙⲉⲩⲧ-	ⲙⲟⲩⲟⲩⲧ	ⲟⲓ̈†	ⲁⲓ̈ⲁⲓ̈
ⲙⲉϣⲧ̄-	ⲙⲟⲩϣⲧ̄	ⲟⲩⲁⲁⲃ†	ⲟⲩⲟⲡ
ⲙⲉϩ-, ⲙⲉϩ†	ⲙⲟⲩϩ	ⲟⲩⲉⲥⲧⲱⲛ†	ⲟⲩⲟⲥⲧⲛ̄
ⲙⲏⲉⲓ⸗	†	ⲟⲩⲉⲧⲟⲩⲱⲧ†	ⲟⲩⲟⲧⲟⲩⲉⲧ
ⲙⲏⲛ†	ⲙⲟⲩⲛ	ⲟⲩⲏⲩ†	ⲟⲩⲉ
ⲙⲏⲣ†	ⲙⲟⲩⲣ	ⲟⲩⲟⲃϣ̄†	ⲟⲩⲃⲁϣ
ⲙⲏϩ†	ⲙⲟⲩϩ	ⲟⲩⲟⲭ†	ⲟⲩϫⲁⲓ̈
ⲙⲟⲕϩ̄†	ⲙ̄ⲕⲁϩ	ⲟϣ†	ⲁϣⲁⲓ̈
ⲙⲟⲕϩ⸗	ⲙⲟⲩⲕϩ̄		
ⲙⲟⲗϩ⸗, ⲙⲟⲗϩ̄†	ⲙⲟⲩⲗϩ̄	ⲡⲁⲡⲉ-	ⲡⲱⲡⲉ
ⲙⲟⲟⲩⲧ†	ⲙⲟⲩ	ⲡⲁⲡⲱ⸗	ⲡⲱⲡⲉ
ⲙⲟⲟⲩⲧ⸗	ⲙⲟⲩⲟⲩⲧ	ⲡⲁⲥ- (cp)	ⲡⲓⲥⲉ
ⲙⲟⲣ⸗	ⲙⲟⲩⲣ	ⲡⲁⲥⲧ⸗	ⲡⲓⲥⲉ
ⲙⲟⲥⲉ†	ⲙⲓⲥⲉ	ⲡⲉⲥ(ⲧ̄)-	ⲡⲓⲥⲉ
ⲙⲟⲧⲛ̄†	ⲙ̄ⲧⲟⲛ	ⲡⲟⲣⲉ†	ⲡ(ⲉ)ⲓⲣⲉ́
ⲙⲟⲩⲧ-	ⲙⲟⲩⲟⲩⲧ	ⲡⲟⲥⲉ†	ⲡⲓⲥⲉ
ⲙⲟϣⲧ⸗, ⲙⲟϣⲧ̄†	ⲙⲟⲩϣⲧ̄	ⲡⲣ̄ⲣⲉ́	ⲡ(ⲉ)ⲓⲣⲉ́
ⲙⲡ̄-	ⲙⲟⲩⲣ		
		ⲣ̄-	ⲉⲓⲣⲉ
ⲛ̄-	ⲉⲓⲛⲉ	ⲣⲁϣⲧ⸗	ⲣⲱϣⲉ
ⲛⲁϣⲧ̄†	ⲛ̄ϣⲟⲧ	ⲣⲉⲕ(ⲧ̄)-, ⲣⲉⲕⲧ⸗	ⲣⲓⲕⲉ
ⲛⲁϥⲧ⸗	ⲛⲓϥⲉ	ⲣⲉϣⲧ̄-	ⲣⲱϣⲉ
ⲛⲁϩ⸗	ⲛⲟⲩϩⲉ	ⲣⲏⲥ†	ⲣⲟⲉⲓⲥ
ⲛⲁϩⲃ̄-, ⲛⲁϩⲃ⸗, ⲛⲁϩⲃ̄†	ⲛⲟⲩϩⲃ̄	ⲣⲟⲕⲉ†	ⲣⲓⲕⲉ
ⲛⲁϩⲙ⸗	ⲛⲟⲩϩⲙ̄	ⲣⲟⲟⲩⲧ†	ⲟⲩⲣⲟⲧ
ⲛⲉϥⲧ⸗	ⲛⲓϥⲉ		
ⲛⲉϩ-, ⲛⲉϩ†	ⲛⲟⲩϩⲉ	ⲥⲁⲁⲧ⸗	ⲥ(ⲉ)ⲓⲛⲉ
ⲛⲉϩⲙ̄-	ⲛⲟⲩϩⲙ̄	ⲥⲁⲛⲁϣⲧ̄†	ⲥⲁ(ⲁ)ⲛϣ̄
ⲛⲉⲭ-	ⲛⲟⲩⲭ(ⲉ)	ⲥⲁⲛⲟⲩϣ⸗	ⲥⲁ(ⲁ)ⲛϣ̄
ⲛⲉϭⲛⲉϭ-	ⲛⲟϭⲛⲉϭ	ⲥⲁⲧ⸗	ⲥⲓⲧⲉ
ⲛⲉϭⲛⲟⲩϭ⸗	ⲛⲟϭⲛⲉϭ	ⲥⲁϩ⸗	ⲥϩⲁⲓ̈
ⲛⲉϭⲥ̄-	ⲛⲟⲩϭⲥ̄	ⲥⲁϩⲉ-	ⲥⲟ(ⲟ)ϩⲉ
ⲛⲏⲩ†	ⲉⲓ	ⲥⲁϩⲉ-	ⲥⲟⲟϩⲉ
ⲛⲏϩ†	ⲛⲟⲩϩⲉ	ⲥⲁϩⲏⲩ†	ⲥⲟⲟϩⲉ
ⲛⲏⲭ†	ⲛⲟⲩⲭ(ⲉ)	ⲥⲁϩⲱ⸗	ⲥⲟ(ⲟ)ϩⲉ
ⲛⲟϥⲣ†	ⲛⲟⲩϥⲣ	ⲥⲁϩⲱ(ⲱ)⸗	ⲥⲟⲟϩⲉ

INDEX OF VERBAL FORMS

cⲃⲃⲏⲧ⸗	cⲃⲃⲉ	ⲧⲁⲙⲉ-	ⲧⲁⲙⲟ
cⲃⲃⲏⲩ(ⲧ)†	cⲃⲃⲉ	ⲧⲁⲙⲓⲉ-	ⲧⲁⲙⲓⲟ
cⲃ̄ⲧⲉ-	ⲥⲟⲃⲧⲉ	ⲧⲁⲙⲓⲏⲩ†	ⲧⲁⲙⲓⲟ
cⲃ̄ⲧⲱⲧ⸗, cⲃ̄ⲧⲱⲧ†	ⲥⲟⲃⲧⲉ	ⲧⲁⲛϩⲉ-	ⲧⲁⲛϩⲟ
ⲥⲉⲡⲥ̄-	ⲥⲟⲡⲥⲡ̄	ⲧⲁⲛϩⲉⲧ-	ⲧⲁⲛϩⲟⲩⲧ
ⲥⲉⲡⲥⲱⲡ†	ⲥⲟⲡⲥⲡ̄	ⲧⲁⲛϩⲏⲩ†	ⲧⲁⲛϩⲟ
ⲥⲉⲧ-	ⲥⲓⲧⲉ	ⲧⲁⲛϩⲏⲩⲧ†	ⲧⲁⲛϩⲟⲩⲧ
ⲥⲉϩ-	ⲥϩⲁï	ⲧⲁ(ⲟ)ⲩⲉ-	ⲧⲁ(ⲟ)ⲩⲟ
ⲥⲉϩⲧ⸗	ⲥϩⲁï	ⲧⲁϣⲉ-	ⲧⲁϣⲟ
ⲥⲏⲧ†	ⲥⲓⲧⲉ	ⲧⲁϩⲉ-	ⲧⲁϩⲟ
ⲥⲏⲩ†	ⲥ(ⲉ)ⲓ	ⲧⲁϩⲉ†	†ϩⲉ
ⲥⲏϩ†	ⲥϩⲁï	ⲧⲁϩⲏⲩ†	ⲧⲁϩⲟ
ⲥⲗ̄ⲥⲗ̄-	ⲥⲟⲗⲥⲗ̄	ⲧⲁϫⲣⲉ-	ⲧⲁϫⲣⲟ
ⲥⲗ̄ⲥⲱⲗ⸗, ⲥⲗ̄ⲥⲱⲗ†	ⲥⲟⲗⲥⲗ̄	ⲧⲁϫⲣⲏⲩ†	ⲧⲁϫⲣⲟ
ⲥⲙⲁⲙⲁⲁⲧ†	ⲥⲙⲟⲩ	ⲧⲃ̄ⲃⲉ-	ⲧⲃ̄ⲃⲟ
ⲥⲙⲛ̄-	ⲥⲙⲓⲛⲉ	ⲧⲃ̄ⲃⲏⲩ†	ⲧⲃ̄ⲃⲟ
ⲥⲙⲛ̄ⲧ⸗	ⲥⲙⲓⲛⲉ	ⲧⲛ̄ⲛⲉⲩ-	ⲧⲛ̄ⲛⲟⲟⲩ
ⲥⲙⲟⲛⲧ̄†	ⲥⲙⲓⲛⲉ	ⲧⲛ̄ⲧⲛ̄-	ⲧⲟⲛⲧⲛ̄
ⲥⲛ̄-	ⲥ(ⲉ)ⲓⲛⲉ	ⲧⲛ̄ⲧⲱⲛ⸗, ⲧⲛ̄ⲧⲱⲛ†	ⲧⲟⲛⲧⲛ̄
ⲥⲟⲃⲕ̄†	ⲥⲃⲟⲕ	ⲧⲟ†	†
ⲥⲟⲡⲥ̄	ⲥⲟⲡⲥⲡ̄	ⲧⲟⲩⲛⲉⲥ-	ⲧⲟⲩⲛⲟⲥ
ⲥⲟⲩⲛ̄-	ⲥⲟⲟⲩⲛ̄	ⲧⲟⲩϫⲉ-	ⲧⲟⲩϫⲟ
ⲥⲟⲩⲧⲛ̄-	ⲥⲟⲟⲩⲧⲛ̄	ⲧⲟⲩϫⲏⲩ†	ⲧⲟⲩϫⲟ
ⲥⲟⲩⲧⲱⲛ⸗, ⲥⲟⲩⲧⲱⲛ†	ⲥⲟⲟⲩⲧⲛ̄	ⲧⲣⲉϣⲣⲱϣ†	ⲧⲣⲟϣⲣⲉϣ
ⲥⲟⲩⲱⲛ⸗	ⲥⲟⲟⲩⲛ̄	ⲧⲣⲟϣ	ⲧⲱⲣϣ̄
ⲥⲡ̄ⲥ-	ⲥⲟⲡⲥⲡ̄	ⲧⲥⲁⲃⲉ-	ⲧⲥⲁⲃⲟ
ⲥⲡ̄ⲥⲡ̄-	ⲥⲟⲡⲥⲡ̄	ⲧⲥⲁⲃⲏⲩ(ⲧ)†	ⲧⲥⲁⲃⲟ
ⲥⲡ̄ⲥⲱⲡ⸗, ⲥⲡ̄ⲥⲱⲡ†	ⲥⲟⲡⲥⲡ̄	ⲧⲥⲉ-	ⲧⲥⲟ
ⲥⲣⲉϥⲣⲱϥ⸗	ⲥⲣⲟϥⲣⲉϥ	ⲧⲥⲏⲩ†	ⲧⲥⲟ
ⲥⲣⲟϥⲧ̄†	ⲥⲣ̄ϥⲉ	ⲧϭⲁ(ⲉ)ⲓⲉ-	ⲧϭⲁ(ⲉ)ⲓⲟ
ⲥϩⲟⲩⲟⲣⲧ̄†	ⲥⲁϩⲟⲩ(ⲉ)	ⲧϭⲁ(ⲉ)ⲓⲏⲩ†	ⲧϭⲁ(ⲉ)ⲓⲟ
ⲥϩⲟⲩⲣ̄-	ⲥⲁϩⲟⲩ(ⲉ)		
ⲥϩⲟⲩⲱⲣ⸗	ⲥⲁϩⲟⲩ(ⲉ)	ϣⲁⲕⲧ⸗	ϣⲓⲕⲉ
		ϣⲁⲣ⸗, ϣⲁⲣ†	ϣⲁⲁⲣⲉ
ⲧⲁⲁ⸗	†	ϣⲃ̄(ⲧ)-, ϣⲃ̄ⲧ⸗	ϣⲓⲃⲉ
ⲧⲁ(ⲉ)ⲓⲉ-	ⲧⲁ(ⲉ)ⲓⲟ	ϣⲉⲕⲧ̄-	ϣⲓⲕⲉ
ⲧⲁ(ⲉ)ⲓⲏⲩ†	ⲧⲁ(ⲉ)ⲓⲟ	ϣⲉⲧϣⲱⲧ-, ϣⲉⲧϣⲱⲧ†	ϣⲟⲧϣ̄ⲧ
ⲧⲁï- (ⲥⲣ)	†	ϣⲓ(ⲕ)ⲧ⸗	ϣⲓⲕⲉ
ⲧⲁⲕⲉ-	ⲧⲁⲕⲟ	ϣⲓⲧ⸗	ϣⲓ
ⲧⲁⲕⲏⲩ(ⲧ)†	ⲧⲁⲕⲟ	ϣⲓⲧⲉ	ϣⲓⲕⲉ
ⲧⲁⲗⲉ-	ⲧⲁⲗⲟ	ϣⲙ̄ϣⲏⲧ⸗	ϣⲙ̄ϣⲉ
ⲧⲁⲗⲏⲩ†	ⲧⲁⲗⲟ	ϣⲛ̄-	ϣⲓⲛⲉ
ⲧⲁⲗϭⲉ-	ⲧⲁⲗϭⲟ	ϣⲛ̄ⲧ⸗	ϣⲓⲛⲉ
ⲧⲁⲗϭⲏⲩ†	ⲧⲁⲗϭⲟ	ϣⲟⲃⲉ†	ϣⲓⲃⲉ

267

ϣoke†	ϣike	ϫaï- (cp)	ϫi
ϣoy(e)-	ϣoyo	ϫap- (cp)	ϫpo
ϣoyeit†	ϣoyo	ϫaci- (cp)	ϫice
ϣoyⲱ=	ϣoyo	ϫact=	ϫice
ϣoyⲱoy†	ϣooye	ϫat- (cp)	ϫⲱ
ϣoϫt̄	ϣotⲱt̄	ϫay- (cp)	ϫi
ϣtam†	ϣtom	ϫe-	ϫo
ϣtr̄tr̄-	ϣtortr̄	ϫepe-	ϫepo
ϣtr̄tⲱp=, ϣtr̄tⲱp†	ϣtortr̄	ϫect̄-	ϫice
		ϫey-	ϫooy
ϥaï- (cp)	ϥi	ϫhy†	ϫo
ϥit=	ϥi	ϫit=	ϫi
		ϫne-	ϫnoy
ϩaló- (cp)	ϩloϭ	ϫoce†	ϫice
ϩapϣ̄- (cp)	ϩpoϣ	ϫpe-	ϫpo
ϩact̄-, ϩact=	ϩice	ϫpie-	ϫpo
ϩepϣ̄-	ϩpoϣ	ϫpiht†	ϫpo
ϩetϩ̄-	ϩotϩ̄	ϫpaeit†	ϫpo
ϩetϩⲱt=, ϩetϩⲱt†	ϩotϩ̄		
ϩeϫϩⲱϫ=, ϩeϫϩⲱϫ†	ϩoϫϩ̄	ϭale-	ϭo(e)ile
ϩeϫϩ̄-	ϩoϫϩ̄	ϭalhy(t)†	ϭo(e)ile
ϩhm†	ϩmom	ϭalⲱoy†	ϭo(e)ile
ϩhy†	ϩe	ϭalⲱ(ⲱ)=	ϭo(e)ile
ϩi-	ϩioye	ϭeet†	ϭⲱ
ϩit=	ϩioye	ϭm̄-	ϭine
ϩkaeit†	ϩko	ϭm̄ϭⲱm=	ϭomϭm̄
ϩolϭ†	ϩloϭ	ϭn̄-	ϭine
ϩopϣ̄	ϩpoϣ	ϭn̄t=	ϭine
ϩoce†	ϩice		
ϩpϣ̄-	ϩpoϣ		

268

textbook*plus*

FREE Resources!

Equipping Instructors and Students with
FREE RESOURCES for Core Zondervan Textbooks

Available Resources for Basics of Sahidic Coptic

Study Resources

- Answer key for exercises
- Additional biblical and extrabiblical readings
- Expanded lexicon
- Full color verb paradigm charts

*How To Access Resources

- Go to www.ZondervanAcademic.com
- Click "Sign Up" button and complete registration process
- Find books using search field or browse using discipline categories
- Click "Teaching Resources" or "Study Resources" tab once you get to book page to access resources

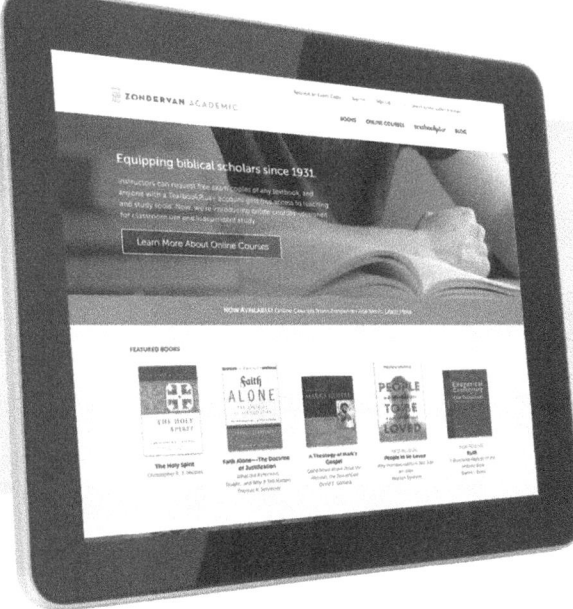

www.ZondervanAcademic.com

Zondervan Language Basics

Basics of Akkadian

A Complete Grammar, Workbook, and Lexicon

Gordon P. Hugenberger, with Nancy L. Erickson

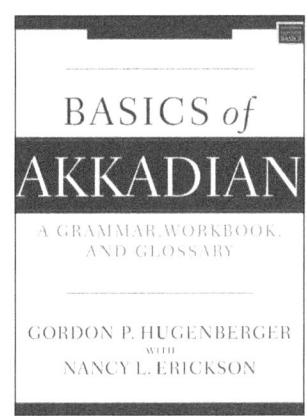

Basics of Akkadian: A Complete Grammar, Workbook, and Lexicon is a one-semester introductory textbook to the Akkadian language. The grammar provides students with essential tools in order to quickly grasp the Akkadian language and move into translation. Designed around the Laws of Hammurabi, each chapter includes:

- Explanation of grammatical points
- Signs that need to be learned
- Vocabulary
- Exercises

Short contributions that highlight the unique significance of learning Akkadian for the studies of the Hebrew Bible are also included throughout the grammar. By the end of the grammar, students will have acquired all the necessary tools to either pursue additional studies of the Akkadian language or to utilize the information gained for better understanding the cognitive environment of the biblical world and to engage thoughtfully and carefully with Akkadian literature.

ZondervanAcademic.com/LanguageBasics

Zondervan Language Basics

Basics of Ancient Ethiopic

A Complete Grammar, Workbook, and Lexicon

Archie T. Wright

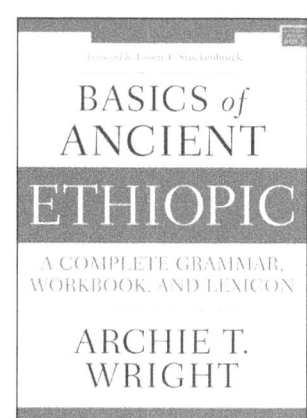

Basics of Ancient Ethiopic by Archie Wright introduces students to the basic grammar of ancient Ethiopic (Ge'ez) while approaching the language through its wider cultural and literary context, and its historical legacy.

As part of the widely-used Zondervan Language Basics series of resources, Wright's Ethiopic grammar is a student-friendly introduction. It helps students learn by:

- Minimizing technical jargon
- Providing only the information needed to learn the basics
- Breaking the grammar of language down into manageable and intuitive chunks
- Illustrating the grammar in question by its use in rich selections from ancient Christian and the Second Temple Jewish books of 1 Enoch and Jubilees
- Providing grammar, readings, exercises, and a lexicon all in one convenient volume

Basics of Ethiopic provides an ideal first step into this important language and focuses on getting the student into texts and translation as quickly as possible.

ZondervanAcademic.com/LanguageBasics

Zondervan Language Basics

Basics of Latin

A Grammar with Readings and Exercises from the Christian Tradition

Derek Cooper

Basics of Latin: A Grammar with Readings and Exercises from the Christian Tradition by Derek Cooper introduces students, independent learners, and homeschoolers to the basics of Latin grammar with all readings and exercises taken from texts in the Christian tradition. This grammar is organize into eight parts, each equipping students with skills needed to master a particular grammatical concept. *Basics of Latin* provides an ideal first step into this important language and focuses on getting the student into texts and translation as quickly as possible.

ZondervanAcademic.com/LanguageBasics

Zondervan Language Basics

Basics of Arabic

A Complete Grammar, Workbook, and Lexicon

Ayman S. Ibrahim

Basics of Arabic by Ayman Ibrahim is an introductory grammar, workbook, and lexicon for learning Modern Standard Arabic. Designed for students approaching Arabic for the first time the book provides them with all the tools necessary to develop skills in reading and writing Arabic. Students will learn Arabic grammar and vocabulary and be able to translate key Arabic passages from biblical and qur'anic texts.

Each lesson includes:

- A thorough and understandable introduction to a particular grammatical feature in Arabic
- List of vocabulary to be memorized
- Exercises for practice and reinforcement of key concepts

Basics of Arabic will help readers:

- Recite the Arabic alphabet
- Read and pronounce Arabic words
- Learn the Arabic noun and verbal system
- Understand syntax for writing and reading sentences

Additional translation exercises and a complete lexicon are included at the back of the book. Ideal for students, missionaries, independent learners, and homeschoolers this accessible guide give readers a clear and understandable introduction to this important language.

ZondervanAcademic.com/LanguageBasics